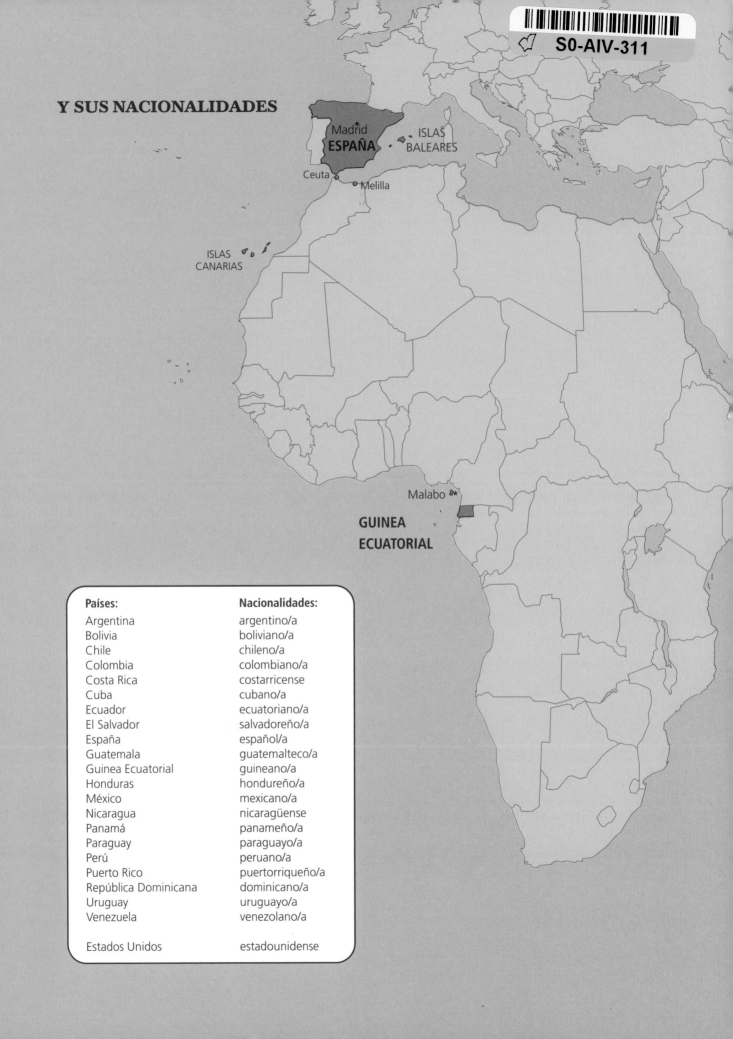

Y SUS NACIONALIDADES

ESPAÑA
Madrid
ISLAS BALEARES
Ceuta
Melilla

ISLAS CANARIAS

Malabo

GUINEA ECUATORIAL

Países:	Nacionalidades:
Argentina	argentino/a
Bolivia	boliviano/a
Chile	chileno/a
Colombia	colombiano/a
Costa Rica	costarricense
Cuba	cubano/a
Ecuador	ecuatoriano/a
El Salvador	salvadoreño/a
España	español/a
Guatemala	guatemalteco/a
Guinea Ecuatorial	guineano/a
Honduras	hondureño/a
México	mexicano/a
Nicaragua	nicaragüense
Panamá	panameño/a
Paraguay	paraguayo/a
Perú	peruano/a
Puerto Rico	puertorriqueño/a
República Dominicana	dominicano/a
Uruguay	uruguayo/a
Venezuela	venezolano/a
Estados Unidos	estadounidense

Annotated Instructor's Edition

¡Vívelo!

Beginning Spanish

Dolly J. Young
The University of Tennessee

Jane E. Berne
The University of North Dakota

Pablo Muirhead
Milwaukee Area Technical College

Claudia Montoya
Midwestern State University

WILEY

John Wiley & Sons, Inc.

VICE PRESIDENT AND EXECUTIVE PUBLISHER	Jay O'Callaghan
DIRECTOR, MODERN LANGUAGES	Magali Iglesias
SENIOR DEVELOPMENTAL EDITOR	Elena Herrero
PROJECT EDITOR	Glenn A. Wilson
ASSOCIATE DIRECTOR OF MARKETING	Jeffrey Rucker
MARKETING MANAGER	Tiziana Aime
MARKET SPECIALIST	Elena Casillas
ASSOCIATE EDITOR	Maruja Malavé
SENIOR PRODUCTION EDITOR	William A. Murray
EDITORIAL PROGRAM ASSISTANT	Lisha Perez
SENIOR PHOTO EDITOR	Jennifer MacMillan
SENIOR ILLUSTRATION EDITOR	Anna Melhorn
SENIOR MEDIA EDITOR	Lynn Pearlman
MEDIA PROJECT MANAGER	Margarita Valdez
CREATIVE DIRECTOR	Harry Nolan
COVER DESIGN	Jim O'Shea
PHOTO MONTAGE	Norm Christiansen
COVER IMAGES	(left to right) Jeremy Woodhouse/Age Fotostock America, Inc.; Nick Dolding/Taxi/Getty Images, Inc.; Emilio Ereza/Age Fotostock America, Inc.; Andy Sotiriou/Age Fotostock America, Inc.; Brand X Pictures/Getty Images, Inc.; Fan: Wiley Archive

This book was set in Berthold Baskerville by Curriculum Concepts International and printed and bound by Courier/Kendallville.

ISBN: 978-0-471-72776-7
BRV ISBN: 978-0-470-55649-8
AIE ISBN: 978-0-470-55497-5

Printed in the United States of America

10 9 8 7 6 5 4 3 2 1

I was born in Austin, Texas and embrace the deep cultural roots that bind me to my bilingual and bicultural upbringing. I was inspired to teach by my high school Spanish teacher. I majored in Spanish and then Latin American Studies at the University of Texas and then taught in a Bilingual Education junior high program where I taught Texas History, ESL and Reading. This began my journey into materials development and sparked my interest in how languages are learned and culture is experienced by adult learners. Having also tasted French and Portuguese, my love of learning took me back to the University of Texas to obtain a Ph.D. in FLE with a concentration in Spanish Applied Linguistics, and later to study-abroad experiences in Portugal, France, Spain and Mexico. I aspire to create bridges between and among cultures, and between research and practice. This textbook privileges cultural aspects of language learning informed by SLA research and theory and represents my commitment to beginning language learners. After all, that is where we create life-long learners and lovers of Spanish.

I dedicate this book to mother Gloria and my son Philip, who was consistently understanding and supportive during the many years it took to write this book.

Dolly Jesusita Young

I fell in love with Spanish from the moment I began studying it in high school. My passion for the Spanish language and for the cultures that live it has followed me throughout my career and my life. I was born in Minneapolis, MN and raised in Eden Prairie, MN. After studying Spanish for four years in high school, I spent a year in Tehuacán, Puebla, Mexico as a participant in a Rotary Club youth exchange program. Upon my return to the U.S., I enrolled at Carleton College in Northfield, MN, where I majored in Spanish. While at Carleton, I had the opportunity to spend a semester studying in Córdoba, Spain. When I graduated from Carleton, I taught Spanish at St. Stephen's Episcopal School in Austin, TX for three years. I then pursued graduate studies in Spanish at the University of Illinois at Urbana-Champaign, where I received both MA and PhD degrees in Spanish Applied Linguistics. Since 1992 I have taught a variety of Spanish courses at all levels at the University of North Dakota in Grand Forks, ND. For me, the opportunity to share my love of Spanish with my students and watch their language skills develop is very fulfilling. This book, *Vívelo*, is the culmination of more than 20 years working with adult learners of Spanish.

I am pleased and proud to dedicate it to my parents, Donald and Harriet Berne.

Jane E. Berne

I was born in Arequipa, Peru to parents who instilled a sense of pride in my cultural roots. They did so by maintaining Spanish at home in the U.S. and making sure we spent extensive time at home in Peru, just like my wife and I do with our two children. This passion for languages and cultures has led me to spend extensive time in various parts of the Spanish-speaking world as well as to live in Germany and Indonesia. I have taught Spanish from the college to the middle school levels, experiences which led me to complete a doctorate in education at the University of Wisconsin-Milwaukee.

First and foremost, I am a classroom teacher passionate about bridging the often elusive gap between theory and practice. I teach at Milwaukee Area Technical College, where I thoroughly enjoy creating a connected community of learners on the path toward linguistic and cultural proficiency. Secondly, I am passionate about my research which has led me to explore the inextricable link between language and culture. This connection comes alive in *¡Vívelo!*, a text born from Dolly Young's vision, and one I was excited to embrace.

Dedico este libro a Jackie y a nuestros hijos Santiago y Gabriela y a mis padres, Richard e Isabel. Los quiero muchísimo.

Pablo Muirhead

I grew up in Puebla, Mexico, listening to the old bolero records my parents loved to play and enjoying the diverse cuisine of Mexico's central area. Multiple trips from north to south and east to west in Mexico taught me much about the ethnic and cultural diversity contained within just one country. It is my hope that all students using this book will acquire a true interest in the cultural diversity of the Spanish-speaking world.

I studied my bachelor's degree in Linguistics and Hispanic Literature in Mexico, and years later completed my graduate studies in the United States. Although the main focus of my studies was Latin American literature, through my nearly 20 years of teaching experience I have always understood the critical importance of the first years in the process of learning a second language and the vital role of early positive cultural experiences. It is for this reason that I enthusiastically agreed to help author this book.

I want to dedicate my efforts to my teacher Gloria and my friends Angélica and Tesha.

Claudia Montoya

ACKNOWLEDGEMENTS

The *¡Vívelo!* authors gratefully acknowledge the contributions of the many individuals who were instrumental in making this first-edition project possible.

First, we gratefully acknowledge the indispensable contributions of past and present members of the Wiley team: Helene Greenwood for her work in the important and early stages of the project; Elena Herrero for her on-going devotion and hands-on contributions to all aspects of the project, including her participation in the script-writing and on-site filming of the DVD; Lisha Perez, for her extensive work in lining up reviewers and focus group participants; Magali Iglesias for the expertise she brings and her role in carrying out this project into the future; and Jay O'Callaghan for his constant encouragement and support. Special gratitude is extended to Glenn A. Wilson, whose countless hours of attention to *¡Vívelo!* went above and beyond the call and were indispensible to the completion of this project. We also thank Antonio Blas Pérez Nuñez for developing the excellent activities for the *¡En directo!* sections.

We also want to thank Tiziana Aime, Marketing Manager for Modern Languages, Elena Casillas, Market Specialist, and Jeffrey Rucker, Associate Director of Marketing, for their enthusiasm, creativity, and brilliant work in developing an advertising program that will convey *¡Vívelo!* message to colleagues and universities across the nation.

We are grateful to Anna Melhorn, Senior Illustration Editor, and Jennifer MacMillan, Senior Photo Editor, for their excellent work in selecting magnificent illustrations and photographs for *¡Vívelo!*; to Lynn Pearlman, Senior Media Editor, and Margarita Valdez, Media Project Manager, who are responsible for the text's highly innovative and technologically relevant media ancillaries; and to Bill Murray, Senior Production Editor, for coordinating all of the technical aspects of production.

We express our sincere gratitude to Curriculum Concepts International for their skillful management of the project: Candy Rodó, Executive Director; Kevin Adkins, Editor; Maureen O'Connor, Production Manager; Nancy Figueiredo and Frank Ferri, Designers, who worked with us so diligently through the various and challenging stages of production.

We thank Rebecca Taub for her fine work in creating the exams and self-tests. We are grateful to Sheila Basulto Tarifa for both the internet activities and PowerPoint slides. We extend our gratitude also to Kimberley Sallee for the test bank; to Carmen García for the Wimba voice tool questions; and to Mary Jane Kelley for the video activities.

For their candid commentary and creative ideas, we wish to thank the following reviewers and contributors:

Tomás Ruiz-Fabrega, *Albuquerque TVI Community College;* Ingetraut Rut Baird, *Anderson University;* Stacey Powell, *Auburn University;* Phillip Johnson, *Baylor University;* Elena González Ros, *Brandeis University;* María Dolores Costa, *California State University, Los Angeles;* Eduardo Barros-Grela, *California State University, Northridge;* Judy Getty, *California State University, Sacramento;* Carlos Andrés, *California State University, Stanislaus;* Carlos Valdez, *Carleton University;* Pascal Rollet, *Carthage College;* Cindy Espinosa, *Central Michigan University;* Alejandra Rengifo; *Central Michigan University;* Jorge Koochoi, *Central Piedmont Community College;* Juana Sylvia Nikopoulos, *Central Piedmont Community College;* Irena Stefanova, *City College of San Francisco;* Roger Simpson, *Clemson University;* Ana Girón Collin, *County Community College;* Patricia Harrigan, *Community College of Baltimore County;* Chris DiCapua, *Community College of Philadelphia;* Yolanda Hernández, *Community College of Southern Nevada, Cheyenne;* Tony Rector-Cavagnaro, *Cuesta College;* José López-Marrón, *CUNY Bronx Community College;* Patricia Davis, *Darton College;* Richard McCallister, *Delaware State University;* Eduardo Jaramillo, *Denison University;* Aurea Diab, *Dillard University;* Joanne Philip Lozano, *Dillard University;* Michael Schinasi, *Eastern Carolina University;* Jerome Mwinyelle, *East Tennessee State University;* José Varela

Eastern, *Kentucky University;* Chary-Sy Copeland, *Florida A&M University;* Sandra Kregar, *Florida State University;* Adela Borrallo-Solís, *Georgetown College;* Ronald Leow, *Georgetown University;* Ana Cruz; *Georgia Institute of Technology;* Dyana Ellis, *Georgia Southern University;* Dolores Rangel, *Georgia Southern University;* Rafael Falcón, *Goshen College;* Jeff Samuels, *Goucher College;* Héctor F. Espitia, *Grand Valley State University;* Miryam Criado, *Hanover College;* Angela Cresswell, *Holy Family University;* Josephine Books, *Inver Hills Community College;* Julie Wilhelm, *Iowa State University;* Samuel Sommerville, *Johnson County Community College;* Mary Copple, *Kansas State University;* Adriana Natali-Sommerville, *Kansas University;* Timothy Benson, *Lake Superior College;* Nancy Barclay, *Lake Tahoe Community College;* Laurie Huffman, *Los Medanos College;* Kate Grovergrys, *Madison Area Technical College, Madison;* Deborah Mistron, *Middle Tennessee State University;* Tere Gilles, *Montana State University, Billings;* Gail Ament, *Morningside College;* Ronna Feit, *Nassau Community College;* Jeff Longwell, *New Mexico State University;* Yuly Asención Delaney, *Northern Arizona University;* Nicholas Concepción, *Northern Illinois University;* Hilary Landwehr, *Northern Kentucky University;* María López Morgan, *Northwest Florida State College;* Sue Pechter, *Northwestern University;* Mary Jane Kelley, *Ohio University;* Virginia Hojas, *Ohio University;* John Deveny, *Oklahoma State University, Main Campus;* Inma Álvarez, *Open University;* Victor Slesinger, *Palm Beach Community College;* Judith Richards, *Park University;* Jennifer Garson, *Pasadena City College;* Robin Bower, *Pennsylvania State University;* Kit Decker, *Piedmont Virginia Community College;* Enrica Ademagni, *Purdue University;* Peggy Patterson, *Rice University;* Daria Cohen, *Rider University;* U. Theresa Zmurkewycz, *Saint Joseph's University;* Laura Ruiz-Scott, *Scottsdale Community College;* Robert Lesman, *Shippensburg University of Pennsylvania;* Charlene Grant, *Skidmore College;* Carol Snell-Feikema, *South Dakota State University;* Covadonga Arango-Martín, *Southern Connecticut State University;* Heidy Carruthers, *Southern Illinois University, Edwardsville;* Alice A. Miano, *Stanford University;* Elizabeth Lansing, *State University of New York, Albany;* Silvia Álvarez-Olarra, *Temple University;* Norma Corrales-Martin, *Temple University;* Cheryl Bevill, *Tennessee State University;* Carmen García, *Texas Southern University;* Leticia Romo, *Towson University;* Thomas Capuano, *Truman State University;* Danion Doman, *Truman State University;* Ari Zighelboim, *Tulane University;* Amy George-Hirons, *Tulane University;* Juliet Falce-Robinson, *University of California, Los Angeles;* Dina Fabery, *University of Central Florida;* María Montalvo, *University of Central Florida;* Noel Fallows, *University of Georgia;* Teresa Pérez-Gamboa, *University of Georgia;* Luisa Kou, *University of Hawaii, Manoa;* R. Joseph Rodríguez, *University of Houston;* Aymará Boggiano, *University of Houston;* Melanie Waters, *University of Illinois, Urbana-Champaign;* Rosalinda Silva-Alemany, *University of Louisiana at Lafayette;* Regina Roebuck, *University of Louisville;* Carla Martínez, *University of Memphis;* Eugenio Ángulo, *University of Miami;* Michelle Orecchio, *University of Michigan;* Luis Beláustegui, *University of Missouri, Kansas City;* María Beláustegui, *University of Missouri, Kansas City;* Bethany Sanio, *University of Nebraska, Lincoln;* Patricia Baker, *University of North Carolina, Asheville;* Michelle Bettencourt, *University of North Carolina, Asheville;* María Moratto, *University of North Carolina, Greensboro;* Marcia Payne Wooten, *University of North Carolina, Greensboro;* Jiyoung Yoon, *University of North Texas;* María Arenillas, *University of Notre Dame;* Linda Grabner Travis, *University of Pennsylvania;* Claudia Ferman, *University of Richmond;* Natalie Wagener, *University of Texas, Arlington;* Delia Montesinos, *University of Texas, Austin;* Karen Rubio, *University of Tulsa;* Joan Fox, *University of Washington;* Bridgette Gunnels, *University of West Georgia;* Isabel Álvarez, *University of Wisconsin, Oshkosh;* Samira Chater, *Valencia Community College;* Aida Díaz, *Valencia Community College;* Yolanda González, *Valencia Community College;* Rachel Chiguluri, *Vanderbilt University;* Arthur Sandford, *Ventura College;* Elizabeth Calvera, *Virginia Polytechnic Institute and State University;* Marilyn Kiss, *Wagner College;* Rebekah Morris, *Wake Forest University;* Marisa Barragan-Peugnet, *Washington University, St. Louis;* Candy Henry, *Westmoreland Community College;* Maripaz García, *Yale University;* M. Lourdes Sabe-Colom, *Yale University;* Serge Ainsa, *Yavapai College.*

PREFACE

¡Vívelo! offers a fresh approach to beginning Spanish based on a solid foundation of what second language acquisition research tells us about how students acquire and assimilate language and cultural competence. It is a holistic, culturally rich, task-driven program with engaging input and realistic expectations of what beginning learners can achieve in a first college Spanish course.

¡Vívelo! pays close attention to the role of affect in the foreign language learning process by emphasizing what students know and can readily do with language, and by going beyond exposing them to the products and practices of other cultures to explore, compare, and embrace the perspectives they come from. It is designed strategically to ensure that beginning students of Spanish, even with a limited amount of language, can understand and make themselves understood well enough to function at levels parallel to their cognitive abilities and in a culturally appropriate manner.

Main Pedagogical Features

A task-driven program, rich in content. In our native language, we read and listen to learn, and we speak and write to share our experiences, express our feelings, and voice our opinions. **¡Vívelo!** treats college learners like adults who are capable of thinking at higher cognitive levels even with their limited proficiency in Spanish. While students need practice, they are also capable of interacting on a real, meaningful level. Students are more motivated to learn Spanish by engaging in authentic language functions, such as gathering and sharing information for the purpose of doing something with it. We consistently include interactive activities such as signature searches, information-gap exercises, and interviews to encourage negotiation of meaning with a purpose. And in **¡Vívelo!** students do not just learn Spanish; they explore content from an array of disciplines. In *Capítulo 5*, for example, while they learn vocabulary for colors, clothing, body parts, and prepositions of location, students are also learning how to think critically about fashion, what it is, what it does, and how it can be interpreted. The content-rich, task-driven, and problem-solving nature of this program encourages long-term retention and life-long learning habits because the focus is on authentic purposes of communication instead of short-term, superficial learning.

The language students know. Our program makes strategic use of cognates and context to introduce students to the topics they will explore. Each *Investigación* begins with *Adelante*, which presents a list of easily recognizable cognates and near–cognates with activities that establish context and engage students in a meaningful way right from the start. Cognates are then consistently used throughout the chapter to continue the contextual thread as new language is introduced.

The language students need. We refrain from including the full range of explicitly framed grammar structures that most first-year textbooks include. For example, the subjunctive is not omitted but we limit its coverage and emphasize comprehension over production because the subjunctive is a cognitively complex structure that is ultimately acquired late. By encouraging students to link the verb form *vaya* to its meaning (go), we facilitate comprehension even without an explicit awareness of this advanced grammar concept. A student will more readily comprehend the sentence *Yo quiero que mi amigo vaya con ustedes* than *Le doy la mochila que le tengo guardada a mi amigo*, even though the former is in the subjunctive and the latter is not. Time-consuming instruction of advanced structures may lead to superficial, short-term performance on fill-in-the-blank tests, but it takes class time away from problem-solving communicative tasks that help students internalize structures that are more within the reach of their developing linguistic system. Time is better spent on topics that help students make form-meaning connections using structures without which there is a breakdown in communication, such as object pronouns and constructions with *se*. The scope and sequence thus gives priority to those structures without which communication is impeded, and forms that offer the greatest flexibility of self-expression with the least cognitive effort. For example, we introduce the present perfect to refer to past actions, before we introduce the preterit because the present perfect is cognitively less complex.

Processing instruction. When developing the scope and sequence of topics, and the tasks and activities in this program, we took into account the principles of input processing, processing instruction, and structured output and speaking tasks. For example, through processing instruction research we know that students process language based on communicative value. Consequently, for grammar, we design practice activities that draw students' attention to the meaning inherent in forms, such as the change in meaning that comes with verb forms (present, future, past) or with the information contained in the verb, such as person and number. We emphasize making form-meaning connections and move tasks from recognition to structured output. In other words, when students are asked to produce, the tasks are structured to ensure linguistic and lexical support.

Culture integration. **¡Vívelo!** maximizes the role of culture by integrating it throughout each chapter's various sections. Cultural content is woven into anything from vocabulary presentations and practice activities to grammar exercises, and explored explicitly in *Vívelo: Cultura* and *Contextos y perspectivas* where students engage in the construction and deconstruction of perspectives about culture from the L1 to L2 and vice versa. Critical cultural awareness is achieved by encouraging students to reflect on perceptions of their own cultures and cultures of the Spanish-speaking world. The breakdown of ethnocentric interpretations and a suspension of enthnocentricism is a principle objective of **¡Vívelo!**

Low–Anxiety Classroom Community. Willingness to communicate is essential for successful language deve-lopment. For students to feel willing to communicate, risk must be minimized in the classroom. Familiarity at the individual and social level lowers risk. **¡Vívelo!** attempts to create a familiar, social classroom environment through highly interactive, dialogic tasks and the *Retrato de la clase* writing tasks which have students collect and record information about their class community. A comfort zone is established with cognates at the beginning of each *Investigación,* and community is built from the many tasks throughout each *Capítulo* that have students collect, record, and share information about themselves and their classmates.

Empowerment and accountability. The heavy emphasis on content and experiential learning in **¡Vívelo!** both empowers students and holds them accountable in various ways. For example, the content of the *Retrato de la clase* is integrated into writing exercises or classroom compositions. If students are conscientiously collecting and recording information at the times indicated in the book, they will have the content they need to write more extensively and can be asked to focus on organization, grammar, and composition skills. Just by being attentive to what people say in class, students have control over this component of the program. **¡Vívelo!** builds accountability via the *Retrato de la clase* assignments. By holding students accountable for the information they learn in and out of class, and by asking students to do something with information they have gathered and shared, we place the emphasis on *what is* said and *why,* and not just *how* it is said.

Beyond the classroom. For students to see language learning as useful, they must move beyond the classroom. **¡Vívelo!** supports broadening the language learning experience by linking content in the book to real world, up-to-date knowledge, experiences and events via online connections. Students explore geography through Google Earth, climate via actual and authentic weather predictions, artistic expressions via accessible websites that showcase works of art, etc. We promote learning experiences through community tasks, such as interviewing native Spanish speakers in the community or on campus. We explore Spanish-language cinema to promote critical cultural awareness and intercultural competence.

Learning styles. ¡Vívelo! takes into account a variety of learning styles. We vary the types of textbook and activities manual tasks to provide a balanced appeal to different learning styles so that all students are given opportunities to learn in ways that will be most successful for them. In addition, the instructor annotations often give suggestions on how a given activity might be modified or followed-up on to appeal to specific learning styles.

Learning strategies. ¡Vívelo! offers reading strategies, communicative strategies, and other L2 learning strategies along with many of the input selections and activities throughout the book to effectively arm students with cognitive and metacognitive tools for L2 development.

Our Approach to the Basics: Vocabulary, Grammar, and Culture

In the course of ¡Vívelo!'s development, we have been motivated by reviewers' enthusiastic appreciation of how well vocabulary, grammar, and culture are integrated and interwoven throughout the program. These basic elements of language instruction work in harmony to create a rich, coherent context in each *Investigación* and *Capítulo*.

Vocabulary. Each *Investigación* begins with a section called *Adelante* that gives a list of easily recognizable cognates and near–cognates that students use in activities that begin to establish context for the *Investigación*. "Cognates" in *Adelante* are not strictly words that are spelled alike and have similar meanings in Spanish and English, but also include words that share the same root as their English equivalent and related words whose meanings may vary somewhat in the two languages. Clear context in the activities and facile recognition of most items provides a comfortable environment for students as they begin exploring the *Investigación* topic in general terms. Following this work with cognates, a short, engaging reading selection begins to move things from the conceptual to the concrete and provides the context for beginning to introduce new vocabulary. *Palabras clave* introduces new, thematic vocabulary in a visual context and by way of synonym associations, brief definitions, and example sentences or exchanges, entirely in Spanish. Items presented in one chapter may be reintroduced in another in a new context. Throughout each chapter, *Expresiones útiles* boxes appear when there is an opportunity to introduce high-frequency expressions that might be used in any variety of contexts. At the end of each *Investigación*, a *Vocabulario* section collects thematic vocabulary in the form of a list with English equivalents. The list is organized into *Vocabulario esencial*, containing the most high-frequency vocabulary necessary for communication at the beginning level, and *Otras palabras y expresiones*, containing items that students may or may not assimilate into their working vocabulary at this level, but are likely to recognize in context. There is also a reminder on the vocabulary lists to review the cognates in *Adelante* and a cross-reference to a list of all of the cognates appearing in the *Investigación*, in an appendix at the end of the book.

Grammar. As mentioned, our approach to grammar focuses on topics that help students make form-meaning connections using structures without which there is a breakdown in communication, and we give priority to forms that offer the greatest flexibility of self-expression with the least cognitive effort. *Estructuras clave* focuses on form and function, and often asks students to make observations about how a particular structure works before presenting the "rules". We recognize that many students are not comfortable with grammar terminology, so we explain concepts clearly before presenting forms and rules. For example, before presenting direct object pronouns, we establish that a direct object answers the question *what?* or *whom?*.

We place heavy importance on establishing form-meaning connections. In early chapters, for instance, students learn and practice the meaning of new verbs in the infinitive before they begin to conjugate them. Thus, when they begin to conjugate verbs their full attention is on the association of the various endings with the appropriate person. *Vívelo: Lengua* focuses on simple forms and constructions used for a specific function or purpose and is presented as such with titles like *Expressing possession, Giving instructions with infinitives, Describing actions: Adverbs ending in −mente*, etc. As in *Estructuras clave,* form-meaning connections are of central importance.

Culture. Culture is integrated throughout each *Investigación* in *Adelante* reading selections, activities, grammar explanation examples, etc., and is the focus of the *Vívelo: Cultura* and *Contextos y perspectivas* sections. *Vívelo: Cultura* introduces cultural phenomena and information in the form of brief essays and excerpts from many real-life sources. In early chapters, topics are presented in Spanish wherever they can be with accessible language, or in English when they are more complex. Beginning in *Capítulo 5,* all *Vívelo: Cultura* sections are presented in Spanish. *Contextos y perspectivas* explores the Investigación topic in a Hispanic context through an examination of both the Hispanic perspective and the students' home culture perspective. Video segments and their associated activities in *En directo* (found in the chapter-ending *¡Vívelo!* section) open a window on manifestations of culture throughout the Spanish-speaking world.

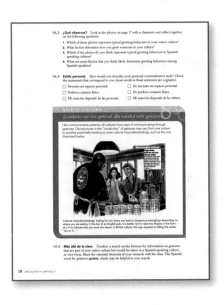

SECTION BY SECTION GUIDE

You will learn This section introduces the study objectives for each *Investigación* and activates student's background knowledge with a set of thematic questions.

Adelante This section begins with simple lists of topically relevant cognates. Cognates include words of recognizable origin even if not spelled like their English counterparts, and words that are related in meaning to English words but may not correspond one-to-one. Following this list, students work with the cognates in a few heavily recognition-oriented activities. ▼

A brief reading selection follows. The aim of the reading and its activities is to further introduce and contextualize cognates and begin introducing new, topical/thematic vocabulary in context. ▼

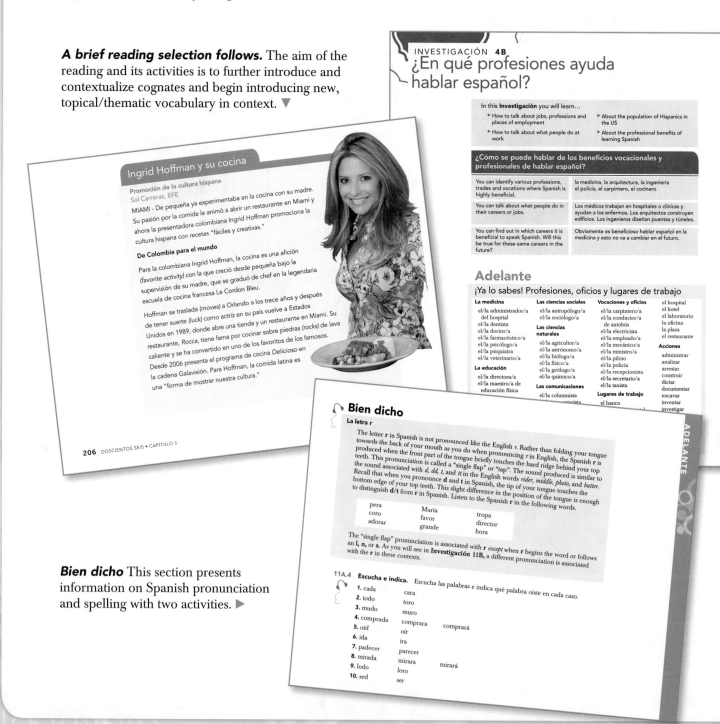

Ingrid Hoffman y su cocina

Promoción de la cultura hispana
Sol Carreras, EFE

MIAMI - De pequeña ya experimentaba en la cocina con su madre. Su pasión por la comida le animó a abrir un restaurante en Miami y ahora la presentadora colombiana Ingrid Hoffman promociona la cultura hispana con recetas "fáciles y creativas."

De Colombia para el mundo

Para la colombiana Ingrid Hoffman, la cocina es una afición (favorite activity) con la que creció desde pequeña bajo la supervisión de su madre, que se graduó de chef en la legendaria escuela de cocina francesa Le Cordon Bleu.

Hoffman se traslada (moves) a Orlando a los trece años y después de tener suerte (luck) como actriz en su país vuelve a Estados Unidos en 1989, donde abre una tienda y un restaurante en Miami. Su restaurante, Rocca, tiene fama por cocinar sobre piedras (rocks) de lava caliente y se ha convertido en uno de los favoritos de los famosos. Desde 2006 presenta el programa de cocina Delicioso en la cadena Galavisión. Para Hoffman, la comida latina es una "forma de mostrar nuestra cultura."

206 DOSCIENTOS SEIS • CAPÍTULO 5

INVESTIGACIÓN **4B**
¿En qué profesiones ayuda hablar español?

In this **Investigación** you will learn…

- ► How to talk about jobs, professions and places of employment
- ► About the population of Hispanics in the US
- ► How to talk about what people do at work
- ► About the professional benefits of learning Spanish

¿Cómo se puede hablar de los beneficios vocacionales y profesionales de hablar español?

You can identify various professions, trades and vocations where Spanish is highly beneficial.	la medicina, la arquitectura, la ingeniería el policía, el carpintero, el cocinero
You can talk about what people do in their careers or jobs.	Los médicos trabajan en hospitales o clínicas y ayudan a los enfermos. Los arquitectos construyen edificios. Los ingenieros diseñan puentes y túneles.
You can find out in which careers it is beneficial to speak Spanish. Will this be true for these same careers in the future?	Obviamente es beneficioso hablar español en la medicina y esto no va a cambiar en el futuro.

Adelante

¡Ya lo sabes! Profesiones, oficios y lugares de trabajo

La medicina	Las ciencias sociales	Vocaciones y oficios	
el/la administrador/a del hospital	el/la antropólogo/a el/la sociólogo/a	el/la carpintero/a el/la conductor/a	el hospital el hotel
el/la dentista		de autobús	el laboratorio
el/la doctor/a	**Las ciencias naturales**	el/la electricista	la oficina
el/la farmacéutico/a		el/la empleado/a	la plaza
el/la psicólogo/a	el/la agricultor/a	el/la mecánico/a	el restaurante
el/la psiquiatra	el/la astrónomo/a	el/la ministro/a	
el/la veterinario/a	el/la biólogo/a	el/la piloto	**Acciones**
	el/la físico/a	el/la policía	administrar
La educación	el/la geólogo/a	el/la recepcionista	analizar
el/la directora/a	el/la químico/a	el/la secretario/a	arrestar
el/la maestro/a de		el/la taxista	construir
educación física	**Las comunicaciones**		dictar
	el/la columnista	**Lugares de trabajo**	documentar
		el banco	excavar
			inventar
			investigar

Bien dicho

La letra r

The letter **r** in Spanish is not pronounced like the English *r*. Rather than folding your tongue towards the back of your mouth as you do when pronouncing *r* in English, the Spanish **r** is produced when the front part of the tongue briefly touches the hard ridge behind your top teeth. This pronunciation is called a "single flap" or "tap". The sound produced is similar to the sound associated with *d*, *dd*, *t*, and *tt* in the English words *rider*, *middle*, *photo*, and *butter*. Recall that when you pronounce **d** and **t** in Spanish, the tip of your tongue touches the bottom edge of your top teeth. This slight difference in the position of the tongue is enough to distinguish **d/t** from **r** in Spanish. Listen to the Spanish **r** in the following words.

pera	María	tropa
coro	favor	director
adorar	grande	hora

The "single flap" pronunciation is associated with **r** *except* when **r** begins the word or follows an **l**, **n**, or **s**. As you will see in **Investigación 11B**, a different pronunciation is associated with the **r** in these contexts

11A.4 Escucha e indica. Escucha las palabras e indica qué palabra oíste en cada caso.

1. cada	cara	
2. todo	toro	
3. mudo	muro	
4. comprada	comprara	comprará
5. oíd	oír	
6. ida	ira	
7. padecer	parecer	
8. mirada	mirara	mirará
9. lodo	loro	
10. sed	ser	

Bien dicho This section presents information on Spanish pronunciation and spelling with two activities. ►

Palabras clave This section introduces new, thematic vocabulary in a visual context and by way of synonym associations, brief definitions, example sentences or exchanges, etc., entirely in Spanish. There are often two or three *Palabras clave* presentations in an *Investigación*, each with an activity set that follows. ▼

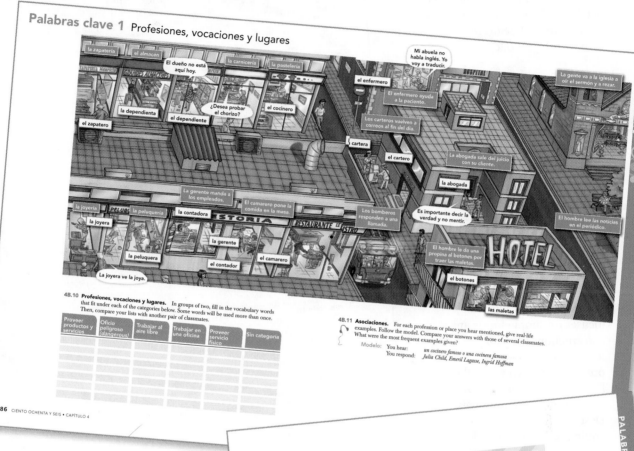

Palabras clave 1 Profesiones, vocaciones y lugares

4B.10 Profesiones, vocaciones y lugares. In groups of two, fill in the vocabulary words that fit under each of the categories below. Some words will be used more than once. Then, compare your lists with another pair of classmates.

Proveer productos y servicios	Oficio peligroso (dangerous)	Trabajar al aire libre	Trabajar en una oficina	Proveer servicio físico	Sin categoría

4B.11 Asociaciones. For each profession or place you hear mentioned, give real-life examples. Follow the model. Compare your answers with those of several classmates. What were the most frequent examples given?

Modelo: You hear: *un cocinero famoso o una cocinera famosa*
You respond: *Julia Child, Emeril Lagasse, Ingrid Hoffman*

¡Atención! This section is comprised of a brief presentation of several false cognates followed by one or two short activities. ▶

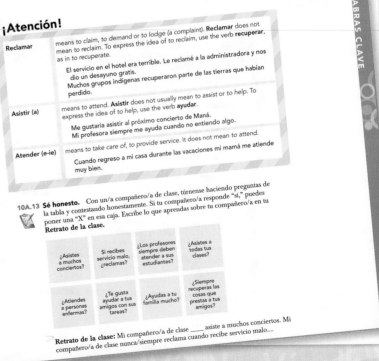

¡Atención!

Reclamar	means to claim, to demand or to lodge (a complaint). **Reclamar** does not mean to reclaim. To express the idea of to reclaim, use the verb **recuperar**, as in to recuperate.
	El servicio en el hotel era terrible. Le reclamé a la administradora y nos dio un desayuno gratis.
	Muchos grupos indígenas recuperaron parte de las tierras que habían perdido.
Asistir (a)	means to attend. **Asistir** does not usually mean to assist or to help. To express the idea of to help, use the verb **ayudar**.
	Me gustaría asistir al próximo concierto de Maná.
	Mi profesora siempre me ayuda cuando no entiendo algo.
Atender (e-ie)	means to take care of, to provide service. It does not mean to attend.
	Cuando regreso a mi casa durante las vacaciones mi mamá me atiende muy bien.

10A.13 Sé honesto. Con un/a compañero/a de clase, túrnense haciendo preguntas de la tabla y contestando honestamente. Si tu compañero/a responde "sí," puedes poner una "X" en esa caja. Escribe lo que aprendas sobre tu compañero/a en tu **Retrato de la clase.**

¿Asistes a muchos conciertos?	Si recibes servicio malo, ¿reclamas?	¿Los profesores siempre deben atender a sus estudiantes?	¿Asistes a todas tus clases?
¿Atiendes a personas enfermas?	¿Te gusta ayudar a tus amigos con sus tareas?	¿Ayudas a tu familia mucho?	¿Siempre recuperas las cosas que prestas a tus amigos?

Retrato de la clase: Mi compañero/a de clase _____ asiste a muchos conciertos. Mi compañero/a de clase nunca/siempre reclama cuando recibe servicio malo....

Estructuras clave *Estructuras clave* focuses on form and function, and often asks students to make observations about how a particular structure works before presenting the "rules". There are between one and three *Estructuras clave* sections in an *Investigación,* each with an activity set that follows. ▶

ESTRUCTURAS CLAVE

Estructuras clave 2

Comparisons of equality and inequality

WILEY **PLUS**
Go to *WileyPLUS* and review the tutorial for this grammar point.

Equality

To talk about equality in terms of *quality*, Spanish uses **tan** + *adjective* + **como** *(as...as).* **Tan** and **como** do not change forms, but the adjective must agree with what it is describing.

Esta galería es tan variada como esa.
Dalí es tan conocido como Picasso.
Swanson no es tan famoso como Hopper.

This gallery is as varied as that one.
Dalí is as well known as Picasso.
Swanson is not as well known as Hopper.

To talk about equality in terms of *quantity*, Spanish uses **tanto/-a/-os/-as** + *noun* + **como** *(as much/many...as).* **Tanto** is an adjective and must agree with the noun it describes.

Javier Bardem no tiene tanto dinero como Paris Hilton.
Sonia Solanilla no tiene tantos cuadros como Carmen Lomas Garza.
No hay tantas galerías en Nashville como en la Ciudad de Nueva York.

Javier Bardem does not have as much money as Paris Hilton.
Sonia Solanilla doesn't have as many paintings as Carmen Lomas Garza.
There aren't as many galleries in Nashville as (there are) in New York City.

Inequality

To make comparisons of inequality in terms of quality, Spanish uses **más/menos** + *adjective* + **que** *(more/less...than),* and to make comparisons of inequality in terms of quantity, **más/menos** + *noun* + **que** *(more/less/fewer...than).*

Las pinturas son más interesantes que las fotografías.

Paintings are more interesting than photos.

El programa *Heroes* es más violento que el programa *Brothers and Sisters*.

The program Heroes is more violent than the program Brothers and Sisters.

El teatro tiene menos espectadores que el cine.

The theater has fewer spectators than the cinema.

To express *more than* or *fewer than* with numbers, use **más/menos de** + *number.*

El museo exhibe más de diez cuadros de Dalí.
Hay menos de cien obras en la galería.

The museum is exhibiting more than ten Dalí paintings.
There are fewer than a hundred works in the gallery.

8B.22 ¿Estás de acuerdo?

Paso 1: Lee los siguientes enunciados y escribe *Sí,* si estás de acuerdo o *No,* si no lo estás. Luego, busca a un/a compañero/a cuyas *(whose)* respuestas sean, en su mayoría, iguales a las tuyas. Trabaja con ese/a estudiante en el segundo paso en la página 386.

—— Mi clase de español es más interesante que mis otras clases.
—— Montar en bicicleta es más económico que manejar un auto.
—— Comer en casa es más barato *(inexpensive)* que comer en un restaurante.
—— Las películas son más entretenidas que los programas de televisión.
—— La música de Jay Z me gusta más que la música de Eminem.
—— Los libros son más interesantes que las revistas *(magazines).*
—— Las fotos son más bonitas que los videos.
—— Hacer mi tarea es más divertido que pasar tiempo en Facebook.
—— El fútbol es más divertido que el béisbol.
—— Los tacos son menos populares que la pizza.
—— Mi profesor/a es más alto/a que yo.

INVESTIGACIÓN 8B • TRESCIENTOS OCHENTA Y CINCO **385**

Vívelo: Lengua This box focuses on simple forms and constructions used for a specific function or purpose and is presented as such with titles like Expressing possession, Giving instructions with infinitives, Describing actions: Adverbs ending in –mente, etc. ▼

VÍVELO: LENGUA

Expressing superlatives

Superlatives express ideas such as *the biggest, the youngest, the tallest, the smartest, the most beautiful, the least expensive,* etc. Spanish uses the following construction:

el/la/los/las ___*(noun)* **más/menos** + *adjective.*

The noun may be omitted when it is understood through context or to avoid repetition. To indicate the field of comparison, such as *in the world, in the class, in my family,* etc. Spanish uses the preposition **de**, not **en**.

El país más grande del mundo es Rusia mientras que la Ciudad del Vaticano es el más pequeño.
La Miss EE.UU. y la Miss América son las mujeres más bonitas de este país.
El género literario menos estudiado de todos es el ensayo.

There are some irregular superlatives that do not use **más** or **menos**:

el/la mayor	los/las mayores	*the oldest* (people), *the greatest* (magnitude)
el/la menor	los/las menores	*the youngest* (people), *the least* (magnitude)
el/la mejor	los/las mejores	*the best*
el/la peor	los/las peores	*the worst*

Ricardo es el menor de su familia. Tiene tres hermanos mayores.
Las mejores películas del año son nominadas para los premios Óscar y las peores son nominadas para los premios Golden Raspberry.

Enlaces This is a short section with one or two activities that calls attention to connecting words/expressions that students will see in the *Contextos* reading that immediately follows on the next page. ▶

Contextos y perspectivas *Contextos* explores an aspect of the *Investigación* theme in a reading selection that highlights a Hispanic perspective on that theme, followed by activities that confirm students' comprehension and have them process the information contained in the selection. *Perspectivas* continues the thematic thread established by the *Contextos* reading and is comprised of activities designed to foster personal expression and exploration/comparison of cultural perspectives on that theme. ▲

Vocabulario This is a summary listing of all of the thematic vocabulary introduced in the chapter. Words and expressions appear in list form with their English equivalents. A reminder to review the cognates presented at the beginning of the *Investigación* appears at the end of the list. ▶

Enlaces

A veces es necesario hacer conexiones entre una cláusula y otra de una oración. Esto se hace con palabras como **quien, cuyo, y que,** entre otras.

8B.25 Relaciones dentro de las oraciones. Adivina lo que significa la palabra subrayada en las siguientes oraciones. Luego, comprueba tus respuestas con la clase.

who   whose   that

_____ 1. Hoy en día los descendientes de los peregrinos (*pilgrims*), <u>quienes</u> inmigraron a Plymouth Rock en el siglo XVII, todavía viven allí.

_____ 2. Muchos hispanos, <u>cuyos</u> padres heredaron (*inherited*) tierra en Texas bajo el gobierno mexicano, perdieron (*lost*) su tierra cuando Texas obtuvo su independencia en 1836.

_____ 3. Un mural es una obra de arte <u>que</u> expresa conceptos o ideas en forma de collage y <u>que</u> se hace en una pantalla o una pared (*wall*) dentro o fuera de un edificio.

8B.26 Enlaces. Empareja el significado según el contexto de la palabra subrayada y las palabras en inglés, abajo. Luego, comprueba tus respuestas con al menos otros dos compañeros de clase.

Contextos

11A.30 De la gasolina a los biocombustibles. Previamente leíste un artículo sobre la subida del precio de la gasolina. Ahora, leerás cómo la solución podría ser desastrosa también en "Todos contra los biocombustibles". Después de leer el artículo, indica con un/a compañero/a de clase si las oraciones a continuación son ciertas o falsas. Busquen información en el artículo que justifique sus respuestas.

Cierto Falso

□ □ 1. La producción de biocombustibles afecta a los países pobres de una manera positiva.

□ □ 2. El costo de la comida ha bajado debido a la producción de biocombustibles.

□ □ 3. Los biocombustibles están hechos de plantas u otras materias vegetales.

□ □ 4. Según varias organizaciones internacionales, el costo de la comida se considera un problema grave.

□ □ 5. Los problemas económicos actuales se originaron en Estados Unidos.

□ □ 6. Todos están a favor de la producción de biocombustibles.

□ □ 7. Los países pobres pueden verse afectados negativamente por los cambios del clima.

□ □ 8. La producción de biocombustibles no tiene ninguna consecuencia negativa.

Todos **contra** los biocombustibles

La energía del futuro

Se habla mucho en las noticias de la fabricación de biocombustibles como la fuente de energía del futuro. Sin embargo, la sustitución de petróleo por biocombustibles puede generar otros problemas. Según varios informes de la organización humanitaria Oxfam, el aumento del uso de biocombustibles podría tener consecuencias negativas para los países más pobres del planeta.

504 QUINIENTOS CUATRO • CAPÍTULO 11

Perspectivas

11A.31 ¡Reacciona! En grupos de tres, determinen si están de acuerdo o no con las siguientes declaraciones. Luego, analicen sus respuestas como clase.

¿Estamos de acuerdo?

Sí No

□ □ 1. Cualquier avance tecnológico será inútil (*useless*) si no encontramos formas limpias y seguras de producir energía.

□ □ 2. Hay un efecto dominó global con respecto a la solución de la crisis de energía. Lo que puede ser una solución para un país puede dañar a otro.

□ □ 3. Los países pobres del mundo están a la merced de (*at the mercy of*) los países ricos.

□ □ 4. El descubrimiento de fuentes de energía nuevas yace (*lies*) en los recursos inexplorados que se pueden encontrar en países pobres.

□ □ 5. Los estadounidenses tendrán que cambiar su modo de vida basado en la conveniencia para ser como la gente de otros países desarrollados.

□ □ 6. La energía nuclear será la solución de los problemas de energía del futuro.

□ □ 7. Explorar el océano en busca de petróleo sería la mejor solución para la crisis de energía.

□ □ 8. Los países en vías de desarrollo han contribuido a la crisis de energía tanto como los países desarrollados.

□ □ 9. La necesidad de encontrar nuevas fuentes de energía debe predominar sobre la protección del medio ambiente.

□ □ 10. La economía global quedará completamente destruida si no encontramos nuevas fuentes de energía.

Basándose en las respuestas, ¿tienen ustedes una perspectiva optimista o pesimista sobre la energía del futuro?

□ optimista   □ pesimista

¿Qué piensa la clase en general?

Vocabulario: Investigación A

Vocabulario esencial

Sustantivos

el aeropuerto	*airport*
el boleto/billete	*ticket*
el/la agente de viajes	*travel agent*
el avión	*airplane*
la autopista	*highway*
el barco	*boat*
la bicicleta	*bicycle*
la calle	*street*
el camión	*truck*
el carro/coche	*car*
la carretera	*road*
las cifras	*numbers; figures*
la ciudad	*city*
el cohete	*rocket*
el crucero	*cruise ship*
la desventaja	*disadvantage*
la estación de autobuses	*bus station*
el ferrocarril	*train*
el ingreso	*income*
la maleta	*bag/luggage*
el paisaje	*landscape*
el promedio	*average*
el tráfico	*traffic*
la vela	*sail*
la ventaja	*advantage*
el vuelo (de ida y vuelta)	*(round trip) flight*

Adjetivos

caro/a	*expensive*
corto/a	*short*
lento/a	*slow*
lleno/a	*full*
vacío/a	*empty*

Verbos

alcanzar	*to reach*
andar adelantado	*to be fast*
andar atrasado	*to be slow*
aprovechar	*to take advantage of*
caminar	*to walk*
cansarse a uno	*to tire one*
demorar(se)	*to delay; to become delayed*
dirigir(se)	*to direct; to head for*
facturar el equipaje	*to check in luggage*
hacer fila	*to wait in line*
hacer escala	*to have a layover*
hacer las maletas	*to pack the bags*
ir a pie	*to go by foot*
llevar a	*to take to; to lead to*
manejar/conducir el carro	*to drive the car*
montar en bicicleta	*to ride a bike*
pasar por aduana	*to go through customs*
tener lugar	*to take place*
tener sueño	*to be sleepy*
volar	*to fly*

Otras palabras y expresiones

ajuste	*adjustment*
arrebatar	*to seize*
biocombustible	*biofuel*
caña de azúcar	*sugar cane*
combustible	*fuel*
crudo/a	*raw*
dañar	*to damage*
desplazar	*to displace*
desviar	*to deviate*
escasez	*scarcity*
fatigar	*to tire*
felicidad	*happiness*
inalámbrico/a	*wireless*
inútil	*useless*
lejano	*far*
llantas	*tires*
materia prima	*raw material*
mirada	*look*
muro	*wall*
padecer	*to suffer (an illness)*
peinarse	*to comb your hair*
propósito	*purpose*
recibo	*receipt*
recorrer	*to cover, travel*
retrasarse	*to run late*
rueda	*wheel*
sondeo	*survey*
tarifa	*fee*
vapor	*steam*

Cognados

Review the cognates in *Adelante* and the false cognates in *¡Atención!* For a complete list of cognates, see Appendix 4 on page 605.

506 QU…   INVESTIGACIÓN 11A • QUINIENTOS SIETE 507

Vívelo: Cultura This box explores a cultural phenomenon either generally linked to the chapter topic or more tightly linked to an immediately following activity. ▶

Expresiones útiles This box appears when there is an opportunity to introduce high-frequency expressions that might be used in any variety of contexts and which are relevant for an immediately adjacent activity. ▼

VÍVELO: CULTURA
Reflejos de la tierra, por Diana N. González

Sonia Solanilla Morales (1975-), nacida en Penonomé, provincia de Coclé, Panamá, a través de su plástica (sus obras de arte) y creatividad, reivindica la riqueza cultural panameña y su infinito amor hacia la naturaleza. Confiesa ser una mujer orgullosa (*proud*) de sus raíces (*roots*) y agradecida con la vida. Su talento se dejó ver desde niña y una vez finalizados sus estudios secundarios decide profesionalizarse. Estudió Arte y Decoración en la Facultad de Arquitectura Española en Madrid (1975) y en la Escuela Nacional de Artes Mateo Inurria en Córdoba, España (1982).

La adquisición de estos conocimientos la llevó a personalizar su obra pictórica con gran fuerza cromática y con un demostrado equilibrio entre el realismo de sus personajes y la fascinación de su contexto basado en lo cotidiano (*the day-to-day*). Para ella, su obra trasciende de lo estético para poner al descubierto (*uncover*) el misterio que habita en el interior de sus personajes.

"En mis creaciones podrán ver el retrato de gente común, la vegetación voluptuosa y mágica, el estilo colorista e intenso que reflejan la tierra". Su deseo es presentar al espectador un conjunto emotivo y técnicamente

Fine art photo of painting by Son

...bados sus sentimientos diarios,
...cotidianas, a lo fantástico en la
...to y a lo maravilloso de cada de

EXPRESIONES ÚTILES
Preguntas y expresiones para la clase

Tengo una pregunta.	*I have a question.*
No entiendo.	*I don't understand.*
Repita, por favor.	*Say that again, please.*
Necesito más tiempo, por favor.	*I need more time, please.*
¿Está bien?	*Is it okay?*
¿Cómo se dice... en español?	*How do you say... in Spanish?*
¿Cómo?	*What? (Used when you didn't hear what was said to you.)*
¿Hay tarea?	*Is there homework?*
¿Para cuándo es?	*When is it due?*
¿Qué página?	*What page?*
Lo siento.	*I'm sorry.*
¿Qué significa...?	*What does... mean?*

DICHOS

Entre padres y hermanos no metas tus manos.	*Don't come between family members.*
De tal palo, tal astilla.	*Like father, like son.*

Dichos This box presents Spanish sayings and proverbs along with their English counterparts. ▲

Conéctate This box prompts students to explore the internet to access authentic content relevant to adjacent information and activities. ▶

www

¡Conéctate!
Would you like to see the world in just a few clicks? Download the free program Google Earth. Start out by typing in your address and see a satellite picture of where you live. Now venture out and explore some Spanish-speaking countries. Zoom in and look at the topography, vegetation, architecture. What countries did you explore? How do their features compare to where you live?

¡Vívelo! This section appears at the end of the chapter and includes conversational, writing, and video activities. *En vivo,* with one speaking activity and one writing activity engages students in meaningful, purposeful tasks. Writing activities, included from *Capítulo 3* on, guide students step-by-step through the process of organizing their thoughts, writing a draft, and revising and polishing their work. *En directo* exposes students to various people and places in the Spanish-speaking world. Activities check students' comprehension of the video segment and invite them to share their own thoughts on the themes explored. ▼

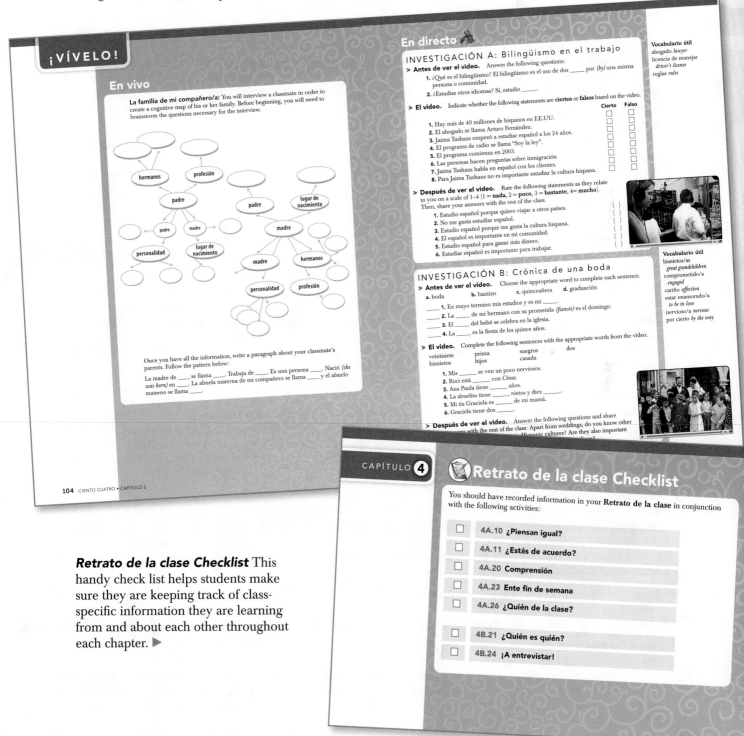

Retrato de la clase Checklist This handy check list helps students make sure they are keeping track of class-specific information they are learning from and about each other throughout each chapter. ▶

THE COMPLETE PROGRAM

To receive a review or desk copy of any of these program components, please contact your local Wiley sales representative or call our Sales Office at 1.800.237.2665.

▶ **Student Textbook**
Packaged with Textbook Audio CD
978-0-471-72776-7
The textbook is organized into twelve *Capítulos,* each of which is divided into two identically structured and thematically complementary *Investigaciones,* and culminates in the *¡Vívelo!* section which incorporates lively speaking activities, writing tasks, and video activities designed to give students a forum to put to use the language they have learned to creatively use.

▶ **Annotated Instructor's Edition**
Packaged with Textbook Audio CD
978-0-470-55497-5
The Annotated Instructor's Edition contains side notes with suggestions for teaching, meaningful structural exercises, suggestions for varying or expanding communicative activities, and audio scripts for aural input recorded on the accompanying CD. These annotations are especially helpful for first-time instructors.

▶ **Activities Manual**
978-0-471-72777-4
The Activities Manual links reading and writing, builds vocabulary, practices grammar, and helps students develop personal expression and composition skills through a variety of written and aural activities. Some activities are self correcting and the answer key appears at the end of the Activities Manual. Listening strands for the aural activities are available on the Lab Audio Program, or digitally in WileyPLUS.

▶ **Lab Audio Program**
978-0-470-50954-8
The Lab Audio Program is coordinated with the Activities Manual. The audio program is available on CD and also digitally in WileyPLUS for students and instructors. The audio transcript is included on the book Companion Site and in WileyPLUS.

▶ **¡Vívelo! Video**
978-0-470-58107-0
The *¡Vívelo! video* consists of text-specific and culturally-oriented segments correlated to activities in the chapter ending *¡Vívelo!* section. Throughout the segments, students will watch real-life interactions between native speakers of Spanish in the U.S. and abroad, in professional or social settings, in order to explore cultural topics presented in the textbook. The video is complimentary for instructors and can be purchased by students. It is also available digitally in Wiley*PLUS.*

This online teaching and learning environment integrates the entire digital textbook with the most effective instructor and student resources to fit every learning style. With Wiley*PLUS,* students achieve concept mastery in a rich, structured environment that's available 24/7, and instructors personalize and manage their course more effectively with assessment, assignments, grade tracking, and more. WileyPLUS can complement your current textbook or replace the printed text altogether.

▶ **Electronic Activities Manual**
WileyPLUS Premium offers an electronic version of the Activities Manual with its written and aural activities. This electronic version allows instructors to assign work to students that will be automatically graded as well as work that can be manually graded by the professor. *WileyPLUS* Premium also contains a gradebook that allows instructors to view class statistics in a variety of ways and that provides students with individual feedback. The electronic Activities Manual can be accessed from any computer with an Internet connection.

▶ **Book Companion Web Site for Students**
www.wiley.com/college/young/
The Book Companion Site for students contains complimentary self-tests, internet discovery activities, and audio flash cards.

▶ **Book Companion Web Site for Instructors**
www.wiley.com/college/young/
The Web site for instructors features online instructor resources including Word and computerized versions of the testing program and digital test audio files. It also includes the digital Lab Audio files, and online PowerPoint presentations for all sections of the chapters, answer keys for the Activities Manual and audio transcripts of the Lab Audio, sample syllabi, and guidelines for using the video.

CAPÍTULO 1   Los compañeros y la clase

CONTENTS

CONTENTS

CONTENTS

WILEY PLUS

In this preliminary **Investigación** you will learn:

- ▶ How to greet people in culturally appropriate ways
- ▶ How to ask questions to learn more about people
- ▶ How to get to know your classmates by sharing information
- ▶ How to refer to people and objects that have already been mentioned

What kind of information do you sometimes share with people when you first meet them?

You can ask people their names in culturally appropriate ways. You can offer your name in return.	¿Cómo se llama usted? ¿Cómo te llamas? Yo me llamo …
You can ask classmates how old they are. You can tell someone your age too.	¿Cuántos años tiene usted? ¿Cuántos años tiene ella? ¿Cuántos años tiene él? Tengo dieciocho años.
You can ask people where they are from. In return you can offer the same information about yourself.	¿De dónde es usted? ¿De California? ¿De dónde eres tú? Soy de Indiana. Soy de Venezuela. Soy de Nashville.
You can ask someone their telephone number and give your own.	¿Cuál es tu número de teléfono? Mi número de teléfono es el (555) 539-9110.

WILEY
PLUS

You will find
PowerPoint presentations
for use with *Saludos y
despedidas* in *WileyPLUS*.

Paso 1: Saludos y despedidas
(Greetings and good-byes)

SUGGESTION: You may want to walk around the room greeting students, asking for their name. Try to remember students' names. Then, tell the students that they have 10 minutes to learn the names of their classmates. Before anyone can actually give their name, however, they must be asked *¿Cómo te llamas?* Responses should begin *Me llamo...* or *Soy...* After 10 minutes, test student memories to see who can actually remember their classmates' names.

TEACHING TIP: Ask students what they think the difference is between *¿Cómo se llama usted?* and *¿Cómo te llamas?* based on the illustrations. Likewise, ask what they think the difference is between *Encantado* and *Encantada*. You can use these questions to introduce briefly the concepts of register (formality/informality) and gender, which students will explore more in depth later in the *Investigación preliminar* and in *Capítulo 1*.

IP.1 **A conocernos.** Greet two of the classmates seated near you and ask them their names. Then, introduce one of them to the other. Be sure to say goodbye to each other, in Spanish, at the end of class.

IP.2 **Hola y adiós.** Work with two classmates you don't know to create a brief skit in which you find out each other's names and how each other is doing, then take leave of each other. Use a variety of greetings and goodbyes in your skit, and be prepared to perform it in front of the class.

WILEY
PLUS

You will find
PowerPoint presentations
for use with *Los números
de 0 a 100* in WileyPLUS.

Paso 2: Los números de 0 a 100

cero	0	diecisiete	17	treinta y cuatro	34
uno	1	dieciocho	18	treinta y cinco	35
dos	2	diecinueve	19	treinta y seis	36
tres	3	veinte	20	treinta y siete	37
cuatro	4	veintiuno	21	treinta y ocho	38
cinco	5	veintidós	22	treinta y nueve	39
seis	6	veintitrés	23	cuarenta	40
siete	7	veinticuatro	24	cuarenta y uno	41
ocho	8	veinticinco	25	(etcétera)	…
nueve	9	veintiséis	26	cincuenta	50
diez	10	veintisiete	27	sesenta	60
once	11	veintiocho	28	setenta	70
doce	12	veintinueve	29	ochenta	80
trece	13	treinta	30	noventa	90
catorce	14	treinta y uno	31	cien	100
quince	15	treinta y dos	32		
dieciséis	16	treinta y tres	33		

TEACHING TIP: Give students five minutes to get as many of their classmates' phone numbers as possible by asking *¿Cuál es tu número de teléfono?* They should give them in the grouping most common in Latin America, as described in *Vívelo: Lengua.* Ask students to keep these phone numbers for a task later in this chapter. If students are not comfortable sharing their phone numbers, tell them they can make one up.

IP.3 TEACHING TIP: You will need to provide phone numbers for Activity IP.3. We suggest you identify frequently used numbers, such as the main office of the language department, the financial aid office, the main office of campus police, the advising center, or whatever numbers you deem important for students.

VÍVELO: LENGUA

Expressing phone numbers

The way Spanish-speakers group numbers when saying a telephone number may be different from your native-language convention. You might see 2-34-51-78 or 2.34.51.78. In Spanish this phone number would be uttered as **dos, treinta y cuatro, cincuenta y uno, setenta y ocho.** It is common for Spanish-speakers to say **el** before the numbers when giving their phone number, as in this exchange:

—¿Cuál es su número de teléfono?
—Es el dos, treinta y cuatro, cincuenta y uno, setenta y ocho.

IP.3 **Números de teléfono.** Listen as your instructor reads you telephone numbers that may come in handy in the future. Write the office or place on the left and the phone number on the right.

Oficina o lugar	Número de teléfono
1.	
2.	
3.	
4.	

Paso 3: Los datos personales
(Personal information)

WILEY **PLUS**

You will find PowerPoint presentations for use with *Los datos personales* in *WileyPLUS*.

Sustantivos (*Nouns:* Concepts, people, and things.)

el código postal
el compañero/la compañera de clase
la nacionalidad
el número del celular/móvil
el nombre

la dirección electrónica
la dirección residencial
el origen
la profesión
la relación

soltero/a

casado/a

divorciado/a

viudo/a

COGNATES: These words are cognates. Ask students to tell you what each item means without remarking that there are no translations given. Respond enthusiastically to good guesses, and underscore the importance of using cognates as a means toward comprehension. The two *investigaciones* that comprise each *capítulo* following this *Investigación preliminar* begin with a section called *Adelante* that presents a list of cognates. In *¡Vívelo!*, "cognates" are not strictly words that are spelled alike and have the same meaning in Spanish and English, but also words that share the same root as their English equivalent and related words whose meanings may vary somewhat in the two languages. Clear context in the activities and facile recognition of most items provides a comfortable environment for students as they begin exploring the *investigación* topic in general terms.

Los datos

Nombre: _Juan_	Apellido paterno: _Valdez_	Apellido materno: _García_

Edad: _19_

País de origen: _Estados Unidos_

Estado: _Texas_

Código postal: _78704_

Ciudad de residencia: _Austin_

Sexo: ☑ masculino ☐ femenino

Profesión: ☑ estudiante ☐ profesor/a

Estado civil: ☑ soltero/a ☐ casado/a ☐ divorciado/a ☐ viudo/a

Correo electrónico: _jvaldez@correo.com_

Teléfono residencial: _(213) 447 3219_

Teléfono celular/móvil: _(221) 358 6790_

ORIENTATION: DISCOVERY LEARNING. Research indicates that discovery learning may increase retention of information/vocabulary. On the basis of the completed form, ask students if they can guess what the following vocabulary words mean: *el apellido, la edad, la ciudad, el correo, el país, el estado, el estado civil*. Underscore the importance of context in discovering the meaning of the new words.

IP.4 **Tus datos personales.** Fill out this blank form with your own personal data, then exchange your filled out form with a classmate. Be prepared to share some of your classmate's information with the rest of the class.

Nombre: _____	Apellido paterno: _____	Apellido materno: _____

Edad: _____

País de origen: _____

Estado: _____

Código postal: _____

Ciudad de residencia: _____

Sexo: ☐ masculino ☐ femenino

Profesión: ☐ estudiante ☐ profesor/a

Estado civil: ☐ soltero/a ☐ casado/a ☐ divorciado/a ☐ viudo/a

Correo electrónico: _____

Teléfono residencial: _____

Teléfono celular/móvil: _____

IP.5   Suscríbete.

Paso 1:   Interview a classmate to obtain the specific information indicated on two of the subscription forms below. Write down your partner's information, then switch roles to complete two subscription forms each. Then, share the completed forms to ensure the information is correct.

> Modelo: Estudiante 1 reads and says: *Apellido*
> Estudiante 2 says: *Smith*
> Estudiante 1 writes: *Smith* next to the word "Apellido" on the form.

WILEY PLUS
IP.5 INSTRUCTOR'S RESOURCES You will find reproducible magazine subscription forms in your Instructor's Resources.

a

b

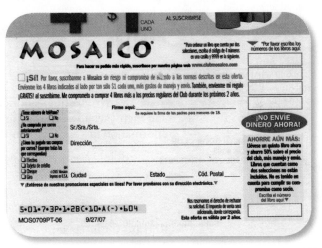

c

d

IP.5 TEACHING TIP: Point out that when filling out a form it is not necessary to use full questions like *How old are you?* One might simply ask, *Age?* But during a normal conversation questions and answers should be clear. Ask students to face each other so that they have to request the information orally as opposed to showing each other the forms and providing the answers without any type of solicitation.

Paso 2: Escucha e identifica. You will hear several questions about which forms require certain pieces of information. Identify the form being asked about in each question. **¡Ojo!** There may be more than one question about a given form. Verify your responses as a class.

Suscripción

	a	b	c	d			a	b	c	d
1.	☐	☑	☐	☐	4.		☐	☐	☑	☐
2.	☑	☐	☐	☐	5.		☐	☐	☐	☑
3.	☐	☐	☑	☐	6.		☐	☑	☐	☐

Go to *WileyPLUS* and review the tutorial for this grammar point.

VÍVELO: LENGUA

Expressing possession I: *Mi/mis, tu/tus, su/sus*

Use the following to express possesion as in **Mi número de teléfono es...** (*My phone number is...*).

mi	*my*
tu	*your* (informal)
su	*his/her, your* (formal)

Use **mis, tus** and **sus** to express possession of more than one thing.

Mis amigos son inteligentes.	*My friends are intelligent.*
Tus clases son interesantes.	*Your classes are interesting.*
Sus estudiantes son de Bolivia.	*His, Her, Your students are from Bolivia.*

TEACHING TIP: Present the possessive adjectives in a way that requires student participation and provides them with a lot of comprehensible input. Take things off of your desk, or out of your bag, and say things like, *Es mi libro., Son mis lápices.,* etc. Then ask students if the items you mentioned belong to them (e.g. *¿Es tu libro? ¿Son tus lápices?*). Take this a step further by taking an item from several students in your class, and then asking them randomly, *¿Es tu calculadora?* The idea is to make this interactive, and to get students to begin answering using *mi/mis/tu/tus/su/sus* correctly. Students may find it easier to express possession with *nuestro/a/os/as* later on by first using these more transparent forms. This exercise will also start to familiarize students with some of the classroom vocabulary they will study in *Capítulo 1* and the present tense of *ser*.

IP.6 **¡A escribir!**

Paso 1: Write a brief summary of your **datos personales** using the **modelo** below and then exchange your summary with a classmate. Write your classmate's personal information in your **Retrato de la clase.**

> Modelo: *Nombre: Cristina.*
> *Origen: Soy de Florida.*
> *Correo electrónico: Mi correo electrónico es cristina2@correo.com.*
> *Número de teléfono: Mi número de teléfono es el....*

Retrato de la clase:
Nombre: _____.
Origen: Mi compañero/a de clase es de _____.
Correo electrónico: Su correo electrónico es _____.
Número de teléfono: Su número de teléfono es el _____.

Paso 2: Now, compare your notes with three other classmates and summarize your findings in your **Retrato de la clase.**

Retrato de la clase: La mayoría *(majority)* de la clase es de _____. La mayoría de la clase es de sexo ☐ masculino ☐ femenino. Hay _____ estudiantes en la clase de español.

RETRATO DE LA CLASE. Explain to students that now and then they will need to record information about students or about the entire class in a notebook they should title *Retrato de la clase*. In addition to helping create a learner-centered environment, another goal of this class profile is for students to have information they can use for various purposes. Placing a value on information that classmates share sends the message that Spanish is being used not only for "practice," but to actually convey information for a purpose. Each of the subsequent chapters has a *Retrato de la clase* checklist at the end that indicates for which activities students should have recorded information.

IP.7 **Para conocernos mejor.** Share some information about yourself and find out some things about a classmate and your instructor.

A. Complete these statements with **mi** or **mis**, and indicate whether, for you, each statement is **cierto** *(true)* or **falso** *(false)*. Then, share your responses with a classmate.

	Cierto	Falso
1. _____ amigos son inteligentes.	☐	☐
2. _____ mejor *(best)* amigo es estudiante.	☐	☐
3. _____ profesores son responsables.	☐	☐
4. _____ profesor de español es bueno.	☐	☐
5. _____ primer *(first)* nombre es común.	☐	☐

B. Ask a classmate the following questions using **tu** or **tus**. Indicate his/her responses as **Sí** or **No**.

	Sí	No
1. ¿Es _____ mamá de Perú?	☐	☐
2. ¿Son _____ padres *(parents)* de Estados Unidos?	☐	☐
3. ¿Es _____ papá de Canadá?	☐	☐
4. ¿Es grande *(big)* _____ familia?	☐	☐

C. Ask your instructor the following questions using **su** or **sus**. Indicate his/her responses as **Sí** or **No**.

	Sí	No
1. ¿Es interesante _____ rutina diaria?	☐	☐
2. ¿Son tímidos _____ estudiantes?	☐	☐
3. ¿Es agradable _____ profesión?	☐	☐
4. ¿Son optimistas _____ colegas?	☐	☐

www **¡Conéctate!**
What magazines do you like? Search for some of the magazines you like online. Is there a Spanish version of the magazine? Is the website available in Spanish as well? Can you subscribe online in Spanish?

IP.7 TEACHING TIP: Students are likely to be unfamiliar with a lot of the vocabulary used in Activity IP.7. Point out that these words are cognates and that they should be able to understand them without difficulty. Challenge students to tell you what *Es de...* and *Son de...* mean. Ask how they figured it out as a lead-in to talking about context. Remark again on the importance of cognates and context in learning Spanish, and foster a feeling of accomplishment among your students for being able to understand the statements in this activity. Working with cognates will be an important first step in each *Investigación* in subsequent chapters.

Paso 4: Asking questions

Preguntas (*Questions*)	Respuestas (*Answers*)
¿Cuántos?/¿Cuántas? (*How many?*)	
¿Cuántos años tiene usted? (*How old are you?*)	Tengo ___ años. (*I am ___ years old.*)
¿Cuántos años tienes tú?	
¿Cuántas personas hay en la clase?	Hay veinte personas.
¿Cuántos objetos hay en la clase?	Hay veinte objetos.
¿De dónde? (*From where?*)	
¿De dónde es usted?	Soy de Argentina.
¿De dónde eres tú?	
¿Dónde? (*Where?*)	
¿Dónde vive usted? (*Where do you live?*)	Vivo en Puerto Rico.
¿Dónde vives tú?	
¿Cuál? (*Which, What?*)	
¿Cuál es su número de teléfono?	Mi número de teléfono es…
¿Cuál es tu número de teléfono?	

Notice two primary features when writing or reading sentences that ask questions. First, questions in Spanish require an inverted question mark (¿) at the beginning and a regular question mark at the end. Second, every interrogative word requires a written accent over the first or second vowel. As you learn interrogative words, learn where the written accent falls.

IP.8 **¿Qué dices?** In pairs, match each question in Spanish to the task (**función**) it respresents. Two of the questions will not have a corresponding task in English. If your group finishes early, take turns asking and answering the questions in Spanish.

Preguntas

__5__ **a.** ¿Cuál es tu teléfono?

__10__ **b.** ¿Cuántos años tienes?

__1__ **c.** ¿Cuántos años tiene?

__6__ **d.** ¿Cuál es su correo electrónico?

__8__ **e.** ¿De dónde eres?

__2__ **f.** ¿Cuántos estudiantes hay en la clase?

____ **g.** ¿Cuál es su teléfono?

__3__ **h.** ¿Cómo te llamas?

__9__ **i.** ¿Cómo se llama?

__7__ **j.** ¿Cuál es tu teléfono celular/móvil?

____ **k.** ¿De dónde es?

__4__ **l.** ¿Cuántas mujeres hay en la clase?

Funciones

1. Ask someone how old he/she is (formal).

2. Ask someone how many students are in your class.

3. Ask someone for his/her name (informal).

4. Ask someone how many women are in your class.

5. Ask someone for his/her phone number (informal).

6. Ask for someone's e-mail (formal).

7. Ask a friend for his/her cell phone number.

8. Ask a friend what country he/she is from.

9. Ask someone you do not know for his/her name.

10. Ask a friend how old he/she is.

IP.9 **Para conocer a Elizabeth Vargas.** Read the description of the ABC reporter, anchor, and host of the news program *20/20*. Then, listen to several questions about her and write down your answers. Confirm your answers with several classmates.

Elizabeth Vargas es reportera del programa de investigación *20/20*. Nació *(she was born)* en Paterson, Nueva Jersey, el 6 de septiembre de 1962. Es expresiva, independiente, interesante y muy inteligente. Su padre es puertorriqueño y su madre es irlandesa-americana.

1. _____   4. _____

2. _____   5. _____

3. _____

IP.10 **¿Quién es el estudiante más joven de la clase?** Find out who is the youngest student in class by asking each classmate, **¿Cómo te llamas?** and **¿Cuántos años tienes?** Make a list to keep notes of your answers. Write your classmate's first name or initials. Record that information in your **Retrato de la clase.**

> Modelo: E1: *¿Cómo te llamas?*   E2: *Me llamo Eva Méndez.*
> E1: *¿Cuántos años tienes?*   E2: *Tengo veinte años.*

Retrato de la clase: El/La estudiante más joven *(youngest)* se llama _____.

IP.11 **Si la respuesta es... la pregunta es...** Write the question (formal) for each of the answers given below. Compare your questions with those of two other classmates.

> Modelo: You read: *Estoy bien, gracias.*
> You write: *¿Cómo está?*

¿De dónde es usted? **1.** Soy de Costa Rica.

¿Cuál es su teléfono móvil? **2.** Mi teléfono móvil es 45-987-45-78.

¿Cuántos años tiene? **3.** Tengo 21 años.

¿Cuántos estudiantes hay en la clase? **4.** Hay 25 estudiantes en la clase.

¿Cómo se llama usted? **5.** Soy María Salas.

IP.12 **Libreta de direcciones.** You have acquired some information about your classmates based on previous tasks. Create a chart like the sample below with the information you have up to now. Keep this information in your **Retrato de la clase.**

Mi clase de español				
Nombre	¿De dónde es?	Edad	Número de teléfono	Dirección electrónica

IP.13 **¡A analizar!** Examine the information in your completed **Libreta de direcciones** from Activity IP.12. Then, answer the following questions based on it. Afterwards, check your answers as a class.

¿Cómo se llama...

... el estudiante más joven *(youngest)*/mayor *(oldest)* de la clase?

... el estudiante con el correo electrónico más misterioso/con más letras/con más números?

¿Cuántos estudiantes no son de este estado/país *(country)*?

¿Cuántos estudiantes son mujeres y cuántos son hombres?

En términos generales, ¿cómo se caracteriza esta clase?
¿Es mayormente estadounidense *(from the US)* o es mayormente internacional?

IP.9 AUDIO SCRIPT AND ANSWERS: 1. ¿Cómo se llama? (Elizabeth Vargas), 2. ¿De dónde es? (de Nueva Jersey), 3. ¿De dónde es su papá? (de Puerto Rico), 4. ¿Cuál es su profesión? (reportera), 5. ¿Cómo es ella? (Accept any of the following: expresiva, independiente, interesante, inteligente.)

IP.9 SUGGESTION: Draw students' attention to how Elizabeth Vargas' date of birth is expressed in Spanish— *el (día) de (mes) de (año).*

IP.10 TEACHING TIP: Tell students that they do not need to provide their true ages. As a follow-up to the question, ask *¿Quién es el estudiante más joven de la clase?* Ask for specific ages to narrow down the possibilities, such as *¿Quién tiene diecisiete años?*

It is important for students to keep all information they have gathered from classmates. The more information they have available, the less class time will be needed to complete the task.

IP.11 TEACHING TIP: Have five volunteers write questions for items 1–5 on the board. Go over their questions as a class. Draw attention to the upside down question mark and the accented vowel. Have students repeat the exercise, this time with an informal context.

WILEY
PLUS

IP.12 INSTRUCTOR'S RESOURCES: You will find a reproducible chart for use in completing this activitiy in your Instructor's Resources.

IP.13 TEACHING TIP: Ask several questions to offer more language input and invite students to look over their charts e.g. *¿Es Kyle de Texas?* Instruct students to keep their charts from IP.12 and answers to IP.13 and place them in their *Retrato de la clase* for future use.

WILEY
PLUS

You will find PowerPoint presentations for use with *Subject pronouns* in *WileyPLUS*.

Paso 5: Subject pronouns

Pronouns are words we use to replace a noun in order to avoid naming that noun over and over again. For example, once the conversation establishes that we are talking about Alex Rodríguez and Oscar De la Hoya, instead of saying Alex and Oscar we say *they*. Instead of saying *You, Shanna, Robert and I*, we use the subject pronoun *we*. Once the subject of a sentence has been established, we replace it with a subject pronoun. Examine the subject pronouns for English and Spanish in the chart below.

Yo	*I*
Tú (Informal/familiar) **Usted (Ud.)*** (formal)	*You*
Él, Ella	*He, She, It*
Nosotros, Nosotras	*We*
Vosotros, Vosotras (informal in Spain) **Ustedes (Uds.)*** (formal in Spain/both formal and informal in Latin America)	*You, Y'all*
Ellos, Ellas	*They*

*Since the verb forms for **usted** (*you* singular, formal) and **ustedes** (*you* plural, formal) are the same as the third person singular (**él/ella**) and the third person plural (**ellos/ellas**), respectively, verb charts in *¡Vívelo!* will group them together. Note that the abbreviations **Ud.** and **Uds.** are always capitalized in Spanish.

Which language has more subject pronouns? Based on the chart, what subject pronouns in Spanish refer to females only? What subject pronouns refer to males only? What subject pronouns indicate formality?

When referring to a group of females, use **ellas.** When referring to a group composed of males, or males and females, use **ellos.** Follow the same guidelines for using **vosotros/vosotras** and **nosotros/nosotras.**

ORIENTATION: The section entitled *Vívelo: Cultura* appearing throughout each *Investigación* offers cultural information and poses questions that stimulates students' thinking and reflection and develops their intercultural awareness. Beyond discussing these sections in class, consider having students journal on the topics. You should also seek out students' responses to how their individual cultures perceive some of these topics, as "US culture" is not monolithic.

VÍVELO: CULTURA

Tú y usted

Just as there are formal and less formal gestures and customs related to greeting, Spanish has a linguistically appropriate formal and an informal way of addressing people. Depending on the country, it is customary to use **usted** with a new acquaintance or to show respect, as in **¿Cómo se llama usted?** Sometimes **usted** is used with almost everyone in order not to be interpreted as disrespectful. Only after asking permission, particularly in a formal context, should you use the **tú** form. In some Spanish-speaking countries, such as Spain, the use of **usted** among peers is not as common as it used to be. In most Latin American countries however, one should assume this is the convention because it is best to err on the side of being overly respectful than vice versa.

In Argentina and Uruguay, the pronoun **vos** is generally used instead of **tú**. In some other places, such as parts of Chile, Guatemala, and Honduras, to name a few, **tú** is used in some informal contexts while **vos** signifies an even greater level of intimacy or informality. In Latin America, **ustedes** is the plural form used in both formal and informal contexts, while in Spain, the informal **vosotros/vosotras** is used as the plural of **tú**. A good strategy is to pay attention to how native speakers deal with the use of **usted, tú, vos,** and **vosotros/vosotras**. As you will see in *Capítulo 1*, each of these ways of addressing people uses its own particular verb forms.

IP.14 **Correspondencias.** Listen to several references to specific people. Then, match the subject pronouns in a–e that could be used instead of the names. The first one is done for you as a model. Verify your answers with a classmate.

<u>5</u> **a.** él   <u>4</u> **d.** ellas

<u>2</u> **b.** ellos   <u>3</u> **e.** nosotros

<u>1</u> **c.** ella

IP.15 **Repita, por favor.** Listen to several statements and write the number of each statement next to its corresponding question. One of the questions will not correspond to any of the statements you will hear; leave it blank. The first one is done for you as a model. Verify your answers with a classmate.

Repita, por favor….

<u>3</u> **a.** ¿Cuántos años tiene ella?   <u>4</u> **e.** ¿De dónde eres tú?

<u>6</u> **b.** ¿Cuántos años tenemos nosotros?   <u>5</u> **f.** ¿Qué es usted?

<u>2</u> **c.** ¿Qué son ellos?   <u>___</u> **g.** ¿Cuántos años tiene él?

<u>___</u> **d.** ¿Qué somos nosotros?

IP.16 **¿Relación formal o informal?** Can you discern the characteristics that distinguish a formal from an informal greeting in your native culture? Based on your native culture, indicate as a class whether the relationship between the people in each photo is formal or informal.

¿Es la relación entre estas personas formal o informal? ¿Cómo lo sabes? *(How do you know?)*

2.

1.

3.

WILEY PLUS

You will find PowerPoint presentations for use with *Subject pronouns* in *WileyPLUS*.

IP.14 AUDIO SCRIPT:
1. Rosario Dawson, 2. Eduardo Yáñez y Pablo Montero, 3. Los estudiantes de la clase, tú y yo, 4. Jessica Alba and Cristina Aguilera, 5. Juan Carlos

IP.15 AUDIO SCRIPT: 1. Antonio tiene 51 años. 2. Chelsea Clinton y Prince Andrew son estudiantes. 3. María Luisa tiene 50 años. 4. Amigo, soy de Perú. 5. Soy profesora. 6. María, tú y yo tenemos 17 años.

IP.16 FOLLOW-UP: Factors that can influence greeting behaviors include context, such as formal or informal, the type of relationship that exists between people, i.e., friends, acquaintances, strangers, the social and economic status of the involved parties, etc. The native culture of your students may not be the same. Make sure to explore similarities and/or unique behaviors based on the diversity of cultures represented in your class.

Vocabulario: Investigación preliminar

Vocabulario esencial

Hola	*Hi*
Buenos días	*Good morning, Good day*
Buenas tardes	*Good afternoon*
Buenas noches	*Good night*
¿Cómo se llama usted?	*What is your name?* (formal)
¿Cómo te llamas?	*What is your name?* (familiar/informal)
Me llamo…	*My name is…*
Soy…	*I am…*
¿Cómo está usted?	*How are you?* (formal)
¿Cómo estás?	*How are you?* (informal)
Bien. ¿Y usted?	*Fine, and you?*
Regular	*So-so, Okay*
Mal	*Bad, not well*
Le presento a Javier.	*This is Javier.* (formal)
Te presento a Javier.	*This is Javier.* (informal)
Mucho gusto	*Nice to meet you*
Encantado/a	*Delighted to meet you*
Igualmente	*Likewise*
Hasta pronto	*See you soon*
Hasta mañana	*See you tomorrow*
Hasta luego	*See you later*
Nos vemos	*See you later*
Adiós	*Goodbye*
Chau/chao	*Goodbye*
¿Cuántos años tiene usted?	*How old are you?* (formal)
¿Cuántos años tienes tú?	*How old are you?* (informal)
Tengo… años.	*I am… years old.*
¿De dónde es usted?	*Where are you from?* (formal)
¿De dónde eres tú?	*Where are you from?* (informal)
Soy de…	*I am from…*
¿Dónde vive usted?	*Where do you live?* (formal)
¿Dónde vives tú?	*Where do you live?* (informal)
Vivo en…	*I live in…*
¿Cuál es su número de teléfono?	*What is your phone number?* (formal)
¿Cuál es tu número de teléfono?	*What is your phone number?* (informal)
Mi número de teléfono es…	*My phone number is…*
¿Cuántos/as… hay?	*How many… are there?*
Hay	*There is/are…*

apellido	*last name*
el código postal	*zip/postal code*
el compañero/ la compañera de clase	*classmate*
la nacionalidad	*nationality*
el celular/el móvil	*cell phone*
el nombre	*name*
la dirección (electrónica)	*(email) address*
el origen	*origin*
la profesión	*profession*
la relación	*relationship*

Be sure to study the numbers on page 4.

Los compañeros y la clase

WILEY PLUS

INVESTIGACIÓN 1A
¿Cómo eres y qué te gusta hacer?

ADELANTE

► ¡Ya lo sabes! Palabras descriptivas y acciones
► Ways to greet others
Bien dicho: Los sonidos del alfabeto

PALABRAS CLAVE

► Las actividades

ESTRUCTURAS CLAVE

► The verb *ser*

VÍVELO: LENGUA

► Expressing preferences about activities: *Me/te/le gusta*
► Expressing origin with *ser*

VÍVELO: CULTURA

► ¡Cuidado con los gestos!

CONTEXTOS Y PERSPECTIVAS

Los malentendidos culturales

INVESTIGACIÓN 1B
La clase de español y la universidad

ADELANTE

► ¡Ya lo sabes! Actividades en clase
► La educación

Bien dicho: Linking sounds in Spanish *(Enlaces)*

PALABRAS CLAVE

► Acciones de la clase
► En la clase
► Lugares en la universidad

ESTRUCTURAS CLAVE

► Nouns: Number and gender
► Definite and indefinite articles

VÍVELO: LENGUA

► Expressing "there is/there are": *Hay*
► Expressing ownership with *ser*

VÍVELO: CULTURA

► El papel de la Iglesia
► Los malentendidos culturales

CONTEXTOS Y PERSPECTIVAS

Sistemas educativos

¡VÍVELO!

En vivo:
¡Ay, caramba!

En directo:
A: ¡Bienvenido al mundo hispano!
B: Una visita a la UNAM

¿Cómo eres y qué te gusta hacer?

In this **Investigación** you will learn:

- ▶ How to talk about personality traits
- ▶ More about greeting behaviors among Spanish speakers
- ▶ How to talk about various activities and preferences regarding those activities
- ▶ About the Spanish alphabet and spelling
- ▶ How to express where you or someone else is from

How can you get to know your classmates better?

You can inquire about someone's personality and express your own.	¿Cómo es usted? ¿responsable? ¿independiente? ¿Cómo es ella? ¿optimista? ¿inteligente? ¿Cómo es él? ¿cómico? ¿sociable? Soy perfeccionista y tímida.
You can ask someone to spell his/her name, if necessary.	¿Cómo se deletrea? Mi nombre se deletrea *ele-u-i-ese-a*.
You can ask someone if he/she likes to do various activities, and tell him/her what you like to do.	¿Te gusta jugar al fútbol? Me gusta tocar la guitarra.

ORIENTATION: Each chapter is divided into two *Investigaciones*. At the beginning of each *Investigación*, a chart will list the language goals or functions on the left and sample usage in Spanish on the right. Draw your students' attention to this preview of the language and content of the *Investigación*.

Adelante

¡Ya lo sabes! Palabras descriptivas y acciones

The words below are called cognates because the Spanish and English equivalents resemble each other. For example, *important* in English is **importante** in Spanish. Your comprehension in Spanish will grow exponentially by learning how to be a strategic language learner: recognizing cognates is also the first step in facilitating Spanish literacy.

ADELANTE: The vocabulary introduced in *Adelante* should not be used as a word list for students to memorize. Instead, these words allow students to work beyond their limited proficiency in Spanish and lower anxiety about not being able to understand things. Keep in mind that expansion of students' repertoire of vocabulary for comprehension purposes is a major objective of this section.

TEACHING TIP: Draw attention to the adjectives that end in *–o/–a*. Without going into extensive detail, lead students to discover that nouns in Spanish are either masculine or feminine, and that *–o* endings are used for adjectives describing masculine nouns and *–a* for adjectives describing feminine nouns, as in *Hannah Montana es fotogénica y Peyton Manning es fotogénico*. Inform stu-

atlético/a	perfecto/a	completar
cómico/a	pesimista	comunicar
complicado/a	respetuoso/a	estudiar
emocional	responsable/irresponsable	expresar
estable/inestable	sociable	pronunciar
extrovertido/a	tímido/a	
fotogénico/a		
generoso/a		
independiente		
inteligente		
introvertido/a		
optimista		
perfeccionista		

dents that cognates may be easier to recognize in writing than orally. This is because the stress may not fall on the same syllables in Spanish as English. Consequently, to practice recognizing Spanish cognates expressed orally, they will need to complete listening tasks in the text and Activities Manual. Hearing the cognates as they are pronounced in Spanish will greatly facilitate how quickly they will be able to recognize them in class next time.

1A.1 **Tu personalidad.** How would you describe yourself? Indicate the four words that best describe you. Then, ask individual classmates **¿Cómo eres?** *(What are you like?)* until you find someone with responses most similar to yours. The next time you need a partner, work with this person.

> Modelo: E1: *¿Cómo eres?*
> E2: *Soy. . .*

☐ atlético/a   ☐ cómico/a   ☐ complicado/a   ☐ emocional

☐ estable   ☐ inestable   ☐ extrovertido/a   ☐ introvertido/a

☐ optimista   ☐ pesimista   ☐ perfeccionista   ☐ respetuoso/a

☐ responsable   ☐ irresponsable   ☐ tímido/a   ☐ independiente

1A.2 **¿Cómo es?** Listen to the descriptions of several famous people and indicate whether each statement is **cierto** *(true)* or **falso** *(false)*. Then, list at least three other famous people and write an adjective that describes each. Share your names and descriptions with the class to see which famous people were selected and how they were described. How would you respond to your classmates' descriptions? Are they **ciertas** or **falsas**?

> Modelo: You hear: Paris Hilton es materialista.
> You indicate: Cierto

	Cierto	Falso			Cierto	Falso
1.	☐	☑		5.	☑	☐
2.	☑	☐		6.	☐	☑
3.	☑	☐		7.	☑	☐
4.	☐	☑		8.	☐	☑

Ways to greet others

You have practiced appropriate language for greeting people and taking leave in Spanish. Greetings, however, involve physical gestures that correspond to the linguistic ones. Look at these photos that capture various greeting behaviors.

a.

c.

b.

d.

1A.1 TEACHING TIP: In reviewing the answers to this task, ensure that students hear the correct pronunciation from you.

1A.1 TEACHING TIP: After students have completed this activity, process it with the class. Consider asking individual students *¿Cómo eres?* After several students have answered, ask the class *¿Cómo es él/ella?* Do this in order to practice the vocabulary and learn more about your students. This activity also serves to introduce the expressions for "What are you like?" and "I am..." and begins to use subject pronouns, such as *yo, tú, él,* and *ella* without having to go into elaborate explanations.

1A.2 AUDIO SCRIPT: 1. Robin Williams es tímido. 2. Barack Obama es responsable. 3. Peyton Manning es atlético. 4. Beyoncé es inestable. 5. Sponge Bob es cómico. 6. Hanna Montana es introvertida. 7. Queen Latifah es independiente. 8. Angelina Jolie es pesimista.

1A.2 TEACHING TIP: Ask students to provide the names of the famous people they came up with and write them on the board. Then, ask *¿Cómo es (name)?* and repeat back student responses using *Sí, él es...* or *ella es...* so that students hear this repeated and associate the question *¿Cómo es...?* with *él/ella* in contrast to the previous use of *¿Cómo eres tú?*

1A.3 **¿Qué observas?** Look at the photos on page 17 with a classmate and reflect together on the following questions.

1. Which of these photos represent typical greeting behaviors in your native culture?
2. What factors determine how you greet someone in your culture?
3. Which of the photos do you think represent typical greeting behaviors in Spanish-speaking cultures?
4. What are some factors that you think likely determine greeting behaviors among Spanish speakers?

1A.4 **Estilo personal.** How would you describe your personal communicative style? Check the statements that correspond to you (most words in these sentences are cognates).

☐ Necesito mi espacio personal.   ☐ No necesito mi espacio personal.

☐ Prefiero contacto físico.   ☐ No prefiero contacto físico.

☐ Mi reacción depende de las personas.   ☐ Mi reacción depende de la cultura.

VÍVELO: CULTURA

¡Cuidado con los gestos! *(Be careful with gestures)*

Like communicative patterns, all cultures have ways of communicating through gestures. Discrepancies in the "vocabulary" of gestures may vary from one culture to another potentially leading to cross-cultural misunderstandings, such as the one illustrated below.

Malentendido cultural

Según dónde, pedir dos cervezas entraña peligro
En la barra de un pub inglés es preferible no alzar dos dedos en forma de V para indicar que queremos un par de tragos. Ese signo en un país anglosajón equivale a decirle al camarero "¡vete a ...!".

Cultural misunderstandings: Asking for two beers can lead to dangerous entanglings depending on where you are asking. In the bar of an English pub, it is better not to raise two fingers in the form of a V to indicate that you want two beers. In British culture, this sign equates to telling the waiter "Go to H…"

1A.5 **Más allá de la clase.** Conduct a search on the Internet for information on gestures that are part of your native culture but would be taboo in a Spanish-speaking culture, or vice-versa. Share the essential elements of your research with the class. The Spanish word for *gestures* is **gestos**, which may be helpful in your search.

Bien dicho

El alfabeto

Even though the alphabet in Spanish looks like the English alphabet, the names of the letters are pronounced differently. The letters in parenthesis *(ch, ll)* are treated as separate letters in dictionaries published before approximately 1998. If you have an older dictionary, be aware, for example, that there might be a section for words starting with *ch* after the words that begin with *cu*.

a	*a*	j	*jota*	r	*ere*
b	*be*	k	*ka*	rr	*erre*
c	*ce*	l	*ele*	s	*ese*
(ch	*che)*	(ll	*elle)*	t	*te*
d	*de*	m	*eme*	u	*u*
e	*e*	n	*ene*	v	*ve, uve**
f	*efe*	ñ	*eñe*	w	*doble ve, uve doble*
g	*ge*	o	*o*	x	*equis*
h	*hache*	p	*pe*	y	*i griega*
i	*i*	q	*cu*	z	*zeta*

* Also used are *ve baja, ve corta*. When spelling out loud, speakers often use *"v de vaca/b de burro"* or *"b grande"* and *"v chica"* to distinguish between the letters b/v.

1A.6 **¿Cómo se deletrea el apellido?**   You will hear the spelling of several surnames in Spanish. Write the number that corresponds to the spelling of each name on the blank next to it. The first one is done for you as a model.

_5_	Rulfo	_3_	Neruda	_6_	Acevedo
_2_	Sosa	_4_	Zamora	_1_	Soler

1A.7 **¿Cuál es su apellido?**   Write your last name backwards on a piece of paper. Then, in pairs, take turns spelling your name backwards to each other in Spanish but in the chart below write the true last name of your partner under the first letter that begins his/her last name. Repeat this process with two other classmates. Then, as a class, confirm all last names under each letter.

Modelo: E1 says: *Mi apellido es "ese e ene o jota".*
          E2 writes: *"s e n o j"*, then says *Jones* and writes *Jones* in the box with the letter "j".

A	B	C	D	E
F	G	H	I	J
K	L	M	N	O
P	Q	R	S	T
U	V	W	X	Y
Z				

TEACHING TIP: As you review the pronunciation of the Spanish alphabet, take a moment at the appropriate letter to mention key pronunciation items, such as *h* not being pronounced in Spanish, the letter *v* being pronounced in Spanish as [b] and the letter *z* in Spanish being pronounced as [s], except in Spain. Additional practice will appear in later *Investigaciones*. You also might want to point out that the Spanish sounds for the letters *p, t* and *k* contain no puff of air, or aspiration, as they do in English. In addition, point out that the pronunciation of some letters may change depending on the region.

TEACHING TIP: A recording of the alphabet is available on the Audio CD and online, but you may want to model pronunciation of the alphabet in class.

1A.6 AUDIO SCRIPT: 1. ese-o-ele-e-ere, 2. ese-o-ese-a, 3. ene-e-ere-u-de-a, 4. zeta-a-eme-o-ere-a; 5. ere-u-ele-efe-o; 6 a-ce-e-uve-e-de-o (also a-ce-e-ve-e-de-o)

1A.7 TEACHING TIP: Spelling names backwards prevents students from simply guessing the last letters of someone's name without hearing the letters pronounced.

WILEY
PLUS 1A.7
INSTRUCTOR'S RESOURCES: You will find a reproducible chart for use with this activity in your Instructor's Resources.

Palabras clave 1 Las actividades

TEACHING TIP: Point out that *fútbol* in Spanish is the equivalent of *soccer* in American English. For American style football, they should use *fútbol americano*. Also point out that Spanish uses *jugar* as the equivalent of *to play* with sports and games, but uses *tocar* as the equivalent of *to play* with musical instruments. Consider acting out the meaning of the words so that students can call out the verb in Spanish. Ask students for other ways to act out the meaning of the words and then give a time limit and place them in pairs to see how many they can act out within the time you give. Remember, if we attach a gesture to a word, we can retain it longer.

caminar

bailar salsa

nadar en el mar

cocinar hamburguesas

llamar a un amigo

correr en el parque

dibujar

escribir tu nombre

visitar a los amigos

escuchar música

hablar por teléfono

tocar un instrumento

1A.8 INSTRUCTOR'S RESOURCES: You will find a reproducible chart for this activity in your Instructor's Resources.

1A.8 RECYCLING: By identifying the least number of people for each activity, numbers get recycled and the meaning of the activity is also verified.

1A.8 Categorías. Create a chart like the one below. Look at the verbs illustrated above and place them into the appropriate categories in your chart. Then, to the right of each activity, indicate the least number of individuals that can participate in it. A few have been done as models. Check your lists with two other classmates for differences and share those with the class.

Acciones sedentarias	Acciones físicas o deportivas	Actividades creativas o intelectuales	Otras
comer pizza (1)	*levantar pesas (1)*	*dibujar (1)*	*llamar a un amigo (2)*

1A.8 ANSWERS: Acciones sedentarias: hablar por teléfono (2), escribir (1), mirar la televisión (1), comer pizza (1), jugar videojuegos (1), escuchar música (1). Acciones deportivas o físicas: caminar (1), bailar (1), nadar (1), levantar pesas (1), andar en bicicleta (1), jugar deportes (1), correr en el parque (1). Actividades creativas o intelectuales: escribir (1), dibujar (1), tocar un instrumento (1), cantar (1). Otras: cocinar (1), tomar agua (1), comer pizza (1), visitar a amigos (2), llamar a un amigo (2). Note that some answers may vary.

jugar deportes

andar en bicicleta

el tenis

el fútbol

levantar pesas

comer pizza

el béisbol

tomar agua

mirar la tele
(la televisión)

jugar videojuegos

cantar

manejar

1A.9 **Asociaciones.** With a partner, match each activity in column A with something associated with that activity in column B following the model. Review your responses with the class.

A

1. _c_ cantar
2. _h_ llamar a un amigo
3. _b_ bailar
4. _g_ comer
5. _c_ andar en bicicleta
6. _f_ mirar un documental
7. _j_ escribir
8. _d_ jugar deportes
9. _a_ tocar un instrumento musical
10. _i_ nadar

B

a. guitarra, piano, flauta
b. salsa, merengue, cumbia, reguetón
c. en un parque
d. el tenis, el fútbol
e. Christina Aguilera
f. el televisor, la computadora
g. frutas, hamburguesas, tomates
h. por teléfono, walkie talkie, Skype
i. en el mar *(sea)*
j. una novela

1A.9 TEACHING TIP: MULTIPLE INTELLIGENCES. Before beginning activity 1A.9, tap into students' kinesthetic intelligence by having them take turns acting out the vocabulary in column A with a partner, eliciting responses (e.g. student A acts out eating, and student B says *comer*).

VÍVELO: LENGUA

Expressing preferences about activities: *Me/te/le gusta*

¿Qué le gusta hacer?	*(What do you like to do?) (formal)*
¿Qué te gusta hacer?	*(What do you like to do?) (informal)*
¿Le gusta bailar?	*(Do you like to dance?) (formal)*
¿Te gusta bailar?	*(Do you like to dance?) (informal)*
Sí, me gusta bailar.	*(Yes, I like to dance.)*
No, no me gusta bailar.	*(No, I do not like to dance.)*

 Go to *WileyPLUS* and review the tutorial for this grammar point.

1A.10 ¿Qué le gusta hacer? For each of the activities you hear, write the name of someone commonly associated with the activity. Then, share your responses with the class. Were there any activities for which no one thought of a name?

> Modelo: You hear: *Le gusta cantar.*
> You write: *David Archuleta* (or whatever singer comes to mind)

1A.11 ¡A conocer a Sandra Cisneros! Read the short passage about a popular Mexican-American writer in the United States. Then, infer from the passage her likes and dislikes. Share your inferences with the rest of the class.

Sandra Cisneros, novelista y poeta estadounidense, nació *(was born)* en Chicago, Illinois el 20 de diciembre de 1954. Su padre era *(was)* mexicano y su madre era méxico-americana. Es famosa por escribir sobre la experiencia latina en Estados Unidos. Su colección de cuentos más famosa, **La casa en Mango Street** *(The House on Mango Street)* vendió *(sold)* más de dos millones de copias. Vive en San Antonio, Texas. Le gusta preparar platos deliciosos para su familia y sus amigos. También le gusta la música de los Texas Tornadoes, Los Lonely Boys y Tish Hinojosa. Le gusta observar a la gente *(people)* y una cosa que le gusta mucho es caminar en el parque.

A Sandra Cisneros...

☐ 1. Le gusta cantar.	☑ 6. Le gusta escribir.
☑ 2. Le gusta observar a personas.	☐ 7. Le gusta bailar.
☐ 3. Le gusta correr.	☑ 8. Le gusta escuchar música.
☑ 4. Le gusta cocinar.	☐ 9. Le gusta visitar a amigos.
☐ 5. Le gusta dibujar.	☑ 10. Le gusta caminar.

1A.11 TEACHING TIP: Do you have avid readers among your students? Invite them to check out *The House on Mango Street,* read one of the stories in it, and then share it with the class. Are any of your students already familiar with the book? Have them share with the class what they remember about it. Connecting Spanish to other disciplines, such as literary studies, is part of the Standards for Foreign Language Learning because it makes the language experience more real.

1A.12 Nuestras actividades favoritas.

Paso 1: Complete the following statement about what you like to do. Write the complete statement in your **Retrato de la clase** and on a slip of paper to turn in to the instructor.

> **Retrato de la clase** Mis actividades favoritas son _____, _____ y _____.
> *(List as many as you want.)*

Paso 2: **Firma aquí.** Now find out what your classmates like to do in their free time. Create a chart like the one below. For each of the activities listed, ask **¿Te gusta _____?** plugging the name of the activity into the blank. Respond to your classmates' questions with **Sí, me gusta _____. / No, no me gusta _____.** If your classmate answers in the affirmative, say, **Firma aquí, por favor** pointing to the blank. If he or she says no, move on to the next person. See who can collect the most signatures in the time allotted.

¿Te gusta...	Firma aquí
1. ...comer pizza?	_____
2. ...escuchar música?	_____
3. ...correr en el parque?	_____
4. ...cocinar?	_____
5. ...nadar?	_____
6. ...jugar deportes?	_____
7. ...escribir poemas?	_____
8. ...mirar la televisión?	_____
9. ...bailar?	_____
10. ...andar en bicicleta?	_____

Paso 3: **Resultado de la encuesta.** Your instructor will investigate the results of the 'Our favorite activities' survey (in Spanish, of course) by asking **¿A quiénes les gusta comer pizza?** Keep a tally of the results in a chart like the one below.

Actividad	Número de personas	Actividad	Número de personas
1. comer pizza	_____	**6.** jugar deportes	_____
2. escuchar música	_____	**7.** escribir poemas	_____
3. correr en el parque	_____	**8.** mirar la televisión	_____
4. cocinar	_____	**9.** bailar	_____
5. nadar	_____	**10.** andar en bicicleta	_____

Paso 4: **Resumen** In your **Retrato de la clase**, write the following to summarize the general preferences of your classmates and compare your own preferences from *Paso 1* with the class trend.

> **Retrato de la clase** En general, las actividades preferidas de mis compañeros de clase son _____, _____, _____ y _____.

1A.12 INSTRUCTOR'S RESOURCES You will find a reproducible chart in your Instructor's Resources.

ORIENTATION: It is not necessary at this point to go into any explanation about the construction *A quién le gusta* or *A quiénes les gusta*. Students should not have trouble understanding the questions if you provide a model. The more they hear these constructions (even without fully understanding them gramatically), the easier they may be able to comprehend them and their grammatical foundation later. Extend this activity further by asking questions such as *¿Dónde te gusta comer pizza? ¿en* (name of local pizzeria) *o en Pizza Hut?*

1A.12 TEACHING TIP: Point out to students that the *Retrato de la clase* documents information related to individual students in class or to general characteristics of the class. Remind them that the information that they share with classmates is important not only because they will have the opportunity to use it in future activities or assessments, but because the classroom community is important. At this point, students are limited to writing practice in the form of lists. As their vocabulary and exposure to Spanish increases, so will the writing practice. The *Retrato de la clase* also serves as writing practice.

¡Atención!

Introducir	means *to introduce* or *put an object inside of another*. It is not used in the sense of *introducing someone* or *something for the first time*. In this context, use **presentar**. Debes introducir la llave *(key)* en la puerta *(door)*. La profesora presenta el material nuevo. Mamá, te presento a mi amigo Tomás.
Nota	can be a *musical note, a footnote, marginal note* or other secondary information, but in the academic environment, **nota** also frequently means *grade* as in to have good grades. To refer to *notes* that are taken in class, the word **apuntes** is usually used, e.g. **tomar apuntes**. In the Americas, tomar notas is also used. To convey the idea of *writing something down*, use the verbs **apuntar** or **anotar**. Me gusta recibir buenas notas en los exámenes. Durante la clase, los estudiantes toman muchos apuntes (muchas notas). Es importante apuntar información en el *Retrato de la clase*.

¡ATENCIÓN! Each *Investigación* contains a section titled *¡Atención!* which highlights words that could be misused or misinterpreted by English-dominant students of Spanish.

1A.13 ANSWERS: 1. presentar, 2. nota, 3. tomar apuntes, 4. notas

1A.13 Asociaciones. Choose from the following words and phrases the one that best represents each scene below. One of the options will not be used.

nota   notas   introducir   presentar   tomar apuntes

1. _____

2. _____

3. _____

4. _____

Estructuras clave 1 The verb *ser*

Go to *WileyPLUS* and review the tutorial for this grammar point.

The verb *ser*

You have been using the verb **ser** to talk about your classmates, famous people, and even yourself, as in **Soy de...**, or **Mi número es...** Let's look at the verb **ser** more formally. Why do you suppose **soy** is the form of **ser** you use to talk about yourself, while you use **eres** and **es** to talk about other people and things?

In Spanish, as well as in English, the subject of a sentence needs to combine with a certain form of the verb. For example, in English we ensure that the subject pronoun *I* is used with *am* rather than *is* or *are*. Spanish also must ensure that the verb is in the appropriate form, or conjugation, to agree with the subject. As you can see, there are a few more conjugations in Spanish than in English. Examine the chart below. Which subject pronouns in Spanish share the same forms of **ser**?

You will find PowerPoint presentations for use with *Estructuras clave* in *WileyPLUS*.

ANSWER: Hopefully a few students will point out that *él/ella* and *usted* have the same verb forms and that *ellos/ellas* and *ustedes* also share the same verb form.

Yo	**soy**	*I am*
Tú	**eres**	*You (informal) are*
Él/ella Usted	**es**	*He/she is, You (formal) are*
Nosotros/as	**somos**	*We are*
Vosotros/as (used only in Spain)	**sois**	*You (plural) are*
Ellos/Ellas Ustedes	**son**	*They are, You (plural) are*

1A.14 Cierto o falso. Read the sentences below and indicate whether each statement is **cierto** or **falso** on the line next to it. If you do not know the subjects, replace them with ones you do know as long as they are clearly true or false.

> Modelo: You see: *Britney Spears es una persona complicada.*
> You write: *Cierto*

Falso _____ **1.** Bart Simpson es inteligente.

Cierto _____ **2.** Eddie Murphy, Whoopi Goldberg y George López son cómicos.

Cierto _____ **3.** En la clase, nosotros somos respetuosos.

Cierto _____ **4.** *(To a classmate)* Tú eres estudiante de español.

Falso _____ **5.** En realidad, soy estudiante de francés.

Cierto/Falso **6.** Brad Pitt, Tom Cruise y Owen Wilson son hombres extrovertidos.

(Have students defend their answers.)

1A.14 RECYCLING: This is a good opportunity to practice the importance of recognizing when to use what pronoun. For the sentences that do not already have a pronoun, ask students to circle the person/people being spoken about and write the pronoun they could substitute.

Students will not be tested on how much pop culture from their native language they know, nor should they feel uniformed because of any lack of familiarity with pop culture. We use US pop culture references to make tasks more interesting. We also introduce Hispanic celebrities (intellectual as well as popular) in the same way.

1A.15 ¿Quién habla?   In groups of three, match each of the following statements to the person who is most likely to have said it, but first provide the appropriate conjugation of the verb **ser** in the blanks. **¡Ojo!** Not all characters will be used.

a. Shrek
b. Dumbo
c. SpongeBob SquarePants
d. Lois Lane
e. Fat Albert

f. Doc, Gruñón *(Grumpy)* y Dormilón *(Sleepy)*
g. Charlie Brown (Carlitos)
h. Bart Simpson
i. Tigger
j. El Pingüino

___i___ **1.** "Yo _____soy_____ Tigre y mi amigo es Pooh".

___f___ **2.** "Nosotros _____somos_____ los enanos *(dwarfs)* en Blanca Nieves *(Snow White)*".

___d___ **3.** "Usted _____es_____ el reportero del Metrópolis y también _____es_____ mi héroe".

___b___ **4.** "Yo _____soy_____ un elefante".

___a___ **5.** "Fiona, tú _____eres_____ mi amor eterno".

___h___ **6.** "Homer _____es_____ mi padre pero no _____es_____ inteligente".

___j___ **7.** "Batman y Robin _____son_____ mis enemigos mortales".

___g___ **8.** "Snoopy _____es_____ mi mascota *(pet)*".

1A.16 READING STRATEGY: Scanning is an important skill to develop. Let students know that they can begin understanding written items in Spanish without knowing all the words. In *Paso 2*, have students focus on scanning the dialogs for key information that would help them answer the questions.

1A.16 TEACHING TIP: As you review the answers, you could ask students to role play the dialogs in the way they were meant to be spoken in the films.

1A.16 ANSWERS PASO 2:
1. Buscando a Nemo, 2. Los piratas del Caribe, 3. Harry Potter y la piedra filosofal, 4. Parque Jurásico, 5. El sexto sentido, 6. El Señor de los Anillos, 7. Harry Potter y la piedra filosofal

1A.16 ¿Te gusta el cine?

Paso 1: **¿Cómo se llama la película?** Are you a movie buff? Work with two other classmates to match the following movie titles in English to the corresponding title in Spanish. The first one has been done for you. Look in **Paso 2** for some clues if you have difficulty. If no one in your group has seen the movie or can figure out the answer, just do as many as you can.

___b___ **1.** La leyenda del Zorro
___d___ **2.** Buscando a Nemo
___a___ **3.** El laberinto del fauno
___f___ **4.** Harry Potter y la piedra filosofal
___h___ **5.** El Señor de los Anillos
___e___ **6.** Los piratas del Caribe
___i___ **7.** El diablo se viste de Prada
___g___ **8.** El sexto sentido
___c___ **9.** Parque Jurásico

a. Pan's Labyrinth
b. The Legend of Zorro
c. Jurassic Park
d. Finding Nemo
e. Pirates of the Caribbean
f. Harry Potter and the Philosopher's Stone
g. The Sixth Sense
h. The Lord of the Rings
i. The Devil Wears Prada

Paso 2: Remain in your same groups. Each of the following dialogs occurs in one of the movies listed above. Circle all forms of **ser** in the conversations and try to name the movie that corresponds to each dialog. You are not expected to understand everything in the dialogs. Focus on scanning to guess the name of the movie. Check your responses with another group.

—Hola, y ¿quién eres tú?
—Yo soy Nemo.
—Hola, me llamo Marlin.
—¡Ahhhh! ¿Quién es?

—¡Soy yo, Marlin!
—¿Eres mi conciencia?
—Sí, Dori, soy tu conciencia. ¿Cómo estás?

1. _____

–Soy el Capitán Jack Sparrow.

–Mucho gusto, capitán.

–Capitán. Me llamo Will Turner. Ella es la señorita Swan.

2. _____

–¿Quién eres tú? ¿Te conozco?

–Hola, ¿qué tal? Soy Ron. ¿cómo te llamas?

–¡Imbécil! Soy Draco. Mi familia es muy importante.

3. _____

–¡Corran! ¡Corran!

–¿Es el tiranosaurio?

–¡No! ¡Son los velocirraptores!

4. _____

–¿Quién es?

– (silencio…) Es un fantasma. Yo veo *(see)* fantasmas.

5. _____

–Precioso, mi precioso

–No, Gollum, no es tu precioso…. Es necesario destruir el anillo *(ring)*.

6. _____

–¿Qué somos Hagrid?

–Ustedes son magos.

–Tú y Ron son residentes de Gryffindor pero ellos son residentes de Slytherin.

7. _____

1A.17 ¿Te gusta o no te gusta?

Paso 1: Make a list of movies you have seen and indicate whether you like the movie or not.

Lista de títulos	Me gusta	No me gusta
1. _____	☐	☐
2. _____	☐	☐
3. _____	☐	☐
4. _____	☐	☐
5. _____	☐	☐

Paso 2: La película es… Las películas son… With a classmante, categorize the movies based on the genres provided below. Then, as a class indicate which genres of movies were the most popular. Write your observations in your **Retrato de la clase.**

Es una película…   romántica/violenta/de horror/de suspenso/de acción/animada.

Es…   una comedia/una tragedia/un musical/un drama.

   Retrato de la clase Las películas más populares son las… (e.g., comedias y de acción).

1A.17 TEACHING TIP:
The more you can create meaningful interaction in Spanish around the vocabulary/gramatical structures incorporated in a chapter, the more authentic the experience becomes. To find out what genre of movies are most popular, ask for the names of the movies listed under *"Me gusta."*

VÍVELO: LENGUA

Expressing origin with *ser*

We have been using the verb **ser** in Spanish to express an identity or characteristic of a person place or thing, but **ser** is also used to tell where one is from as you saw in the *Investigación preliminar*. Remember, there are different verb forms for each subject (or subject pronoun). Some examples of **ser** used to express origin are **Shakira *es* de Colombia** and **Thalía y Gael García Bernal *son* de México.**

1A.18 ¿De dónde son estas personas u objetos? With a partner, try to complete the unfinished sentences below based on what you may already know about these people. Then, confirm your answers based on the information in the map:

1. La familia de Aarón Sánchez es de _____*México*_____.

2. Fidel Castro es de _____.

3. "Los Lonely Boys" son de _____.

4. Benicio del Toro es de _____.

5. Ricky Martin y Daddy Yankee son de _____.

6. Juanes es de _____.

7. Enrique Iglesias es de _____.

8. La familia de Benjamin Bratt es de _____.

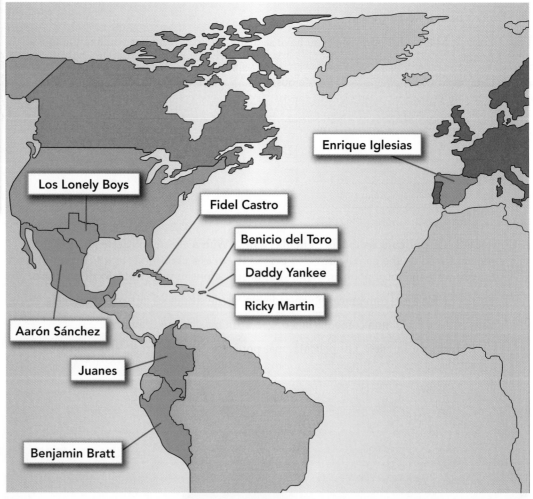

¡Conéctate!
Would you like to see the world in just a few clicks? Download the free program Google Earth. Start out by typing in your address and see a satellite picture of where you live. Now venture out and explore some Spanish-speaking countries. Zoom in and look at the topography, vegetation, architecture. What countries did you explore? How do their features compare to where you live?

Go to *WileyPLUS* and review the tutorial for this grammar point.

1A.19 ¿De dónde son? You have learned where your classmates are from. Yet in a mobile and global society, their parents could be from elsewhere. Ask the question **¿De dónde son tus padres?** to as many classmates as you can in the time specified by your instructor and keep track of the various states or countries. To answer this question, respond **Son de…** Create a chart like the one below to keep track of your classmates' responses and summarize your findings in your **Retrato de la clase.**

Nombre del compañero	País de origen de sus padres
_____	_____
_____	_____
_____	_____

> **Retrato de la clase:** La mayor parte de los padres de mis compañeros de clase son de_____. Algunos son de _____ y _____. En general, hay/no hay mucha diversidad entre el origen de los padres y sus hijos.

DICHOS

Conócete a ti mismo.	*Know thyself.*
Más vale malo conocido que bueno por conocer.	*Better the devil you know than the one you don't.*

Enlaces

The *Enlaces* section introduces you to words that provide cohesion to a paragraph or even within a sentence. By learning to use these words and phrases, you will be able to communicate more effectively even with limited proficiency in Spanish. The words on the left are used in context on the right. Read the sentences to determine the meaning of these helpful phrases.

A propósito	Two men have just been introduced and just before they depart, one of them says **"A propósito, ¿cómo se llama tu secretaria?"**
O sea	The instructor has announced six pages of homework and then says **"O sea, terminen el Capítulo 2 del libro."**
Es decir	Three students are introducing themselves and when one of them responds **"Soy la Señora Martínez,"** another student asks: **"¿Es decir que usted es casada?"**

1A.20 ¿Qué quiere decir? Based on the contextual cues above, write the phrase in Spanish next to its corresponding English phrase.

1. In other words ____O sea____

2. By the way ____A propósito____

3. That is to say ____Es decir____

1A.19 TEACHING TIP: Students may not be able to write these conclusions in Spanish without some guidance. This guided writing task will help them recognize how to form general statements about their class.

1A.19 TEACHING TIP: If your classroom has a computer with an LCD projector download the free program Google Earth. When going over where students' parents are from, go to those places on Google Earth. If students are not already familiar with this program, it is highly likely that they will be very enthusiastic after this activity. For your visual learners, this will drive home how global their communities are.

ENLACES: The section titled *Enlaces* is a part of every *Investigación* to help students connect their ideas more naturally. Often students learn lists of vocabulary and grammatical points, but are unable to string together sentences. The vocabulary presented in *Enlaces* is manageable and encourages students to expand their Spanish. Often the items selected for presentation in *Enlaces* appear in context within the immediately following *Contextos y perspectivas* section.

1A.20 For question 3, you may accept *o sea* and *es decir* interchangeably, and explain that *o sea* is more often used in informal conversation, and *es decir* both in more formal conversation and in writing.

1A.21 Estás muy cerca.

Paso 1: Read the passage below related to general Hispanic cultural norms. Then, explain the statements that follow in *Paso 2*.

The amount of space established by people as they interact with each other can vary from culture to culture and can be influenced by an individual's personality, the nature of a relationship, and established cultural norms. Researchers have argued that Latin Americans establish less spatial distance and are more contact-oriented than North Americans or Europeans. Even within specific cultures, however, significant differences in behavior can exist.

Paso 2: How does this passage explain the following two statements?

Spacial distance can be misinterpreted as being cold or aloof or pushy and aggressive, depending on the individual's native culture.

A study conducted in Costa Rica, Panamá and Colombia on the question of spatial distance and contact orientations indicated that there were significant differences in behavior between Central and South Americans.

1A.22 Malentendidos culturales. With two other classmates, read the situations below and explain why the misunderstandings in each situation occurred.

1. (**Primera situación**) Marco, a Peruvian college student, is introduced to Jim and Carly, who live in his dorm. He shakes Jim's hand and then proceeds to shake Carly's hand and leans in and gives her a light kiss on the cheek. Carly is a bit taken aback. Jim feels that Marco is coming on to his girlfriend and gets tense.

2. (**Segunda situación**) Dan is on a semester abroad in Santiago, Chile. His Spanish is quite strong. His first week in his new setting, he is invited to a party. Upon arriving, he greets everyone with the appropriate form of ¿**Cómo estás/está?** but he maintains a lot of physical space between himself and his hosts. His hosts feel that he is very distant and impersonal.

3. (**Tercera situación**) Kwame has just returned from spending a year abroad in Latin America where he grew very accustomed to the **abrazos** and **besos** *(kisses)* used as part of their greetings. Upon bumping into old friends, he proceeds to greet them with light hugs and kisses. He finds his old friends taken aback by his behavior.

What is a comfortable distance for you when talking with a stranger or someone you have only recently met?

Perspectivas

This situation looks like the situation Kwame faces in Activity 1A.22. How would your friends react if you were to greet them with **abrazos** or **besos**?

1A.23 ¿Estereotipo o realidad?

Paso 1: Gaining perspectives means understanding the source of practices and products of a people's culture. Remember what you learned about greetings in the *Investigación preliminar* and read this short and generalized description of how people in Spanish-speaking cultures greet one another. Then, reflect on what these practices may indicate about Hispanic cultures. The triangle following the passage represents three interconnected parts of culture: *products, practices,* and *perspectives.* Use it to understand what the description tells you about Hispanic cultures.

Physical contact is very important in the Spanish-speaking world when friends greet one another. When two male friends greet each other it's proper to shake hands and give each other a hug. When two female friends, or male and female friends meet, it's common to give each other a kiss on the cheek.

Product: Greetings

Practice
Guys will shake each other's hands and give each other a hug. Guys and girls, as well as girls, will greet with a kiss on the cheek and a hug.

Perspective
What do this product and practice indicate about cultural perspective?

PERSPECTIVAS: Following students' exploration of Hispanic perspectives on a particular topic in *Contextos, Perspectivas* provides a framework for examining one's own cultural perspectives on that topic with activities that foster self-expression and cultural comparison.

1A.23 TEACHING TIP: Ask student volunteers to model these different ways of greeting one another with fellow classmates.

1A.23 ANSWERS: Possible answers will be along the following lines of thought: Perspectives of the Spanish-speaking world: Physical touch and contact is valued. It is important to physically acknowledge the presence of a friend. Practice and Perspective of the student's own culture: Answers will likely vary. In any generalization, however, remind students that there are factors in most cultures that can influence greeting behaviors, such as context, formal or informal, the type of relationship that exists between people, i.e., friends, acquaintances, strangers, the social and economic status of the involved parties, etc.

Paso 2: How do you greet friends in your culture? What do these practices tell you about your cultural perspectives? Complete a similar cultural triangle, but this time focused on your own cultural background. When you are finished, share your personal analyses in small groups. Was there common ground in the descriptions you shared? How much variation was there?

Product: Greetings

Practice
How do you greet friends in your culture?

Perspective
What do this product and practice indicate about cultural perspective?

Greeting with a kiss on the check is common among many cultures. Does your family or the family of a friend follow this cultural practice? Is it just among family members, or also among other people with the same cultural background?

Vocabulario: Investigación A

Vocabulario esencial

Sustantivos

el/la amigo/a	friend
el béisbol	baseball
la casa	house
la computadora	computer
los deportes	sports
el fútbol	soccer
el mar	sea
la música	music
el nombre	name
el parque	park
el teléfono	telephone
la televisión	television
el tenis	tennis
el videojuego	video game

Verbos

andar en bicicleta	to go bike riding
bailar	to dance
caminar	to walk
cantar	to sing
cocinar	to cook
comer	to eat
correr	to run, to go running
dibujar	to draw
escribir	to write
escuchar	to listen to, to hear
hablar	to speak, to talk
jugar	to play (sports, games)
levantar pesas	to lift weights
llamar	to call
mirar	to watch, to look at
nadar	to swim
ser	to be
tocar	to play (an instrument), to touch
tomar	to drink (a beverage), to take
visitar	to visit
vivir	to live

Otras palabras y expresiones

el aficionado	fan
el amor	love
el anillo	ring
aquí	here
conocer	to know (be familiar with)
la cosa	thing
el cuento	story
(el) cuidado	care, be careful
deletrear	to spell
deportivo	sports related
el documental	documentary
estadounidense	U.S. citizen
el espacio	space
firmar	to sign
la gente	people
el gesto	gesture
el hombre	man
más allá	beyond
la mascota	pet
nacer	to be born
el resumen	summary
el sentido	sense
también	also
vender	to sell
me/te/le gusta ___	I/you/he, she, you (formal) like to ___ (Lit. ___ is pleasing to me/you/him/her.)

Cognados

Review the cognates in *Adelante* and the false cognates in *¡Atención!*. For a complete list of cognates, see Appendix 4 on page 605.

La clase de español y la universidad

In this **Investigación** you will learn:

▶ How to talk about activities and objects in the classroom

▶ How to express to whom something belongs

▶ How to refer to some places around the university

▶ How to refer to people and things the listener is already focused on

How can you talk about your classroom and your school?

You can describe the objects in the classroom.	En la clase hay libros, mesas, escritorios, ventanas, asientos, pizarras, tiza, plumas, lápices, marcadores, cuadernos, mochilas, diccionarios….
You can describe activities in the classroom and on campus.	Leer, escribir, escuchar, hablar, conversar, contestar, responder, repetir, preguntar, explicar, mirar, señalar, abrir, cerrar, levantar la mano…
You can identify buildings and places on campus.	La biblioteca, el gimnasio, la parada de autobús, el laboratorio, la cafetería, la librería, el edificio de la administración…
You can point out specific objects or refer to them in more general terms.	¿La mesa o una mesa? ¿La pluma o una pluma? ¿Las alumnas o unas alumnas? ¿Los libros o unos libros?

GOALS: Read through the functions as a class ensuring students' comprehension. As you read through, use cognates (*e.g. describir, identificar, objeto, indicar, etc.*) to restate in Spanish what students can do.

Adelante

¡Ya lo sabes! Actividades en clase

TEACHING TIP: TOTAL PHYSICAL RESPONSE (TPR). Attaching a gesture to a word is an excellent way of ensuring long-term retention of vocabulary. Most of the above verbs can be acted out in class. The meaning expressed with gestures alongside the cognates associated with the verbs should provide clues to the meaning of the verbs without having to use English.

conversar	con el profesor, con un amigo en la cafetería
copiar	el vocabulario, el alfabeto
descubrir	los planetas en el espacio
estudiar	el vocabulario, la lección, la historia, las ciencias, las matemáticas
explorar	el espacio, el universo, la galaxia, una región tropical
necesitar	a un amigo, estudiar, dinero *(money)*
observar	las fotos en la pantalla *(screen)*
preparar	el informe, el reportaje, la información
repetir	el secreto, el alfabeto, el número de teléfono
resolver	el problema, el conflicto
usar	la computadora para preparar el informe
académico/a	La universidad es una institución académica.
avanzado/a	Hay estudios básicos y estudios avanzados.
innovador/a	La tecnología innovadora revoluciona la educación.
diferente	Mi compañero ofrece una solución/opinión diferente.

1B.1 **Las clases de hoy.** With a classmate, read the following sentences and select the best option from the list to complete each sentence. Two of these cognates don't appear in the list in *Adelante,* but you should be able to understand their meaning based on the context. Share your responses with the class.

innovadoras   académicos   virtual   diferente   área común   avanzada

1. La clase es muy difícil porque es una clase _____.   *avanzada*

2. Los profesores son _____.   *académicos*

3. Las invenciones populares son _____.   *innovadoras*

4. No es repetitivo. Es _____.   *diferente*

5. La cafetería es un _____.   *área común (not given in list)*

6. La clase _____ no necesita un salón físico.   *virtual (not given in list)*

1B.2 **Se asocia más con...** Listen to several statements about activities that take place in class and indicate whether each would most frequently be associated with the instructor, the student or both, following the model. Verify your responses as a class.

	Profesor	Estudiante	Ambos *(both)*
1.	☐	☑	☐
2.	☐	☑	☐
3.	☐	☐	☑
4.	☐	☐	☑
5.	☐	☑	☐
6.	☐	☐	☑
7.	☑	☐	☐
8.	☑	☐	☐

1B.2 AUDIO SCRIPT: 1. estudiar para un examen, 2. copiar el vocabulario, 3. preparar una presentación, 4. resolver un conflicto en la clase, 5. conversar con compañeros de clase, 6. explorar la Internet, 7. repetir las instrucciones, 8. observar a los estudiantes

1B.3 **¡A emparejar!** With a partner, one of you will read the first five words in Column A and the other will select the word from Column B best associated with each word, following the model. Then, reverse roles for the last five words. **¡Ojo!** As you read the words in Column A, note that the syllables that are stressed in each word are in bold. (For cognates, the stress does not necessarily fall on the same syllable as it does in English). Verify your answers with another group of classmates.

1B.3 TEACHING TIP: The syllables are bolded in Column A to indicate where the oral stress resides in these words since it may not be the same as in English. An alternative approach to this activity would be to read the statements in Column B to the class as opposed to having the class read them to each other. In this way students can make sound and meaning associations at the same time. The words in column A are cognates and can be found in the vocabulary list at the end of *Investigación 1B*.

Modelo: E1 reads: *resol**ver***
E2 selects:*Se asocia con (It's associated with) un conflicto, un problema o una crisis.*

	A		B
i	**1.** el **cam**pus		**a.** Es la jerarquía estructural de una institución.
d	**2.** explo**rar**		**b.** Se asocia con palabras y definiciones.
g	**3.** el pro**gra**ma		**c.** Se asocia con notas y melodías.
f	**4.** el **cur**so		**d.** Es sinónimo de "experimentar" o "descubrir."
e	**5.** la informa**ción**		**e.** Se asocia con "contenido," "datos" y "comunicación."
c	**6.** la **mú**sica		**f.** Es sinónimo de "la clase."
b	**7.** el diccio**na**rio		**g.** Se asocia con comedia, documental, serie televisiva.
j	**8.** el **ma**pa		**h.** Se asocia con el básquetbol.
h	**9.** el gim**na**sio		**i.** Es el sitio *(place)* físico de la universidad.
a	**10.** la administra**ción**		**j.** Es una imagen de la geografía de una región o un continente.

En la mayor parte de los países hispanos los estudiantes en escuelas (*schools*) públicas y privadas usan uniformes escolares para reducir el impacto de las diferencias socio-económicas y otras distracciones. ¿Es esto común en la cultura de tu país?

1B.4 **La educación.** Before reading the passage in Spanish below, indicate your responses to the following questions.

Sí	No	
☐	☐	**1.** Does your native culture value education?
☐	☐	**2.** Are students required to attend school?
☐	☐	**3.** Does the government give high priority to education?
☐	☐	**4.** Does your family give high priority to education?
☐	☐	**5.** Does your native culture work on the assumption that no matter how economically deprived one is, a good education can be a way out of poverty and socioeconomic problems?

Los valores culturales

No todas las culturas permiten el acceso a una buena vida socio-económica con base en (*based on*) una buena educación. Aunque (*Even though*) muchas culturas hispanas promueven (*promote*) la educación como una forma de combatir la pobreza (*poverty*), la división entre las clases sociales persiste en muchos países hispanos. Un ejemplo son las telenovelas (*soap operas*) de Univisión, Galavisión, Telemundo, etcétera, en que los personajes de diferentes clases sociales se enamoran (*fall in love*) pero comparten un destino fatal por pertenecer a diferentes grupos sociales. Esta forma de inflexibilidad social está cambiando (*changing*) pero todavía existe implícitamente en la cultura popular. ¿Cuál es la relación entre las barreras socio-económicas y la educación formal en tu cultura nativa?

1B.5 TEACHING TIP: This reading might lead to a discussion about how open U.S. society (or the native culture of students) really is. Ask students, *¿Qué disminuye* (decreases) *las divisiones de clase en tu país nativo? ¿Persisten las divisiones sociales en tu país a pesar de una buena educación formal?* Problematize this further by asking students whether or not society in the U.S. truly values education as a way to provide upward mobility for all students. There are often vast disparities in the quality of education that students in economically weak neighborhoods and more affluent areas receive.

1B.5 **Un paso más.** With a classmate, indicate which of the statements below are upheld in the reading passage. Then, verify your responses as a class.

☑ **1.** Hay divisiones de clase en la sociedad de muchos países hispanos.

☐ **2.** Las divisiones de clase están basadas en la educación.

☑ **3.** Las divisiones de clase están basadas en el nivel socio-económico.

☑ **4.** Persisten las divisiones sociales a pesar de (*in spite of*) una buena educación formal.

Bien dicho

Linking sounds in Spanish

In this section, we want you to learn how to adjust your listening strategies so that you can increase your listening comprehension. When you listen to a native Spanish-speaker, you may find it difficult to identify and understand even words that you may know. Why is this? In English, we insert a brief pause between the words in a phrase and this allows us to sense where each word begins and ends. For example, consider the difference between *nitrate* and *night rate*. Both sequences are pronounced exactly the same, with the exception of the brief pause between *night* and *rate*, and it is this pause that allows us to distinguish between them. Spanish speakers do not insert a pause between words in a phrase and this can make it difficult for non-native speakers to distinguish the individual words that make up the phrase. What they may perceive instead is an unbroken string of sounds. For example, the phrase **Me llamo Anita** may be perceived as **"mellamoanita"**. With practice and increasing exposure to Spanish, your ear will eventually adjust to this phenomenon, but until then, we will practice omitting pauses between the words in the useful phrases for the classroom given in *Expresiones útiles* below.

1B.6 **Práctica de pronunciación.** In groups of three, take turns saying these phrases and questions without pauses. Use what is between brackets as a pronunciation guide, emphasizing the syllables in bold. Provide feedback to each other.

1. ¿Hay tarea? [ai-ta-**re**-a]
2. ¿Para cuándo es? [pa-ra-**kwan**-do-es]
3. ¿Qué página? [ke-**pa**-hi-na]
4. Necesito más tiempo, por favor. [ne-se-**si**-to-más-**tiem**-po-por-fa-**bor**]
5. Lo siento. [lo-**sien**-to]
6. Repita, por favor. [re-**pi**-ta-por-fa-**bor**]
7. ¿Cómo se dice en español? [**ko**-mo-se-**di**-se-nes-pa-**ñol**]
8. ¿Qué significa "tengo"? [ke-sig-ni-**fi**-ka-**ten**-go]

EXPRESIONES ÚTILES
Preguntas y expresiones para la clase

Tengo una pregunta.	*I have a question.*
No entiendo.	*I don't understand.*
Repita, por favor.	*Say that again, please.*
Necesito más tiempo, por favor.	*I need more time, please.*
¿Está bien?	*Is it okay?*
¿Cómo se dice… en español?	*How do you say… in Spanish?*
¿Cómo?	*What?* (Used when you didn't hear what was said to you.)
¿Hay tarea?	*Is there homework?*
¿Para cuándo es?	*When is it due?*
¿Qué página?	*What page?*
Lo siento.	*I'm sorry.*
¿Qué significa…?	*What does… mean?*

1B.7 **¿Cuál es la pregunta?** With a partner, match each question in Column B with its corresponding answer in Column A. Confirm your matches and your pronunciation with another group or as a class.

A

___f___ **1.** Sí, muy bien.

___g___ **2.** Sí, estudiar el vocabulario de la lección uno.

___h___ **3.** Significa "no básico".

___d___ **4.** Es para mañana.

___e___ **5.** Página veinticinco.

___a___ **6.** Repito: Escribe.

___b___ **7.** Se dice tarea.

___c___ **8.** blah, blah, blah (unintelligible string of words)

B

a. Repita, por favor.

b. ¿Cómo se dice *homework* en español?

c. ¿Cómo?

d. ¿Para cuándo es?

e. ¿Qué página?

f. ¿Está usted bien?

g. ¿Hay tarea?

h. ¿Qué significa "avanzado"?

1B.6 VISUAL SUPPORT: Consider writing these commonly used phrases on cardstock paper and hanging them around the room or putting them on a PowerPoint slide presentation running during the class session. This will make it more likely for students to reference these phrases quickly. Additionally, this will help you keep the class in Spanish.

TEACHING TIP: Music is a wonderful way of highlighting how Spanish is pronounced. Have students read the lyrics while listening to a song. Draw their attention to the lack of a glottal stop. You may even invite them to sing a line or two of the song when they hear it. This is not only a good way of providing other examples of this phenomenon, but it also begins to expose them to music of the Spanish-speaking world.

1B.7 TEACHING TIP: You can intentionally mumble or give the wrong page number to students to encourage them to use these phrases. In the future, engage students in using these phrases in class. The frequency of use will help students learn these useful phrases more effectively.

Palabras clave 1 En la clase

TEACHING TIP: You may want to introduce many of these words by touching the objects available in your classroom and pronouncing the words in Spanish. For example, go to the door and say *Es una puerta*. Go to a chair and say *Es una silla*. Do 5–6 examples at a time and then ask students to confirm statements such as *Es una silla* as you touch the door. Students should respond *No* (or *Sí* if you touch a chair). Then, repeat the procedure with another 5–6 words.

VOCABULARY: Encourage students to establish a method that helps them keep track of the vocabulary they learn. They may want to write down the words they learn in their notebook/folder, and write a description of the word, or include an image that represents it. Many may feel the propensity to write the translation. You may consider encouraging them to use one of the other strategies to avoid students overly relying on translation.

1B.8 RECYCLING: This activity recycles vocabulary from *Investigación A*.

el salón de clase

la ventana

el estudiante

la compañera de clase

la silla /el asiento

lugares en la universidad

la residencia estudiantil

la biblioteca

el edificio

1B.8 **Asociaciones.** Circle the word that least associates with the action or place indicated. Then, verify your responses with a classmate.

1. saludar:	la profesora	el estudiante	(la grabadora)	la compañera de clase
2. escribir:	en el cuaderno	(en la ventana)	en la pizarra	en la hoja de papel
3. leer *(to read)*:	el libro	(el escritorio)	la prueba	la respuesta
4. mover:	la mochila	la silla	la mesa	(la pregunta)
5. mirar:	el mapa	la pantalla	la pizarra	(el concepto)
6. dibujar con:	(la mochila)	el lápiz	la pluma	la tiza
7. caminar en:	el edificio	(la página)	el salón de clase	la residencia estudiantil
8. en la biblioteca:	las mesas	los asientos	las sillas	(las pruebas)

el proyector

la puerta

la prueba

el mapa

la pizarra

la profesora

la mochila

la grabadora

la página

la tiza

el escritorio

el cuaderno

la mesa

el lápiz

el libro

la pluma

la hoja de papel

¿EXAMEN
NOMBRE
FECHA

VÍVELO: LENGUA

Expressing "there is" and "there are": *Hay*

Hay, in Spanish, is not what horses eat. It is the equivalent of *There is…* or *There are…* in English. It is pronounced similar to the English word "eye" but with the shorter more crisp sound characteristic of Spanish vowels. Remember, the **h** in Spanish is silent.

1B.9 **¡A escribir!**   Write as many sentences as you can using any of the new vocabulary words under **El salón de clase** or **Lugares en la universidad.** Some must be obviously false and some must be true. Use **hay** to write sentences about what is or is not in your classroom, for example. Read at least one of your sentences to the class. The class will guess whether the sentence is true or false.

1B.9 TEACHING TIP:
Make sure students understand that they must write a sentence that can be verified as true or false. If they write *Me gusta el lápiz* there is no way the class can verify that statement. On the other hand, if they write, *Hay una biblioteca en la clase de español,* the class can respond to this statement as being *falso.* Repeat students' statements to the class to model correct agreement since students have not been formally introduced to concept of gender and number agreement.

WILEY PLUS

1B.10 **¿Qué hay en el salón de clase?** Working with a classmate, take turns asking and answering questions about the number of people and objects in the classrooms pictured below. One of you asks and answers questions based on drawing A, the other asks and answers questions based on drawing B. Then, make a list of the differences between the two classrooms. Afterwards, verify your responses by looking at each other's drawings.

Modelo: E1: *¿Hay tres ventanas en el salón de clase?*
E2: *No, hay cuatro ventanas.*

A

B

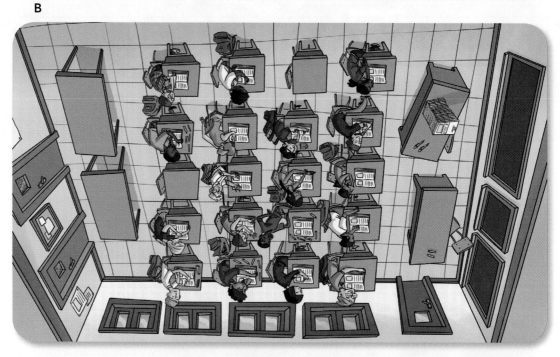

¡Conéctate!

Open up http://officedepot.com and click on the *Español* icon. Make a list of school supplies that you would like to buy. What kinds of things would you purchase? What new vocabulary did you learn that may not have been presented in the text? Can you find other websites where you can see school supply catalogs in Spanish?

Palabras clave 2 Acciones de la clase

abrir · trabajar · cerrar · hacer la tarea · señalar · leer · levantar la mano · hacer preguntas · contestar · tomar apuntes · aprender

WILEY PLUS

You will find PowerPoint presentations for use with *Palabras clave* in *WileyPLUS*. Along with the regular PowerPoint slide corresponding to this *Palabras clave* illustration, your Instructor's Resources include an additional slide in which the labels have been replaced with names. This allows you to ask questions or make true/false statements about these activities as a way of working with the vocabulary. For example, you might ask *¿Quién lee un libro?* or *¿Arturo toma apuntes?*

TEACHING TIP: TOTAL PHYSICAL RESPONSE (TPR). Most of the above verbs can be acted out in class. The following are examples of the type of comprehensible input and gestures that you can offer your students: *Abre tu libro. Abre tu libro rápidamente. Abre tu libro en la página cinco.* (Gesture: start with your palms together, and then have them open while the sides of your hands continue touching...like a book.)

1B.11 TEACHING TIP: To make this a production activity, ask students to tell you the activities that instructors are most likely to do and those that they are most likely to do.

1B.11 ¿El profesor o el estudiante? With a classmate, indicate whether each action below is more typical of a student or an instructor. Then, confirm your answers with the rest of the class.

	Estudiante	Profesor
1. aprender el vocabulario	☑	☐
2. escribir en la pizarra	☐	☑
3. contestar preguntas	☑	☑
4. levantar la mano	☑	☐
5. hacer preguntas	☑	☑
6. leer la explicación	☑	☐
7. usar la tiza	☐	☑
8. mirar la pantalla	☑	☐
9. tomar apuntes	☑	☐
10. copiar los apuntes de un compañero de clase	☑	☐

1B.12 AUDIO SCRIPT:
1. observar al estudiante, 2. abrir la puerta, 3. contestar una pregunta, 4. levantar la mano, 5. escuchar la pregunta, 6. hacer la tarea, 7. tomar apuntes, 8. estudiar español

VÍVELO: CULTURA: The *¡Vívelo: Cultura!* passages function as a point of departure for exploring cultural phenomena. The information they provide can be applied cumulatively in the *Contextos y perspectivas* section at the end of the *Investigación,* or can be explored independently of that section. In either case, students should be encouraged to explore the validity of cultural generalizations, irrespective of whether the content offers a historical, social or cultural perspective.

SUGGESTION: One of the Five National Standards for Foreign Language Learning is *Communities.* The goal of this standard is to get students to put the knowledge they learn into practice by connecting with a community. Ask students if they have any friends, neighbors, classmates, etc., who were brought up in Latin America with whom they can chat about the cultural information shared in this *Vívelo: Cultura* section. Have them pursue these conversations and then report their findings back to the class. How reflective was this information of their friend's experiences? What did they learn?

1B.12 Sinónimos o antónimos. Read the phrases below. For each of these phrases, you will hear a corresponding phrase. Indicate whether the phrase you hear expresses a similar or an opposite meaning to the one you read, following the model. Verify your responses as a class.

Sinónimo	Antónimo	
☑	☐	**1.** mirar al estudiante
☐	☑	**2.** cerrar la puerta
☐	☑	**3.** hacer una pregunta
☑	☐	**4.** señalar con la mano
☐	☑	**5.** leer la pregunta
☑	☐	**6.** trabajar en la tarea
☐	☑	**7.** ofrecer apuntes
☑	☐	**8.** aprender español

VÍVELO: CULTURA

El papel de la Iglesia (*The role of the Church*)

What is the connection between Church and State in your native culture? Until their independence from Spain, and to some extent even after that, education in Latin American countries was controlled by the Catholic Church. In colonial times, education by the Church was denied to all natives and later to **mestizos** (mixed-blooded population). When the colonies won their independence, little changed because of the lack of attention given to public education. Today, public education is made available in Hispanic countries, but some educational systems still maintain a heavily authoritarian philosophy toward education, particularly in rural areas. For example, discipline is strict in elementary schools and high schools, but more lax in colleges and universities. At the elementary and high school levels, the education process emphasizes passing examinations. Traditionally, students were taught conformity and obedience to authority rather than how to act independently and solve problems, although this is changing. In Spanish, to be **bien educado** refers more to being *well mannered* than to being schooled in math, grammar, and so on.

¡Conéctate!

Check out the discussions on the separation of church and state taking place at http://au.org. What topics are being discussed?

¡Atención!

Bachillerato	refers to secondary school or high school; to talk about a *bachelor* (an umarried male) use the word **soltero**; to express a *bachelor's degree* in Spanish, use the word, **licenciatura**. A person holding a *bachelor's degree* is a **licenciado/a**. Para asistir a la universidad es necesario completar el bachillerato. Después de 4 ó 5 años en la universidad, se recibe la licenciatura. Fernando Colunga no tiene esposa. Es soltero.
Carpeta	means *binder* (as in three-ring binder) that you fill with loose papers; the carpet on the floor is **la alfombra** in Spanish. La tarea está en mi carpeta. Las máquinas de Hoover o Dyson son para las alfombras.
Colegio	means *secondary* or *high school*, and may be used for primary school as well. When you talk about *college* you need the word **universidad**. Los estudiantes de 15 a 18 años asisten al colegio. La Universidad Nacional Mayor de San Marcos está en Lima, Perú.
Dormitorio	means *bedroom*; a *dormitory* like where you live when you go to boarding school or college is **una residencia estudiantil** in Spanish. En mi casa hay cuatro dormitorios. Muchos estudiantes viven en residencias estudiantiles.
Facultad	is used like English uses *school* or *college* to refer to a subdivision of a university. Where in English we say *School of Medicine* and *College of Humanities*, Spanish uses **Facultad de Medicina** and **Facultad de Humanidades**. The *faculty*, as in the collective of professors, is **el profesorado**. La Facultad de Filosofía y Letras ofrece clases de lenguas. El profesorado de la universidad protesta contra (*against*) las acciones de la administración.

NOTE: Language is not static. It is constantly evolving and words take on new meanings as is evidenced by the interaction between English and Spanish in the US among heritage speakers and recent immigrants. For instance, the word *carpeta* in "standard" Spanish means binder, but in some circles in US Spanish, it has taken on the meaning of *alfombra*.

1B.13 ¡A emparejar! Match the first half of each sentence to its most logical conclusion. Check your work with a classmate.

a. …en mi carpeta de biología. ¡Ay, caramba!

b. …"universidad".

c. …hay un sofá y un televisor.

d. …graduarse de la escuela secundaria.

e. …la Facultad de Humanidades y Ciencias Sociales.

- e **1.** Él es profesor de
- d **2.** Terminar el bachillerato es
- c **3.** En el dormitorio de mi mamá
- a **4.** Hay tarea para mi clase de español
- b **5.** "Colegio" no es sinónimo de

1B.13 EXTENSION ACTIVITY. Write down the phrases in 1B.13 on index cards. Use these as pairing cards. Randomly distribute them and have each student find a person with the connecting card (e.g. a student with *La profesora necesita* looks for someone with *…un salón de clase con ventanas.*)

Estructuras clave 1 Nouns: Number and gender

WILEY PLUS
Go to *WileyPLUS* and review the tutorial for this grammar point.

WILEY PLUS

You will find PowerPoint presentations for use with *Estructuras clave* in *WileyPLUS*.

TEACHING TIP: Write the words *ventana, biblioteca, clase,* and *reloj* on the board. Then signal with your fingers *dos* and add an *–s* or *–es* to these words to illustrate how plural nouns are formed. Write the word *lápiz* on the board and write the plural form *lápices* and say *Hay palabras con formas irregulares en el plural.* You may practice a few more nouns that they have learned.

Number

You have learned to name common classroom objects and have even expressed the number of various objects in a classroom. Did you figure out exactly what to do to make a distinction between one item (a singular noun) or more than one item (a plural noun)? The following are the patterns for making nouns plural.

Words that end in **–e**, **–a**, or **–o** need only to have an **–s** added to make them plural.

1 estudiant**e** ⟶	2 estudiante**s**
1 puert**a** ⟶	3 puerta**s**
1 libr**o** ⟶	4 libro**s**

Words that end in a consonant require the addition of **–es**.

1 hote**l** ⟶	2 hotel**es**
1 relo**j** ⟶	2 reloj**es**

Words that end in **–z**, change the **z** to **c** along with the addition of **–es**.

1 lápi**z** ⟶	6 lápi**ces**
1 lu**z** ⟶	5 lu**ces**

Gender

As you have learned new nouns, you have learned them with either **el** or **la** in front of them. You will learn more about these little words called articles in *Estructuras clave 2*. In the meantime, do you have a sense of why **el** is used with some nouns while **la** is used with others?

Nouns in Spanish are considered either masculine or feminine. Most nouns ending in **–o** are masculine, and most nouns ending in **–a** are feminine, although there are some exceptions such as **el mapa** (m.) or **la mano** (f.).

If a noun does not end in an **–o** or **–a**, pay close attention to the noun's gender, such as **el hotel** (m.), **la luz** (f.), **el lápiz** (m.), **la clase** (f.), when you learn it. As you continue learning Spanish, you will notice other patterns that indicate noun gender. For example, words that end in **–ción/ sión** or **–dad** are feminine.

In general, the gender of a particular noun is a purely grammatical phenomenon. However, nouns ending in **–e** that refer to people, such as **estudiante** can be masculine or feminine according to the gender of the person they refer to. **El estudiante** is a male student, **la estudiante** is a female student.

Masculine nouns	**Feminine nouns**
el libro	la puerta
el compañero	la letra
el estudiante	la estudiante
el nombre	la clase
el origen	la profesión
el código	la nacionalidad

1B.14 ¿Cuántos hay? Work in groups of three. Make a chart like the one below and write the name of each person in your group across the top. Ask each classmate in your group how many of the following items he/she usually carries to class or has in his/her backpack and insert that number under the classmate's name. If an item is totally preposterous (there's no way anyone would carry it in their backpack), write X. Add up the totals for each item and write them in Spanish. Check with each other to make sure you all have the same answers. When you have finished, assemble all the items on a desktop so the instructor can check your work. Then, write your results in your **Retrato de la clase.**

WILEY
PLUS

1B.14 INSTRUCTOR'S RESOURCES You will find a reproducible chart in your Instructor's Resources.

Modelo: E1: *¿Cuántos cuadernos hay en tu mochila?*
E2: *Hay dos cuadernos.*

	_____ (Nombre)	_____ (Nombre)	_____ (Nombre)	Total (Escribe el número con palabras.)
lápices				
mesas				
plumas				
marcadores				
ventanas				
cuadernos				
libros				

Retrato de la clase: Hay dos lápices y una pluma en la mochila de _____
Hay un cuaderno y cuatro libros en la mochila de _____

1B.15 ¿Qué hay y qué falta (is missing)?

Paso 1: Work with a partner, each choosing one of the cards below. First, *Estudiante 1* reads the five sentences on his/her card and *Estudiante 2* draws a classroom with the objects named. Then, *Estudiante 2* gives the partial drawing to *Estudiante 1* and reads the sentences on his/her card while *Estudiante 1* draws the remaining items to complete the classroom scene. When your scene is complete, compare it with another group's to check that they contain the same number of each item.

1B.15 ALTERNATE/ EXTENSION ACTIVITY. Make statements about your own classroom and have students say whether they are *cierto* or *falso. En esta clase, hay....* Have students design their ideal classroom. Then have them describe it to a partner without showing it to him/her. The partner needs to draw the items mentioned. When they finish, they should check to make sure that all the items were included. They can then reverse roles.

Estudiante 1

1. Hay ocho asientos.

2. Hay dos pizarras.

3. Hay cinco estudiantes.

4. Hay dos mesas.

5. Hay tres computadoras.

5. Hay un escritorio.

4. Hay cuatro libros.

3. Hay un profesor.

2. Hay una puerta.

1. Hay tres ventanas.

Estudiante 2

Paso 2: Pair up with a different partner to determine what else each of your classrooms might need. Express it in Spanish and add it to the drawing. As a class, select the most original classroom drawing.

Modelo: E1: *La clase necesita dos estudiantes más.*
E2: (draws an additional two students)

Estructuras clave 2 Definite and indefinite articles

Without necessarily knowing it, you have already been using articles in Spanish. In English, to refer to someone or something in particular you would use *the* before the word. *The* means that you are referring to a person, place or thing that is "known" as in *You know* the *backpack I bought yesterday? It already has a hole in it!* If, however, you want to refer to someone or something in general, you would use *a* or *an*, such as in *What I need is* a *new backpack*. These are called the definite article (referring to something known) and indefinite article (referring to something in general). Can you tell from the examples below which of the Spanish articles would be the definite and which the indefinite articles? What are some additional patterns you note in the use of these articles? Can you distinguish which articles indicate masculine gender, and which indicate feminine gender?

El estudiante inteligente	*The intelligent student* (the one who won a scholarship)
Los estudiantes inteligentes	*The intelligent students* (the ones who won a scholarship)
La tecnología innovadora	*The innovative technology* (a specific innovation such as the iPhone)
Las tecnologías innovadoras	*The innovative technologies* (referring to specific ones, such as iPhone and Satelite tracking)
Un estudiante inteligente	*An intelligent student* (anyone who fits certain criteria for being intelligent)
Unos estudiantes inteligentes	*Some intelligent students* (several students who fit the criteria for being intelligent, but no specific names in mind.)
Una tecnología innovadora	*An innovative technology* (any technology that is groundbreaking)
Unas tecnologías innovadoras	*Some innovative technologies* (without actually referring to specific ones)

	Definite Articles		Indefinite Articles	
	Masculine	Feminine	Masculine	Feminine
Singular	el	la	un	una
Plural	los	las	unos	unas

The article used with a given noun matches, or "agrees" with that noun in terms of gender and number.

1B.16 ¿Es lógico? As you hear several statements, determine whether the speaker refers to a specific object or person, or not. The second time you hear each statement, indicate whether it is logical (**lógico**) or illogical (**ilógico**). Follow the model, then verify your answers as a class.

	¿Específico?	Lógico	Ilógico			¿Específico?	Lógico	Ilógico
1.	☑ Sí ☐ No	☑	☐		5.	☐ Sí ☑ No	☐	☑
2.	☑ Sí ☐ No	☑	☐		6.	☐ Sí ☑ No	☑	☐
3.	☐ Sí ☑ No	☑	☐		7.	☑ Sí ☐ No	☐	☑
4.	☐ Sí ☑ No	☑	☐					

1B.17 ¿Qué es necesario para...? Interview a classmate in Spanish to find out what is needed to complete each action below. The answers will include actions, things, places, and a description. Take turns asking questions and providing answers. Make note of your answers, and verify them with the rest of the class.

Modelo: E1: *¿Qué es necesario para hacer la tarea?*
E2: *el libro, un lápiz o una pluma y un cuaderno*

¿Qué es necesario para...

1. ... escribir en la pizarra? (cosa) una tiza
2. ... tomar apuntes en un cuaderno? (cosa) un lápiz o una pluma
3. ... aprender el vocabulario, la gramática y los conceptos culturales de esta clase? (cosa) el libro de español
4. ... hacer una pregunta en clase? (acción) levantar la mano
5. ... contestar una pregunta? (cosa) la respuesta
6. ... transportar los libros, las plumas, los cuadernos y los lápices? (cosa) una mochila
7. ... proyectar palabras e imágenes en una pantalla? (cosa) un proyector
8. ... escribir con tiza? (cosa) una pizarra
9. ... conversar? (persona) un compañero de clase
10. ... prepararse para una clase? (acción) hacer la tarea
11. ... aprender los varios significados de una palabra en español? (cosa) un diccionario
12. ... explorar el mundo? (cosa) un mapa
13. ... conectarse a la Internet? (cosa) una computadora
14. ...comer en una escuela? (lugar) una cafetería
15. ... practicar básquetbol? (lugar) un gimnasio
16. ... entrar a un edificio? (cosa) una puerta

1B.17 ALTERNATE ACTIVITY: As an alternative to the above format of having students work with a partner, consider inviting them to walk around the classroom and ask these questions of various classmates.

VÍVELO: LENGUA

Expressing ownership with *ser*

You have learned to describe something or someone using a form of **ser** as in **Clark Kent es un héroe** or **Nosotros *somos* estudiantes.** You also learned that a form of **ser** is used to express where you or someone else is from, as in **Yo *soy* de Argentina** and **Ella *es* de Texas.**

Ser is also used to express ownership, as in **La capa *es* de Batman.** The context of the sentence will dictate how the form of **ser** is being used.

El libro **es** de ella.

La mochila **es** de él.

La pluma **es** del presidente de la compañía.

Los libros **son** de la estudiante.

Los lápices **son** de ellos.

To ask to whom something belongs, use the question **¿De quién es...?**

—**¿De quién es** el libro?

—**Es de** mi compañero de clase.

Go to *WileyPLUS* and review the tutorial for this grammar point.

TEACHING TIP: Provide students with many comprehensible examples of this use of *ser*. Take into account what belongings your students have with them and use that to ask questions: *¿De quién es la computadora? ¿Es de Jim? ¿De quién es el iPhone? ¿Es de Angelique? ¿De quién son los libros de filosofía? ¿Son de Armando? ¿De quién son las revistas? ¿Son de Jenny?*

1B.18 Es de/son de.   Select the most appropriate caption for each of the pictures below. Then, check your answers with another classmate.

<u> 3 </u> El libro es de Gloria Estefan.

<u> 1 </u> El escritorio es del Presidente.

<u> 2 </u> La silla es del director.

<u> 4 </u> El organizador es de la marca Blackberry.

<u> 5 </u> La pizarra es de la profesora.

1.

2.

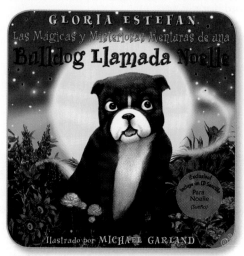

3.

4.

5.

1B.19 ¿De quién son estas cosas? Indicate to whom each item in the drawing belongs. Verify your responses with the class.

Modelo: *El libro es de Ahmed.*

1B.20 ¿De quién son? As a class, guess the item that most likely belongs to each figure below. Then, share with the class the number of correct responses your group guessed.

Modelo: You read: La canción "Dame más gasolina"
You say: *La canción es de Daddy Yankee.*

Robert Rodríguez   Carlos Santana   Pablo Neruda y Robert Frost
Sandra Cisneros   Penélope Cruz   Reina Isabel de Castilla
Oscar de la Renta   Barry Bonds y Babe Ruth

1. El libro *La casa en Mango Street*   **5.** El mapa de España

2. Los poemas   **6.** El premio Óscar

3. Los bates   **7.** La película *Spy Kids*

4. La guitarra   **8.** El perfume

Enlaces

Después de	is an expression used with a sequence of actions to indicate that one action follows another.
En cambio	is an expression indicating that an alternative point of view follows.

1B.21 Adivina. Based on the above hints, can you match which of the translations below corresponds to each of these expressions?

1. __b__ después de   **a.** On the other hand
2. __a__ en cambio   **b.** Afterward

1B.19 ANSWERS: 1. El lápiz es de Enrique., 2. La mochila es de Mark., 3. La pluma es de Irma., 4. El cuaderno es de Sofía., 5. La tiza/El libro es de la profesora Sosa.

1B.20 ORIENTATION: This activity is done as a class to increase the chances that a student will know one or two of these people. The activity is not to test whether they know or do not know these people, but it can be used to introduce these names to the students. If you are confident that students will not know these names, you can give the class hints, such as *Pablo Neruda es poeta, Bonds es atleta, Cisneros es escritora, Cruz es actriz, Santana es músico, Rodríguez es director de cine,* etc.

1B.20 ANSWERS: 1. El libro es de Sandra Cisneros (contemporary Latina writer), 2. Los poemas son de Pablo Neruda (Chilean poet) y Robert Frost, 3. Los bates son de Barry Bonds y Babe Ruth, 4. La guitarra es de Carlos Santana (Latino guitarist since the 1970's), 5. El mapa de España es de la Reina Isabel de Castilla (Spanish queen who funded Columbus' voyage to the New World), 6. El premio Óscar es de Penélope Cruz (Spanish actress who won the Oscar in 2009 for Best Supporting Actress), 7. La película es de Robert Rodríguez (Mexican-American film maker noted for *Desperado* and *Once Upon a Time in Mexico*), 8. El perfume es de Oscar de la Renta (Dominican fashion designer).

1B.22 **Un sistema educativo.**

Paso 1: With a classmate, study the flowchart titled *El sistema educativo de México* to determine how the Mexican educational system works.

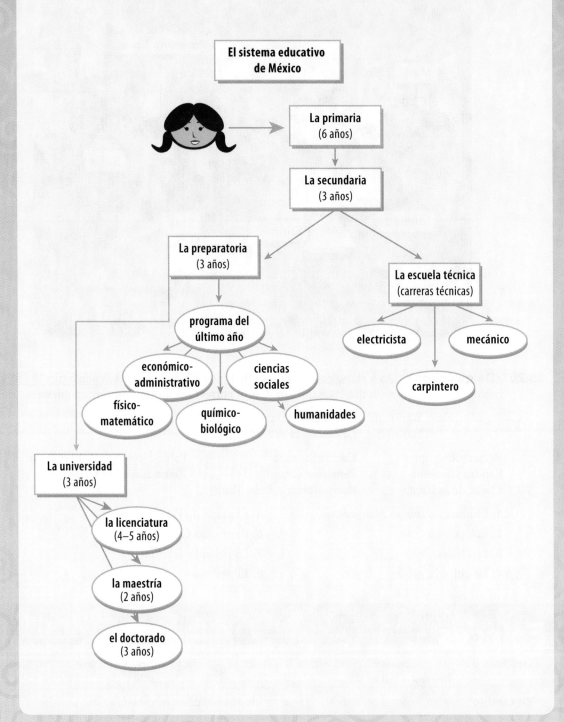

Paso 2: **Ahora en palabras.** On the basis of the information in the diagram, work with a partner to fill in the blanks with the appropriate information. Then, check your responses with the class.

En México, un niño asiste a seis años de ¹___primaria___. Los jóvenes asisten a tres años de ²___secundaria___. **Después de** terminar la secundaria, hay que elegir *(choose)* entre la ³___preparatoria___ y la escuela ⁴___técnica___. Optar por la escuela técnica implica prepararse para electricista, ⁵___mecánico/carpintero___, o ⁶___carpintero/mecánico___. **En cambio**, optar por la preparatoria implica prepararse para la ⁷___universidad___. En el último año de "la prepa," los estudiantes eligen entre varios programas académicos para especializarse antes de llegar a la universidad. La educación universitaria consiste en tres etapas: la ⁸___licenciatura___ que dura de cuatro a cinco años, la maestría que dura dos años y finalmente, el doctorado que dura tres años y es el grado más alto *(highest)*.

WILEY
PLUS

1B.22 INSTRUCTOR'S RESOURCES: For comparison with other Spanish-speaking countries, you will find additional information on Educational Systems in Spain and Latin America in your Instructor's Resources.

STANDARDS: COMMUNITIES. Have students talk with a friend, neighbor, classmate, etc. who was brought up in a different country to find out how their educational systems compare and contrast to the US system. Perhaps students in your class were brought up in another country and can share their experiences at this time, even if it is not in a Spanish-speaking country.

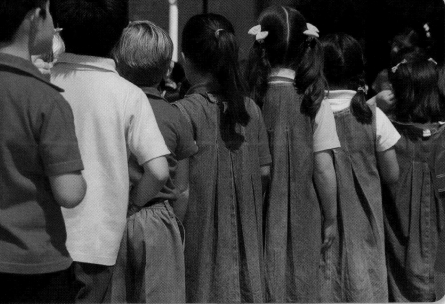

Estos niños de México están en la primaria.

En el último año de "la prepa", los estudiantes mexicanos deciden su carrera universitaria.

Perspectivas

1B.23 **El sistema escolar de tu país.** Now that you have learned about the educational system in Mexico, you will consider how it differs from that of the US. Using the flowchart from *Contextos* as a model, diagram the educational system of the US (or your native country if it is not the US). Then use the Spanish paragraph in 1B.22 as a model for expressing how your educational system works. Share your ideas with the class. Is there one primary model or were there variations?

VÍVELO: CULTURA

Los malentendidos en contextos escolares

Understanding how culture frames collective behavior can provide insights that quickly breakdown stereotypes. Traditionally, showing respect to adults or authority figures has been highly valued in Hispanic cultures. For example, children in Hispanic cultures are socialized to not interrupt conversations between adults; they must wait until the end of the conversation to speak up. As a result, when children are asked to interact with teachers and other adults in a US school setting their lack of experience comes across to some as an inability to demonstrate knowledge effectively. Teachers who are not aware of the socialization process of Hispanic children might conclude erroneously that the child is shy or language delayed. Consider the negative impact that not understanding these cultural differences can have on Latino children.

Estos chicos están en la primaria en Perú. ¿Crees que el sistema peruano es similar al de México? Investígalo en la Internet.

1B.24 **Malentendidos dentro del contexto escolar.**

Paso 1: Based on the information in *¡Vívelo: Cultura!* and throughout this *Investigación*, work in groups of three to discuss the cultural misunderstanding at play in the following scenario. How might Diego's teacher handle the situation?

Situación: Diego's parents came to the United States on a work visa. Diego's father is in management and will reside in the US for five years. Diego is in the third grade and is an above average student. However, after his first full week of school in the US, students are making fun of him because he responds to adults with "Yes sir," and "Yes Mrs. Parker." They think he is awkward because he never speaks while the teacher is talking, speaks only when spoken to, always raises his hand, and addresses adults formally.

Paso 2: Based on what you have learned about education in Latin America in general, identify other potential cross-cultural miscommunications (between your native culture and Hispanic cultures) within an education context.

Vocabulario: Investigación B

Vocabulario esencial

Sustantivos

el asiento	*seat*
la biblioteca	*library*
la carrera	*career, major*
el/la compañero /a de clase	*classmate*
el cuaderno	*notebook*
el edificio	*building*
el escritorio	*desk*
el/la estudiante	*student*
la grabadora	*recorder*
la hoja de papel	*sheet of paper*
el lápiz	*pencil*
el libro	*book*
el lugar	*place*
el mapa	*map*
la mesa	*table*
la mochila	*backpack*
la mujer	*woman*
el mundo	*world*
la oficina	*office*
la página	*page*
la pizarra	*blackboard, whiteboard*
la pluma	*pen*
el proyector	*projector*
la prueba	*test, quiz*
la puerta	*door*
el reloj	*clock/watch*
la residencia estudiatil	*student dorm*
el salón de clase	*classroom*
la silla	*chair*
la tiza	*chalk*
la universidad	*university*
la ventana	*window*

Adjetivos

bueno/a	*good*
grande	*big*
malo/a	*bad*
pequeño/a	*small*
todo/a	*all*
último/a	*last*
útil	*helpful, useful*

Verbos

abrir	*to open*
aprender	*to learn*
asistir	*to attend*
cambiar	*to change*
cerrar	*to close*
contestar	*to answer*
hacer la tarea	*to do homework*
hacer preguntas	*ask questions*
leer	*to read*
levantar la mano	*raise your hand*
llegar	*to arrive*
necesitar	*to need*
saludar	*to greet*
señalar	*to point out*
significar	*to mean*
terminar	*to finish*
tomar apuntes	*take notes*
trabajar	*to work*

Adverbios

antes	*before*
después	*after*
mañana	*tomorrow*

Otras palabras y expresiones

el abrazo	*hug*
alto/a	*tall*
el/la alumno/a	*student*
ambos	*both*
el año	*year*
a pesar de	*in spite of*
aunque	*even though*
el beso	*kiss*
bien educado/a	*well mannered*
las ciencias sociales	*social science*
compartir	*to share*
con base en	*based on*
educativo/a	*educational*
en cambio	*on the other hand*
enamorarse	*to fall in love*
el éxito	*success*
(el/la) joven	*young/young person*
la licenciatura	*bachelor's degree*

la maestría	*master's degree*
el malentendido	*misunderstanding*
el marcador	*marker*
mejorar	*to improve*
la pantalla	*screen*
por favor	*please*
Tengo una pregunta.	*I have a question.*
No entiendo.	*I don't understand.*
Repita, por favor.	*Repeat, please.*
Necesito más tiempo.	*I need more time.*
¿Está bien?	*Is it okay?*
¿Cómo se dice… en español?	*How do you say… in Spanish?*
¿Cómo?	*What?*
¿Hay tarea?	*Is there homework?*
¿Para cuándo es?	*When is it due?*
¿Qué página?	*What page?*
Lo siento.	*I'm sorry.*
¿Qué significa… ?	*What does… mean?*
Hay…	*There is/There are…*
¿Qué hay?	*What is there?*
¿Qué falta?	*What is missing?*
¿Oyes bien?	*Do you hear well?*
¿Qué es necesario para…?	*What is necessary for…?*

Cognados

Review the cognates in *Adelante* and the false cognates in *¡Atención!*. For a complete list of cognates, see Appendix 4 on page 605.

¡VÍVELO!

En vivo

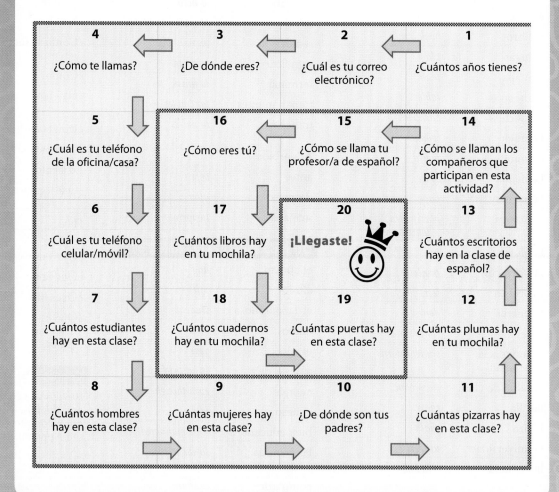

¡Ay, caramba! In groups of four, play the game **¡Ay, caramba!** according to the instructions below.

Cómo jugar a ¡Ay, caramba!:

1: Roll a die (**un dado**) or draw a number from 1–6.

2: Move the number of spaces indicated on the die (from 1–6 only) and answer the corresponding question on the board.

3: If you answer correctly, the next person gets a turn.

4: If you answer incorrectly, you say **¡Ay, caramba!** and move back two spaces, and the next person gets a turn.

4	3	2	1
¿Cómo te llamas?	¿De dónde eres?	¿Cuál es tu correo electrónico?	¿Cuántos años tienes?

5	16	15	14
¿Cuál es tu teléfono de la oficina/casa?	¿Cómo eres tú?	¿Cómo se llama tu profesor/a de español?	¿Cómo se llaman los compañeros que participan en esta actividad?

6	17	20	13
¿Cuál es tu teléfono celular/móvil?	¿Cuántos libros hay en tu mochila?	¡Llegaste!	¿Cuántos escritorios hay en la clase de español?

7	18	19	12
¿Cuántos estudiantes hay en esta clase?	¿Cuántos cuadernos hay en tu mochila?	¿Cuántas puertas hay en esta clase?	¿Cuántas plumas hay en tu mochila?

8	9	10	11
¿Cuántos hombres hay en esta clase?	¿Cuántas mujeres hay en esta clase?	¿De dónde son tus padres?	¿Cuántas pizarras hay en esta clase?

TEACHING TIP: Students need a die to play this game. Alternatively, to indicate how many movements forward are allowed, students could draw from a stack of numbered cards or draw slips of paper with the numbers 1–6 on them from a bag. Remind students that they can provide fake telephone numbers if they choose not to give that information.

WILEY PLUS

INSTRUCTOR'S RESOURCES: You will find a reproducible copy of the game board in the Instructor's Resources.

ORIENTATION. At the end of every *Capítulo*, there will be a section titled *¡Vívelo!* where the language comes to life through lively speaking activities in *En vivo* and video input and exercises in *En directo*. This section is designed as somewhat of a culminating activity for students to put their new language skills to use. Writing activities are included from *Capítulo 4* on.

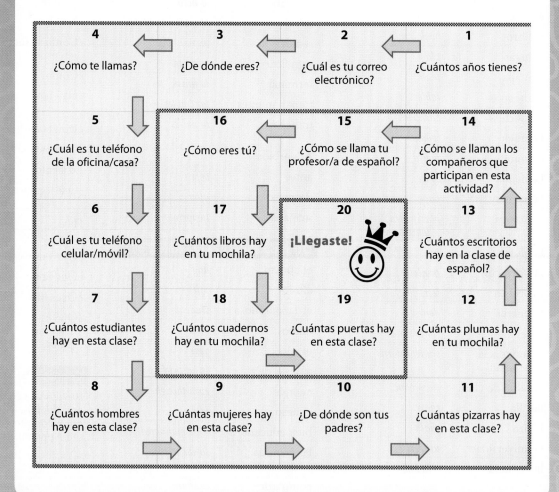

En directo

INVESTIGACIÓN A: Video: ¡Bienvenido al mundo hispano!

> **Antes de ver el video.** Answer the following questions:

1. ¿De dónde eres? Soy de _____ .
2. ¿Cuál es tu nacionalidad? Soy _____ .
3. ¿De dónde son tus padres? Mis padres son de _____ .

> **El video.** Which countries are mentioned in the video?

	Sí	No		Sí	No
Argentina	☑	☐	Guatemala	☑	☐
Bolivia	☐	☑	España	☑	☐
Colombia	☑	☐	México	☑	☐
Chile	☐	☑	Paraguay	☐	☑
Cuba	☑	☐	Perú	☑	☐
Ecuador	☑	☐	Puerto Rico	☐	☑
Estados Unidos	☐	☑	Uruguay	☑	☐
Honduras	☐	☑	Venezuela	☐	☑

> **Después de ver el video.** Think about your own answer to the following question, then discuss and compare your answers with the rest of the class: How do you greet and take leave of your friends and relatives?

Vocabulario útil
mejilla *cheek*
beso *kiss*
abrazo *hug*

WILEY PLUS

You will find a variety of resources for use with *En vivo* in *WileyPLUS,* such as a transcript of the video segment, a translation of that transcript, and guidelines for implementing the *En vivo* activities.

INVESTIGACIÓN B: Video: Un paseo por la UNAM

> **Antes de ver el video.** **¿Cómo es tu universidad?** Select the best words from the list to describe your college or university.

grande	pública	motivados	malos	muchos
pequeña *(small)*	privada	buenos	pocos	extranjeros *(foreign)*

Mi universidad es _____. Hay _____ estudiantes _____ y los profesores son _____.

> **El video.** Indicate whether the following statements are **ciertos** or **falsos** based on the video.

	Cierto	Falso
1. La UNAM está en la capital de México.	☑	☐
2. Hay más de 369,000 estudiantes.	☐	☑
3. Es la universidad pública más grande del mundo.	☐	☑
4. Mazaki es coreana.	☐	☑
5. Robert es de Australia.	☑	☐
6. Muchos estudiantes sólo estudian español.	☑	☐
7. Las clases de español son grandes y trabajan mucho en grupos pequeños.	☑	☐
8. Elliot dice que las personas que saben dos lenguas ganan más dinero en Estados Unidos.	☐	☑

> **Después de ver el video.** Think about your own answer to the following question, then discuss and compare your answers with the rest of the class: ¿Dónde está tu universidad? ¿Cuántos estudiantes hay en tu universidad? ¿Hay estudiantes de otros países? ¿De qué nacionalidad son? ¿Cómo es tu clase? ¿Y los profesores?

TEACHING TIP: Encourage student conversation with simple questions such as *¿Hay gestos físicos que acompañan los saludos con tus amigos? ¿con tu familia? Cuando les preguntas a tus amigos cómo están, ¿siempre dicen "Bien" o te cuentan lo que pasa en sus vidas?*

Vocabulario útil
de todas partes
 from everywhere
solamente *only*
después *after, later on*
ahorita *now*
mejorar *to improve*

ADDITIONAL ACTIVITY: Say or write these sentences on the board and have students complete them with the appropriate words from the video: *1. El español es el idioma oficial en ___ países. 2. En Perú los amigos se saludan con un ___ en la mejilla. 3. Los viejos amigos se saludan con un ___.* Answers: 1. 21, 2. beso, 3. abrazo

Retrato de la clase Checklist

WILEY
PLUS

TESTING PROGRAM:
You will find a complete
testing program for use
with *¡Vívelo!* in
WileyPLUS.

You shoud have recorded information in your **Retrato de la clase** in conjunction
with the following activities:

☐ **1A.12 Nuestras actividades favoritas**

☐ **1A.17 ¿Te gusta o no te gusta?**

☐ **1A.19 ¿De dónde son?**

☐ **1B.14 ¿Cuántos hay?**

Más allá de la clase

WILEY PLUS

INVESTIGACIÓN **2A**	INVESTIGACIÓN **2B**
### ¿Qué estudias y para qué?	### ¿Me presentas a tu familia?

ADELANTE
- ▶ ¡Ya lo sabes! Las carreras y las materias
- ▶ Guía de la universidad

Bien dicho: Linking between words

ADELANTE
- ▶ ¡Ya lo sabes! La familia, la personalidad y el carácter
- ▶ La familia real española

Bien dicho: Yes/No questions

PALABRAS CLAVE
- ▶ Las materias, las especializaciones y las carreras

PALABRAS CLAVE
- ▶ La familia

ESTRUCTURAS CLAVE
- ▶ Conjugating verbs: *Yo* and *tú* forms
- ▶ *Estar*

ESTRUCTURAS CLAVE
- ▶ Conjugating verbs: *Él, ella,* and *usted* forms
- ▶ Adjectives

VÍVELO: LENGUA
- ▶ Expressing possession II

VÍVELO: CULTURA
- ▶ Las universidades
- ▶ Estudiar en el extranjero

VÍVELO: CULTURA
- ▶ El tamaño de la familia
- ▶ Los apellidos
- ▶ Los hijos

CONTEXTOS Y PERSPECTIVAS
La angustia estudiantil

CONTEXTOS Y PERSPECTIVAS
El compadrazgo

¡VÍVELO!

En vivo:
La familia de mi compañero/a

En directo:
A: Bilingüismo en el trabajo
B: Crónica de una boda

¿Qué estudias y para qué?

In this **Investigación** you will learn:

▶ How to talk about professions and careers

▶ How to talk about the classroom and the campus

▶ How to express time

▶ How to talk about your weekly schedule

¿Qué estudias y para qué?

You can investigate what someone studies. You can answer questions about what you study.	¿Qué estudias? ¿Qué carrera estudias? ¿enfermería? ¿periodismo? ¿arte? Estudio biología.
You can talk about the university campus.	La biblioteca está al lado del teatro. La Facultad de Medicina está al lado del estadio.
You can find out what time it is. You can tell what time it is.	¿Qué hora es? Es la una. Son las dos. Es mediodía.
You can ask when a class begins. You can say when your classes meet.	¿A qué hora es la clase? Mi clase de biología es los lunes, miércoles y viernes a las 10:00 de la mañana.
You can ask about someone else's schedule. You can explain your schedule to someone else.	¿Cómo es tu horario? Mis clases son los lunes, miércoles y viernes por la mañana.
You can talk about your personality in order to explain what classes you like best or your choice of major/ future career.	En general, no me gusta la química. Me gusta el arte porque estimula la imaginación.

TEACHING TIP: Ask students to place a check mark by the courses that are required for their major. Since most of the cognates have more than three syllables you may want to practice recognition of the cognates by using them in a sentence and having students place an X next to the ones they hear, i.e, *Se asocian las plantas con la agricultura; Se asocia Don Quijote con la literatura española; Se asocia Dell y Apple con la tecnología; Se asocia el PowerPoint con la comunicación visual.*

Adelante

¡Ya lo sabes! Las carreras y las materias

la administración	la biología	la geografía	la programación
la agricultura	las ciencias	la geología	la psicología
la anatomía	la ciencia política	la historia	la religión
la antropología	la comunicación visual	el latín	la sociología
las artes gráficas	la ecología	la literatura	el teatro
las artes plásticas	la economía	las matemáticas	la tecnología
la arquitectura	la filosofía	la medicina	la terapia física
la astronomía	la física	la música	

2A.1 El mapa cognitivo.   With a classmate, use the graphic organizer to organize the different majors according to the general areas of study to which they pertain.

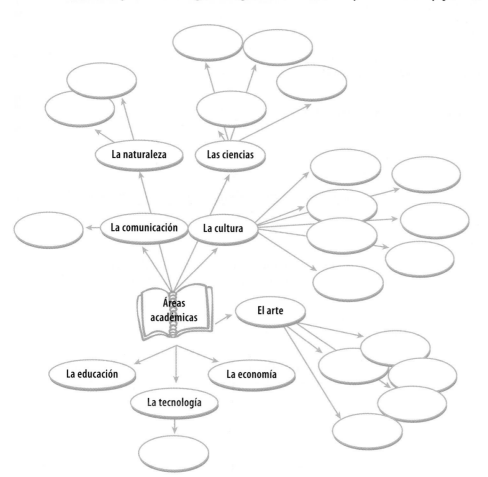

2A.1 INSTRUCTOR'S RESOURCES: A PowerPoint slide of this semantic map, completed, is provided in your Instructor's Resources.

2A.2 Las carreras y las materias.   Read the list of names below. Match each statement you hear about these famous people's fields of study with the appropriate name following the model. Verify your answers as a class.

1. __i__   **a.** Galileo Galilei
2. __d__   **b.** Leonardo daVinci
3. __b__   **c.** Margaret Mead
4. __c__   **d.** Ludwig van Beethoven
5. __g__   **e.** Sigmund Freud
6. __h__   **f.** Karl Marx
7. __f__   **g.** C.S. Lewis
8. __e__   **h.** la Clínica Mayo
9. __i__   **i.** Frank Lloyd Wright
10. __a__   **j.** Bill Gates

2A.2 AUDIO SCRIPT: 1. Se asocia con las computadoras y la tecnología. 2. Se asocia con la música y la composición. 3. Se asocia con la física, la anatomía, la ingeniería mecánica, pero principalmente con el arte. 4. Se asocia con la antropología. 5. Se asocia con la literatura filosófica, espiritual y religiosa. 6. Se asocia con la medicina. 7. Se asocia con la economía, la sociología y la política. 8. Se asocia con la psicología. 9. Se asocia con la arquitectura. 10. Se asocia con la astronomía.

EXPRESIONES ÚTILES

Para mí means *for me*.
Para ti means *for you (informal)*.

For other persons, use **para** with the words you learned as subject pronouns: **usted, él, ella, nostros, vosotros, ustedes, ellos, ellas.**

No es necesario para ti pero es necesario para mí.
Para ella no es necesario estudiar pero sí es necesario para él.
Para nosotros la clase de español es interesante.

Para ser means *in order to be… .*

Para ser doctor, es necesario estudiar por muchos años.

2A.3 TEACHING TIP:
You may wish to call attention to the *modelo* and explain simply that *¿Te interesa…?* works similarly to *¿Te gusta…?*. Avoid any lengthy grammatical explanation at this level.

2A.3 TEACHING TIP:
For Paso 2, ask the class *¿Cuál es el promedio para la tecnología?* and write the number on the board to obtain a general average once all groups have reported their results. Then report to the class *Entonces, el promedio para la tecnología es….* *Y para la comunicación es….* This will more easily enable students to write the results in their *Retrato de la clase.*

2A.3 ORIENTATION: BUILDING COMMUNITY.
Throughout the text, there are many activities developed to not only build students' communicative skills but to also foster a sense of interdependency among students. Remind students that their voices matter. As the instructor, you should make note of where students' interests fall, and do not fall, in order to better connect with them.

2A.3 ¿Te interesa?

Paso 1: In groups of three, find out each other's interest level in the general fields below. On a scale of 1–5, 1 being the least interesting and 5 being the most, rank your interest in each field of study.

Modelo: E1: *¿Te interesa la historia?*
E2: *Para mí, es un tres.*

Campos generales	Yo	Compañero/a 1	Compañero/a 2	Promedio (*Average*)
La tecnología				
La comunicación				
La cultura				
La economía				
La educación				
La naturaleza				
El arte				
Las ciencias básicas				
La medicina				

Paso 2: As a class, determine the least and most popular interest areas and write your results in your **Retrato de la clase.**

Retrato de la clase: Los cursos más populares de la clase son ___, ___ y ___.

DICHOS

Vivir para ver y ver para saber.	*Live and learn.*
Quien poco sabe poco teme.	*Ignorance is the mother of imprudence.*
Para aprender, nunca es tarde.	*You are never too old to learn.*

VÍVELO: CULTURA

Las universidades

Universities in Spain and Latin America share common basic characteristics because Latin American institutions inherited many of their qualities from Spain. During the colonial era, the purpose of the university was either to train students to be civil servants, products of the public universities, or to serve ecclesiastically in the Catholic Church, products of the private universities. This type of university system dominated Latin America until the twentieth century when higher education began to take on its main unique feature: university autonomy. With university autonomy came the notion of students participating in the decision-making process related to university administration and the growth of an institution that also participated in the social advancement of Latin America.

Even then, many universities in Latin America were modeled after European institutions which had two fundamental orientations, one was vocational and the other nationalistic. The public universities emphasized training students to become professionals, such as lawyers, engineers, doctors and the private institutions emphasized a general education to the few elite that could afford them. Traveling and studying abroad, mainly in Europe, was a privilege of the small elite. Combined, these institutions formed what has been called the intelligentsia of Latin America until the end of the twentieth century. In the twentieth century, for those who could study abroad, they increasingly opted to study in the United States. They returned to their homelands with new knowledge from North American and European scholars, but only marginally effected real change at home because of their small numbers. It was not until after WWII that the concept of international cooperation among institutions became the new model for institutions of higher education. University exchanges between Latin American and North American or European universities were intended to foment the economic growth and development of Latin America. Scholarship and exchange programs, technical assistance, research and development grants increased. Today, study abroad exchanges are significant experiences for students of most universities around the world. Find out what study-abroad opportunities exist at your school.

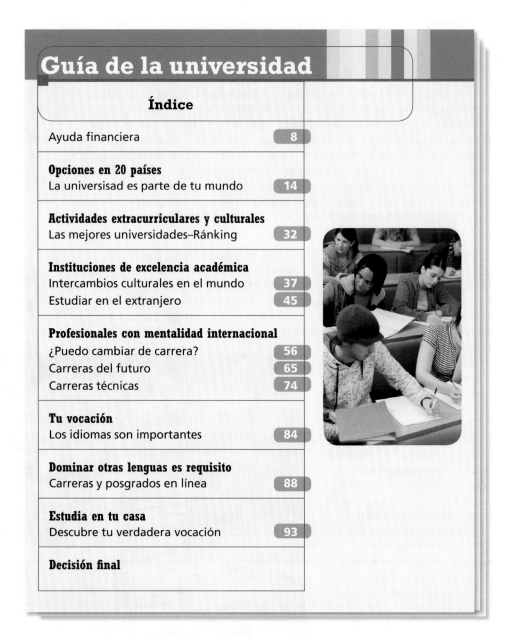

Guía de la universidad

Índice

2A.4 TEACHING TIP:
When you go over the answers, probe further by asking students how they arrived at their answers and what they associated with the phrases. This is another opportunity to draw attention to the fact that students know more than they might realize because of the cognates present.

2A.4 Guía de la universidad.   Scanning for information is an excellent reading strategy. Scan the Table of Contents to determine on what page you would find the following:

1. rankings of the best institutions of higher learning — p. 32

2. information on alternative careers of the future — p. 65

3. information on scholarships, financial aid and grants — p. 8

4. an article on the benefits of knowing a second language — p. 84

5. information on exchange or study abroad programs — p. 37

Bien dicho

Linking between words

As mentioned in *Investigación 1B,* in English we use a brief pause to separate words when we speak. For example, say the phrases *me either* and *her aunt* three times slowly and notice what happens in the back of your throat. In order to signal the boundary between the two words in each phrase, the back of your tongue rises and briefly touches the back of the roof of your mouth, momentarily interrupting the flow of air. This phenomenon does not naturally occur in Spanish. In other words, the spaces we see between words in written Spanish are not signaled in speech. This explains why two vowels in Spanish are pronounced either as a single vowel, as in the case of **a + a** or with a smooth transition between them, as in the case of **a + e.** The lack of a pause between the words in these phrases is called *linking,* or **enlace** in Spanish.

Writing	Speech
la agricultura	lagricultura
la astronomía	lastronomía
la educación	laeducación
la economía	laeconomía

Words seem to be linked even when there are consonants separating them. This is particularly true when a word ending in a consonant is combined with another word beginning with a vowel.

el español	elespa**nyol**
Hablan inglés	**a**blanin**gles**
La historia es interesante	lais**to**rya**es**intere**sa**nte

The syllables in bold indicate where the spoken stress should fall. Remember that the letter **h** is not pronounced in Spanish.

2A.5 **Práctica de pronunciación.** With a partner, take turns practicing **enlaces** while pronouncing the following sentences. You will notice that we have provided 'alternate' spelling to remind you of the sounds represented by the alphabet in Spanish. We have also indicated the stressed syllables in bold type.

1. ¿Qué hora es?   ke**o**raes
2. Estudio antropología.   estu**dy**oantropolo**hi**a
3. Nicolás estudia alemán.   niko**la**sestudyalale**man**
4. ¿Puedes estudiar español conmigo?   **pwe**desestu**dy**arespa**nyol**com**mi**go
5. Se habla español en esta clase.   se**a**blaespa**nyol**e**nes**ta**kla**se
6. Buenos Aires es una ciudad increíble.   bweno**sai**re**se**sunasyu**da**dinkreible
7. El Álamo está en San Antonio.   e**la**lamoes**taen**sanan**to**nyo
8. Paco desea estudiar inglés aquí.   **pa**kode**se**aestu**dya**rin**gle**saki

2A.6 **Dictado.** You will hear several sentences in Spanish. On a separate sheet of paper, write exactly what you hear. Keep in mind that you will not hear pauses between words. Listen to each sentence at least a couple of times before trying to write what you hear.

2A.6 AUDIO SCRIPT: 1. Soy estudiante de artes plásticas. 2. El profesor es inteligente y dedicado. 3. Estudio antropología y arquitectura. 4. Historia es una clase interesante. 5. Hay veinticinco estudiantes en el salón.

2A.6 FOLLOW-UP: Have volunteers write sentences 1 through 5 on the board, or on a transparency. Go over them as a class. Your students may not get the accent marks quite yet. That is okay. For the time being, point out that written accents indicate a deviation from an established pattern and remind us where to put the emphasis.

Palabras clave 1 Las materias, las especializaciones y las carreras

La hora del día

Es la 1:16 pm.
Es la una y dieciséis de la tarde.

Es la 1:25 am.
Es la una y veinticinco de la mañana.

Son las 4:05 pm.
Son las cuatro y cinco de la tarde.

Son las 9:06 pm.
Son las nueve y seis de la noche.

Es la 1:50 pm.
Son las dos menos diez de la tarde.

Son las 5:53 am.
Son las seis menos siete de la mañana.

Son las 12:00 de la noche.
Es (la) medianoche.

Son las 12:00 del día.
Es (el) mediodía.

Las fuerzas armadas

El mercadeo

La ingeniería

La administración de empresas

El periodismo

El desarrollo infantil

El derecho

La contabilidad

BANCO CENTRAL

Preguntas	Respuestas
¿Qué hora es? *What time is it?*	Es la una/Son las dos en punto. *It's one o'clock/It's two o'clock exactly (on the dot).*
¿A qué hora empieza la clase? *(At) What time does class begin?*	Empieza a las 8:00 de la mañana. *It begins at 8:00 in the morning.*

Use **y media** to express half past the hour, and **y cuarto** or **menos cuarto** for a quarter past or a quarter until the hour, respectively:

Llego a la universidad a las ocho y media.	*I get to the university at eight thirty (half past eight).*
Tenemos clase a las nueve y cuarto.	*We have class at nine fifteen (quarter past nine).*

When giving exact times in the morning, afternoon or at night, use the preposition **de**:

Son las dos de la mañana.	*It is two in the morning.*
Es la una de la tarde.	*It is one in the afternoon.*

To express more generally "in the morning, afternoon, evening" or "at night," use **en** and to express a part of the day as the time period "during" which you do something, use **por**:

En la mañana tengo una clase.	*In the morning I have one class.*
Estudio por las mañanas.	*I study in the morning.*

SUGGESTION: You may wish to tell students that they are likely to hear *y treinta* and *y quince/menos quince* as well as *y media* and *y cuarto/menos cuarto.*

2A.7 WARM-UP: Write five times on the board and label a–e, such as a. 1:30, b. 1:00, c. 1:45, d. 3:30, e. 7:15. Then, give the times in Spanish in random order and have students indicate the time that corresponds to what you said.

2A.7 AUDIO SCRIPT: 1. Son las ocho y veinte. 2. Son las cuatro y media. 3. Son las siete y catorce. 4. Son las once y media. 5. Son las tres menos once. 6. Son las tres y veintiuno. 7. Son las seis y ocho. 8. Son las cinco y media. 9. Son las dos menos veintidós.

2A.7 **¿Qué hora es?** Indicate which clock below represents each time you hear by writing that statement's number next to the corresponding clock.

 3

 4

 6

 8

 9

 7

 2

 5

 1

2A.8 AUDIO SCRIPT: 1. La clase de introducción a la programación comienza a las once y veinte. 2. La clase de economía comienza a las diez y veinticinco. 3. La clase de contabilidad comienza a las cinco y cuarto. 4. La clase de administración de empresas comienza a las siete menos cuarto. 5. La clase de francés comienza a las nueve y diez. 6. La clase de literatura comienza a las ocho y media.

2A.8 TEACHING TIP: If you feel this task is too difficult for your students, write the names of the courses on the board and ask students to identify the time of the class as they hear each sentence.

2A.8 **¿Cuál es?** You will hear statements about several classes and the times they begin. As you hear each statement, write the class mentioned and then indicate which clock shows the time it begins following the model.

 a

 b

 c

 d

 e

 f

	Clase	Comienza a las
1.	Introducción a la programación	f
2.	Economía	d
3.	Contabilidad	b
4.	Administración	c
5.	Francés	e
6.	Literatura	a

Los días de la semana

lunes	martes	miércoles	jueves	viernes	sábado	domingo
	1	2	3	4	5	6
7	8	9	10	11	12	13

Note that the days of the week are not capitalized, and the names of the days don't change in the plural, except for **los sábados** and **los domingos.** To express the idea of something happening *routinely* on a given day of the week, use **los.** To express the idea of a single event happening on a given day of a particular week, use **el.**

Tengo clase de biología los lunes y los miércoles.	*I have biology on Mondays and Wednesdays.*
Los sábados trabajo en la biblioteca.	*On Saturdays, I work in the library.*
Tengo un examen de biología el miércoles.	*I have a biology exam on (this coming) Wednesday.*

EXPRESIÓN ÚTIL

¿Qué tienes que hacer?

tener que	must, to have to (do something)

Los estudiantes tienen que estudiar y practicar para aprender un segundo idioma.
Students must/have to study and practice to learn a second language.

2A.9 **¿Qué día de la semana?** As you hear the details of where Señor López has to be on certain dates in September, indicate which days of the week correspond. Follow the model and check your work with a partner.

SEPTIEMBRE

lunes	martes	miércoles	jueves	viernes	sábado	domingo
		1	2	3	4	5
6	7	8	9	10	11	12
13	14	15	16	17	18	19
20	21	22	23	24	25	26
27	28	29	30			

1. *el miércoles y el jueves*
2. el lunes, el martes y el miércoles
3. el martes y el miércoles
4. el martes, el miércoles, el jueves, el viernes y el sábado
5. el domingo, el lunes y el martes

www **¡Conéctate!**
Visit http://expedia.es and search for a round-trip flight from where you live to a country you would like to visit. Are there certain *días* and *horas* that are cheaper to fly than others? Compare flights with the same connections that differ only in *días* and *horas.* Share this comparison with your classmates.

CULTURAL INFORMATION: Draw attention to the order of the days on the calendar. Spanish-language calendars typically start the week on Mondays, whereas English-language calendars typically start the week on Sundays. Point out that in Hispanic cultures, Sundays are often reserved for family activities.

TEACHING TIP: For listening comprehension practice for days of the week, read students a definition and ask them to provide the corresponding day in Spanish, such as *generalmente el primer día de trabajo o de clases (lunes); en general, el día de estar con familia y el día de descanso (domingo); el día en que no hay clases ni trabajo (sábado); el segundo día de la semana laboral/ escolar (martes); el quinto o el último día de la semana laboral/ escolar (viernes); el tercer día de la semana laboral/ escolar (miércoles); el cuarto día de la semana laboral/escolar (jueves).* For *primer, segundo, tercer, cuarto, quinto,* hold up number of fingers to indicate the meaning of the ordinal numbers.

2A.9 TEACHING TIP: As you proceed, make sure to recycle this vocabulary. It is easy to begin the class by asking students ¿Qué día es?, ¿Qué día es mañana? or ¿Qué hora es?, ¿A qué hora termina la clase?

2A.9 AUDIO SCRIPT: 1. El Señor López tiene que estar en San Francisco el primero y el dos de septiembre. 2. Tiene que estar en San José, Costa Rica del 6 al 8. 3. Tiene que estar en Caracas, el 14 y el 15. 4. Tiene que estar en Bogotá, Colombia del 21 al 25. 5. Tiene que estar en Ecuador del 26 al 28 de septiembre.

2A.10 El horario de Claudia.   With a classmate, read Claudia's university schedule to answer the following questions. Then, verify your responses as a class.

1. ¿Qué carrera estudia Claudia?   ☐ Estudia ingeniería.

☐ Estudia idiomas extranjeros.

☐ No es posible determinar qué estudia.

2. ¿Qué días de la semana y cuántas horas trabaja Claudia?

3. ¿Cuántas horas de laboratorio a la semana tiene Claudia?

4. ¿Cuándo tiene Claudia tiempo completamente libre durante la semana?

5. ¿Cuándo estudia Claudia en la biblioteca durante la semana?

6. ¿Tiene Claudia un régimen sistemático para almorzar?

El horario de Claudia

	lunes	martes	miércoles	jueves	viernes
8:00-8:50	Biología – Facultad de Ciencias	8:30-10:00 Laboratorio de Biología	Biología – Facultad de Ciencias	8:30-10:00 Laboratorio de Biología	Biología – Facultad de Ciencias
9:05-9:55	Historia – Facultad de Humanidades		Historia – Facultad de Humanidades		Historia – Facultad de Humanidades
10:10-11:00	Música – Departamento de Música	Estudiar en la biblioteca	Música – Departamento de Música	Estudiar en la biblioteca	Música – Departamento de Música
11:15-12:15	Estudiar en la biblioteca		Estudiar en la biblioteca		Estudiar en la biblioteca
12:20-1:10	Comer en la cafetería	Comer en la cafetería	Comer en la cafetería	Comer en la cafetería	Comer en la cafetería
1:20-2:20	Inglés – Facultad de Humanidades	Trabajo 1:30–5:30	Inglés – Facultad de Humanidades	Trabajo 1:30–5:30	Inglés – Facultad de Humanidades
2:30-3:30					
3:35-5:35	Trabajo		Trabajo		Trabajo

2A.11 ¿Dónde está Claudia?   You will hear several statements about Claudia's whereabouts at certain times. Look for her on the illustration on page 69 at the indicated time. If the statement correctly describes where she is on the map, circle *cierto* (See column A). If not, circle *falso* and write where she actually is (See column B). Take notes if you need to. Lastly, look at Claudia's schedule in Activity 2A.10 and write down in the last blank (See column C) where she is supposed to be at the indicated times. Follow the model, then verify your responses with classmates. **¡Ojo!** You will hear the expression **cerca de,** meaning *near*. Use this expression in your responses as is relevant.

A **B** **C**

1. cierto/(falso)   Está *en la cafetería*.   ¿Dónde tiene que estar? *en la clase de biología*

2. (cierto)/falso   Está _____.   ¿Dónde tiene que estar? en la clase de historia

3. cierto/(falso)   Está *cerca del teatro*.   ¿Dónde tiene que estar? en la clase de música

4. (cierto)/falso   Está _____.   ¿Dónde tiene que estar? en la facultad de ciencias

5. cierto/(falso)   Está *en el parque*.   ¿Dónde tiene que estar? en la biblioteca

6. (cierto)/falso   Está _____.   ¿Dónde tiene que estar? en la clase de inglés

2A.12 El horario más exigente. You want to find out who in class has the most demanding schedule. Ask five students the following questions and write their answers down. Then, compare your answers as a class to determine which students' schedules are the most demanding and write that information in your **Retrato de la clase.**

	Nombre	Nombre	Nombre	Nombre	Nombre
1. ¿Cuántas clases tienes este semestre?					
2. ¿Cuáles son los días de la semana que tienes clases?					
3. ¿Qué día y a qué hora empieza tu primera *(first)* clase?					
4. ¿Qué día y a qué hora termina tu última *(last)* clase?					
5. ¿Trabajas? ¿Cuántas horas a la semana trabajas?					
6. ¿Qué días de la semana trabajas?					
7. ¿A qué hora empiezas a trabajar?					
8. ¿A qué hora terminas de trabajar?					

Retrato de la clase: _____ y _____ son los estudiantes con los horarios más complicados de la clase.

2A.12 TIME MANAGEMENT: In order to best manage the time spent on the interview, you may want to establish a limit of three minutes to interview each classmate. You may also want to let students know when their time is up so that they begin working with someone else. They may not be done with the interview, but this will ensure that there is a flow and that students conduct the needed interviews.

WILEY PLUS

2A.12 INSTRUCTOR'S RESOURCES You will find a reproducible chart for this activity in your Instructor's Resources.

EXPRESIONES ÚTILES

Para hablar del horario

primera/o	Mi primera clase del día es a las 8:00 de la mañana.
última/o	Mi última clase del día es a las 4:30 de la tarde.
comienza	Mi primera clase del día comienza a las 8:00 de la mañana.
termina	Mi última clase del día termina a las 5:30 de la tarde.

2A.13 ¿Qué preguntas son necesarias? What questions would you need to know how to ask to find out your classmate's exact schedule? Check the most appropriate questions.

- ☑ ¿Qué clases tienes este semestre?
- ☑ ¿Qué días tienes clases?
- ☑ ¿A qué hora es tu clase de ____?
- ☐ ¿Cómo se llama tu profesor/profesora de español?
- ☑ ¿Qué días tienes que trabajar?
- ☑ ¿A qué hora tienes que estar en el trabajo?
- ☐ ¿Cuál es tu teléfono?
- ☑ ¿Qué compromisos *(commitments)* tienes este semestre?

2A.14 Tu propio horario. With a partner, arrange the questions from the previous activity (only the appropriate ones) so they make sense as interview questions. Then, take turns interviewing each other in Spanish to test whether you can recreate each other's schedule. When finished, compare schedules. Did you get each other's schedules right? Write your partner's schedule in your **Retrato de la clase.**

VÍVELO: LENGUA

Expressing preferences with nouns: Me/te/le gusta(n)

You have learned to talk about what people like or do not like to do using **me, te,** or **le** with the verb form **gusta. Me gusta, te gusta,** and **le gusta** correspond to what *I* , *you* (informal), or *he/she* or *you* (formal) like, respectively.

When referring to *things* one likes, as opposed to what one likes to do, the verb form will either be singular **(gusta)** or plural **(gustan)** depending on the noun(s) referred to.

—¿Te **gustan** los libros de Danielle Steel?
—Sí. Me **gusta** mucho su última novela.

Since **le gusta** expresses what *he* or *she* likes and what *you* (formal) *like*, you may may add **a él, a ella,** or **a usted,** for clarification. Likewise add **a** with a person's name when mentioning what a specific person likes.

¿A usted le gustan las clases de ciencia?   *Do you like science classes?*
A Juan le gusta el actor Tom Cruise,   *Juan likes the actor Tom Cruise,*
pero a Laura no le gusta.   *but Laura doesn't.*

2A.15 **¿Te gusta...?** Work with a classmate to interview each other with questions that begin with **¿Te gusta/gustan...** and end with the things and activities numbered 1-12. When each of you has interviewed the other, note which of the questions you responded to similarly. Then, share with the class the ones you had in common. Determine the most popular activities among all students in the class and write them in your **Retrato de la clase.**

2A.15: EXTENSION. ACTIVITY: You may want to model similar questions highlighting the meaning of *me da igual* (I'm indifferent) and *para nada* (not at all). Some more colloquial equivalents for *me da igual* are "(It) doesn't matter" and "Whatever".

¿Te gusta/gustan...?	Sí. Me gusta/ gustan mucho.	Me da igual. *(I'm indifferent.)*	No. No me gusta/gustan para nada *(at all).*
1. ...estudiar en la biblioteca?			
2. ... hablar español en clase?			
3. ...aprender español?			
4. ...la poesía?			
5. ...escuchar música country?			
6. ...escuchar música rock?			
7. ...el jazz?			
8. ...escuchar música clásica?			
9. ...bailar?			
10. ...ver la tele?			
11. ...las películas de terror?			
12. ...leer libros de historia?			

Retrato de la clase: Las actividades más populares de la clase son ____, ____ y ____.

VÍVELO: CULTURA

Estudiar en el extranjero

As an adult, the best way to learn a foreign language and learn about the cultures of people who speak the language is to begin with formal instruction and then spend time in countries where the language is spoken. There is a great variety of programs for study abroad. Some last four to six weeks in the summer. Some are for an entire summer, a semester, or a full academic year. Many colleges and universities sponsor their own study-abroad programs and will often issue credits based on participation in another college's or university's program. There are also many independent language institutes abroad. Seek out information about your institution's study-abroad programs and talk about credit and non-credit options with your academic advisor.

When studying abroad, the best way to learn about the culture is by living with a family. Conversing with family members is a good way to practice what you know. If invited, participate in family celebrations, traditions, and customs as a way to gain insights into the culture.

2A.16 ¡Antes de leer!

Paso 1: The following is an advertisement about various opportunities for studying abroad or studying a foreign language. Read it over to get a general idea of what each section emphasizes.

¡Viajestudios te da la bienvenida!

En Viajestudios tienes un recurso único si te interesa estudiar en el extranjero. Tenemos centros de enseñanza en varios países del mundo y ofrecemos gran variedad de programas de estudio y opciones de alojamiento. Los estudiantes que participan en nuestros programas vienen de todas partes del mundo. Así que, además de aprender sobre la cultura del país que visitas, compartes la experiencia con una comunidad internacional.

Base de datos para estudiar en el extranjero

Tenemos centros de enseñanza en todas partes del mundo. Ofrecemos programas de estudio de idiomas y una variedad de mini-cursos sobre temas culturales. Consulta nuestra base de datos para informarte sobre los programas y los eventos importantes en nuestros centros.

Comunidad internacional

Participa en la comunidad internacional donde vives. Nuestros centros organizan eventos para juntar a personas de diferentes culturas en programas de intercambio cultural.

Perspectivas del mundo

Aquí los participantes en nuestros programas ponen fotos y escriben breves comentarios sobre su experiencia y sobre los eventos importantes en los países que visitan.

Intercambio de idiomas

Puedes participar en nuestros programas sin salir de tu país o ni siquiera salir de tu casa. En Internet ofrecemos visitas virtuales de muchos lugares y tenemos un programa de intercambio de idiomas. Puedes conectarte con personas en otros países o en tu propia ciudad.

Intercambio de familias

Tienes la opción de vivir en un apartamento o una residencia estudiantil con otros participantes en el programa, o puedes optar por vivir con una familia anfitriona para experimentar una auténtica vida cotidiana. Si quieres ser estudiante de intercambio o si quieres invitar a tu familia a ser familia anfitriona, ¡contáctanos!

Viajestudios

Paso 2: Read the ad again. Can you guess the meaning of the following words based on the context in the passage and in the sentences? Check your guesses with a classmate.

mundo
familia anfitriona
intercambio

www ¡Conéctate!

Visit your school's website to find out what study abroad options are available. If you would like to broaden your search options, check out http://studyabroad.com and search for programs by country or school. What did you find? Does your school offer a program that might interest you? Are there other programs that piqued your interest?

Paso 3: Indicate which section of the ad in a–e below is likely to have specific information about what you hope to get out of the study-abroad experience based on the statements numbered 1–5. Read the descriptions in the ad that correspond to each section.

2A.17 PASO 2: ANSWERS. mundo *world,* familia anfitriona *host family,* intercambio *exchange*

a. Base de datos para estudiar en el extranjero

b. Comunidad internacional

c. Perspectivas del mundo

d. Intercambio de idiomas

e. Intercambio de familias

_c_ **1.** Deseo investigar los eventos y las culturas de todo el mundo.

_b_ **2.** Deseo hablar con personas de otras culturas en mi ciudad o país.

_e_ **3.** Deseo participar como estudiante o familia anfitriona en un programa de intercambio.

_a_ **4.** Deseo investigar programas para estudiar en el extranjero según *(according to)* varios criterios.

_d_ **5.** Deseo practicar el español en la Internet con personas en otras partes del mundo.

¡Atención!

Publicidad	can mean *publicity* but also means *advertising.*
	El mercadeo y la publicidad son dos aspectos de los negocios.
Asignatura	does not mean signature; it means *subject* as in the subjects one studies.
	¿Cuántas asignaturas estudias este semestre?
Firma	does not mean firm; it means *signature.* The verb for *to sign* is **firmar.** To refer to *a firm* in the sense of a company, use **la empresa.** A law firm is often called **un bufete de abogados.** If you want to describe something as *firm,* use the adjective **firme.**
	Las firmas de los médicos son ilegibles. **El documento necesita la firma del presidente de la empresa.** **El presidente de la empresa firma todos los documentos importantes.**

2A.17 Escoger y escribir. Fill in each blank with the most appropriate word based on the context of the statement. Then check your work with a partner.

1. Mis ___asignaturas___ este semestre son biología, química, matemáticas e inglés.

2. Este libro lleva la ___firma___ de la autora. Es una copia especial.

3. Me gusta que el profesor responda de una manera ___firme___ a las preguntas. Así *(That way)* no tengo dudas.

4. Para trabajar en una empresa grande de Madison Avenue en Nueva York, es necesario estudiar ___publicidad___.

5. Los abogados trabajan en un ___bufete (de abogados)___.

Estructuras clave 1 Conjugating verbs: *Yo* and *tú* forms

PLUS
Go to *WileyPLUS* and review the tutorial for this grammar point.

PLUS

You will find PowerPoint presentations for use with *Estructuras clave* in *WileyPLUS*.

TEACHING TIP: The practice exercises that follow focus on *yo* and *tú* forms. Explain to students that they will not be expected to produce these verbs properly conjugated immediately. Rather, they should begin drawing their attention to how verbs change and whether they recognize these patterns. Shortly, they will be expected to use them.

What have you noticed about the verbs you have learned to express various activities? What are the different forms of those verbs you have used to express *who* does a particular activity?

In Spanish there are three verb categories, sometimes called "conjugations", identified by their infinitive endings: **–ar**, **–er**, and **–ir.** Much like in English where you must use the form *call* with *I* and *calls* with *she,* the subject or subject pronoun dictates which personal ending a verb uses. Using the appropriate personal ending according to the subject is called conjugating the verb. While English usually has only two verb endings, e.g. call/calls, eat/eats, sleep/sleeps, Spanish has several verb endings in each of the three verb categories. We will focus here on the **yo** and **tú** verb endings for **–ar**, **–er**, and **–ir** verbs.

In the present tense, the **yo** form of all **–ar**, **–er**, and **–ir** verbs ends in **–o.** For **–ar** verbs, the **tú** form ends in **–as,** while for **–er** and **–ir** verbs it ends in **–es.** See the chart that follows.

–ar			**–er**		**–ir**	
hablar	(yo)	habl**o**	comer	com**o**	vivir	viv**o**
	(tú)	habl**as**		com**es**		viv**es**
bailar		bail**o**	correr	corr**o**	resistir	resist**o**
		bail**as**		corr**es**		resist**es**
nadar		nad**o**	ver	ve**o**	escribir	escrib**o**
		nad**as**		v**es**		escrib**es**
escuchar		escuch**o**	leer	le**o**	describir	describ**o**
		escuch**as**		le**es**		describ**es**
llamar		llam**o**				
		llam**as**				
levantar		levant**o**				
		levant**as**				

2A.18 ¿Quién lo dice? Indicate who makes the following statements. Check your work with a classmate and then the rest of the class. The first one has been done for you as a model.

_C_ **1.** "Practico fútbol americano todos los días".　　　**a.** J. K. Rowling

_f_ **2.** "Con frecuencia visito a mi familia en México".　　**b.** El increíble Hulk

_e_ **3.** "Canto la canción 'Dame más gasolina'".　　　**c.** Peyton Manning

_a_ **4.** "Escribo los libros de Harry Potter".　　　　**d.** Johnny Depp

_d_ **5.** "Me llamo Captain Jack Sparrow".　　　　**e.** Daddy Yankee

_g_ **6.** "Nado en los Juegos Olímpicos".　　　　**f.** Salma Hayek

_b_ **7.** "Levanto autobuses y trenes con facilidad".　　**g.** Michael Phelps

2A.19 ¿Y tú? Finish the following five sentences about yourself. Then share your responses with a classmate. Here are some phrases to help.

en la cafetería	e-mail	en el lago *(lake)*	en una discoteca	frecuentemente
en el parque	en una piscina	en un bar	jazz, hip hop,	todos los días
poemas	*(swimming pool)*	en un club	música clásica,	*(every day)*
novelas	en el océano	en casa *(home)*	rock, country	nunca *(never)*

1. Escribo...
2. Bailo...
3. Como...
4. Nado...
5. Escucho...

EXPRESIONES ÚTILES

También y tampoco

También is the Spanish equivalent to expressions like *also, too, as well,* and **tampoco** is the opposite, as in *not...either, neither.*

—Yo tengo una clase de física.	*I have a physics class*
—Yo también tengo una clase de física.	*I also have a physics class.*
—Yo no hablo francés.	*I do not speak French.*
—Yo tampoco.	*Me either. (Neither do I.)*

2A.20 Entrevistas. An interview is the best way to get to know someone.

Paso 1. Work with a classmate you have not worked with previously and take turns asking each other the questions below. Your goal is to determine how many of the activities below you and your partner have in common. Keep a list and write those activities in your **Retrato de la clase.**

Modelo: E1: *¿Nadas, corres o levantas pesas?*
E2: *Yo nado y corro, pero no levanto pesas.*
E1: *Yo también corro, pero no levanto pesas y tampoco nado.*
Actividades en común: *correr*

1. ¿Nadas, corres o levantas pesas?
2. ¿Bailas los viernes por la noche?
3. ¿Escuchas música hip-hop? ¿country? ¿clásica?
4. ¿Estudias en la casa o en la biblioteca?
5. ¿Escribes poemas?
6. ¿Lees el periódico todos los días?
7. ¿Vives en una residencia estudiantil, un apartamento o en casa de tus padres?
8. ¿Comes en restaurantes más que en casa?

Retrato de la clase: _____ y yo tenemos las siguientes actividades en común: _____, _____ y _____.

2A.19 POSSIBLE ANSWERS: 1. Escribo poemas, novelas, e-mail; 2. Bailo en un bar, en una discoteca, en un club; 3. Como en la cafetería, en casa, en el parque; 4. Nado en el océano, en la piscina, en el lago; 5. Escucho jazz/*hip hop*/música clásica/rock/*country* frecuentemente/todos los días/nunca.

2A.19 FOLLOW-UP: Recast some students' answers to ensure their understanding. For example, ask *¿A quién le gusta escuchar música jazz en un bar?* Students respond, "Juan" or "A Juan" (They are likely to omit the preposition.) You say *"Sí, a Juan le gusta escuchar música jazz...* You don't need to explain the use of the preposition *a,* just expose students to its use so that later they will connect the explanation of indirect object pronouns and *gustar* type verbs to what they have heard you model in class.

2A.20 TIME MANAGEMENT: This activity will take considerable time—15 minutes for the interviews and 5-10 minutes to do the follow-up and write their findings in *Retrato de la clase*— so plan accordingly. Make sure you help the students stay on task by giving them a definite time limit (*Tienen 15 minutos*) and informing them as they go (*Faltan 10 minutos*). As a follow-up to this activity, tally which of the activities most students had in common and list them on the board.

Estructuras clave 2 The verb *estar*

WILEY PLUS
Go to *WileyPLUS* and review the tutorial for this grammar point.

WILEY PLUS
[ ] You will find PowerPoint presentations for use with *Estructuras clave* in *WileyPLUS*.

2A.21 AUDIO SCRIPT AND ANSWERS: 1. [Male speaker] Trabajo con muchos actores y actrices para hacer filmes (películas). 2. [Female speaker] Uso la computadora diariamente y leo mucho sobre la informática. 3. [Male speaker] Veo y analizo la estructura de la torre Eiffel. 4. [Female speaker] Nado diariamente para una competencia. 5. [Female speaker] Compro artefactos de Machu Picchu y leo mucho sobre los incas. 6. [Female speaker] Escucho los síntomas físicos de muchos pacientes. 7. [Male speaker] Veo a muchos pacientes cada día y escucho sus problemas. 8. [Female speaker] Estudio para mis clases y leo muchos libros aquí.

2A.21 TIME MANAGEMENT: Give students one minute to read through the options in *a–h* so that they can anticipate the type of information they will hear each speaker give.

2A.22 SUGGESTIONS: Walk around the room to verify weaker students' sentences. Call on a handful of students (preferably those who tend to not participate much) to read one of their sentences to the class. The class will respond with *cierto* or *falso*.

Estar, like **ser,** means *to be* but each of these verbs is used in unique ways. For example, you have used the verb **estar** to respond to the question **¿Cómo estás?** *(How are you?).* You have learned to say **Estoy bien,** or **No estoy bien,** or **Estoy mal.** In this context, **estar** is used to express a mental or physical state. **¿Cómo?** is the question word most used with **estar** when referring to mental or physical state. You will learn more about this use of **estar** in an upcoming chapter.

The verb **estar** is also used for expressing the location of things.

La medicina está en la farmacia.	*The medicine is in the pharmacy.*
La instructora está en la clase.	*The instructor is in class.*
El criminal está en la cárcel.	*The criminal is in jail.*

¿Dónde? is the question word most used with **estar** to refer to location.

¿Dónde está el libro?	*Where are the books?*
¿Dónde están los estudiantes?	*Where are the students?*

Estar		
yo	**estoy**	Estoy en una clase de español.
tú	**estás**	¿No estás en el aeropuerto?
él/ella/usted	**está**	Él no está en su apartamento.
nosotros/as	**estamos**	Estamos en la biblioteca.
vosotros/as	**estáis**	¿Estáis en el parque?
ellos/ellas/ustedes	**están**	Los ingenieros están en San Francisco.

2A.21 ¿Dónde están? For each statement you hear about what people do in the course of their work, indicate what you would guess about the speaker's occupation and where he/she is located. The first one is done for you as a model.

_2_ **a.** Usted es profesora de informática y está en un laboratorio de computación.

_1_ **b.** Usted es director de cine y está en Los Ángeles.

_5_ **c.** Usted es turista y está en Perú.

_7_ **d.** Usted es psicólogo y está en su oficina.

_8_ **e.** Usted es estudiante y está en una biblioteca.

_4_ **f.** Usted es atleta y está en las Olimpiadas.

_6_ **g.** Usted es enfermera *(nurse)* y está en una clínica.

_3_ **h.** Usted es arquitecto y está en París.

2A.22 Cierto o falso. Write two sentences using the verb **estar,** one that is undeniably true and one that is undeniably false. Then select one of the sentences to read to the class. The class will guess whether the sentence is true or false.

Modelo: 1. Estoy en Madrid. (falso)
2. Estoy en la clase de español. (cierto)

2A.23 Las facultades.

Paso 1: Test how much you and your classmates understand about how various academic *departments* fit into the various *colleges* (**facultades**) of a large university by answering the following questions with respect to the ten colleges of **La Universidad Universal.**

Facultades de la Universidad Universal

Facultad de Economía y Negocios
Facultad de Educación
Facultad de Arte y Arquitectura
Facultad de Ciencias Exactas y Naturales

Facultad de Ciencias Sociales

Facultad de Medicina
Facultad de Humanidades
Facultad de Comunicaciones
Facultad de Tecnología y Ciencias Aplicadas
Facultad de Ciencias Políticas y Relaciones Internacionales

1. ¿En qué facultad está el Departamento de Física?
2. ¿En qué facultad está el Departamento de Publicidad?
3. ¿En qué facultad está el Departamento de Administración de Empresas?
4. ¿En qué facultad está el Departamento de Ingeniería?
5. ¿En qué facultad está el Departamento de Enfermería?
6. ¿En qué facultad está el Departamento de Lenguas Modernas?

Paso 2: Now find out which **facultades** and **departamentos** are most common among your classmates and their friends, using the structure of **La Universidad Universal.** Pose *each* of the questions below to *two* different classmates, and make note of their answers on a separate sheet of paper. Then, have each of them write their initials on your sheet. When you have obtained two answers for each question, analyze the results to determine which **facultades** and **departamentos** are most cited. Analyze your results as a class and write them up in your **Retrato de la clase.**

1. ¿En qué departamento está tu especialización?

2. ¿En qué facultad estás tú?

3. ¿En qué facultad está tu mejor amigo/a?

4. ¿En qué departamento está la especialización de tu mejor amigo/a?

Retrato de la clase: La mayor parte de los estudiantes de la clase de español y sus amigos/as están en la Facultad de _____ y la Facultad de _____. Los departamentos más populares son el departamento de _____ y el departamento de _____.

Enlaces

2A.24 Leer y escribir. Read the sentences below and select the connecting word that most logically completes each sentence.

además	*in addition*
esencialmente	*essentially*
a continuación	*following*

1. Los lunes, miércoles y viernes Pepito tiene clase de biología y de historia. <u>Además</u> tiene música e inglés.

2. <u>A continuación</u> hay una lista de personas que necesitan invitaciones: Juan, Laura, Carmen, Arturo.

3. Ellos son compañeros de la universidad. Participan en muchas actividades y tienen muy buenas notas. <u>Esencialmente</u> son excelentes estudiantes.

2A.23 PASO 1: ANSWERS. La facultad de... 1. Ciencias Exactas y Naturales, 2. Comunicaciones, 3. Economía y Negocios, 4. Ciencias Exactas y Naturales, 5. Medicina, 6. Humanidades

2A.23 PASO 1: This activity prepares students to answer more personalized questions in Paso 2 and also sensitizes them to general university structures. Confirm students' understanding of *negocios* as "business" given the context.

2A.23 PASO 2: TEACHING TIP. Facilitate the whole-class analysis by asking a question like *¿Quiénes están en la Facultad de Humanidades?* Then, ask one of the students who responds affirmatively *¿En qué departamento está tu especialización?,* and follow up by asking the whole class *¿Quién más está en el departamento de...?* Note the most popular *departamentos* and *facultades* on the board.

FUNCTIONAL OUTCOMES:
The central question that frames this Investigación is "¿Qué estudias y para qué?" Explore whether students can now address this question and how they would go about it. Have them review the chart on the first page of this Investigación.

2A.25 La angustia estudiantil. This selection reports research on stress in university students in Spain. Do the factors that cause stress in university students in Spain also cause stress in university students in the US? Read the article below with that question in mind.

CONTEXTOS: READING STRATEGY. For *Contextos*, remind students that they know the main idea of the text (stress in Spanish university students). They should put their reading strategies (skimming and looking for contextual clues) to practice as they try to interpret the meaning of the text. Have them share their findings with a partner before you entertain a class discussion on what the major points were.

El estrés de los estudiantes

A continuación hay once situaciones potencialmente generadoras de mucho estrés en los estudiantes dentro del contexto académico español. Las cuatro primeras están relacionadas específicamente con las clases:

1. Tomar un examen
2. Presentar trabajos en clase
3. Responder a una pregunta del profesor, hacer preguntas, participar en coloquios, etc.
4. Estar en salones de +200 personas

Además, hay otros siete factores con potencial de producir estrés:

5. Excesivo número de créditos, trabajos obligatorios, etc.
6. Hablar con el profesor en sus horas de oficina
7. No tener el tiempo para poder hacer las actividades académicas (tiempo insuficiente para hacer los trabajos académicos)

8. Competitividad entre compañeros
9. Trabajos obligatorios de la clase (Buscar el material necesario, escribir el trabajo, etc.).
10. Hacer la tarea
11. Trabajar en grupo

La lista **a continuación** presenta las siete cosas que causan más estrés en los estudiantes españoles según el orden de importancia que tienen para ellos. **Esencialmente,** las situaciones en esta última lista están relacionadas con la organización de tiempo y del horario.

1. No tener el tiempo para poder realizar las actividades académicas
2. Tarea académica excesiva
3. Tomar un examen
4. Presentar trabajos en clase
5. Trabajos obligatorios de la clase
6. La tarea de estudio
7. Responder a una pregunta del profesor, hacer preguntas, participar en coloquios, etc.

¿Dónde estudias tú?

¿Te gusta estudiar solo/a o con amigos?

¿Es estresante para ti hacer una presentación en clase?

Perspectivas

2A.26 **Experiencia personal.** Each of the stressors that made the "Top 7 list" in the *Contextos* reading selection received an average score of from 3.33–4.37 on a scale of 1–5, indicating highly perceived stress on the part of the students. Which, if any, of the situations below cause stress for you? Rate each from 1–5 (1 = least stress; 5 = most stress). Compare your answers with those of a couple of classmates. How do your experiences of these situations compare to the experiences of students in Spain?

1   2   3   4   5   **1.** Tomar un examen

1   2   3   4   5   **2.** Presentar trabajos en clase

1   2   3   4   5   **3.** Responder a una pregunta del profesor, hacer preguntas, participar en coloquios, etcétera

1   2   3   4   5   **4.** Estar en salones de más de *(more than)* 200 personas

1   2   3   4   5   **5.** Excesivo número de créditos, trabajos obligatorios, etcétera

1   2   3   4   5   **6.** Ir a la oficina del profesor en horas de tutoría

1   2   3   4   5   **7.** Tiempo insuficiente para hacer los trabajos académicos

1   2   3   4   5   **8.** Competitividad entre compañeros

1   2   3   4   5   **9.** Trabajos obligatorios de la clase (buscar el material necesario, escribir el trabajo, etcétera)

1   2   3   4   5   **10.** La tarea de estudio (tarea para hacer en la casa)

1   2   3   4   5   **11.** Trabajar en grupo

What situations produce the most stress in your native culture? If similar to those of students in Spain, can you offer reasons for the similarities? If different, investigate why. For example, in many university level classes in Spain, many professors expect students to take one sole exam at the end of the semester and their performance on that exam determines their grade for the course.

2A.26 NOTE: This is not as thorough a scientific method as the one followed in the cited study but it will give your students a general idea of how they might compare to the Spaniards. Questions on the cited study included whether the stress was just mildly perceived, caused physiologic responses, induced cognitive awareness or caused nervous motor response (tics, twitches, etc.).

2A.26 FOLLOW-UP: Conduct an informal scan of the class to see how they scored the different categories.

2A.26 SUGGESTION: In developing students' intercultural communicative competence, it is helpful to have them compare and contrast their culture with the cultures they are studying. Have students investigate aspects of the Spanish university experience that may factor into differences in how each cultural group experiences similar situations.

WILEY **PLUS**

2A.26 INSTRUCTOR'S RESOURCES: Your Instructor's Resources provide a model Venn Diagram to reproduce and hand out or project in class. It will help organize comparative information visually.

Vocabulario: Investigación A

Vocabulario esencial

Sustantivos

la administración de empresas	business administration
la carrera	career, major
la computación	computer science
la contabilidad	accounting
el derecho	law
el desarrollo infantil	child development
los días de la semana	days of the week
lunes	Monday
martes	Tuesday
miércoles	Wednesday
jueves	Thursday
viernes	Friday
sábado	Saturday
domingo	Sunday
la enfermería	nursing
la especialización	specialty
el examen	test
la facultad	university school or college
las fuerzas armadas	armed forces
la hora del día	time of day
la mañana	morning
el mediodía	noon
la medianoche	midnight
la tarde	afternoon
la noche	night
el horario	schedule
el idioma	language
la informática	computer science
la ingeniería	engineering
la materia	school subject
el mercadeo	marketing
el periodismo	journalism
el trabajo social	social work

Adjetivos

extranjero/a	foreign
primero/a	first

Verbos

comenzar	to start
desear	to wish, want
estar	to be
nadar	to swim
ver	to see
vivir	to live

Otras palabras y expresiones

la base de datos	database
el campo	field
la ciudad	city
con frecuencia	frequently
conmigo	with me
empezar	to start
la entrevista	interview
la empresa	company
el/la enfermero/a	nurse
escoger	to choose
exigente	demanding
el intercambio	exchange
las lenguas modernas	modern languages
más de/más que	more than
la naturaleza	nature
el negocio	business
la publicidad	advertising
realizar	to do, achieve
según	according to
tampoco	neither
¿Cuál es?	Which one is it?
¿Qué hora es?	What time is it?
para mí	for me
para ti	for you
para ser	in order to be
¿Te interesa?	Does it interest you?
tener que	must, to have to

Cognados

Review the cognates in *Adelante* and the false cognates in *¡Atención!*. For a complete list of cognates, see Appendix 4 on page 605.

¿Me presentas a tu familia?

In this **Investigación** you will learn:

▶ How to refer to family relationships

▶ How to describe people

▶ How to talk about what you do

▶ How to express what someone else does

▶ How to further express likes and dislikes

¿Cómo puedes hablar de tu familia?

You can talk about your family members.	Tengo tres hermanas y un hermano. Tengo una hermana menor y un hermano mayor. Mi abuelo paterno está muerto.
You can describe your family members.	Mi mamá es simpática y mi papá es estricto. Mi abuela es viuda y es muy paciente.
You can describe what you do or ask someone you know what he/she does.	Por las mañanas corro con mi hermano. ¿Corres por las mañanas o por las tardes?
You can express the likes and dislikes of your family members.	A mi hermano no le gusta leer los libros de John Grisham. A mi hermana, le gusta ver la tele. A mí me gusta jugar deportes.

TEACHING TIP: The adjectives in *Adelante* are taken from those used in the Myers-Briggs personality test and are used to characterize general personality types. Ask students *¿Cómo te percibes?* and have them circle or write the words that they most associate with their own personality. Tell them to write those words on a piece of paper and then find a classmate that has written most of the same words by asking *¿Eres... jovial? ¿puntual?* etc. Once they find the classmate with whom they have the most traits in common, ask them to partner with that person in some of the activities in this *Investigación*.

Adelante

¡Ya lo sabes! La familia, la personalidad y el carácter

la adolescencia	aventurero/a	humilde	original
el bautismo	carismático/a	impaciente	paciente
la ceremonia religiosa	creativo/a	impulsivo/a	pacifista
la comunión	condescendiente	individualista	persistente
la familia extendida	convencional	inocente	persuasivo/a
la familia nuclear	convincente	intolerante	reservado/a
la graduación	cooperativo/a	irresponsable	sereno/a
la infancia	cordial	irreverente	sincero/a
el matrimonio	determinado/a	jovial	sociable
el papá/la mamá	decidido/a	moderno/a	sumiso/a
agresivo/a	diplomático/a	motivado/a	tolerante
arrogante	espiritual	obediente	tradicional
	expresivo/a	obstinado/a	valiente

2B.1 **El horóscopo válido.** Indicate your astrological signs and those of your family members based on when they were born. Then, write the adjectives that would need to be included in your family members' horoscopes to be true. Lastly, compare the adjectives you wrote for each astrological sign with those your classmates wrote for the same sign. What do your findings suggest about astrological signs as predictors of personality type?

1. Yo soy _____.

2. Mi mamá es _____.

3. Mi papá es _____.

4. Mi hermano *(brother)* _____.

5. Mi hermana *(sister)* _____.

Aries (21 marzo–19 abril)	**Tauro** (20 abril–20 mayo)	**Géminis** (21 mayo–20 junio)	**Cáncer** (21 junio–22 julio)
Leo (23 julio–22 agosto)	**Virgo** (23 agosto–22 septiembre)	**Libra** (23 septiembre–22 octubre)	**Escorpión** (23 octubre–21 noviembre)
Sagitario (22 noviembre–21 diciembre)	**Capricornio** (22 diciembre–19 enero)	**Acuario** (20 enero–18 febrero)	**Piscis** (19 febrero–20 marzo)

2B.2 **Definiciones.** Listen to the definitions of various personality types and select which type corresponds to each definition following the model. Verify your answers with the class.

1. _g_   **a.** irreverente
2. _c_   **b.** sumiso/a
3. _d_   **c.** sociable
4. _f_   **d.** obstinado/a
5. _b_   **e.** intolerante
6. _e_   **f.** creativo/a
7. _a_   **g.** pacifista

2B.1 PREVIEW: Months of the year are introduced as *Palabras clave* in the next chapter. Activity 2B.1 offers a preview of these words, all but one of which, *enero*, are cognates. Students should have no trouble understanding the months in this activity, and will find themselves on familiar ground when they begin learning new vocabulary in *Investigación 3A*.

2B.1 FOLLOW-UP: Ask students how similar the adjectives were based on astrological signs. Then, ask students ¿*Leen su horóscopo?* For students who answer *Sí*, ask them how often, such as ¿*Con frecuencia o a veces?* Ask them ¿*Dónde lees tu horóscopo? ¿en revistas o en la Internet?*

2B.2 AUDIO SCRIPT: 1. Es una persona que no es violenta. 2. Es una persona que tiene muchos amigos. 3. Es una persona persistente o que no es flexible. 4. Es una persona con ideas originales. 5. Es una persona obediente y dócil. 6. Es una persona que no es tolerante. 7. Es una persona que no respeta a nadie.

2B.3 TEACHING TIP: Tell students to feel free to substitute significant figures in their lives in lieu of parents, such as guardians. Ask them, however, to cross out *mamá* and *papá* and write the names of their figures instead.

2B.3 SUGGESTIONS: Students will be learning about agreement between adjectives and nouns explicitly later in this chapter. Until then, feel free to model correct agreement to allow them the opportunity to learn the rule implicitly.

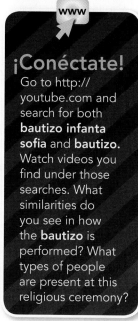

¡Conéctate!

Go to http://youtube.com and search for both **bautizo infanta sofia** and **bautizo.** Watch videos you find under those searches. What similarities do you see in how the **bautizo** is performed? What types of people are present at this religious ceremony?

2B.3 **¿Cómo es tu familia?**

Paso 1: Indicate whether you associate the following words with your own personality, and then with your mother, your father, or neither. Then, write a brief description of your parents in your **Retrato de la clase.**

	Yo soy	Mi mamá es	Mi papá es	Nadie (*No one*) es
1. solitario/a	☐	☐	☐	☐
2. sociable	☐	☐	☐	☐
3. persistente	☐	☐	☐	☐
4. obediente	☐	☐	☐	☐
5. moderno/a	☐	☐	☐	☐
6. expresivo/a	☐	☐	☐	☐
7. optimista	☐	☐	☐	☐
8. rebelde	☐	☐	☐	☐
9. obstinado/a	☐	☐	☐	☐
10. flexible	☐	☐	☐	☐
11. estable	☐	☐	☐	☐
12. condescendiente	☐	☐	☐	☐
13. impulsivo/a	☐	☐	☐	☐
14. compulsivo/a	☐	☐	☐	☐

Paso 2: Examine your answers in *Paso 1* to answer the question "Who are you most like?" and write your answers in your **Retrato de la clase.**

> **Retrato de la clase:** Mi mamá es ___ y yo también. Mi papá es ___ y yo también. Soy más como mi mamá/papá.

La familia real española

Like Great Britain, Spain maintains the historical tradition of having a royal familiy. The royal familiy is highly regarded and well-respected in Spain.

Desde el 22 de noviembre de 1975, el rey (*king*) de España es Juan Carlos I. Su esposa (*wife*) es la Reina Sofía y ellos tienen tres hijos (*children*): Elena, Cristina, y Felipe. La Infanta (*princess*) Elena es la hija mayor y tiene dos hijos. La Infanta Cristina está casada (*married*). Su esposo es Don Iñaki Urdangarín, el Duque de Palma de Mallorca. Felipe, el Príncipe de Asturias, es el heredero de la Corona de España (*crown prince/heir apparent*). Letizia, la Princesa de Asturias, es la esposa de Felipe y ellos tienen dos hijas.

2B.4 **¿Qué recuerdas tú de la familia real española?** After reading the preceding paragraph about the Spanish royal family, listen to several statements about the family and indicate whether each is **cierto** or **falso.** Listen again and correct any false statements.

	Cierto	Falso
1.	☑	☐
2.	☑	☐
3.	☑	☐
4.	☑	☐
5.	☐	☑
6.	☐	☑

Bien dicho

Yes/No questions

Pitch patterns in English and Spanish are similar and at the same time different. For example, pitch patterns at the end of yes/no questions rise in both Spanish and English signaling that what's spoken is a yes/no question. While pitch rises in both languages, it rises slightly higher in English.

English

Do you feel okay?

Spanish

¿Estás bien?

Spanish and English have different pitch patterns in questions that require more than a yes or no answer. Pitch falls in Spanish questions while it rises in English questions.

Where is your mother?

¿Dónde está tu mamá?

2B.5 **¿Qué tipo de pregunta es?** Indicate whether each of the following questions should rise or fall at the end in Spanish. Then, verify your answers as a class.

	↑	↓
1. ¿Estás bien?	☑	☐
2. ¿Cómo se llama el bebé que bautizan?	☐	☑
3. ¿Están los amigos de tu hermano en la ceremonia?	☑	☐
4. ¿Quién eres tú?	☐	☑
5. ¿Es grande tu familia?	☑	☐

2B.6 **Entrevista breve.** With a partner, determine whether or not the tone should rise or fall at the end of each question. After confirming your responses as a class, interview your partner, taking note of his/her responses.

1. ¿Cómo se llaman tus padres?
2. ¿Cuántas clases tienes este semestre?
3. ¿Tocas un instrumento musical?
4. ¿Escuchas la radio?
5. ¿Cuál es tu programa de televisión favorito?
6. ¿Practicas un deporte?
7. ¿Dónde estudias normalmente?
8. ¿Te gusta bailar?

2B.4 STANDARDS: CONNECTIONS AND COMPARISONS. Ask students if they know what type of government Spain has and how that might compare to their government. Do we have "royalty" in the US? Do certain celebrities receive the kind of treatment that royalty in other countries might receive?

2B.4 AUDIO SCRIPT: 1. El rey de España se llama Juan Carlos. 2. Sofía es la mamá del Príncipe de Asturias. 3. El papá de Elena, Cristina y Felipe es el rey de España. 4. Elena, Cristina y Felipe son adultos y tienen familias también. 5. Cristina está divorciada. (Falso. Cristina está casada). 6. Felipe, el Príncipe de Asturias, no es papá. (Falso. Tiene dos hijas).

2B. 4 MULTIPLE INTELLIGENCES: VISUAL/SPATIAL. Tap into your students' visual strengths by having them draw a family tree of the Spanish royal family. Consider allowing them to reference this as they hear the statements.

2B.5 ANSWERS: To verify answers, either read the questions modeling the terminal pitch or ask students to read the questions with the correct terminal pitch.

2B.6 WARM-UP: Before the interview, review student responses regarding rising or falling pitch and model pronunciation of each question. After the interview, continue to model pronunciation as you ask 3-4 students to report on their partners' responses to each question.

2B.6 ANSWERS: Pitch rises: 3, 4, 6, 8. Pitch falls: 1, 2, 5, 7.

Palabras clave 1 La familia

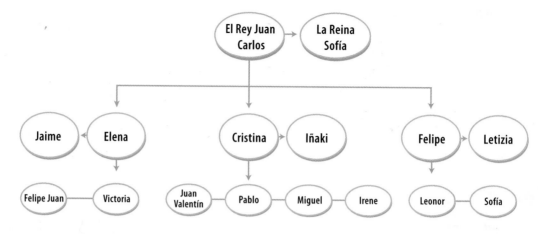

ORIENTATION: PROCESSING INSTRUCTION. An underlying methodology of this text is processing instruction, which focuses on providing students with comprehensible input they need to manipulate. When presenting the Spanish royal family use input like the descriptions above, but push it further by moving into questions (e.g. *¿Cómo se llama el hijo de Juan Carlos y Sofía?*).

La familia nuclear

el padre	El **padre** de Elena, Cristina y Felipe se llama Juan Carlos.
la madre	La **madre** de Elena, Cristina y Felipe es la Reina Sofía.
el/la esposo/a	La **esposa** de Felipe es Letizia.
el marido	El **marido** de Cristina es Iñaki.
el/la hijo/a	El **hijo** de Elena y Jaime es Felipe Juan.
el/la hermano/a	La **hermana** de Felipe Juan se llama Victoria.

La familia extendida

el/la abuelo/a	El **abuelo** de Felipe Juan, Juan Valentín, Pablo y Miguel es Juan Carlos.
el/la primo/a	Los **primos** de Leonor y Sofía son los hijos de sus tías Elena y Cristina.
el/la tío/a	El Príncipe Felipe es el **tío** de los hijos de sus hermanas.
el/la nieto/a	La Reina Sofía tiene ocho **nietos**: cuatro nietos y cuatro nietas.
el/la sobrino/a	Los **sobrinos** del Príncipe Felipe son los hijos de sus dos hermanas.

Descripciones útiles de la familia

la pareja	dos personas unidas
el/la niño/a	una persona muy joven; lo contrario de adulto
el/la hijo/a único/a	una persona que no tiene hermanos ni hermanas
menor	el/la hijo/a más joven de la familia
mayor	el/la hijo/a más grande (en edad) de la familia
el/la soltero/a	una persona que no está casada ni tiene pareja
el/la difunto/a	una persona muerta *(dead)*
el/la viudo/a	una persona que no tiene esposo/a porque él/ella está muerto/a
casado/a	unido/a con otra persona en el matrimonio
divorciado/a	separado/a del esposo/de la esposa mediante un proceso legal

2B.7 AUDIO SCRIPT AND ANSWERS: 1.Casado es lo contrario de divorciado. 2. Mi hermano es el sobrino de mis padres. 3. El hijo de mi abuelo es mi primo. 4. La hermana de mi madre es mi tía. 5. El hijo de mis tíos es mi sobrino. 6. Mi abuelo está muerto; mi abuela es viuda. 7. La hija de mi hijo es mi nieta. 8. Tengo un hermano y una hermana; soy hija única. 9. El esposo de mi hermana es mi tío. 10. El hermano de mi padre es mi tío.

2B.7 FOLLOW-UP. Have students correct the false statements.

2B.7 Las relaciones familiares. Indicate whether each statement you hear about family relationships is **cierto** or **falso** following the model.

	Cierto	Falso			Cierto	Falso
1.	✓	☐		**6.**	✓	☐
2.	☐	✓		**7.**	✓	☐
3.	☐	✓		**8.**	☐	✓
4.	✓	☐		**9.**	☐	✓
5.	☐	✓		**10.**	✓	☐

amar

Mi padre **ama** a mi madre.

ayudar

Marisa **ayuda** a su padre.

cuidar

Los padres **cuidan** a su hija.

proveer

Los padres **proveen** una casa a sus hijos.

reunir

Es importante **reunir** a toda la familia para celebrar un matrimonio.

unir

El ministro **une** a los esposos en una boda (ceremonia del matrimonio).

2B.8 **¿Lógico o ilógico?** Working with a partner, determine whether the following statements are logical or illogical following the model, and correct the illogical statements. Then, check your statements with another pair of classmates.

	Lógico	Ilógico
1. Los padres reúnen a la familia en la casa.	☑	☐
2. Los niños cuidan a los adultos.	☐	☑
3. Los doctores ayudan a sus pacientes.	☑	☐
4. El esposo ama a su esposa.	☑	☐
5. El alumno ayuda a la maestra con la tarea.	☐	☑
6. Los profesores proveen información inútil a sus estudiantes.	☐	☑

2B.8 ANSWERS: Lógico: 1, 3, 4, ; Ilógico: 2 (Los adultos cuidan a los niños)., 5 (La maestra ayuda al alumno). 6 (Los profesores proveen información útil).

2B.8 EXTENSION ACTIVITY: Have students develop their own statements (logical and illogical) using the same vocabulary. They can read them in groups and decide whether they are logical or illogical.

EXPRESIONES ÚTILES

Otros miembros de la familia

el padrastro	*stepfather*
la madrastra	*stepmother*
el/la hermanastro/a	*step brother*
el/la hijastro/a	*step child*
el/la medio hermano/a	*half brother/half sister*
el/la suegro/a	*father-/mother-in-law*
el/la cuñado/a	*brother-/sister-in-law*
el yerno	*son-in-law*
la nuera	*daughter-in-law*

2B.9 **¿Cómo se llama?** Match the words in column A to their corresponding definitions in column B. Then, verify your responses with a classmate.

A	B
__i__ **1.** el suegro y la suegra	**a.** la persona casada con tu hermano/hermana
__d__ **2.** el/la medio hermano/a	**b.** el esposo de tu hija
__c__ **3.** la madrastra	**c.** la esposa de tu padre, pero no tu madre biológica
__b__ **4.** el yerno	**d.** tu hermano/a de parte de tu padre o de tu madre, pero no hijo/a de los dos
__g__ **5.** la nuera	**e.** el esposo de tu madre, pero no tu padre biológico
__f__ **6.** el/la hermanastro/a	**f.** el/la hijo/a de tu padrastro o tu madrastra
__e__ **7.** el padrastro	**g.** la esposa de tu hijo
__h__ **8.** el/la hijastro/a	**h.** el/la hijo/a de tu esposo/a, pero no tu hijo/a biológico/a
__a__ **9.** el/la cuñado/a	**i.** los padres de tu pareja

VÍVELO: LENGUA

Expressing possession II

You have learned to express *my, your, his, her,* and *their* using **mi/mis, tu/tus,** and **su/sus.** Remember that which of these possessives to use depends on the possessor **(yo, tú, él/ella, usted, ellos/ellas, ustedes)** and whether to use the singular or plural form depends on the thing or things possessed. These possessives do not change according to gender.

Because **su** and **sus** may each refer to number of possessors **(él/ella, usted, ellos/ellas, ustedes)**, they can be ambiguous. For clarity, a different format may be used to express possession in these cases.

el/la/los/las + thing possessed + **de** + possessor

El tío de él es de España y el tío de ellos es de Italia.
La tía de ustedes es de Francia y la tía de ella es de México.
Los primos de Juana son de Italia.
Los primos de Juana y Carlos son de Italia.
Las primas de ellos son de Alemania (*Germany*).
Las primas de mi padre son de Alemania.

Nuestro/nuestra/nuestros/nuestras

To express *our,* Spanish uses the word **nuestro/a** to talk about a single thing possessed, and **nuestros/as** to talk about more than one thing possessed.

Nuestro padre es de Argentina.
Nuestra madre es de Perú.
Nuestros padres son de Latinoamérica.
Nuestras tías son de Guatemala.

Notice that the possessive adjective **nuestro/a/os/as** must agree in both gender and number with the noun it is modifying. In Spain, where vosotros/as is used as the informal *you* plural, **vuestro/a** and **vuestros/as** follow this same pattern.

WILEY PLUS Go to *WileyPLUS* and review the tutorial for this grammar point.

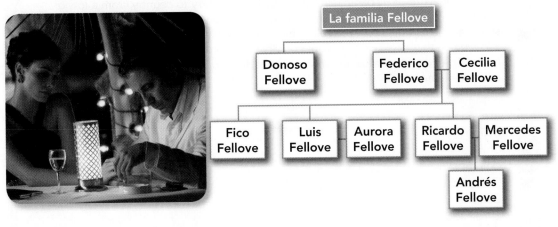

2B.10 **La ciudad perdida.** With a partner, examine the family tree of the Fellove family and complete the passage below with the appropriate vocabulary. Read over the resulting description of the Fellove family, consulting the family tree diagram to help you understand the relationships between the family members.

La familia de Fico *(nickname for Federico)* Fellove es de La Habana. El ¹ ___padre___ de Fico se llama Federico y su **madre** se llama Cecilia. Federico es el ² ___esposo___ de Cecilia. Fico no es **hijo único** porque Federico y Cecilia tienen tres ³ ___hijos___. Fico es el **hijo mayor,** o el **primogénito,** Luis es el **hijo del medio** y Ricardo es el **hijo** ⁴ ___menor___. Luis y Ricardo son los **hermanos** de Fico. Federico y Cecilia no tienen **hijas;** por eso, Fico no tiene **hermanas.** Donoso Fellove es el ⁵ ___hermano___ de Federico y es el **tío** de Fico. Fico no tiene **tías.** Fico es ⁶ ___soltero___. No tiene **esposa.** Luis y Ricardo están **casados.** La ⁷ ___esposa___ de Luis se llama Aurora y la **esposa** de Ricardo se llama Mercedes. Aurora y Mercedes son las ⁸ ___cuñadas___ de Fico y son las **nueras** de Federico y Cecilia. Federico es el **suegro** de Aurora y Mercedes y Cecilia es su ⁹ ___suegra___. Ricardo y Mercedes tienen un **hijo** que se llama Andrés. Andrés es el ¹⁰ ___nieto___ de Federico y Cecilia. Federico es el ¹¹ ___abuelo___ de Andrés y Cecilia es su **abuela.** Andrés es el ¹² ___sobrino___ de Fico y Luis y ellos son sus **tíos.** Aurora es la ¹³ ___tía___ de Andrés.

2B.11 **¿Cómo se llama?** Look at the Fellove family tree and match each description you hear with the name of the corresponding Fellove family member following the model.

___6___ **a.** Ricardo

___4___ **b.** Mercedes

___3___ **c.** Aurora

___1___ **d.** Federico

___2___ **e.** Donoso

___5___ **f.** Cecilia

2B.12 **Descripciones.** With a classmate, answer the following questions on the basis of the description of the Fellove family in Activity 2B.10. Then, confirm your answers with the class.

1. ¿De dónde es la familia Fellove? — de La Habana, Cuba

2. ¿Cómo se llaman los padres de Fico? — Federico y Cecilia

3. ¿Donoso es el cuñado o el primo de Cecilia? — Donoso es el cuñado de Cecilia.

4. ¿Cuántos hermanos tiene Fico? — Fico tiene dos hermanos.

5. ¿Quién es el hijo menor? — Ricardo

6. ¿Fico es un hombre casado o soltero? — soltero

7. ¿Mercedes es la cuñada o la esposa de Ricardo? — Mercedes es la esposa de Ricardo.

8. ¿Cómo se llama el nieto de Federico y Cecilia? — Andrés.

2B.10 NOTE: The film *The Lost City,* released in 2006, depicts the lives of various members of the Fellove family who were living in Havana, Cuba in the late 1950's during the revolution that deposed Fulgencio Batista and brought Fidel Castro to power. The main character of the film is Fico Fellove, who owns El Trópico, a prominent nightclub in Havana. The Fellove family is extremely close and the family members are very loyal and devoted to one another; however, during the course of the film, various family members are caught up in the revolution and its aftermath with tragic consequences. The film stars Andy García, who also directed. García himself left Cuba with his family in 1961, when he was 5 years old. Consequently, this film represents a very personal and emotional story for him.

2B.10 TEACHING TIP: Have students go over their answers with another group. Remind them that often their classmates are the best "teachers" in the classroom as they often come up with new and unique ways of explaining things.

2B.11 AUDIO SCRIPT AND ANSWERS: 1. El padre de Fico se llama... (d. Federico), 2. El hermano de Federico es... (e. Donoso), 3. La esposa de Luis es... (c. Aurora), 4. La madre de Andrés es... (b. Mercedes), 5. La abuela de Andrés es... (f. Cecilia), 6. El sobrino menor de Donoso es... (a. Ricardo).

2B.11 MULTIPLE INTELLIGENCES: Visual/Spatial. Encourage students to look at the family tree as they hear the descriptions.

El tamaño de la familia (Family size)

The average size of Hispanic families varies from country to country, from a low of 2.9 members in Spain to over 6 in Nicaragua, and can depend on socio-economic status and location, urban or rural. The average family size in the United States is 3.2. Do you think family size in your country varies on the basis of similar factors, i.e., socio-economic status, urban versus rural location? What other factors might influence family size?

VÍVELO: CULTURA: Have students research the most current statistics they can find on the Internet.

El tamaño típico de familias de países hispanos

Argentina	3.5
Bolivia	4.7
Chile	4
Colombia	4.3
Costa Rica	5
Cuba	4
El Salvador	5.1
España	2.9
Estados Unidos	3.14
Guatemala	4.4
Honduras	5.2
México	4.5
Nicaragua	6.7
Panamá	5.4
Paraguay	4.8
Perú	5.1
Puerto Rico	3.5
República Dominicana	3.9
Uruguay	4.4
Venezuela	6

2B.13 Comprensión. Complete the following statements based on the information in *Vívelo: Cultura*. Then, confirm your answers with the class.

1. Los países con las familias más grandes son <u>Nicaragua</u> y <u>Venezuela</u>.

2. Los países con las familias más pequeñas son <u>España</u> y <u>Estados Unidos</u>.

3. Las variables que influyen el tamaño de la familia son…

☑ la situación económica de la familia.

☑ si la familia vive en un área rural o urbana.

☐ el grupo étnico.

☐ el nivel *(level)* de educación.

2B.14 TEACHING TIP: Call students' attention to the *tú*-form *Tienes* in the model. Have them tell you what the corresponding *yo*-form is. Avoid any lengthy discussion of stem-changing or irregular verbs at this point.

2B.14 Juntos forman la familia. You will interview a classmate and record the information in the chart on p 91. Before beginning, brainstorm with your partner the questions you will need to do the interview. The first is done for you as a model. Then, conduct the interview. Include your findings in your **Retrato de la clase.**

1. Persona: _____ *¿Tienes madrastra?* _____

2. Nombre: _____

3. Edad: _____

4. Personalidad: _____

5. Lugar de residencia: _____

	1. Persona	2. Nombre	3. Edad	4. Personalidad	5. Lugar de residencia
madrastra					
padrastro					
hermano/a					
hermanastro/a					
medio hermano					
media hermana					

2B.14 RECYCLING. This activity recycles question words.

2B.14 ANSWERS: 1. ¿Tienes...?, 2. ¿Cómo se llama...?, 3. ¿Cuántos años tiene?, 4. ¿Cómo es?, 5. ¿Dónde vive?

Retrato de la clase: Mi compañero de clase se llama ___. No tiene madrastra ni padrastro. Tiene dos hermanos y una hermana. Sus hermanos se llaman ___ y ___. Su hermano/a se llama ___. ____ es cómico/cómica/inteligente y vive en ____.

2B.15 ¿Quién de la clase...? Interview your classmates to see to whom in the class each of the statements might apply. If a classmate responds **Sí** to a question, ask him/her to sign on the appropriate line. Try to talk to as many people as possible. In your questions, be sure to use the **tú** form of the verbs **tener (tienes)** and **ser (eres).** And because these are yes/no questions, also make sure to use a rising pitch as indicated in *Bien dicho*. Write your findings in your **Retrato de la clase.**

¿Quién de la clase...	Firma aquí, por favor.
1. es hijo/hija única?	_____
2. es casado/a?	_____
3. tiene más de cuatro hermanos?	_____
4. tiene madrastra en otra ciudad?	_____
5. tiene sobrinos?	_____
6. es el/la menor de la familia?	_____
7. tiene parientes en varios estados *(states)*?	_____
8. tiene un abuelo viudo?	_____

Retrato de la clase: Mi compañero de clase, ____ , es hijo único. Mi compañera de clase, ____, tiene madrastra en otra ciudad. Mis compañeros de clase, ____ y ____, tienen sobrinos.

2B.15 TEACHING TIP: To recycle intonation patterns in Spanish, before having students begin this activity, ask them how they would go about finding out if their classmates had "un abuelo viudo" in terms of asking the question. In order to draw attention to the intonation needed to ask questions, read the following statements to them and ask them to indicate if they are *preguntas* or *oraciones.* Make sure to use proper intonation. *¿Tienes un abuelo muerto? Tienes un abuelo muerto. Tienes un pariente que es profesor. ¿Tienes un pariente que es profesor?*

2B.15 SUGGESTION: Without going into a detailed grammatical explanation, point out that Spanish does not generally use indefinite articles with nouns following the verb *tener* unless the notion of count is relevant or the noun is modified. For example, *Tengo hermanos* versus *Tengo una hermana muy inteligente.*

2B.16 Definiciones. Listen to several definitions and indicate the word being described following the model. Verify your responses with a classmate's.

1. _a_	**a.** el amor	
2. _g_	**b.** la adolescencia	
3. _b_	**c.** la ceremonia religiosa	
4. _c_	**d.** el bautismo	
5. _e_	**e.** la comunión	
6. _d_	**f.** el matrimonio	
7. _h_	**g.** la infancia	
8. _f_	**h.** la graduación	

2B.16 AUDIO SCRIPT AND ANSWERS: 1. Es una emoción muy positiva hacia otra persona, muchas veces romántica. 2. Es el período que se asocia con los bebés y los niños. 3. Es el período que asociamos con personas de 13-18 años. 4. Es un evento que ocurre en un centro religioso. 5. Es el ritual cristiano que simboliza el sacrificio de Jesucristo. 6. Es el ritual cristiano para admitir a una persona en la comunidad cristiana. 7. Es la ceremonia que indica que una persona termina los estudios. 8. Es la unión legal de dos personas, generalmente un hombre y una mujer.

2B.16 STANDARDS: COMPARISONS. Have students compare and contrast the ritual of the "bautismo" with similar practices in their culture.

2B.17 PASO 1: TEACHING TIP. The reading selection in Activity 2B.19 uses much of the vocabulary of this *Investigación* and confirms in Spanish the content students read in English is the last *Vívelo: Cultura*. Students should understand this Spanish passage with little difficulty. When going over the descriptions of family in *Paso 1*, ask questions for further understanding. For example: *¿Tu familia tiene reuniones frecuentes? ¿Qué tipo de celebraciones religiosas celebra tu familia? ¿Es importante recibir ayuda financiera? ¿Cuáles son más importantes, las fiestas familiares con la familia extendida o las fiestas con la familia nuclear?*

2B.17 PASO 2: TEACHING TIP. Before they do a careful reading, have them read the statements in 2B.18 so that they know what is important to understand in the passage.

2B.17 **El valor de la familia.**

Paso 1: Antes de leer. Select four items from the list below that you might use in describing the concept of "family" in your native culture. As a class, tally the most cited items.

- ☐ unidos
- ☐ familias grandes
- ☐ familias extendidas
- ☐ familias nucleares
- ☐ reuniones frecuentes
- ☐ celebraciones religiosas
- ☐ fiestas familiares
- ☐ ayuda médica
- ☐ ayuda financiera
- ☐ ayuda moral
- ☐ inculcar *(instill)* buenos modales *(manners)*
- ☐ respetar la autoridad

Paso 2: Estrategia de lectura. Read the highlighted words in the article, *El valor de la familia,* and say what you think the article will be about.

El valor de la familia

"La economía impacta a la familia moderna o contemporánea".

Tradicionalmente, **la familia** es la unidad social más **importante** de la **sociedad hispana**. El término *familia* normalmente va más allá de la familia nuclear. La **típica familia hispana** no sólo incluye a los padres y sus hijos sino que también **incluye a la familia extendida**, los tíos, primos, abuelos y compadres. Los **individuos** de una **familia** tienen la **responsabilidad** de **ayudar** a otros **miembros** de la familia **con problemas** financieros, desempleo *(unemployment)*, pobres condiciones de salud y otros problemas de la vida. Las familias hispanas **se reúnen frecuentemente** para celebrar fiestas, cumpleaños, bautismos, primeras comuniones, graduaciones y bodas. Las familias hispanas **inculcan en** sus **niños** la **importancia del honor**, de los **buenos modales**, de **respetar** la **autoridad** y a las personas **mayores**.

La economía impacta a la familia moderna o contemporánea. Cuando el padre y la madre tienen que trabajar para sobrevivir o cuando ambos tienen carreras, los hijos están menos supervisados y es más difícil inculcar los valores tradicionales en los niños.

■

2B.18 Comprensión del artículo. With a classmate, indicate whether each of the following statements is **cierto** or **falso,** based on *El valor de la familia*. Then, underline the sentence in the article that supports your answers. Confirm your answers with two other classmates.

Cierto	Falso	
☑	☐	**1.** La familia es la unidad social más importante en la cultura hispana.
☐	☑	**2.** La familia hispana se limita a la familia nuclear.
☑	☐	**3.** Una persona tiene la responsabilidad moral de ayudar a los miembros de su famila.
☐	☑	**4.** Las familias hispanas no se reúnen frecuentemente.
☑	☐	**5.** El honor es un valor importante en las familias hispanas.
☐	☑	**6.** Los niños hispanos no aprenden a respetar la autoridad.

2B.18 STANDARDS: COMPARISONS. Ask students which of the statements also apply to their native culture.

2B.18 LEARNING STRATEGY: Highlight the importance of students talking through their answers. For this, and for other activities, it is important to recognize the importance of learning from one another. Stress the fact that often classmates can explain things in a way that is more comprehensible to them than even the textbook or the instructor.

¡Atención!

Pariente	does not mean parent but rather *relative* (**padres** are parents). Los padres de Andrés Fellove se llaman Ricardo y Mercedes. Los parientes incluyen a los abuelos, los tíos y los primos.
Familiar	does not mean familiar. It means *having to do with the family.* Something familiar in the sense of being "known" is **conocido/a** in Spanish. Para unas personas, las relaciones familiares son complicadas. Benicio del Toro es un actor puertorriqueño conocido.
Tranquilo	can mean *tranquil* but also can mean *quiet* and *relaxed* when referring to people. El parque es un lugar tranquilo. Ernestito es un niño tranquilo.
Unido/a	can mean *united* as in **Estados Unidos**, but also can mean *close* when referring to family relationships. When referring to close friendships, **íntimo** is used. The adjective **cercano** usually refers to closeness in terms of physical space. La familia Fellove está muy unida. Lana y Lois son amigas íntimas.

2B.19 ¿La palabra correcta? Determine whether the bold faced word in each statement below is used correctly based on context. If the word is incorrect, supply the correct word. Then, check your answers with a classmate.

1. "Cielito Lindo" es una canción *(song)* mexicana muy **familiar**.

2. Roberto y Ricardo son amigos **cercanos** de mi hermano.

3. Mis primos organizan una reunión **familiar** durante el Día de la Independencia.

4. Hoy Mariana no está nerviosa; está muy **tranquila**.

5. Los **parientes** de mis primos son mis tíos.

6. Mis hermanos y yo estamos muy **unidos**.

2B.19 ANSWERS: Correct: 3, 4, 6; Incorrect: 1 (conocida), 2 (íntimos), 5 (padres)

2B.19 FOLLOW-UP: Go over the answers as a large group once students have had a chance to work with a classmate.

Estructuras clave 1 Conjugating Verbs: *Él, ella,* and *usted* forms

WILEY PLUS

Go to *WileyPLUS* and review the tutorial for this grammar point.

WILEY PLUS

You will find PowerPoint presentations for use with *Estructuras clave* in *WileyPLUS*.

SUGGESTIONS: Invite students to pay more attention to verb endings. Remind them that being a good detective, noticing things and seeing patterns, will help them pick up these linguistic nuances.

In *Investigación A* you learned that pairing a subject or subject pronoun with its appropriate form of the verb is called *conjugating* the verb. You have been using the **–o** ending for verbs whose subject is **yo,** and the **–as** or **–es** ending for verbs whose subject is **tú.** What endings have you been using for **él, ella,** and **usted**?

Now, we will look at the forms for **él, ella** and **usted (Ud.)** more formally so you can talk about what your family, an individual family member, a friend, or any other individual does. You will also be able to ask someone what he/she does in a formal context. Note that the abbreviation **Ud.** is used often in writing, and always capitalized.

The chart below illustrates the regular verb endings for **–ar, –er,** and **–ir** verbs when the subject is **él, ella,** or **usted.**

-ar		-er		-ir	
hablar	habl**a**	comer	com**e**	abrir	abr**e**
bailar	bail**a**	correr	corr**e**	escribir	escrib**e**
nadar	nad**a**	ver	v**e**	vivir	viv**e**
escuchar	escuch**a**	leer	le**e**		
llamar	llam**a**	hacer	hac**e**		
levantar	levant**a**	beber	beb**e**		

In short, for **–ar** present tense regular verbs, drop the final **–r** for the correct conjugation, and for **–er** and **–ir** verbs, drop the final **–er/–ir** ending and end the verbs with an **–e.** Note that if the subject is named or known, you don't use the pronoun.

Él habla con mi padre.	*He is speaking with my father.*
Ella baila con su esposo.	*She is dancing with her husband.*
¿Tiene usted nietos?	*Do you (formal) have grand children?*
Laura vive en México. Habla español.	*Laura lives in Mexico. She speaks Spanish.*

2B.20 TEACHING TIP: Remind students to pay attention to the endings. This would be a good time to ask them whether or not they think that pronouns are not used as often as they are in English. Tell them that based on the endings, it is clear who is being talked about, thus limiting the usage of pronouns.

2B.20 RECYCLING: This activity recycles previously learned verbs.

2B.20 ¿Quién hace la acción? Read the verbs and indicate whether **yo, tú** or **usted** is the subject.

		yo	tú	usted
1.	dibujo	☑	☐	☐
2.	cantas	☐	☑	☐
3.	influye	☐	☐	☑
4.	aprendes	☐	☑	☐
5.	abro	☑	☐	☐
6.	nada	☐	☐	☑
7.	como	☑	☐	☐
8.	cuida	☐	☐	☑
9.	escribes	☐	☑	☐
10.	lee	☐	☐	☑

2B.21 ¿La clase o el tiempo libre?   Listen to several statements describing the activities of a typical student and determine whether each activity is more likely done in class or in his/her free time. What other activities can you describe in Spanish that might be done in class or in your free time?

2B.21 AUDIO SCRIPT: 1. Levanta la mano., 2. Toca el piano., 3. Escucha a la profesora., 4. Corre., 5. Toma apuntes., 6. Se reúne con su familia., 7. Escribe una composición., 8. Hace preguntas.

	En la clase	En el tiempo libre
1.	☑	☐
2.	☐	☑
3.	☑	☐
4.	☐	☑
5.	☑	☐
6.	☐	☑
7.	☑	☐
8.	☑	☐

2B.22 EXTENSION ACTIVITY: Using the verbs listed, have students write other possible sentences.

2B.22 Las conexiones más lógicas.   Match the verbs in column **A** with the most logical complement in column **B.** Then, check your work with two other classmates.

	A		B
e	**1.** Baila…	**a.**	…su programa favorito.
h	**2.** Anda…	**b.**	…videojuegos.
a	**3.** Mira …	**c.**	…la tarea de francés.
g	**4.** Escribe…	**d.**	…con sus amigos en un restaurante.
f	**5.** Come…	**e.**	… salsa con su novio.
b	**6.** Juega…	**f.**	…pizza.
d	**7.** Se reúne…	**g.**	…mensajes electrónicos.
c	**8.** Hace…	**h.**	…en bicicleta.

¿Haces tú alguna de estas actividades? ¿Qué haces tú los fines de semana?

2B.23 Las acciones de los parientes.   Choose a family member (parent, spouse, child, sibling, in-law, grandparent, aunt, cousin, etc.) and on a separate sheet of paper, write four sentences describing what he/she does or does not do. When you are finished, form a group with other people who have written about the same family member and compare activities. Do your family members do the same things or not? Are there any outrageous family members?

> Modelo: *Mi madre habla mucho.*
> *Mi madre toca la guitarra.*
> *Mi madre no escucha música rap.*
> *Mi madre…*

2B.24 ¿Qué hace la persona ideal?   In groups of 3 or 4, discuss the following idealized people and write 3–4 sentences describing what each person does. The descriptions for each group will then be compiled to generate a single description of each idealized person for the entire class.

1. El padre/La madre ideal

2. La pareja ideal

3. El/La estudiante ideal

4. El/La amigo/a ideal

2B.25 TEACHING TIP:
Allow groups to work on their descriptions providing the following model if necessary: *El/La profesor/a ideal respeta a los estudiantes. Ayuda a los estudiantes. Comunica bien la información. Es extrovertido/a.* Then, ask each group to write its description of each idealized person on the board. Cases where particular statements/ideas are repeated should be indicated. Process the results with the classes. The following questions will help spark discussion: *¿Son similares/diferentes las descripciones? ¿Qué persona ideal respeta a sus estudiantes? ¿Hay personas ideales en sus vidas?*

2B.25 SUGGESTION: Call attention to the way a whole family is named in the model.

2B.26 INSTRUCTOR'S RESOURCES: You will find a reproducible chart for Activity 2B.26 in your Instructor's Resources.

2B.25 Es la familia...   In small groups, describe a well-known real or fictional family, such as a family from a TV program, a movie, or a well-know family such as the Kennedys, etc., without mentioning family members' names. Use family vocabulary and adjectives to describe the family members' personalities or character traits. Share the group descriptions with the class and the class will try to identify the family.

> Modelo: Group describes: *El padre es muy irresponsable. Tiene una esposa tradicional y tres hijos. Su hijo es rebelde. Su hija mayor es inteligente y …*
>
> Class responds: *La familia Simpson o Los Simpson*

2B.26 A contestar las preguntas.   Ask the following questions to a student in class until he/she can respond **"Sí"** to a question. Have him/her write his/her initials on your chart. Once a classmate has signed their initials, move on to ask another classmate the questions until he/she can respond **"Sí"** and initial the box. Repeat the process until you have intials in each box in your chart. As a class, find out which students do certain things well and write the findings in your **Retrato de la clase.**

¿Dibujas bien?	¿Cantas bien?
¿Haces la tarea de español diariamente?	¿Corres rápido?
¿Llamas a tu familia por teléfono frecuentemente?	¿Escribes bien?
¿Tienes muchos amigos?	¿Aprendes a hablar español?
¿Nadas bien?	¿Comes mucho?
¿Escuchas las noticias (news) diariamente?	¿Visitas a tu familia con frecuencia?
¿Bailas bien?	¿Lees rápidamente?
¿Comes bien?	¿Juegas un deporte?

Retrato de la clase: Mi compañero de clase _____, dibuja bien pero no canta bien. _____ no lee rápidamente pero escucha las noticias diariamente…

¡CONÉCTATE! Assign this *¡Conéctate!* as a homework assignment by having students share their individual results. Keep these in mind as you move forward with your students.

¡Conéctate!

As you talk about your personal interests in this *Investigación*, reflect on how your own strengths in learning may lead you to specific interests. Just as we all have different interests, we have different learning styles. To learn more about your own, type in "multiple intelligence test" in your favorite search engine (e.g. http://google.com, http://yahoo.com). Find an online test where you will receive immediate feedback and complete it. Does there seem to be a relationship between your interests and your strengths? What did you find out about your own learning styles?

Estructuras clave 2 Adjectives

 WILEY PLUS

You will find PowerPoint presentations for use with *Estructuras clave* in *WileyPLUS*.

In *Capítulo 1* you learned about the need for articles to agree in number and gender with the nouns they modify and you learned how to make singular nouns plural. What other words that you have been using seem to change depending on the noun they are associated with?

Adjectives in Spanish also have to agree in number and gender with the nouns they modify. Descriptive adjectives in Spanish generally follow the noun they modify, unlike in English where adjectives typically precede the noun.

	Masculine	Feminine
Singular	el niño **respetuoso** el padre **moderno**	la niña **respetuosa** la madre **moderna**
Plural	los niños **respetuosos** los padres **modernos**	las niñas **respetuosas** las madres **modernas**

El libro negro está en la mesa.	*The black book is on the table.*
Los libros negros están en la mesa.	*The black books are on the table.*
La mochila negra es de Juan.	*The black backback belongs to Juan.*
Las mochilas negras son de Juan.	*The black backpacks belong to Juan.*

You will generally find the masculine singular form of the adjective in lists such as a dictionary or glossary, and these typically end in **−o**, **−e**, or a consonant. Adjectives that end in **−o** in their masculine form, drop the **−o** and use **−a** in the feminine. The masculine plural form ends in **−os** and the feminine plural in **−as.**

El libro negr**o**	La mochila negr**a**
Los libros negr**os**	Las mochilas negr**as**

Adjectives that end in **−e** in their masculine singular form also end in **−e** in their feminine singular form. These adjectives end in **−es** in the plural for both genders.

el chico inteligent**e**	la chica inteligent**e**
los chicos inteligent**es**	las chicas inteligent**es**

Like adjectives that end in **−e,** most adjectives that end in a consonant typically share the same form when they describe both masculine and feminine nouns. To make these adjectives plural, simply add **−es** after the consonant.

el libro popula**r**	la clase popula**r**
los libros popula**res**	las clases popula**res**

However, adjectives that end in **−dor / −ol / −ón** in their masculine form add an **−a** for the feminine form. Plural forms add **−es** for masculine or **−as** for feminine.

el escritor conserva**dor**	los escritores conserva**dores**
la escritora conserva**dora**	las escritoras conserva**doras**
el profesor españ**ol**	los profesores español**es**
la profesora españ**ola**	las profesoras español**as**
el amigo barrig**ón** *(big bellied)*	los amigos barrig**ones**
la amiga barrig**ona**	las amigas barrig**onas**

2B.27 ¿A quién describe? Decide whether each word you hear describes Orlando Bloom or Penélope Cruz following the model. Then decide whether each description is true or not.

	Orlando	Penélope
1.	☐	☑
2.	☑	☐
3.	☑	☐
4.	☐	☑
5.	☑	☐
6.	☑	☐
7.	☐	☑
8.	☐	☑

2B.28 ¿Cómo son los famosos? In small groups, think of a celebrity (actor, singer, musician, politician, author, comedian, athlete, etc.) and write a short description of him/her. You may include physical characteristics, personality traits and activities associated with your celebrity as well as information about any family members you are aware of. Be sure to keep in mind subject/verb agreement and noun/adjective agreement as you prepare your description. A spokesperson for your group will read your description aloud and the class will guess whom you are describing.

Modelo: Group reports: *Es de Nueva York. Su familia es puertorriqueña. Es extrovertida, talentosa y sociable. Canta y baila. También es actriz. Es Selena en la película* Selena. *Su esposo se llama Marc Anthony.*

Class responds: *Jennifer López (J-Lo)*

2B.29 Los compañeros de cuarto.

Paso 1: You and a partner are roommates and are looking for a third person to move in and form your new family of friends. Prepare a short advertisement describing the type of person you would like to have as the third roommate. Once you have agreed on your ad, make sure that it is polished. Then, write your ad on the white/black board.

Modelo: *¿Eres jovial, paciente, responsable y organizado/a? ¿Te gusta la música de Enrique Iglesias? ¿Te gusta el programa "American Idol"? ¿Te gusta correr en el parque, nadar en el océano, jugar deportes…? Si tu respuesta es sí, llama al 333-4444.*

Paso 2: Now, imagine you are looking for an apartment share and take a few minutes to walk around and read all of the groups' ads on the board to see which ad most interests you. Write a short description explaining which ad is the best fit for you, and why.

2B.29 STANDARDS: PRESENTATIONAL MODE. The presentational mode of communication is one of the three modes addressed by the standards. What distinguishes this mode from the others (interpersonal and interpretive) is the fact that it is polished and edited. Use this activity to focus students' attention on this standard.

DICHOS

Entre padres y hermanos no metas tus manos.	*Don't come between family members.*
De tal palo, tal astilla.	*Like father, like son.*

Enlaces

2B.30 ¿Puedes conectar las ideas?
Determine the meaning of the bold faced word or phrase according to the context of the sentences. Choose from the following options.

along with	but rather

_____ **1.** El concepto de la familia en la cultura hispana no se limita a la familia nuclear, **sino que** incluye a los miembros de la familia extendida.

_____ **2.** Las familias hispanas inculcan en sus hijos la importancia del honor **junto con** los buenos modales *(manners)*.

2B.30 ANSWERS: 1. but rather, 2. along with

2B.31 ¿Puedes conectar las ideas?
Choose between **sino que** and **junto con** to connect the ideas in the following sentences.

1. Las familias hispanas no sólo se reúnen para celebrar eventos especiales, _____ los individuos de la familia tienen la responsabilidad moral de ayudar a otros miembros de la famila.

2. _____ los abuelos y los tíos, los padrinos forman parte de la familia extendida de los latinoamericanos.

2B.31 ANSWERS: 1. sino que, 2. junto con

FUNCTIONAL OUTCOMES:
The central question that frames this *Investigación* is *"¿Cómo puedes hablar de tu familia?"* Explore whether students can now address this question and how they would go about it. Have them review the chart on the first page of this *Investigación*.

CONTEXTOS: PRE-READING ACTIVITY. Follow up on the last activity by brainstorming with the students about godparents in US culture, writing their comments and ideas on the black/white board or overhead transparency in Spanish as they provide the information to you.

2B.32 El compadrazgo. You have read about the important role that family relationships play in Hispanic cultures. Another type of social support system common in many Latin American countries is called **el compadrazgo,** which refers to the relationship between godparents and parents. Essential to **el compadrazgo** are **los padrinos** *(godparents)* (**el padrino** and **la madrina**). What comes to mind when you think of godparents? With what context(s) are godparents associated in US culture? Do you have godparents or sponsors? What is their role? What is your relationship with them?

El compadrazgo

El compadrazgo evolved from the Catholic rite of baptism and represents the combination of Hispanic and indigenous traditions in addition to an indigenous interpretation of Christian precepts. Today, **el compadrazgo** is an important system for social support in many parts of Latin America. **El compadrazgo** is found in large cities, in rural areas and at all socio-economic levels. Traditionally, **el compadrazgo** begins when the parents of a newborn choose the **padrinos** of the baby for the baptism. Now, the parents of the baby and the godparents are **compadres. El compadrazgo** also is part of other Catholic rites that require godparents such as the first communion, confirmation and marriage. However, **el compadrazgo** is not limited to religious celebrations because there are various secular occasions for which honorary godparents are named such as **quinceañeras** and graduations.

Not all, but most Hispanics are culturally or actively practicing Catholics. In addition to the marriage ceremony and the act of communion, the celebration of baptism is an important ritual in the church.

The choice of **padrinos** and **compadres** is very important because traditionally **el compadrazgo** does not simply refer to the relationship between godparents and godchildren (**los ahijados**) but it also implies a series of social, financial and even professional obligations between the **compadres.** In some cases, a relative is chosen to be the godfather or godmother. This serves to reinforce family ties. In other cases, friends or neighbors are chosen as godparents and this serves to reinforce community ties and also to resolve or eliminate potential conflicts because, traditionally, the relationship between **compadres** should be very formal and respectful. Another possibility is to choose one's boss at work or a person from a higher socio-economic group. This allows relationships between different professional and socio-economic levels to be established. In these cases, more well off **compadres** help the less well off **compadres.** For example, they often protect or guarantee the job of the less well off **compadre** or they pay the expenses of the family, including those related to the children's education. In return, less well off **compadres** owe their benefactors a great deal of loyalty. Without the **compadrazgo** system, many children would not receive an education and more families would suffer from poverty.

Perspectivas

2B.34 En tu familia. In groups of three, share answers to the following questions. Then, compare the family and social networks of various cultures represented in your group with that of **el compadrazgo.**

1. ¿Quién paga los gastos *(pays the expenses)* de la familia cuando tus padres no pueden?
2. ¿Quién paga los gastos de la educación de tu familia?
3. ¿Qué obligaciones sociales tiene tu familia con otra gente (no de tu familia)?
4. ¿Qué celebra tu familia y con quién?
5. ¿Quién ayuda a tu familia a obtener trabajos?
6. ¿Quién participa en las celebraciones de tu familia?
7. ¿A quién llaman cuando tienen problemas o conflictos en la familia?
8. ¿Quién ayuda a tu familia a mudarse *(to move)* de una casa o ciudad a otra?

2B.34 SUGGESTION: Ask students to share some of their observations with the class.

VÍVELO: CULTURA
Los apellidos

Many Spanish-speakers use two last names—their father's last name, followed by their mother's maiden name. Both **el apellido paterno** and **el apellido materno** are commonly used in official or important documents, but many people use only their father's last name in everyday situations. When a woman gets married, she may keeps her father's paternal surname, followed by **de**, and add her husband's last name for social purposes, but generally does not legally change her name.

Look at the invitation to María Gracia's and Eduardo's first communion celebration. Their father's (paternal) last name is Cervantes, and their mother's maiden name (paternal last name) is Escamilla. What was their godmother's maiden name before she married Héctor Cruz?

VÍVELO: CULTURA: RECYCLING: Recycle previously learned material, such as surnames, time, etc. For example, in Spanish ask students the names of the two children based on the communion invitation (first names and last names). Ask at what time the ceremony takes place. Ask students if they can figure out who the godparents *(los padrinos)* will be.

Recuerdo de la Primera Comunión de los niños

María Gracia y Eduardo Cervantes Escamilla

efectuada el día 18 de Diciembre de 1977, a las 8.00 horas, en la Iglesia de la Soledad (Unidad Vicente Budib) oficiada por el R. P. Salvador Carrera.

Sus Padrinos:

Héctor Cruz Santillana

Dalila Contreras de Cruz

El compadrazgo has its roots in religious tradition, with godparents playing a significant role in events marking a child's spiritual development such as receiving the sacrament of holy communion. Nowadays the relationship is both spiritual and secular.

Los hijos

Hispanic cultural values put the family at the center of society. It seems that everyone loves children and children are included in all social activities. Parties and dinners always include the children. They accompany their parents to church services, weddings, funerals, movies, the theater, and the symphony. More well-to-do adults are likely to have a live-in housekeeper/babysitter and thus are able to leave children at home while doing the shopping and running errands.

Children are introduced to adults that they are not acquainted with and are taught to shake hands and greet respectfully those to whom they are presented. They are expected to say good-bye to everyone before leaving a social gathering just as the adults do, and their presence is always acknowledged with affectionate words and gestures.

Members of the extended family often share living quarters. Aging parents often live with their married children and grandchildren. Students might live for a while at a relative's home while attending college when the campus is closer to the relative's house than to their own.

Hispanic families typically stay in close contact with each other in spite of geographical distance. Many immigrants to the US feel a responsibility to financially assist other family members who remain in the country of origin. Family loyalty is evident everywhere from the emphasis put on **El Día de las Madres** to the effort made to attend all weddings, graduations, **quinceañeras** and other birthday celebrations, and funerals of family members.

La celebración de los quince años es de origen mexicano y es exclusivamente para las mujeres. Cuando una niña cumple *(turns)* quince años, se convierte en mujer; para celebrar la transformación de niña a mujer, hay una ceremonia de agradecimiento *(thanksgiving)* en la iglesia. Después de la ceremonia religiosa hay una gran fiesta en donde la quinceañera baila con sus acompañantes el vals de quince años.

Vocabulario: Investigación B

Vocabulario esencial

Sustantivos

el/la abuelo/a	grandfather/grandmother
la boda	wedding
el cumpleaños	birthday
el/la cuñado/a	brother/sister-in-law
el difunto/a	dead person
la edad	age
el/la esposo/a	husband/wife
el/la hermanastro/a	stepbrother/stepsister
el/la hermano/a	brother/sister
el/la hijastro/a	stepchild
el/la hijo/a	son/daughter
el/la hijo/a único/a	only child
la iglesia	church
la madrastra	stepmother
la madre	mother
la madrina	godmother
el marido	husband
el matrimonio	marriage
el/la medio hermano/a	half brother/half sister
el/la nieto/a	grandson/granddaughter
el/la niño/a	boy/girl
la nuera	daughter-in-law
el padrastro	stepfather
el padrino	godfather
el padre	father
la pareja	couple
el/la primo/a	cousin
el/la sobrino/a	nephew/niece
el/la suegro/a	father/mother-in-law
el/la tío/a	uncle/aunt
el yerno	son-in-law

Adjetivos

casado/a	married
divorciado/a	divorced
mayor	older
menor	younger
muerto/a	dead
soltero/a	not married
viudo/a	widowed

Verbos

amar	to love
ayudar	to help
cuidar	to take care of
estar enamorado/a	to be in love

Otras palabras y expresiones

el/la abogado/a	lawyer
beber	to drink
el/la bisnieto/a	great grandchild
los buenos modales	good manners
el cariño	affection
la carta	letter
cercano	close
el/la chico/a	guy/gal
comprometido/a	engaged, commited
el desempleo	unemployment
la fiesta	party
el gasto	expense
el/la heredero/a	heir
el/la hijo/a del medio	middle child
inculcar	to instill
la licencia de manejar	driver's license
el lugar de nacimiento	place of birth
mediante	through
mudarse	to move
nadie	no one, nobody
pobre	poor
por cierto	by the way
porque	because

el/la primogénito/a	first child
proveer	provide
recordar	to remember
reunir	to gather
la salud	health
sobrevivir	to survive

Cognados

Review the cognates in *Adelante* and the false cognates in *¡Atención!*. For a complete list of cognates, see Appendix 4 on page 605.

En vivo

La familia de mi compañero/a: You will interview a classmate in order to create a cognitive map of his or her family. Before beginning, you will need to brainstorm the questions necessary for the interview.

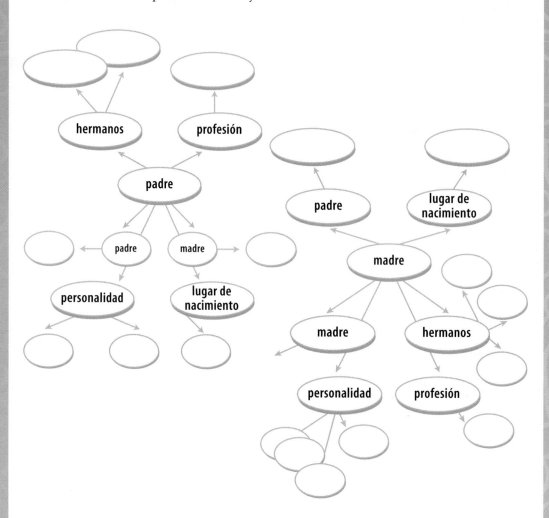

FOLLOW-UP: Have students interview a Spanish speaker or someone in another Spanish class to obtain this information.

Once you have all the information, write a paragraph about your classmate's parents. Follow the pattern below:

La madre de _____ se llama _____. Trabaja de _____. Es una persona _____. Nació *(she was born)* en _____. La abuela materna de mi compañero se llama _____ y el abuelo materno se llama _____.

DICHOS: Ask students *¿Con qué dichos te identificas?*

INVESTIGACIÓN A: Bilingüismo en el trabajo

> **Antes de ver el video.** Answer the following questions:

1. ¿Qué es el bilingüismo? El bilingüismo es el uso de dos _____ por *(by)* una misma persona o comunidad.
2. ¿Estudias otros idiomas? Sí, estudio _____.

> **El video.** Indicate whether the following statements are **ciertos** or **falsos** based on the video.

	Cierto	Falso
1. Hay más de 40 millones de hispanos en EE.UU.	☑	☐
2. El abogado se llama Arturo Fernández.	☐	☑
3. Jaima Tushaus empezó a estudiar español a los 24 años.	☑	☐
4. El programa de radio se llama "Soy la ley".	☐	☑
5. El programa comienza en 2003.	☑	☐
6. Las personas hacen preguntas sobre inmigración	☑	☐
7. Jaima Tushaus habla en español con los clientes.	☑	☐
8. Para Jaima Tushaus no es importante estudiar la cultura hispana.	☐	☑

> **Después de ver el video.** Rate the following statements as they relate to you on a scale of 1–4 (1 = **nada**, 2 = **poco**, 3 = **bastante**, 4= **mucho**). Then, share your answers with the rest of the class.

1. Estudio español porque quiero viajar a otros países. ( )
2. No me gusta estudiar español. ( )
3. Estudio español porque me gusta la cultura hispana. ( )
4. El español es importante en mi comunidad. ( )
5. Estudio español para ganar más dinero. ( )
6. Estudiar español es importante para trabajar. ( )

Vocabulario útil
abogado *lawyer*
licencia de manejar *driver's license*
reglas *rules*

ANSWERS: 1. lenguas / idiomas, 2. answers will vary

FOLLOW-UP: Have students interview a Spanish speaker or someone in another Spanish class to obtain this information.

INVESTIGACIÓN B: Crónica de una boda

> **Antes de ver el video.** Choose the appropriate word to complete each sentence.

a. boda   **b.** bautizo   **c.** quinceañera   **d.** graduación

___d___ **1.** En mayo termino mis estudios y es mi _____.
___a___ **2.** La _____ de mi hermano con su prometida *(fiancée)* es el domingo.
___b___ **3.** El _____ del bebé se celebra en la iglesia.
___c___ **4.** La _____ es la fiesta de los quince años.

> **El video.** Complete the following sentences with the appropriate words from the video.

veintisiete   prima   suegros   dos
bisnietos   hijos   casada

1. Mis _____ se ven un poco nerviosos.
2. Roci está _____ con César.
3. Ana Paula tiene _____ años.
4. La abuelita tiene _____ nietos y diez _____.
5. Mi tía Graciela es _____ de mi mamá.
6. Graciela tiene dos _____.

> **Después de ver el video.** Answer the following questions and share your answers with the rest of the class: Apart from weddings, do you know other important events or celebrations in Hispanic cultures? Are they also important in your culture? What celebrations are important in your culture?

Vocabulario útil
bisnietos/as *great grandchildren*
comprometido/a *engaged*
cariño *affection*
estar enamorado/a *to be in love*
nervioso/a *nervous*
por cierto *by the way*

ANSWERS: 1. suegros, 2. casada, 3. dos, 4. veintisiete / bisnietos, 5. prima, 6. hijos.

Retrato de la clase Checklist

WILEY PLUS

TESTING PROGRAM:
You will find a complete testing program for use with *¡Vívelo!* in *WileyPLUS*.

You should have recorded information in your **Retrato de la clase** in conjunction with the following activities:

- ☐ **2A.3** **¿Te interesa?**
- ☐ **2A.12** **El horario más exigente**
- ☐ **2A.14** **Tu propio horario**
- ☐ **2A.15** **¿Te gusta…?**
- ☐ **2A.20** **Entrevistas**
- ☐ **2A.23** **Las facultades**

- ☐ **2B.3** **¿Cómo es tu familia?**
- ☐ **2B.14** **Juntos forman la familia**
- ☐ **2B.15** **¿Quién de la clase…?**
- ☐ **2B.26** **A contestar las preguntas**

El mundo hispano

INVESTIGACIÓN **3A**
¿En dónde se habla español en el mundo?

ADELANTE
▶ ¡Ya lo sabes! Geografía y nacionalidades
▶ La diversidad de España

Bien dicho: La acentuación y los acentos escritos

PALABRAS CLAVE
▶ ¿Qué tiempo hace?
▶ Los meses del año
▶ La geografía
▶ Las preposiciones
▶ Los números mayores de 100

ESTRUCTURAS CLAVE
▶ Conjugating verbs: Plural forms
▶ Demonstrative adjectives and pronouns

VÍVELO: LENGUA
▶ Tag questions
▶ Expressing years in Spanish

VÍVELO: CULTURA
▶ Los países del Caribe
▶ Las estaciones y el clima en el hemisferio sur
▶ Aspectos importantes de la geografía de América del Sur

CONTEXTOS Y PERSPECTIVAS
Una panorámica de la región

¡VÍVELO!

En vivo:
¿Has aprendido a ubicar los países?
Ser hispano: Representaciones visuales

INVESTIGACIÓN **3B**
¿Qué significa ser hispano? ¿Qué es la hispanidad?

ADELANTE
▶ ¡Ya lo sabes! Las comunidades
▶ ¿Hispano o latino?

Bien dicho: La acentuación y el significado de las palabras

PALABRAS CLAVE
▶ Cosas que pasan en la ciudad

ESTRUCTURAS CLAVE
▶ The present perfect tense

VÍVELO: LENGUA
▶ Expressing "to know": *Saber* and *conocer*

VÍVELO: CULTURA
▶ El español de América del Sur
▶ Los hispanos en EE.UU.
▶ Los jóvenes: Tercera parte de la población hispana

CONTEXTOS Y PERSPECTIVAS
Una comunidad transnacional

En directo:
A: 1492: intercambio de dos mundos
B: ¿Qué significa ser hispano?

¿En dónde se habla español en el mundo?

In this **Investigación** you will learn:

▶ The location of Spanish-speaking countries and capitals and how to indicate nationality

▶ How to express weather conditions and describe geography/topography

▶ How to express years in Spanish

▶ How to comprehend comparisons in Spanish

¿Cómo puedes hablar de los países en donde se habla español?

You can identify the Spanish-speaking countries of the world.	¿Hablan español los brasileños? ¿Hablan español los argentinos? ¿Hablan español los estadounidenses?
You can talk about geographical location.	México está al sur de Estados Unidos y Canadá está al norte.
You can describe some of the prominent geographical features of Spanish-speaking countries.	Hay desiertos, selvas y montañas en Perú. Hay mucha costa en Chile. Hay lagos grandes en Bolivia y Argentina.
You can describe the climate of various places.	Cuando es verano en el hemisferio norte, es invierno en el hemisferio sur. Hace mucho frío en el sur de Chile. El clima de California es muy templado.
You can express the year of independence of countries.	La independencia de Estados Unidos fue el 4 de julio de 1776.

NOTE: While the majority of the adjectives of nationality presented here are cognates, we realize that some may be challenging, for example *alemán* or *escocés*. You may want to point out *Alemania* or *Escocia* on a map so that students connect the adjectives of nationality with their corresponding countries. You may also use comprehensible input such as *Los escoceses son de Escocia. Escocia es una de las islas británicas* or *Los alemanes son de Alemania. Alemania tiene ciudades importantes como Munich, Berlín, Hamburgo y Frankfurt.* The purpose of exposing the students to nationalities is not for them to memorize all of them, but to make intelligent guesses or recognize nationalities when they hear or see them. In terms of content, working with nationalities connects students with geography almost immediately.

Adelante

¡Ya lo sabes! Geografía y nacionalidades

el continente	la laguna	el este	el sur
el desierto	el océano	el noreste/el nordeste	el sureste
la frontera	la península	el noroeste	el suroeste
el golfo	la región	el norte	
el hemisferio	el valle	el oeste	

afgano/a	árabe	bengalí	canadiense
albanés/a	argentino/a	boliviano/a	checo/a
alemán/a*	armenio/a	brasileño/a	chileno/a
angoleño/a	australiano/a	búlgaro/a	chino/a
argelino/a**	austríaco/a	camboyano/a	colombiano/a

*alemán, *German*   **argelino, *Algerian*

coreano/a	guatemalteco/a	kuwaití	(o boricua)****
costarricense	guyanés/a**	liberiano/a	rumano/a
(o tico/a)*	haitiano/a	lituano/a	ruso/a
croata	holandés/a**	maltés/a**	salvadoreño/a
cubano/a	hondureño/a	mexicano/a	senegalés/a**
danés/a**	húngaro/a	marroquí	serbio/a
dominicano/a	indio/a***	nepalí	sudanés/a**
ecuatoriano/a	indonesio/a	neozelandés/a**	sueco/a
egipcio/a	iraní	nicaragüense	taiwanés/a**
escocés/a**	iraquí	nigeriano/a	tailandés/a**
eslovaco/a	irlandés/a**	noruego/a	turco/a
español/a	israelí	pakistaní	ucraniano/a
estadounidense	italiano/a	panameño/a	ugandés/a**
etíope	jamaicano/a (Spain)	paraguayo/a	uruguayo/a
filipino/a	jamaiquino/a	peruano/a	venezolano/a
finlandés/a**	(Latin America)	polaco/a	vietnamita
francés/a**	japonés/a	polinesio/a	zambiano/a
ghanés/a**	jordano/a	portugués/a**	
griego/a	keniano/a	puertorriqueño/a	

*__Tico/a__ is a more common way of referring to a __costarricense.__ Much like someone from Australia is called an Aussie instead of an Australian.

These nationalities carry a written accent when they end in **–s. When they end in **–a,** the written accent is omitted.

***The formal way of referring to someone from India is __indio/a.__ However, very few Spanish speakers use __indio/a__ to refer to someone from India. The word __hindú__ is used, despite the fact that millions of people in India practice Islam among other religions.

****Often, __boricua__ is used instead of __puertorriqueño/a.__ It comes from __taíno,__ the indigenous language of Puerto Rico, and derives from __Borinquén,__ the name the natives gave the island before the Spanish renamed it Puerto Rico.

Note that nationalities are not capitalized in Spanish. Many adjectives of nationality end in **–o** or **–és** when they describe men, and end in in **–a** or **–esa** when they describe women.

3A.1   **No pertenece.**   Working with a partner, select the word that does not belong to the indicated category. Then, verify your answers as a class.

1. naturaleza: el desierto   la laguna   el océano   (la línea)
2. masas de agua: (el valle)   el océano   la laguna   el golfo
3. direcciones: (esta)   oeste   noroeste   norte
4. lenguas: francés   español   japonés   (estadounidense)
5. nacionalidades: peruano   (anciano)   cubano   ecuatoriano
6. países: Argentina   Venezuela   (Iberia)   Bolivia
7. países del hemisferio norte: México   (Chile)   Canadá   Estados Unidos
8. países del hemisferio sur: Bolivia   Ecuador   (España)   Uruguay

3A.1 SUGGESTION: Read the category and have the students respond aloud so that you repeat the word with the correct pronunciation.

3A.2 Terminología geográfica. Using the vocabulary in *Adelante,* fill in the blank with the appropriate word in Spanish, following the model. Verify your responses with a classmate.

1. Estados Unidos tiene seis _____*penínsulas*_____ pequeñas, la más grande es la de Florida.

2. El _____desierto_____ más famoso del mundo se llama Sáhara y está en África.

3. Estados Unidos tiene _____frontera_____ con dos países, Canadá y México.

4. Israel, Iraq, Irán y Afganistán son países que están en una _____región_____ muy conflictiva.

5. En California el _____valle_____ de Napa es muy famoso por su producción de vino.

6. En el continente americano existen tres _____golfos_____, dos son de México y uno es de Estados Unidos y está en Alaska.

7. México está al _____sur_____ de Estados Unidos y al _____norte_____ de Guatemala.

8. Chile, Bolivia, Argentina y Uruguay son países del _____hemisferio_____ sur.

3A.3 Los países y la nacionalidad. How many continents are there? In the US, students are taught that there are seven continents. In much of the rest of the world, students are taught that there are six continents, in which North and South America are considered one (**las Américas**). Using the six-continent categorization that students in other countries use, create a chart to group the nationalities above. Underline all of the nationalities representing a Spanish-speaking country. Review your answers with several classmates.

África	Las Américas	Asia	Antártida	Australia	Europa

3A.4 ¿Cuánto sabes del mundo y de geografía? You will hear specific examples of geographic features, languages and nationalities. Match each example with the corresponding term, following the model.

1. ___*f*___ **a.** un océano
2. ___h___ **b.** un desierto
3. ___a___ **c.** un golfo
4. ___g___ **d.** una lengua
5. ___c___ **e.** una nacionalidad
6. ___e___ **f.** un continente
7. ___d___ **g.** una nación
8. ___i___ **h.** una península
   i. una sierra

3A.5 **Cierto o falso.** Look at the map and indicate whether each statement is **cierto** or **falso.** Then, check your work with two other classmates.

Cierto	Falso		
☑	☐	**1.**	México está al sur de Estados Unidos.
☑	☐	**2.**	Baja California y Yucatán son penínsulas mexicanas.
☑	☐	**3.**	Miami está al norte de la Ciudad de Panamá.
☐	☑	**4.**	Las naciones con fronteras al sur de México son Guatemala y Nicaragua.
☐	☑	**5.**	La isla de Jamaica está al norte de Cuba.
☐	☑	**6.**	La República Dominicana está al oeste de Haití.
☑	☐	**7.**	El continente de América del Sur está al sureste de Estados Unidos.
☐	☑	**8.**	Costa Rica está al norte de Colombia.
☑	☐	**9.**	El Salvador está al sur de Honduras.
☐	☑	**10.**	Cancún está directamente al norte de Panamá.

3A.6 **Las nacionalidades originales.** Do you know the nationality of these famous people? Write one sentence to state where each person is from, then write a second sentence describing each person's nationality, following the model. **¡Ojo!** Nationality is expressed with adjectives. Be sure to use the correct **–o** or **–a** ending, depending on whether you're describing a man or a woman.* Write down the names of any classmates who knew the countries and nationalities of all of these people in your **Retrato de la clase.**

*Note exception: **español,** not españolo

mexicano/a   español/a   puertorriqueño/a   cubano/a   colombiano/a
dominicano/a   argentino/a   venezolano/a   chileno/a

Modelo: Thalía
Thalía es de México. Es mexicana.

1. Pau Gasol
2. Manu Ginóbili
3. Salma Hayek
4. Fidel Castro

5. Gael García Bernal
6. Penélope Cruz
7. Antonio Banderas
8. Ricky Martin

9. Shakira
10. Juanes
11. Felipe Calderón
12. Hugo Chávez

13. Eduardo Nájera
14. Evita Perón
15. Sammy Sosa
16. Michelle Bachelet

Retrato de la clase: Mis compañeros/as ____, ____ y ____ conocen a todas las personas.

La diversidad de España

Los españoles hablan castellano, es decir, español. España está en la Península Ibérica, en Europa. ¿Qué otro país está en la Península Ibérica? Portugal. ¿Es el español la lengua principal de Portugal? No, en Portugal la lengua, o el idioma, principal es el portugués.

El mapa distingue las diferentes regiones de España. España es un país con mucha diversidad. La identidad regional es muy importante y aunque *(even though)* todo el mundo habla español, varias regiones tienen también su propio *(own)* idioma como por ejemplo el vasco, el gallego o el catalán. Por eso, "La marcha real", el himno nacional *(national anthem)* de España, no tiene palabras sino sólo música.

TEACHING TIP: To verify comprehension of this passage, ask students to indicate the location of the various provinces in Spain: *¿Dónde está Andalucía? ¿En el norte? ¿El este? ¿El sur? ¿El oeste? ¿Dónde está Galicia? ¿Dónde está Cataluña? ¿Dónde está Madrid? ¿Dónde está el País Vasco? ¿Dónde está Asturias?*

SUGGESTIONS: Point out that *el idioma* and *la lengua* are synonyms and will surface often.

3A.7 **Cierto o falso.** Indicate whether each statement you hear about Spain is **cierto** or **falso** based on what you read. Verify your responses as a class.

	Cierto	Falso
1.	☐	☑
2.	☑	☐
3.	☐	☑
4.	☐	☑
5.	☑	☐
6.	☐	☑

3A.7 AUDIO SCRIPT: Have students correct false statements. 1. España está en la península de Yucatán en el Caribe. 2. En España, la mayoría de la población habla castellano. 3. España está en una península y no hay otros países en la península. 4. España está en América Latina. 5. El himno nacional de España no tiene palabras. 6. No se hablan otras lenguas en España.

3A.8 **De preguntas generales a perfiles personales.**

Paso 1: Answer the following questions as they relate to you. Then, interview a classmate using these same questions and write down his/her responses. Be prepared to present your classmate's responses to the class.

1. ¿Cuántas personas conoces que no son estadounidenses? ¿De dónde son?

2. ¿Cuántas lenguas hablas?

3. ¿En qué hemisferio vive tu familia?

4. ¿Cuál es tu nacionalidad?

5. ¿Cuál es la nacionalidad de algunos de tus parientes?

6. ¿Vive tu familia cerca *(near)* del océano, en una península o en un valle?

7. ¿Cuál es tu persona favorita de la lista de personas que hay en *Actividad 3A.6*?

8. ¿Cuáles son las nacionalidades de tus amigos más cercanos *(closest)*?

Paso 2: Use the information you gathered from your classmate to tell the rest of the class about him/her, and listen as everyone describes his/her partner. Write a summary of the class results of *Paso 1* in your **Retrato de la clase.**

Retrato de la clase: Hay _____ personas en la clase que tienen amigos que viven en otros continentes. Hay _____ estudiantes que hablan otra lengua. Hay _____ estudiantes con familias que viven en el hemisferio del sur.

3A.8 SUGGESTION: Keep a tally of any quantitative information, so that some general conclusions may be drawn from the results for *Paso 2.*

VÍVELO: CULTURA:
Throughout the early chapters of the book, *Vívelo: Cultura* appears sometimes in English and sometimes in Spanish. Wherever possible through the use of a high number of cognates, simple syntax, and limited glossing, the cultural topics are explored in Spanish.

VÍVELO: CULTURA

Los países del Caribe

When Europeans first came to the islands of the Caribbean in the 15th century, the islands were inhabited by three distinct indigenous groups: the Ciboney, the Taíno, and the Carib peoples. All had migrated into the Caribbean region from northern South America at different times. The Spanish were the first Europeans to explore and colonize the islands. They began to settle the islands now called the Greater Antilles soon after Christopher Columbus landed in the Bahamas in 1492. They made no serious effort to colonize the Lesser Antilles, which were small and not strategically important, mainly because they had abundant opportunities on the Greater Antilles and later on the mainland of North and South America. Today, Venezuela controls about 70 Lesser Antilles islands, including Margarita Island.

Several Caribbean countries are comprised of a number of small islands, grouped by geography and separated by a colonial past. Politically the Caribbean is home to 13 independent nations and a number of dependencies, territories, and possessions of several European countries. The Republic of Cuba, consisting of the island of Cuba and several nearby islands, is the largest island nation. Haiti and the Dominican Republic, two other independent nations, occupy Hispaniola, the second largest island in the archipelago. Jamaica is the third and Puerto Rico, a US commonwealth, is the fourth largest island of the archipelago.

3A.9 Comprensión. Determine whether each statement is **cierto** or **falso.** Correct any false statements and share your responses with a classmate.

Cierto	Falso	
☑	☐	**1.** Los españoles son los primeros europeos que colonizan las islas del mar Caribe.
☐	☑	**2.** Las Antillas Menores eran muy importantes para los colonizadores.
☐	☑	**3.** Venezuela es una isla en la región del Caribe.
☑	☐	**4.** En la región del mar Caribe existen muchos países independientes.
☑	☐	**5.** Las islas del mar Caribe se caracterizan por la fragmentación política.
☐	☑	**6.** Haití es el país más grande de la región del Caribe.

Bien dicho

La acentuación y los acentos escritos

While cognates help your understanding of Spanish, you have noticed that words that look similar in Spanish and English are pronounced quite differently. Note that in English the natural stress in the word *color* falls on the next-to-last syllable: *col-or*. In the Spanish word **color**, on the other hand, natural stress is on the last syllable: **co-lor**.

In general, natural stress in Spanish tends to fall on either the last syllable or the next-to-last syllable. If the word ends in a vowel or the consonants **n** or **s**, natural stress falls on the next-to-last syllable: **es-cu-chan, per-so-nas.** If the word ends in any other consonant, stress falls on the last syllable: **ar-ti-fi-cial, ex-pre-sar.**

A written accent mark is used to signal that a word doesn't follow this pattern: **es-tás, Mar-tí-nez.** Any word you hear that places stress on a syllable other than the last or next-to-last will require a written accent on the vowel in the stressed syllable, e.g., **jóvenes, plásticos, pájaro** *(bird).*

3A.10 El acento en español. As you hear each of the following words pronounced correctly underline the stressed syllable. Verify your answers with a classmate.

1. las palmas
2. las figuras
3. reflexionar
4. el escándalo
5. el cigarro
6. representar
7. serio
8. el televisor
9. la expresión
10. plástico
11. el bebé
12. la sensualidad
13. observar
14. los objetos
15. la computadora
16. la forma

3A.11 ¿Se requiere acento escrito o no? Listen to the following words to determine whether or not they require a written accent, and if so, write it in. Verify your answers with a partner and then alternate pronouncing the words.

1. profesores
2. motivan
3. hindu
4. telefono
5. Isabel
6. actriz
7. region
8. libertad
9. Tomas
10. caracter
11. memorandum
12. capitalismo
13. logica
14. dificil
15. conversar
16. maquinas

3A.10 AUDIO SCRIPT AND ANSWERS: 1. las pal-mas, 2. las fi-gu-ras, 3. re-fle-xio-nar, 4. el es-cán-da-lo, 5. el ci-ga-rro, 6. re-pre-sen-tar, 7. se-rio, 8. el te-le-vi-sor, 9. la ex-pre-sión, 10. plás-ti-co, 11. el be-bé, 12. la sen-sua-li-dad, 13. ob-ser-var, 14. los ob-je-tos, 15. la com-pu-ta-do-ra, 16. la for-ma

3A.11 TEACHING TIP: To draw students' attention to polysyllabic words, have them physically punch the air, or tap their desk as each syllable is spoken. After saying a word, ask them ¿*Cuántas sílabas tiene?* and follow up by asking them ¿*Y dónde está el acento?* To help them out, you can ask ¿*Está en la última sílaba? ¿la penúltima sílaba? ¿la primera sílaba?* This type of exchange will help the bodily-kinesthetic and linguistic learners better understand where accents are placed.

3A.11 AUDIO SCRIPT: 1. profesores, 2. motivan, 3. hindú, 4. teléfono, 5. Isabel, 6. actriz, 7. región, 8. libertad, 9. Tomás, 10. carácter, 11. memorándum, 12. capitalismo, 13. lógica, 14. difícil, 15. conversar, 16. máquinas

Palabras clave 1 ¿Qué tiempo hace?

TEACHING TIP: Have students tell you which months comprise each season as a way of getting them comfortable with this vocabulary.

SUGGESTION: Survey the months students were born to ascertain which month students celebrate their birthday, i.e., *¿En qué mes celebras tu cumpleaños?*

TEACHING TIP: Show pictures featuring a variety of weather scenarios as you review vocabulary to bind the meaning of the word to the concept. Do comprehension checks by asking *¿Qué tiempo hace?* and forcing a choice (e.g. *¿Hace calor o hace frío?*). The answers would depend on the pictures.

Hace buen tiempo. Hay pocas nubes y está seco. La temperatura es de 60 grados. Está templado.

Está despejado. Hace sol. Hace calor pero está húmedo.

Hace fresco. Hace viento. Llueve.

Está nublado. Hace mal tiempo. Nieva.

la tormenta	Hay tormenta cuando hay muchas nubes, llueve con fuerza y hace mucho viento.
el terremoto	La falla *(fault)* de San Andrés causa muchos terremotos en California.
el huracán	Hay muchos huracanes en la costa del golfo.
el tornado	Son vientos violentos en un patrón *(pattern)* circular.
el maremoto	El maremoto de 2004 devastó muchos países de Asia.
el relámpago	Es un resplandor instantáneo producido por una descarga eléctrica.
el trueno	Es el "boom" que ocurre después del relámpago.
la inundación	Es un desastre natural causado por un exceso de agua.
los chubascos	Son lluvias fuertes *(strong)* que pueden causar inundaciones.

www ¡Conéctate!

What is the weather like where you live? What is it like in Spain or Peru? Visit http://espanol.weather.com to compare and contrast the weather where you live with the weather in various cities around the Spanish-speaking world. Prepare a brief weather report about three places in Latin America or Spain, in addition to where you live. Share this with your class.

Los meses del año

enero	julio
febrero	agosto
marzo	septiembre
abril	octubre
mayo	noviembre
junio	diciembre

Notice that, like days of the week, months are not capitalized in Spanish.

3A.12 ¿En qué mes ocurre? For each event you hear mentioned, indicate in what month that event typically occurs, following the model. Verify your answers with a classmate.

1. _febrero_
2. _julio_
3. _agosto/septiembre_
4. _diciembre_
5. _mayo_
6. _junio_
7. _marzo_
8. _enero_

3A.13 Asociaciones. Match each natural disaster in column B to its corresponding description in column A. Then, check your work with a classmate.

A	B
_b_ **1.** viento fuerte, violento y circular sobre los llanos *(plains)*	**a.** el maremoto
_e_ **2.** movimiento violento de la tierra *(earth)*	**b.** el tornado
_d_ **3.** vientos fuertes, lluvias fuertes, relámpagos	**c.** el huracán
_a_ **4.** subida *(surge)* rápida del océano a la costa	**d.** la tormenta
_c_ **5.** vientos fuertes y lluvias torrenciales	**e.** el terremoto

3A.14 El clima de tu región. For each weather description you hear, say what months of the year that weather would be likely where you live, following the model.

1. _en julio y en agosto_
2. _____
3. _____
4. _____
5. _____
6. _____
7. _____
8. _____

3A.12 AUDIO SCRIPT: 1. el Día de San Valentín, 2. el Día de la Independencia, 3. el primer día de clase, 4. el fin del semestre escolar en el otoño, 5. el Día de las Madres, 6. el Día de los Padres, 7. el Día de San Patricio, 8. el primer día del Año Nuevo.

3A.12 FOLLOW-UP: As you go over the answers for Activity 3A.12, have students associate each holiday or event with a particular season. Ask, for example, *¿El día de las Madres es en invierno?* to elicit *No. Es en primavera.* Likewise, you might ask questions about the weather typical of these days, e.g. *¿Hace calor o hace frío el primer día de clase?*

3A.14 AUDIO SCRIPT: 1. Hace sol. 2. Está húmedo. 3. Hace fresco. 4. Llueve mucho. 5. Hay tormentas terribles. 6. Es seco. 7. Hace mucho, mucho viento. 8. Hace calor.

3A.15 Condiciones actuales. With a partner, examine the weather conditions for Bogotá, Colombia, posted on the website below and answer the questions. Then, check your work with the rest of the class.

1. In which direction are the winds blowing?
2. How humid is it?
3. What is the weather like?
4. What is the temperature?
5. What is the visibility range?

VÍVELO: CULTURA
Las estaciones y el clima en el hemisferio sur

Una gran parte de América del Sur está en el hemisferio sur. Esto significa que en estos países, las estaciones (*seasons*) y el clima son opuestos (*opposite*) a las estaciones y el clima del hemisferio norte. Por ejemplo, cuando es verano en Estados Unidos y México, es invierno en Argentina y Uruguay. Cuando es primavera en España, es otoño en Bolivia. Observa que la palabra *ecuador* (*equator*) es también el nombre de un país sudamericano.

3A.16 ¿Qué estación es? For each date and capital city, indicate the season. Then, verify your answers with a classmate.

1. el 3 de julio en Madrid, España — verano

2. el 24 de enero en Santiago, Chile — verano

3. el 15 de octubre en Asunción, Paraguay — primavera

4. el 10 de febrero en Tegucigalpa, Honduras — invierno

5. el 7 de noviembre en San José, Costa Rica — otoño

6. el 30 de abril en Lima, Perú — otoño

3A.17 El país y el clima más atractivo.

Paso 1: The map below describes the general climates of Central and South America. In groups of three, describe the general climate for as many Latin American countries as possible.

Modelo: *En el suroeste de Chile, hay una zona polar. También hay una zona templada y el invierno es seco. Al norte de esta zona templada, hace mucho calor porque hay un desierto.*

Paso 2: Find out which country each member of your group would like to live in based on the weather. The question to ask is **¿En qué país te gustaría vivir?** Write the responses in your **Retrato de la clase.**

Retrato de la clase:
___ prefiere vivir en ____. ___ prefiere vivir en ___ y yo prefiero vivir en ____.

www

¡Conéctate!
Is there a particular country in Latin America that you would like to learn more about? Check out http://lanic.utexas.edu/subject/countries/ and click on a country, or countries, that interest you. Navigate the related websites. Prepare a list of five good websites and include what topics they cover. Share this list with your class.

3A.17 TEACHING TIP: One group member could be responsible for identifying the country, the other for identifying the climate based on the color-coded legend and the third could write the sentences for the group.

3A.17 EXTENSION ACTIVITY: Have students describe some general weather patterns for regions in their native country and share them with the class to see if they agree (when possible).

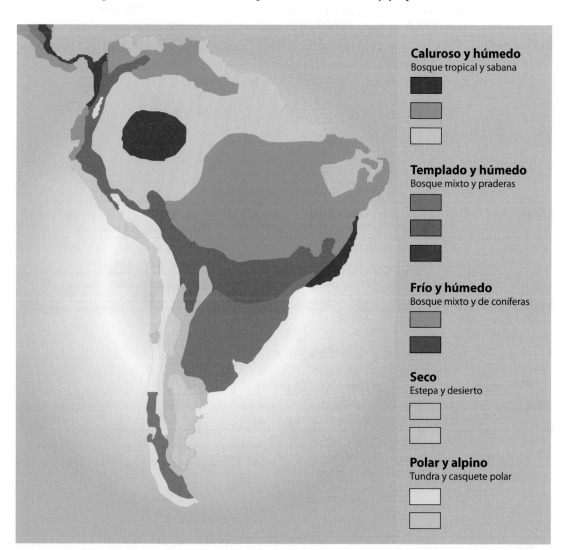

Caluroso y húmedo
Bosque tropical y sabana

Templado y húmedo
Bosque mixto y praderas

Frío y húmedo
Bosque mixto y de coníferas

Seco
Estepa y desierto

Polar y alpino
Tundra y casquete polar

EXPRESIONES ÚTILES:
Comparisons in Spanish can be made with a few simple phrases. While it is not difficult to process comparisons for meaning, it is more difficult to produce comparisons because each type of comparison must take into account issues of agreement. In later chapters, the specific rules related to comparisons will be offered. For now, emphasis is placed on comprehension of these expressions, not necessarily on production.

3A.18 AUDIO SCRIPT: 1. Hay más habitantes en Bogotá, Colombia, que en Montevideo, Uruguay. 2. Hay menos habitantes en Buenos Aires, Argentina, que en Quito, Ecuador. 3. Hay tantos habitantes en La Paz, Bolivia, como en Managua, Nicaragua. 4. La ciudad de Lima, Perú, está más poblada que la Ciudad de México. 5. San José, Costa Rica, es más grande que Caracas, Venezuela. 6. Hay tantos habitantes en San Juan, Puerto Rico, como en Asunción, Paraguay.

EXPRESIONES ÚTILES

Para hacer comparaciones

más ... que	El clima de Chicago es más extremo que el clima de Los Ángeles.
more ... than	*The weather in Chicago is more extreme than the weather in Los Angeles.*
menos ... que	En verano el calor en Cancún es menos intenso que en Tucson.
less ... than	*During the summer the heat in Cancún is less intense than in Tucson.*
tantos ... como	No hay tantos habitantes en San Antonio como en Dallas.
as much/many ... as	*There are not as many people in San Antonio as in Dallas.*
tan ... como	Washington D.C. no es tan grande como Los Ángeles.
as ... as	*Washington D.C. is not as large as Los Angeles.*

WILEY PLUS Go to *WileyPLUS* and review the tutorial for this grammar point.

3A.18 Ciudades de América Latina. Read the statistics below. You will hear some information comparing the population of capital cities in Latin America. Indicate whether each statement you hear is **cierto** or **falso** following the model, based on the statistics presented below.

	Cierto	Falso		Cierto	Falso
1.	☑	☐	4.	☐	☑
2.	☐	☑	5.	☐	☑
3.	☑	☐	6.	☐	☑

Capital y población		
América del Sur	**América Central**	**El Caribe**
Argentina Buenos Aires: 6.6 millones	Costa Rica San José: 346,799	Cuba Habana: 2.4 millones
Bolivia La Paz: 1.6 millones	El Salvador San Salvador: 496,000	Puerto Rico San Juan: 434,374
Chile Santiago: 5.8 millones	Honduras Tegucigalpa: 894,000	República Dominicana Santo Domingo: 2.0 millones
Colombia Bogotá: 4.4 millones	México México (D.F.): 8.5 millones (22 millones zona metropolitana)	
Ecuador Quito: 1.9 millones	Nicaragua Managua: 1.6 millones	
Paraguay Asunción: 1.4 millones	Panamá Panamá: 1.8 millones	
Perú Lima: 7.9 millones	Guatemala Guatemala: 1.3 millones	
Uruguay Montevideo: 1.2 millones		
Venezuela Caracas: 3.2 millones		

VÍVELO: LENGUA

Tag questions

A tag question is the word or phrase that attempts to confirm, verify or deny the previous statement. In Spanish the most common tag questions are **¿no?** and **¿verdad?**.

Los españoles son los primeros europeos que colonizan las islas del mar Caribe, ¿verdad?
The Spaniards were the first Europeans to colonize the Caribbean Islands, right?

Hace frío, ¿no?
It's cold, isn't it?

3A.19 **Escuchar y luego decir.** This partner activity will help you practice the countries and capitals. Decide who is person A and who is person B. Person A starts off by saying the name of one of the countries in the right-hand column of his/her card. Person B then finds the corresponding capital, which will be in the left-hand column on his/her card, and proceeds to say the name of the country to its right. Person A then finds that country's capital on his/her card and reads the country to its right, and so on. Check off each country and capital as it is mentioned and continue until you have all the boxes checked on your cards.

Modelo: Person A: *¿Perú?*
Person B: *La capital de Perú es Lima. ¿Y la de Paraguay?*
Person A: *La capital de Paraguay es…*

A	
☐ Bogotá	☐ Perú
☐ Panamá	☐ Argentina
☐ Tegucigalpa	☐ Nicaragua
☐ La Paz y Sucre	☐ Ecuador
☐ Asunción	☐ Venezuela
☐ San José	☐ Cuba
☐ Santo Domingo	☐ Guatemala
☐ Santiago	☐ Uruguay

Chile ☐	Buenos Aires ☐
Colombia ☐	Guatemala ☐
Panamá ☐	Habana ☐
La República Dominicana ☐	Quito ☐
Costa Rica ☐	Managua ☐
Paraguay ☐	Lima ☐
Bolivia ☐	Montevideo ☐
Honduras ☐	Caracas ☐
B	

WILEY
PLUS

3A.19 INSTRUCTOR'S RESOURCES: Use the maps provided in your Instructor's Resources to review the locations of countries and capital cities. Note major lakes, rivers, mountains, etc. as well. Remind students that they may be tested on some of this information.

3A.19 SUGGESTION: Confirm answers using tag questions, such as *La capital de Argentina es Buenos Aires, ¿verdad?, La capital de Cuba es Habana, ¿no?*

3A.19 INSTRUCTOR'S RESOURCES: You will find reproducible cards for use with Activity 3A.19 in your Instructor's Resources.

Palabras clave 2 Los números mayores de 100

100	cien/ciento	700	setecientos/as
200	doscientos/as	800	ochocientos/as
300	trescientos/as	900	novecientos/as
400	cuatrocientos/as	1,000	mil
500	quinientos/as	14,582	catorce mil quinientos ochenta y dos
600	seiscientos/as	150,000	ciento cincuenta mil

100	cien/ciento	700	setecientos/as

Use **cien** when simply counting and before a noun when you are describing an even hundred. Use **ciento** when describing more than a hundred of a given noun.

Tengo cien dólares pero necesito ciento noventa y ocho dólares para comprar un GPS para mi carro.	*I have one hundred dollars but I need a hundred and ninety-eight dollars to buy a GPS for my car.*

Use the feminine form of multiples of 100 when describing a feminine noun.

Entre su colección de quinientos mapas, Jorge tiene doscientas páginas que describen la historia de los mapas.	*Among his collection of five hundred maps, Jorge has two hundred pages that describe the history of the maps.*

VÍVELO: LENGUA

Expressing years in Spanish

Up through the twentieth century, years are expressed differently in English and Spanish. While English speakers express 1898 as *eighteen ninety-eight*, Spanish speakers say **mil ocho cientos noventa y ocho.** With the twenty-first century under way, many English speakers say *two thousand ten* just as Spanish speakers say **dos mil diez.** Look at the Spanish examples of how these significant years are expressed.

1492 Cristóbal Colón viaja a las Américas en mil cuatrocientos noventa y dos.
1776 Se firma la Declaración de Independencia de Estados Unidos en mil setecientos setenta y seis.
1939 Comienza la Segunda Guerra Mundial en mil novecientos treinta y nueve.
2008 Los Juegos Olímpicos se celebran en Beijing en dos mil ocho.

3A.20 FOLLOW-UP:
Verify answers by asking students *¿Qué ocurrió en 2005? ¿Y en 1989?*, etc. In this way students hear years and can provide answers in Spanish.

3A.20 ¿En qué año? Do you remember the year the following natural disasters occurred? Match each natural disaster with the corresponding year.

_c_	**1.** 1985	**a.** el maremoto del sureste de Asia y de las islas Filipinas
_f_	**2.** 1989	**b.** el huracán Katrina y la devastación de Nueva Orleáns
_d_	**3.** 1992	**c.** el gran terremoto y la devastación de la Ciudad de México
_e_	**4.** 1993	**d.** el huracán Andrew que destruyó la costa de la Florida
_a_	**5.** 2004	**e.** las grandes inundaciones del río Mississippi
_b_	**6.** 2005	**f.** el gran terremoto que devastó las ciudades de San Francisco y Oakland

3A.21 La independencia de una nación. Work with a partner, each choosing a card below. Each card gives the date of independence of some countries, but not others. Take turns telling each other on what day and year each country gained independence. Write the information you hear from your partner on your card and he/she will do the same until both cards are complete.

WILEY PLUS

3A.21 INSTRUCTOR'S RESOURCES: Blank cards and a copy of a completed chart are available in your Instructor's Resources.

Modelo: Estudiante A: *La fecha de la independencia de Argentina es el 9 de julio de 1816.*
Estudiante B: writes *9 de julio de 1816* on his/her card.

A	
País	**Fecha de independencia**
Argentina	9 de julio de 1816
Bolivia	
Chile	
Costa Rica	15 de septiembre de 1821
Cuba	
República Dominicana	27 de febrero de 1844
El Salvador	
Estados Unidos	4 de julio de 1776
Guatemala	
Honduras	15 de septiembre de 1821
México	16 de septiembre de 1810
Nicaragua	
Paraguay	14 de mayo de 1811
Perú	
Uruguay	
Venezuela	5 de julio de 1811

B	
País	**Fecha de independencia**
Argentina	
Bolivia	6 de agosto de 1825
Chile	18 de septiembre de 1810
Costa Rica	
Cuba	20 de mayo de 1902
República Dominicana	
El Salvador	15 de septiembre de 1821
Estados Unidos	
Guatemala	15 de septiembre de 1821
Honduras	
México	
Nicaragua	15 de septiembre de 1821
Paraguay	
Perú	28 de julio de 1821
Uruguay	25 de agosto de 1825
Venezuela	

Palabras clave 3 La geografía

el mar

la playa

el bosque

el lago

el árbol

las montañas

la piedra

la tierra

la selva

el río

VÍVELO: CULTURA

Aspectos importantes de la geografía de América del Sur

1. La geografía física de Sur América está dominada por las montañas de los Andes en el este y el área del Amazonas en el norte centro. El resto del territorio es una meseta.

2. La mitad del territorio y de la población está concentrada en un país: Brasil.

3. La población de América del Sur está concentrada en la periferia del continente. En el interior del continente la población está separada por distancias muy grandes, pero recientemente en algunas áreas hay una gran expansión de la población.

4. La interconexión entre los estados del área aumenta constantemente. La integración económica es una motivación importante, particularmente en la parte sur de Sudamérica.

5. En la región, las diferencias y contrastes económicos son muy grandes, en el territorio en general y dentro de cada país en particular.

6. La diversidad cultural existe en todos los países del área y generalmente es expresada regionalmente.

7. La expansión urbana desproporcionada continúa siendo una característica de la región, y el nivel de urbanización es hoy en día similar al nivel de desarrollo en Estados Unidos y Europa.

Las frases preposicionales

El pájaro está sobre la piedra.

El pájaro está encima de la piedra.

El pájaro está arriba del árbol.

La serpiente está debajo de la tierra.

El pájaro está al lado del árbol.

El pájaro está a la derecha de la piedra.

El pájaro está a la izquierda de la piedra.

3A.22 ¡A emparejar!   Match the following English renderings of the content in *Vívelo: Cultura* using the numbers of the corresponding statements there. The first one is done for you as a model. Then, verify your responses with a classmate.

Major Geographical Qualities of South America

___4___ *Interconnections among the states of the realm (South America) are improving rapidly. Economic integration has become a major force, particularly in southern South America.*

___3___ *South America's population remains concentrated along the continent's periphery. Most of the interior is sparsely peopled (sparsely populated), but sections of it are now undergoing significant development.*

___6___ *Cultural pluralism exists in almost all of the realm's countries, and is often expressed regionally.*

___2___ *One half of the continent's area and one-half of the population are concentrated in one country—Brazil.*

___7___ *Rapid urban growth continues to mark much of the South American realm (continent), and the urbanization level over all is today on a par with the levels in the United States and Europe.*

___5___ *Regional economic contrasts and disparities, both in the realm (continent) as a whole and within individual countries, are strong.*

___1___ *South America's physiography is dominated by the Andes Mountains in the west and the Amazon Basin in the central north. Much of the remainder is plateau country (an expansive plateau).*

TEACHING TIP: Use TPR to help students learn the meanings of prepositions of location. Place a book or other object on, next to, under... a desk and say *El libro está encima del escritorio., El libro está al lado del escritorio.,* etc. Then switch to questions as you place the object, ¿*El libro está encima del escritorio?,* etc.

3A.22 EXTENSION ACTIVITY: Ask students to write some *cierto/falso* statements in Spanish based on the content of the reading. Then, call on volunteers to read their statements and the class will respond to them as *cierto* or *falso.*

3A.23 Mi casa en Bariloche. Complete this description of a home in Bariloche, Argentina, with the appropriate prepositions. ¡Ojo! Not all of the prepositions will be used.

a la derecha	encima de	al lado de
a la izquierda	sobre	debajo de

Vivo cerca de Bariloche, en el sur de Argentina. Mi casa está_____ una montaña con
₁

vistas panorámicas. Desde la casa, miro hacia el sur. _____ está la vasta extensión
₂

de la Patagonia y_____ están los Andes y la frontera con Chile. _____ de la casa,
₃ ₄

hay un pequeño lago donde voy a pescar *(to fish)* con mis amigos en el verano, o sea

en diciembre, enero y febrero. En el invierno hacemos mucho esquí. Hay mucha nieve

_____ las pistas *(trails)* de junio a octubre.
₅

¡Atención!

Monte	when used as a noun means *forest* or *woodland*, and in some Latin American countries indicates *wilderness*. The verb **montar** means *to mount*, as in to post (something) or in the sense of mounting a horse.
	En los montes hay serpientes venenosas, animales salvajes y poca agua. Vamos a montar las fotos en la página de Internet. Mi padre monta a caballo cuando va al monte.
Suceso	does not mean to succeed. It means *event*, *incident*, something that happened or an *occurrence*. To express to succeed in Spanish, use **tener éxito**.
	Los sucesos anticoloniales provocaron las guerras de independencia. Para tener éxito como vaquero *(cowboy)* es importante tener un caballo inteligente.
Surgir	means to *emerge*, *arise*, *appear* or *come out* and does not mean to *surge*. To express to surge in Spanish, use **levantarse** or **entrar/salir/avanzar**.
	Después de la independencia de muchos países latinoamericanos, surge una serie de dictaduras violentas. Durante un maremoto, las olas del oceano se levantan hacia la playa. Después del concierto, el público sale en masa por las puertas del auditorio.

3A.24 ¿Cuál es la palabra? Write the word that is being described in each sentence. Review the words in *¡Atención!* to confirm your answers.

_____suceso_____ **1.** Se refiere a un momento en que ocurre algo memorable.

_____monte_____ **2.** Se refiere a una región de tierra con árboles, bosque y la naturaleza en su forma más pura.

_____montar_____ **3.** La profesora pone *(to put)* la tarea de la clase en nuestro sitio de *Blackboard*.

_____surgir_____ **4.** Es una acción que indica que algo aparece o se hace evidente.

_____tener éxito_____ **5.** Es importante hacer algo bien en el trabajo para recibir un aumento de salario.

Estructuras clave 1 Conjugating verbs: Plural forms

You have already learned to conjugate verbs in the **yo** and **tú** forms, and in the form for **él, ella,** and **Ud.** Have you discerned the pattern for talking about what more than one person does? To conjugate verbs for **ellos/ellas** *(they)*, or **Uds.** *(you, plural)*, use **–an** as the ending for **–ar** verbs, and **–en** as the ending for **–er** and **–ir** verbs.

hablar	ellos/ellas/Uds. habl**an**	comer	ellos/ellas/Uds. com**en**
cantar	ellos/ellas/Uds. cant**an**	escribir	ellos/ellas/Uds. escrib**en**
bailar	ellos/ellas/Uds. bail**an**	vivir	ellos/ellas/Uds. viv**en**

You have likely figured out that to talk about what you and other people (**nosotros/nosotras**) do, you use **–amos** for **–ar** verbs, **–emos** for **–er** verbs, and **–imos** for **–ir** verbs.

hablar	nosotros/nosotras habl**amos**
comer	nosotros/nosotras com**emos**
escribir	nosotros/nosotras escrib**imos**

In Spain, and only in Spain, the subject pronoun **vosotros/vosotras** functions as the plural form of **tú.** Its endings are **–áis** for **–ar** verbs, **–éis** for **–er** verbs, and **–ís** for **–ir** verbs.

hablar	vosotros/vosotras habl**áis**
comer	vosotros/vosotras com**éis**
escribir	vosotros/vosotras escrib**ís**

Exercises and activities throughout *¡Vívelo!* use **ustedes** as the plural *you*, both in formal and informal contexts, as is typical of Spanish speakers outside of Spain. You do not need to use the **vosotros** forms, but you should be able to recognize them.

Summary of verb conjugations: Present tense

	–ar verbs	–er verbs	–ir verbs
yo	–o	–o	–o
tú	–as	–es	–es
él/ella/Ud.	–a	–e	–e
nosotros/as	–amos	–emos	–imos
vosotros/as	–áis	–éis	–ís
ellos/ellas/Uds.	–an	–en	–en

3A.25 Es lógico. Match each sentence's subject from column A with its most logical completion in Column B. Then, provide the correct form of the verb according to that subject. Check your work as a class.

A

___b___ **1.** Las tormentas

___e___ **2.** Los árboles

___a___ **3.** Los ríos y lagos

___f___ **4.** Las montañas

___c___ **5.** Las ciudades con playas

___d___ **6.** Los pastos *(pastures)*

B

a. (ofrecer) __ofrecen__ energía eléctrica para las ciudades.

b. (causar) __causan__ inundaciones.

c. (promocionar) __promocionan__ el turismo.

d. (ayudar) __ayudan__ a los agricultures y a los rancheros.

e. (proteger) __protegen__ contra el sol.

f. (proveer) __proveen__ minerales importantes.

3A.25 TEACHING TIP: When you check answers as a class, have students read the sentences instead of you. This makes the class seem less teacher centered.

WILEY PLUS

Go to *WileyPLUS* and review the tutorial for this grammar point.

WILEY PLUS

You will find PowerPoint presentations for use with *Estructuras clave* in *WileyPLUS*.

3A.26 ¡Ay, caramba! In groups of four, play *¡Ay, caramba!* according to the instructions below.

1. Roll the die or draw a number from 1–6.

2. Move the number of spaces on the die (up to six moves allowed) and answer the question on the board.

3. If you answer correctly, the next person gets a turn.

4. If you answer incorrectly, move back three spaces, and the next person gets a turn.

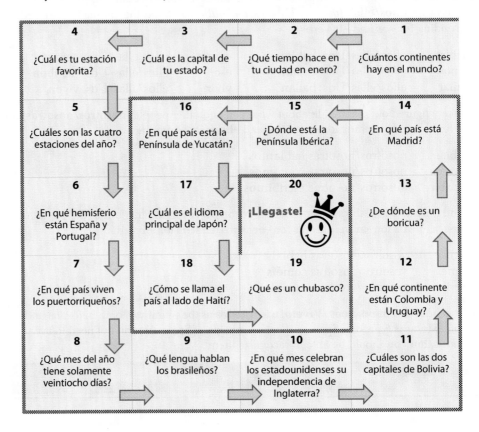

3A.27 ¿Estás o no estás de acuerdo?

Paso 1: Indicate whether you agree (**Estoy de acuerdo**) or disagree (**No estoy de acuerdo**) with each of the following statements. Then, find a classmate who responded most like you and share your perspectives with the class.

Modelo: *Nosotros/as pensamos (o no pensamos) que estamos a punto de destruir el planeta.*

	Estoy de acuerdo	No estoy de acuerdo
1. Estamos a punto de destruir el planeta.	☐	☐
2. Queremos estudiar menos y salir más.	☐	☐
3. Tenemos que proteger nuestras libertades.	☐	☐
4. Deseamos trabajar juntos para eliminar la violencia.	☐	☐
5. Hacemos lo necesario para mantener los bosques.	☐	☐
6. Necesitamos mantener nuestras fronteras nacionales.	☐	☐
7. Participamos en partidos políticos más que nuestros padres.	☐	☐
8. Heredamos *(we inherit)* muchas costumbres de las generaciones anteriores.	☐	☐

Paso 2: With a partner, or in groups of three, write two sentences that make a statement about "us" as a nation, class, group of males/females, students, etc. At least one of your statements must be true, and one false. Be creative in coming up with sentences that will make your classmates wonder whether they are true or not. Read your statements to the class so that your classmates can guess if they are true or false.

Estructuras clave 2 Demonstrative adjectives and pronouns

WILEY+
PLUS
Go to *WileyPLUS* and review the tutorial for this grammar point.

WILEY+
PLUS

You will find PowerPoint presentations for use with *Estructuras clave* in *WileyPLUS*.

Words such as *this, that, these,* and *those,* which we use to distinguish one noun from others like it *(this book, not that book),* convey an element of distance from the speaker, or speakers. These are called demonstrative adjectives. We think of *this* and *these* as indicating something either literally or figuratively close-by, and we think of *that* and *those* as indicating something farther away. One pair of adjectives describes singular nouns *(this/that),* and another pair describes plural nouns *(these/those).*

Demonstrative adjectives in Spanish work similarly. Just as in English, Spanish uses a singular demonstrative adjective to distinguish a single noun (**este libro**), and a plural demonstrative adjective to distinguish a plural noun (**estos libros**). Remember that in Spanish, however, the adjective not only agrees with the noun in number, but also in gender. Another difference in Spanish is a third level of proximity. Note the Spanish demonstrative adjectives in the chart below and their usage in the examples.

Demonstrative adjectives						
Noun	Close		Far		Farther	
árbol (masc. sing.)	este	árbol	ese	árbol	aquel	árbol
silla (fem. sing.)	esta	silla	esa	silla	aquella	silla
árboles (masc. pl.)	estos	árboles	esos	árboles	aquellos	árboles
sillas (fem. pl.)	estas	sillas	esas	sillas	aquellas	sillas

Estas montañas son más altas que esas montañas.	*These mountains are higher than those mountains.*
Esas palmeras crecen más rápido que aquellos pinos.	*Those palm trees (over there) grow faster than those pine trees (way over there).*

Once it's known what nouns we're talking about, we often use expressions such as *this one, these, that one,* and *those* instead of naming the noun each time we mention it. Spanish does this with demonstrative pronouns. Demonstrative pronouns look exactly like the demonstrative adjectives only they are not followed by a noun, they replace the noun. The noun has to be established prior the demonstrative pronoun's use. As you see, the number (singular/plural) and the gender (masculine/feminine) of the demonstrative pronoun used depends on the number and gender of the noun it replaces.

TEACHING TIP: You may want to point out that students are likely to see demonstrative pronouns with a written accent on them because a written accent mark used to be required.

Necesitamos plantar este árbol, no ese.	*We need to plant this tree not that one.*
Esta película me gusta, esa no.	*I like this movie, not that one.*
Prefiero aquellos árboles y tú prefieres estos.	*I like those trees and you like these.*

To refer to a whole concept, idea, situation, etc. *(i.e. That really bothers me)* or to refer to a noun whose nature is unknown *(i.e. What's that in your hand?),* Spanish uses what are called the "neuter" demonstrative pronouns **esto, eso,** and **aquello.**

Hace sol y está despejado. Eso me gusta.	*It's sunny and clear. I like that.*
¿Qué es aquello al lado del árbol? No veo bien.	*What is that over by the tree? I can't see well.*

**3A.28 EXTENSION
ACTIVITY:** You can role play this activity by positioning students in different parts of the classroom to illustrate the distance from the speaker. Assign one student the role of the instructor and another, the role of the visitor, both of whom stand at the front of the room. Assign other students a number 1–6 representing each of the comments made and have them stand toward the front, the middle, or the back of the room according to the comment that describes them.

3A.28 ¿De quién habla?   An instructor makes the following comments to a visitor who will be teaching the class next semester. Match each comment to the best explanation of who the instructor is talking about. Then, check your answers as a class.

____d___ **1.** Aquel estudiante es muy inteligente pero no estudia mucho.

____g___ **2.** Este estudiante no asiste a clase y nunca hace su tarea.

____c___ **3.** Esas estudiantes no escuchan bien y luego tienen muchas preguntas.

____b___ **4.** Aquellas estudiantes no hablan mucho pero comprenden bien la lección.

____f___ **5.** Estos estudiantes desean aprender español y estudian el vocabulario.

____e___ **6.** Aquella estudiante habla español muy bien.

a. refers to several male students near the speaker, but not too close

b. refers to several female students farthest away from the speaker

c. refers to several female students not too far from the speaker but not too close

d. refers to a male student farthest from the speaker

e. refers to a female student farthest from the speaker

f. refers to several male students very near the speaker

g. refers to a male student very near the speaker

3A.29 TEACHING TIP:
Make sure to reiterate to students that when they work with a partner or in groups they should help each other understand why there is one appropriate answer. Sometimes, students are able to offer explanations that are easier to understand because they come from similar perspectives.

3A.29 ¡Fíjate bien!   In pairs, read the comments below that were made by the student in the art gallery and identify which painting she is referring to in each statement. Then, confirm your responses with another pair of classmates.

	A	B	C
1. Me gustan esas montañas porque son muy altas.		✓	
2. Me gusta aquel río porque es rápido.			✓
3. Me gustan estos árboles porque están en un bosque.	✓		
4. Me gusta esta escena porque hace buen tiempo.	✓		
5. Me gusta aquella escena también porque tiene muchos colores.			✓

3A.30 Los pronombres demostrativos. Complete each sentence with the appropriate demonstrative pronoun according to the cue. In pairs, alternate giving and explaining answers (e.g., one partner takes even-numbered items and the other takes the odd-numbered items). Then, compare your responses with another pair of classmates.

1. Este coche es muy bonito, pero _____aquel_____ (farther away) es más rápido.

2. La profesora pregunta, "¿Qué es _____esto_____ (near speaker)?"

3. Carlos no va a comprar aquellos libros. Va a comprar _____esos_____ (not so near speaker).

4. ¿Qué mochila prefieres, _____esta_____ (near speaker) o _____esa_____ (not so near speaker)?

5. ¿Cuáles son las fotos de María, _____estas_____ (near speaker) o _____aquellas_____ (farther away)?

6. No estoy de acuerdo contigo. _____eso_____ (something you said to me) no me gusta.

7. Tomás: Esa guitarra es de Manuel.
Rebeca: Y _____aquella_____ (farther away), ¿de quién es?

8. Este reloj es de la marca Citizen y _____ese_____ (not so near speaker) es de Rolex.

Enlaces

These expressions will help you understand transitions between one idea and another and to make smooth transitions yourself.

Es más	is an expression used to signal that additional information follows.
A la vez	is an expression used to indicate simultaneous actions.
En cuanto a	is an expression used to indicate reference to a previous theme, topic or comment.

3A.31 ¿Puedes conectar las ideas? Determine the meaning of the bold faced word or phrase according to the context of the sentences. Choose from the following options.

In addition   At the same time   With respect to

___With respect to___ **1. En cuanto** a la densidad, en las áreas rurales de Argentina y Chile, no es muy alta. El 85% de la población se concentra en las áreas urbanas.

___In addition___ **2.** La migración de Guatemala hacia México es un problema grave así como lo es la migración de México hacia Estados Unidos. **Es más,** la migración entre los países afecta a la población y el desempleo.

___at the same time___ **3.** Los pobres que viven en las periferias de las megaciudades no tienen agua y **a la vez** no tienen trabajos para poder comprar agua potable.

FUNCTIONAL OUTCOMES:
The central question that frames this *Investigación* is *"¿Cómo puedes hablar de los países en donde se habla español?"* Explore whether students can now address this question and how they would go about it. Have them review the chart on the first page of this *Investigación*.

You have learned some things about Latin America's geography and climate in this chapter. Little has been said, however, about the human geography of Latin America. In the following article, you will learn how physical and human geography effect changes in society and potentially in history.

3A.32 Antes de leer. Before you read the article carefully, read each question below and match it to the corresponding question in English. Then, use these questions to focus your attention when you read the article.

___b___ **1.** ¿Cuáles son los países más poblados de América Latina?

___e___ **2.** ¿Cuáles son los países que sufren mayor riesgo *(risk)* de terremotos?

___c___ **3.** ¿Dónde vive la mayoría de la gente de América Latina y el Caribe, en regiones rurales o urbanas?

___a___ **4.** ¿Cuáles son las características de la gente pobre de América Latina y el Caribe?

___d___ **5.** ¿Qué tendencias aumentan *(grow)* a causa de la alta densidad en las regiones de la periferia de las ciudades y megaciudades de América Latina y el Caribe?

___f___ **6.** ¿Están preparados los centros poblados de América Latina y el Caribe para afrontar desastres naturales?

a. What are the characteristics of the poor people of Latin America and the Carribbean?

b. Which are the most populated countries in Latin America?

c. Do the majority of the people of Latin America and the Caribbean live in rural regions or urban regions?

d. What tendencies increase as a result of the high density of people that live on the periphery of big cities or mega cities?

e. Which are the countries that are most at risk to suffer an earthquake?

f. Are the populated areas of Latina America and the Caribbean prepared to handle natural disasters?

Un panorama de la región

En cuanto a la geografía humana, los diez países más poblados del continente americano incluyendo el norte son Argentina, Brasil, Canadá, Colombia, Chile, Ecuador, Estados Unidos, México, Perú y Venezuela– constituyen el 89% de la población total de hemisferio occidental *(Western)*. Con la excepción de Argentina, Brasil y Canadá, esta población se encuentra en las regiones más vulnerables a desastres naturales de origen tectónico. Recuerden *(recall)* el terremoto de la Ciudad de México del 19 de septiembre de 1985 donde ocurrió un terremoto de 8.1 grados de intensidad en la escala de Richter y al día siguiente ocurrió otro terremoto de 7.5 grados.

El 75% de la población de América Latina y el Caribe se concentra en las ciudades, a veces formando megaciudades (ciudades con más de 5 millones de habitantes). La infraestructura de servicios de estas ciudades resulta inadecuada y los recursos básicos son limitados. Es importante saber que más de la mitad *(half)* de los residentes urbanos de las grandes ciudades de América Latina viven en condiciones de pobreza. **Es más,** la mayoría vive en la periferia de las grandes ciudades. La población indígena, 30 millones en América Central y del Sur, representa una parte importante de las poblaciones rurales y urbanas pobres y continúa migrando a las ciudades. La estructura social de las zonas rurales puede perderse *(be lost)* en el proceso de migración. **A la vez,** la densidad poblacional y la inestabilidad de las zonas pobres de las ciudades son factores relevantes en el impacto de un desastre y pone en alto riesgo a la gente.

En las afueras *(outskirts)* de las grandes ciudades, la infraestructura llega mucho más tarde que la población.

3A.33 Comprensión. In groups of three, indicate whether each of the following statements is **cierto** or **falso** based on *Un panorama de la región*. Challenge any false statements with a direct quote from the reading. Then, compare your responses with another group.

Cierto	Falso	
☐	☑	**1.** La mayoría de los países latinoamericanos vulnerables a terremotos están en la región andina.
☐	☑	**2.** La población de los países latinoamericanos se concentran en áreas rurales porque trabajan en la agricultura.
☐	☑	**3.** Las poblaciones indígenas de América Latina son respetadas y protegidas por sus contribuciones a la cultura y su importancia en la historia del continente.
☑	☐	**4.** La migración de pobres a los centros urbanos es principalmente económica; no hay suficientes trabajos en las regiones rurales.
☑	☐	**5.** No hay suficientes servicios (agua, electricidad) para la población que vive en periferia de las ciudades grandes.

Perspectivas

3A.34 ¿Cuánto sabes de la geografía física y humana de tu país nativo?

Paso 1: Hopefully, you know as much about your own country as you have learned about Latin America in this chapter. In groups of two, list in Spanish as many geographical features as possible in your native country. Include the names of rivers, mountain ranges, forests, lakes, peninsulas, flatlands, deserts, etc.

Modelo: *Las montañas Smoky están al este del país. En el oeste están las montañas Rocky….*

Paso 2: Is the tendency of the general population in your country to migrate to big cities? Do the poorest people live on the outskirts of the big cities? What groups of people tend to be the poorest in your country? (For answers to these questions, use the linguistic models in the reading above).

Modelo: *Soy de North Dakota. La población no es muy grande, sobre todo en las regiones rurales.*

3A.35 Observaciones generales. Discuss each of these statements with a partner and indicate which statements you find accurate based on what you have learned. Share your responses with the rest of the class.

- ☑ La población latinoamericana es tan diversa como la población estadounidense.
- ☐ Hay tantos indígenas en Estados Unidos (en proporción a la población general) como en América Latina.
- ☑ En Estados Unidos tanto como en América del Sur, la mayor parte de la población está en las grandes ciudades.
- ☑ En Estados Unidos tanto como en América Latina, hay grupos étnicos que sufren injusticia y que son víctimas de prejuicios.
- ☑ Hay tanta diversidad de climas en Estados Unidos como en América Latina.
- ☐ Hay más personas en el mundo que hablan español que inglés.
- ☑ En América Latina tanto como en Estados Unidos hay distintas clases socioeconómicas.

Vocabulario: Investigación A

Vocabulario esencial

Sustantivos

el agua *(f.)*	*water*
el árbol	*tree*
el bosque	*forest*
el fin de semana	*weekend*
la geografía	*geography*
la estación	*season*
el huracán	*hurricane*
la inundación	*flooding*
el invierno	*winter*
el lago	*lake*
la lluvia	*rain*
el mar	*sea*
la montaña	*mountain*
los meses del año	*months of the year*
enero	*January*
febrero	*February*
marzo	*March*
abril	*April*
mayo	*May*
junio	*June*
julio	*July*
agosto	*August*
septiembre	*September*
octubre	*October*
noviembre	*November*
diciembre	*December*
la nube	*cloud*
el número	*number*
la ola	*wave*
el otoño	*autumn*
la playa	*beach*
la población	*population*
el pronóstico	*forecast*
la primavera	*spring*
el relámpago	*lightning*
el río	*river*
el terremoto	*earthquake*
el tiempo	*weather*
la tierra	*land; ground*
el tornado	*tornado*
la tormenta	*storm*
el trueno	*thunder*

la selva	*jungle*
el verano	*summer*
el viento	*wind*

Adjetivos

actual	*current*
bonito/a	*pretty*
cada	*each*
distinto/a	*different*
fuerte	*strong*
otro/a	*another*
salvaje	*wild*

Verbos

comprar	*to buy*
crecer	*to grow*
llover	*to rain*
viajar	*to travel*

Preposiciones

a la derecha de	*to the right of*
a la izquierda de	*to the left of*
al lado de	*next to*
arriba de	*above*
debajo de	*below*
encima de	*on top of*
sobre	*on top of, over*

Otras palabras y expresiones

aumentar	*to grow*
el chubasco	*heavy shower*
la búsqueda	*search*
la carretera	*road, highway*
el coche	*car*
la falla	*fault*
la fuerza	*strength, power*
la guerra	*war*
el/la habitante	*inhabitant*
los llanos	*plains*
el maremoto	*seaquake*
la masa de agua	*body of water*
la meseta	*plateau*
el pájaro	*bird*
la palmera	*palm tree*
el pasto	*pasture*

la piedra	*stone*
el pino	*pine tree*
relevante	*important*
reflexionar	*to reflect*
saber	*to know*
salir	*go out*
suficiente	*enough*
el trabajo	*job*
la verdad	*thruth*
a veces	*sometimes*
¡Claro que no!	*Of course not!*
es decir	*that is to say*
Estoy de acuerdo.	*I agree.*
más que	*more than*
menos que	*less than*
No estoy de acuerdo.	*I don't agree.*
¿no?	*isn't it?*
¿Qué tiempo hace?	*What's the weather like?*
tan… como	*as… as*
tanto… como	*as much/many… as*
¿verdad?	*right?*

Cognados

Review the adjectives that describe nationality on pages 108–109. Learn those nationalities that are relevant for you and the people in your life.

Review the cognates in *Adelante* and the false cognates in *¡Atención!*. For a complete list of cognates, see Appendix 4 on page 605.

¿Qué significa ser hispano?
¿Qué es la hispanidad?

In this **Investigación,** you will learn:

- About the diversity of ethnic and racial groups that form the Spanish-speaking world

- About indigenous languages of South America

- How to express what has happened up to a given moment in the present

¿Cómo se puede hablar de lo que es ser hispano?

You can investigate the meaning of the term Hispanic.	¿Quiénes son "hispanos"? ¿Cuál es la diferencia entre "hispano", "latino", y "latinoamericano"?
You can investigate what it means to be Hispanic.	¿Ser hispano significa hablar español? ¿Significa vivir en un país donde el primer idioma es el español?
You can talk about the different varieties of Spanish.	Las diferencias entre el español de España y el español de Colombia son interesantes.
You can describe your personal experiences with regard to Hispanic culture and the Hispanic community.	He escuchado el español de Puerto Rico. He comido tacos picantes pero deliciosos.

TEACHING TIP: Have students identify the words in list that belong to the same word families as the following ones: *ignorante, estatal, injusto, libre, diferente, percibir, existir, diferir, descender, la violencia, la posibilidad, el desempleo.* This sensitizes students to the concept of word families.

TEACHING TIP: Ask questions such as *¿Qué conservamos? ¿Qué percibimos? ¿Qué empleamos?* etc. Some answers might include *conservar el territorio, percibir sonidos,* etc. Remind students that these words are cognates, and should be easy for them to understand.

Adelante

¡Ya lo sabes! Las comunidades

el acento	el/la inmigrante	diferente	conservar
el/la anglosajón/a	la libertad	(in)evitable	contratar
la comunidad	la mayoría	(in)existente	eliminar
el descendiente	la percepción	mutuo/a	emplear
el desempleo	la polémica	(im)posible	generar
el dialecto	el respeto	territorial	inmigrar
el estado	el territorio	violento/a	percibir
la (in)existencia	la violencia		resolver
el grupo étnico			
la (in)justicia			
la ignorancia			
la inmigración			

3B.1 **Completar la idea.** Read the definitions or incomplete descriptions in 1–8 below, then match each definition or description with its corresponding word from *Adelante* in a–i. The first one is done for you as a model. **¡Ojo!** One of the terms will not fit any of the descriptions. Verify your responses with the class.

a. emplear **d.** mayoría **g.** comunidad

b. injusticia **e.** inmigrantes **h.** conservar

c. dialecto **f.** la polémica **i.** resolver

_i_ **1.** La acción de descubrir una solución a un problema es…

_c_ **2.** La manera de hablar de una comunidad, en una región, o de un grupo de personas es su…

_d_ **3.** Cuando hay 10 personas en total y 8 personas votan por un candidato y 2 votan por otro candidato, decimos que el grupo de 8 representa el consenso o la…

_e_ **4.** Las personas que salen de su país original para vivir en otro país se llaman…

_a_ **5.** Otra palabra para "usar" es…

_b_ **6.** La discriminación reduce las oportunidades que tiene una persona; es una…

_f_ **7.** Otra forma de decir "el problema" es…

_h_ **8.** Otra palabra para "mantener" es…

3B.2 **Trabajadores inmigrantes.** Working with a classmate, complete each statement below with the appropriate word from list. Then, working alone, indicate whether you agree (**Sí. Estoy de acuerdo.**) or disagree (**No. No estoy de acuerdo.**) with each statement. Finally, compare your responses with your classmate's, then with the responses of the rest of the class and write your results in your **Retrato de la clase.**

contratan generan inmigrantes

inevitable descendientes mutuo

Sí **No**

☐ ☐ **1.** Las compañías _____ a inmigrantes para formar su base laboral.

☐ ☐ **2.** Muchos hispanohablantes que viven hoy día en Texas, Nuevo México, California y Arizona son _____ de mexicanos que vivían allí antes de la Guerra de 1848.

☐ ☐ **3.** En algunas regiones hay un respeto _____ entre los nativos y los inmigrantes.

☐ ☐ **4.** En otras regiones, la inmigración y las contribuciones de los inmigrantes_____ debates intensos y feroces.

☐ ☐ **5.** En realidad, el fenómeno de los indocumentados existe porque la necesidad de mano de obra *(work force)* es _____ en un país como Estados Unidos.

Retrato de la clase: La mayoría de la clase está de acuerdo con las siguientes declaraciones:… La mayoría de la clase no está de acuerdo con las siguientes declaraciones:…

3B.3 **¿Qué o quién?** With a classmate, complete the following statements logically. Then, share your responses with the class.

1. Una persona violenta es…

2. Una acción inevitable es…

3. Algo injusto es…

4. Un territorio polémico es…

5. Un estado con mucho territorio es…

6. Un grupo étnico es…

7. Un dialecto fuerte existe en…

8. Una descendiente de un hispano famoso es…

3B.2 ANSWERS: 1. contratan, 2. descendientes, 3. mutuo, 4. generan, 5. inevitable

3B.2 FOLLOW-UP: Write headings *Estoy de acuerdo* and *No estoy de acuerdo* on the board. After checking student responses, tally the number of students that disagreed with a sentence. Students will not have enough language proficiency to support their opinions but let them know that the class will return to this issue later in the book. For the time being, ask students to write in their *Retrato de la clase* the number of students that disagreed with specific sentences.

3B.4   Antes de leer:

Paso 1: **Ideas principales.** Reading the first sentence of each paragraph of a text will often give you a good idea of what the whole text is about. Read the first sentence of each paragraph in *¿Quiénes son los hispanos?* and write down what you think the main idea of each paragraph might be.

Paso 2: Indicate whether each statement below expresses a main idea or a supporting detail (**un detalle**). Check your responses with two other classmates.

Idea principal	Detalle	
☐	☑	**1.** …hace alusión directa a la herencia *(heritage)* española…
☐	☑	**2.** …se refiere a los países de habla española y a la exclusión de los países de Latinoamérica de habla portuguesa o francesa…
☑	☐	**3.** …los hispanos son gente muy diversa…
☐	☑	**4.** Los hispanos pueden ser de descendencia europea, indígena, asiática o africana…
☐	☑	**5.** Pueden tener sus orígenes en España…

NOTE: The main point of this reading is to sensitize students to the fact that not all of Latin America consists of Spanish-speakers, that the term *Latin America* refers to countries where a romance language is spoken (derived from Latin). Lastly, that *Hispanic* refers to countries where Spanish is the main language. In this textbook, we use *Hispanic* to refer to Spanish speakers, irrespective of nationality or ethnicity. You may point out to students that some people find the term *Hispanic* offensive for a variety of reasons. For some, it connotes Spanish colonialism and suggests a dismissal of indigenous populations with their own languages. Others take offense because it is a term that the US government developed to group the growing Spanish-speaking population in the US in the 1970s.

SUGGESTION: Sometimes grouping students so that they can help each other understand the passage is an effective reading technique, particularly for longer passages.

¿Hispano o latino?

La palabra *hispano* provoca mucha polémica entre las personas de diferentes nacionalidades latinoamericanas; pues definir quién es hispano es más difícil de lo que parece *(than it seems)*. ¿Quién es español, quién es latino y quién es hispano? La palabra *español* describe a una persona de España y la palabra *latino* se usa para describir a una persona que habla una lengua derivada del latín; de esta manera, los italianos, los bolivianos,

los rumanos, los españoles, los franceses, los colombianos, etcétera., son considerados latinos. *Hispanoamérica* nombra colectivamente a los países que fueron colonias de España y que hablan español en la actualidad. El término *Latinoamérica* incluye a todos los países del continente americano que fueron colonizados por un país latino. Por eso Latinoamérica incluye a Brasil donde se habla el portugués, y Haití, Martinica y la Guayana Francesa, donde se habla francés.

El uso del término *hispano* se ha generalizado, por lo menos en Estados Unidos, para definir a la persona que es descendiente de una familia de alguno de los países hispanohablantes. El término puede provocar reacciones variadas. Muchas personas piensan que *hispano* hace referencia a la colonización española y no considera la individualidad de cada país. *Hispano* no es un término racial ya que existen hispanos de todas las razas, tampoco es un término cultural ya que cada país tiene una cultura diferente. El término realmente es lingüístico porque define a las personas por el idioma que hablan. Sin embargo muchos "hispanos" de tercera generación ya no hablan español y ellos mismos prefieren ser considerados simplemente como americanos.

Como aprendimos en la investigación anterior, los hispanos no son de una sola nacionalidad ni de una sola cultura. Al contrario, los hispanos son gente muy diversa. Los hispanos pueden ser de descendencia europea, indígena, asiática, africana o cualquier mezcla *(mix)* de estas, y pueden tener sus orígenes en España, México o alguno de los países hispanohablantes del Caribe, de Centroamérica o de América del Sur.

3B.5 Comprensión.

Indicate whether each statement you hear is **cierto** or **falso** based on *¿Hispano o latino?* Then, check your responses as a class.

	Cierto	Falso
1.	☑	☐
2.	☐	☑
3.	☐	☑
4.	☑	☐
5.	☐	☑

Bien dicho

La acentuación y el significado de las palabras

The stress we place on words can make a difference in meaning. For example, if you say **hablo**, with the stress on the next to the last syllable (it ends in a vowel), you are saying *I speak*. If you say, however, **habló**, and place the stress on the last syllable, you are saying (someone) *spoke*. Placing the stress on the right syllable in a word can also make the difference in how "foreign" you sound, especially with respect to cognates.

You learned about placing the stress on the appropriate syllable in Spanish in *Investigación* 3A. When you see words in writing, you can tell whether they follow the regular stress pattern or not by the absence or presence of a written accent mark. Just as it is important to place stress correctly when you're speaking, writing, or reading, it is important to recognize where the stress falls when you're hearing Spanish.

3B.6 Piénsalo bien.

How would you pronounce the following words? Confirm your pronunciation with a classmate, then listen to the pronunciation on the recording.

1. el café instantáneo
2. el teléfono celular
3. la palabra esdrújula
4. el laboratorio de computación
5. el contestador automático
6. la cultura hispánica
7. las investigaciones científicas exploratorias
8. la iconografía

3B.7 ¿Qué palabra oyes?

You will hear a series of statements. As you listen to the sentences, indicate which of the two words you heard in each case. Then, verify your answers as a class.

1.	☐ hable	*(Speak!)*	☑ hablé	*(I spoke)*
2.	☑ límite	*(boundary)*	☐ limité	*(I limited)*
3.	☐ término	*(term)*	☑ termino	*(I finish)*
4.	☐ saco	*(I get)*	☑ sacó	*(He got)*
5.	☑ río	*(river)*	☐ rió	*(She laughed)*
6.	☑ busque	*(Look for!)*	☐ busqué	*(I looked for)*

3B.5 AUDIO SCRIPT: 1. Los hispanos son descendientes de personas que hablan español. (Cierto), 2. Hispanoamérica incluye países que fueron colonias de Portugal y Francia. (Falso. Sólo incluye países que fueron colonias de España), 3. El español es el idioma principal de todos los países de Latinoamérica (Falso. Hablan portugués en Brasil y francés en otros países.), 4. Latinoamérica incluye el territorio de Brasil. (Cierto), 5. El término *hispano* es aceptado por todos. (Falso. Algunos piensan que es ofensivo.)

3B.7 AUDIO SCRIPT: 1. Hablé con mi mamá el sábado pasado. 2. La frontera es el límite entre dos países. 3. Siempre termino la tarea antes de clase. 4. Sacó una A en el examen de español. 5. El río Amazonas pasa por Perú y Brasil. 6. Busque la definición en el diccionario.

3B.7 TEACHING TIP: Focus on syllables. To draw attention to the way in which words are divided into syllables, have students punch/tap out the syllables as you state them. This will help them recognize where the second-to-last and last syllables are.

Palabras clave 1 Cosas que pasan en la ciudad

SUGGESTION: You may choose to explore the scene by sections. For example, you can begin by highlighting the section in the drawing you wish to look at first and say, a. ¿El joven tira la basura a la calle? ¿Sí o no? (No, tira la basuara al basurero.), b. La huelga ocurre porque quieren mantener la libertad de prensa, ¿cierto o falso?, c. ¿Creen que los dos hombres van a pelear? ¿Sí o no?, d. ¿La luz señala que las personas deben o no deben cruzar la calle? e. El alcalde habla con el reportero. ¿Cierto o falso?, f. El ingeniero habla con el reportero. ¿Cierto o falso?, g. La chica ofrece una encuesta. ¿Sí o no?, h. ¿La huelga apoya la violencia o es pacífica?, i. El pueblo está en el estado de Colorado. ¿Cierto o falso?, j. Parece que hay mucho desempleo en este pueblo. ¿Cierto o falso?

3B.8 **Repaso de verbos con gestos y movimientos.** Take turns with a partner acting out the meaning of the verbs in the list below in random order. As one of you acts out a word, the other guesses, then vice versa and so on. Check off each action guessed correctly until you've guessed six items. Your instructor may ask you to guess additional items as well.

3B.8 LEARNING STYLES: Students with tactile learning style preferences will favor total physical response as a way to learn.

☐ caminar	☐ bailar	☐ nadar	☐ levantar pesas	☐ andar en bici
☐ correr	☐ cocinar	☐ hablar	☐ escribir	☐ dibujar
☐ llamar	☐ tocar	☐ saludar	☐ comer	☐ mirar
☐ visitar	☐ conversar	☐ copiar	☐ entrar	☐ estudiar
☐ pegar	☐ saltar	☐ explorar	☐ observar	☐ silenciar
☐ abrir	☐ levantar la mano	☐ leer	☐ sacar	☐ señalar
☐ trabajar	☐ escuchar	☐ cantar	☐ proteger	☐ ignorar
☐ expresar	☐ tirar	☐ ayudar	☐ cuidar	☐ guardar
☐ tirar	☐ agarrar	☐ jalar	☐ elegir	☐ levantar

3B.9 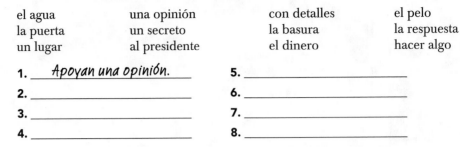 **¿Qué hacemos con…?**   For each question you hear, choose the most logical response from the items below and write a sentence to answer the question, following the model. Check your answers with those of a classmate.

el agua	una opinión	con detalles	el pelo
la puerta	un secreto	la basura	la respuesta
un lugar	al presidente	el dinero	hacer algo

1. _Apoyan una opinión._   5. _____

2. _____   6. _____

3. _____   7. _____

4. _____   8. _____

3B.10 **Asociaciones.**   With a classmate, take turns reading the phrases and statements below and identifying the vocabulary word best associated with each. Confirm your answers with the rest of the class.

> Modelo: E1: *Escuchar a alguien hablar sobre un tema*
> E2: *el discurso*

1. Muchas personas que no trabajan en señal de protesta
2. El político más importante de una ciudad
3. La falta *(lack of)* de trabajo
4. El 15 de abril cada año
5. Normas que limitan y controlan para mantener el orden civil
6. Una calle por donde los carros viajan rápidamente
7. Texas, California, Nueva Jersey
8. Una conversación basada en una serie de preguntas
9. Los demócratas y los republicanos
10. Preguntas para muchas personas sobre asuntos particulares

3B.11 **Adivina cierto o falso.**   Using words from *Palabras clave*, write two sentences using two different verbs. One sentence must be obviously true and the other sentence should be obviously false. Read one sentence to the class so they may guess whether it is true or false.

VÍVELO: LENGUA

Expressing "to know": *Saber* and *conocer*

Saber and **conocer** are two verbs that mean *to know* in English. In Spanish, a distinction is made between *to know* in the sense of knowing a fact, pieces of information, or how to do something **(saber)**, and *to know* in the sense of being acquainted or familiar with a person, place, or thing **(conocer)**.

Saber		Conocer	
Yo sé	Nosotros/as sabemos	Yo conozco	Nosotros/as conocemos
Tú sabes	Vosotros/as sabéis	Tú conoces	Vosotros/as conocéis
Él, ella, Ud. sabe	Ellos, ellas, Uds. saben	Él, ella, Ud. conoce	Ellos, ellas, Uds. conocen

¿Sabe usted de dónde es la profesora?
¿Sabes hablar francés?
¿Sabes tocar el piano?

¿Conoces tú la Ciudad de Nueva York?
¿Conocen ustedes al presidente de la universidad?

 PLUS Go to *WileyPLUS* and review the tutorial for this grammar point.

3B.12 ¿Saber o conocer? Complete each question using **saber** or **conocer** depending on the context and what notion of *to know* is being expressed. **¡Ojo!** Make sure to conjugate the verb according to its subject or use the infinitive when called for. Then, interview a classmate using these questions with all of the verbs in the **tú** form.

1. ¿ <u>Sabe</u> usted dónde está Buenos Aires?

2. ¿ <u>Conoces</u> tú a una persona hispana famosa?

3. ¿ <u>Sabe</u> usted cómo se llama el líder de Cuba?

4. ¿ <u>Conoce</u> usted personalmente al presidente de la universidad?

5. ¿ <u>Sabes</u> tú cuántos años tiene el/la instructor/a de la clase de español?

6. ¿Crees que es importante <u>saber</u> información personal del presidente?

3B.13 ¿Cómo se dice? You and a classmate have been asked to help interpret some questions in the school counselor's office for a family that recently arrived from Guatemala. How would you ask the following questions?

> Modelo: "Ask the parents if they know how to speak English."
> *¿Saben hablar inglés?*

El consejero dice:

1. "Ask the parents if they know their full address."

2. "Ask the parents if they know a doctor."

3. "Ask the student if he/she knows someone in the class."

4. "Ask the student if he/she knows how to read in English."

5. "Ask the parents if they know how to write in Spanish."

3B.12 FOLLOW-UP: After students interview their classmate, ask the class how many of their partners answered Sí to questions 1, 2, and 3. These students may have retained more "facts" or know more about Latin America than the rest of the class, irrespective of how proficient or not they are in Spanish.

3B.13 ANSWERS: 1. ¿Saben su dirección?, 2. ¿Conocen a un doctor?, 3. ¿Conoces a alguien en la clase?, 4. ¿Sabes leer en inglés?, 5. ¿Saben escribir en español?

3B.13 SUGGESTION: Point out that this is a realistic situation, reflective of one that non-Spanish speakers can face on a regular basis. Encourage students to reflect on their day-to-day experiences. Are there times when speaking Spanish would ebenefit them?

VÍVELO: CULTURA

El español de América del Sur

Spanish is part of what **la hispanidad** is but it is also part of what makes Hispanic cultures so diverse. For example, the Spanish spoken in Medellín, Colombia, is different from the Spanish spoken in Bogotá. While all Spanish-speakers can understand each other, there are differences in pronunciation, intonation and regional expressions. Hundreds of words from indigenous languages have enriched the Spanish spoken throughout Latin America. Today these words often form a part of the general Spanish lexicon. It should be noted that the indigenous languages these words come from belong to distinct, unrelated families, so that an **aguacate** (*avocado*) in Mexico and Central America becomes a **palta** in the Andes.

Although Spanish speakers today generally have little difficulty understanding each other, the following variants represent some extreme divergences:

	Little boy	Bus	Blond
México	chamaco	camión	güero
Guatemala	patojo	camioneta	canche
El Salvador	cipote	camioneta	chele
Panamá	chico	chiva	fulo
Colombia	pelado	autobús	mono
Argentina	pibe	colectivo	rubio
Chile	cabro	micro	rubio
Cuba	chico	guagua	rubio

VÍVELO: CULTURA: Ask students if they can think of examples of this lexical diversity in English. For example, in the US, a colloquial way of expressing going to the bathroom is "going to the john" and in England, the same is expressed as "going to the loo"; what might be a "pop" in one part of the US is a "soda" somewhere else.

Some of these words are rooted in Spanish while some are from the indigenous languages of the respective areas. The fact that there are differences of this sort is to be expected in a language population whose cultures are so diverse. International Spanish-language media both familiarizes people from different areas with each other's regional vocabulary and at the same time promotes universal understanding among Spanish speakers.

In Cuba and Puerto Rico, the word **guagua** means **autobús**.

¡Atención!

Diferir	looks like different but it means *to defer* as in *to postpone*, synonymous with **postergar,** and *to differ* or *be different*. To refer to the idea of *to make different*, use the verb **distinguir.** La universidad difiere sus planes de construir un nuevo estadio de fútbol americano. Los dos carros difieren en el precio. El uso de regionalismos distingue el español de un país del español de otro.
Compromiso	looks like compromise but it really means *commitment* as in an *obligation*. To refer to the idea of *to compromise*, use the expression **llegar a un acuerdo.** Quiero ir a México en julio pero ya tengo un compromiso. Mis amigos van a visitarme por un mes. Los bancos llegaron a un acuerdo gracias al gobierno.
Decepción	would appear to mean *deception* but it really means *disappointment*. As such, the verb **decepcionar** means *to disappoint*. A synonym for **decepcionar** is **desilusionar.** To refer to the idea of deceiving someone, use the verb **engañar.** ¡Qué decepción! Estoy muy triste porque no he recibido la beca *(scholarship)* para estudiar en Argentina. Mi amigo engaña a su novia con otra mujer.

3B.14 Definiciones. Read the following sentences and choose the correct word that could be substituted to convey the same meaning. Then, check your responses as a class.

a. diferir   **b.** un compromiso   **c.** engañar   **d.** decepcionar

___b___ **1.** Juan tiene *planes.*

___d___ **2.** Silvia no quiere *desilusionar* a sus amigas pero no va a jugar más fútbol.

___a___ **3.** Santiago va a *postergar* sus planes para viajar a Nicaragua hasta diciembre durante las vacaciones.

___c___ **4.** No es bueno *decir cosas falsas* a las personas que amas.

Estructuras clave 1 The present perfect tense

The present perfect tense expresses actions that *have happened* in the past with respect to the present moment. It is a compound tense. That is to say, it is composed of two parts, an auxiliary, or "helping" verb and a participle, which is a special form of the verb conveying most of the meaning.

—¿Qué **has estudiado**?   — *What have you studied?*
—**He estudiado** la geografía latinoamericana.   — *I have studied Latin American geography.*

Note that in English, the present tense of the auxiliary verb *to have* is used with the past participle of a verb (often called "the *-ed* form"). Likewise in Spanish, the present tense of the auxiliary verb **haber** *(to have)* is used with a past participle. See below for the conjugation of **haber** and examples of the past participles of familiar Spanish verbs.

haber +		past participle	
yo	**he**	com**ido**	*(I have eaten.)*
tú	**has**	habl**ado**	*(You have spoken.)*
él/ella/usted	**ha**	le**ído**	*(He/She has read, You have read.)*
nosotros/as	**hemos**	visit**ado**	*(We have visited.)*
vosotros/as	**habéis**	mir**ado**	*(You all have watched.)*
ellos/ellas/ustedes	**han**	bail**ado**	*(They have danced, You have danced.)*

Regular past participles in Spanish follow the pattern shown above. The past participle of **-ar** verbs ends in **-ado,** and the past participle of **-er** and **-ir** verbs ends in **-ido.**

Notice in the examples above and below that it is the auxiliary verb that agrees with the subject. The past participle remains unchanged no matter who is performing the action. To make a present perfect statement negative, place **no** before the conjugated form of **haber.**

— ¿**Has preparado** la comida?   — *Have you prepared the food?*
— No, **no he preparado** la comida.   — *No, I have not prepared the food.*

Irregular past participles		
There are a handful of irregular past participles. They include the following.		
decir	**dicho**	Siempre he dicho la verdad.
hacer	**hecho**	No he hecho la tarea hoy.
escribir	**escrito**	He escrito varios poemas.
ver	**visto**	No he visto los Andes.
volver	**vuelto**	He vuelto a estudiar en la biblioteca.
morir	**muerto**	Mi abuela ha muerto.
romper	**roto**	Hemos roto la ventana con la pelota de béisbol.
poner	**puesto**	He puesto mis libros en la mochila.
cubrir	**cubierto**	¿Has cubierto las plantas para protegerlas del frío?
descubrir	**descubierto**	Nunca se ha descubierto la fuente *(fountain)* de la juventud.
abrir	**abierto**	¿Has abierto la puerta para tu abuela?

WILEY PLUS
Go to *WileyPLUS* and review the tutorial for this grammar point.

WILEY PLUS
You will find PowerPoint presentations for use with *Estructuras clave* in *WileyPLUS*.

SUGGESTION: Most texts do not introduce the perfect tenses until much later. The perfect tenses are not fully acquired early on even though the structure is not complex. The purpose of introducing it early in *Vívelo* is to expand comprehension in Spanish. You may want to note that in Spain they use the present perfect more than the preterite to express events in the past.

TEACHING TIP: Ask students to read the statements and agree or disagree with them. This will allow students to connect the meaning of the past participle to its irregular form.

3B.15 ¿Quién? Interview a classmate to see how much trivia he/she knows. Write down his/her answers, then verify them with other classmates' responses to see if there was anyone in class who answered all questions correctly.

1. ¿Quién ha cantado con J-Lo?
2. ¿Quiénes han jugado al béisbol para los Yankees de Nueva York?
3. ¿Qué equipos universitarios han ganado muchos partidos?
4. ¿Qué actrices han tenido gemelos?
5. ¿Qué actores han vivido en España?

EXPRESIONES ÚTILES

Para hablar de la frecuencia

In Spanish, the following words and expressions describe the frequency of an action.

siempre	Siempre corro en el parque por las mañanas. *I always run in the park during the morning.*
nunca	Nunca he viajado a España. *I have never been to Spain.*
jamás	Jamás he conocido a una persona como usted. *I have never met a person like you.*
a veces	A veces tenemos que hablar en español en clase. *Sometimes we have to speak in Spanish in class.*
con frecuencia	Leo con frecuencia las explicaciones del libro. *I often read the explanations in the book.*
de vez en cuando	Me gusta ir al cine de vez en cuando. *I like to go to the movies once in a while.*

3B.16 ¿Qué has hecho? ¿Con qué frecuencia?

Paso 1: What have you done to prepare for Spanish class this week? Indicate which responses are most true for you. Then, as a class investigate whether or not anyone has managed to check all statements.

Esta semana...

☐ he estudiado el vocabulario.

☐ he leído las explicaciones de gramática del libro.

☐ he tomado apuntes.

☐ he hablado con alguien en español.

☐ he aprendido algo nuevo sobre las culturas hispanas.

☐ he memorizado las conjugaciones de los verbos.

Paso 2: Interview a classmate to see how often he/she completes the same tasks in general. Use the words/phrases in *Expresiones útiles* to respond to the questions when your classmate interviews you. Compare your classmate's responses in *Paso 1* indicating what he/she has done this week to his/her answers in *Paso 2* to determine if this week was a typical week. Then, as a class, determine which tasks are completed most and least frequently.

> Modelo: E1: *¿Con qué frecuencia estudias el vocabulario?*
> E2: *Siempre estudio el vocabulario antes de clase.*

¿Con qué frecuencia...?

a. estudiar el vocabulario antes de clase

b. leer las explicaciones de gramática del libro

c. tomar apuntes en clase

d. hablar con alguien en español

e. aprender mucho sobre las culturas hispanas

f. memorizar las conjugaciones de los verbos

3B.17 Antes de leer. Read each of these statements and select the answer you think is correct. Then, go over your results with a partner before going over them as a class.

1. ____ La mayoría de los hispanos en Estados Unidos (EE.UU.) son de ___

a. Norteamérica **b.** Sudamérica **c.** El Caribe

2. ____ Los hispanos en EE.UU. están principalmente en California, Texas y Florida.

a. Cierto **b.** Falso

3. ____ El suroeste de EE.UU. antes era de México.

a. Cierto **b.** Falso

4. ____ La población hispana en EE.UU. en el 2000 era el ___ de la población total.

a. 5.5% **b.** 43.7% **c.** 12.5%

VÍVELO: CULTURA

Los hispanos en EE.UU.

Antes considerados como un grupo regional, los hispanos hoy en día se encuentran *(are found)* por todo Estados Unidos. Desde el momento en que el noroeste de México pasó a ser *(became)* el suroeste de Estados Unidos (1848), una gran porción de la población mexicana se convirtió en extranjera en su propia tierra y Estados Unidos comenzó a ser *(began being)* en parte un país de habla hispana.

La población hispana aumentó *(grew)* dramáticamente durante la década de 1990. En el año 1990 la población era *(was)* de 22.4 millones, el 9 por ciento de la población de Estados Unidos. En el año 2000 era de 35.3 millones, el 12.5 por ciento de la población del país.

En el año 2006, la distribución de la población hispana en los Estados Unidos era:

		% total de la población hispana
Total	44,252,278	
Mexicano	28,339,354	64.0
Puertorriqueño	3,987,947	9.0
Cubano	1,520,276	3.4
Dominicano	1,217,225	2.8
Centroamericano	3,372,090	7.6
Sudamericano	2,421,297	5.5
Otro	3,394,089	7.7

3B.17 ANSWERS: 1. a (la mayoría es de México), 2. b (están en todas partes de Estados Unidos), 3. a (Sí, estados como California, Arizona, Nuevo México, Texas eran parte de México), 4. c

3B.17 READING STRATEGY: The purpose of the *Antes de leer* activities is to expose students to the main ideas in the text. Now have them go through the reading highlighting the main points.

VÍVELO: CULTURA: Encourage students to reread the passage after you have gone through the answers. They should notice an increase in their comprehension.

3B.18 Comprensión. With the same partner from 3B.17, identify the line(s) or parts of *Vívelo: Cultura* that refer to the topics listed below. Then, compare your responses with another pair of classmates.

1. Population growth
2. US takeover of Mexican land
3. Mexican influences
4. Population distribution

3B.19 Una entrevista. Interview a classmate using the statements below. All statements must be answered honestly. Then summarize in your **Retrato de la clase** your classmate's dedication to learning Spanish based on his/her answers with supporting details.

1. ¿Has viajado a algún país latinoamericano?
2. ¿Has leído alguna novela de Isabel Allende?
3. ¿Has hablado en español con una persona bilingüe?
4. ¿Has ido al cine a ver una película española?
5. ¿Has escuchado un programa de radio en español?
6. ¿Has participado en una conversación en español?
7. ¿Has escrito una carta en español?
8. ¿Has visto una frontera física que separa un país de otro país como la cerca *(fence)* que está entre Texas, Arizona, Nuevo México, California y México?

Retrato de la clase: _____ sinceramente desea aprender español. Por ejemplo, ha viajado a México, Perú, Chile y España.

3B.20 ¡A leer para entender! The following *Vívelo: Cultura* is about the composition of the Hispanic population in the United States. Scan the passage for the responses to the questions below and jot down the answers. Then, in groups of three re-read the passage more carefully and verify your answers.

1. What percent of the Hispanic population in the United States was born in the United States?
2. What percent of the population of Hispanics in the United States is comprised of people who are less than 18 years old?
3. Are there more Spanish speakers who do not speak English than those who do?
4. What happens to the Spanish language by the third generation of Hispanics?
5. What areas in the United States have had unexpected increases in the Hispanic population?
6. Do younger Hispanics in the US identify themselves culturally as Hispanic or as Americans?

VÍVELO: CULTURA

Los jóvenes: Tercera parte *(one third)* de la población hispana

El 34.8% de la población hispana de Estados Unidos es menor de 18 años y aproximadamente el 60% del total de la población hispana nació *(was born)* en Estados Unidos. Los hispanos nacidos en Estados Unidos tienen una conexión menor con el español y para la tercera generación de hispanos el español ya no es su primer idioma. Es importante reconocer que sólo uno de cada doce hispanos no habla inglés. Es decir, 14 millones de hispanos hablan inglés y 1.5 millones no. Frecuentemente los descendientes de hispanos se americanizan hasta tal punto que culturalmente mantienen valores hispanos pero lingüísticamente ya no son bilingües. El bilingüismo se mantiene con la continuación de inmigrantes que sólo hablan español, con las visitas regulares a sus parientes que están en países hispanos y con las familias hispanas que desean conservar su herencia cultural a través de los medios de comunicación. Por ejemplo, la radio en español florece *(flourishes)* en áreas donde los hispanos eran casi inexistentes, tales como Charlotte, North Carolina, Kansas City, Missouri y Providence, Rhode Island. Un problema grave de los hispanos de tercera generación es que culturalmente son hispanos (por las tradiciones heredadas de sus padres y abuelos) mientras que lingüísticamente son americanos, porque solamente hablan inglés, situación que causa una crisis de identidad más fuerte de lo normal durante la adolescencia.

3B.21 Cierto o falso. With a classmate, determine whether each of the following statements is *cierto* or *falso*. Verify your responses with the rest of the class.

Cierto	Falso	
☑	☐	**1.** Within the Hispanic US population, 34% are 18 years or younger.
☑	☐	**2.** 60% of the Hispanic population in the US was born in the US
☐	☑	**3.** One in twelve Hispanics in the US speaks English.
☐	☑	**4.** The Hispanic population typically quits speaking Spanish by the second generation because they assimilated into the English-speaking culture.
☑	☐	**5.** There are nine times more Hispanics who speak English in the US than who do not.
☑	☐	**6.** Hispanic populations in the US have increased significantly in unexpected states.
☑	☐	**7.** The media in the US plays a role in preserving the Spanish language and culture.
☐	☑	**8.** Hispanic youth often face identity issues when they are culturally Hispanic and also speak Spanish fluently.

3B.21 ANSWERS: 1. Cierto, 2. Cierto, 3. Falso (one in twelve does not speak English), 4. Falso (A loss of Spanish is typically more visible by the third generation due to many factors), 5. Cierto, 6. Cierto, 7. Cierto, 8. Falso (Identity issues surface when they do not speak Spanish.)

www ¡Conéctate!
Visit the National Public Radio (NPR) program, Latino USA, at http://latinousa.org. Listen to the most recent show. What topics were being discussed? Did you gain new perspectives as a result? Share your thoughts with your classmates.

Enlaces

3B.22 ANSWERS: 1. such as, 2. in fact, 3. including, 4. such as

Point out to students that *tales como* is the plural of *tal como*. You can also ask them to guess what the singular form would be.

Making links within sentences and between paragraphs is a sign of good writing. In addition, your comprehension is facilitated when you recognize words and phrases that add cohesion to a text.

3B.22 Enlaces. The phrases *such as, in fact* and *including* are useful for making links within sentences and between sentences. Can you figure out the Spanish equivalent of each of these phrases by paying attention to the context in the following sentences? Verify your responses as a class.

1. Hay muchas celebridades transnacionales **tales como** Enrique Iglesias, Shakira, Salma Hayek, Antonio Banderas y Penélope Cruz.
2. La nueva tecnología, **inclusive** la tecnología tradicional de los medios de comunicación, ayuda a ampliar la popularidad de los artistas transnacionales.
3. Hay más hispanos en Estados Unidos que hablan inglés que los que no hablan inglés. **De hecho,** hay 12 hispanos que hablan inglés por cada 1 que no lo habla.
4. Un artista transnacional, **tal como** Rubén Blades, apoya la unidad entre los hispanos.

tales como	=	such as
de hecho	=	in fact
inclusive	=	including

FUNCTIONAL OUTCOMES:
The central question that frames this *Investigación* is *"¿Cómo se puede hablar de lo que es ser hispano?"* Explore whether students can now address this question and how they would go about it. Have them review the chart on the first page of this *Investigación*.

3B.23 Contextos. The following passage explains the vision shared by many Hispanic celebrities for a transnational community. What does this actually mean? Read this passage for some insight into what a transnational community is, who is included and what unifies them. Then, indicate whether each statement below is supported or not by the passage by underlining the supporting information in the reading and writing the number of the statement next to it. If the statement is not supported by information in the passage, indicate the language in the text that contradicts the statement.

> En la canción "Plástico," Rubén Blades evoca una visión de una comunidad transnacional de los países de América Latina, **inclusive** de los latinos de Estados Unidos. La comunidad transnacional de una "raza unida" latina no es una referencia exclusiva de la canción de Blades. **De hecho,** es también el discurso de un número importante de actores y cantantes, **tales como** Jennifer López y Ricky Martin, con preocupaciones sociales que piensan que están unidos por el alma *(soul)*, la imaginación y los sentimientos de diversas poblaciones de todo el territorio de este continente llamado América.

1. No hay muchos actores o cantantes que piensen como Blades.

2. Aunque los hispanos del mundo son diversos por varias razones, Blades piensa que hay sentimientos que unen a todos los hispanos.

3. Blades no incluye a los hispanos de EE.UU. como parte de esta comunidad hispana transnacional.

4. Los sentimientos, el alma, y la imaginación de los hispanos unen a todos los hispanos del mundo y por eso usan el término comunidad "transnacional".

Rubén Blades

Perspectivas

3B.24 **¿Es posible tener una comunidad transnacional?** Now, with another classmate, read the next passage that questions whether a transnacional community is possible. Read to understand why some question this. Note whether the passage ends on a positive or negative note. Once you have read the passage, discuss your understanding with your partner before you attempt to respond to the statements in Activity 3B.25.

Un análisis de la opinión de algunas celebridades hispanas cuestiona qué tan inclusiva es la identidad hispana cuando están involucrados 22 países. Por ejemplo, Salma Hayek descalificó a Jennifer López como "latina" porque nació en Nueva York y habla español con acento. Ricky Martin habla inglés sin acento y mantiene su identidad puertorriqueña, o boricua, con ferocidad. La americanización de López representa a la mayoría de hispanos que nacen en EE.UU. que tratan de conservar lo que pueden de su cultura latina. Por un lado, los hispanos de otros países los descalifican como hispanos naturales y los anglosajones los descalifican como verdaderos americanos y los perciben como forasteros *(foreigners)*. Sabemos que no existe una sola identidad hispana; la identidad de los hispanoamericanos es más compleja. Lo que es seguro es que el poder adquisitivo *(buying power)* de los hispanoamericanos, en combinación con el número de inmigrantes, tiene como consecuencia una demanda de todo lo hispano en EE.UU. Lo que sí tienen todos los hispanos en común es que no tienen que sacrificar sus raíces *(roots)* culturales, como sus predecesores. De hecho, en un mundo cada vez más global, ser bilingüe, bicultural, transcultural o transnacional será una ventaja en el nuevo milenio.

www

¡Conéctate!

What celebrities do you know from the Spanish-speaking world? Check out http://peopleenespanol.com to get to know some of these individuals. Did you know some of them already? What did you learn? Make a list of three individuals and include statements in Spanish about who they are and why they are being mentioned.

3B.25 **¿Estás o no estás de acuerdo?** In groups of three, indicate whether you agree or disagree with the following statements.

Hablando de las tendencias sociales del mundo y los ciclos históricos de las civilizaciones:

Sí **No**

1. El cuestionamiento *(questioning)* de las identidades nacionales es consecuencia de la globalización en el mundo.

2. El rechazo *(rejection)* de los mexicoamericanos, cubanoamericanos, y puertorriqueños de la diáspora (puertorriqueños que no viven en la isla) por parte de los mexicanos, cubanos o puertorriqueños indica que va a ser difícil obtener una comunidad transnacional.

3. Siempre van a existir personas que excluyan o rechacen *(reject)* a otros grupos para sentirse superiores, pero esto no representa la opinión de la mayoría de la población.

4. La cuestión de transnacionalismo o transculturalismo es producto del declive *(decline)* de la identificación exclusiva de los ciudadanos estadounidenses con un estado nacional.

5. El rechazo a los inmigrantes en EE.UU. va a provocar que los inmigrantes no se integren a la sociedad estadounidense como las generaciones previas.

6. El fenómeno de una identidad global hispana contradice el aumento de identidades locales donde la población se identifica más con su comunidad local que con una identidad nacional.

7. Los países hispanoamericanos son diversos y cada nación es distinta. Estas diferencias no van a permitir una identidad transnacional.

8. No existe una identidad cultural común en EE.UU.

9. En el futuro, la lucha de clases sociales va a ser más importante que la lucha de civilizaciones.

10. Las guerras aumentan la identidad nacional de un país.

11. La civilización occidental está en declive demográfica y económicamente.

Haciendo *skate* delante de una iglesia en El Viejo San Juan

Vocabulario: Investigación B

Vocabulario esencial

Sustantivos

el acontecimiento	*event*
el/la alcalde/sa	*mayor*
la basura	*garbage*
la beca	*scholarship*
la comida	*food*
el dinero	*money*
el discurso	*speech; discourse*
la encuesta	*survey*
la entrevista	*interview*
la falta	*lack of*
el gobierno	*government*
la huelga	*worker's strike*
la lucha	*struggle*
la mezcla	*mix, blend*
el/la novio/a	*boyfriend/ girlfriend*
la pelea	*fight*
el pueblo	*town; people*

Verbos

agarrar	*to grab*
cubrir	*to cover*
conocer	*to know*
elegir	*to choose*
entender	*to understand*
guardar	*to keep*
jalar	*to pull*
mantener	*to maintain*
luchar	*to fight for something*
pegar	*to hit*
pelear	*to fight*
pensar	*to think*
resolver	*to solve*
saber	*to know*
saltar	*to jump*
señalar	*to point at something*
tirar	*to throw (away)*
volver	*to return*

Adverbios

antes de	*before*
contra	*against*
después de	*after*
jamás	*never*
mientras	*while*
nunca	*never*
siempre	*always*

Otras palabras y expresiones

adivinar	*to guess*
el alma *(f.)*	*soul*
anterior	*previous*
el asunto	*issue*
atento	*careful; considerate*
construir	*to build*
el consultorio	*office*
convertirse	*to become*
la explicación	*explanation*
fundar	*to found*
el/la gemelo/a	*twin*
indígena	*indigenous; Native American*
la mano de obra	*workers*
parecer	*to appear to be*
el partido	*game*
el precio	*price*
la raíz	*root*
rechazar	*reject*
reconocer	*recognize*
el sentimiento	*feeling*
el siglo	*century*
tratar	*to try*
triste	*sad*
ubicar	*to locate*
la ventaja	*advantage*
verdadero/a	*true*

al contrario	*on the contrary*
a través de	*through*
con frecuencia	*frequently*
de esta manera	*in this way*
de vez en cuando	*once in a while*

en la actualidad	*currently*
en realidad	*actually*
lo que es seguro	*what is certain*
pasar a ser	*to become*
por ejemplo	*for example*

Cognados

Review the cognates in *Adelante* and the false cognates in *¡Atención!*. For a complete list of cognates, see Appendix 4 on page 605.

¡VÍVELO!

En vivo

¿Has aprendido a ubicar los países? With a partner, insert the pieces of the puzzle grouped in A and B for a complete map outline of the countries of Central and South America and Spain and show what you know. Then, write in the names of the countries and their capitals. No English may be used to complete this task.

Modelo: *Yo tengo Nicaragua. Está en Centroamérica. Nicaragua está entre Costa Rica y Honduras. Su capital es Managua.*

Grupo A

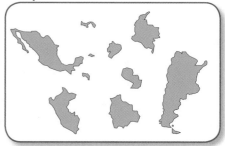

Grupo B

 Ser hispano: Representaciones visuales. The focus of this *Capítulo* has been on discussing the rich and complex nature of the Hispanic world and **los hispanos.** Create a visual representation that illustrates this diversity. You could use any of the following formats:

• collage   • painting   • Powerpoint   • other?

Prepare a written description to support your visual representation. You can do this is any variety of ways (captions, narration, etc.). Consider the vast vocabulary you learned, the topics you read about and the complexities around this topic. We recommend the following process:

Paso 1: Prepare visual representation.

Paso 2: Write a first draft of your written description.

Paso 3: Have a classmate critique your written description in terms of overall content. (Do the ideas flow? Is your presentation interesting?)

Paso 4: Write a second draft.

Paso 5: Have a classmate critique your second draft, this time looking for accuracy. (Do subjects and verbs agree? Do adjectives agree with the nouns they're describing? Are words spelled correctly?)

Paso 6: Write the final draft.

INVESTIGACIÓN A: Video: 1492: intercambio de dos mundos

> **Antes de ver el video.** Choose the best answer or completion for each item.

1. ¿En qué año llegan los españoles a América?
  a. 1483
  b. 1482
  c. 1492 ⟵

2. Los españoles introducen en América…
  a. los tomates.
  b. los caballos. ⟵
  c. la religión.

3. Uno de los conquistadores españoles más conocidos es…
  a. Simón Bolívar.
  b. Hernán Cortés. ⟵
  c. Pau Gasol.

4. El español es idioma oficial en…
  a. 10 países.
  b. 15 países.
  c. 21 países. ⟵

> **El video.** Indicate whether the following statements are **cierto** or **falso** based on the video.

Cierto	Falso	
☐	☑	**1.** Los Reyes Católicos, Isabel y Alfonso, expulsan en 1492 a los árabes y a los judíos que no se convierten al catolicismo.
☐	☑	**2.** Cristbal Colón llega a América el 2 de octubre de 1492.
☑	☐	**3.** La Hispaniola es la primera colonia fundada por Colón.
☐	☑	**4.** La iglesia no convierte a los indígenas al catolicismo.
☑	☐	**5.** Los españoles introducen las papas, el maíz y el tabaco en Europa.
☐	☑	**6.** Los criollos más famosos son Simón Bolívar y Francisco Pizarro.

Vocabulario útil

sufrir	*to suffer*
expulsar de	*to expel from*
a través de	*through*
edificio	*building*
mezcla	*mix / blend*
criollo	*born in the New World of European parents*
conservar	*to keep*
siglo	*century*

> **Después de ver el video. ¿Estás de acuerdo o no estás de acuerdo?** Discuss each of these statements with a partner and indicate whether you agree or disagree with them: 1) En general, la llegada de los europeos a América es un acontecimiento histórico pacífico *(peaceful).* 2. La llegada de los españoles a América es positiva para los indígenas porque aprenden a leer y a escribir.

INVESTIGACIÓN B: Video: ¿Qué significa ser hispano?

> **Antes de ver el video.** What aspects of culture do you think Spanish-speaking people share regardless of country of residence or origin? In your opinion, is there a difference between the terms **hispano** and **latinoamericano**? Discuss your answers with your classmates.

> **El video.** Choose the best word or phrase to complete or respond to each statement based on the video.

1. Según la antropóloga, las personas que viven en Hispanoamérica se identifican como…
  a) latinoamericanos.   **b)** hispanos. ⟵   **c)** Las dos son correctas.

2. El término _____ se refiere al idioma que se habla.
  a) latino   **b)** hispano ⟵   **c)** latinoamericano

3. Los dos aspectos principales que identifican a los latinoamericanos son…
  a) la religión y el idioma.   **b)** la raza y el idioma.   **c)** la cultura y el idioma. ⟵

4. En Latinoamérica hay muchas razas.
  a) cierto ⟵   **b)** falso

Vocabulario útil

en realidad	*actually*
orgullosamente	*proudly*

> **Después de ver el video.** Answer the following questions and discuss them with the rest of the class: *¿Qué significa la palabra* mestizo*? ¿Crees que Estados Unidos es un país mestizo? ¿Por qué?*

Retrato de la clase Checklist

WILEY
PLUS
You will find a complete testing program for use with *¡Vívelo!* in *WileyPLUS*.

You should have recorded information in your **Retrato de la clase** in conjunction with the following activities:

☐	**3A.6**	**Las nacionalidades originales**
☐	**3A.8**	**De preguntas generales a perfiles personales**
☐	**3A.17**	**El país y el clima más atractivo**
☐	**3B.2**	**Trabajadores inmigrantes**
☐	**3B.19**	**Una entrevista**

El mundo hispano en tu vida

¿Qué contacto tienes tú con el mundo hispano?

In this **Investigación** you will learn…

▶ How to talk about various forms of entertainment

▶ How to express actions that include yourself and others

▶ About the influence of Hispanic culture in US society

▶ How to express actions that happen, are happening and will happen

¿Cómo puedes hablar del contacto que tienes con el mundo hispano?

You can describe what you like to do for entertainment.	Me gusta bailar, ir al cine y cantar karaoke. Prefiero leer libros de ciencia ficción que de ficción.
You can express where and with whom you like to do these activities.	Me gusta salir con mis amigos. Muchas veces comemos en restaurantes y luego bailamos en una discoteca.
You can express where you go to have fun.	Voy a las montañas para pensar y descansar. Vamos a los partidos de fútbol americano los sábados.
You can describe what happens, is happening and will happen.	Pienso mucho en mi familia aquí en la universidad. Mañana no visito a mis padres porque mis amigos y yo tenemos que terminar un proyecto.

TEACHING TIP: Ask personalized questions that provide more input with these words while inviting students to share their own opinions and experiences. Give examples and input for items like *las noticias, la telenovela, las caricaturas, la publicidad, sostener,* etc. which students will readily associate with common English words, but whose meaning in Spanish they will grasp with context.

REACHING MULTIPLE LEVELS: For advanced students, or false beginners, consider having them create a story using many of the new vocabulary words. For true beginners, consider asking students to group the words into the following categories: *cosas que me gustan mucho, cosas que me gustan un poco, cosas que no me gustan.*

Adelante

¡Ya lo sabes! Música televisión y noticias

la animación	la música salsa	la telenovela	actuar
las caricaturas	las noticias	la tragedia	afectar
el canal	el piano	la trompeta	influenciar
la ciencia ficción	el pop		informar
la columna	el programa de deportes	con frecuencia	mantener
la comedia	la publicidad	enorme	obtener
la discoteca	la radio	feroz	proyectar
el documental	el/la reportero/a	futurístico/a	reportar
el drama	la serie policíaca	rápido/a	servir
la guitarra	el teatro	raramente	sostener
el jazz			

4A.1 ¡A organizar!   You will hear words from *Adelante* given in random order. As you hear each word, write it under the appropriate category heading in the chart below. Each word can be used under only one category. Compare your lists with those of two other classmates.

La música	La televisión	La diversión	Palabras descriptivas	Acciones

4A.2 Asociaciones.   You will hear incomplete statements about various authors, entertainers, and media. As you hear each statement, provide the word from *Adelante* that logically completes it, following the model. Verify your answers with a classmate.

1. _____ *piano* _____
2. _____ guitarra _____
3. _____ canales _____
4. _____ telenovela _____
5. _____ ciencia ficción _____
6. _____ tragedia _____
7. _____ jazz _____
8. _____ teatros _____

4A.3 A emparejar.   Match the phrases in column **A** to those in column **B** to form the most logical statements. Then, compare your responses with a classmate.

A

_b_ **1.** Escuchar música rock cuando estudias…

_a_ **2.** Es la obligación de los padres y las madres…

_c_ **3.** La figura mitológica de Átlas sirve para…

_d_ **4.** América Ferrera…

_e_ **5.** El periódico *(newspaper) The Washington Post*…

B

a. mantener económicamente a sus hijos.

b. puede afectar negativamente la concentración.

c. sostener al mundo.

d. actúa en la serie *Betty la fea*.

e. informa al público del Distrito de Columbia.

4A.4 La diversión y el entretenimiento.   With a classmate, select the most appropriate word from the list below to fill in the blank, following the model. Verify your responses with another pair of classmates.

feroces	con frecuencia	documentales	programas de deportes
pop	reportero	futurístico	columna

1. El canal ESPN ofrece muchos _programas de deportes_.
2. En el canal Discovery hay muchos _documentales_.
3. Britney Spears, Pee Wee y Shakira cantan música _pop_.
4. El filme *La guerra de las galaxias* es _futurístico_.
5. Muchas personas escuchan música _con frecuencia_.
6. En las caricaturas hay animales tímidos y también _feroces_.
7. Muchos periódicos tienen una _columna_ editorial.
8. Un corresponsal es también un _reportero_.

4A.1 AUDIO SCRIPT: Words from *Adelante* read in random order

4A.1 TEACHING TIP: Have students tally how many words they matched to each category and compare their numbers with other partner groups. As a class, go over the words they placed under different categories, focusing implicitly on their pronunciation.

WILEY
PLUS

4A.1 INSTRUCTOR'S RESOURCES: You will find a blank chart for use with Activity 4A.1 as well as a filled-in chart for use as an answer key in your Instructor's Resources.

4A.2 AUDIO SCRIPT: 1. Billy Joel y Elton John tocan bien el… 2. A Carlos Santana le gusta tocar la… 3. El Food Network y HGTV son… 4. *Betty la fea* es una… 5. Las novelas de Ray Bradbury y de Isaac Asimov son de… 6. La obra *Hamlet* de Shakespeare es una… 7. Duke Ellington, Herbie Hancock y Wynton Marsalis son especialistas de la música… 8. En la Avenida Broadway en Nueva York hay muchos…

4A.3 NOTE: CELEBRITY NAMES: To avoid confusion and provide good modeling for beginning students, written accent marks are retained on Spanish celebrity names whether or not the named celebrity uses a written accent mark in his/her professional life. America Ferrera's name generally appears without a written accent mark in English publications, for example.

4A.5 SUGGESTION:
Encourage students to put themselves in contexts where Spanish is spoken, such as going to parties where Hispanic music is played, watching some Spanish-language TV, listening to Spanish-language radio, getting to know Spanish-speakers. The more they become involved with the Spanish-speaking community, either directly or indirectly, the more quickly they will learn Spanish.

4A.5 **¡Toma la prueba!** Interview a classmate to determine how much contact he/she has with the Hispanic world. Each **Sí** answer is worth 1 point. Add up the points and then read your classmate his/her results.

	Sí	No
1. ¿Te gusta ver películas hispanas como *Diarios de motocicleta* y *El laberinto del fauno?*	☐	☐
2. ¿Sabes quién es Alex Rodríguez?	☐	☐
3. ¿Asistes a fiestas de cumpleaños donde hay una piñata?	☐	☐
4. ¿Comes tacos, burritos o sándwiches de "wrap"?	☐	☐
5. ¿Lees libros de autores hispanos?	☐	☐
6. ¿Miras el programa de Carlos Mencía o George López?	☐	☐
7. ¿Escuchas música hispana?	☐	☐
8. ¿Sabes qué es *Betty la fea?*	☐	☐
9. ¿Conoces a algún político hispano famoso?	☐	☐
10. ¿Bailas salsa o cumbia?	☐	☐
11. ¿Viajas a países hispanos?	☐	☐
12. ¿Sabes quién es Frida Kahlo?	☐	☐
13. ¿Tienes música de Christina Aguilera, Enrique Iglesias, J. Lo, Marc Anthony, Shakira u otro cantante hispano?	☐	☐
14. ¿Sabes quiénes son Fidel Castro, Evo Morales o Hugo Chávez?	☐	☐
15. ¿Sabes quién es Jorge Ramos?	☐	☐

Total de puntos _____

Resultados:
11–15 puntos La cultura hispana te rodea (*surrounds you*).
7–10 puntos La cultura hispana es una parte de tu vida.
4–9 puntos La cultura hispana es una pequeña (*small*) parte de tu vida.
1–3 puntos ¡No vives en este planeta!

Las telenovelas en Latinoamérica

El género de la telenovela tiene su origen en las radionovelas de la década de 1940, patrocinados (*sponsored*) por las compañías de jabón (*soap*) como Palmolive y Lever Brothers. Hoy en día, los latinoamericanos son grandes maestros de la telenovela. El tremendo interés del público y de los patrocinadores resulta en producciones costosas de alta calidad que se ven (*are seen*) en todas partes del mundo. Como la industria cinemática en Latinoamérica es relativamente pequeña, es en las telenovelas que los actores y a las actrices tienen la oportunidad de ser verdaderas "estrellas".

Como las *soap operas* de Estados Unidos, las telenovelas normalmente se presentan los cinco días de la semana. Pero a diferencia de las *soap operas* estadounidenses que se dan durante el día, las telenovelas se presentan típicamente en la noche cuando hay más televidentes (*viewers*). Otra diferencia es que las *soap operas* parecen seguir sin fin (*go on forever*) mientras que las telenovelas en Latinoamérica tienen normalmente unos 75 ó 100 episodios en total. Es decir, se presentan por un período de entre tres y seis meses con un final climático que nadie quiere perder (*to miss*).

4A.6 **¿Latinoamérica o Estados Unidos?** With a classmate, determine whether each statement below describes Latin America or the US with respect to soap operas.

	Latinoamérica	Estados Unidos
1. Las telenovelas no son tan populares como otros tipos de programas.	☐	☑
2. Sus telenovelas tienen una distribución mundial.	☑	☐
3. No es tan prestigioso salir en una telenovela como salir en el cine.	☐	☑
4. Las telenovelas se presentan por un tiempo limitado, por ejemplo seis meses.	☑	☐
5. Las telenovelas más populares se presentan por la noche.	☑	☐

Bien dicho

Las vocales

Every syllable in Spanish will contain a vowel. The five vowels in Spanish are **a, e, i, o,** and **u.** Spanish vowels are shorter in duration and more staccato-like (without an elongation or glide at the end) than vowels in English. These vowels are also pronounced without much variation. To correctly pronounce the Spanish vowels, you will need to drop your lower jaw a bit more than you are used to for the **a,** close your jaw some and pull your lips as if to smile to pronounce the **e** and the **i,** round your lips to correctly pronounce the **o,** and pucker them to pronounce the **u.** Practice the vowel sounds with your instructor applying these descriptors.

4A.7 **¿Español o inglés?** You will hear several words pronounced. As you hear each word, decide whether the speaker is saying a Spanish word or an English word based on the sound of the vowels.

	Español	Inglés
1.	☐	☑
2.	☑	☐
3.	☑	☐
4.	☑	☐
5.	☑	☐
6.	☐	☑
7.	☐	☑
8.	☑	☐

4A.8 **¡A pronunciar!** With a classmate, take turns reading the following statements aloud, concentrating on the appropriate pronunciation of the vowels. Provide feedback to your partner when a vowel is elongated or the physical mouth movements are not visible. When you have finished, switch sentences and repeat the activity.

1. El género de música que más me gusta es la salsa.

2. El fútbol es un deporte popular en América del Sur.

3. Las películas de horror son muy violentas.

4. Es fácil comprar películas en iTunes.

5. Héctor Galán produce documentales sobre los latinos.

6. Rafael Nadal es uno de los mejores tenistas del mundo.

7. Gerardo Rosales toca varios instrumentos de percusión.

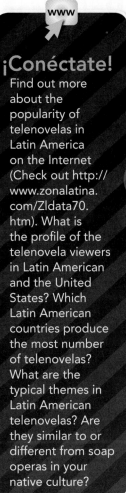

¡Conéctate!
Find out more about the popularity of telenovelas in Latin America on the Internet (Check out http://www.zonalatina.com/Zldata70.htm). What is the profile of the telenovela viewers in Latin American and the United States? Which Latin American countries produce the most number of telenovelas? What are the typical themes in Latin American telenovelas? Are they similar to or different from soap operas in your native culture?

PRONUNCIATION PRACTICE: Write out the vowels in large script on the board. After students have heard you pronounce A-E-I-O-U, have them pronounce the vowels as you point to them in random order. This can be a fast-paced activity that offers students a lot of practice. Drive home the point that unlike English, vowels in Spanish are always pronounced the same. You can do this by pointing to words that may already be visible to them and have them initially pronounce the vowels before saying the entire word (e.g., E-A-O, Es-pA-ñOl).

4A.7 AUDIO SCRIPT: 1. too, 2. tú, 3. (Spanish) me, 4. mí, 5. sí, 6. see, 7. key, 8. aquí

4A.7 FOLLOW-UP: After going over the answers, you may want to write each of the words on the board and play the recording again so that students who are strong visual learners will get more out of this activity.

Palabras clave 1 El ocio (leisure)

el baile	La salsa y el merengue son bailes populares.
el cine	La televisión, la radio, el teatro y el cine sirven para divertir al público.
la ciudad	La Ciudad de México es la segunda más poblada del mundo.
el dinero	Depositamos dinero en el banco.
el entretenimiento	La televisión es el medio de entretenimiento más popular.
la obra maestra	*Don Quijote de la Mancha* es la obra maestra de Miguel de Cervantes.
el poder	Los políticos y los ricos tienen todo el poder.
la película	*Diarios de motocicleta* es una película sobre Che Guevara.
el reguetón	La música reguetón, originalmente de Puerto Rico, es una combinación de rap, hip hop y música reggae, y es muy popular entre la juventud.

Verbos

TEACHING TIP: Total Physical Response may be used with these verbs quite easily. Give students a minute to think about how they would use gestures to evoke the verb, then have them attempt linking specific gestures to verbs in the list.

cambiar	Todas las sociedades y las culturas cambian y evolucionan con el tiempo.
divertir	Las películas cómicas divierten al público.
enfatizar	Los actores enfatizan las palabras clave en el guión *(script)*.
entrenar	Para ser un buen atleta, hay que entrenar mucho.
ir de compras	A Paris Hilton le gusta ir de compras frecuentemente por Rodeo Drive.
llorar	El público llora al final de una escena trágica.
mezclar	Para hacer una ensalada mixta es necesario mezclar el tomate y la lechuga *(lettuce)*.
pedir	Es importante pedir ayuda *(help)* cuando sufres de estrés o de depresión.
reír	Adam Sandler y Jack Black hacen reír a mucha gente porque son muy cómicos.
tener éxito	Si deseas tener éxito, tienes que trabajar mucho.
traer	Cuando hago fiestas, yo preparo la comida *(food)* y mis amigos traen las bebidas *(drinks)*.
viajar	Muchos turistas europeos viajan a España.
volver	Después de viajar mucho, me gusta volver a casa.

4A.9 MULTIPLE INTELLIGENCES: Tap into students' *kinesthetic intelligence* by having them write down the words in the word bank of activity 4A.8 in their notebooks or on a sheet of paper. Then, have them close their books. As you say the words in the lists from items 1–6, have students touch the word that describes each list. After doing this several times, have students practice in pairs.

4A.9 Asociaciones. Select the word that associates best with each of the lists in items 1–6, following the model. Compare your answers with a classmate.

películas	obras maestras	la ciudad
bailes	el dinero	el entretenimiento

el dinero 1. el peso, el dólar, el sucre, el euro

la ciudad 2. el centro, el tráfico, ir de compras, los bancos

películas 3. *El señor de los anillos*, *Batman: El caballero de la noche*, *Crónicas de Narnia*

bailes 4. la salsa, la cumbia, el cha cha cha, el reguetón

el entretenimiento 5. el teatro, el cine, la televisión, los deportes

obras maestras 6. *La noche estrellada* (Starry Night) de Van Gogh, *Romeo y Julieta* de Shakespeare, *Sopa Campbell's* de Andy Warhol

 www ¡Conéctate!
Visit http://batanga.com which has streaming radio stations in approximately two dozen genres. Listen to various stations and share your likes/dislikes with the class (e.g. *Me gusta el rock clásico, especialmente el grupo Soda Stereo. No me gusta la música reguetón.*).

4A.10 ¿Piensan igual? Complete the following sentences with people's names or with program titles. The first one is done for you as a model, but you can also provide your own favorite actor. Compare your completed statements with a classmate's, and then with the statements from the whole class. How many blanks were filled the same way? Record the most common names and titles in your **Retrato de la clase.**

1. _Tom Cruise_ siempre tiene éxito con sus películas.

2. _____ compra y compra porque tiene más dinero de lo que necesita.

3. Me gusta ver el programa _____ porque hace reír al público.

4. Yo lloro mucho cuando veo películas como _____ y _____.

5. Creo *(I believe)* que aumenta la popularidad de la música hispana porque mis amigos compran música de _____ y _____.

6. _____ cambia su apariencia en muchas de sus películas.

7. _____ entrena a atletas para las olimpiadas.

8. A _____ le gusta volver a España después de hacer sus películas.

Retrato de la clase: Según la clase, ____ siempre tiene éxito. ____ , ____ y ____ compran mucho porque son ricos. La comedia más popular para la clase es ____ ….

4A.10 FOLLOW-UP: Investigate what the most common or popular answers were for your class. For example, how many students in the class answered "Paris Hilton" for item 2? Survey the class for the most common responses and write them on the board.

EXPRESIONES ÚTILES

nadie *(no one)*	No hay nadie en la clase. Los estudiantes están en el gimnasio.
nada *(nothing)*	Nada importa más que la familia y los amigos. No me gusta nada el programa *Judge Judy*.
ninguno/a *(none)*	Ningún* grupo étnico es superior a otro. Ninguno de ustedes es del planeta Marte.
alguno/a/os/as *(some, any)*	Algunas discotecas sirven bebidas sin alcohol pero la mayoría sirve bebidas alcohólicas. ¿Hay algún* estudiante de Perú en la clase?

*When *ninguno* or *alguno* modifies a singular masculine noun, it is shortened to *ningún* or *algún*.

4A.11 ¿Estás de acuerdo? Respond to the following statements by indicating that you agree or disagree with the statement. Compare your responses with a classmate's, and write your comparisons in your **Retrato de la clase.**

Estoy de acuerdo	**No estoy de acuerdo**	
☐	☐	1. El ocio está relacionado con la decadencia de la sociedad.
☐	☐	2. El poder es más importante que el dinero.
☐	☐	3. Ningún grupo social tiene mucho poder económico y político.
☐	☐	4. Me gusta la música que mezcla ritmos de varias culturas.
☐	☐	5. Pedir dinero a los padres después de los 30 años de edad es aceptable.

Retrato de la clase: Mi compañero/a ____ y yo estamos de acuerdo con que el ocio… No estamos de acuerdo con que el poder…

4A.11 WARM-UP: Before doing this activity, have students read the graffiti *"El dinero anestesia corazones"* which came from a wall in Segovia, Spain. Ask them, *¿Están de acuerdo?* Point out that a lot of graffiti in the Spanish-speaking world revolves around political issues and soccer.

Palabras clave 2 ¿Qué pasa en el centro?

MULTIPLE INTELLIGENCES. Reach your visual learners by projecting a large image of the new vocabulary. Use the visual to add support to comprehensible input you offer your students.

TEACHING TIP: List on the board or project the English equivalents of several items from *Palabras clave*. Act out their meanings in random order and have students call out the Spanish word. As students call out the Spanish word, place a check mark next to or cross out its English equivalent on the board.

Sale del teatro a fumar.

Para entrar en el teatro, el hombre **empuja** la puerta.

El joven **grita** porque hay mucho **ruido**.

Las muchachas **vienen** en otro taxi.

Los espectadores desean **seguir** al hombre a sus asientos pero es difícil.

La mujer **sonríe** porque está contenta.

almorzar
En EE.UU. almorzamos al mediodía.

Dormimos ocho horas esta noche.

dormir

empezar
Empezamos las carreras con un disparo *(shot)*.

encontrar
Cuando estamos en el parque encontramos muchas flores bonitas.

¡En este teatro siempre conseguimos buenos asientos!

conseguir

pensar
Pensamos en nuestra familia en la Navidad.

¿Dónde están mis llaves?

perder
Perdemos las cosas
cuando estamos
ocupados.

¡Podemos ganar!

poder

traer
Traemos un sándwich
a la oficina cuando no
podemos salir a comer.

4A.12 ¿Quiénes lo hacen? Read items a–f below. You will hear a list of people that execute the actions in these statements. Indicate which action is most likely executed by each person or group of people you hear mentioned. Then, check your responses as a class. The first one is done for you as a model.

1. __f__   **a.** Tiran la pelota *(ball).*
2. __b__   **b.** Pelean por dinero.
3. __e__   **c.** Dibujan los mapas del mundo.
4. __c__   **d.** Señalan los errores.
5. __a__   **e.** Gritan mucho.
6. __d__   **f.** Sonríen sin saber por qué.

4A.13 Escoger la palabra. With a classmate, match the descriptions in a–e with the corresponding verbs in 1–10, following the model. Then, verify your answers with your classmates.

  __d__ **1.** empujar   **a.** Es más aceptado en el hockey que en otros deportes.

  __a__ **2.** pelear   **b.** Cuando levantas tu voz y más personas pueden oír *(hear).*

  __e__ **3.** seguir   **c.** Es obtener algo.

  __b__ **4.** gritar   **d.** Los papás hacen esto a sus niños en sus cochecitos *(strollers).*

  __f__ **5.** dibujar   **e.** Cuando conduces *(you drive)* tu auto, es importante hacer esto con las leyes *(laws).*

  __j__ **6.** señalar   **f.** Es similar a pintar pero sin colores.

  __i__ **7.** saltar   **g.** Cuando algo (música, voces, máquinas) está a un volumen alto.

  __c__ **8.** conseguir   **h.** Las personas positivas y felices hacen esto con mucha frecuencia.

  __h__ **9.** sonreír   **i.** A muchos niños les gusta hacer esto en sus camas.

  __g__ **10.** el ruido   **j.** Es sinónimo de *indicar.*

4A.12, 4A.13 RECYCLING: Along with verbs presented in *Palabras clave,* activities here recycle verbs whose meanings were learned in *Capítulo 3.*

4A.12 AUDIO SCRIPT AND ANSWERS: 1. los bebés, 2. los boxeadores, 3. los entrenadores, 4. los geógrafos, 5. los jugadores de vólibol, 6. los profesores de idiomas

4A.12 TEACHING TIP: It is important to take into account "wait time" when eliciting responses from your students. This will prevent the same few students from always volunteering answers.

4A.13 ALTERNATE ACTIVITY: Write the verbs and sentences on index cards and pass them out, one per student. Then, have students match themselves up (one word–one description/definition). For large classes, divide the class into two groups each with the same verbs and sentences.

EXPRESIONES ÚTILES

The following phrases are used to express obligation and correspond to English phrases like *have to*, *must*, *ought to*, and *should*, when used with an infinitive.

Tener que + infinitive	Tenemos que limitar las horas que vemos la televisión.
Hay que + infinitive	Hay que visitar a nuestra familia de vez en cuando *(occasionally)*.
Deber + infinitive	Debemos apoyar *(support)* a nuestros amigos.

4A.14 ANSWERS: Card A: 1. el/la entrenador/a, 2. el/la alcalde/alcaldesa, 3. el padre, 4. el/la tenista, 5. los participantes de *Dancing with the Stars,* 6. la modelo. Card B: 1. el/la niño/a de seis años, 2. los participantes de *American Idol,* 3. el/la criminal, 4. el/la policía, 5. el/la adolescente, 6. el/la estudiante universitario/a

WILEY
PLUS

4A.14 INSTRUCTOR'S RESOURCES: You will find blank cards for use with Activity 4A.13 in your Instructor's Resources. Completed cards are also available for use as an answer key.

4A.14 Los deberes. In groups of two, select card **A** or card **B** so that each of you has a different card. Read the **declaraciones** on your card to your partner who will provide the answer for you to write in the **respuesta** column of your card and viceversa. Check your completed cards with those of another group.

A		
los participantes de *American Idol*	el/la adolescente	el/la criminal
el/la niño/a de seis años	el/la policía	los estudiantes universitarios
Declaraciones		**Respuestas**
1. Tiene que gritar mucho.		
2. Debe conseguir la mayoría de votos.		
3. Tiene que pensar en su familia.		
4. Para tener éxito, tiene que practicar tenis cada día.		
5. Deben saber bailar bien.		
6. Siempre trae lápiz labial *(lipstick)*.		

B		
el/la alcalde/alcaldesa	el padre	el/la tenista
los participantes de *Dancing with the Stars*	el/la entrenador/a	la modelo
Declaraciones		**Respuestas**
1. Debe dormir en su cama.		
2. Tienen que cantar bien.		
3. No siempre dice la verdad.		
4. No debe perder su arma.		
5. Debe volver a su casa cada noche.		
6. Tienen que empezar el semestre en enero.		

4A.15 TEACHING TIP: You may want to model what is meant by the reference to false sentences. For example, if a student writes, *Tiro el papel en el basurero,* the sentence is logistically possible. It cannot, however, be judged as true or false. On the other hand, *En Blockbuster no hay películas* could be judged false since it is clearly illogical.

4A.15 Cierto o falso. Write two sentences, each using one of the words from the word list below. Make one sentence true and the other false. Read one of your sentences to the class to see if they guess correctly whether what you're saying is **cierto** or **falso.**

señalar	gritar	el dinero	conseguir
tirar	saltar	empujar	el ruido

¡Atención!

Periódico	does not mean periodically. Instead, it means *newspaper*. To express the meaning of *periodically* in Spanish, use **de vez en cuando.**
	El periódico *The New York Times* es muy famoso. Yo leo ese periódico de vez en cuando.
Ensayo	means *essay*, but it can also mean *rehearsal*. **Ensayar** means *to rehearse*.
	El profesor asignó un ensayo sobre los efectos de la inmigración. El club dramático tiene un ensayo esta tarde. Es importante ensayar antes de una presentación.
Lectura	does not mean lecture. Instead, it means *reading*. The Spanish word **conferencia** is used to refer to a *lecture*. A *conference* is often called a **congreso** in Spanish.
	La lectura para mañana es el capítulo 5. Me gusta asistir a las conferencias sobre la ecología. En noviembre siempre hay un congreso de profesores de lenguas.
Oficio	does not mean office. Instead, it means *occupation, profession, trade* or *vocation*. An *office* in Spanish is **oficina.**
	El oficio de carpintero es respetable y ventajoso *(advantageous).* Los empleados llegan a la oficina a las 8:30 de la mañana.
Noticia	does not mean notice. Instead, it means *news item* or *information*. In Spanish, **anuncio, aviso** or **cartel** means *notice*, and **llamar la atención** or **notar** means *to notice.*
	La noticia más importante del siglo XXI es la destrucción de las Torres Gemelas en Nueva York el 11 de septiembre de 2001. El anuncio indica cuándo y dónde es el concierto.

¡ATENCIÓN!: You may want to point out that *aviso* and *anuncio* may refer to any type of notice—printed, spoken, posted, etc., while *cartel* typically refers to a notice in the sense of a sign or poster.

4A.16 ¿Te corresponde o no? Choose the correct words according to the context and then indicate whether the following statements apply to you or not. Afterwards, as a class, tally the results.

¿Me corresponde?

Sí   No

1. Escribo muchos ~~ensayos~~/**carteles** para mis clases. ☐ ☐
2. Escucho ~~las noticias~~/**los avisos** en la radio. ☐ ☐
3. Quiero trabajar en **un oficio**/~~una oficina.~~ ☐ ☐
4. Leo **el anuncio**/~~el periódico~~ todos los días. ☐ ☐
5. No asisto a clase ~~de vez en cuando~~/**periódico.** ☐ ☐
6. Yo **noticio**/~~noto~~ que mis compañeros estudian mucho. ☐ ☐
7. Asisto a ~~las conferencias~~/~~las lecturas~~ que ofrece la universidad con frecuencia. ☐ ☐
8. Hago todas ~~las lecturas~~/**las noticias** para mis clases diariamente. ☐ ☐

4A.16 EXTENSION ACTIVITY: After students have completed this activity, have them walk around the classroom interviewing one another about the same topics. Draw their attention to how they would need to change the sentences in order to ask appropriate questions (e.g. *Escucho las...* would become *¿Escuchas las...?*)

Estructuras clave 1 Usage of the present tense

TEACHING TIP: As you present this section, give many examples and have students shout out whether the statement refers to something that happens, will happen or is happening. For example, you say *El domingo juegan los Giants de Nueva York y los Colts de Indianápolis.* Your students shout out, "will happen." Other sentences might be the following: *Leo libros en mi tiempo libre.* (happens); *Ahora mismo escribo una carta.* (is happening), etc. Remember, the more structured input we offer our students, the more they will have to hold onto in order to gain confidence in the language.

After going over this, have students put the main concepts into their own words by sharing these concepts with a partner. Often, the best teacher is a fellow student. The more opportunities we provide for students to grasp a concept, the more likely it is that they will grasp it.

We are using *ahora mismo* to reinforce the use of the present tense to express actions in progress. You may want to point out that in some varieties of Spanish, *ahora mismo* may indicate near future action.

4A.17 SUGGESTION: To further challenge more advanced students, ask them to come up with sentences with each word/phrase.

Look at the English equivalents of the present-tense Spanish sentence that follows. What observations do you have about how the present tense is used in Spanish?

Camino a la universidad.	*I walk to the university.*
	I am walking to the university.
	I will walk to the university.

The present tense may function to express an action in the simple present, to indicate an action in progress at the time the speaker makes the statement, or to express future action. The context in which a statement is made will usually indicate the appropriate interpretation. Moreover, words such as **mañana** *(tomorrow)*, **todos los días** *(every day)*, and **ahora mismo** *(right now)* are also indicators of how the speaker is using the present tense.

Ahora mismo salgo de la casa.	*I am leaving the house right now.* (action in progress)
En dos días salgo para Europa.	*In two days, I will leave for Europe.* (action in near future)
Salgo con mis amigos frecuentemente.	*I go out with my friends often.* (routine action)

4A.17 Estrategias. Read the list of words/phrases below and organize them according to the function of the present tense they would most likely cue.

| mañana | en un momento | frecuentemente | a las 9 de esta noche |
| siempre | ahora mismo | raramente | en este momento |

Cues routine action	Cues near future	Cues action in progress
siempre	mañana	ahora mismo
frecuentemente	en un momento	en este momento
raramente	a las 9 de esta noche	

4A.18 ¿Cuál es la interpretación más lógica? Select a classmate with whom you have not worked in the past and read the sentences below together. Then, identify how the present tense verb is functioning in that particular sentence, following the model. Use *Pres* to indicate that the present tense verb is functioning as the simple present tense (for routine or generalized actions), *Prog* to indicate the verb is functioning to communicate an action in progress, or *Fut* to indicate the verb is functioning to indicate a future action. Verify your answers as a class.

Prog **1.** En este momento, completamos la actividad 4A.18.

Fut **2.** Shakira tiene un concierto en Houston en dos semanas.

Pres **3.** Normalmente, Thalía no come chocolates.

Pres **4.** Muchas personas famosas, como Cristina y Oprah, quieren ayudar a la gente.

Fut **5.** Isabel Allende piensa escribir una novela nueva.

Pres **6.** Sammy Sosa vuelve a su casa cada noche para estar con su familia.

4A.19 Ahora tú. Use the following cues as a guide to create complete sentences. Then, indicate whether each sentence you created uses the present tense to express a future action, an action in progress, or a simple, generalized action. Review your answers with the class.

> Modelo: Más tarde/yo/hacer/tarea/español
>
> *Más tarde hago la tarea de español.* (future action)

1. hoy en día / mucho / países / hispano / tener / economías / frágil

2. ¿que / día / empezar / Copa del Mundo?

3. nosotros / viajar / Barcelona / próximo / año

4. clase / jugar / *Jeopardy* / dos / días

5. ¿cuántas / hora / dormir / niños / cada / noche?

4A.19 ANSWERS: 1. Hoy en día muchos países hispanos tienen economías frágiles. (simple present), 2. ¿Qué día empieza la Copa del Mundo? (future action), 3. Nosotros viajamos a Barcelona el próximo año. (future action), 4. La clase juega *Jeopardy* en dos días. (future action), 5. ¿Cuántas horas duermen los niños cada noche? (simple present)

4A.19 TEACHING TIP: Assign students to write a sentence on the board as soon as you see they have completed the assignment so that you can check accuracy with the whole class. Students may not have enough language proficiency to know to insert the articles, prepositions, maintain agreement in subjects and adjectives, etc. By reviewing together, this becomes an effective grammar instruction/input for them.

VÍVELO: CULTURA

Los valores (*values*) culturales

El valor del individuo no se evalúa de la misma manera en todas las culturas. Algunos piensan que los anglosajones tienden (*tend to*) a evaluar a la persona basándose en sus éxitos (*successes/achievements*), sus posesiones y sus cualidades exteriores como la buena apariencia, la profesión y las habilidades que posee. En contraste, en la cultura hispana, se valoran otras cosas menos materiales como los lazos (*ties*) familiares, los modales (*manners*) y la capacidad de tomar decisiones. El cariño (*affection*) y la hospitalidad que se extienden a los familiares y a los amigos reflejan el valor que tienen para los hispanos. Las cosas con una estructura rígida se perciben como mecánicas o frías, sin valor humano. Cualquier cultura que quiera tener relaciones con el mundo hispano no debe creer que este punto de vista representa una desventaja (*disadvantage*) sino que debe considerarlo como uno de los aspectos más importantes y admirables de la cultura hispana.

Claro está. No todos los hispanos piensan igual así como no todos los anglosajones piensan igual. Comparamos aquí las perspectivas más frecuentemente asociadas con las culturas hispanas y con las anglosajonas. ¿Piensas que estas generalizaciones tienen validez?

VÍVELO: CULTURA: Ask students to brainstorm their thoughts on what personal and social characteristics are valued by US culture (not necessarily personally). As students provide words and phrases in English, write them on the board in Spanish. This exercise will help prepare students for the upcoming reading in Spanish about what Hispanic cultures value.

4A.20 Comprensión. From the perspective offered in *Vívelo: Cultura*, characterize the statements below as applying to Anglo-Saxon (**A**) or Hispanic (**H**) cultural tendencies. Then, compare your responses with a classmate's and indicate whether you agree or disagree with each statement. Write down any statements about which there is consensus in your **Retrato de la clase.**

_____ **1.** La vocación o la profesión que tenemos determina nuestro valor social.

_____ **2.** Valoramos la casa grande y lujosa (*luxurious*).

_____ **3.** Valoramos al individuo más que lo que tiene.

_____ **4.** Valoramos a la familia más que el trabajo.

_____ **5.** Enfatizamos más lo humano y menos la eficiencia del sistema.

_____ **6.** Prestamos atención a los buenos modales.

_____ **7.** Notamos los éxitos del individuo.

Retrato de la clase: Según la clase, los ___ tienden a enfatizar el trabajo prestigioso mientras que (*while*) los ___ tienden a…

4A.20 ANSWERS: Based on students' opinions and experiences, answers will vary. These are possible answers based on the reading. 1. A, 2. A, 3. H, 4. H, 5. H, 6. H, 7. A. Make sure to process these answers with the class, as the discussion that ensues will be more valuable than simply accepting these answers as fact.

Estructuras clave 2 The verb *ir*

PROCESSING INSTRUCTION. One of the principles of this text is to provide students with comprehensible input so they can acquire vocabulary and grammatical structures. Take this opportunity to talk about yourself and in doing so, provide students with a lot of input. You may want to write your plans on the board, such as: *Voy a ir al cine esta noche. / El viernes, mis amigos y yo vamos a ir a un concierto. / Este fin de semana voy a leer un libro nuevo. etcétera.* Share your plans with your students, drawing their attention to the *ir a + infinitive* structure. Eventually you will want to ask them what their plans are. The next activity will provide further input in context so that students can begin recognizing and using this structure.

The verb **ir** is irregular in the present tense.

yo	**voy**
tú	**vas**
él/ella/usted	**va**
nosotros/nosotras	**vamos**
vosotros/vosotras	**vais**
ellos/ellas/ustedes	**van**

Ir can be used to indicate movement towards a destination, or movement from one place to another. The destination is often indicated with a prepositional phrase introduced by **a** *(to)*.

Alejandro González Iñárritu **va a** Nueva York con Guillermo del Toro para hablar de un nuevo proyecto cinematográfico.

Alejandro González Iñárritu is going to New York with Guillermo del Toro to talk about a new film project.

Los padres de Bob Menéndez **van a** Nueva Jersey.

Bob Menéndez's parents are going to New Jersey.

VÍVELO: LENGUA

Expressing future actions

You have seen that the present tense can express what's going to happen in the future, often with an adverbial phrase that indicates the future time frame. Another common way Spanish speakers express future actions is with **ir + a + *infinitive*** which is equivalent to the English *to be going to* + verb.

¿Qué **vas a hacer** este fin de semana?

What are you going to do this weekend?

Esta noche, ellos **van a ver** *Bajo la misma luna.*

Tonight, they are going to see Under the Same Moon.

El sábado, la profesora **va a leer** las composiciones.

On Saturday, the professor is going to read the compositions.

En mayo, **vamos a asistir** al concierto de Daddy Yankee.

In May, we are going to attend the Daddy Yankee concert.

4A.21 ¿Adónde van estas personas? Based on these people's situations, say where they are going.

_d_ **1.** Tu compañero/a de cuarto necesita estudiar.   **a.** Vas de compras.

_c_ **2.** Tus amigos quieren tomar algo.   **b.** Vamos al cine.

_e_ **3.** Tú quieres ver una película.   **c.** Van a un café.

_b_ **4.** Nosotros queremos ver una película.   **d.** Va a la biblioteca.

_a_ **5.** Yo necesito ropa *(clothes)* nueva.   **e.** Voy al cine.

4A.22 La agenda de mañana. Think about what the following people are going to do tomorrow and complete the **ir + a** expression with an appropriate infinitive/infintive phrase. Consult with three or four classmates and note any similarties or differences.

1. El presidente de EE.UU. va a…
2. El/La profesor(a) de español va a…
3. Los profesores de esta universidad van a…
4. Mis padres van a…
5. Mis compañeros de clase y yo vamos a…
6. Yo voy a…

4A.23 Este fin de semana. Poll six classmates and your instructor to find out what they are going to do at different times in the future, as indicated by the questions below. What is the most unusual response you received? After tallying the responses of the entire class, note the results in your **Retrato de la clase.**

	_____	_____	_____	_____	_____	_____	Prof.
¿Qué va(s) a hacer este fin de semana?							
¿Qué va(s) a hacer en el verano?							
¿Qué va(s) a hacer dentro de 10 años?							

Retrato de la clase: Muchos estudiantes de la clase van a… El/la profesor/a va a…

VÍVELO: CULTURA

La vida nocturna

¿Y tú qué haces para divertirte *(to have fun)* los fines de semana por la noche? En los países hispanos la vida nocturna varía de país a país, de ciudad a ciudad y de pueblo a pueblo. En las ciudades principales de España como en Madrid, por ejemplo, la gente va al centro de la ciudad para reunirse *(to get together)* con los amigos. A los españoles les gusta mucho **la marcha,** palabra que se usa en España para describir la acción de caminar con los amigos de bar en bar bebiendo y comiendo **tapas,** pequeñas porciones de comida como jamón, queso *(cheese)*, aceitunas *(olives)* y pan *(bread)*. Los españoles disfrutan *(enjoy)* mucho de la conversación, la bebida y la comida durante toda la noche hasta el amanecer *(dawn)*. En España la gente también va a discotecas y les gusta cantar karaoke.

En las ciudades principales de México y en la capital del país, los jóvenes salen a bailar a las discotecas o clubes o se reúnen a beber en un **antro** *(slang for* cantina *or* bar*)*. Los chicos salen en grupo, con sus amigos, y generalmente la diversión comienza a las once de la noche. Después de bailar por varias horas, la gente come para minimizar los efectos del alcohol. En México, la comida típica después de una noche de **pachanga** *(slang for* fiesta *or* diversión*)* son los tacos, el menudo o el **pozole***. Las personas que quieren continuar la fiesta hasta el amanecer van a escuchar la música de los mariachis en las plazas públicas.

Las costumbres en otros países hispanohablantes son similares. Los jóvenes se reúnen con sus amigos en un lugar céntrico. Después de conversar y tomar algo, los muchachos salen a bailar a discotecas o bares. Típicamente salen a bailar a las once o las doce de la noche. La fiesta puede continuar hasta las cinco o seis de la mañana. Un aspecto de la vida nocturna muy importante en toda Hispanoamérica es que una fiesta sin baile no es fiesta.

***Pozole** and **menudo** refer to a traditional hearty soup or stew made with hominy. **Pozole** can refer to the hominy itself or to a version of the stew that uses pork. **Menudo** refers specifically to a version of the stew made with beef tripe (stomach).

4A.22 TEACHING TIP: Providing students with a lot of input leads to them gaining confidence and demonstrating better accuracy when they provide their output (their speaking). As a follow-up, ask several students to report on their own responses and on the results of their discussions with classmates.

WILEY PLUS

4A.23 INSTRUCTOR'S RESOURCES: A reproducible chart for use with Activity 4A.23 is available in your Instructor's Resources.

4A.23 TEACHING TIP: As students are interviewing each other, walk around the room and listen to their questions and answers. When you hear students responding with only the infinitive, model the appropriate response using *ir + a*. For example, if you hear *"salir con mis amigos"*, say *"Voy a salir con mis amigos"*.

VÍVELO: CULTURA: Before students read this text, ask them questions about what they do on Friday or Saturday nights, their nightlife practices. For example, *¿A qué hora sales con tus amigos los fines de semana? ¿A dónde van? ¿Qué hacen? (bailan, comen, escuchan música, juegan videojuegos, navegan en la Internet, etcétera.) ¿A qué hora les gusta volver a sus casas? etcétera*. After reading the passage on *La vida nocturna*, ask students what practices are shared amongst cultures and how things differ.

Estructuras clave 3 Stem-changing verbs

WILEY PLUS

Go to *WileyPLUS* and review the tutorial for this grammar point.

WILEY PLUS

You will find PowerPoint presentations for use with *Estructuras clave* in *WileyPLUS*.

TEACHING TIP: Make sure to review the meaning of the infinitive verbs in the chart using gestures to evoke specific infinitives. The less cognitive space students use focusing on the meaning of the infinitives, the more cognitive space they can dedicate to learning/remembering their stem-changing forms.

You have been using different verb endings according to the subject of the verb. Have you noticed any other changes in some verbs? Take **preferir** for example. Look at the difference in the verb stem, rather than the ending, between **yo prefiero** and **nosotros preferimos.** We will now look more closely at verbs that maintain the regular verb endings but have changes in their verb stems.

Here we present three types of verb stem changes. Since you have practiced the meaning of most of these verbs, you will find it easier to focus on the stem changes. As you look at the sample sentences below, note which subject forms *do not* carry the stem change.

e ⟶ ie Verbs with an **e** in the stem that changes to **ie**	**Querer** *(to want)* Yo **qu*ie*ro** ir a mi clase de español. ¿Tú también **qu*ie*res** ir? Mi amigo **qu*ie*re** ir. ¡Todos **queremos** ir! ¿Vosotros **queréis** ir al cine? Mis amigos **qu*ie*ren** ir también.	Additional e ⟶ ie verbs cerrar pensar divertir perder empezar preferir
o ⟶ ue Verbs with an **o** in the stem that changes to **ue**	**Dormir** Yo **d*ue*rmo** bien. Y tú, ¿**d*ue*rmes** bien? Y Ud. ¿**d*ue*rme** bien? No todos **dormimos** bien. ¿Vosotras **dormís** bien? Mis padres **d*ue*rmen** bien.	Additional o ⟶ ue verbs almorzar mover volver contar *(to count)* poder jugar* *Note that with *jugar* the change is *u* ⟶ *ue*.
e ⟶ i Verbs with an **e** in the stem that changes to **i**	**Repetir** Yo **rep*i*to** el vocabulario. Y tú, ¿**rep*i*tes** el vocabulario? Y ella, ¿**rep*i*te** el vocabulario? No todos **repetimos** el vocabulario. Vosotros **repetís** después de la profesora. Ellos no **rep*i*ten** el vocabulario.	Additional e ⟶ i verbs pedir seguir servir conseguir *(to obtain)*

If you noted that the verb forms for **nosotros/nosotras** and **vosotros/vosotras** do not have the change in their stem, you are correct!

4A.24 AUDIO SCRIPT: 1. Prefiere escuchar ópera en lugar de bailar salsa o reguetón. 2. Empieza a cantar en inglés con la canción "La vida loca." 3. Perdemos nuestros libros si no tenemos mochila. 4. Cierran las puertas del concierto de Juanes cuando él empieza a cantar. 5. Muchos del público piensan que soy fea.

4A.24 ¿Quién? First, read the options a–e below. You will hear statements about these people or groups of people. As you hear each statement, determine which person or group of people it refers to. The first one is done for you as a model. Verify your answers as a class.

1. ___*c*___   **a.** La policía y los guardias
2. ___c___   **b.** Nosotros los estudiantes
3. ___b___   **c.** Ricky Martin
4. ___a___   **d.** El personaje de "Betty" (América Ferrera)
5. ___d___   **e.** Plácido Domingo

4A.25 ¿Quién dice eso? In groups of three, match the following statements with the celebrities who would most likely make them. Verify your responses with another group of classmates.

4A.25 TEACHING TIP: By increasing the group size, you increase the chance of at least one student recognizing a name from the list in a–h. Before having students match personalities to statements, ask students to tell how they know these famous figures.

a. Benjamin Bratt

b. Marysol Castro

c. Rosario Dawson

d. George López y Constance Marie

e. Carlos Mencia

f. Los Lobos

g. Álex Rodríguez (A-Rod)

h. Roselyn Sánchez y Enrique Murciano

___e___ **1.** Me divierto mucho en mi programa de Comedy Central.

___f___ **2.** Nos movemos al ritmo de *La Bamba*.

___h___ **3.** Encontramos a muchas personas que desaparecen en nuestro programa *Without a Trace*.

___b___ **4.** No duermo mucho porque trabajo en *Good Morning America*.

___g___ **5.** Derek Jeter juega conmigo en el equipo de los Yankees.

___c___ **6.** ¿Quieres ver mis películas *He Got Game, Sin City* y *Rent*?

___d___ **7.** En nuestro programa representamos a una familia mexico-americana.

___a___ **8.** Yo salgo en muchos episodios del programa *Law and Order*.

4A.26 ¿Quién de la clase? Survey your classmates to find out to whom in the class each statement applies. If your classmate responds **Sí**, ask him or her to sign on the appropriate line. Be sure to ask the questions in the **tú** form, and you should respond using the **yo** form when you are asked a question. Tally the number of positive responses for each item and record the results in your **Retrato de la clase.**

Modelo: E1: *¿Almuerzas en el Centro Estudiantil de la universidad?*
E2: *Sí, almuerzo allí.* or *No, no almuerzo allí.*

¿Quién de la clase...

1. almuerza en el Centro Estudiantil? _____

2. duerme menos de siete horas normalmente? _____

3. puede tocar el piano? _____

4. juega al tenis? _____

5. prefiere bailar más que escuchar música? _____

6. quiere viajar a la Argentina? _____

7. sirve comida en un restaurante? _____

8. vuelve a casa antes de la medianoche los sábados? _____

Retrato de la clase: La mayoría de los estudiantes de la clase de español almuerza en ____. Duerme más de/menos de ____ horas. Toca/No toca el piano. Etcétera.

4A.27 TEACHING TIP:
Most of the vocabulary used here is familiar or easily gleaned from context. Help students with any challenging words. Limit students to no more than three initials from the same person in order to encourage them to talk to many classmates. You may want to have them work at this until most students have completed most of the board, or wait until you have had several students complete a *bingo* line. For Bingo winners, reward them in some way.

WILEY
PLUS

4A.27 INSTRUCTOR'S RESOURCES: A reproducible "Bingo" card for Activity 4A.27 is available in your Instructor's Resources.

4A.27 Bingo. Learn more about your classmates by turning these statements into questions. As your classmates answer affirmatively, have them initial the corresponding box. Make sure to talk to as many people as possible and to turn the statements into questions. Once you have initials from classmates in a complete horizontal, vertical, or diagonal row, hold up your paper and say **"¡Bingo!"**.

Cree que el precio de la gasolina va a aumentar mucho este año.	Escucha reguetón en la radio.	Tiene que entrenar con su equipo más de dos veces por semana.	Cambia de lugar en el cine si hay personas cerca que hablan.	Trae su celular a clase todos los días.
No es de esta ciudad.	Va al cine todas las semanas.	Cree que el dinero no es lo más importante en la vida.	Cree que esta ciudad no tiene suficiente entretenimiento.	No tiene mucho éxito con las matemáticas.
Cree que es normal reírse del humor de George López.	Divierte a sus amigos con su sentido de humor.	GRATIS	No le gusta ir de compras.	Sus padres enfatizan la importancia de ganar mucho dinero.
No trae su tarea a clase todos los días.	Viaja con bastante frecuencia.	Quiere viajar a un país hispanohablante.	Su familia escucha cumbias.	Nunca pide dinero a sus padres.
Entrena con sus amigos.	Le gusta mezclar ingredientes diferentes en una ensalada.	Le gustan las películas románticas.	Llora con las escenas tristes de las películas.	Vuelve a casa después de esta clase.

4A.28 Completar la narración.

Paso 1: With a classmate, fill in the blanks with the correct conjugation of the verb provided.

Cuando necesito dinero, yo (encontrar) __encuentro__ a mi mamá. Yo le (pedir) __pido__
                                           1   2
unos 500 dólares y (querer) __quiero__ el dinero en dólares y no euros. Cuando llegan
                                 3
mis amigos, (nosotros) (pensar) __pensamos__ que somos ricos y vamos a un restaurante
                                      4
muy chévere *("cool")*. Nosotros (pedir) __pedimos__ los platos más caros *(expensive)*.
                                              5
No importa cuándo (cerrar) __cierra__ el bar porque (nosotros) (seguir) __seguimos__
                                6   7
pidiendo cervezas. Cuando (yo) (empezar) __empiezo__ a repetir las palabras de mi
                                               8
amigo, sé que es hora de volver a casa. Todos __tomamos__ (tomar) un taxi y (regresar)
                                                      9
__regresamos__ a mi casa después de las dos de la mañana. Yo siempre me (divertir) __divierto__
     10   11
mucho cuando estoy con mis amigos. ¿Y tú?

Paso 2: Select the most logical conclusions to the above passage.

☐ El párrafo describe a un joven típico.

☐ El párrafo describe el comportamiento de un estudiante irresponsable.

☐ El párrafo describe el comportamiento de un adulto responsable.

☐ El párrafo describe a un joven religioso.

VÍVELO: LENGUA

Expressing destination and origin: *A* y *de*

The meaning of some verbs can change depending on the preposition that follows them. For example, when verbs that convey motion precede **a**, the motion is directed *to* or *toward* a destination. When these verbs precede **de,** the motion is directed *from* a point of departure or place of origin.

A: Destination *(to, toward)*

salir a	**Salimos al** restaurante para comer los viernes por la noche.
venir a	Mis amigos **vienen a** mi casa para ver una película.

De: Point of departure/place of origin *(from)*

salir de	Ellos **salen de** clase cuando el profesor termina de hablar.
venir de	Mi mamá **viene de** Bolivia. Es boliviana.

Pay close attention to the prepositions following verbs as they can really impact the meaning of a sentence.

4A.29 Adivina. Can you guess the meaning of the following phrases just based on the preposition used? Verify your answers with a classmate.

1. Mis amigos *vienen de* Ecuador.
☑ come from
☐ come to

2. Mis amigos *vienen a* Los Ángeles este verano.
☐ are coming from
☑ are coming to

3. Jenny *sale a* las discotecas los fines de semana.
☑ goes out to
☐ leaves from

4. Mi perro *sale de* mi casa todos los días.
☐ goes out to
☑ leaves from

Enlaces

These expressions provide cohesion within or between sentences and paragraphs.

por eso	Para tener éxito, los inmigrantes en Estados Unidos deben aprender inglés. **Por eso** muchos de ellos estudian inglés por la noche después de trabajar.
en otras palabras	Los hijos de inmigrantes en Estados Unidos empiezan a integrarse en la cultura estadounidense; **en otras palabras** empiezan a formar una cultura entre su cultura nativa y la cultura estadounidense.
por esa razón	La tercera generación de hijos de inmigrantes frecuentemente no habla español porque la asimilación a la cultura estadounidense es completa. **Por esa razón,** estas generaciones no se identifican con la cultura hispana, que es la cultura de sus abuelos.

4A.30 Enlaces. Read the sentences above that provide a context for the *Enlaces* expressions. Then, determine which of the expressions corresponds to each of these English phrases. Verify your responses with the class.

1. for this reason _____

2. said another way _____

3. that is why _____

ENLACES: Share with students the impact that these *expresiones* can have on how native speakers interpret their communication skills. They will be able to express themselves much better if they begin incorporating these expressions.

4A.30 ANSWERS: 1. por esa razón, 2. en otras palabras, 3. por eso. You may want to accept *por eso* and *por esa razón* interchangeably for items 1 and 3. You may also want to challenge students to give you another English equivalent for *en otras palabras,* literally, "in other words".

4A.31 **Antes de leer.** Read the title of the following article and briefly scan it to predict the nature of its content. Indicate what you think this article will be about.

- ☑ The influence of Hispanic culture on US culture
- ☐ The popularity of US culture in Mexico
- ☐ The coming together of two cultures along the Mexico-Texas border

La presencia latina se siente más y más en Estados Unidos

En Estados Unidos, por un lado hablamos de un "melting pot" y, por otro lado, la cultura estadounidense refleja los valores anglosajones. En la actualidad, la importancia de la cultura latina es considerable en Estados Unidos y su influencia es cada vez mayor. **Por eso,** ahora hablamos de las influencias latinas en la cultura de Estados Unidos. Por ejemplo, Marc Anthony y la salsa son de Nueva York. **Por esa razón,** él cree que es ridículo tener que buscar sus discos en la sección "internacional" en las tiendas de música.

Sabemos que lo latino tiene mucho éxito en Estados Unidos. La música reguetón no sólo es popular entre los latinos, sino que ahora se escucha en las estaciones de radio más populares. Si quieres bailar salsa, es fácil encontrar una discoteca donde puedes salir a bailar con tus amigos. **En otras palabras,** el interés por lo latino aumenta y la cultura latina tiene mucho éxito. Hay muchos beneficios por el aumento de la influencia latina en la cultura estadounidense. Pero también hay resistencia a las cosas nuevas o diferentes. Esta resistencia puede causar xenofobia que resulta en sentimientos anti-inmigrantes y anti-hispanos. Lo bueno es que ahora no sólo hay artistas latinos que cantan en inglés y español, sino que también hay artistas estadounidenses, como Beyoncé, que cantan en español para llegar a un público más numeroso.

Concierto de Juanes en Milwaukee

4A.32 Después de leer. Answer the following questions as a class based on the reading on page 178.

1. ¿Es la cultura latina parte de la cultura estadounidense?

2. ¿Por qué se frustra Marc Anthony cuando tiene que buscar sus álbumes en las tiendas de música?

3. ¿Cuáles son dos géneros de música mencionados en el artículo?

4. La resistencia a culturas "diferentes" puede causar diferentes consecuencias. ¿Cuáles son?

5. ¿Se resiste Beyoncé a cantar en español?

Donde tu vives, ¿dónde hay letreros (*signs*) en inglés y español? ¿Qué dicen?

Perspectivas

4A.33 **Las fotos revelan.** In *Contextos*, we explored Hispanic influences in US culture. What about US cultural influences in Hispanic cultures? Examine these photos to determine where US influences can be seen in Hispanic countries and discuss them as a class. Then, bring images or examples of other US influences on Hispanic cultures to the next class session.

4A.33 TEACHING TIP: Ask students what influences US culture might have on people around the world. Share with them that often the rest of the world knows a lot about us but we, as a country, do not know as much about our neighbors. Share with them that having movies and TV shows in English helps people in other countries develop their English skills.

Vocabulario: Investigación A

Vocabulario esencial

Sustantivos

el baile	*dance*
el cine	*cinema*
la ciudad	*city*
el dinero	*money*
la diversión	*fun*
el entretenimiento	*entertainment*
la ley	*law*
la llave	*key*
el ocio	*leisure*
la película	*movie*
el ruido	*noise*
las noticias	*news*
la plaza	*square*

Adjetivos

caro	*expensive*
cerca	*close*
contento	*happy*
fácil	*easy*
feliz	*happy*
próximo	*next*

Verbos

almorzar	*to have lunch*
cambiar	*to change*
cerrar	*to close*
conseguir	*to obtain*
contar	*to count*
divertir	*to entertain*
dormir	*to sleep*
empezar	*to start*
empujar	*to push*
encontrar	*to find*
ganar	*to win; to earn*
gritar	*to scream*
ir	*to go*
ir de compras	*to go shopping*
jugar	*to play*
llorar	*to cry*
mezclar	*to mix*
mover	*to move*
pedir	*to ask for*
pensar	*to think*

perder	*to lose*
poder	*to be able to*
querer	*to want*
reír	*to laugh*
repetir	*to repeat*
seguir	*to follow*
servir	*to serve*
sonreír	*to smile*
tener éxito	*to succeed*
traer	*to bring*
viajar	*to travel*
volver	*to return*

Adverbios

ahora	*now*
tarde	*late*

Otras palabras y expresiones

alguno/a	*some, any*
apoyar	*to support*
el campeonato	*championship*
la ciudadanía	*citizenship*
conducir	*to drive*
el corazón	*heart*
creer	*to believe*
descansar	*to rest*
el disparo	*shot*
la desventaja	*disadvantage*
el/la entrenador/a	*trainer*
el equipo	*team*
la flor	*flower*
fumar	*to smoke*
la juventud	*youth*
la meta	*goal*
poder	*power*
la publicidad	*advertising*
el punto	*point*
el punto de vista	*point of view*
rodear	*to surround*
el sentido de humor	*sense of humor*
sostener	*to support; to hold*
ahora mismo	*right now*
de la misma manera	*in the same way*

de vez en cuando	*occasionally*
deber + *infinitive*	*should + infinitive*
hay que	*to have to*
mientras que	*while*
por ejemplo	*for example*
prestar atención	*pay attention*

Cognados

Review the cognates in *Adelante* and the false cognates in *¡Atención!*. For a complete list of cognates, see Appendix 4 on page 605.

¿En qué profesiones ayuda hablar español?

In this **Investigación** you will learn…

▶ How to talk about jobs, professions and places of employment

▶ How to talk about what people do at work

▶ About the population of Hispanics in the US

▶ About the professional benefits of learning Spanish

¿Cómo se puede hablar de los beneficios vocacionales y profesionales de hablar español?

You can identify various professions, trades and vocations where Spanish is highly beneficial.	la medicina, la arquitectura, la ingeniería el policía, el carpintero, el cocinero
You can talk about what people do in their careers or jobs.	Los médicos trabajan en hospitales o clínicas y ayudan a los enfermos. Los arquitectos construyen edificios. Los ingenieros diseñan puentes y túneles.
You can find out in which careers it is beneficial to speak Spanish. Will this be true for these same careers in the future?	Obviamente es beneficioso hablar español en la medicina y esto no va a cambiar en el futuro.

TEACHING TIP: Have students call out names of well-known people in various professions to verify the meaning of the vocabulary word, i.e., Sigmund Freud (*psiquiatra*), Anderson Cooper (*reportero, comentarista, corresponsal*), Carl Sagan (*astrónomo*). Students will likely be able to recognize the words in these categories with ease, while struggling with the pronunciation. To model good pronunciation, read through the various professions as you elicit responses (i.e. *¿Saben el nombre de un lingüista famoso?*)

Ask students questions, such as *¿Hay profesores en la universidad o en la plaza? ¿Hay médicos en una clínica o en un banco? ¿Hay atletas en un gimnasio o en un hotel? ¿Hay secretarias en una oficina o en una farmacia?*, etc. as a way to have them hear the pronunciation of the vocabulary words in meaningful contexts before working with them.

Ask students, *¿Quién arresta? (¿un policía o un médico?) ¿Quién excava? (¿un recepcionista o un antropólogo?) ¿Quién inventa? (¿un científico o un taxista?)*

Adelante

¡Ya lo sabes! Profesiones, oficios y lugares de trabajo

La medicina

el/la administrador/a del hospital
el/la dentista
el/la doctor/a
el/la farmacéutico/a
el/la psicólogo/a
el/la psiquiatra
el/la veterinario/a

La educación

el/la directora/a
el/la maestro/a de educación física

Las letras y las humanidades

el/la filósofo/a
el/la lingüista

Las ciencias sociales

el/la antropólogo/a
el/la sociólogo/a

Las ciencias naturales

el/la agricultor/a
el/la astrónomo/a
el/la biólogo/a
el/la físico/a
el/la geólogo/a
el/la químico/a

Las comunicaciones

el/la columnista
el/la comentarista
el/la corresponsal
el/la fotógrafo/a
el/la reportero/a

Vocaciones y oficios

el/la carpintero/a
el/la conductor/a de autobús
el/la electricista
el/la empleado/a
el/la mecánico/a
el/la ministro/a
el/la piloto
el/la policía
el/la recepcionista
el/la secretario/a
el/la taxista

Lugares de trabajo

el banco
el centro comercial
la clínica
la compañía
el consultorio
la corte
la farmacia

el hospital
el hotel
el laboratorio
la oficina
la plaza
el restaurante

Acciones

administrar
analizar
arrestar
construir
dictar
documentar
excavar
inventar
investigar
observar
organizar
plantar
reservar

4B.1 **¡A categorizar las palabras!** As a class, indicate with which category each of the following words is associated.

la bióloga
el carpintero
el centro comercial
la clínica
el conductor de autobús

la dentista
la doctora
la electricista
el hospital
el banco

el piloto
el químico
el recepcionista
la secretaria
el taxista

El transporte	La oficina	Los servicios de salud *(health)*
El comercio	La construcción	El laboratorio

4B.1 ANSWERS: El transporte: el conductor de autobús, el piloto, el taxista; La oficina: el recepcionista, la secretaria; Los servicios de salud: la clínica, la dentista, la doctora, el hospital; El comercio: el centro comercial, el banco; La construcción: el carpintero, la electricista; El laboratorio: la bióloga, el químico

WILEY
PLUS

4B.1 INSTRUCTOR'S RESOURCES: You will find a reproducible chart for Activity 4B.1 in your Instructor's Resources.

4B.2 **No pertenece.** Indicate which word does not belong in the list based on the categories provided. Then check your work as a class.

1. la universidad
☐ la profesora
☑ el piloto
☐ el laboratorio
☐ el gimnasio

2. la profesión
☑ el gimnasio
☐ la veterinaria
☐ el corresponsal
☐ la lingüista

3. la farmacia
☐ las vitaminas
☐ la medicina
☐ la pasta dental
☑ la corte

4. el banco
☑ las medicinas
☐ el dinero
☐ los depósitos
☐ los cheques

5. poner en orden
☐ ordenar
☐ organizar
☑ observar
☐ enumerar

4B.2 FOLLOW-UP: As you go over the answers offer students more comprehensible input. The following questions are examples of what you might ask: *¿Cuántos gimnasios hay en esta universidad? ¿Alguien quiere ser veterinaria/o? ¿Qué vitaminas son populares?* etc. The objective is to give students a chance to hear these words pronounced in context.

4B.3 **Lógico o ilógico.** You will hear several statements. As you listen to each statement, indicate whether it is **lógico** or **ilógico.** Then, compare your responses with those of a classmate.

	Lógico	Ilógico		Lógico	Ilógico
1.	☐	☑	**4.**	☑	☐
2.	☐	☑	**5.**	☐	☑
3.	☐	☑	**6.**	☑	☐

4B.3 AUDIO SCRIPT AND ANSWERS: 1. Los doctores trabajan en restaurantes. 2. Los profesores trabajan en la plaza. 3. Los biólogos trabajan en la clase. 4. Los recepcionistas trabajan en hoteles. 5. Los policías trabajan en las farmacias. 6. Los veterinarios trabajan en las clínicas para animales.

4B.3 FOLLOW-UP: As you go over the answers, refer to the illogical statements and ask students follow-up questions like *Entonces, ¿dónde trabajan los doctores?*

4B.4 **¿Ya sabes qué hacen?** With a classmate, select the most appropriate verb to complete each statement below. **¡Ojo!** Remember to conjugate the verb according to the subject of the sentence. Compare your responses with those of two other students.

contestar
observar

documentar
plantar

investigar
dictar

arrestar
excavar

1. El/La policía _____ arresta _____ a individuos acusados de delitos *(crime)*.

2. El/La reportero/a __ investiga/documenta __ los sucesos históricos y los incidentes notables.

3. El dueño *(owner)* de la compañía _____ dicta _____ las cartas a su secretaria.

4. El agricultor _____ excava _____ la tierra para plantar verduras *(vegetables)*.

5. El/La recepcionista _____ contesta _____ el teléfono.

6. El/La psiquiatra _____ observa _____ a sus pacientes.

4B.4 EXPANSION: As you go through the answers, ask additional questions related to these statements (e.g. *¿Qué más hace el recepcionista?*)

EXPRESIONES ÚTILES

Expresiones útiles con *para*

Para ser...   *In order to be...*

Para ser doctora, es necesario estudiar biología y anatomía.
Para ser mecánico, uno tiene que saber mucho de los autos.

Estudiar para...   *To study to be...*

Queremos diseñar casas, así que estudiamos para arquitectos.
Si te gustan las lenguas, puedes estudiar para lingüista.

Trabajar para...   *To work for (be employed by)...*

Soy farmacéutico y trabajo para CVS.
Paco estudia para piloto y quiere trabajar para American Airlines.

4B.5 EXPANSION: As you go over the answers with students, create further opportunities to use the items these professions use (e.g. ¿Qué otra profesión usa herramientas?)

4B.5 **Para trabajar.**   Take turns with a partner asking each other the questions below. Use the drawings and words next to them to answer the questions. Then, verify your answers with the rest of the class.

Modelo: E1: *¿Qué usa la profesora para su trabajo?*
          E2: *Para su trabajo, la profesora usa un libro (g) o una computadora (h).*

a.
el taxi

b.
el aceite para el auto

c.
el avión

d.
el carro

e.
las herramientas

f.
el autobús

g.
el libro

h.
la computadora

1. ¿Qué usa el plomero para su trabajo? e
2. ¿Qué usa el policía para su trabajo? d
3. ¿Qué usa el taxista para su trabajo? a
4. ¿Qué usa el piloto para su trabajo? c
5. ¿Qué usa el conductor de autobús para su trabajo? f
6. ¿Qué usa el mecánico para su trabajo? b e

4B.5 ORIENTATION: The words introduced with the illustrations in Activity 4B.5 are given solely for the purpose of providing context for recognition of the various occupations. These items are not intended as new vocabulary to be assimilated at this time.

4B.6 **Orgullos hispanos.** Complete the following sentences with the most appropriate word. Then, compare your answers with at least three other classmates. As a class, report the items with the most varied answers.

1. Walter Clement Álvarez es doctor y escribe libros de medicina. Para ser doctor/a, es necesario ser…

   ☐ atractivo

   ☐ elegante

   ☑ paciente

¿En qué lugares es necesario un anuncio como este?

2. El mexicano Carlos Fuentes escribe novelas y cuentos y es conocido por todo el mundo. Para ser escritor/a, es necesario ser…

   ☐ metódico

   ☑ imaginativo

   ☐ malévolo

Have students say where they would expect to see a sign like this: en un restaurante, en un hospital, en un laboratorio, en una clínica…

3. Judith Baca es artista y profesora en UCLA. Para ser profesora, es necesario ser…

   ☐ agresiva

   ☐ vulnerable

   ☑ interesante

4. Ken Salazar es un político hispano en EE.UU. Para ser político, es necesario ser…

   ☐ tenso

   ☐ famoso

   ☑ inteligente

5. Rubén García se asocia con el FBI. Para ser agente o detective, es necesario ser…

   ☐ social

   ☑ metódico

   ☐ ambicioso

EXPRESIONES ÚTILES

trabajar a tiempo completo   *to work full time*

Es muy difícil trabajar a tiempo completo y también ser estudiante universitario.

trabajar a tiempo parcial   *to work part time*

Muchos restaurantes emplean estudiantes que trabajan a tiempo parcial.

dejar de + *infintivo*   *to stop* (doing something)

Para dejar de llegar tarde al trabajo, compra un despertador (*alarm clock*).

despedir a   *to dismiss/to fire*

Nadie desea despedir a una madre soltera.

Jorge Ramos

Before reading the following passage about Jorge Ramos, scan the words and phrases that are highlighted in bold to get a general idea about the type of information that the passage contains.

Jorge Gilberto Ramos Ávalos no nació en Estados Unidos. Nació en México. Ramos **es bilingüe** y es considerado uno de "los 25 hispanos más influyentes de Estados Unidos" (revista *Time*). La revista *Latino Leaders* dice que **es uno de "los 10 latinos más admirados en Estados Unidos"** y uno de los "101 líderes de la comunidad hispana". *People en Español* lo incluye en su lista de los **100 latinos de mayor influencia en Norteamérica.** Es el personaje de la televisión en español en Estados Unidos que más tiempo ha estado en el aire de manera ininterrumpida en un mismo programa noticiero y todavía trabaja para Univisón a tiempo completo.

Ramos, el mayor de una familia de cinco hermanos, **llega a** la ciudad de **Los Ángeles** como estudiante en enero de 1983. Ahí comienza su aventura estadounidense. Ya en Estados Unidos, **estudia** un curso especializado en **televisión y periodismo** (*journalism*) de la Universidad de California en los Ángeles (**UCLA**) y más tarde obtiene **una maestría en relaciones internacionales** de la **Universidad de Miami.** Desde **1991 vive en Miami.**

Como **locutor** (*newscaster*) **del programa de noticias de Univisión,** Ramos ha cubierto (*covered*) **cinco guerras** (El Salvador, el Golfo Pérsico, Kosovo, Afganistán e Irak), numerosos eventos históricos —los actos terroristas del 11 de septiembre de 2001, la caída (*fall*) del muro de Berlín, el fin del apartheid en Sudáfrica, la desintegración de la Unión Soviética, cumbres (*summits*) iberoamericanas, movimientos guerrilleros en Chiapas y Centroamérica, elecciones en casi todo el continente— y **desastres naturales,** incluyendo la catástrofe causada por el huracán Katrina. **Escribe** una **columna** semanal **en más de 40 diarios del hemisferio** (que distribuye *The New York Times Syndicate*) y participa en el sitio de la Internet en español más grande en Estados Unidos (www.univision.com). Hasta hoy ha escrito **nueve libros** y ha ganado más de **15 premios** (*awards*).

READING STRATEGY:
Remind students that they do not need to understand everything in order to get the gist of the reading. They should look for words they know, cognates and how unfamiliar vocabulary is used in context. Encourage them to make an outline of the main points of the reading.

4B.7 AUDIO SCRIPT AND ANSWERS: 1. Jorge Ramos es originalmente de EE.UU. (Falso. Es de México.), 2. Jorge Ramos es un periodista, locutor y autor famoso. 3. Jorge

4B.7 **Jorge Ramos.** You will hear several statemtents about Jorge Ramos. Based on what you read about him, indicate whether each statement is **cierto** or **falso.** Correct any false statements.

	Cierto	Falso
1.	☐	☑
2.	☑	☐
3.	☑	☐
4.	☐	☑
5.	☑	☐

Ramos nunca deja de documentar los eventos importantes del mundo. 4. Jorge Ramos escribe para periódicos como el National Enquirer. (Falso. Escribe una columna semanal en más de 40 diarios del hemisferio.), 5. Jorge Ramos es un líder hispano en EE.UU.

4B.7 TEACHING TIP: Encourage students to complete this activity on their own before going back to the reading. Once they have finished, they can look at the reading and make changes. After you have gone through the answers as a class, see how they did on each successive turn.

🎧 Bien dicho

Más sobre las vocales

In *Investigación 4A* you learned about the five vowels in Spanish. These vowels can be divided into strong vowels and weak vowels. The strong vowels are **a, e** and **o.** The weak vowels are **i** and **u.** A strong vowel and a weak vowel, or two weak vowels may work together in a syllable to form a single sound called a diphthong. A written accent mark over the weak vowel in a pair signals that no diphthong is formed, and the vowels belong to different syllables. A written accent mark over the strong vowel in a diphthong simply indicates that stress falls on that syllable of the word.

Diphthong (Same syllable, single sound)	**No diphthong** (Different syllables, separate sounds)
ciencia ⟶ ci**ēn**-cia	día ⟶ d**ī-a**
agua ⟶ ā-g**ua**	Raúl ⟶ ra-**ūl**
Europa ⟶ **eu**-rō-pa	guía ⟶ gu**ī-a**
oigo ⟶ **ōi**-go	
farmacéutico ⟶ far-ma-c**ēu**-ti-co	
ciudad ⟶ c**iu**-dād	

4B.8 🎧 **¿Hay diptongo o no?**   Repeat each word as you hear it pronounced. Then indicate whether the word has a diphthong or not. If there is no diphthong, write an accent mark over the appropriate stressed **i** or **u.** Verify your responses with a classmate.

	¿Diptongo? Sí No			**¿Diptongo?** Sí No
1. oír	☐ ☑	**7.** baúl	☐ ☑
2. cuota	☑ ☐	**8.** reina	☑ ☐
3. ciudad	☑ ☐	**9.** pausa	☑ ☐
4. reíste	☐ ☑	**10.** me gradúo	☐ ☑
5. mío	☐ ☑	**11.** farmacia	☑ ☐
6. luego	☑ ☐	**12.** grúa	☐ ☑

4B.9 **Busquen los diptongos.**   With a classmate, locate the diphthongs in the following sentences. Then take turns reading the sentences, concentrating on the appropriate pronunciation of the vowels and diphthongs. Provide feedback to your classmate when a vowel is elongated or the diphthong is missing. Switch roles and repeat the activity. Can you guess what these names have in common? **¡Ojo!** One of the sentences does not contain diphthongs.

1. Cristina Saralegui nunca despide a sus empleados leales.

2. Cristina tiene su propio programa en la cadena Univisión.

3. Elizabeth Vargas es una corresponsal de tiempo parcial y locutora de la cadena ABC.

4. Juan García es psicólogo y descubrió la aversión condicionada al sabor *(taste).*

5. Adriana Ocampo es geóloga y estudia el impacto de asteroides en la Tierra.

6. Ellen Ochoa es astronauta y voló en el transbordador espacial tres veces.

7. Severo Ochoa es bioquímico y ganó un premio Nobel por sus investigaciones.

8. Luis Álvarez es físico y él también ganó un premio Nobel por su trabajo.

4B.9 RECYCLING: Linking. Students learned about linking between words in Capítulo 2. You may want to have them identify places in the sentences in Activity 4B.9 where vowels end and begin adjacent words, and in each situation determine whether there is a single vowel sound *(cadena ABC)*, a smooth transition between separate vowel sounds *(despide a sus empleados)*, or a diphthong *(cadena Univisión)*.

NOTE: One of the goals throughout this text is to introduce students to issues of pronunciation and intonation. Take advantage of this to begin drawing attention to diphthongs.

4B.8 TEACHING TIP: When drawing attention to how words are divided into syllables, have students punch out each syllable. After pronouncing a word, with them repeating and punching out the syllables, ask them how many syllables there are. Follow up by asking which syllable is stressed. This will help you draw attention to accent marks, and to make a distinction between the words that have diphthongs and those that do not.

4B.9 ANSWERS: 1. Cristina Saralegui nunca despide a sus empleados leales. 2. Cristina t**ie**ne su prop**io** programa en la cadena Univis**ió**n. 3. Elizabeth Vargas es una corresponsal de t**ie**mpo parc**ia**l y locutora de la cadena ABC. 4. J**ua**n García es psicólogo y descubr**ió** la avers**ió**n condic**io**nada al sabor *(taste).* 5. Adr**ia**na Ocampo es geóloga y estud**ia** el impacto de aster**oi**des en la T**ie**rra. 6. Ellen Ochoa es astron**au**ta y voló en el transbordador espac**ia**l tres veces. 7. Severo Ochoa es b**io**químico y ganó un prem**io** Nobel por sus investigac**io**nes. 8. L**ui**s Álvarez es físico y él tamb**ié**n ganó un prem**io** Nobel por su trabajo.

4B.9 SUGGESTION: You may want to have students listen and repeat the sentences before beginning the activity on their own.

Palabras clave 1 Profesiones, vocaciones y lugares

TEACHING TIP: Ask students to develop gestures or act out the meaning of the verbs as a way to review these verbs. Also, instead of having students refer to the end of the chapter for the English translations of the words, have them work in groups to guess the meaning of the word on the basis of its use in these sentences.

4B.10 TEACHING TIP: Walk around the room and interact with students as they categorize the new vocabulary.

4B.10 Profesiones, vocaciones y lugares. In groups of two, fill in the vocabulary words that fit under each of the categories below. Some words will be used more than once. Then, compare your lists with another pair of classmates.

Proveer productos y servicios	Oficio peligroso *(dangerous)*	Trabajar al aire libre	Trabajar en una oficina	Proveer servicio físico	Sin categoría

Mi abuela no habla inglés. Yo voy a traducir.

La gente va a la iglesia a oír el sermón y a rezar.

el enfermero

El enfermero ayuda a la paciente.

Los carteros vuelven a correos al fin del día.

la cartera

el cartero

La abogada sale del juicio con su cliente.

la abogada

Es importante decir la verdad y no mentir.

Los bomberos responden a una llamada.

El hombre lee las noticias en el periódico.

El hombre le da una propina al botones por traer las maletas.

el botones

las maletas

4B.11 Asociaciones. For each profession or place you hear mentioned, give real-life examples. Follow the model. Compare your answers with those of several classmates. What were the most frequent examples given?

Modelo: You hear: *un cocinero famoso o una cocinera famosa*
You respond: *Julia Child, Emeril Lagasse, Ingrid Hoffman*

4B.11 AUDIO SCRIPT AND POSSIBLE ANSWERS. Answers will vary: 1. un abogado famoso o una abogada famosa (e.g., Johnny Cochran, Michelle Obama), 2. una joyería (e.g., Zales, Shaw's), 3. un periódico (e.g., *The Washington Post, The Chicago Tribune, The Miami Herald*), 4. una iglesia (e.g., St. Paul's Cathedral, Westminster Abbey), 5. una zapatería (e.g., D.S.W., Payless), 6. un almacén (e.g., Sears, Macy's, Loehman's), 7. un peluquero famoso o una peluquera famosa (e.g., Vidal Sassoon, Nick Arrojo), 8. un banco (e.g., Chase, Wachovia), 9. una pastelería (e.g., Dunkin Donuts), 10. una farmacia (e.g., Eckerds, Walgreens, CVS)

4B.11 EXTENSION ACTIVITY: Have students form partners and decide who is person A and B. Instruct person B not to look at the board while A sees three new vocabulary words you put on the board (e.g. *un periódico, un banco, una farmacia*). They have to get their classmate to say those words without using the words themselves. They will have to make reference to them or describe what takes place there. This activity helps students develop their circumlocution skills. Reverse roles after 45 seconds so that both students have a chance to play each role.

4B.12 ANSWERS: When reviewing answers as a class, have students call out the words not the letters.

4B.12 Acciones ilógicas. Select the word from the list that cannot be used logically with the underlined verb. The first one is done for you as a model. Check your answers with those of a classmate.

_a_ **1.** <u>hacer</u> **a.** la radio **b.** la tarea **c.** la lectura **d.** el trabajo

_d_ **2.** <u>poner</u> **a.** el lápiz **b.** el libro **c.** la pluma **d.** la lluvia

_d_ **3.** <u>salir</u> **a.** de la clase **b.** a comer **c.** al parque **d.** a la mesa

_d_ **4.** <u>traer</u> **a.** la mochila **b.** el papel **c.** el cuaderno **d.** el matrimonio

_c_ **5.** <u>oír</u> **a.** el mensaje **b.** la música **c.** la foto **d.** la conversación

_d_ **6.** <u>probar</u> **a.** el chorizo **b.** el café **c.** la pizza **d.** la propina

4B.13 ANSWERS: 1. el/la enfermero/a, 2. el/la cocinero/a, 3. el/la camarero/a, 4. el/la recepcionista, el botones, 5. el/la abogado/a, 6. el/la joyero/a

4B.13 ADAPTATION STRATEGIES: Provide the list of professionals for *struggling students* to choose from on the board. Have *stronger students* extend this activity further by creating their own possible quotes to match to one of the professionals.

4B.13 ¿Quién lo dice? With a classmate, take turns reading to each other the quotes below to identify the professional saying it.

> Modelo: E1: "La dirección de esta carta no es correcta. Esta persona no vive aquí".
> E2: *el cartero*

1. "Abra la boca, por favor. Quiero tomarle la temperatura".

2. "Tengo que ponerle más sal a la sopa porque no tiene mucho sabor *(flavor)*".

3. "¿Desean ustedes más té, café o agua?"

4. "Su habitación es la número 235 y es una habitación de no fumar".

5. "El policía arrestó a mi cliente sin motivo".

6. "Señor, creo que a su esposa le gustan las perlas de Mallorca y aquí tengo algunos collares de perlas a unos precios muy razonables".

4B.14 Conceptos culturales.

Paso 1: In groups of three, read the following two passages to determine which passage has the following sentence as its main idea: **Es muy importante que los profesores de español enseñen más que vocabulario y gramática.** Verify your answer with the rest of the class.

Selección A
Muchos estudiantes internacionales que estudian en la universidad en Estados Unidos vuelven a sus países de origen para trabajar. Sin embargo, en ocasiones, han absorbido la cultura estadounidense hasta el punto en que tienen problemas para adaptarse a las condiciones de trabajo en sus propios países. Este es el caso de los médicos africanos que trabajan en hospitales públicos o privados. Muchos de ellos estudian en Europa o Estados Unidos y adquieren valores occidentales que contrastan con la diversidad cultural y religiosa de sus comunidades. Esto causa dificultades en la interacción médico-paciente porque los conceptos de enfermedad y salud, así como los tratamientos medicinales son muy diferentes de una cultura a otra.

Selección B
Aprender un idioma es un proceso más complejo y profundo que aprender reglas gramaticales y aspectos lingüísticos. Para poder comprender el significado total de las palabras es importante también conocer la cultura que define y da un significado a las palabras. Para ser un buen estudiante de español, o de cualquier otro idioma, se necesita tener la mente abierta y receptiva para comprender muy bien la relación entre el idioma y la cultura.

Paso 2: Check the summaries below that correspond to passages A and B above. One summary may be relevant to both passages. Share your responses with a classmate.

Selección

A   B   A y B

☑   ☐   ☐   **1.** The passage discusses the difficulties that western-trained physicians encounter when working in Africa due to differences in how health and illness are viewed from the western and African perspectives.

☐   ☑   ☐   **2.** The passage addresses the importance of training professors who teach languages to analyze and understand how certain behaviors are a reflection of the culture; for it is only with this type of training that these professors can lead their students to a higher level of intercultural competence.

☐   ☐   ☑   **3.** In today's increasingly multilingual and multicultural societies, knowledge of the language alone is not sufficient for working successfully with individuals from other cultures and countries. It is important to supplement this knowledge with cultural competence: the knowledge or awareness of the values, practices and behaviors associated with particular cultures.

4B.15 ¿Cómo se perciben estas profesiones?   With a classmate interview four native Spanish-speakers about how certain professions and occupations are perceived in their native countries. You may ask, **"¿Cómo se percibe la profesión de ___ en su país?"** Create a chart like the one below for each native speaker you interview. You may notice significant differences in the perspectives of people from different countries, for example, a waiter in Spain is considered a good long-term profession while in other cultures (i.e. US) it is seen as a temporary position, ideal for college students, for example. Compare your findings and then share them with the class. Are there any generalizations possible from the class results?

Nombre: _____	País de origen: _____			
¿Cómo se percibe la profesión de…?	Es respetado.	Se percibe como perezoso (lazy).	Se percibe como muy trabajador.	No es respetado.
abogado/a				
piloto				
cartero/a				
camarero/a				
peluquero/a				
dependiente/a				
enfermero/a				
botones				
contador/a				
joyero/a				
policía				
carnicero/a				

4B.15 STANDARDS: COMMUNITIES. This activity leads students into the community where the language is spoken. In the community, students use the new vocabulary to find out native speakers' perceptions about the professions. Not only will they be communicating in Spanish, but they will be learning perspectives that different cultures hold, an important aspect of the Standards.

4B.14 STANDARDS: COMMUNICATION. This activity is excellent practice for developing students' *interpretive mode* of communication as they are asked to make meaning out of a written message. Encourage students to focus on the gist of the reading as they go through this activity. There are certainly words and grammatical features that are beyond them, but by focusing on words they know, cognates and their context, they should experience success.

4B.14 FOLLOW-UP: Standards for Foreign Language Learning explicitly state that language learning is "knowing how, when and why to say what to whom." This is a great opportunity for you to share with the class your personal experiences with any intercultural misunderstandings you may have had.

WILEY
PLUS

4B.15 INSTRUCTOR'S RESOURCES: You will find reproducible charts for use with Activity 4B.15 in your Instructor's Resources.

4B.15 PREPARATION: Allow students an appropriate amount of time to complete this activity. Depending on your location, students may not have the access to native speakers that they might in other areas. If they can only interview one native speaker, encourage them to do so. Have them prepare their questions in advance and encourage them to think of how they want to represent their findings.

VÍVELO: LENGUA

Expressing location: A summary

In Spanish, the verb **estar** is used with prepositional phrases to express the location of people, things, places (e.g., buildings, cities, states, countries) and other entities (e.g., your college/university).

Estar +

arriba de	*above*	en	*in/on/at*
al lado de	*next to*	encima de	*on top of*
cerca de	*close to*	enfrente de	*facing/across from*
debajo de	*below/underneath*	entre	*between*
delante de	*in front of*	fuera de	*outside of*
dentro de	*inside of*	lejos de	*far from*
detrás de	*behind*	sobre	*over, on top of*

El nombre del teatro está **arriba de** la puerta.
La taquilla *(box office)* está **enfrente del** cine.
Los actores están **dentro del** teatro.
La entrada está **detrás de** la taquilla.
La farmacia está **entre** la peluquería y la zapatería.
La Universidad de North Dakota está **en** Grand Forks.
Australia está **lejos de** Estados Unidos.

4B.16 El centro. Working with a classmate, one of you using map A and the other map B, take turns asking each other questions in Spanish to identify the unlabeled places. Then, compare your versions of the completed downtown map.

Modelo: E1: *¿Dónde está la iglesia en la Calle 4?*
E2: *Está enfrente del hospital.*

¿Dónde está...?
el hotel
la peluquería
la carnicería
el banco
la pastelería
el hospital
el almacén

¿Dónde está...?
el restaurante
la farmacia
el correo
la bodega *(corner store)*
la iglesia

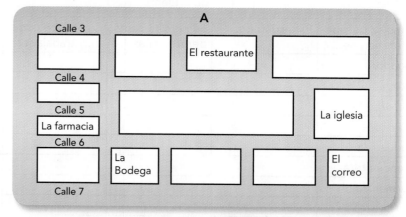

¡Atención!

Honestidad	Usually means decency, *modesty* and *decorum*. To express *honesty* as in the notion of telling the truth in Spanish, use the word **sinceridad**.
	Para una relación sólida, hay que establecer sinceridad y ser una persona honesta.
	Una persona virtuosa y modesta se comporte *(behaves)* con honestidad.
Notorio/a	means *well-known*, noted, renowned and also obvious or evident. To express the idea of *notorious* in Spanish, use **infame** or **de mala fama**.
	Las películas de Pedro Almodóvar son notorias y respetadas.
	Augusto Pinochet y Francisco Franco son ejemplos de dictadores infames.
Conveniente	does not mean convenient. Instead, it means *appropriate, proper,* or *suitable*. To express *convenient* in Spanish, use **oportuno, bien situado, útil** or **práctico**.
	La persona conveniente para mi hijo tiene que ser inteligente.
	Cuando estamos enfermos no es oportuno tener visitas.

4B.17 ¿Puedes encontrar el error? Determine whether or not the underlined words are used correctly. If not, rewrite the sentence with the correct words. Verify your answers with a classmate.

1. Las telenovelas venezolanas son <u>de mala fama</u> porque son <u>populares</u> en muchos países.

2. Los teléfonos celulares son muy <u>convenientes</u>.

3. <u>La honestidad</u> describe a una persona que siempre dice la verdad.

4. No es un momento <u>conveniente</u> para hablar con usted porque tengo que ir a otra reunión. ¿Podemos hablar más tarde?

5. Ese criminal <u>notorio</u> ha cometido crímenes violentos y crueles.

6. <u>La sinceridad</u> es una característica de las personas con buenos modales *(manners)*.

VÍVELO: CULTURA

Los estados con grandes poblaciones hispanas

Hay más hispanohablantes en México que en todos los países de Latinoamérica. En segundo lugar está Colombia y en tercer lugar está Argentina y luego España. En quinto lugar está Estados Unidos. Los estados con el mayor número de hispanos son los que aparecen en la lista a continuación. ¿Puedes adivinar el orden de estos estados, del 1 al 10 con respecto al número de hispanos? California es el primero.

2	**Texas**	3	**Florida**
5	**Arizona**	10	**Carolina del Norte**
4	**Nueva York**	7	**Nueva Jersey**
6	**Illinois**	1	**California**
9	**Nuevo México**	8	**Colorado**

4B.17 ANSWERS: 1. Las telenovelas venezolanas son notorias ..., 2. Los teléfonos celulares son muy útiles/prácticos, 3. La honradez/La sinceridad describe..., 4. No es un momento oportuno ..., 5. Ese criminal infame ..., 6. La honestidad es una característica...

4B.17 TEACHING TIP: Have students write the sentences on the board so that you may correct them together as a class. Often students do not pay attention to corrections you make on paper. To encourage them to attend to the corrections, offer students an incentive to correct errors in sentences.

VÍVELO: CULTURA: Students are likely to guess that California and Texas are the top two states for Hispanic population. If they're struggling with the rankings, you may want to provide some statistics to help them: CA 12,146,508; TX 8,269,407; FL 3,300,333; NY 2,881,409; AZ 1,711,429; IL 1,533,767; NJ 1,221,616; CO 918,899; NM 841,285; NC 571,307.

VÍVELO: CULTURA, SUGGESTION: By providing the following information in Spanish, you may preview ordinal numbers, which will be presented explicitly later in the program. *En primer lugar está California. En segundo lugar está Texas. En tercer lugar está Florida. En cuarto lugar está Nueva York. En quinto lugar está Arizona. En sexto lugar está Illinois. En séptimo lugar está Nueva Jersey. En octavo lugar está Colorado. En noveno lugar está Nuevo México. En décimo lugar está Carolina del Norte.*

Estructuras clave 1 Present tense of verbs with **yo** form changes

TEACHING TIP: Before reading this explanation, have students explain to their partner what the stem of a verb is. To make sure that they all understand this concept ask them to raise one hand if they have a grasp of what it is, and two hands if they also want to share their explanations. This will serve as a visible clue as to how many of your students understand this concept. As you go through the explanations shared, check back to see if students are all on the same page. To drive home the point of what a stem is, you may want to vertically write a verb on the board and draw some petals at the top to represent a flower. This visual may help any student struggling with the idea of the stem being at the beginning of the verb.

You may want to encourage students to think of these verbs as the "go-go verbs" to help them remember the *yo* form.

MULTIPLE INTELLIGENCES: MUSICAL. Give students a few minutes to come up with a rhyme, song or poem using at least five of the *–go* verbs in the *yo* form. Consider offering them extra credit if they volunteer to perform their creation for the class. Prepare to be impressed with their creativity.

In previous chapters and in *Investigación A*, you have studied regular verbs and verbs that have certain stem-changes in all forms except **nosotros** and **vosotros.** Have you noticed other verb forms that seem to have a change particular to a grammatical person?

Here, we will examine verbs whose **yo** form ends in **–go.** Look at the conjugations of some common verbs below:

	hacer	**poner**	**salir**
yo	ha**go**	pon**go**	sal**go**
tú	haces	pones	sales
él/ella/usted	hace	pone	sale
nosotros/nosotras	hacemos	ponemos	salimos
vosotros/vosotras	hacéis	ponéis	salís
ellos/ellas/ustedes	hacen	ponen	salen

Note that some verbs with **yo** forms ending in **–go** also have the **e ⟶ ie** stem-change you studied in *Investigación A* in the forms for other persons.

	venir	**tener**
yo	ven**go**	ten**go**
tú	vi**e**nes	ti**e**nes
él/ella/usted	vi**e**ne	ti**e**ne
nosotros/nosotras	venimos	tenemos
vosotros/vosotras	venís	tenéis
ellos/ellas/ustedes	vi**e**nen	ti**e**nen

You are familiar with several verbs related to **tener** which also follow this pattern: **mantener, sostener, obtener.**

The verbs **oír** and **traer** follow the basic pattern of verbs whose **yo** form ends in **–go,** but have other irregularities as well.

	oír	**traer**
yo	oi**go**	trai**go**
tú	oyes	traes
él/ella/usted	oye	trae
nosotros/nosotras	oímos	traemos
vosotros/vosotras	oís	traéis
ellos/ellas/ustedes	oyen	traen

4B.18 ¿A qué profesión se refiere? In an interview, certain statements would be appropriate depending on the job. For which job candidates would the statements below be most appropriate? With a partner, take turns reading each other the statements below and providing the name of the appropriate professional.

Modelo: E1: Tengo un diploma del Instituto Culinario.
E2: *un cocinero*

1. Traigo los últimos modelos en cuero *(leather)* de Italia.

2. Soy preciso cuando trabajo con números.

3. Siempre digo la verdad.

4. Sirvo la comida con una sonrisa.

5. Respeto la privacidad de mis pacientes.

6. Vengo preparado para caminar diariamente.

4B.18 ANSWERS: Answers may vary. Accept all logical answers. 1. el/la zapatero/a, 2. el/la contador/a, 3. el/la mi-nistro/a, el/la abogado/a, 4. el/la camarero/a, 5. el/la psicólogo/a, el/la enfermero/a, 6. el/la cartero/a.

4B.19 ¿Quién lo dice? The following well-known Hispanics have made the statements below. With a classmate, match each statement to the person who is most likely to have made it.

a. Desi Arnaz, dueño de un club cubano en *I Love Lucy.*

b. Ricardo Chivara, esposo de Eva Longoria en el programa *Desperate Housewives.*

c. Henry Cisneros, ex-alcalde de San Antonio y ex-miembro del gabinete del Presidente Clinton.

d. María Hinojosa, conocida como corresponsal de asuntos urbanos de CNN. Hoy en día es conductora del programa *Latina USA* y corresponsal de *NOW,* una revista de noticias de PBS.

<u>a</u> **1.** "Traigo conmigo la música para el espectáculo *(show)* del viernes por la noche".

<u>b</u> **2.** "No ves, mi amor, el divorcio no es la solución para nuestros problemas".

<u>d</u> **3.** "Anuncio de emergencia…El gobierno manda una evacuación. Un huracán está en el golfo de México y las ciudades de Brownsville y Corpus Christi están bajo una orden de evacuación".

<u>c</u> **4.** "El gobierno existe para servir al público y por eso deseo construir casas para las familias pobres que no ganan suficiente dinero para compar una casa".

4B.20 A hacer oraciones lógicas. First, complete each sentence fragment with the appropriate **yo** form of the verb. Then, combine each fragment in column A with a fragment from column B to create a logical statement. Finally, indicate which of the completed statements is true for you and share your responses with the rest of the class

A	B
1. Cuando yo (hacer) _____ la tarea	no (oír) _____ la construcción por la ventana.
2. Si (poner) _____ la música	para (salir) _____ con mis amigos.
3. Ya no (tener) _____ tiempo	cuando (salir) _____ a comer con mi familia.
4. Si (mantener) _____ buenas notas	(obtener) _____ un título universitario.
5. Siempre (salir) _____ a comer	(recibir) _____ buenas notas.
6. Nunca (traer) _____ dinero	con mi familia los viernes.

4B.20 ANSWERS: 1. Cuando yo hago la tarea, recibo buenas notas. 2. Si pongo la música no oigo la construcción por la ventana. 3. Ya no tengo tiempo para salir con mis amigos. 4. Si mantengo buenas notas obtengo un título universitario. 5. Siempre salgo a comer con mi familia los viernes. 6. Nunca traigo dinero cuando salgo a comer con mi familia.

4B.21 ¿Quién es quién? On a sheet of paper, answer the following questions about yourself using **siempre, nunca, a veces, de vez en cuando, con frecuencia** or **raramente.** Then, ask a classmate the same question and make a note of his/her answers in your **Retrato de la clase.**

> Modelo: ¿Haces tu tarea en la Internet?
> *Raramente hago la tarea en la Internet.*

1. ¿Sales con tus padres los fines de semana?

2. ¿Dices cosas sin *(without)* pensar?

3. ¿Traes café a clase?

4. ¿Vienes tarde a clase?

5. ¿Tienes amigos en otra universidad?

6. ¿Mantienes contacto con los amigos de la secundaria?

7. ¿Haces muchas cosas con tu familia?

8. ¿Sales a bailar salsa?

Retrato de la clase: Mi compañero/a de clase _____ a veces hace su tarea en la Internet. No sale nunca con sus padres los fines de semana. Etcétera…

4B.21 RECYCLING: This activity recycles adverbs of frequency.

4B.21 FOLLOW-UP: When students have completed the activity, process it as a class. For example, you can ask them, *¿Quién tiene amigos en otra universidad?* After several answers have been shared, flip the question around by asking them, for example, *¿Qué sabemos de Jim?* This will invite them to pay closer attention to what their classmates have to say.

Estructuras clave 2 Other irregular verbs in the present tense

TEACHING TIP: Encourage students to keep track of these grammatical points in their notebooks for easy reference. Often, when we write something down, we are more likely to remember it.

Some irregular verbs are less easily categorized. The verbs below have been grouped based on the pattern they have in common. Can you figure out each group's pattern?

Construir, destruir, and **contribuir** add a **y** to the stem before the personal endings (except in the **nosotros/as** and **vosotros/as** forms).

construir	destruir	contribuir
construyo	destruyo	contribuyo
construyes	destruyes	contribuyes
construye	destruye	contribuye
construimos	destruimos	contribuimos
contruís	destruís	contribuís
construyen	destruyen	contribuyen

Conocer, producir, and **traducir** have a **c ⟶ zc** change in the **yo** form.

conocer	producir	traducir
conozco	produzco	traduzco
conoces	produces	traduce
conoce	produce	traduces
conocemos	producimos	traducimos
conocéis	producís	traducís
conocen	producen	traducen

Ver, leer, and **dar** are also conjugated like **ir.**

ver	leer	dar
veo	leo	doy
ves	lees	das
ve	lee	da
vemos	leemos	damos
veis	leéis	dais
ven	leen	dan

4B.22 NOTE: Even if students do not know who these individuals are, the descriptions should provide the context so they can match them to the statements.

4B. 22 ¿Quién lo dice? With a partner, read the following statements and identify who from the list of options below is likely to have made these statements.

Declaraciones

___d___ **1.** "Leo la radiografía y veo que el paciente necesita una tercera operación para reconstruir la mano".

___a___ **2.** "Voy a ver al paciente para darle una inyección de antibióticos".

___e___ **3.** "Construyo objetos con mis manos y les doy explicaciones muy detalladas a los televidentes".

___c___ **4.** "No conozco a este asesino *(murderer)* pero vamos a detener a su esposa para ver si ella habla".

___b___ **5.** "Yo no produzco la evidencia porque la evidencia ya está allí. Voy a convencer a todos en esta corte de la culpabilidad *(guilt)* del acusado".

Personajes

a. Judy Reyes hace de enfermera en el programa *Scrubs.*

b. Óscar Zeta Acosta fue abogado, activista y novelista.

c. Roselyn Sánchez hace de agente de FBI en *Without a Trace.*

d. Sara Ramírez hace de doctora y cirujana *(surgeon)* ortopédica en *Grey's Anatomy.*

e. Bob Vila es carpintero y ex-conductor del programa *This Old House.*

4B.23 La construcción de la oración. With another classmate, use the elements given to write a complete and logical sentence. Make sure to insert any articles or prepositions.

1. Pedro Almodóvar / producir / películas / excelente.
2. Jorge Ramos / dar / noticias / programa / Univisión.
3. Bob Vila / construir / mesa.
4. huracán / destruir / edificios / parques / centros.
5. Judy Reyes / ver / Roselyn Sánchez / muchos / lugares / Los Ángeles.

4B.24 ¡A entrevistar! Interview a classmate using the following questions. Create a chart like the one below and jot down his/her answers. Then, write a brief summary of what you learned about that classmate, share it with the rest of the class, and include it in your **Retrato de la clase.**

Entrevista de _____	
¿Qué lees?	
¿Adónde vas de vacaciones con tu familia este verano?	
¿Conoces a una persona famosa?	
¿Traduces de tu idioma nativo al idioma que aprendes?	
¿Destruyes a un amigo cuando se transforma en enemigo?	
¿Cómo contribuyes a tu clase de español?	

Retrato de la clase: Mi compañero/a de clase _____ lee _____. Su familia va a _____ este verano. No conoce a nadie famoso….

4B.25 Para estas profesiones, ¿cuáles son los beneficios de hablar español? With three other classmates, discuss what the benefits of knowing Spanish will offer the following professions in the United States in the future.

Modelo: *Los doctores van a tener más pacientes hispanohablantes.*

1. los doctores
2. los dependientes
3. los psicólogos
4. los escritores
5. los policías
6. los contadores
7. los abogados
8. los sociólogos

Enlaces

4B.26 ¿Puedes conectar las ideas? Conecta las ideas en las oraciones de abajo usando la expresión apropiada. Luego, comprueba tus respuestas con la clase.

even   according to   in the face of

according to **1. Según** proyecciones realizadas por el Instituto Cervantes de España, para el año 2050, 96 millones de personas hablarán español en Estados Unidos.

even **2.** Es un buen objetivo tratar de dominar otro idioma, **incluso** puede ayudarle a una persona a conseguir un buen trabajo.

in the face of **3. Ante tal** perspectiva, más de ocho millones de estudiantes norteamericanos van a clases de español.

4B.23 ANSWERS: 1. Pedro Almodóvar produce películas excelentes. 2. Jorge Ramos da las noticias para un programa de Univisión. 3. Bob Vila construye una mesa. 4. El huracán destruye los edificios y parques de los centros. 5. Judy Reyes ve a Roselyn Sánchez en muchos lugares de Los Ángeles.

4B.23 TEACHING TIP: Remind students to pay special attention to the changes in verbs as well as any connectors that might be needed to smooth out the sentences. You may want to complete the first sentence together as a class.

WILEY PLUS

4B.24 INSTRUCTOR'S RESOURCES: A reproducible chart for use with Activity 4B.24 is included in your Instructor's Resources. Students do not need to ask the questions in this order, and can certainly adapt them if they feel it necessary.

4B.25 TEACHING TIP: Give students time to prepare their lists of benefits. Provide (on board, overhead transparency, large sheets of paper) three category headings: «Personal» «Cultural» «Social». Record students' responses under the appropriate heading as they are given, or have a representative of each group record the group's responses, before beginning the discussion. Review and tally students' responses. Comment on similarities and differences.

4B.27 ¿Cuántos europeos hablan más de un idioma? Scan the list of the percentage of Europeans in various demographic groups that speak a second language. As a class, discuss which groups have the highest/lowest percentage of speaking a second language. What patterns do you notice?

Hablar un segundo idioma es común en Europa

En Europa un 50% de la población puede sostener una conversación en una segunda lengua. Incluso personas de todos los niveles socioeconómicos pueden hablar un segundo idioma y a veces un tercer y cuarto idioma. Los idiomas más populares en Europa son el inglés, el francés, el alemán y el español. Examina la tabla de abajo con datos específicos. Ante tales datos, es lógico que EE.UU. sea percibido como un país monolingüe.

Grupos socio-demográficos que hablan un segundo idioma	
hombres	52%
mujeres	47%
estudiantes	79%
gerentes *(managers)*	73%
trabajadores *(no laboral)*	54%
personas que trabajan por su propia cuenta *(self-employed)*	52%
obreros manuales *(manual workers)*	46%
obreros sin trabajo	47%
personas de casa	36%
jubilados *(retired)*	26%
personas de 15-24 años de edad	69%
personas de 25-39 años de edad	58%
personas de 40-54 años de edad	47%
personas de 55 + años de edad	35%

With a partner, answer the following questions:

1. ¿Por qué creen que tantos europeos hablan otro idioma?
2. ¿Pueden explicar la distribución? (Por ejemplo: Se nota que los jóvenes y los profesionales son los que más hablan otro idioma.)
3. En Estados Unidos, ¿creen que los resultados serían semejantes o diferentes? ¿Por qué?

Perspectivas

The following passage mentions that more than 8 million students in the US are taking Spanish classes. Can you think of reasons to explain why so many students are taking Spanish? Do your reasons correspond to the information in the text below?

¿Se habla español?

Según proyecciones realizadas por el Instituto Cervantes de España, para el año 2050, 96 millones de personas van a hablar español en Estados Unidos (EE.UU.). No hay duda que saber dos idiomas ayuda en la carrera de una persona, tanto hoy como en el futuro. El mercado necesita personal multilingüe. Ante tal perspectiva más de ocho millones de estudiantes norteamericanos toman clases de español. Muchos quieren estudiar la lengua para desempeñar bien *(perform well)* su trabajo, así como para comunicarse con los empleados y clientes que hablan español.

Dentro de pocos años EE.UU. va a ser el segundo país en el mundo con el mayor número de hispanohablantes después de México. Esto significa que muchos jóvenes hispanos dominarán el español y el inglés. Ellos van a ser los verdaderos bilingües del futuro porque para ser completamente bilingüe hay que aprender el idioma de joven o estudiarlo en la universidad y luego ir al extranjero por una temporada. Lo más importante es ser persistente.

VÍVELO: CULTURA: We need to remember that the reason Spanish instructors have more students than people teaching other languages is because of its relevance in today's society. Most students in our beginning-level Spanish classes just want to develop a certain basic level of Spanish proficiency. Poll your students to see why they are taking Spanish.

4B.28 **¿Qué comprendiste de la lectura?** Working with a partner, answer the following questions based on the reading. Check your answers with another group. Do you agree with the passage's assertions with respect to questions 5 and 6? Why or why not? Be prepared to discuss and justify your responses.

1. Para el año 2050, ¿cuántas personas van a hablar español en Estados Unidos?
2. ¿Para qué quieren estudiar español algunas personas?
3. En pocos años, ¿en qué lugar va a estar Estados Unidos en cuanto al número de hablantes de español?
4. ¿Quiénes van a ser los verdaderos bilingües del futuro?
5. ¿Cuáles son las dos maneras de ser bilingüe?
6. ¿Cuál es la característica más importante para las personas que quieren ser bilingües?

4B.28 ANSWERS: 1. 96 millones, 2. para desempeñar bien su trabajo y para comunicarse con los empleados y clientes, 3. Va a estar en segundo lugar después de México. 4. los jóvenes hispanos, 5. aprender el idioma de joven o estudiarlo en la universidad y luego ir al extranjero, 6. ser persistente / la persistencia

4B.29 SUGGESTION: As students explore these themes from the movies, you may want to share personal instances of cultural misunderstandings. Drive home the importance of being able to gain new perspectives and how that can lessen misunderstandings. Also, you can talk about how the film industry helps to propagate cultural, social, racial and economical stereotypes.

4B.29 Las películas también enseñan. As you begin studying languages it is important to become a cultural observer. Much can be learned about appropriate behaviors and perspectives by being observant. Cinema can present a variety of perspectives. Watch a movie related to the themes in this chapter, such as *Spanglish, Live-in Maid,* or *Crónicas* with the following questions in mind. Some information about these films appears below, but you may find other films as well.

- What professions in the film benefited from knowing Spanish or another foreign language?
- What lessons were learned about the importance of other cultures' perspectives?
- What perspectives or cultural understandings would have helped reduce the misunderstandings?

Films	Lessons Learned	Perspectives Needed

Spanglish

This film highlights various social and cultural issues that surround a family in California. The movie is robust with cultural misundertandings and language barriers.

Cama adentro

This film explores the unique relationship between a domestic employee and her employer in Argentina. The relationship depicted in this movie reflects the unique dynamics common between employer and domestic employee in many Hispanic cultures.

Crónicas

Look on the Internet for an interview John Leguizamo had with NPR about *Crónicas.* Then rent and watch the movie to address how what he says in the interview is reflected in the film. (**¡Ojo!** This movie is a suspense/thriller and not for the faint-hearted.)

Vocabulario: Investigación B

Vocabulario esencial

Sustantivos

el/la abogado/a	lawyer
el/la agricultor/a	farmer
el almacén	store
el botones	bellhop
los bomberos	firefigthers
el/la camarero/a	waiter/waitress
la carnicería	butcher shop
el/la carnicero/a	butcher
el/la cartero/a	letter carrier
el/la cirujano/a	surgeon
el/la cocinero/a	cook
el/la contador/a	accountant
el correo	mail
el/la dependiente/a	clerk
el/la enfermero/a	nurse
el/la gerente	manager
el/la joyero/a	jewelry seller or repairer
la maleta	suitcase
la pastelería	bakery
el/la peluquero/a	barber/hairdesser
la peluquería	barber shop/ hairdressing salon
el/la zapatero/a	shoe seller or repairer
la zapatería	shoe shop/store

Adjetivos

abierto/a	open
enfermo	sick
jubilado	retired
perezoso/a	lazy

Verbos

conocer	to know
contribuir	to contribute
construir	to construct
dar	to give
destruir	to destroy
hacer	to do
leer	to read
oír	to hear
poner	to put
producir	to produce
salir	to leave; to go out
tener	to have
traducir	translate
traer	to bring
venir	to come
ver	to see

Preposiciones

cerca de	near
delante de	in front of
dentro de	inside of
detrás de	behind
en	in, on, at
enfrente de	across from, facing
entre	between
fuera de	outside of
lejos de	far from

Otras palabras y expresiones

adquirir	to acquire
el/la asesino/a	murderer
avanzar	to advance
el autobús	bus
el avión	airplane
la bodega	corner store
la cadena	chain
la calle	street
el centro comercial	shopping mall
la confitería	cake shop
el consultorio	office
la corte	court
la culpabilidad	guilt
el delito	crime
desempeñar	to perform (a task or job)
despertador	alarm clock
el diario	daily newspaper
diseñar	design
el/la dueño/a	owner
la enfermedad	illness
enseñar	to teach
el espectáculo	show

el hogar	home
la iglesia	church
la joya	jewel
el juicio	trail
leal	loyal
la mente	mind
mentir	to lie
mandar	to order, to command
las letras (educación)	liberal arts
el noticiero	newscast
los obreros manuales	manual workers
el oficio	trade
la propina	tip, gratuity
la reunión	meeting
la revista	magazine
rezar	to pray
el sabor	taste
la salud	health
la temporada	season
el título universitario	college degree
la vecindad	neighborhood
a continuación	following
dejar de + infinitive	to stop (doing something)
despedir a	to dismiss, to fire
estudiar para	to study to be
para ser	in order to be
poner en orden	to put in order
sin embargo	however
trabajar a tiempo completo	to work full time
trabajar a tiempo parcial	to work part time
trabajar para	to work for (be employed by)

Cognados

Review the cognates in *Adelante* and the false cognates in *¡Atención!*. For a complete list of cognates, see Appendix 4 on page 605.

En vivo

 Las carreras de los/as compañeros/as de clase. First, answer these questions for yourself, then poll ten classmates to find out what their career plans are: What career are they going to pursue and why?

Modelo: E1: *¿Para qué carrera estudias? Y ¿por qué?*
            E2: *Estudio para arquitecto porque soy creativo y quiero diseñar casas.*

Nombre	¿Para qué carrera estudias? ¿Por qué?	¿Vas a usar el español en tu profesión? ¿Cómo?
Yo		

 ¡Tanto tiempo! Imagine that you are a few years out of college and are working in a full-time job. You have found on Facebook an old friend who was in a high school Spanish class with you and want to update them on your job, lifestyle, and use of Spanish in your career. Write him/her an e-mail that includes the following information and that would allow them to conclude whether you work to live or live to work.

* your current job and what you do in it
* what you like about it
* how you use your Spanish in your current job
* how much free time you have
* how you spend your free time

Follow these steps to compose your e-mail.

Begin your e-mail with **Querido/a…**

Paso 1: Think of a potential job you want in the future. Imagine you are there in that job and describe at least 4 things you do in your typical work day.

Paso 2: Think about what you like doing in that job and list at least 3 things.

Paso 3: Think about the situations/occasions in that job that would provide opportunities for you to use Spanish. Include at least two situations/occasions.

Paso 4: Describe your work hours and how much time you actually have free.

Paso 5: Describe what you like to do in your free time.

Finish by signing, **Atentamente,…**

En directo

INVESTIGACIÓN A: Ser inmigrante no es fácil

> **Antes de ver el video.** Answer these questions and compare your answers with your classmates: ¿Hay inmigrantes donde vives o estudias? ¿De dónde vienen? ¿Tienes contacto con algún inmigrante?

> **El video.** Indicate if the following statements are **ciertos** or **falsos** based on the video.

	Cierto	Falso
1. Olga viene de México.	☐	☑
2. Francisco es colombiano y tiene diez hermanos.	☐	☑
3. Olga huyó de la violencia en su país.	☑	☐
4. Francisco ganaba 150 dólares al mes.	☐	☑
5. Francisco está feliz porque ayudó a su familia.	☑	☐
6. María Cristina y su familia fueron víctimas de la contaminación por plomo.	☑	☐
7. Para Vladimir fue fácil dejar a su familia, amigos y costumbres.	☐	☑
8. Samuel ha compartido su cultura con muchos estadounidenses.	☑	☐

> **Después de ver el video.** Answer the following questions and share your answers with the rest of the class: ¿Crees que es fácil para un inmigrante adaptarse a un nuevo país? ¿Por qué? En tu opinión, ¿crees que se puede aprender algo de los inmigrantes? (En mi opinión, creo que (no) se puede aprender… su cultura, su folclor, su lengua, sus costumbres, etcétera.) En el futuro, ¿quieres vivir en algún otro país? ¿Dónde?

Vocabulario útil
plomo *lead*
contaminación *pollution*
un montón *a lot*
desperdiciar *to waste*

INVESTIGACIÓN B: CLUES ayuda a inmigrantes

> **Antes de ver el video.** Si llegas a un nuevo país para vivir, ¿qué es lo más importante para ti? Combine elements from the two columns to say what's logically important.

___d___ **1.** Aprender el idioma…   **a.** para viajar.

___c___ **2.** Conseguir un empleo…   **b.** donde vivir.

___b___ **3.** Tener un hogar…   **c.** para ganar dinero.

___a___ **4.** Tener un modo de transporte…   **d.** para comunicarme.

> **El video.** Choose the best option to complete each statement based on the video.

1. CLUES es una organización de __c__ dedicada a ayudar a la comunidad hispana.
a) personas   **b)** hispanos   **c)** voluntarios

2. Ayuda a los inmigrantes a conseguir un empleo, un __b__ y un modo de transporte.
a) trabajo   **b)** hogar   **c)** casa

3. Tan pronto como llega un inmigrante a CLUES, le aconsejan que tome clases de __c__.
a) lengua   **b)** manejar   **c)** inglés

4. Un inmigrante puede asistir a __a__ para saber cómo escribir el "resumé" y la carta de presentación.
a) talleres   **b)** clases   **c)** programas

5. Hoy tengo una cita con el consejero de __b__ que me va a ayudar a conseguir un trabajo.
a) CLUES   **b)** empleo   **c)** formación

> **Después de ver el video.** Answer the following questions with a partner, then share your answers with the class: Los inmigrantes que llegan a tu país, ¿hablan el idioma? ¿En qué trabajan?

Vocabulario útil
tan pronto como *as soon as*
taller *workshop*
consejera de empleo *career counselor*
voluntario/a *volunteer*

TEACHING TIP: As a warm-up for watching the video, ask students to think about these questions: *En tu opinión, ¿es necesario ayudar a los inmigrantes a integrarse mejor en su nuevo país? ¿Por qué? ¿Conoces alguna organización que ayude a los inmigrantes?*

Retrato de la clase Checklist

WILEY PLUS

TESTING PROGRAM:
You will find a complete testing program for use with *¡Vívelo!* in *WileyPLUS*.

You should have recorded information in your **Retrato de la clase** in conjunction with the following activities:

- [ ] **4A.10 ¿Piensan igual?**
- [ ] **4A.11 ¿Estás de acuerdo?**
- [ ] **4A.20 Comprensión**
- [ ] **4A.23 Ente fin de semana**
- [ ] **4A.26 ¿Quién de la clase?**

- [ ] **4B.21 ¿Quién es quién?**
- [ ] **4B.24 ¡A entrevistar!**

Lo que influye en la formación de una cultura y sociedad

¿Por qué comes lo que comes?

In this **Investigación** you will learn:

▸ How to talk about a variety of foods

▸ How to indicate your preferences with regard to food

▸ How to order food at a restaurant

▸ How to avoid repetition when talking about something already mentioned

▸ How food and culture are connected

¿Cómo se puede hablar de las comidas y bebidas?

You can identify foods and beverages.	¿Es comida o bebida? ¿Es fruta? ¿verdura? ¿carne? ¿postre? ¿Se come para el desayuno? ¿el almuerzo? ¿la cena? ¿Es comida mexicana?
You can indicate your preferences with regard to food and beverages.	¿Te gusta o no te gusta esa comida o bebida? ¿Cuál es tu comida o bebida favorita? ¿Con qué frecuencia la comes? ¿la bebes?
You can avoid repetition when you talk about foods and beverages.	¿Te gusta la fruta? ¿Cuándo la comes? ¿Te gusta el café? ¿Lo bebes por la mañana o antes de estudiar?

Adelante

¡Ya lo sabes! Para hablar de comidas y bebidas

la banana*	el chocolate	las legumbres	el plato	el té
el bistec	la ensalada	el limón	la pizza	el tomate
el brócoli	el espagueti	la mayonesa	el restaurante	el vinagre
el café	las espinacas	el melón	la sal	el yogur
el cereal	la fruta	la mermelada	el salmón	
el chile	la hamburguesa	la pasta	la sopa	

delicioso/a   fresco/a

cremoso/a   nutritivo/a

* In some Spanish-speaking regions, the word *plátano* is used to refer to a banana, but *el plátano* is more specifically a plantain, which is shaped like a banana but, when ripe, it is dark yellow and eventually turns black.

5A.1 **¿A qué categoría pertenece?** En parejas, miren la lista de cognados y hagan una tabla con las palabras que correspondan a cada una de estas categorías. Comprueben *(verify)* sus respuestas *(responses)* con otra pareja.

Frutas	Proteínas	Carbohidratos
Bebidas	Verduras *(Vegetables)*	Condimentos

TEACHING TIP: As you go over the cognates in *¡Ya lo sabes!*, you may consider asking students questions so that they produce these cognates in their answers, such as *¿Qué condimento es blanco (white) y cremoso? ¿Qué cosas de la lista son deliciosas? ¿Qué comidas no son nutritivas? ¿Qué comidas son cremosas? ¿Qué comidas son grasosas? ¿Cuáles son algunas comidas saladas? ¿Qué comidas prefieres frescas?* When appropriate, repeat their answers for two purposes—to make sure all students in the class hear the answers, and to provide the correct pronunciation of these cognates in meaningful contexts.

WILEY PLUS

5A.1 INSTRUCTOR'S RESOURCES You will find a reproducible chart for Activity 5A.1 in your Instructor's Resources.

5A.1 ANSWERS: Frutas: limón, melón, tomates, Bebidas: café, té, chocolate; Carbohidratos: cereal, espagueti, pasta, pizza; Proteínas: bistec, salmón, hamburguesa; Verduras: brócoli, espinacas, ensalada; Condimentos: mayonesa, mermelada, sal, chile.

5A.2 **Asociaciones.** Como clase, mencionen los alimentos que asocian con cada una de las marcas de abajo. Sigan el modelo.

1. Godiva   *el chocolate*
2. Hardy's, McDonalds la hamburguesa
3. Special K los cereales

4. Dannon el yogur
5. Domino's, Papa John's la pizza
6. Campbell's la sopa

7. Lipton el té
8. Hunt's los tomates

5A.2 ORIENTATION: This is not a written activity. Students should simply call out the type of food associated with each item.

5A.2 TEACHING TIP: Remind students that all cognates are listed by chapter at the end of the book. As you go through the answers, ask students if they can think of other food items that would fit in each category. Their answers will give you an idea of how much vocabulary they may already know.

5A.3 **Categorías.** Con un/a compañero/a de clase, túrnense *(take turns)* para asociar las comidas y los restaurantes con una de las categorías de la lista. Luego, comprueben sus respuestas con otros dos compañeros de clase.

Modelo: **Your classmate reads:** la champaña
You write: *Las bebidas alcohólicas*

Categorías:

las sopas
la comida rápida
las verduras
el pescado *(fish)*
los restaurantes
las frutas

los condimentos
las bebidas con cafeína
las bebidas alcohólicas
las carnes *(meats)*
los postres *(desserts)*
los carbohidratos

1. los carbohidratos : las pastas, los espaguetis
2. las bebidas con cafeína : el té, el chocolate, el café
3. las sopas : de pollo, de tomate, de verduras
4. los restaurantes : Applebee's, Chili's, Outback Steakhouse
5. la comida rápida : Wendy's, Sonic, Burger King
6. las frutas : las bananas, las peras, los tomates, los melones
7. las verduras : el brócoli, los espárragos, las espinacas
8. las carnes : el filete, el jamón *(ham)*

5A.4 **Busca la palabra correcta.** Vas a escuchar descripciones asociadas con comidas y bebidas. Consulta la lista de **Para hablar de comidas y bebidas** de la pág. 204 y escribe la palabra asociada con cada descripción según el modelo. Comprueba tus respuestas con la clase.

1. *el té*
2. la hamburguesa
3. un restaurante
4. la mayonesa
5. las espinacas
6. delicioso
7. el cereal
8. la banana

5A.4 AUDIO SCRIPT: 1. Es una cosa que beben los ingleses, tradicionalmente por la tarde. 2. Es el tipo de sándwich que se asocia con McDonald's y Burger King. 3. Es un lugar adonde vamos para sentarnos a comer. 4. Es una salsa que se pone en un sándwich. 5. Es una verdura que se asocia con Popeye. 6. Es un adjetivo que describe una cosa que nos gusta mucho comer. 7. Es una cosa que normalmente se come por la mañana, por ejemplo Cheerios o Wheaties. 8. Es una fruta tropical larga y amarilla que se asocia con los gorilas.

5A.4 STANDARDS: COMMUNICATION/ INTERPRETIVE MODE. This activity helps practice students' receptive skills. To adapt this for students who are stronger visual learners, you may want to provide a word bank on the board. This will help limit what students must focus on while listening to the descriptions.

5A.5 **Encuentra a una persona.** Pregúntales a tus compañeros de clase sobre sus preferencias. Si un/a compañero/a responde afirmativamente, pídele *(ask him/her)* que firme tu hoja. Comparte *(share)* tus resultados con la clase y escríbelos en tu **Retrato de la clase**.

> Modelo: ¿Quién en la clase bebe café cuando tiene que estudiar?
> E1: *¿Bebes café cuando tienes que estudiar?*
> E2: *Sí, bebo café.*
> E1: *Firma aquí, por favor.*

¿Quién en la clase...

1. bebe café cuando tiene que estudiar? _____

2. es vegetariano/a? _____

3. come yogur por la mañana? _____

4. trae un sándwich para comer al mediodía? _____

5. come sopa cuando hace frío? _____

6. prefiere no comer muchos carbohidratos? _____

7. no come salmón? _____

8. come pizza una vez a la semana o más? _____

Retrato de la clase: _____, _____, _____ beben café cuando tienen que estudiar.

Ingrid Hoffman y su cocina

Promoción de la cultura hispana
Sol Carreras, EFE

MIAMI - De pequeña ya experimentaba en la cocina con su madre. Su pasión por la comida le animó a abrir un restaurante en Miami y ahora la presentadora colombiana Ingrid Hoffman[7] promociona la cultura hispana con recetas "fáciles y creativas."

De Colombia para el mundo

Para[2] la colombiana Ingrid Hoffman, la cocina es una afición *(favorite activity)* con la que creció desde pequeña[3] bajo la supervisión de su madre, que se graduó de chef en la legendaria escuela de cocina francesa Le Cordon Bleu.

[4]Hoffman se traslada *(moves)* a Orlando a los trece años y después de tener[5] suerte *(luck)* como actriz en su país vuelve a Estados Unidos en 1989, donde abre[6] una tienda y un restaurante en Miami. Su restaurante, *Rocca*, tiene fama por cocinar sobre piedras *(rocks)* de lava caliente y se ha convertido en uno de los favoritos de los famosos. Desde 2006 presenta el programa de cocina *Delicioso* en la cadena Galavisión.[8] Para Hoffman, la comida latina es una "forma de mostrar nuestra cultura."

5A.6 **La cultura hispana comienza con la comida.** Vas a escuchar varios enunciados *(statements)* sobre el artículo de la página 206. Por cada enunciado, subraya en la lectura la información que corresponde y decide si lo que se dice es cierto o falso. Escribe el número del enunciado al lado de la información. Compara tus respuestas con la clase.

Modelo: You hear: **1.** La madre de Hoffman asistió a una escuela de cocina en Francia.

You underline: …se graduó de chef en la escuela de cocina francesa…

You write: **1.** *Cierto* next to that information.

Bien dicho

Los sonidos que producen las letras *s*, *c*, y *z*

In most varieties of Spanish, the letter **s** and the letter **z** have the same sound and that sound corresponds to the English *s* sound.

la zanahoria	la ensalada	la sopa	el sándwich

In most varieties of Spanish, the letter **c** when followed by the vowels **e** and **i** also corresponds to the English *s* sound.

el cereal	el tocino	cenar	delicioso

In Spanish, when a **c** is followed by the remaining vowels, **a**, **o**, and **u**, or by the consonants **l** or **r**, the sound produced is like the English *k*.

el café	la cuchara	comer	el microondas

The only time the *z* sound of English–a sort of "buzz"–is heard in Spanish is when the letters **s** or **z** come before the following consonants: **b, v, d, g, y, n, ñ, m, l, r,** and **rr.** Examples include words like **desde** *(from)* and **mismo** *(same)*. Due to linking, this same pheonomenon also occurs between words as in the phrases: **esos vinos blancos** [esozbinozblankos] and **los garbanzos** [lozgarbansos].

5A.7 **¿Cómo se pronuncia?** En parejas, decidan si la s o la z en negrita en las siguientes palabras se pronuncian como la *s* en inglés o pueden tener el zumbido *(buzz sound)* más característico de la *z* en inglés. Luego, practiquen la pronunciación y comenten cómo lo hace cada uno.

1. los mariscos z sound **3.** las manzanas s sound **5.** la pasta s sound **7.** sus legumbres z sound

2. mis fresas s sound **4.** las paletas s sound **6.** sus cereales s sound **8.** las cebollas s sound

5A.8 **¡A practicar!** Con un/a compañero/a, túrnate para pronunciar las siguientes oraciones. Comenten entre ustedes cómo pronuncian los sonidos asociados con las letras **c, s** y **z,** en particular en las palabras identificadas a la izquierda de cada oración. Cuando terminen, intercámbiense las oraciones y repitan la actividad.

1. zapatos   Tengo muchos zapatos negros.

2. catorce   Mi hermanito tiene catorce años.

3. Fernández   El profesor Fernández enseña español.

4. cine   Vamos al cine todos los sábados.

5. rasgos   Los valles y las mesetas son rasgos geográficos.

6. crema   Prefiero tomar mi café con crema.

7. silencio   Durante un examen, los estudiantes trabajan en silencio.

8. hacemos   Siempre hacemos la tarea antes de clase.

5A.6 AUDIO SCRIPT: 1. La madre de Hoffman asistió a una escuela de cocina. 2. Ingrid Hoffman es alemana. 3. La madre de Hoffman le enseña a cocinar. 4. Hoffman vive en los EE.UU. cuando tiene dos años. 5. Hoffman tiene experiencia como actriz en Colombia antes de ser famosa en los EE.UU. 6. Hoffman tiene un restaurante en Orlando. 7. Hoffman promociona comidas fáciles. 8. Hoffman cree que ofrece al mundo un componente de la cultura hispana: la comida.

5A.6 ANSWERS: 1. cierto, 2. falso, (es colombiana), 3. cierto, 4. falso, (en Colombia), 5. cierto, 6. falso (en Miami), 7. cierto, 8. cierto.

5A.8 TEACHING TIP: Circulate among the groups to check pronunciation. You may then want to have the entire class repeat the sentences. When going over the answers, remind students to pay careful attention to spelling as they learn new words, since the /s/ sound can be represented in various ways.

Palabras clave 1 En la cocina: Las comidas y las bebidas*

WILEY PLUS

You will find PowerPoint presentations for use with *Palabras clave* in *WileyPLUS*.

TEACHING TIP: Bring in real or fake fruits and vegetables or draw simple images of some foods on the board and express your personal food preferences. For example, point to an apple and say *Me gustan las manzanas, pero no me gustan las uvas. Prefiero el café con leche y azúcar. No me gustan las zanahorias pero sí me gusta el apio.*

TEACHING TIP: Point out the blue category labels: *Condimentos, carnes, pescados y mariscos, postres, frutas, verduras y legumbres.* Have students tell you which items from the drawing belong to each category.

Labels in image: Condimentos, el arroz, el trigo, el maíz, el aceite, la pimienta, la miel, la sal, Cereales, las salchichas, el azúcar, Carnes, el pan, Pescados y mariscos, el pollo, el bistec, los camarones, el tocino, el pastel, las chuletas de puerco/cerdo, el hielo, las uvas, los calamares, Postres, Frutas, las fresas, las naranjas, las galletas, los plátanos, las manzanas

5A.9 TEACHING TIP: Consider offering the following as a homework assignment: Have students write eight additional statements, using Activity 5A.9 as a model. In the next class session, have them exchange statements with a partner and complete an activity like 5A.9. This additional practice will give students a chance to manipulate the new vocabulary on their own.

5A.9 ¿Probable o improbable? Lee los enunciados de abajo e indica si cada uno es **probable** o **improbable**. Prepárate para explicarle a un/a compañero/a de clase tus respuestas.

	Probable	Improbable
1. Un vegetariano come pollo.	☐	☑
2. Una persona que está a dieta come mucho helado.	☐	☑
3. Un bebé bebe leche.	☑	☐
4. El arroz es una comida fundamental en China.	☑	☐
5. Un francés bebe más cerveza que vino.	☐	☑
6. Las naranjas se cultivan *(are grown)* en Alaska.	☐	☑
7. Una persona pone sal en su café.	☐	☑
8. Sirven calamares en un restaurante elegante.	☑	☐

*The words *cocina* and *comida* can have a variety of meanings. *La cocina* may refer to the kitchen in the sense of a physical space. It may also refer to the act of cooking or to a particular type of food much the way "cuisine" is used in English. *La comida* refers to food in a general sense, but may also mean "meal".

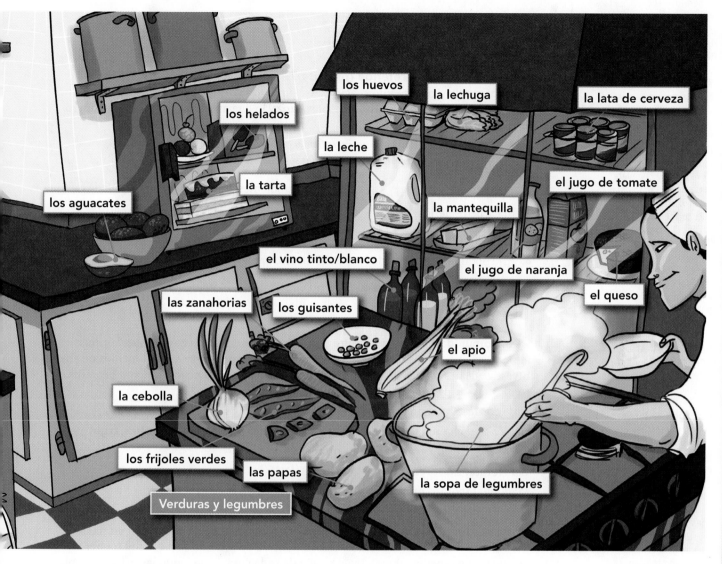

los huevos
la lechuga
la lata de cerveza
los helados
la leche
el jugo de tomate
la tarta
la mantequilla
los aguacates
el vino tinto/blanco
el jugo de naranja
el queso
las zanahorias
los guisantes
el apio
la cebolla
los frijoles verdes
las papas
la sopa de legumbres
Verduras y legumbres

5A.10 Busca la definición correcta. Con un/a compañero/a de clase, túrnense para leer las definiciones de abajo y emparejar cada definición con la palabra correspondiente. Comprueben sus respuestas con el resto de la clase.

5A.10 TEACHING TIP: Have students verify their answers with another pair of students before going over them as a large group.

a. la manzana   c. la fresa   e. los frijoles verdes   g. el hielo
b. el tocino   d. la papa   f. el cilantro   h. el aguacate

_e_ **1.** Es una legumbre verde y larga que contiene frijoles *(beans)* pequeños adentro.

_b_ **2.** Trozos *(pieces)* de carne de puerco que se comen por la mañana con huevos.

_f_ **3.** Una planta de color verde parecida al perejil *(parsley)* que se asocia con comidas hispanas.

_g_ **4.** Es agua que se ha hecho sólida en un congelador *(freezer)*.

_a_ **5.** Es la fruta que se asocia con Adán y Eva.

_c_ **6.** Una fruta roja y pequeña que asociamos con el verano.

_d_ **7.** Una fuente *(source)* de carbohidratos que asociamos con el estado de Idaho.

_h_ **8.** Es el ingrediente principal del guacamole.

5A.11 AUDIO SCRIPT: 1. Es el líquido blanco que beben los bebés. 2. Es la comida de Mickey Mouse. 3. Es la comida de Bugs Bunny. 4. Es la comida de Winnie the Pooh. 5. Es la bebida favorita de Homer Simpson. 6. Se asocian con las marcas Keebler y Oreo.

5A.11 TEACHING TIP: Have students refer to the illustration in *Palabras clave* as they complete Activity 5A.11. You may want to add visual support to the audio input by writing a narrowed-down list of possible answers on the board. Students need to hear, see and comprehend these new vocabulary words often before being asked to produce them.

5A.13 ALTERNATE ACTIVITY: If your students aren't likely to find several native Spanish-speakers to interview, have them do Internet key-word searches using each of the English words in 5A.13, followed by a comma and the name of a Spanish-speaking country. Have them try each word with three different countries selected randomly. Be sure to tell them that they may not understand everything that appears on each Spanish-language website that comes up in their searches, but they should be able to discover what word is used in a particular country to describe the selected food item. The variety of words for various food items is revisited in an upcoming *Vívelo: Cultura*. See page 216.

5A.11 ¿Qué es? Escribe la comida que corresponde a la descripción que escuches. Sigue el modelo.

1. *la leche*
2. el queso
3. las zanahorias
4. la miel
5. la cerveza
6. las galletas

5A.12 ¿Cuál es tu comida preferida (favorite)? Entrevista a un/a compañero/a de clase para obtener la siguiente información. Asegúrate *(be sure)* de crear preguntas para la entrevista según el modelo. Resume *(summarize)* lo que aprendas sobre tu compañero/a en tu **Retrato de la clase.**

> Modelo: E1: *¿Cuáles son tus ingredientes preferidos en una ensalada?*
> E2: *Mis ingredientes preferidos son el tomate, las espinacas, la lechuga y el queso.*

1. Tu ensalada preferida
2. Tu carne preferida
3. Tu postre preferido
4. Tus condimentos preferidos
5. Tus ingredientes preferidos en una ensalada de fruta
6. Tus ingredientes preferidos en una sopa
7. Tu jugo preferido
8. Tu bebida preferida

Retrato de la clase: La bebida preferida de ___ es ___. Su jugo preferido es ___, etcétera.

5A.13 ¡A la comunidad hispana! Entrevista a diferentes personas cuyo *(whose)* primer idioma sea el español sobre las palabras que usan para referirse a los alimentos de abajo. Investiga cuáles son las palabras que se usan en sus países. Luego, compara tus resultados con los de varios compañeros de clase.

Pork: **cerdo, chancho, cochino, lechón, puerco**
Green beans: **chaucha, ejote, judía verde, perona, poroto verde, vaina, frijol verde**
Strawberry: **fresa, fresón, frutilla, metra**
Corn: **elote, maíz, choclo**
Peach: **melocotón, durazno**

5A.14 Abastecedores (Caterers). Con otros dos compañeros de clase, creen un menú para *uno* de los siguientes eventos. Deben ponerse de acuerdo *(agree)* en el número de personas que esperan, el menú y el precio de cada cosa, incluyendo las bebidas, el plato principal y el postre. ¡Traten de ponerse de acuerdo en español!

El menú es para:
☐ una cena de una compañía donde algunos *(some)* de los invitados son vegetarianos
☐ una comida para ocho jugadores de póker
☐ una cena formal para una familia
☐ una cena romántica para dos personas
☐ una cena para estudiantes que anticipan un viaje a España
☐ una cena para profesores de un congreso *(conference)* en Argentina
☐ otro: _____

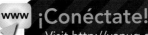

www ¡Conéctate!
Visit http://yanuq.com to find exquisite recipes from Peru. Identify one or two recipes that contain food that you like. What recipe would you like to prepare? How much time would it take? What are you waiting for?

5A.14 TEACHING TIP: You may want to assign each of the suggested menus to a particular group. If your classroom does not have the technology to allow students' menus to be displayed for the whole class, have each group make enough copies of their menu so that the rest of the class can review the menus and vote on the best based on categories, such as the best prices, the most delicious menu, the most creative menu, etc. Then, these menus can be used for role-playing as if at a restaurant.

Palabras clave 2 ¿Cómo pones la mesa?

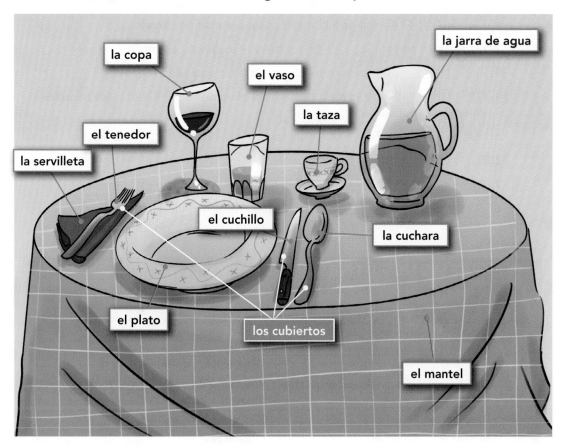

WILEY PLUS

You will find PowerPoint presentations for use with *Palabras clave* in *WileyPLUS*.

TEACHING TIP: Bring in props (e.g. a napkin, silverware, etc.) to present this new vocabulary. Set a table in plain view of the students as you name the items at hand. To offer students more input, ask questions such as *¿Necesitas una copa de vino para tomar café? ¿Qué necesitas para tomar sopa?*

En el restaurante

el/la cocinero/a	la persona que prepara la comida
el/la camarero/a	la persona que sirve la comida
el/la cliente	la persona que come en un restaurante
la cuenta	el costo total de la comida que se paga al restaurante
dejar la propina	un porcentaje de la cuenta que el cliente deja *(leaves)* para el camarero
el plato principal	el componente más importante de una comida
servir	traerles la comida a los clientes

5A.15 ¿Qué o quién es? Túrnate con un/a compañero/a para leer los siguientes enunciados el uno al otro y decir la palabra de vocabulario correspondiente. Comprueben sus respuestas con otros compañeros de clase.

> Modelo: E1: *Soy la cosa que indica el costo de la comida en un restaurante.*
> E2: *la cuenta/el menú*

1. Soy la persona que sirve la comida en un restaurante. → el/la camarero/a

2. Soy la cosa que usamos para servir agua. → la jarra

3. Soy el cubierto que corta *(cuts)* la carne. → el cuchillo

4. Soy el cubierto que recoge *(picks up)* la carne del plato para comerla. → el tenedor/la cuchara

5. Soy la cosa que contiene el vino para beberlo. → la copa

6. Soy la cosa donde ponen la comida para servirla a los clientes. → el plato

7. Soy la cosa que cubre *(covers)* y protege la mesa. → el mantel

8. Soy la persona que va a un restaurante a comer. → el/la cliente

5A.15 TEACHING TIP: Use activity 5A.15 to develop partnering cards for your students. On slips of paper have each statement (1-8) and on separate slips of paper, the answers. Randomly pass these sheets out to students and have them find the person with the matching slip of paper.

5A.16 ¿Cuál es la palabra? Escribe la palabra de vocabulario que mejor complete cada oración según el modelo. Compara tus respuestas con las de un/a compañero/a de clase.

1. Las __servilletas__ son de tela *(cloth)* en los restaurantes elegantes.

2. El camarero prepara la ____cuenta____ cuando los clientes terminan de comer.

3. El ____cocinero____ prepara la comida según la preferencia de los clientes.

4. El ____postre____ llega a la mesa después del plato principal. A veces *(sometimes)* es dulce *(sweet)* y delicioso.

5. Las botellas de agua hoy en día reemplazan *(replace)* las ____jarras____ de agua en la mesa.

6. La ____taza____ es para beber té o café.

7. Usamos una ____cuchara____ para comer sopa.

8. El cliente deja la ____propina____ sobre la mesa antes de salir del restaurante.

EXPRESIONES ÚTILES

As in the United States, interactions between customers and servers in restaurants in Hispanic countries include a number of set or predetermined polite expressions. People use these expressions to be polite in social situations as well.

¿Qué le(s) gustaría?	*What would you like?*
¿Qué desea(n) de comer/beber/postre?	*What would you like to eat/to drink/for dessert?*
¿Desea(n) algo más?	*Would you like anything else?*
Me gustaría…/Quisiera…	*I would like. . .*
Nos gustaría…/Quisiéramos…	*We would like. . .*
Tráigame… por favor	*Please bring me. . .*
Tráiganos… por favor	*Please bring us. . .*
Buen provecho	*Enjoy your meal (both when the food is served and when you leave the table while others are still eating).*
Con permiso	*Excuse me (when leaving the table or needing to pass through a crowded area).*
Perdón	*Excuse me / I'm sorry (when you make a mistake, you drop something, you bump into someone, etc.).*
Te invito.*	*It's my treat or It's on me.*

*__Te invito…__ can also mean simply *I invite you. . .* to a party or other event. In the context of dining out, it is generally an offer to pay the bill.

5A.17 En el restaurante. En grupos de tres, preparen una conversación entre un camarero y dos clientes en un restaurante y representen *(act out)* la escena para el resto de la clase. Usen varias palabras de vocabulario relacionadas con comidas, bebidas, servicios de mesa *(tableware)* y especialmente las expresiones de cortesía de **Expresiones útiles.**

Palabras clave 3 En la cocina: Los aparatos y las acciones

WILEY **PLUS**

You will find PowerPoint presentations for use with *Palabras clave* in WileyPLUS.

batir	combinar ingredientes enérgicamente o con movimientos rápidos
calentar (e-ie)	subirle *(raise)* la temperatura a la comida
congelar	poner la comida en un lugar frío para mantener su forma sólida
cortar	usar un cuchillo para hacer trozos pequeños de fruta, carne o legumbres
cubrir	poner algo sobre la comida para protegerla
derretir (e-i)	la acción de transformarse de sólido a líquido
freír (e-i)	calentar la comida en aceite de oliva u otro tipo de aceite
hervir (e-ie)	calentar un líquido al punto de que se mueva rápidamente
hornear	cocinar algo en el horno
mezclar	combinar varios ingredientes
pelar	quitar la parte exterior de una fruta o una verdura

5A.18 TEACHING TIP: Model how you would portray the action of *mezclar*. Hold your hands in front of you and rotate your wrists several times as if you were tossing a salad.

5A.18 MULTIPLE INTELLIGENCES: BODILY/KINESTHETIC. This activity is particularly helpful for students who remember better by attaching a gesture to a word.

5A.18 Comunicar sin hablar. En grupos de tres, dibujen varias palabras de vocabulario y/o hagan gestos físicos o con las manos que transmitan el significado de esas palabras. Luego, compartan con la clase los gestos y dibujos, sin decir a qué palabra se refieren, mientras sus compañeros de clase responden con la nueva palabra.

5A.19 AUDIO SCRIPT: 1. el agua para hacer pasta, 2. la mantequilla en el sartén, 3. la pizza, 4. las papas de McDonald's, 5. la banana o el plátano, 6. los huevos

5A.19 EXTENSION ACTIVITY: Have students create a semantic map with the verbs and foods they most commonly use. This association will serve as an additional tool to help them remember the vocabulary.

5A.20 TEACHING TIP: Point out that students do not need to understand every word in the description, but rather just get the gist in order to find the right match.

TEACHING TIP: Ask students what foods are associated with specific traditions in their native or background culture. Do they know the source or origin of these traditions?

5A.19 ¿Con qué comidas y bebidas se asocian estos verbos? Vas a escuchar una lista de varias cosas relacionadas con comidas y bebidas. Identifica el verbo que asocia con cada palabra o frase. El primero se muestra como modelo. Compara tus respuestas con la clase.

_____5_____ **a.** pelar _____3_____ **c.** hornear _____1_____ **e.** hervir

_____6_____ **b.** batir _____4_____ **d.** freír _____2_____ **f.** derretir

5A.20 Busca la palabra apropiada. Con un/a compañero/a de clase, túrnate para leer las descripciones de abajo y seleccionar la palabra que mejor corresponda a cada descripción. Una de las palabras no se usa. La primera se muestra como modelo.

a. la parrilla **c.** derretir **e.** mezclar **g.** cortar

b. cubrir **d.** el horno **f.** el microondas **h.** el sartén

___C___ **1.** El antónimo de congelar.

___h___ **2.** El tipo de olla que se usa para freír la comida.

___a___ **3.** La cosa que usamos para preparar la comida al aire libre (e.g., en el patio de la casa).

___f___ **4.** El aparato eléctrico que usamos para calentar la comida rápidamente.

___d___ **5.** La parte de la cocina que usamos para preparar un pastel de cumpleaños *(birthdays)* u otro postre.

___e___ **6.** Lo contrario de separar los ingredientes.

___g___ **7.** El verbo que significa dividir algo en trozos o separar algo con un cuchillo.

VÍVELO: CULTURA

La cocina: ¡Vivan las diferencias!

El mundo de habla hispana es muy vasto. Aunque el idioma español es una fuerza unificadora entre 21 países, la cocina es muy diferente entre los países hispanohablantes. Hay una gran variedad de platos en las diferentes regiones. Esto depende de la cultura y de las influencias locales. Por ejemplo, en México los tamales eran *(were)* una comida común entre los indígenas porque durante las guerras *(wars)* entre tribus, el tamal era nutritivo y fácil de transportar. Hoy en día son tan variados como lo es el sándwich. En esta foto, la familia se reúne a untar *(to spread)* la masa *(dough)* de los tamales en las hojas de maíz *(corn husks)* donde luego se ponen los ingredientes, tales como carne, queso y chiles, entre otros. También se pueden preparar usando una hoja de plátano.

No toda la comida hispana es picante *(spicy)* y no todas las tortillas se asocian con el burrito o el taco. En España, la tortilla es un plato de huevos, papas y cebolla que es similar al omelette.

Además, como han visto en la Actividad 5A.13 de la página 210, los nombres de una misma *(same)* comida pueden ser diferentes en diferentes países. Por ejemplo, en Perú, Chile y Ecuador, al maíz se le llama "choclo". Lo que en inglés son *noodles* en algunas partes de Sur América son "tallarines" y en otras son "fideos". Algunas comidas son comunes en muchas regiones, por ejemplo, el arroz con pollo, la carne de cerdo y el pescado. A pesar de *(in spite of)* las diferencias entre las comidas de los diferentes países, varias comidas tradicionales de España han influido en la cocina de Latinoamérica. Un ejemplo es el bacalao *(cod fish)*, que es nativo de aguas frías y sin embargo *(nonetheless)* se come mucho en el Caribe y en México.

VÍVELO: LENGUA

Giving instructions with infinitives

In Spanish, it is very common to use the infinitive of the verb when giving instructions or directions in writing. One context where this is frequently seen is in recipes (**las recetas**). It is also seen on signs or other public announcements.

Añadir la sal.	*Add the salt.*
Mezclar la sal y la pimienta.	*Mix the salt and pepper.*
Batir los huevos.	*Beat the eggs.*
Pelar y cortar las zanahorias.	*Peel and cut the carrots.*
Dejar los huevos hervir unos minutos.	*Let the eggs boil for a few minutes.*
No fumar.	*No smoking.*
Salir por la puerta de atrás.	*Exit by the back door.*

TEACHING TIP: Encourage students to make at least five signs with similar infinitive commands that they will write on index cards and place in their own kitchens.

5A.21 ¿Qué se prepara? Trabaja con un/a compañero/a de clase para emparejar cada comida o bebida con la descripción de cómo prepararla. Sigan el modelo.

a. ensalada   **d.** pizza   **g.** tortilla española

b. limonada   **e.** sándwich de jamón y queso   **h.** vino

c. papas fritas   **f.** sopa de pollo

___h___ **1.** Hay que hacer jugo de uvas. Luego, hay que dejar fermentar el jugo y ponerlo en botellas. Se puede servir después de varios años.

___c___ **2.** Hay que pelar las papas y luego cortarlas. Después, hay que calentar aceite en una sartén. Luego, poner las papas en el aceite caliente…

___b___ **3.** Es necesario cortar varios limones y sacar el jugo de ellos. Después, mezclar el jugo de los limones con agua y azúcar. Entonces, se sirve fría.

___d___ **4.** Primero, hacer una masa *(dough)* y darle forma de un círculo. Luego poner salsa de tomate y salchichas encima *(on top of)* de la mesa. Después, cubrir todo con mucho queso. Finalmente, es necesario hornearlo unos veinte minutos.

___g___ **5.** Primero, cortar y freír varias papas y una cebolla. Luego mezclar las papas y la cebolla con los huevos y calentarlo todo en la sartén por unos minutos.

___e___ **6.** Untar *(to spread)* dos rebanadas de pan con mayonesa. Después, cortar un poco de jamón y un poco de queso. Finalmente, poner el jamón y el queso entre los rebanadas de pan.

___a___ **7.** Primero, lavar, pelar y cortar varias verduras y legumbres. Luego combinar las verduras y legumbres. Servir este plato antes del plato principal.

___f___ **8.** Hervir un pollo en agua hasta formar un consomé. Después, sacar el pollo del consomé y cortarlo. Luego combinar el pollo con varias verduras, poner la mezcla en el consomé y permitir que se cocine.

5A.22 Hazte famoso/a por un minuto. En grupos de tres, creen su propio segmento de video (al estilo de Rachael Ray o Ingrid Hoffman). El segmento de video debe ilustrar en español cómo preparar, paso por paso, algún tipo de plato. Uno de ustedes se puede encargar *(take charge)* de la grabación *(filming)*, otro de la explicación y el tercero de la demostración de lo que dice la persona que habla. Por ejemplo, si la persona que habla dice "Tomar una zanahoria del refrigerador. Cortar la zanahoria,…", la persona que hace la demostración debe sacar una zanahoria del refrigerador y cortarla. Miren *Vívelo: Lengua* en la página 218 y usen adverbios en sus explicaciones.

5A.22 TEACHING TIP Encourage students to use *hay que* with infinitives and to use adverbs in their segments.

5A.22 STANDARDS: COMMUNICATION/ PRESENTATIONAL MODE. What distinguishes this mode from the others (interpersonal and interpretive) is the fact that it is polished and edited. Make sure that students have ample time to meet outside of class to prepare for this activity.

5A.22 ALTERNATE ACTIVITY If your students don't have easy access to a video camera, have them prepare their cooking demo as a role play to perform in front of the class.

TEACHING TIP: Bring in a copy of Elvis Crespo's hit *Suavemente* to expose students to the formation of adverbs. As an extension activity, have them write their own verse using new vocabulary (e.g. *cocínalo lentamente*).

VÍVELO: LENGUA

Describing actions: Adverbs ending in *–mente*

Adverbs in Spanish are often formed by adding **–mente** to the feminine singular form of the adjective. These forms are the equivalent of English adverbs that end in *–ly*.

rápido ⟶ rápidamente
lento ⟶ lentamente
atento ⟶ atentamente

claro ⟶ claramente
suficiente ⟶ suficientemente
general ⟶ generalmente

¡Atención!

copa	refers to a *wine glass* or *champagne flute*. It can also mean *drink* as in **Vamos a tomar una copa** *(Let's go for a drink)*. A cup is **una taza** in Spanish. Con un bistec, me gusta tomar una copa de vino tinto. Para beber café, se usa una taza.
vaso	refers to *a glass* for drinking water, juice, milk, etc. A *vase* in English is a **florero** in Spanish. Es recomendable tomar ocho vasos de agua cada día. Las rosas están en el florero.
crudo	is an adjective meaning *raw*. The Spanish words **vulgar** and **grosero** are equivalents for the English *crude*. No es buena idea comer pollo crudo. Esos chicos son muy vulgares porque usan palabras groseras.
régimen	can refer to *regime* in the context of government. In the context of food, however, it refers to a specified *diet* as in **Tengo que seguir un régimen que controla la diabetes** *(I have to stay on a specific diet that controls my diabetes)*. To talk about *being on a diet* in the sense of eating light in general, use **estar a dieta**. El régimen de South Beach es muy popular. Alfonso ha bajado de peso porque está a dieta y hace ejercicio.

5A.23 TEACHING TIP: Make sure to remind students to complete the sentences before deciding whether or not they agree with them.

5A.23 ¿Estás de acuerdo? Completa cada enunciado con la palabra apropiada de la lista. Una de las palabras no se usa. Cuando completes los enunciados, indica si estás de acuerdo (Sí) o no estás de acuerdo (No) con cada uno. Comprueba tus respuestas con las de un compañero de clase y luego con toda la clase. ¿Hay enunciados con los cuales la clase no está de acuerdo?

cruda   copa   taza
vaso   régimen   dieta

	Sí	No
1. Cuando alguien hace un brindis *(a toast)*, es grosero no alzar *(to raise)* la _____copa_____.	☐	☐
2. Es peligroso *(dangerous)* comer carne _____cruda_____.	☐	☐
3. Se sirve el té en una _____taza_____.	☐	☐
4. El _____régimen_____ del Dr. Atkins es saludable.	☐	☐
5. Prefiero usar un _____vaso_____ de cristal y no de plástico.		

Estructuras clave 1 Direct objects and direct object pronouns

WILEY **PLUS**
Go to *WileyPLUS* and review the tutorial for this grammar point.

Look at these Spanish sentences, focusing on what Ingrid Hoffman prepares, and whom she visits.

Ingrid Hoffman prepara **la ensalada**.	*Ingrid Hoffman prepares the salad.*
Ingrid Hoffman visita **a sus primos**.	*Ingrid Hoffman visits her cousins.*

What does Ingrid Hoffman prepare? She prepares *the salad*. Whom does she visit? She visits *her cousins*. These are direct objects. A direct object is a noun that receives the action of a verb. It answers the question "What?" or "Whom?".

When the direct object of a verb is a person, Spanish introduces that person with what is known as the personal **a** or **la a personal**. It has no equivalent in English, but serves as a marker which signals that the direct object of the verb is a person. When both the subject and the direct object of the verb are people, the **a personal** helps us determine who is the subject and who is the direct object.

Pronouns in general allow for shorter, more economical communication since they avoid the need to repeat the same noun over and over again. Instead of saying, for example,

Ingrid Hoffman prepara **la ensalada** y luego lleva **la ensalada** a la casa de sus primos.

we can say…

Ingrid Hoffman prepara **la ensalada** y luego **la** lleva a la casa de sus primos.

WILEY **PLUS**

You will find PowerPoint presentations for use with *Estructuras clave* in *WileyPLUS*

Direct object pronouns			
me *me*		**nos** *us*	
te *you*		**os** *you* (pl. informal. Spain)	
lo *it* (masc.)	*him / you* (masc. formal)	**los** *them* (masc.)	*you* (pl.)
la *it* (fem.)	*her / you* (fem. formal)	**las** *them* (fem.) *you* (pl. fem.)	

Compare these short paragraphs to see how direct object pronouns make for smoother, more economical communication.

Without direct object pronouns	With direct object pronouns
Ingrid Hoffman prepara **la ensalada**. Luego pone **la ensalada** en el refrigerador hasta que sea la hora de llevar **la ensalada** a la casa de sus primos. Ingrid Hoffman quiere mucho a **sus primos** y ve a **sus primos** con frecuencia.	Ingrid Hoffman prepara **la ensalada.** Luego **la** pone en el refrigerador hasta que sea la hora de llevar**la** a la casa de sus primos. Ingrid Hoffman quiere mucho **a sus primos** y **los** ve con frecuencia.
Ingrid Hoffman prepares the salad. Then she puts the salad in the refrigerator until it's time to take the salad to her cousins' house. Ingrid Hoffman loves her cousins and sees her cousins often.	*Ingrid Hoffman prepares the salad. Then she puts it in the refrigerator until it's time to take it to her cousins' house. Ingrid Hoffman loves her cousins and sees them often.*

Position of direct object pronouns

Note the position of the direct object pronouns in the sentences below. While English puts the direct object pronoun after the verb (e.g., puts it, take it, sees them), in Spanish, the direct object pronoun precedes a conjugated verb.

¿La ensalada? Ingrid Hoffman **la** prepara.	*The salad? Ingrid Hoffman prepares it.*
¿Sus primos? Ingrid Hoffman **los** visita.	*Her cousins? Ingrid Hoffman visits them.*

When the verb is not conjugated, and instead is used in the infinitive form, the pronoun is attached to the end of the infinitive.

Ingrid Hoffman quiere mucho a sus primos.	*Ingrid Hoffman loves her cousins.*
Para ella es importante ver**los** con frecuencia.	*It is important to her to see them often.*
Corta las zanahorias antes de poner**las** en la ensalada.	*She cuts the carrots before putting them in the salad.*

When the verb expression is comprised of a conjugated verb and an infinitive working together, the direct object pronoun may precede the conjugated verb or be attached to the infinitive.

¿Sus primos? Ingrid Hoffman quiere ver**los** hoy. ⎫	*Her cousins? Ingrid Hoffman wants to*
¿Sus primos? Ingrid Hoffman **los** quiere ver hoy. ⎭	*see them today.*

5A.24 Eva Longoria.   Trabajen en parejas para determinar si Eva Longoria es el sujeto o el objeto directo del verbo en los siguientes enunciados. Luego, indiquen si los enunciados son probables o dicen la verdad.

		Sujeto	Objeto	¿Es probable? ¿Es verdad?
1.	Eva Longoria ha ido a Europa.	☑	☐	☐
2.	Teri Hatcher y Felicity Huffman conocen a Eva Longoria	☐	☑	☐
3.	Eva Longoria ha comido en restaurantes elegantes.	☑	☐	☐
4.	Eva Longoria ha preparado muchos platos hispanos.	☑	☐	☐
5.	He escuchado a Eva Longoria cantar.	☐	☑	☐
6.	Eva Longoria come enchiladas picantes.	☑	☐	☐
7.	Admiro a Eva Longoria.	☐	☑	☐
8.	Eva Longoria ha usado un vestido de Carolina Herrera.	☑	☐	☐

5A.25 ¿Cómo se interpreta?   Con un/a compañero/a de clase, lee cada una de las oraciones de abajo e indiquen si la interpretación A o B es la interpretación correcta. Sigan el modelo.

		A	**B**
1.	Lo invito.	☑ *I invite him.*	☐ *He invites me.*
2.	La beben.	☑ *They drink it.*	☐ *She drinks it.*
3.	La conocemos.	☐ *She knows us.*	☑ *We know her.*
4.	Los visitas.	☐ *They visit you.*	☑ *You visit them.*
5.	Me miras.	☐ *I look at you.*	☑ *You look at me.*
6.	Nos comprenden.	☐ *We understand them.*	☑ *They understand us.*
7.	Te adoro.	☑ *You adore me.*	☐ *I adore you.*
8.	Las comen.	☐ *She eats them.*	☑ *They eat them.*

5A.26 ¿Qué dibujo representa la idea? Lee cada una de las siguientes oraciones e indica cuál de los dos dibujos representa mejor el significado. Compara tus respuestas con las de un/a compañero/a de clase.

1. Juan las ve.

2. Yo la como.

3. Ellos los fríen.

4. Tú nos oyes.

5. Nosotros lo bebemos.

6. La cocinera las pela.

5A.26 TEACHING TIP: Before they begin the activity, have students identify the object nouns in each drawing, with a focus on number and gender: 1. la chica/las chicas, 2. el sándwich/la pizza, 3. los huevos/el huevo, 4. nosotros/yo, 5. la cerveza/el vino, 6. los aguacates/las naranjas.

VÍVELO: STANDARDS: COMMUNITIES. Ask students to interview Spanish-speakers in the community (or online) about what they would call a mid-morning snack and what they consider to be light snack foods in their native countries, as well as about some of their favorite *tapas* or *botanas*. Have students report back their findings.

VÍVELO: CULTURA

Algo para picar (*Something to munch on*)

La merienda Es una comida ligera (*light*) que se come antes del almuerzo o de la cena.

Las tapas Este fenómeno gastronómico y cultural de España es popular en muchas ciudades norteamericanas. Se refiere a una variedad de aperitivos (*appetizers*) que se sirven en los bares y restaurantes acompañados de vino o cerveza. Entre los aperitivos hay diferentes variedades de quesos y jamones, así como aceitunas (*olives*) y papas. Las tapas se sirven en porciones individuales en platos pequeños y se comen tradicionalmente en la tarde entre la hora en que termina el trabajo y la cena. El concepto de "ir de tapas" es muy similar al concepto del *happy hour* en Estados Unidos.

Las botanas Son el equivalente mexicano de las tapas españolas. Las personas van a un "botanero" para tomar algo y disfrutar de aperitivos como chalupas, tostadas, taquitos, guacamole y salsa. Usualmente las personas se reúnen en los botaneros para ver un partido de fútbol o algún otro evento deportivo.

¿Qué comes tú cuando quieres algo para picar?

TAPAS

Patatas bravas	3.00 €
Alitas de pollo	6.00 €
Calamares a la romana	10.00 €
Sepia	7.50 €
Champiñones	6.00 €
Patatas dos salsas	6.50 €
Tortilla de patata	10.00 €
Montadito de jamón	6.00 €
Ración de chorizo	7.50 €
Morcilla	7.50 €
Ración de aceitunas	3.70 €
Empanada de atún	5.70 €
Croquetas de ibérico	6.95 €
Huevos rotos con jamón	6.90 €
Salpicón	3.00 €
Gazpacho	3.00 €
Tosta de angulas	4.50 €
Tosta de salmorejo	3.30 €

5A.27 ¡A leer una receta! Lee la siguiente receta y presta mucha atención a los pronombres de objeto directo en negrita. Luego, completa los espacios en blanco de abajo, tomando como base la lectura. Comprueba las respuestas con la clase.

Deléitate con un desayuno dominicano
Mangú dominicano

Por Ángela María González, Univisión Online

El mangú es una especie de puré hecho a base de plátano verde. Hay dominicanos que comen mangú a la hora del almuerzo y hay quienes **lo** comen a la hora de la cena. Pero lo clásico es comer**lo** en el desayuno, acompañado con huevos o con salchichón. Prueba *(taste)* este delicioso plato y prepára**lo** para saber cómo sólo los dominicanos saben hacer**lo**.

"Generalmente el mangú se hace con plátano verde majado *(mashed)*, pero hay quienes prefieren hacerlo con plátano maduro y es igual de rico pero tiene un sabor más dulce. El mangú se acompaña tradicionalmente con huevos fritos, salchichón o queso blanco. No puede faltar la cebolla por encima del mangú", dice la dominicana Liza Díaz-Pinzón. Jesús Santana, sub chef del restaurante "La Tortuga," del Punta Cana Beach Resort en Punta Cana, República Dominicana, te ofrece su versión del desayuno típico dominicano que incluye el rico mangú:

Ingredientes:

2 huevos	1 plátano verde
1 cucharadita de aceite	sal al gusto
2 trozos de tocino	1 cucharadita de mantequilla
3 salchichas	1 taza de agua hervida

- Colocar *(Place)* los huevos en un recipiente.
- En un sartén poner el aceite y vertir los huevos.
- Freír los huevos 2 minutos y voltear**los** para cocinar**los** por ambos lados.
- Cocinar el tocino al horno 3 minutos.
- Poner las salchichas al horno 5 minutos.
- Pelar el plátano y hervir**lo** en agua 25 minutos hasta que esté blandito.
- Licuar**lo** y añadir la sal, la mantequilla, el agua y el aceite.
- Servir el plátano y poner un poco de cebolla por encima.
- Acompañar con los huevos, las salchichas y el tocino.

Elige la respuesta que mejor completa cada oración.

__d__ **1.** El mangú es un plato típico de …

a. México   **b.** Ecuador   **c.** Nicaragua   **d.** La República Dominicana

__a__ **2.** El mangú se asocia tradicionalmente con …

a. el desayuno   **b.** la merienda   **c.** la cena   **d.** las tapas

5A.28 Ordenar cronológicamente. Usando números del 1–6, indica el orden correcto de los pasos de la receta. Luego, comprueba tus respuestas con un/a compañero/a de clase.

__5__   Cubrir el puré de plátano con cebolla.

__1__   Freír los huevos en un sartén.

__3__   Pelar y hervir el plátano.

__6__   Servir el mangú con los huevos, el tocino y las salchichas.

__2__   Cocinar el tocino y las salchichas al horno.

__4__   Combinar el plátano con sal, mantequilla, agua y aceite después de licuarlo.

5A.29 Adivina. Lee el siguiente pasaje para tener una idea general de qué trata *(what it's about)*. Luego con un/a compañer/a de clase, vuelve a leerlo y por cada pronombre de objeto directo subrayado, indica el objeto al que se refiere el pronombre. El primero se muestra como modelo.

Pelo las papas antes de cocinar<u>las</u>^{1}. <u>Las</u>^{2} pongo en una olla para hervir<u>las</u>^{3}. Veo que están listas *(ready)* cuando <u>las</u>^{4} puedo cortar fácilmente con un tenedor. Luego, <u>las</u>^{5} saco de la olla y <u>las</u>^{6} pongo en la sopa. Además de las papas, añado *(I add)* otros vegetales a la sopa. <u>Los</u>^{7} añado lentamente, y cuando no hay más que añadir a la sopa y está lista, <u>la</u>^{8} como.

1. _las papas_   3. las papas   5. las papas   7. otros vegetales
2. las papas   4. las papas   6. las papas   8. la sopa

5A.30 ¿A qué o a quién se refiere?   Empareja el pronombre de objeto directo de cada oración con el nombre al que más lógicamente se refiere.

<table>
<tr><td>a</td><td>1. Bugs Bunny <u>las</u> come siempre.</td><td>a. las zanahorias</td></tr>
<tr><td>c</td><td>2. Los estudiantes <u>la</u> comen mucho.</td><td>b. a ti</td></tr>
<tr><td>h</td><td>3. Mi mejor amigo/a <u>me</u> conoce bien.</td><td>c. la pizza</td></tr>
<tr><td>b</td><td>4. <u>Te</u> invitamos a cenar.</td><td>d. las uvas</td></tr>
<tr><td>e</td><td>5. Mi padre <u>lo</u> abraza *(hugs)*.</td><td>e. a mi hermano</td></tr>
<tr><td>f</td><td>6. <u>Nos</u> visitan frecuentemente.</td><td>f. a nosotros</td></tr>
<tr><td>d</td><td>7. <u>Las</u> usan para producir vino.</td><td>g. los camarones</td></tr>
<tr><td>g</td><td>8. <u>Los</u> pido cuando voy a Red Lobster.</td><td>h. a mí</td></tr>
</table>

5A.31 Entrevista a un/a compañero/a.   Entrevista a un/a compañero/a de clase usando las siguientes preguntas y apunta sus respuestas. Comparte con la clase cualquier respuesta inusual y luego escríbela en tu **Retrato de la clase.**

1. ¿Quién lava los platos en tu casa?
2. ¿A qué hora preparas la cena?
3. ¿Cuándo pones la mesa?
4. ¿Abres las latas de comida con un aparato electrónico (un abrelatas) o manualmente?
5. ¿Pides café cuando vas a un restaurante?
6. ¿Quién nos protege de la comida venenosa *(poisonous)*?
7. ¿Pagas la cuenta cuando sales a comer con tu novio/a?
8. ¿Bebes bebidas alcohólicas?

5A.30 TEACHING TIP: This activity could be useful for pairing students. On slips of paper, write down the ten sentences and possible answers. Randomly pass them out to students. Have students find the person with the correct match and remain with that person for the next activity.

Enlaces

además de ——→ *in addition to* ——→ Además de preparar comida china, a mi amigo le gusta preparar comida dominicana.

según parece →*apparently* ——→ Según parece Ingrid Hoffman es conocida en todo el mundo hispano.

mientras que →*while/whereas* ——→ Mientras que muchos mexicanos todavía duermen la siesta, los estadounidenses no duermen lo suficiente.

5A.32 ¿Puedes conectar las ideas?   Conecta las ideas en las oraciones de abajo usando la expresión apropiada. Luego, verifica tus respuestas con la clase.

1. Según parece   el tomate contiene vitaminas que combaten el cáncer.

2. Mientras que   muchos de mis amigos quieren estudiar en otros países, otros amigos no quieren salir de su estado.

3. Además de   ver fútbol americano en la televisión, también me gusta ver fútbol de las ligas europeas.

FUNCTIONAL OUTCOMES:
The central question that frames this *Investigación* is "*¿Cómo se puede hablar de las comidas y bebidas?*" Explore whether students can now address this question and how they would go about it. Have them review the chart on the first page of this *Investigación*.

5A.33 TEACHING TIP:
Ask students to read one paragraph at a time and then verify what they have comprehended with the entire group before moving on to the next paragraph. If time is limited, ask all members of the group to read the first paragraph and then each member reads about one mealtime and explains it to the rest of the group.

5A.33 Lo que influye en las prácticas culinarias. En grupos de tres, lean el siguiente texto sobre la influencia del clima en las horas de comer en España y por consiguiente en Latinoamérica. Luego, contesten las preguntas que le siguen.

Las horas de comer en los países hispanos

¿Alguna vez has pensado cómo el clima de una región influye en las prácticas culturales? España tiene una larga historia. Muchos de sus edificios son muy antiguos y fueron construidos en una época en la que el aire acondicionado no existía. Son estructuras sólidas y funcionales que en la actualidad sirven como oficinas de gobierno y negocios (*businesses*), y muchos todavía no tienen aire acondicionado. Es por esta razón que entre las 2:00 y las 4:00 p.m., cuando hace más calor en el día, algunos negocios cierran sus puertas y la gente va a su casa para hacer la comida más importante del día, el almuerzo. Esta tradición fue heredada (*inherited*) por los países latinoamericanos y muchos aún la conservan.

El desayuno Durante la semana es una comida ligera (*light*) que se consume antes de ir a la escuela o al trabajo, y generalmente consiste en café, té caliente o chocolate con pan tostado, panecillos (*sweet rolls*) o cereal. En el fin de semana, sin embargo, el desayuno para muchas familias es un evento social y se cocinan diferentes platos dependiendo de la región.

El almuerzo El término se refiere a la comida del mediodía, generalmente entre la 1:00 y las 3:00 p.m. En algunas regiones "la comida" es sinónimo del almuerzo. Este es el alimento (*food*) principal del día y puede consistir en varios platos (*courses*): primero sopa, arroz o pasta, luego carne, pescado o pollo con legumbres o verduras y finalmente un postre, como flan, arroz con leche, etcétera. En algunos lugares las personas salen del trabajo o de la escuela para ir a casa a comer y regresan por la tarde después de terminar la comida.

La cena Se come en la noche, usualmente entre las 8:00 y las 9:00 p.m. y a veces más tarde, especialmente en el caso de un evento especial como un banquete o una boda. En algunos lugares la cena es sencilla y generalmente consiste en las sobras (*leftovers*) del almuerzo.

Preguntas:

1. ¿Qué come la gente en el desayuno y más o menos a qué hora?

2. ¿Qué come la gente en el almuerzo y más o menos a qué hora?

3. ¿Qué come la gente en la cena y más o menos a qué hora?

4. ¿Cuáles son algunos factores que motivan el establecimiento de estas tradiciones españolas?

Perspectivas

5A.34 Productos y prácticas. El texto de **Contextos** ofrece una explicación de cómo las prácticas culinarias de una cultura pueden establecerse. En la lectura de **Perspectivas** van a leer acerca de un factor que puede alterar las prácticas culinarias.

Paso 1: Culturas en contacto. Lee el artículo sobre factores actuales que motivan cambios en las prácticas de una cultura con respecto a la comida. Luego, indica si los enunciados que siguen son ciertos o falsos según lo que dice el artículo. Corrige los enunciados falsos. Comprueba tus respuestas con otros compañeros de clase.

Costumbres saludables

En casa de mi abuela chilena, las frutas que comemos vienen de los árboles en su jardín. Siempre hay risa *(laughter)* en la cocina y en la casa. **Según parece,** los investigadores han descubierto que estas y otras costumbres latinas nos mantienen saludables *(healthy)*.

Los estudios demuestran que los latinos que mantienen las costumbres de sus países de origen tienen mayor salud física y emocional que aquellos que se "americanizan". En 1998, por ejemplo, el National Women's Health Information Center reportó que los nuevos inmigrantes de México tenían tasas *(rates)* más bajas de cáncer, depresión y abuso de alcohol o drogas que los nacidos en Estados Unidos. Otro estudio publicado el año pasado en *Archives of General Psychiatry* mostró que los inmigrantes nacidos en México tienen una tasa mucho menor de desórdenes mentales que los nacidos *(born)* en Estados Unidos.

Lamentablemente, los estudios también demuestran que muchas de las tradiciones saludables que los latinos traen de sus países de origen se dejan atrás *(behind)* cuando se asimilan a la cultura estadounidense.

"Nuestra cultura es sumamente valiosa", dice Luz Álvarez Martínez, directora ejecutiva del National Latina Health en Oakland, California. "Enseñamos a las jóvenes a mantener su cultura. Es importante adaptarse al nuevo país manteniendo los aspectos de la vieja cultura que las mantienen saludables".

Los alimentos

La dieta tradicional latina, a diferencia de la estadounidense, es rica en alimentos que previenen el cáncer, la diabetes y las enfermedades cardíacas. Estos alimentos incluyen granos enteros *(whole grains)*, frutas frescas y frijoles, y son ricos en vitaminas A y C, ácido fólico y calcio. **Además de** estos beneficios, contienen fibra y poca grasa *(fat)*. Sin embargo, el Hispanic Health and Nutrition Examination Survey encontró que los latinos de segunda generación en EE.UU. prefieren una dieta estadounidense, baja en frutas y verduras. Además, las tortillas de maíz son reemplazadas por las de harina *(flour)*, que son menos nutritivas, y las comidas caseras *(home-cooked)* a menudo *(often)* son reemplazadas por comidas rápidas.

	Cierto	Falso
1. Mantener las costumbres de su país de origen puede afectar positivamente la salud mental y física de los inmigrantes latinos.	☑	☐
2. Los inmigrantes latinos recientes tienen más problemas de salud que los latinos nacidos en los Estados Unidos.	☐	☑
3. La dieta latina tradicional es mala para la salud cardíaca.	☐	☑
4. La dieta estadounidense es menos nutritiva que la dieta latina tradicional.	☑	☐
5. Los latinos de la segunda generación prefieren la comida casera a la comida rápida.	☐	☑

Paso 2: Por otro lado. En grupos, contesten la siguiente pregunta. Luego, compartan sus perspectivas con la clase.

¿Qué tradiciones culinarias estadounidenses han adoptado los latinos como parte de su cultura alimentaria convencional?

5A.34 ANSWERS: Cierto: 1, 4; Falso: 2 (Los latinos nacidos en Estados Unidos tienen más problemas de salud que los inmigrantes latinos recientes.) 3 (La dieta latina tradicional es buena para la salud cardíaca.) 5 (Los latinos de la segunda generación prefieren la comida rápida a la comida casera.)

Vocabulario: Investigación A

Vocabulario esencial

Sustantivos

la aceituna	olive
el alimento	food
el almuerzo	lunch
el arroz	rice
la bebida	beverage
el bistec	beef steak
el aceite	oil
el aguacate	avocado
el apio	celery
el azúcar	sugar
el calamar	squid
las carnes	meats
el/la camarero/a	waiter/waitress
los camarones	shrimp
la cebolla	onion
la cena	dinner
el cereal	cereal
la cerveza	beer
la chuleta de puerco/cerdo	pork chop
el/la cliente	client
la cocina	kitchen, cooking, stove
el/la cocinero/a	cook
la comida	food
los condimentos	condiments
la copa	wine glass
los cubiertos	utensils
la cuchara	spoon
el cuchillo	knife
la cuenta	check
el desayuno	breakfast
las fresas	strawberries
los frijoles	beans
los frijoles verdes	green beans
la fruta	fruit
las galletas	cookies
la grasa	fat
el (horno de) microondas	microwave oven
los huevos	eggs

la jarra de agua	pitcher of water
el jugo	juice
la leche	milk
las legumbres	legumes
la mantequilla	butter
el mantel	tablecloth
la manzana	apple
los mariscos	seafood
la miel	honey
la naranja	orange
la olla	pot
el pan	bread
el pastel	cake
el pescado	fish
la pimienta	pepper
la papa	potato
la parrilla	grill
los plátanos	plaintains
el plato	dish
el plato principal	entreé
el pollo	chicken
el postre	dessert
el queso	cheese
el restaurante	restaurant
la salchicha	sausage
la salsa	sauce
el/la sartén	pan
la servilleta	napkin
la sopa	soup
la tarta	pie
la taza	cup
el tenedor	fork
el tocino	bacon
el tomate	tomato
el vaso	glass
las verduras	vegetables
el vino blanco/tinto	white/red wine
la zanahoria	carrot
la uva	grape

Adjetivos

blando/a	soft
caliente	hot
dulce	sweet
frío	cold
picante	spicy
saludable	healthy

Verbos

almorzar	to have lunch
añadir	to add
batir	to beat, to whisk
calentar	to heat up
cenar	to have dinner
congelar	to freeze
cortar	to cut
cubrir	to cover
cultivar	to grow
dejar	to leave
derretir	to melt
freír	to fry
hervir	to boil
hornear	to bake
mezclar	to mix
pelar	to peel
sacar	to take out

Otras palabras y expresiones

los granos enteros	whole grains
la hoja de maíz	corn husk
la lata	can
lento/a	slow
ligero/a	light
listo/a	ready
la masa	dough
la merienda	afternoon snack
el panecillo	sweet roll
pagar	to pay
las papas fritas	french fries
peligroso/a	dangerous
los rasgos	traits

la rebanada	slice
la receta	recipe
la recipiente	container
recoger	to pick up
el trozo	piece
acabar de + infinitive	just + verb
al aire libre	outdoors
a menudo	often
a pesar de	in spite of
algo para picar	something to munch on
Buen provecho	Enjoy your meal.
Con permiso.	Excuse me.
dejar la propina	to leave a tip
¿Desean algo más?	Would you like anything else?
Me gustaría…/ Quisiera	I would like…
Nos gustaría…/ Quisiéramos	We would like…
paso por paso	step by step
Perdón.	Excuse me./ I'm sorry.
poner la mesa	to set the table
ponerse de acuerdo	to agree on something
¿Qué le(s) gustaría?	What would you like?
¿Qué desea(n) de comer/beber/postre?	What would you like to eat/drink/ for dessert?
Te invito.	It's my treat./It's on me.
Tráigame… por favor.	Please bring me…
Tráiganos… por favor.	Please bring us…

Cognados

Review the cognates in *Adelante* and the false cognates in *¡Atención!*. For a complete list of cognates, see Appendix 4 on page 605.

¿Por qué llevas lo que llevas?

In this **Investigación** you will learn:

▶ How to describe clothing and accessories

▶ How to talk about what you wear and when

▶ How to shop for others

▶ About who and what influences what we wear

¿Qué se puede decir de la ropa?

You can describe the clothes that you are wearing.	¿Qué ropa llevas? ¿De qué color es? ¿Se asocia más con hombres o con mujeres? ¿Es para situaciones formales o informales?
You can talk about when you wear certain clothing items and where you purchase your clothing.	¿Qué ropa prefieres llevar a clase? ¿a una cita? ¿Dónde compras la ropa?
You can indicate to whom or for whom you do something.	¿Tu mamá te regala ropa? ¿Le prestas ropa a tu hermano/a? ¿a tu compañero/a de cuarto? ¿Quién nos dice qué debemos llevar?

Adelante

TEACHING TIP: For some of this vocabulary, you may be able to point to someone wearing sandals and say *las sandalias*, followed by *Las sandalias son de la colección de Prada.* Explain that both *las prendas* and *la ropa* indicate "clothing." *Las prendas* can also be used to refer to jewelry.

¡Ya lo sabes! Las prendas y la ropa

las sandalias de la colección de Prada
el suéter de cachemir de estilo clásico
los *jeans* versátiles
los zapatos *(shoes)* de tenis
el sombrero de colores brillantes
las botas de color neutro
los pijamas de franela *(flannel)*

la chaqueta sofisticada
los accesorios de moda *(in style)*
los pantalones de lino
la blusa de estilo moderno
la silueta perfecta
la calidad de la tela *(fabric)* es buena

5B.1 **Asociaciones.** Empareja *(match)* cada descripción con la ropa que describe. Compara tus respuestas con las de un/a compañero/a de clase. Sigue el modelo.

a. el sombrero   **c.** las botas   **e.** las sandalias
b. los pijamas   **d.** los zapatos de tenis   **f.** los pantalones

___*e*___ **1.** una prenda que se asocia con el verano

___c___ **2.** un artículo que se asocia con el frío

___a___ **3.** un artículo que nos protege del sol

___d___ **4.** un artículo que llevamos para jugar deportes

___b___ **5.** una prenda que llevamos para dormir

___f___ **6.** una prenda más formal que los *jeans* que llevamos en las piernas *(legs)*

5B.2 **Completar la oración.** Con un/a compañero/a de clase, completen cada oración de abajo. Comprueben sus respuestas con el resto de la clase.

1. Nike y Adidas son dos marcas *(brands)* famosas de ___zapatos de tenis___.

2. Los ___jeans___ son "el uniforme" de los jóvenes.

3. Cuando voy a esquiar, llevo una ___chaqueta___.

4. La franela es una tela que asociamos con los ___pijamas___.

5. Cuando hace frío, preferimos llevar un ___suéter___.

6. Las ___botas___ son buenas para caminar en la nieve.

7. Cuando vamos a la playa, llevamos unas ___sandalias___.

8. Usamos un ___sombrero___ para protegernos del sol.

Dos diseñadores famosos

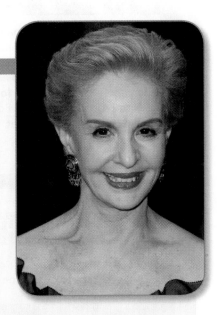

Carolina Herrera

Es de Venezuela y es una de las diseñadoras de mayor éxito *(success)* en Estados Unidos y Latinoamérica. En 1980, presentó su primera colección de moda; en 1986, sus primeras creaciones para novia; y en 1988 su primer perfume – ya tiene seis, tanto para mujeres como para hombres. Ha disfrutado de una carrera meteórica en la que se ha ganado el respeto del mundo de la moda.

Herrera ha logrado *(achieved)* la aprobación de celebridades como Jacqueline Kennedy Onassis y Renée Zellweger. Diseñó el vestido de novia *(wedding dress)* de Caroline Kennedy, la hija de John Fitzgerald Kennedy. Como creadora, ha sabido interpretar perfectamente las preferencias y las necesidades de una mujer amante del lujo *(luxury)* y la elegancia sin exceso. Como empresaria *(entrepreneur)*, ha podido construir poco a poco una compañía sólida que exporta a todo el mundo.

Narciso Rodríguez

Es de Nueva Jersey, de padres cubanos. Graduado de la Academia de Diseño Parsons, Narciso comienza su carrera con grandes figuras como Donna Karan, Anne Klein y Calvin Klein. Su fama aumenta cuando Carolyn Bessette insiste en que él le diseñara el vestido de novia para su matrimonio con John F. Kennedy, Jr. en 1996. Su lista de clientes incluye a Salma Hayek, Sarah Jessica Parker, Rachel Weisz y Sonia Braga. La revista *Time* lo ha nombrado uno de los hispanos más influyentes de Estados Unidos.

5B.3 AUDIO SCRIPT: 1. Es de Venezuela. 2. Es cubano-americano. 3. Se gradúa de la Academia de Diseño Parsons. 4. Empieza su carrera en Nueva York en 1980. 5. Una de sus clientes es Renée Zellweger. 6. Sus diseños son elegantes pero no ostentosos. 7. Diseña el vestido de novia de Carolyn Bessette Kennedy.

TEACHING TIP: Call attention to the fact that *la ropa* is a singular noun and have students associate it with the English word *clothing* instead of *clothes*. Encourage your students to interview Spanish-speakers in the community to learn which clothing vocabulary they associate with certain Spanish-speaking regions.

5B.3 **¿A quién se refiere?** Vas a escuchar varios enunciados sobre estos famosos diseñadores hispanos. Indica si se refieren a Carolina Herrera o a Narciso Rodríguez, basándote en lo que has leído sobre ellos.

	Carolina Herrera	Narciso Rodríguez
1.	☑	☐
2.	☐	☑
3.	☐	☑
4.	☑	☐
5.	☑	☐
6.	☑	☐
7.	☐	☑

VÍVELO: CULTURA

La ropa: Términos variados

El vocabulario de **la ropa** varía de región a región o entre países. En España, **un bolso** *(handbag)* significa lo que es **una cartera** o **una bolsa** para otros hispanohablantes. En México, lo que son **los aretes** *(earrings)* son **los pendientes** en España. **Las gafas**, **los anteojos** o **los lentes** son *eye glasses* o *sun glasses* según la región. **Las lentillas** o **los lentes de contacto** se refieren a *contact lenses*. Lo mismo ocurre en inglés. Por ejemplo, lo que para una persona es *coat*, para otra persona puede ser *jacket*. Es importante saber que existe esta variedad y explorar el vocabulario específico cuando viajen a países hispanohablantes o interactúen con hablantes nativos.

EXPRESIONES ÚTILES

Llevar can mean *to carry*, or *to take*, but when used with apparel, it means *to wear*, as in **Llevo zapatos de tacón a la fiesta.** *(I'm wearing high heeled shoes to the party.)*

5B.4 AUDIO SCRIPT: 1. Llevamos *sandalias* en el invierno. 2. Llevamos *un suéter* cuando hace frío. 3. Llevamos *jeans* en una situación formal. 4. Los hombres llevan *blusas*. 5. Llevamos una chaqueta cuando hace fresco. 6. Llevamos *zapatos de tenis* para hacer ejercicio. 7. Llevamos *pantalones* cuando hace frío. 8. Llevamos *botas* cuando jugamos al básquetbol.

5B.4 **¿Lógico o ilógico?** Indica si cada enunciado que escuchas es **lógico** o **ilógico**. Comprueba tus respuestas con el resto de la clase. Sigue el modelo.

	Lógico	Ilógico
1.	☐	☑
2.	☑	☐
3.	☐	☑
4.	☐	☑
5.	☑	☐
6.	☑	☐
7.	☑	☐
8.	☐	☑

◗ Bien dicho

Los sonidos que producen las letras g, j y x

In Spanish, the letter **g** before the vowels **e** and **i** often corresponds to a sound that is similar to the sound associated with the letter *h* in the English words *hat, ham, heavy,* and *hand.* This is also the sound that corresponds to the letter **j** no matter what follows it. As you may have noticed, the Spanish **j** does <u>not</u> correspond to the sound associated with the letter *j* in English words such as *Joe, pajamas, jeans* or *judge.*

la gente	escoger	el gimnasio	el pijama	el traje

The letter **g** before the vowels **a, o, u,** and the consonants **l** and **r** corresponds to the sound associated with the letter *g* in English words such as *game, gloves, green, gumbo, gold,* and *eagle.*

la gorra	largas	los guantes	agradable	el inglés

As in English, the letter **x** is most often pronounced as the combination of the sounds /k/ and /s/. Compare the cognate pairs *text*/**texto**, *lexical*/**léxico**, *extraordinary*/**extraordinario**, *maximum*/**máximo**.

However, in various place names and other words of indigenous origin from Mexico and Central America, **x** is pronounced like the letter **j** (or the letter **g** when it precedes **e** or **i**).

mexicano	Oaxaca	Xalapa	Xaltepec

NOTE: Certainly there are differences between the way these sounds are articulated in English and Spanish. We compare the Spanish sounds to their approximate counterparts in English because beginner students seldom have a background in phonetics and phonology such that they would understand phonological terminology or IPA transcription.

5B.5 **Escuchar y escribir.** Escucha las palabras y escríbelas según creas que deben escribirse. Luego, comprueba tus respuestas con la clase.

1. tener éxito
2. gente
3. extra
4. gigante
5. extraño
6. mixto
7. gira
8. goma

5B.5 AUDIO SCRIPT: 1. tener éxito, 2. gente, 3. extra, 4. gigante, 5. extraño, 6. mixto, 7. gira, 8. goma

5B.5 TEACHING TIP: You may want to finish this activity with a choral repetition of the words.

5B.6 **¿Como la g inglesa o como la h inglesa?** En parejas, decidan si la **g** en negrita debe pronunciarse con un sonido fuerte *(strong)*, como el que corresponde a la *g* en inglés, o con un sonido suave *(soft)* como el que corresponde a la *h* en inglés. Túrnense para leer las oraciones en voz alta *(aloud)* para practicar la pronunciación.

1. Me **g**usta esta blusa.
2. Estudio psicolo**g**ía.
3. Ten**g**o veintidós años.
4. Somos ve**g**etarianos.
5. El policía diri**g**e el tráfico.
6. ¿Compraste muchos re**g**alos?
7. La **g**ramática es interesante.
8. Muchos **g**itanos *(gypsies)* viven allí.
9. Vamos a visitar In**g**laterra.
10. Debes reco**g**er tus libros.

5B.6 ANSWERS: English g sound (/g/): 1, 3, 6, 7, 9; English h sound (/h/): 2, 4, 5, 8, 10

5B.6 TEACHING TIP: As they practice, encourage students to alternate reading even and odd sentences and then switch so that each partner has the opportunity to pronounce all of the sentences.

Palabras clave 1 ¿Qué ropa llevan?

TEACHING TIP: When presenting this new vocabulary bring in items from home to further support the language input you offer students. As you talk about different items, you can hold the items up for your students to see. Also, tap into what you and your students are already wearing to make connections to the new vocabulary. Any visible support you can offer to add meaning to the vocabulary will be helpful.

los aretes/los pendientes · los lentes · el anillo/la sortija · el cinturón · el abrigo · la falda · el reloj · el vestido · las medias · la cartera/la bolsa · los calcetines · el traje de baño

Para describir el cuerpo y la ropa

el buen gusto	Hay artistas que no tienen buen gusto.
de estatura alta/baja	Los jugadores de básquetbol son de estatura alta, no baja.
engordar	Si comemos mucho chocolate Godiva engordamos.
adelgazar	Si hacemos mucho ejercicio adelgazamos.
suelto/a	Ya que perdió peso, mi amiga tiene mucha ropa suelta.
apretado/a	La ropa apretada no es atractiva.

el paraguas

el traje

la corbata

la gorra

la camisa

el impermeable

el saco

los zapatos de tacón

la bufanda

la camiseta

los guantes

5B.7 **¿Adentro o afuera?** En parejas, túrnense para indicar si cada prenda de ropa se asocia más con llevarse **Adentro** *(indoors)* o **Afuera** *(outdoors)*. Comparen sus respuestas con las de otra pareja de compañeros de clase. Si se asocia la prenda igualmente con llevarse adentro y afuera, indiquen los dos. Sigan el modelo.

5B.7 NOTE: Some items might seem appropriate to students both indoors and outdoors, such as *la corbata*. Have students defend their answers.

		Adentro	Afuera
1.	el abrigo	☐	☑
2.	el pijama	☑	☐
3.	el traje de baño	☐	☑
4.	el impermeable	☐	☑
5.	el vestido	☑	☑
6.	la chaqueta	☐	☑
7.	los calcetines	☑	☑
8.	la corbata	☑	☑

5B.8 **¿Formal o informal?** Vas a escuchar mencionar varias prendas de ropa y accesorios. Indica si cada uno debe considerarse formal o informal. Confirma tus respuestas con un/a compañero/a de clase. Sigue el modelo.

	Informal	Formal
1.	☐	☑
2.	☑	☐
3.	☐	☑
4.	☑	☐
5.	☑	☐
6.	☐	☑
7.	☐	☑
8.	☑	☐

5B.9 **Busca la palabra correcta.** Empareja cada palabra con la definición correspondiente. Comprueba tus respuestas con la clase.

a. el anillo   **e.** el cinturón
b. la bolsa   **f.** la gorra
c. los calcetines   **g.** el impermeable
d. la camiseta   **h.** el traje de baño

___h___ **1.** Es la prenda que llevamos para nadar.

___g___ **2.** Es un abrigo que se lleva cuando llueve.

___a___ **3.** Es el símbolo del matrimonio.

___f___ **4.** Es un sombrero informal.

___c___ **5.** Los llevamos dentro de *(inside)* los zapatos.

___b___ **6.** Las mujeres ponen su dinero, sus llaves, etcétera, dentro de esta cosa.

___e___ **7.** Lo usamos para sostener *(keep up)* los pantalones.

___d___ **8.** Se lleva para hacer ejercicio.

5B.10 **¿En qué se diferencian?** En grupos de tres, determinen si están de acuerdo (**Sí**) o no (**No**) con cada enunciado de abajo. Compartan las conclusiones de su grupo con el resto de la clase.

_____ **1.** Los trajes masculinos tienen pantalones y los trajes femeninos pueden tener una falda.

_____ **2.** Los zapatos masculinos no tienen tacones altos y los zapatos femeninos pueden tener tacones altos.

_____ **3.** Los cinturones masculinos son estrechos *(narrow)* y los cinturones femeninos pueden ser muy anchos *(wide)*.

_____ **4.** Las camisetas masculinas son sueltas y las camisetas femeninas son más apretadas.

_____ **5.** Las camisetas masculinas son de colores neutros u oscuros y las camisetas femeninas son de colores brillantes.

_____ **6.** Los suéteres masculinos son sueltos y los suéteres femeninos son más apretados.

_____ **7.** El traje de baño masculino siempre tiene sólo una pieza y los trajes de baño femeninos pueden tener dos piezas.

5B.11 Las prendas. En parejas, miren el cuadro de abajo y túrnense para describir la ropa de cada individuo de esta pintura.

Frida Kahlo, *El camión* (The Bus), 1929.

VÍVELO: CULTURA

Las prendas y la tradición

En el cuadro de Frida Kahlo, la mujer en el centro lleva un rebozo (*traditional Mexican shawl*) muy común entre las mujeres indígenas. Las mujeres usan el rebozo para cubrir a sus bebés del frío o para llevar productos, ropa, fruta, leña (*wood*), etcétera. El uso principal, sin embargo, es para tener al bebé cerca (*close*) para que siempre sienta el amor y la seguridad de su madre.

En algunos lugares de los Andes, los sombreros sirven para indicar el pueblo de origen de una persona. Por ejemplo, en una de estas fotos, las mujeres llevan un sombrero de la zona del Cusco. En la otra hay sombreros típicos de Chivay, un pueblo en el departamento de Arequipa, Perú. Los sombreros van más allá de indicar el origen de alguien. También pueden indicar si la mujer está casada o no.

¿Hay ciertas prendas tradicionales en tu cultura? ¿Cuáles son?

¡Conéctate!
Open up Google Earth and explore the Andes. Check out the following cities in Peru: Pisac, Ollantaytambo and Urubamba. Did you see differences in the hats people wear? Click on the blue boxes to see pictures of the areas visited.

TEACHING TIP: Ask students if there are particular types of clothing associated with specific traditions in their native or background culture. Do they know the source or origin of these traditions?

5B.12 TEACHING TIP:
Call students' attention
to the *modelo*. You may
want to give some input
with *más de* and *menos
de* comparing quanti-
ties. Comparisons are
presented formally in
Capítulo 8.

5B.12 TEACHING TIP:
Depending on the size
of the class, you should
limit how many signa-
tures students can get per
classmate (e.g. no more
than three signatures
from the same person).
This encourages them to
talk to more people than
they might otherwise.
Invite students to walk
around the classroom to
talk to their classmates.
Then, as a follow-up,
tally students' reponses
and highlight the most
unusual/interesting/hu-
morous findings. Have
students write these in
their *Retrato de la clase.*

5B.12 Tu clóset.

Paso 1: Averigua *(find out)* qué hay en los clósets de tus compañeros de clase. Habla con tantos compañeros como sea posible para averiguar a quién describe cada una de estas oraciones. Crea una tabla como la de abajo y asegúrate de usar preguntas para entrevistar *(interview)* a tus compañeros. Si alguien *(someone)* responde afirmativamente, pídele que firme tu tabla.

Modelo: Tiene más de *(more than)* cinco *jeans.*
          E1: *¿Tienes más de cinco* jeans?
          E2: *Sí*
          E1: *Firma aquí, por favor.*

Tiene más de cinco *jeans.*	No tiene botas.	Tiene más de veinte blusas.	Tiene muchos anillos en las manos.	Tiene un impermeable y un paraguas.
Tiene dos relojes.	No tiene impermeable.	Sólo tiene un par de zapatos.	Tiene pijamas para el invierno y para el verano.	No tiene *jeans.*
Le gusta llevar faldas.	Tiene zapatos de tacón.	Tiene más de un sombrero.	No tiene traje de baño.	Lleva sandalias cuando hace frío.
Tiene guantes para esquiar.	No usa vestidos.	Tiene un sombrero muy grande.	No tiene lentes.	Tiene muchos aretes.
Tiene más de dos cinturones.	Lleva un abrigo hoy.	No tiene paraguas.	No le gustan las corbatas.	Usa calcetines cuando lleva sandalias.

Paso 2: Responde a las siguientes preguntas tú mismo/a *(yourself).* Luego, entrevista a cuatro compañeros de clase para averiguar las últimas prendas que han comprado para ellos mismos o que han recibido como regalo. ¿Hay algunos patrones *(patterns)* que puedas observar? Anota las tendencias *(trends)* en tu **Retrato de la clase.**

	(Nombre)				
¿Cuál es la última prenda que has comprado?					
¿Cuál es la última prenda que has recibido como regalo?					

Retrato de la clase: Muchos compañeros han comprado _____ y ____. Muchos compañeros han recibido ____ y ____ como regalo.

NOTE: Some students may
have been the recipients
of *piropos.* Let students
know that if they do
not want to talk to the
person(s) offering these
unsolicited comments,
the best thing to do is to
ignore the comments and
keep walking. It is often
when someone reacts to a
comment or acknowledges
it that the person making
the remark continues.

VÍVELO: CULTURA

Los piropos

Los piropos son comentarios que una persona le hace a otra para hacerle un cumplido *(compliment).* Algunos piropos pueden ser vulgares u ofensivos, pero tradicionalmente los piropos son creativos y graciosos, y tienen la intención de provocar una sonrisa *(smile).*

Me gustaría ser caramelo para posarme en tus labios y derretirme en tu boca.
I would like to be candy to touch your lips and melt in your mouth.

Me gustaría ser bizco para poder verte doble.
I would like to be cross eyed to be able to see you twice.

EXPRESIONES ÚTILES

To give a compliment about how someone is dressed or looks, the following expressions may be used:

¡Qué vestido más elegante!	What an elegant dress!
¡Me gusta esa blusa!	I like that blouse!
¡Vas muy a la moda!	You are really stylish/in style.
¡El traje de baño te queda muy bien!	The bathing suit fits/suits you really well!
¡Qué guapo/a estás!	You look great! (Literally: How attractive you are!)

5B.13 TEACHING TIP: Students should only need five to eight minutes to prepare for this activity. The actual fashion show should only take about one minute per group/model. Encourage your students to be as descriptive as possible. Consider videotaping the presentations. Students often enjoy watching themselves and their classmates on screen. Moreover, watching and listening to the presentations a second time is a good review.

5B.13 Desfile de modas. En grupos de tres, presenten un desfile de modas. Uno de ustedes es el modelo, mientras los otros dos describen lo que lleva el modelo.

Palabras clave 2 Los colores y las telas

Telas naturales: el algodón, la piel/ cuero

CAMISETAS EN TODOS LOS COLORES: azul, rojo, negro, blanco, amarillo, morado, rosa*, naranja*, verde, marrón*

¡Estilos para todos los gustos!: a cuadros, a rayas, bordado, estampado

la lana

***Rosa** and **naranja** don't have different forms for masculine and feminine. Other words for pink and orange are **rosado/a** and **anaranjado/a** which do have feminine forms. Another word for brown is **café.**

5B.14 EXTENSION
ACTIVITY: Have students
bring in a picture of their
closet with a similar
description of at least ten
items and their colors.

5B.14 **Los colores en español.** Mira los dibujos de abajo que muestran las prendas de ropa de los clósets de Carolina Herrera y Narciso Rodríguez. Luego, con un/a compañero/a, lee las descripciones y empareja las palabras subrayadas *(underlined)* con los carretes de hilo *(spools of thread)* coloreados que ellos representan. Verifiquen sus respuestas con el resto de la clase. **¡Ojo!** Algunas prendas pueden compartir los mismos colores.

Los pantalones de Narciso Rodríguez son grises (1. _gray (d)_). Su camisa es <u>azul</u> (2. _blue (f)_) y la corbata es <u>verde</u> (3. _green (e)_). Tiene unos zapatos <u>de color café</u> (4. _brown (g)_) y una camiseta roja (5. _red (b)_). Su chaqueta es <u>blanca</u> (6. _white (j)_) y el suéter es anaranjado (7. _orange (c)_). Carolina Herrera tiene un vestido <u>rosa</u> (8. _pink (h)_) y una blusa <u>amarilla</u> (9. _yellow (k)_). También tiene una falda <u>gris</u> (10. _gray (d)_) y un abrigo <u>morado</u> (11. _purple (i)_). Sus zapatos de tacón son <u>rojos</u> (12. _red (b)_) y sus botas son <u>negras</u> (13. _black (a)_).

a.   b.   c.   d.   e.   f.

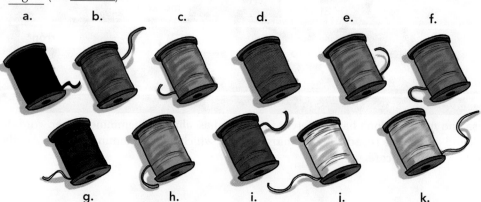

g.   h.   i.   j.   k.

5B.15 ¿Con qué color se asocia? Escucha la descripción de varios colores o combinaciones de colores, e indica qué color se describe. Comprueba tus respuestas con la clase.

1. verde
2. amarillo
3. naranja/anaranjado
4. rojo
5. morado
6. azul
7. negro
8. blanco
9. marrón/café
10. rojo, blanco, azul
11. *will vary*
12. blanco

5B.16 ¿Qué lleva tu profesor(a)? Describe en un párrafo corto lo que tu profesor(a) lleva hoy. Intercambia párrafos con un/a compañero/a de clase y corrijan cada uno el trabajo del otro. Tengan en cuenta que los colores son adjetivos cuando se usan para describir prendas de ropa, así que deben concordar *(match)* con la ropa que describen en género y número (masculino/femenino, singular/plural).

5B.17 Adivina quién es. Escribe una descripción corta pero bien detallada de algo que lleva una persona de la clase. Luego, lee la descripción de manera que tus compañeros puedan adivinar *(guess)* a quién describes.

¡Atención!

Ropa	does not mean *rope*. It refers to *clothing* or *clothes*. *Rope* in English is **cuerda** or **soga** in Spanish. Antes de ir de vacaciones, me gusta comprar ropa nueva. La secadora *(dryer)* no funciona. Vamos a poner una cuerda entre dos árboles para secar la ropa.
Collar	does not mean *collar*. It refers to a *necklace*. *Collar* in English is **cuello** in Spanish. Roberto le ha regalado un collar bonito a su esposa para su cumpleaños. No me gusta este suéter porque el cuello es muy apretado.
Pendiente	can refer to a *pendant*, but as a synonym for **arete**, it also refers to an *earring*. Carlota lleva unos pendientes de diamantes.
Medias	does not mean *medias*, as in modes of communication. It refers to *hose* or *stockings*, usually made of silk or nylon. **Pantimedias** is the word for *pantyhose*. Con un vestido, las mujeres llevan medias en lugar de calcetines.

5B.18 Buscar la definición. Empareja cada palabra con la descripción correspondiente. Comprueba tus respuestas con el resto de la clase.

d 1. joyas pequeñas para las orejas *(ears)*
e 2. prendas de vestir en general
b 3. parte del cuerpo *(body)*
a 4. cadena *(chain)* con perlas
c 5. prendas de nailon para usar con zapatos

a. collar
b. cuello
c. medias
d. pendientes
e. ropa

5B.15 AUDIO SCRIPT: 1. El color que asociamos con las plantas, 2. El color que asociamos con el sol, 3. El color que asociamos con las zanahorias, 4. El color que asociamos con las fresas, 5. El color que asociamos con el jugo de uvas, 6. El color que asociamos con el agua y el cielo, 7. El color que asociamos con la noche, 8. El color que asociamos con la nieve, 9. El color que asociamos con la compañía UPS, 10. Los colores que asociamos con los Estados Unidos, 11. Los colores que asociamos con esta universidad, 12. El color que asociamos con la casa del presidente de los Estados Unidos.

5B.16 TEACHING TIP: Have some students write their descriptions on the board so that you can edit them as a class.

5B.17 TEACHING TIP: Have every student write their name on a scrap of paper. Collect names and randomly pass them out so that each student has someone else's name—this is the classmate he or she will describe. If you have the space, invite your class to stand in a circle as the descriptions are read so that they can better see one another. If you have a smart classroom you can search the web for pictures of models and famous people for the students to describe what they are wearing. You can also use pictures from magazines. To make this activity more fun you may want to ask them to bring a picture of themselves or a family member wearing "interesting" clothes.

PLUS

Go to *WileyPLUS* and review the tutorial for this grammar point.

PLUS

You will find PowerPoint presentations for use with *Estructuras clave* in *WileyPLUS*.

In the previous *Investigación* you learned that the direct object is the person or thing that receives the action of the verb. In the example **Juanes escribe muchas canciones, muchas canciones** is the direct object because it answers the question "What does Juanes write?".

In addition to a direct object, many verbs in Spanish take an indirect object. The indirect object, which is usually a person, expresses *to whom* or *for whom* an action is done. The indirect object pronouns in Spanish are:

Indirect object pronouns	
me *to/for me*	**nos** *to/for us*
te *to for/ you (sg. inform.)*	**os** *to/for you (pl. inform., Spain)*
le *to/for him/her/it/you (sg. form.)*	**les** *to/for them/ you (pl.)*

Verbs that take an indirect object include verbs of communication (e.g. **decir, explicar, escribir, hablar**) and verbs of exchange (e.g. **dar, regalar, prestar**). Note the following examples in English and Spanish.

Bill Richardson **les** da consejos **a sus amigos.**	*Bill Richardson gives advice to his friends.*
Pau Gasol **le** pasa el balón **a Kobe Bryant.**	*Pau Gasol passes the ball to Kobe Bryant.*
Alejandro Sanz **me** habla después de su concierto.	*Alejandro Sanz talks to me after his concert.*
Julieta Venegas **nos** explica por qué canta.	*Julieta Venegas explains to us why she sings.*
Juanes **le** ha escrito una canción **a Shakira.**	*Juanes has written a song for Shakira.*

Note in the last sentence, *a song* is the direct object because it is what Juanes wrote and *Shakira* is the indirect object because Juanes wrote the song *for her*. Note that the indirect object is introduced by the preposition **a** in Spanish and either *to* or *for* in English.

In Spanish, an indirect object pronoun may replace the indirect object introduced by **a**, but that **a**-phrase may be kept if there is no context to clarify to whom the pronoun refers.

¿Qué le ha regalado Marc Anthony a Jennifer López?
Le ha regalado un anillo.
(Context allows "Jennifer López" to be omitted in this case because it is the answer to a question, where "Jennifer López" has already been mentioned.)

Juanes le ha escrito una canción a Shakira.
(The phrase "a Shakira" is not omitted since the referent "le" would not be clear by context.)

Marc Anthony le ha regalado un anillo.
(Gramatically correct, but ambiguous since without context, **le** can refer to any individual.)

When the indirect object is a person or people, the indirect object pronoun is generally used whether or not there is an **a**-phrase introducing that person/those people.

Juanes le ha escrito una canción (a Shakira).

As with direct object pronouns, indirect object pronouns precede a conjugated verb, and are attached to an infinitive verb. When a conjugated verb and an infinitive work together, the pronoun may be placed either before the conjugated verb or attached to the infinitive.

> Marc Anthony le regala el anillo a Jennifer.
> Marc Anthony le va a regalar el anillo.
> Marc Anthony va a regalarle el anillo.

You remember that Spanish uses the **a personal** to introduce direct objects who are people, and you have now learned that **a**-phrases also introduce indirect objects. The best way to determine whether someone is a direct or an indirect object is to remember the questions *whom?* to identify the direct object and *to/for whom?* to identify the indirect object. Another way to determine that a person is the indirect object is to look for the presence of an indirect object pronoun referring to that person.

5B.19 ¿Objeto directo o indirecto? Con un/a compañero/a, lean las siguientes oraciones *(sentences)* sobre Andy García, e indiquen si él es el objeto directo o indirecto del verbo en cada caso. Comprueben sus respuestas con la clase.

Andy García

	Objeto directo	Objeto indirecto
1. Enrique Murciano conoce a Andy García.	☑	☐
2. Emilio y Gloria Estefan visitan a Andy García.	☑	☐
3. Martin Scorsese le ha mandado un guión *(script)* a Andy García.	☐	☑
4. Su esposa le dice "Te amo" *(I love you)* a Andy García.	☐	☑
5. Hemos visto a Andy García en la película *The Lost City*.	☑	☐
6. Sus hijas le regalan muchas corbatas a Andy García.	☐	☑
7. ¿Admiras a Andy García?	☑	☐
8. Muchas mujeres le escriben cartas a Andy García.	☐	☑

5B.20 ¿A quién le va a regalar qué? Uno de los asistentes de Narciso Rodríguez tiene que deshacerse de *(get rid of)* los modelos del año pasado para abrir espacio en el estudio para la nueva colección. Trabaja con un/a compañero/a para indicar a quién le va a regalar qué cosas según el contexto. Sigan el modelo.

a. Les va a regalar varias camisetas.
b. Te va a regalar un impermeable.
c. Le va a regalar un cinturón.
d. Le va a regalar un traje.

e. Nos va a regalar unos vestidos.
f. Les va a regalar unos suéteres de lana.
g. Me va a regalar un traje de baño.
h. Le va a regalar unos aretes de oro *(gold)*.

_f__ **1.** Sus padres van a tomar vacaciones en Alaska.

_h__ **2.** La semana que viene, celebra un aniversario importante con su novia.

_c__ **3.** Su abuelo ha adelgazado mucho y los pantalones le quedan *(fit him)* grandes.

_e__ **4.** Carmina y yo no tenemos nada que ponernos para asistir a una fiesta elegante.

_g__ **5.** Vivo al lado del mar y voy a la playa todos los días.

_d__ **6.** Hernán tiene una entrevista para un trabajo.

_b__ **7.** Tú te mudas *(you are moving)* a Seattle donde llueve mucho.

_a__ **8.** Sus sobrinos tienen 14 y 18 años, y hacen mucho deporte.

Estructuras clave 2 Prepositional pronouns

The pronouns in these phrases are used after most prepositions. With the exception of **mí** and **ti,** these prepositional pronouns are identical in form to their corresponding subject pronouns. They are used to make contrasts, give emphasis, or clarify ambiguity.

Prepositional pronouns	
a mí	A **mí** me gusta el café colombiano, pero a ti no.
a ti	Carlos te va a llamar a **ti** esta noche, no a mí.
a él	A **él** le gustan los frijoles, a ellas no.
a ella	La veo a **ella** todos los días.
a usted	Los estudiantes lo/la admiran a **usted.**
a nosotros/as	A **nosotros/as** nos gusta ir al cine, pero a ellos no.
a vosotros/as	Os queremos invitar a **vosotros/as.**
a ustedes	¿A **ustedes** les gustan las tapas españolas?
a ellos/as	¿Los/Las conoces a **ellos/as**?

Prepositions with **con** *(with)* work a little differently. The special forms **conmigo** and **contigo** correspond to *with me* and *with you* (informal), respectively. Otherwise the same pronouns follow **con** as follow other prepositions.

> −¿Vas a la fiesta **conmigo**?
> −No, no voy **contigo**. Tú vas **con ella** y yo voy **con él.**

5B.21 Completar las oraciones. Empareja el pronombre de objeto indirecto de cada oración con el objeto indirecto al que más lógicamente se refiere. Hay algunas opciones que no se usan. Comprueba tus respuestas con la clase.

a. a los estudiantes   **f.** a nosotros
b. a Kate Moss   **g.** a sus pacientes
c. a mí   **h.** a la profesora
d. a las modelos   **i.** a ti
e. a los niños   **j.** a ustedes

___c___ **1.** Mis padres **me** escriben mensajes por correo electrónico _____.

___d___ **2.** El fotógrafo **les** saca muchas fotos _____.

___h___ **3.** **Le** he entregado *(handed in)* la tarea _____.

___i___ **4.** **Te** presto mi CD de Enrique Iglesias _____.

___e___ **5.** En Halloween, **les** damos dulces *(candies)* _____.

___j___ **6.** ¡Ay, mamá y papá! **Les** estoy diciendo la verdad _____.

___f___ **7.** Susana **nos** ha escrito una carta _____.

___g___ **8.** El doctor **les** recomienda una aspirina _____.

5B.22 **En una tienda de Sevilla.** Lee el siguiente diálogo entre un dependiente y una cliente en una tienda para hombres en Sevilla, España. Trabaja con un/a compañero/a para decidir si cada pronombre en negrita se refiere a la **Cliente**, al **Dependiente**, o al **Novio** de la cliente.

DEPENDIENTE: Buenas tardes, señorita. ¿En qué puedo servir**le**[1]?

CLIENTE: Buenas tardes. Es el cumpleaños de mi novio y busco algo para él. Quiero regalar**le**[2] *(give)* algo muy bonito. ¿**Me**[3] puede recomendar algo?

DEPENDIENTE: Sí, claro. Tenemos unas corbatas muy elegantes. Con mucho gusto **le**[4] muestro *(show)* algunas de ellas.

CLIENTE: No. Mi novio **me**[5] ha dicho que tiene muchas corbatas. Quiero regalar**le**[6] algo más original.

DEPENDIENTE: Pues… Tenemos suéteres de cachemir muy finos.

CLIENTE: Oh, sí. ¡Buena idea! ¿Puede mostrar**me**[7] algunos de ellos?

DEPENDIENTE: Cómo no… Venga conmigo. ¿Qué talla *(size)* usa su novio? ¿De qué color lo prefiere?

CLIENTE: Mi novio usa talla 40 y su color favorito es el rojo.

DEPENDIENTE: Muy bien. Aquí hay varios.

CLIENTE: Prefiero éste. Me lo llevo.

DEPENDIENTE: Muy bien. Pasemos a la caja *(cash register)*.

CLIENTE: ¿Cuánto **le**[8] debo *(owe)*?

DEPENDIENTE: Ese suéter cuesta 150 euros. ¿Cómo lo va a pagar?

CLIENTE: Con tarjeta de crédito. Aquí tiene.

DEPENDIENTE: Muchas gracias.

CLIENTE: **Le**[9] agradezco *(appreciate)* mucho sus recomendaciones.

DEPENDIENTE: No hay de qué. Para servir**le**[10].

Cliente	Dependiente	Novio
1, 3, 4, 5, 7, 10	8, 9	2, 6

5B.23 **Sopa de palabras.** Vas a escuchar varios enunciados que contienen un sujeto, un objeto directo y un objeto indirecto. Completa la tabla con los sujetos y objetos indirectos apropiados de la lista de abajo. Algunas opciones se usan en más de una ocasión. Sigue el modelo.

mis abuelos
a los amigos
el bebé
Carlos
el dependiente
ellos
su hijas
Luisa
tu mamá
María
a mí
a nosotros
su novia
Ricardo
a ti
tú
yo

	Sujeto	Objeto Directo	Objeto Indirecto
	Yo	una falda	*a Luisa*
1.	Carlos	una bufanda	a su novia
2.	yo	muchas cartas	a mis abuelos
3.	tú	esos zapatos	a mí
4.	Ricardo	un sombrero	a ti
5.	ellos	una tarjeta	a nosotros
6.	María	un vestido	a sus hijas
7.	el dependiente	unas sandalias	a mí
8.	yo	un suéter	al bebé

5B.22 TEACHING TIP: Encourage volunteers to model the dialogue for the entire class. Point out that *No hay de qué* is comparable to saying "No problem" in English and *Para servirle* is similar to saying "At your service."

WILEY PLUS

5B.22 and 5B.23 INSTRUCTOR'S RESOURCES: You will find reproducible charts for use with Activities 5B.22 and 5B.23 in your Instructor's Resources.

5B.23 AUDIO SCRIPT: Modelo: Le presto una falda a Luisa. 1. Carlos le quiere regalar una bufanda a su novia. 2. Les escribo muchas cartas a mis abuelos. 3. ¿Me prestas esos zapatos? 4. ¿Te ha dado un sombrero Ricardo? 5. Ellos nos escriben una tarjeta. 6. María les va a comprar un vestido a sus hijas. 7. El dependiente me muestra unas sandalias. 8. Le pongo un suéter al bebé.

5B.24 Salma Hayek asiste a la presentación de los premios Óscar. Con un/a compañero/a, lee la siguiente historia sobre cómo se prepara Salma Hayek para asistir a la ceremonia de los premios Óscar. Conjuga cada verbo o frase verbal. Una vez que hayas conjugado los verbos, inserta el pronombre apropiado de objeto directo o indirecto **lo, los, la, las, le, o les** en la posición apropiada. Luego, comprueba tus respuestas con la clase. **¡Ojo!** Cuando tienes dos verbos, debe conjugarse el primero y dejarse el segundo en el infinitivo.

La actriz Salma Hayek va a asistir a la presentación de los Óscar en Hollywood. El programa de los Óscar es muy popular y millones de personas 1. _____ **mirar** cada año. Salma necesita llevar un vestido y unos zapatos elegantes. Ella interpreta a la pintora mexicana Frida Kahlo en una película y 2. _____ **admirar** mucho, por eso quiere un vestido que represente su estilo. El vestido 3. _____ **ir a diseñar** el diseñador mexicano Eduardo Lucero, pero a Salma 4. _____ **gustar** los zapatos del diseñador español Manolo Blahnik. Ella 5. _____ **poder encontar** en una tienda de Rodeo Drive. También necesita joyas. Salma 6. _____ **preferir comprar** en la tienda de Harry Winston. Los joyeros *(jewelers)* de Harry Winston 7. _____ **recomendar** a Salma un collar y unos aretes de diamantes. Antes de la ceremonia, Salma va a caminar por la alfombra roja *(red carpet)* y su coprotagonista, Alfred Molina, 8. _____ **desear acompañar.** Muchos reporteros van a estar allí. Ellos 9. _____ **querer hacer** muchas preguntas a Salma y a Alfred. Si Salma gana el Óscar, **muchas personas** 10. _____ **ir a decir** a ella "Felicidades".

5B.25 Una entrevista acerca de *(about)* la ropa. Crea una tabla como la de abajo y escribe tus respuestas a las siguientes preguntas. Luego, entrevista a un/a compañero/ a de clase y escribe sus respuestas también. Los dos deben usar el pronombre de objeto directo apropiado en sus respuestas y también considerar dónde debe estar el pronombre en relación con el verbo. Comparte con la clase cualquier semejanza/ diferencia sorprendente o cualquier respuesta inusual, y luego escríbelas en tu **Retrato de la clase.**

	Yo	_____
1. ¿Con qué frecuencia llevas *jeans*?		
2. ¿Dónde prefieres comprar tus zapatos?		
3. ¿Cuándo llevas sandalias?		
4. ¿Para qué actividades debes llevar una camiseta?		
5. ¿Cuándo necesitas llevar tu mejor traje/vestido?		
6. ¿Con qué frecuencia lavas *(wash)* la ropa?		
7. ¿Cuándo llevas ropa informal?		
8. ¿Dónde prefieres comprar tu ropa formal?		

Retrato de la clase: Muchos estudiantes llevan *jeans* con mucha frecuencia. Algunos prefieren comprar su ropa en ____ y otros prefieren comparla en ____ . Etcétera.

www ¡Conéctate!
Visit http://www.elcorteingles.es and click on "Moda". Compare the sales **(las rebajas)** and styles of this well known Spanish department store with the sales and styles in the stores where you live. Does anything seem to be a real bargain **(una ganga)**?

Enlaces

5B.26 **¿Qué significan?**   Determina el significado de las palabras o frases de abajo, de acuerdo al contexto. Confirma tus respuestas con la clase.

a. although
b. to that end
c. for example
d. according to
e. also

___b___ **1. con este fin**   Muchas mujeres quieren parecer *(to appear)* más altas. Con este fin, compran tacones altos.

___e___ **2. también**   Las bufandas y los collares son una manera de crear una imagen individual. También nos permiten variar la imagen según la ocasión.

___a___ **3. aunque**   Aunque hay mucha ropa en las tiendas, muchas personas no saben qué comprar para verse bien.

___c___ **4. por ejemplo**   Hay ropa que todos deben tener; por ejemplo, un pantalón negro y una camisa blanca.

___d___ **5. según**   Según los asesores *(consultants)* de imagen, los hombres deben tener un traje clásico de buena calidad.

5B.27 **Conecta las ideas.**   Con un/a compañero/a, conecta las ideas de las oraciones de abajo, usando la expresión apropiada. Comprueben sus respuestas con la clase.

a. según
b. también
c. con este fin
d. aunque
e. por ejemplo

___a___ **1.** ... mi mamá, cuando hace frío yo debo llevar un abrigo.

___e___ **2.** Diferentes países tienen diferentes costumbres. ..., en Perú es necesario llevar uniforme a la escuela.

___c___ **3.** Muchas escuelas en Latinoamérica quieren mantener una apariencia de igualdad socioeconómica. ..., los uniformes son obligatorios.

___b___ **4.** Para el cumpleaños de mi novio, le regalo pantalones nuevos. ... le regalo una camisa muy elegante.

___d___ **5.** ... no me gustan las bufandas, pero si hace mucho frío llevo una.

5B.26 TEACHING TIP: Encourage students to focus on the context of the sentences to make meaning of these new words. You may want to point out that *según* is not followed by the prepositional pronouns *mí* and *ti*, but rather is followed by the subject pronouns *yo* and *tú*.

5B.27 TEACHING TIP: Encourage students to read over their sentences a couple of times to make sure they make sense before going over the answers as a class.

FUNCTIONAL OUTCOMES:
The central question that
frames this *Investigación*
is "*¿Qué se puede decir de
la ropa?*" Explore whether
students can now address
this question and how
they would go about it.
Have them review the
chart on the first page of
this *Investigación*.

5B.28 ANSWER: Content
applies to both men and
women.

5B.28 Comprensión. Mira el artículo *Claves para vestir bien*. ¿Te da el título alguna indicación de lo que puede tratar el artículo? Lee rápidamente por encima *(skim through)* el artículo para determinar a quién se refiere el contenido y marca la respuesta apropiada.

☐ only to men   ☐ only to women   ☐ to both men and women

READING STRATEGY:
Remind students that
they should look to titles,
subtitles and other sec-
tions within readings to
get a handle on what it
will be about.

TEACHING TIP: In ad-
dition to the reading
strategy just shared,
encourage students to
put their other reading
strategies (skimming and
looking for contextual
clues) to practice as they
try to interpret the meaning of the text.

Claves para vestir bien

Cada mañana, al despertar, nos hacemos la misma pregunta: "¿Qué me pongo?". La imagen es importante porque dice mucho de nosotros, pero vestir bien no es fácil. **Aunque** el buen gusto es innato, las claves *(keys)* fundamentales para llevar prendas apropiadas se pueden aprender. **Con este fin** ha surgido *(arisen)* una profesión de "asesores de imagen". Políticos y actores de cine siguen sus consejos *(advice)*. **Por ejemplo, según** ellos, el estilo masculino se caracteriza por ser clásico. Todo hombre debe tener un traje de buena calidad de color azul marino o gris y para ocasiones más informales uno marrón o beige.

En el caso de las mujeres, es necesario tener un pantalón negro y una blusa blanca: dos piezas que combinan con todo y que resultan adecuadas para cubrir prácticamente cualquier necesidad. Los complementos, como un collar, una bufanda, son el toque que determinará nuestra personalidad y que nos permitirá variar nuestra imagen según la ocasión, aun con ropa idéntica. **También** hay algunos trucos para parecer más altas y delgadas: utilizar vestidos sencillos, sin elementos que ensanchen *(widen)*. Si su deseo es perder unos cuantos kilos visualmente, vestidos lisos con colores oscuros y de telas con caída *(that hang loose)* son la solución.

Collar por Diseños de Jesusa

5B.29 ¿Cuál es la información correcta? Ahora lee el artículo más detenidamente *(slowly)* con un/a compañero/a, para buscar la información necesaria para corregir los siguientes enunciados falsos. Corrijan estos enunciados con información específica.

1. Vestir bien es muy fácil.

2. Los políticos y los actores de cine no se preocupan por su imagen.

3. La moda masculina cambia frecuentemente.

4. Para un evento formal, un hombre puede llevar un traje beige.

5. Una blusa blanca y un pantalón negro sólo son apropiados para llevar al trabajo.

6. No puedes variar la misma ropa según la ocasión.

7. Para parecer más alta, el vestido debe ser complicado y voluminoso.

8. Para parecer más delgada, una mujer debe llevar un vestido blanco.

5B.30 ¿Qué opinas tú de la moda? Indica si estás de acuerdo o no con los siguientes enunciados y piensa por qué. Compara tus respuestas con las del resto de la clase. Anota los resultados en tu **Retrato de la clase.**

	Estoy de acuerdo	No estoy de acuerdo
1. Los modelos de las revistas representan a la gente ordinaria.	☐	☐
2. La ropa de marca *(brand-name clothes)* es un símbolo de estatus socioeconómico.	☐	☐
3. Compro ropa específica porque la gente en la televisión la lleva.	☐	☐
4. Prefiero no seguir la moda sino tener un estilo individual.	☐	☐
5. Es importante llevar la ropa más de moda.	☐	☐
6. La moda cambia tan frecuentemente por razones económicas	☐	☐
7. La ropa de marca es útil y práctica para la vida diaria.	☐	☐
8. Otras personas me dicen qué debo llevar.	☐	☐
9. Estar de moda es más importante que estar cómodo/a *(comfortable).*	☐	☐
10. La ropa de marca es sólo para gente con cuerpos "perfectos".	☐	☐
11. La ropa que llevo determina la imagen que tengo de mí mismo/a.	☐	☐
12. Las prendas y los accesorios comunican el estatus socioeconómico de una persona.	☐	☐
13. Todas las culturas crean una jerarquía social, económica y cultural a través de sus prendas.	☐	☐

Retrato de la clase: La mayoría de la clase piensa que…. Algunos compañeros dicen que…

5B.29 TEACHING TIP: Before students actually refer back to the article, challenge them to see if they can correct these sentences beforehand.

5B.29 ANSWERS: 1. Vestir bien no es fácil. 2. Los políticos y actores de cine buscan los consejos de asesores de imagen. 3. La moda masculina es clásica. 4. Para una ocasión formal, un hombre debe llevar un traje azul marino o gris. Los trajes beige son apropiados para una ocasión más informal. 5. Una blusa blanca y pantalones negros son adecuados para cualquier necesidad. 6. Puedes variar la ropa según la ocasión con complementos como collares y bufandas. 7. Para parecer más alta, el vestido debe ser sencillo. 8. Para parecer más delgada, el vestido debe ser de color oscuro.

5B.30 TEACHING TIP: On one side of the room, hang a sign that reads *Estoy de acuerdo* and on the other side, one that reads *No estoy de acuerdo*. Tell students to imagine there being a continuum between the two statements. Ask them to stand up, read the statements from activity 5B.33, and position themselves somewhere along the continuum that represents their opinion. By promoting physical movement, we not only help students become more active in their learning, but we also make all of our students accountable for participating.

Perspectivas

5B.31 La fuerza de la pertenencia. En la sección anterior, te dieron consejos sobre cómo vestir para verte de lo mejor. ¿Te has preguntado cómo se toman estas decisiones o por qué nos importa la moda?

Paso 1: Con respecto a esto, haz una lluvia de ideas *(brainstorm)* con la clase. Luego, comprueba, con la lista de abajo, los dos factores principales, mencionados en clase, que determinan la moda.

☐ los medios de comunicación   ☐ el deseo de mantener el estatus

☐ el deseo de pertenecer a un grupo   ☐ las tiendas que venden ropa

☐ la publicidad *(advertising)*   ☐ los diseñadores

Paso 2: Como clase, examinen las fotos de abajo. ¿Qué indica la ropa que lleva la gente en relación al papel de la ropa en la sociedad o la cultura? Comprueba los enunciados que reflejen tu perspectiva y comparte tus respuestas con la clase.

☐ El ser humano tiene necesidad de pertenecer a un grupo.

☐ Nuestra identidad consiste en vestir de manera parecida al grupo con el que nos identificamos más.

☐ Mucho del éxito del grupo se exhibe en la forma en que los miembros de ese grupo se visten.

Vocabulario: Investigación B

WILEY PLUS

Vocabulario esencial

Sustantivos

el abrigo	*coat*
el anillo/la sortija	*ring*
el arete/el pendiente	*earrings*
el buen gusto	*good taste*
la bufanda	*scarf*
los calcetines	*socks*
la camisa	*shirt*
la camiseta	*t-shirt*
la cartera/la bolsa	*handbag*
la chaqueta	*jacket*
el cinturón	*belt*
los colores	*colors*
amarillo	*yellow*
azul	*blue*
blanco	*white*
gris	*gray*
marrón	*brown*
morado	*purple*
naranja	*orange*
negro	*black*
rojo	*red*
rosa	*pink*
verde	*green*
la corbata	*tie*
el cuerpo	*body*
la falda	*skirt*
la gorra	*cap*
los guantes	*gloves*
el impermeable	*raincoat*
los lentes	*eyeglasses*
las medias	*pantyhose*
el paraguas	*umbrella*
el reloj	*watch*
la ropa	*clothes*
el saco	*sports jacket*
el sombrero	*hat*
las telas	*fabrics*
el bordado	*embroidery*
el estampado	*print*
el algodón	*cotton*
la franela	*flannel*
la lana	*wool*
la piel/el cuero	*leather*
la seda	*silk*
la talla	*size*
el traje	*suit*
el traje de baño	*bathing suit*
el vestido	*dress*
los zapatos	*shoes*
los zapatos de tacón	*high heels*

Adjetivos

a cuadros	*checkered/plaid*
a rayas	*striped*
ancho/a	*wide*
apreatado/a	*tight fitting*
estrecho/a	*narrow*
fino	*high quality*
suelto/a	*loose fitting*

Verbos

adelgazar	*to lose weight*
delgado/a	*slender*
engordar	*to gain weight*
llevar	*to wear; to take; to carry*

Otras palabras y expresiones

la abertura	*opening*
el/la amante	*lover*
los anteojos	*glasses*
asegurarse	*to make sure*
el/la asesor/a	*advisor*
averiguar	*to find out*
el calzado	*footwear*
la caja	*cash register*
los carretes de hilo	*spools of thread*
el consejo	*advice*
el cuello	*neck*
el cumplido	*compliment*
deber	*to owe*
el desfile de modas	*fashion show*
el/la diseñador/a	*designer*
la estatura	*height*

las gafas	*eyeglasses, sunglasses*
liso	*smooth, even*
el lujo	*luxury*
las mangas	*sleeves*
la manta	*shawl*
el oro	*gold*
oscuro/a	*dark*
la prenda	*garment*
prestar	*to lend*
regalar	*to give as a present*
el regalo	*gift*
la tarjeta	*card*
el tejido	*fabric, knitting*
el toque	*touch*
el vestido de novia	*wedding dress*
voluminoso/a	*bulky*

de moda	*in style*
¡Qué vestido más elegante!	*What an elegant dress!*
¡Me gusta esa blusa!	*I like that blouse!*
¡Vas muy a la moda!	*You are really stylish/in style!*
¡El traje de baño te queda muy bien!	*The bathing suit fits/suits you really well!*
¡Qué guapo/a estás!	*You look great!*

Cognados

Review the cognates in *Adelante* and the false cognates in *¡Atención!*. For a complete list of cognates, see Appendix 4 on page 605.

¡VÍVELO!

En vivo

Entrevistar a un/a compañero/a: Use the information below to create 10 questions that you will use to interview a classmate. After you have interviewed your classmate, share his/her responses with the rest of the class and note them in your **Retrato de la clase.**

> Modelo: ser/color/favorito
> ¿Cuál es tu color favorito?

1. ser/prenda/favorito
2. preferir/sandalia/zapato/tenis
3. preferir tacón/bajo/alto
4. preferir/ropa/formal/informal
5. ropa/preferir/llevar/clase
6. ropa/preferir/llevar/casa
7. ropa/llevar/fiesta
8. ropa/preferir/llevar/invierno
9. ropa/preferir/llevar/hacer/calor
10. comprar/ropa

Retrato de la clase: La prenda favorita de _____ es _____. Prefiere…

Ajustes culinarios. Imagine that you will be studying abroad in a Spanish-speaking country. Part of your immersion will go beyond language and into new foods and customs. As part of having this new experience, you need to prepare yourself for adjustments to your eating schedule and the foods you eat. Write a brief composition indicating how a study-abroad experience can alter your culinary habits and horizons.

Paso 1: Identify the country/city where you will be studying abroad. What do you already know about food/eating schedules there? Use the Internet and/or other sources to explore specific regional cuisine.

Paso 2: Create a list of your current cuisine and mealtime habits and another one for typical cuisine and mealtime habits for the Spanish-speaking country/region/city.

Paso 3: Compare the two lists to determine the changes you will need to make.

Paso 4: Write a draft of your composition explaining the adjustments to the foods and eating schedule that will result from a study-abroad experience there.

Paso 5: Review your draft for spelling and clarity, and pay special attention to your use of object pronouns.

En directo

INVESTIGACIÓN A: Sabores hispanos

> **Antes de ver el video.** Hazle estas preguntas a un/a compañero/a de clase.

    1. ¿Te gusta la comida hispana? ¿Cuál es tu plato favorito?

    2. ¿Sabes qué son las tapas?

> **Al ver el video.** Selecciona la opción correcta según el segmento de video.

1. La gastronomía hispanoamericana es conocida mundialmente por sus…
  a. pescados
  (b.) sabores
  c. carnes

2. El ceviche se cocina con pescado y…
  (a.) limón
  b. verduras
  c. los dos

3. Las empanadas se comen…
  (a.) fritas
  b. crudas
  c. en el desayuno

4. Las tapas pueden comerse…
  a. frías
  b. calientes
  (c.) frías y calientes

5. Para los españoles "ir de tapas" significa…
  a. beber y conversar
  b. comer aperitivos y conversar
  (c.) las dos cosas

> **Después de ver el video.** Comparte tus preferencias sobre la comida con el resto de la clase. Usa las siguientes preguntas para formular tus ideas: ¿Cuáles son tus comidas favoritas? ¿Qué ingredientes llevan? ¿Cuándo las comes?

Vocabulario útil
morcilla *blood sausage*
pulpo *octopus*
gamba (camarón) *shrimp*
al ajillo *fried with garlic*

WILEY PLUS
You will find a variety of resources for use with *En vivo* in WileyPLUS, such as a transcript of the video segment, a translation of that transcript, and guidelines for implementing the En vivo activities.

INVESTIGACIÓN B: El arte del tejido

> **Antes de ver el video.** Empareja cada palabra con su correspondiente definición:

a. zapatos   **b.** falda   **c.** poncho   **d.** pantalón   **e.** chaleco

  _b_ **1.** prenda de vestir que cae desde la cintura sin ceñirse *(to cling)* al cuerpo

  _a_ **2.** calzado *(footwear)* cerrado de piel y elegante

  _d_ **3.** prenda que cubre cada pierna separadamente

  _e_ **4.** prenda de vestir sin mangas *(sleeves)* que se lleva encima de la camisa o blusa

  _c_ **5.** prenda que consiste en una manta *(shawl)* con una abertura *(opening)* para pasar la cabeza

> **Al ver el video.** Indica si los siguientes enunciados son ciertos o falsos:

Cierto	Falso	
☐	☑	**1.** Los tejidos de las comunidades indígenas de los Andes no tienen un alto nivel artístico.
☑	☐	**2.** Los tejedores utilizan fibras naturales de oveja *(sheep)*, llama y alpaca.
☐	☑	**3.** La mujer sólo lleva una blusa, un chaleco y una o más faldas.
☑	☐	**4.** La ropa tradicional sirve para mantener la cultura de las comunidades.

> **Después de ver el video.** Responde a las siguientes preguntas y comparte tus respuestas con el resto de la clase.

    • ¿Puedes describir la ropa tradicional que llevan los hombres y las mujeres?

    • ¿Qué ropa tradicional hay en tu comunidad o lugar de origen? ¿Puedes describirla?

Vocabulario útil
la alpaca *llama*
los patrones *patterns*
sobrevivir *to survive*
tejer *to knit*
el tejido *fabric/textile*
el tinte *tint/dye*
el orgullo *pride*

 Retrato de la clase Checklist

You should have recorded information in your **Retrato de la clase** in conjunction with the following activities:

☐   **5A.5**   **Encuentra a una persona.**

☐   **5A.12**   **¿Cuál es tu comida preferida?**

☐   **5A.31**   **Entrevista a un/a compañero/a**

☐   **5B.12**   **Tu clóset.**

☐   **5B.25**   **Una entrevista acerca de la ropa.**

☐   **5B.30**   **¿Qué opinas tú de la moda?**

☐   **En vivo**

Costumbres sociales y culturales

INVESTIGACIÓN **6A**
¿Qué revelan nuestros hogares?

ADELANTE
- ¡Ya lo sabes! El hogar
- Los múltiples talentos de Eduardo Xol

Bien dicho: Más sobre los diptongos

PALABRAS CLAVE
- La casa y los muebles

ESTRUCTURAS CLAVE
- Combining direct and indirect object pronouns
- The prepositions *por* and *para*

VÍVELO: LENGUA
- Expressing adjectives as nouns: *Lo* and *lo que es*
- Expressing what something is made of

VÍVELO: CULTURA
- El espacio
- Las visitas

CONTEXTOS Y PERSPECTIVAS
- El significado del patio

INVESTIGACIÓN **6B**
¿Se trabaja para vivir o se vive para trabajar?

ADELANTE
- ¡Ya lo sabes! El trabajo y la calidad de vida
- ¿Trabajar para vivir o vivir para trabajar?

Bien dicho: El sonido de la *p*

PALABRAS CLAVE
- El bienestar
- El mundo del trabajo
- El tiempo libre

ESTRUCTURAS CLAVE
- Formal commands
- Informal commands

VÍVELO: LENGUA
- Expressing order: Ordinal numbers
- Expressing preferences: *Repaso y expansión*

VÍVELO: CULTURA
- La siesta
- El vendedor y su cliente
- Los negocios en los países hispanos
- La tiendita

CONTEXTOS Y PERSPECTIVAS
- ¿Trabajar para vivir o vivir para trabajar?

¡VÍVELO!

En vivo:
¿Cómo es tu cuarto?
Los negocios en EE.UU y en Latinoamérica

En directo:
A: El patio andaluz
B: ¿Para qué trabajamos?

¿Qué revelan nuestros hogares?

6A.1 ANSWERS: Tipos de hogares: el condominio/el departamento, el apartamento/el piso, la casa; La sala: el sofá, la chimenea, la lámpara, la planta, el centro de entretenimiento; El exterior de la casa: el jardín, el patio, el balcón, la planta; Los electrodomésticos: el reproductor de DVD, el estéreo, el refrigerador, la tostadora, el televisor de plasma, el radio, el dispensador de agua fría (sólo si es eléctrico), la cafetera

In this **Investigación,** you will learn:

▶ How to talk about the objects that furnish our homes

▶ How to comprehend who does what and for whom in a statement

▶ How to use various object pronouns together in one statement

▶ Patterns of usage for **por** and **para**

▶ How choices in housing are influenced by a society and/or cultures

¿Cómo puedes hablar del hogar, los vecinos o la comunidad?

Puedes identificar los muebles y aparatos que tienes en tu casa.	¿Qué muebles asociamos con la sala? ¿La cocina? ¿El dormitorio? ¿Qué actividades asociamos con la cocina? ¿La cama?
Puedes describir los muebles y aparatos que tienes en tu casa.	¿Tienes casa o apartamento? ¿Qué muebles y aparatos tienes? ¿Cómo son? ¿Dónde están?
Puedes hacer preguntas a tus vecinos.	El estéreo, ¿quién te lo ha comprado? ¿A quién le regalas esas lámparas? El sofá, ¿me lo vendes a buen precio?

Adelante

¡Ya lo sabes! El hogar

el apartamento/ el piso¹	la chimenea³	el jardín	el televisor de plasma
el balcón	la decoración	la lámpara	la tostadora
brillante	el dispensador de	la oficina/el estudio	
la cafetera	agua fría	el patio	adornar
el centro de	los electrodomésticos	la planta	iluminar
entretenimiento	el estéreo	el radio⁴	rentar⁵
el condominio/	el estilo	el refrigerador	
el departamento²	la foto	el reproductor de DVD	
	el garaje	la residencia estudiantil	
		el sofá	

¹*Piso* isn't a cognate, but is given here as a synonym for *apartamento. Piso* means "floor" as well as "apartment" depending on the context. It is most commonly used in Spain.

²A *departamento* can refer to a flat, apartment or condo, in addition to its other meaning as "department".

³*Chimenea* is used to refer to the fireplace in a home and not just the chimney on the roof.

⁴*La radio* is the industry or media, *el radio* is the device. Likewise, *la televisión* is the media, *el televisor* is the device.

⁵The verb *alquilar* means "to rent", but *rentar* (and as a noun, *la renta*) is increasingly being used in Central America, Mexico, the Caribbean and the United States.

6A.1 Busca la categoría correcta. Clasifica las palabras de *Adelante* según las siguientes categorías. Sigue el modelo. Luego, comprueba tus respuestas con la clase.

Los tipos de hogares (*types of homes*)

residencia estudiantil

_____

_____

La sala (*living room*)

_____

_____

El exterior de la casa

_____

_____

_____

Los electrodomésticos

_____

_____

_____

6A.1 RECYCLING: Once students have put the words from *Adelante* into categories, mention some of the kitchen appliances they learned in *Capítulo 5* such as *el refrigerador, la cocina, el microondas* and ask what category those belong to.

6A.2 ¿Cierto o falso? Vas a leer varios enunciados. Indica si cada uno es cierto o falso y corrige los enunciados falsos. Luego, compara tus respuestas con las de la clase.

Cierto	Falso	
☐	☑	**1.** Miramos nuestros programas favoritos en el radio.
☐	☑	**2.** Los balcones están en las cocinas.
☑	☐	**3.** Las chimeneas son románticas.
☐	☑	**4.** Las ventanas sólo adornan el hogar.
☐	☑	**5.** El estéreo es para ver películas.
☐	☑	**6.** Usamos el sofá para cocinar.
☐	☑	**7.** La cafetera es para lavar *(to wash)* la ropa.
☐	☑	**8.** Las tostadoras se asocian con la carne.
☑	☐	**9.** Las lámparas iluminan la casa.
☑	☐	**10.** El garaje es para el carro.

6A.2 ANSWERS: 1. Falso. Miramos nuestros programas favoritos en el televisor. 2. Falso. Los balcones están fuera de la casa. 3. Cierto. 4. Falso. Las ventanas son necesarias para iluminar el cuarto. 5. Falso. Es para escuchar música. 6. Falso. Usamos el sofá para sentarnos. / Usamos el horno (o la cocina) para cocinar. 7. Falso. La cafetera es para hacer el café. 8. Falso. Las tostadoras se asocian con el pan. 9. Cierto. 10. Cierto.

6A.2 EXTENSION ACTIVITY. Have students write their own sentences using the statements in Activity 6A.2 as examples. They can then share them with a partner who needs to decide whether the statements are true or false.

6A.3 ¿Qué palabra es? Con un/a compañero/a de clase, escojan cinco de las palabras a continuación y escriban una pequeña descripción de cada una (sin mencionar la palabra). Intercambien sus definiciones con las de otra pareja e intenten identificar sus palabras. Luego, reúnanse con el otro grupo para comprobar sus respuestas.

> Modelo: E1: *Es una casa compacta que no tiene un jardín muy grande.*
>
> E2: *un condominio*

el televisor de plasma	el jardín	el condominio
el centro de entretenimiento	el estéreo	el patio
el dispensador de agua fría	la lámpara	el radio
los electrodomésticos	la decoración	la tostadora
el balcón		

6A.3 ORIENTATION: This activity helps students develop the important skill of circumlocution, the ability to express something without using the specific word. Give students several minutes to complete this activity.

6A.4 Adivina. Algunas palabras en español sólo están parcialmente compuestas por cognados. Con un/a compañero/a de clase, emparejen las imágenes de los electrodomésticos con su nombre en español en la página 256. Luego, comparen su apariencia y precio en Europa, con la apariencia y precio que tienen en sus países. Compartan sus respuestas con la clase.

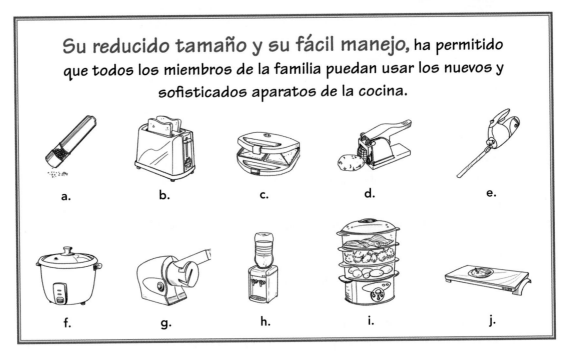

Su reducido tamaño y su fácil manejo, ha permitido que todos los miembros de la familia puedan usar los nuevos y sofisticados aparatos de la cocina.

a.   b.   c.   d.   e.

f.   g.   h.   i.   j.

___h___ **1.** dispensador de agua fría (59,90 euros)

___i___ **2.** olla al vapor (32 euros)

___f___ **3.** arrocera (26 euros)

___d___ **4.** cortapapas (10 euros)

___c___ **5.** sandwichera (15 euros)

___e___ **6.** cuchillo eléctrico (21 euros)

___b___ **7.** tostadora (31 euros)

___a___ **8.** molinillo de pimienta (13 euros)

___g___ **9.** afilador *(sharpener)* eléctrico (13,50 euros)

___j___ **10.** calientaplatos (53 euros)

Los mútiples talentos de Eduardo Xol

Eduardo Xol (se pronuncia "soul") ha tenido una carrera variada e interesante. Nació en el este de Los Ángeles. Fue un prodigio de la música y formó parte de la Orquesta Filarmónica de Los Ángeles y el Conservatorio de Música en la Ciudad de México antes de cumplir 15 años. Después tuvo éxito como bailarín en diferentes películas antes de entrar al programa de Arte Teatral en la Universidad de California en Los Ángeles (UCLA). Después se mudó a México, en donde alcanzó fama como músico pop y también actuó en varias telenovelas. Después de su regreso a Estados Unidos, Xol retomó su gusto por la jardinería, la cual desarrolló gracias a la influencia de su abuela. Estableció su propia empresa de diseño, *Xol Creative*, y ahora es conocido como diseñador de paisajes *(landscape designer)* y ha aparecido con frecuencia como diseñador en el programa televisivo *Extreme Makeover: Home Edition* de la cadena ABC.

6A.5 **Biografía.** Vas a escuchar algunos enunciados sobre Eduardo Xol. Determina, de acuerdo a lo que has leído, si los enunciados siguientes son ciertos o falsos. Luego, comprueba tus respuestas con la clase.

	Cierto	Falso			Cierto	Falso
1.	☐	☑		4.	☑	☐
2.	☑	☐		5.	☐	☑
3.	☐	☑		6.	☑	☐

6A.5 AUDIO SCRIPT:
1. Eduardo Xol nació en México. 2. Eduardo Xol fue un niño prodigio de la música. 3. Eduardo Xol estudió arquitectura en UCLA. 4. Eduardo Xol ha trabajado en varias telenovelas mexicanas. 5. El papá de Eduardo Xol le inspiró su amor por los jardines. 6. Eduardo Xol ha trabajado en el programa *Extreme Makeover: Home Edition.*

6A.5 FOLLOW-UP: Have students correct false statements by citing specific information in the brief biography of Xol.

Bien dicho

Más sobre los diptongos

In *Investigación 4B,* you learned about diphthongs, where two vowels form a single sound within the same syllable. Recall that these combinations of two vowels may consist of a weak vowel and a strong vowel or two weak vowels. The weak vowels are **i** and **u** and the strong vowels are **a, e,** and **o.** You also learned that if **i** or **u** has an accent mark, it is treated as a strong vowel and no diphthong is formed.

Previously, you worked with diphthongs within individual words, such as **pienso, cuatro, aire, reina, nación** and **ciudad.** In this *Investigación,* you will see that diphthongs also occur between words. This phenomenon is related to the concept of *enlace,* which you studied in *Investigaciones 1B* and *2A.* The term *enlace* refers to the lack of pauses between words that characterizes Spanish. When one word ends with a strong vowel and the next word begins with a weak vowel (or vice versa), a diphthong is formed as a result of *enlace.* For example, the following phrases are each pronounced as if they were one word containing a diphthong:

habla inglés	á-bl**ai**n-glés
grupo unido	grú-p**ou**-ní-do
mi amigo	m**ia**-mí-go
tribu indígena	trí-b**ui**n-dí-gena

6A.6 **Dictado.** Vas a escuchar varias frases cortas. Escribe lo que escuches considerando el enlace y la formación de diptongos entre una palabra y otra. Confirma tus frases con un/a compañero/a y luego túrnense para pronunciar las frases.

1. se utilizan	**5.** tribu olmeca	**9.** visito Irlanda
2. mi hermano	**6.** la historia mexicana	**10.** mi horario
3. dialecto uruguayo	**7.** mi apartamento	**11.** aprende italiano
4. casa urbana	**8.** su edad	**12.** tu aparato favorito

6A.7 **¿Cuántos diptongos hay?** Trabajen en parejas y lean cuidadosamente *(carefully)* cada oración para identificar los diptongos que ocurren entre palabras. Escriban cuántos diptongos hay en el espacio al lado de cada oración según el modelo. Luego, túrnense para leer las oraciones en voz alta *(aloud)* y practicar la pronunciación de los diptongos.

1. Tomo un autobús a la universidad cada día. _2_
2. El cuerpo humano me parece increíble. _2_
3. A mi hermana Isabel le interesa cocinar. _3_
4. Su empresa importa comida internacional. _3_
5. Mi abuelo Israel es de Unión en Paraguay. _3_
6. Mi amigo Humberto maneja un coche humilde. _4_
7. Manu Álvarez siempre inventa historias locas. _3_
8. Carlota Uribe usa su horno infrecuentemente. _4_

Palabras clave 1 La casa y los muebles

SUGGESTION: Additional input may consist of questions tying back to any items you may have in the classroom, such as, *¿Cuántas mesas hay en tu apartamento?, ¿Hay armarios en la clase?, ¿Cuántos espejos hay en tu cuarto?*, etc. You could also contrast objects in the house illustrated in *Palabras clave* with the two rooms in Valdez's painting in the chapter opener, such as *¿Quién tiene una escoba en el corredor?*, etc.

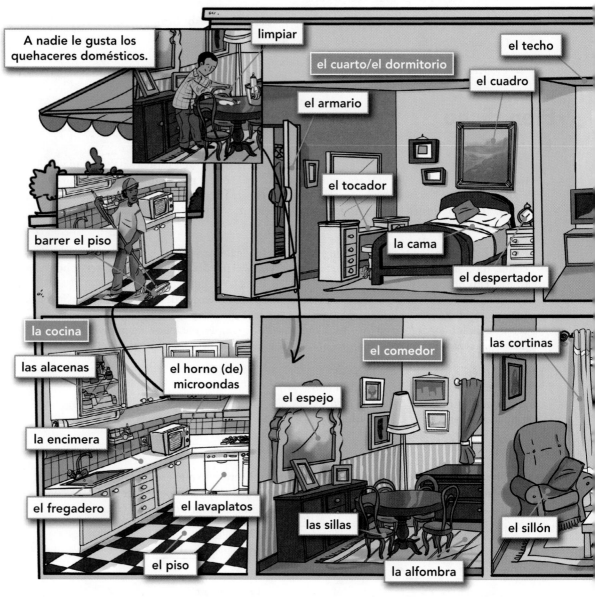

A nadie le gusta los quehaceres domésticos.

limpiar

el cuarto/el dormitorio

el techo

el cuadro

el armario

el tocador

la cama

el despertador

barrer el piso

la cocina

las cortinas

el comedor

las alacenas

el horno (de) microondas

el espejo

la encimera

el lavaplatos

el fregadero

las sillas

el sillón

el piso

la alfombra

6A.8 RECYCLING: This activity recycles prepositions of location.

6A.8 EXTENSION ACTIVITY: Pair students up establishing who is person A and who is person B. Person A finds three items in the illustrated house that he/she will describe in terms of location so that person B can guess the object. Person A has to describe the location of these items while person B guesses the item. Then have them switch roles and do the same.

6A.8 **¿Dónde están?** Con un/a compañero/a, completen estas oraciones usando las frases preposicionales, para indicar dónde se encuentran los objetos de la casa que aparece arriba. Comprueben sus respuestas con la clase.

a la derecha	debajo	entre
a la izquierda	arriba	

1. El cuadro está _____arriba_____ de la cama.

2. El baño está _____debajo_____ de la escalera.

3. El lavamanos está ___a la izquierda___ del inodoro.

4. El estante está ___a la izquierda___ del escritorio.

5. La cama está _____entre_____ el despertador y el tocador.

6. La lavadora está _____debajo_____ de la secadora.

7. La bañera está ___a la derecha___ del inodoro.

8. El comedor está _____entre_____ la sala y la cocina.

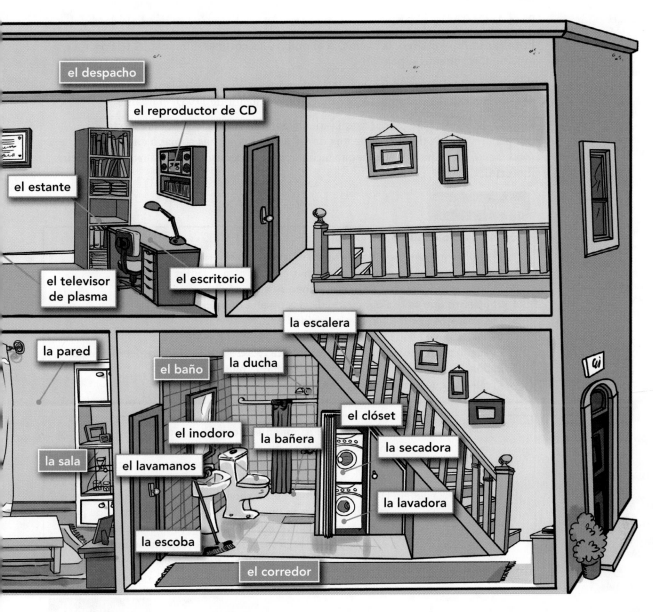

el despacho

el reproductor de CD

el estante

el televisor de plasma

el escritorio

la escalera

la pared

el baño

la ducha

el clóset

el inodoro

la bañera

la secadora

el lavamanos

la sala

la lavadora

la escoba

el corredor

6A.9 **¿Mueble, electrodoméstico o instalación fija?** Vas a escuchar varias palabras. Indica si cada palabra se refiere a un mueble, un electrodoméstico o una instalación fija según el modelo. Luego, comprueba tus respuestas con la clase.

	Mueble	Electrodoméstico	Instalación fija *(fixture)*
1.	☐	☐	☑
2.	☑	☐	☐
3.	☑	☐	☐
4.	☑	☐	☐
5.	☑	☐	☐
6.	☐	☑	☐
7.	☐	☐	☑
8.	☑	☐	☐

6A.9 AUDIO SCRIPT: 1. la ducha; 2. el tocador; 3. la cama; 4. el armario; 5. la mesa; 6. el reproductor de DVD; 7. el fregadero; 8. el escritorio

6A.9 TEACHING TIP: After reading through the list twice, you may choose to show them the words. This will help students who are particularly strong visual learners. Point out to students that flats in Europe often do not have closets but armoires.

WILEY PLUS

6A.10, 6A.11 INSTRUCTOR'S RESOURCES: You will find reproducible cards and a reproducible crossword puzzle for use with Activities 6A.10 and 6A.11 in your Instructor's Resources.

www

¡Conéctate!
Would you like to furnish your room with furniture from *El Corte Inglés*, a popular Spanish department store? Visit http://elcorteingles.es and click on **Hogar**. Check out what type of furniture they have for sale. Keep track of the items that interest you. Were some of the items you learned in this *Investigación* called something else on the website? How much would your dream shopping spree cost? Take into account that you would be paying with euros. Do you know what your total would be in US dollars?

6A.10 ¡Lotería! Con un/a compañero/a de clase, decidan quién es Estudiante A y quién es Estudiante B.

Paso 1: Copien las palabras siguientes al azar *(in random order)* en una hoja de papel.

Estudiante A: el estéreo, la cocina, la alfombra, las cortinas, iluminar, el televisor, la tostadora, el sillón, el espejo

Estudiante B: el despertador, los electrodomésticos, el garaje, el jardín, el reproductor de CD, la residencia estudiantil, la cama, el reproductor de DVD, el estante

Paso 2: Túrnense para leer al azar las definiciones a continuación. Cuando tu compañero/a lea la definición de una de las palabras que has copiado en tu lista, táchala *(cross it out)*. La primera persona que tache tres palabras seguidas *(in a row)* debe decir **¡Lotería!**.

Estudiante A

Definiciones para tu compañero/a:
1. El edificio universitario donde viven muchos estudiantes
2. Un lugar al exterior donde hay muchas flores y otras plantas
3. El lugar donde muchas personas ponen su automóvil
4. El aparato que se usa para ver películas de alta definición
5. Los aparatos que requieren electricidad para funcionar
6. El mueble que se asocia con dormir
7. El aparato que muestra la hora y despierta *(wakes up)* a la familia por la mañana
8. El aparato electrónico que permite escuchar la música de los CD
9. El mueble que usamos para poner los libros

Estudiante B

Definiciones para tu compañero/a:
1. El aparato que se usa para ver nuestros programas favoritos
2. El verbo que asociamos con las luces y las lámparas
3. El aparato que se utiliza para preparar comida caliente
4. El aparato que se asocia con la acción de escuchar música
5. El aparato pequeño que usamos para preparar pan por la mañana
6. Una cosa que refleja la imagen de una persona
7. Un mueble que usamos para descansar, relajarnos, leer el periódico y ver la tele
8. Lo que está sobre el piso y debajo de los muebles en muchas casas
9. Lo que usamos en las ventanas para reducir la luz

6A.11 Crucigrama. Con un/a compañero/a, completen las oraciones siguientes con la palabra más lógica de *Palabras clave* y escríbanla en el crucigrama de la página 259. Luego, comprueben sus respuestas con la clase.

Horizontal
1. La _____ sirve para cubrir el piso.
5. Sirve para colgar *(hang)* los vestidos, los trajes y la ropa formal.
9. Entramos y salimos de la casa por la _____.
10. Los _____ sirven para adornar las paredes.
11. Guardamos *(we keep)* los libros en un _____.
12. Preparamos la comida en la _____.
13. Usamos el _____ para cocinar rápidamente.
15. El _____ es lo opuesto de piso.
16. Después de lavar la ropa, es necesario ponerla en la _____.
17. El _____ es un reloj que tiene alarma.

Vertical

2. Para ver una película, usamos el ____.
3. El lavamanos se encuentra en el ____.
4. Dormimos en la ____.
6. El ____ es el mueble que más asociamos con una oficina.
7. Cuando queremos ver lo que pasa afuera, miramos por la ____.
8. En el comedor, normalmente hay una ____ formal para comer.
14. Recibimos a las visitas en la ____.

6A.11 EXTENSION ACTIVITY: You may want to have students develop their own crossword puzzle with some of the new vocabulary.

6A.12 ¿Cómo es la casa de tu compañero/a?

Paso 1: Responde a las siguientes preguntas sobre tu casa/apartamento. Luego, usando estas preguntas como modelo, entrevista a un compañero/a sobre su casa/apartamento. Puedes crear tus propias preguntas también.

1. ¿Cuántos dormitorios tiene tu casa/apartamento? ¿Cuántos baños?

2. ¿Tu casa/apartamento tiene comedor separado o es parte de la sala o la cocina?

3. ¿De qué color son las paredes de la sala? ¿y las de tu dormitorio? ¿y las de la cocina?

4. ¿Hay un microondas en la cocina? ¿un lavaplatos?

5. ¿Hay una lavadora y una secadora en tu casa/apartamento?

6. ¿Tu baño tiene una ducha separada o es parte de la bañera?

7. ¿Cuántos televisores hay en tu casa/apartamento? ¿Dónde está(n)?

8. ¿Cuántas ventanas hay en la sala? ¿y en tu dormitorio? ¿y en la cocina? ¿Son grandes o pequeñas?

Paso 2: ¿Qué puedes decir de los intereses de tu compañero/a según sus respuestas? Por ejemplo, si tiene muchos estantes con libros es probable que le guste leer. Escribe la información sobre tu compañero en tu **Retrato de la clase.**

Retrato de la clase: Mi compañero/a de clase ____ es muy organizado porque tiene muchos estantes para sus libros. También es ____ porque…

6A.12 SUGGESTION: Tell students that if either/both of them live in a dorm or fraternity/sorority house, to answer the questions with respect to their family home, or their dream home. After completion of task, ask students what they learned about their partner's home space and interests based on this task as a way to recycle vocabulary and as a way to share interesting information about students in class.

VÍVELO: LENGUA

Expressing adjectives as nouns with *lo*

When **lo** is followed by an adjective in Spanish, as in **lo mejor** *(the best thing)* it gives that adjective the quality of a noun.

Lo bueno de estudiar español es aprender acerca de otras culturas.

The good thing about studying Spanish is learning about other cultures.

Lo esencial en la vida es la salud.

The essential thing in life is health.

Be careful not confuse this use of **lo** with its use as a direct object pronoun.

6A.13 TEACHING TIP: Ask students *¿Qué cosas son las más esenciales para la casa?* When you process this activity with students, be prepared for a variety of responses from those who do not need anything to those who seem very materialistic. Ask students why they feel they must have or not have certain items, as in *¿Por qué quieres tener...? ¿Es necesario tener...? ¿Necesitas tener...?* etc.

6A.13 INSTRUCTOR'S RESOURCES: You will find a reproducible chart for use with Activity 6A.13 in your Instructor's Resources.

6A.14 PREPARATION: Choose a room in your own home to describe or make up a room. Provide additional vocabulary as needed. To review learner responses, prepare a completed plan on an overhead transparency or PowerPoint slide to show to the class, or draw the room on the board. To verify students' drawings, have them hold them up at the same time and scan the room to see how they look.

6A.13 Lo más esencial. De todos los muebles y electrodomésticos de tu casa/apartamento/dormitorio, ¿cuáles son los cinco más importantes para ti? Después de anotar tus respuestas, entrevista a cinco compañeros para averiguar *(to find out)* qué consideran lo más esencial. Pregunta, *¿Qué es lo esencial para ti?* Comenta tus resultados con la clase y anota las tendencias generales en tu **Retrato de la clase.**

Nombres	Cosa 1	Cosa 2	Cosa 3	Cosa 4	Cosa 5
Yo					

Retrato de la clase: Según mis compañeros de clase, las cosas más esenciales son ____, ____, ____ y ____. La mayoría de estas cosas son (aparatos electrónicos, muebles, ropa, libros, adornos, etcétera).

6A.14 La casa de tu profesor/a. Escucha a tu profesor/a describir una habitación de su casa. Luego, dibuja lo que escuches en una hoja de papel. Compara tus dibujos con los de un/a compañero/a. Tu profesor/a comprobará tus dibujos.

VÍVELO: LENGUA

Expressing what something is made of

To describe the material something is made of, Spanish uses *ser* **de** + the name of the material.

La encimera es de granito.	*The countertop is made of granite.*
Las alacenas son de madera.	*The cabinets are made of wood.*

Materiales

madera	*wood*
granito	*granite*
acero inoxidable	*stainless steel*
mármol	*marble*
ladrillo	*brick*
piedra	*stone*

6A.15 La habitación ideal. Trabajen en pareja o en grupos de tres, e imaginen que son diseñadores de interiores y arquitectos. Tienen que diseñar una habitación ideal. Escojan entre la sala, la cocina, el dormitorio o el baño, y diseñen la versión ideal de esa habitación. Piensen en los muebles, las instalaciones fijas y los electrodomésticos que puede tener y dónde van a estar. Piensen también en los materiales que van a usar. Comparen su diseño con el de otro grupo que haya escogido el mismo tipo de habitación. ¿En qué se parecen y en qué se diferencian? Muestren sus resultados a la clase.

6A.15 SUGGESTION: In order to ensure a balanced selection of rooms, you may prefer to assign rooms to specific groups, rather than letting each group choose for itself.

VÍVELO: CULTURA: Ask students to write down three of the most interesting/significant statements in *Vívelo: Cultura* and explore these with the class. Ask students if the amount of space in homes in big cities is comparable to the amount of space in homes in smaller cities and towns within their native countries. In Europe in particular, space just about anywhere is at a high premium.

VÍVELO: CULTURA

El espacio

En España y otros países europeos, el espacio es limitado y mucha gente tiende a vivir en apartamentos llamados **pisos.** Muy similares a los de la Ciudad de Nueva York, los pisos europeos no son tan espaciosos como las casas de las afueras *(suburbs)*; los cuartos son más pequeños y los muebles están diseñados para optimizar el espacio y el almacenamiento *(storage)*. Las ciudades europeas son muy antiguas y sus casas fueron construidas con ladrillos, piedras, mármol, granito y otros materiales igual de duraderos *(durable)*. Aunque el espacio sea limitado, la calidad de los materiales puede ser muy alta según los estándares del "Nuevo Mundo". La plomería *(plumbing)*, en cambio, varía de país a país porque tiene que ser reemplazada más frecuentemente que las paredes o los pisos. La madera es escasa y costosa. En Latinoamérica el cemento y la argamasa *(mortar)* son más comunes en la construcción. La madera es menos escasa que en Europa pero es usada más esporádicamente que en Estados Unidos y Canadá, en donde son comunes las casas con marcos *(frames)* y pisos de madera. Además, hay una gran variedad de casas de acuerdo al estatus socioeconómico de la familia. Las diferencias entre los ricos y los pobres es a menudo *(often)* muy extrema. Los más pobres viven en barrios de casas de cartón *(cardboard)* que aumentan con la migración de la gente hacia los centros urbanos.

6A.16 Entrevista. Entrevista a un/a estudiante extranjero/a de un país de habla hispana o a un/a estudiante que haya estudiado en el extranjero. Pídele que describa la casa en la que vivió *(he/she lived)*. Haz un plano o un dibujo de acuerdo a su descripción y tráelo a la clase. ¿Cómo contrastan estos dibujos con las actividades que has hecho hasta ahora, o con la lectura sobre los espacios más pequeños de las viviendas de América Latina y Europa?

6A.17 Promoción de departamentos. Lee la información sobre los departamentos del anuncio que aparece a continuación. Luego, responde a las siguientes preguntas con las palabras en español que aparecen en el anuncio. Comprueba tus respuestas con un/a compañero/a de clase.

1. Are the condominums for sale or for rent?

2. Are they furnished or unfurnished?

3. How many bedrooms are included?

4. Are there utilities included in the monthly rent? If so, which ones?

5. Is the cleaning service included in the monthly rent?

6. The ad is a promotion for a specified number of apartments within a specified amount of time. What are those?

LO MÁS EXCLUSIVO DE MÉXICO

60 departamentos en **renta**, amueblados.
1 y 2 recámaras desde $19,000 mensuales.

PROMOCIÓN VÁLIDA ÚNICAMENTE DURANTE FEBRERO
• Incluye mantenimiento • Internet inalámbrico • Circuito cerrado de TV • Concierge 24 horas
Visitas: 5560-1948 • 5560-1947

¡Atención!

Aspiradora	does not mean aspirator. It refers to a *vacuum cleaner*. The verb *to vacuum* in English is **pasar la aspiradora** in Spanish.
	Los González han comprado una nueva aspiradora.
	Yo paso la aspiradora una vez a la semana.
Cómoda	is not a commode in the sense of toilet. Used as a noun it refers to a *chest of drawers* or *bureau*. *Toilet* is **inodoro** or **excusado** in Spanish. As an adjective, **cómodo/a** means *comfortable*.
	En mi dormitorio, la cómoda está al lado de la cama.
	En mi baño, el inodoro está enfrente del lavabo.
Gabinete	is not cabinet or cupboard in the sense of kitchen storage. It refers to a *cabinet* in the sense of a group of government officials, as "the president's cabinet". *Kitchen cabinet* or *cupboard* in English is **alacena** and **armario** in Spanish. This is also the word for *pantry*.
	El gabinete del Presidente se reúne en la Casa Blanca.
	Guarda los platos en la alacena a la derecha del fregadero.
Planta	can mean *plant* in the sense of greenery or vegetation. However, it can also mean *story* or *floor* of a house or building. When you have a two story house **la planta baja** is the *ground floor* and **la planta alta** is the upper floor. A plant in the sense of a factory is **una fábrica** in Spanish.
	El cuarto de Ramón está en la planta alta de la residencia.
	Hay muchas fábricas en la frontera entre México y Estados Unidos.

TEACHING TIP: Point out to students that languages are constantly undergoing changes and some can be a result of languages coming into contact with each other. Some of the words in the *¡Atención!* section have begun to be commonly accepted in US Spanish with meanings other than their "standard" Spanish meanings. Surrounding these linguistic phenomena are debates as to whether or not something is correct. Lessons in sociolinguistics indicate that this is a natural development in language. For instance, while it might sound "wrong" to a purist that *gabinete* is used to refer to a cabinet instead of *alacena* or that *rentar* is used instead of *alquilar*, the likelihood of these words eventually becoming generally accepted is highly probable.

6A.18 Completa las oraciones. Completa las oraciones siguientes con una de las palabras que aparecen abajo. Usa cada palabra una sola vez. Comprueba tus respuestas con un/a compañero/a de clase.

alacena
fábrica
gabinete
inodoro
planta
plantas
aspiradora
cómoda

1. El presidente consulta con su ___gabinete___ cuando toma decisiones importantes.

2. La sala, el comedor y la cocina están en la ___planta___ baja.

3. Ellos tienen muchas ___plantas___ en el patio.

4. ¿Te gusta esta ___cómoda___ con cuatro cajones *(drawers)*?

5. Para limpiar la alfombra, es necesario tener una ___aspiradora___.

6. La ___fábrica___ de ropa tiene trescientos empleados.

7. Limpiar el ___inodoro___ es un trabajo que muchas personas no quieren hacer.

8. Hay una ___alacena___ pequeña de dos puertas arriba del refrigerador.

6A.18 ALTERNATIVE ACTIVITY: An alternative to Activity 6A.18 would be to write each word and each sentence on its own 3x5 index card and pass out one card per student. Ask students who have cards with incomplete sentences to find the person who has the word that best completes their sentence. Pairs may be challenged if someone else has a better match! Give a specific time limit to ensure they have only enough time to complete the task.

Estructuras clave 1 Combining direct and indirect object pronouns

Up to this point, you have been working with direct and indirect object pronouns individually. However, it is possible to combine both types of object pronouns in the same sentence. When the two pronouns appear in the same sentence, they always appear together and the indirect object pronoun always precedes the direct object pronoun. The rules regarding the placement of the pronouns relative to the verb are the same for two pronouns as for one pronoun. Both pronouns are placed before a single conjugated verb, but if the verb phrase consists of a conjugated verb and an infinitive, the pronouns can either precede the conjugated verb or be attached to the infinitive. In the latter case, a written accent is added above the last syllable of the infinitive in order to maintain the proper stress on the word.

—¿Cuándo te regala rosas tu novio?   —*When does your boyfriend give you roses?*
—Me las regala para mi cumpleaños.   —*He gives them to me for my birthday.*

—¿Cómo prefieres enviarme la foto?   —*How do you prefer to send me the picture?*
—Prefiero enviártela por correo electrónico.   —*I prefer to send it to you via e-mail.*

—¿Con qué frecuencia te mandan dinero tus padres?   —*How frequently do your parents send you money?*
—Me lo mandan cada dos semanas.   —*They send it to me every two weeks.*

Spanish does not allow two pronouns beginning with the letter **l** to appear next to each other. Consequently, the indirect object pronouns **le** and **les** will change to **se** when they precede the direct object pronouns **lo, la, los,** and **las.**

—¿Cuándo le tienen que entregar el informe a la jefa?   —*When do you all have to turn in the report to the boss?*
—**Se** lo tenemos que entregar el viernes.   —*We have to turn it in to her on Friday.*
(**se** replaces **le** referring to **a la jefa**)

—¿Dónde le compras zapatos a tu hijo?   —*Where do you buy shoes for your son?*
—**Se** los compro en Sears.   —*I buy them for him at Sears.*
(**se** replaces **le** referring to **a tu hijo**)

—¿Con qué frecuencia le prestas tu ropa a tu compañero de cuarto?   —*How often do you lend clothes to your roommate?*
—**Se** la presto de vez en cuando.   —*I lend it to him every once in a while.*
(**se** replaces **le** referring to **a tu compañero de cuarto**)

—Profesor, ¿cuándo va a traernos las composiciones?   —*When will you bring us the compositions?*
—Voy a traér**se**las mañana.   —*I will bring them to you tomorrow.*
(se replaces **les** referring to **a ustedes**)

Processing (decoding) questions that use direct and indirect object pronouns together

Comprehending Spanish questions and responses that include object pronouns can be problematic for native English speakers. In English, the typical word order is Subject+Verb+Object, but in Spanish the word order can also be Object+Verb+Subject or Subject+Object+Verb. This flexibility in word order can present challenges in decoding or correctly processing questions and statements that do not follow the English pattern of S+V+O.

Processing and decoding questions introduced by **¿Quién?** *(Who?)* or **¿A quién?** *(To whom?)* is particularly challenging because both refer to people, and we cannot always depend on word order to help us determine who is the subject of the sentence and who is the object. These types of questions require identifying the subject of the question sentence and then determining whether a direct object or indirect object noun or pronoun is necessary in the response. Once the question has been properly decoded, the answers can be fairly straightforward.

Study the following examples and see if you identify any patterns in these types of questions. Remember that the conjugation of the verb in any sentence must reflect the person and number of the subject. For this reason, we have highlighted both the subject and the verb in each sentence. Let's start with the background fact about which the question might be asked:

Jorge Ramos les explica la noticia a Tomás y David.

If we did not know that it was Jorge Ramos who explained the news to Tomás and David, we would have to ask **¿Quién?** as in the exchange below. We know that **les** is the indirect object pronoun that refers to **a Tomás y a David** and **la noticia** is the direct object noun of the sentence. The subject of the question sentence is then **quién** *(who)*.

–¿Quién les explica la noticia a Tomás y a David?	–*Who explains the news to Tomás and David?*

Remember, since Spanish word order can vary in ways that English word order does not, we can respond to this question in several ways.

–Se la explica Jorge Ramos. –Jorge Ramos se la explica. }	–*Jorge Ramos explains it to them.*

Notice that in the first sentence Jorge Ramos comes after the verb and in the second sentence it comes before the verb, yet both convey the same meaning.

Next let's look at a question that asks **¿A quién?** *(To whom?)*. Again, we'll start with the background information about which the question is asked.

Salma Hayek le manda los regalos a Penélope Cruz.

If we did not know to whom Salma Hayek sends the gifts, we would have to ask **¿A quién?** as in the exchange below. We know that **los regalos** is the direct object and that **le** is the indirect object pronoun referring to our unknown recipient.

–¿A quién le manda los regalos Salma Hayek?	–*To whom does Salma Hayek send the gifts?*
–Salma Hayek se los manda a Penélope Cruz. –Se los manda Salma Hayek a Penélope Cruz. –A Penélope Cruz se los manda Salma Hayek. }	–*Salma Hayek sends them to Penélope Cruz*

Again, we can answer the question in several ways in Spanish, but they all convey the same message in English. Notice that when answering the question, **los** replaces **los regalos.** Since both a direct object pronoun and an indirect object pronoun are used together, **se** replaces the **le** from the original question. In natural conversation, the subject is not necessary in the response since it has already been mentioned.

– Se los manda a Penélope Cruz.　　　　　　　–*She sends them to Penélope Cruz.*

To unravel the meaning of a question with **¿Quién?** or **¿A quién?**, and to comprehend the answer to these questions use the following clues to help process sentences correctly in Spanish:

1) The answer to **¿A quién?** will be either the direct or indirect object of the sentence and can be introduced with **a.**

2) Find the subject of the sentence by using the verb form as a clue and determining which noun it agrees with. In the example sentence above about Salma Hayek and Penélope Cruz, **manda** is the verb that signals that the subject has to be singular. Someone sent something. Who did the sending, Salma or Penélope? Because the preposition **a** *(to)* is before Penélope, she must be the receiver of something, so Salma is the subject.

3) Identify the object nouns as direct or indirect. A direct object answers the question *what?* and an indirect object answers the question *to/for whom?* Remember that **lo/la** and **los/las** refer to direct objects, while **le** or **les** signals the indirect object. **Me, te** and **nos** can refer to direct or indirect objects. Finally, remember that **se** replaces **le** or **les** when indirect object and direct object pronouns are used together.

6A.19 RECYCLING: Activity 6A.19 recycles family and clothing vocabulary from previous chapters.

6A.19 ANSWERS:
Answers may vary, but these are the most likely responses. Se lo recomiendo: 1, 3, 5, 8; No se lo recomiendo: 2, 4, 6, 7. Ask students to give their alternative suggestions to the class and also to indicate why particular gifts are or are not appropriate.

6A.19　Un regalo apropiado.　　Imagina que trabajas en una tienda de ropa y Miguel, un joven universitario, va a buscar regalos para varios familiares y amigos. Lee las oraciones a continuación e indica si le recomiendas o no a Miguel el regalo que ha escogido. Cuando no estés de acuerdo con Miguel, piensa en un regalo más apropiado. Compara tus respuestas con las de un/a compañero/a, y describe las semejanzas o diferencias a la clase.

	Se lo recomiendo.	No se lo recomiendo.
1. La gorra **se la** doy a mi hermano menor.	☐	☐
2. La corbata **se la** regalo a mi mejor amiga.	☐	☐
3. Las bufandas **se las** quiero regalar a mis tías.	☐	☐
4. Los pantalones cortos **se los** quiero comprar a mi abuela.	☐	☐
5. El reloj **se lo** compro a mi novia.	☐	☐
6. Las blusas puedo **dárselas** a mis padres.	☐	☐
7. Los pijamas **se los** compro a mis compañeros de cuarto.	☐	☐
8. El suéter prefiero **regalárselo** a mi primo.	☐	☐

6A.20 Me, te, se, nos. Con un/a compañero/a seleccionen la oración que corresponde a la imagen. Comprueben sus respuestas con la clase.

1. **a.** "¿Me las regalas?"
   b. "¿Me las regalan?"

2. **a.** "¿Se la pongo?"
   b. "¿Se los pongo?"

3. **a.** "¿Se los doy?"
   b. "¿Se lo doy?"

el hueso *(bone)*

4. **a.** "¿Te lo van a quitar?"
   b. "¿Te lo va a quitar?"

5. **a.** "¿Nos la compran?"
   b. "¿Nos las compran?"

las blusas

6A.21 TEACHING TIP:
Draw students' attention to the pronouns focusing on gender and number.

6A.21 ¿Cómo se interpreta? En parejas, lean las oraciones cortas que aparecen a continuación e indiquen si la Traducción A o la Traducción B es la interpretación correcta. Luego, comprueben sus respuestas con un/a compañero/a o con toda la clase. **Pista** *(hint)*: Miren el verbo para determinar el sujeto de la oración.

	Traducción A	**Traducción B**
1. Se lo doy.	☑ I give it to him.	☐ He gives it to me.
2. Me las trae.	☐ He brings it to me.	☑ He brings them to me.
3. Nos la regalan.	☑ They give it to us.	☐ We give it to them.
4. Se las ha vendido.	☐ He has sold it to them.	☑ He has sold them to him.
5. Se las ha explicado.	☐ She has explained it to them.	☑ She has explained them to her.
6. Nos los has mandado.	☑ You have sent them to us.	☐ We have sent them to you.
7. Se la compramos.	☑ We buy it for her.	☐ She buys it for us.
8. Te los voy a preparar.	☐ You will prepare them for me.	☑ I will prepare them for you.

6A.22 TEACHING TIP:
Tally student responses so that some general conclusions can be made, such as *La mayoría de la clase pone los zapatos debajo de la cama*. Then, review some generalizations for students' *Retrato de la clase* entries.

6A.22 Más breves.

Paso 1: Trabajando con un/a compañero/a, túrnense para hacerse y contestar las siguientes preguntas. Cuando respondan a una pregunta, usen al menos un pronombre de objeto directo o indirecto. Luego, compartan las respuestas de su compañero/a con la clase.

Modelo: E1: *¿Dónde escuchas música con más frecuencia: en casa, en el carro o en todas partes con tu iPod?*
E2: *La escucho en todas partes con mi iPod.*

1. ¿Dónde compran los muebles de la casa tus padres?

2. ¿Qué les puedes comprar a tus padres para la casa?

3. ¿Cuándo usas el horno?

4. ¿En qué cuarto miras la televisión en tu casa?

5. ¿Dónde pones los zapatos cuando llegas a tu casa?

6. ¿En qué cuarto de tu casa lavas la ropa?

7. ¿Cuántas veces preparas la comida en casa? ¿A quién se la preparas?

8. ¿A quién le prestas tus electrodomésticos?

Paso 2: Después de compartir las respuestas de su compañero/a con la clase, escriban conclusiones generales sobre las tendencias de la clase en su **Retrato de la clase.**

Retrato de la clase: La mayoría de la clase mira la tele en su cuarto, pone los zapatos en…

VÍVELO: CULTURA: This is an opportune moment to highlight the importance of being cultural investigators. This requires students to be perceptive and observant in their surroundings. One of the best ways to know what is appropriate behavior is to interview or observe members of the target culture. They may find that not all "Hispanics" treat visits the way the text indicates. In fact, behaviors and practices vary within countries depending on multiple factors. Additionally, as Hispanics comprise a significant portion of the US, there is obvious overlap between Hispanic and traditional US cultures. It is important that we help our students become cultural investigators.

VÍVELO: CULTURA

Las visitas

Visitar a los amigos o la familia, ya sea en su casa o en la tuya *(yours)*, ha sido un pasatiempo común en la cultura hispana. A diferencia de la tradición cultural en Estados Unidos, las visitas entre hispanos suelen ser *(are usually)* mucho más informales y espontáneas, aunque esto está empezando a cambiar. Especialmente en las ciudades pequeñas, no es necesario llamar con anticipación, como se hace típicamente en Estados Unidos. Frecuentemente estas visitas se llevan a cabo *(will take place)* en la cocina, o en la mesa del comedor, en lugar de *(rather than)* la sala. ¿Cómo son las visitas en tu cultura? ¿Qué es lo culturalmente apropiado?

6A.23 ¿Cuál es la respuesta correcta? Escoge la respuesta correcta para cada pregunta. Comprueba tus respuestas con un/a compañero/a de clase. Prepárate para explicar tus respuestas.

1. ¿A quién le traes una cerveza?

   a. Se la traigo a mi hermano.

   b. Te las traigo a mi hermano.

2. ¿Quién te ha regalado ese libro?

   a. Me lo ha regalado mi abuela.

   b. Me las ha regalado mi abuela.

3. ¿Quién te ha contado ese cuento?

   a. Te lo ha contado mi padre.

   b. Me lo ha contado mi padre.

4. ¿A quién le debemos entregar el informe?

   a. Deben entregárselas al señor Villa.

   b. Deben entregárselo al señor Villa.

5. ¿Quiénes les han recomendado esos restaurantes?

   a. Nosotros se los hemos recomendado.

   b. A nosotros nos los han recomendado.

6A.23 ORIENTATION: In each case, both answer options are grammatically sound statements, but only one of them answers the particular question asked. These questions offer students more opportunities to be exposed to comprehensible input.

6A.24 Una historia familiar. Lee la siguiente conversación entre Thalía y su hija Sabrina. Luego, con un/a compañero/a de clase responde a las preguntas a continuación. Presta atención al uso de los pronombres en negrita. El primero está hecho como modelo. Comprueba tus respuestas con la clase.

THALÍA: Mira, Sabrina. He encontrado muchas fotos viejas. ¿Quieres que **te las** muestre *(show)*?

SABRINA: Sí, mamá. Por favor, muéstra**melas.**

THALÍA: Bueno, hija, aquí están.

SABRINA: Ay, mamá, en esta foto estás muy bonita. ¿Quién **te la** ha sacado?

THALÍA: Pues, **me la** ha sacado tu papá en nuestra luna de miel *(honeymoon)*.

SABRINA: ¿De veras? Y esta foto de mi papá, ¿**se la** has sacado tú?

THALÍA: Sí, pero las fotos de tu papá y yo **nos las** ha sacado un señor que estaba allí.

SABRINA: ¿Y los aretes que llevas en la foto?

THALÍA: **Me los** ha regalado tu abuela. Algún día **te los** voy a regalar a ti para tu boda.

SABRINA: ¡Guau! ¿**Me los** vas a regalar el día de mi boda? Gracias. Y mi papá se ve muy guapo con este sombrero.

THALÍA: Pues, claro. Por eso **se lo** he comprado para su cumpleaños.

SABRINA: ¡Qué gracioso! ¡Cuánto me gusta escuchar historias de la familia! ¿Vas a **contarnos** más historias a mí y a mis hermanos?

THALÍA: Sí, hija. A ustedes **se las** cuento cuando quieran.

1. ¿Qué le quiere enseñar Thalía a Sabrina?

2. ¿Quién le ha sacado una foto a Thalía?

3. ¿Cuándo se la ha sacado?

4. ¿Quién le ha sacado una foto al padre de Sabrina?

5. ¿Quién les ha sacado unas fotos a los padres de Sabrina?

6. ¿Qué le ha regalado la abuela de Sabrina a Thalía?

7. ¿A quién se los va a regalar Thalía algún día?

8. ¿Quién le ha comprado un sombrero al padre de Sabrina?

9. ¿Para que ocasión se lo ha comprado?

10. ¿A quiénes les va a contar Thalía más historias de la familia?

6A.24 ANSWERS: 1. fotos, 2. su esposo, 3. en la luna de miel, 4. Thalía, 5. un señor, 6. unos aretes, 7. a su hija, 8. Thalía, 9. para su cumpleaños, 10. a sus hijos.

6A.24 TEACHING TIP: Have students go over their answers with a classmate. If they have different answers, they should explain to one another how they arrived at their respective choices. Often, when students have to explain their work to a partner, they gain a deeper understanding of it.

Estructuras clave 2   The prepositions *por* and *para*

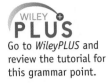

WILEY PLUS
Go to *WileyPLUS* and review the tutorial for this grammar point.

WILEY PLUS

You will find PowerPoint presentations for use with *Estructuras clave* in *WileyPLUS*.

Up to now, you have been introduced formally to a few uses of **por** and **para** and have seen them used throughout this book. The prepositions **por** and **para** often cause difficulties for English speakers learning Spanish because they both can be translated as *for* or *by* in many cases. However, these two prepositions are not interchangeable and they are used with specific meanings in particular contexts. As you examine the examples in the chart below, you will begin to get a feel for the uses of **por** and **para** and you will see that context determines which of the two is appropriate in a given situation.

Use *por*	Use *para*
a. To indicate movement through, along, around, by: Voy a viajar **por** Centroamérica este verano. Caminar **por** la playa es muy romántico. ¿A qué hora pasamos **por** ti? Es necesario entrar **por** la puerta principal.	**a.** To indicate a recipient, as in a gift for someone: Este regalo es **para** mi mamá. Hay una carta **para** ti.
b. To indicate means by which an action is done, such as by means of communication or transportation: ¿Puede usted mandarme los documentos **por** correo electrónico? Ellos prefieren viajar **por** tren.	**b.** To indicate a destination in the sense of "for" or "toward": El tren **para** Barcelona sale a las 8:00 p.m. ¿Qué día salen ustedes **para** Paraguay? Ella camina rápido **para** su casa.
c. To indicate a duration of time, such as for, in, during a specific period of time: Vamos a Puerto Rico **por** dos semanas. Me gusta estudiar **por** la mañana.	**c.** To indicate a deadline or a specific point in time: La composición es **para** el viernes. Es importante terminar el proyecto **para** el 15 de marzo.
d. To indicate cost as in to pay X dollars for something: Venden el coche **por** $1,500. Pagamos $4.00 **por** un café.	**d.** With **trabajar** to express employment: Ellos trabajan **para** su padre. ¿Te gustaría trabajar **para** una compañía multinacional?
e. To indicate exchange, such as in exchange for: Te cambio la manzana **por** la naranja. El regalo es **por** tu ayuda.	**e.** To specify a function or use: Estas copas son **para** vino. La tiza sirve **para** escribir en la pizarra.
f. To indicate a substitution, such as in place of Anita está enferma; así que usted hoy tiene que trabajar **por** ella. Cuando el actor principal tiene laringitis, el suplente (*understudy*) actúa **por** él.	**f.** To indicate a comparison that distinguishes individuals from a group **Para** ser un niño de 10 años, eres muy alto. **Para** ser médico, Jorge no sabe mucho de la anatomía.
g. To indicate an action done on behalf of: Los Gómez han sacrificado mucho **por** sus hijos. Votamos **por** los candidatos de nuestro partido.	**g.** To indicate "in order to" when followed by an infinitive: Ustedes me escuchan con cuidado **para** aprender la pronunciación correcta. **Para** bailar la bamba se necesita una poca de gracia.

h. To indicate the objective of an errand:	h. To indicate a purpose or goal:
Vamos al supermercado **por** leche y pan. Necesito volver a mi cuarto **por** mi libro de español.	El dinero es **para** la comida, no la bebida. Los muebles son **para** usar, no **para** mirar.
i. To indicate a motive for an action, as in because of: El Sr. Suárez ha llegado tarde **por** el tráfico. No pueden jugar afuera **por** la lluvia.	
j. To signal a unit of measure, as in per hour or by the dozen: El límite de velocidad es 88 kilómetros **por** hora. Se venden huevos **por** docena.	

6A.25 ¿Por?   Con un/a compañero/a de clase, lean los enunciados siguientes y escriban la letra que indica el significado o la función de **por** que se indica en la tabla de *Estructuras clave* que aparece arriba. Luego, comprueben sus respuestas con las de otros compañeros de clase. El primero está hecho como modelo.

_h_ **1.** La bebé tiene hambre. Voy al refrigerador por leche.

_b_ **2.** Prefiero viajar a Chile por avión que por autobús.

_a_ **3.** Tengo que caminar por la cocina si quiero ir al jardín.

_e_ **4.** Te cambio esta foto de Penélope Cruz por la de Salma Hayek.

_i_ **5.** Por ser demasiado *(too)* generosa ya no tiene dinero.

_c_ **6.** Voy a Chile por dos semanas.

_j_ **7.** Por cada galón de gasolina, mi carro anda 30 millas.

_d_ **8.** Pagué $800 euros por la secadora.

6A.26 Para.   Con un/a compañero/a de clase, lean los enunciados siguientes y escriban la letra que indica el significado o la función de **para** que se indica en la tabla de *Estructuras clave*. Luego, comprueben sus respuestas con las de otros compañeros de clase.

_c_ **1.** El fregadero es para lavar los platos.

_f_ **2.** Para ser profesor, no tiene muchos libros en su oficina.

_d_ **3.** No queremos trabajar jamás para nuestros padres.

_e_ **4.** El marco *(frame)* es para la foto.

_e_ **5.** La aspiradora es para la alfombra y la escoba es para los pisos de madera.

_c_ **6.** Me van a instalar las alacenas nuevas para el viernes.

_g_ **7.** Para llegar a tu asiento, sigue al hombre de uniforme.

_b_ **8.** El avión para Nueva York sale en dos horas.

6A.27 ¿Por o para? Lee el correo electrónico que Lucero le ha enviado a su primo. Escribe **por** o **para** en los espacios en blanco, según el contexto. Luego, determina si Lucero tiene o no una familia que la apoya. Comprueba tus respuestas con la clase.

| ⇶ Enviar ahora | ✉ Enviar más tarde | ✉ Mensaje nuevo | ⬑ Guardar como borrador | ▯ Suprimir | 📎 Adjuntar documento |

Para/A: [   ]
Cc: [   ]
▶ No hay documento adjunto

Querido primo,

Hemos llegado a Austin y nos hemos instalado en un apartamento de dos dormitorios. ___Para___[1] ser estudiantes la renta mensual es razonable. Salimos de Knoxville ___por___[2] avión a Houston y luego ___para___[3] llegar a Austin rentamos un carro ___por___[4] una semana. Llegamos a Austin muy tarde ___por___[5] el límite de velocidad (55) y ___por___[6] la congestión en San Antonio. Lo bueno es que ___por___[7] cinco horas Guillermo y yo hablamos de nuestra relación, nuestros planes y nuestro futuro. ___Por___[8] cuatro años vamos a vivir en la pobreza pero sabemos que ___para___[9] tener éxito en la universidad tenemos que estudiar muchas horas. ___Por___[10] el amor, somos capaces de todo.

Esta tarde vamos ___por___[11] unos muebles que nos regala la tía Benavides. Más tarde pasamos ___por___[12] el tío ___para___[13] salir a comer. Te escribo mañana si hay novedades (*news*). Hasta entonces.

Tu prima, Lucero

6A.28 Entrevista. Hazle preguntas a un/a compañero/a de clase según las instrucciones a continuación. Luego comparen sus respuestas con las de la otra pareja.

1. Pregúntale por cuánto tiempo va a estar en la universidad hoy.
2. Pregúntale a qué hora sale para la casa.
3. Pregúntale si normalmente entra a su casa por la puerta principal o por otra puerta.
4. Pregúntale para qué ha salido recientemente a la tiendita (convenience store).
5. Pregúntale para qué clases tiene mucha tarea.
6. Pregúntale qué tarea tiene para la próxima clase de español.
7. Pregúntale si mantiene el contacto con sus amigos principalmente por teléfono o por correo electrónico.
8. Pregúntale por dónde camina cuando quiere pasear tranquilamente.
9. Pregúntale cuánto paga normalmente por un galón de gasolina.
10. Pregúntale para quién ha comprado un regalo últimamente y por qué motivo.

DICHOS

Mi casa es tu/su casa.	*Make yourself at home.*
Más cuidado que el jardín de jubilado.	Literally: *Better taken care of than a retired person's garden.*
El casado, casa quiere.	Loosely: *Married people want a home of their own.*

6A.29 Para ti la verdad es... Usando **por** y **para,** escribe tres enunciados sobre ti mismo/a que sean ciertos y dos que sean falsos. Luego, en grupos de tres, léanse unos a otros los enunciados para ver si pueden adivinar cuáles son ciertos y cuáles falsos. Escribe cualquier información importante sobre tus compañeros en tu **Retrato de la clase.**

Enlaces

6A.30 Repaso y más. Determina el equivalente en español de cada una de las palabras o frases en inglés, según el contexto de las oraciones. Luego, comprueba tus respuestas con la clase.

a. according to

b. also

c. from… to

d. both

e. through

<u>a</u> **1. Según** los historiadores, el patio es un concepto muy antiguo.

<u>b</u> **2.** En el patio hay muchas flores y **también** una fuente.

<u>c</u> **3.** Todos los miembros de la familia viven en la misma casa, **desde** los abuelos **hasta** los nietos.

<u>e</u> **4.** Para entrar en sus habitaciones, la familia tiene que pasar **a través** del patio.

<u>d</u> **5. Tanto** los chinos **como** los griegos, los romanos y los árabes construían un patio en sus casas.

6A.31 ¿Puedes conectar las ideas? Conecta las ideas en las oraciones y párrafos que aparecen abajo usando la expresión apropiada. Luego, comprueba tus respuestas con un/a compañero/a de clase.

a. desde… hasta

b. también

c. a través de(l)

d. tanto… como

e. según

<u>c</u> **1.** No se entra a la sala por la puerta principal, sino *(rather)* _____ patio.

<u>a, d</u> **2.** Se emplean varias cosas para adornar el patio, _____ flores _____ una fuente.

<u>b</u> **3.** El patio siempre tiene un piso de baldosa *(tile)* y _____ hay un caño *(pipe)* para evacuar el agua de lluvia.

<u>a, d</u> **4.** _____ los abuelos _____ los padres y los nietos tienen su propia habitación.

<u>e</u> **5.** Las características del patio han cambiado _____ la ecología, la geografía y la cultura de la región.

6A.30 TEACHING TIP: As you read through these statements with students, make sure that they pay attention to the cultural information regarding the *patio.*

6A.31 SUGGESTION: Have students share their answers with a partner before going over the answers as a class. Note that some recycling of previous *enlace* words is included.

FUNCTIONAL OUTCOMES:
The central question that frames this Investigación is *"¿Cómo puedes hablar del hogar, los vecinos o la comunidad?"* Explore whether students can now address this question and how they would go about it. Have them review the chart on the first page of this *Investigación*.

6A.32 **El patio.** ¿Qué imágenes te vienen a la mente cuando escuchas la palabra **patio**? Como clase, piensen en algunas características de los patios. Luego, en parejas lean el siguiente texto sobre lo que es el patio en el mundo hispano.

6A.32 SUGGESTION:
Have students conduct a google image search of "patio" before the next class. Did what they find fall in line with this description of the patio?

El significado del patio

El patio, asociado tradicionalmente con la arquitectura española, no tiene su origen en la Península Ibérica. Tanto los chinos como los incas, los griegos, los árabes y los romanos emplearon el concepto del patio residencial mucho antes de la época moderna. Las características del patio han cambiado según el clima, la geografía y la cultura de la región. Tanto hoy como en el pasado, algunas casas tradicionales tienen un patio, es decir, una zona en el centro de la casa rodeada *(surrounded)* por una serie de puertas que abren a las habitaciones de los residentes. En algunas casas, hay dos plantas *(stories)* que rodean el patio. El patio no tiene techo y el piso con frecuencia es de baldosa *(tile)*, nunca de tierra *(earth/dirt)*, y siempre con desagüe *(drain)* para drenar el agua de lluvia. En las casas más elegantes también hay una fuente *(fountain)* de agua y muchas plantas con flores de colores brillantes que adornan el patio. La fachada *(façade)* de la casa suele ser sencilla *(simple)* y da directamente a *(opens/looks on to)* la calle. A menudo, los residentes sólo pueden entrar a sus habitaciones o a los otros salones de la casa a través del patio.

6A.33 **El papel del patio.** ¿Qué sugiere el papel del patio sobre la cultura hispana? Selecciona los enunciados que pueden ser ciertos sobre la cultura hispana, teniendo en cuenta lo que has aprendido sobre el patio. Luego, comenta tus respuestas con la clase.

☐ El hecho de que las casas tienen un lugar central para reunirse (el patio), confirma que tradicionalmente los hispanos valoran compartir en familia.

☐ Por tener muchas habitaciones que rodean el patio, confirmamos que los miembros de la familia viven en la casa juntos por mucho tiempo.

☐ En el patio los niños tienen un lugar seguro para jugar, confirmando la importancia de los niños y la familia hispana.

☐ Por estar rodeado de habitaciones separadas, el patio enfatiza la importancia del individuo más que de la familia.

☐ El patio ofrece privacidad, lo cual confirma la importancia de obedecer las normas sociales y así mantener la reputación de la familia.

☐ El espacio y ambiente relajante y tranquilo del patio confirma la necesidad de mantener un equilibrio entre el trabajo y la familia.

☐ La importancia de la fachada de las casas hispanas confirma el espíritu competitivo característico de la cultura hispana.

☐ La seguridad que ofrece el patio muestra *(shows)* que la protección de la familia es una preocupación fundamental en la cultura hispana.

6A.33 NOTE: The statements in Activity 6A.33 get at the perspectives associated with the *patio*. Remind students to always dig deeper and try to get to the perspectives associated with different products and practices.

Perspectivas

6A.34 **¿Cómo refleja tu casa tu cultura?** ¿Qué aspectos de **tu** casa reflejan los valores y costumbres asociados con tu cultura? Escribe las respuestas más frecuentes de tus compañeros en tu **Retrato de la clase.**

Retrato de la clase: Tenemos una cocina grande porque mi familia pasa mucho tiempo en la cocina…

¿Cómo son estas casas? ¿Dónde pueden estar? ¿Hay casas con esta arquitectura donde tú vives?

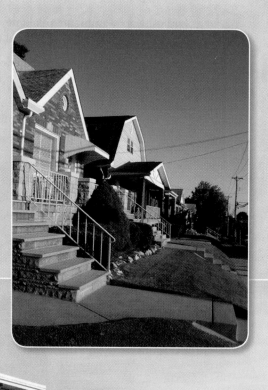

Vocabulario: Investigación A

Vocabulario esencial

Sustantivos

la alfombra	*carpet*
el armario	*closet*
la bañera	*bathtub*
el baño	*bathroom*
la cama	*bed*
la casa	*house*
la cocina	*kitchen*
el comedor	*dining room*
la cortina	*curtain*
el clóset	*closet*
el corredor	*hallway*
el cuadro	*painting*
el cuarto	*room*
el despacho	*office, study*
el despertador	*alarm clock*
el dormitorio	*bedroom*
la ducha	*shower*
los electrodomésticos	*appliances*
el escritorio	*desk*
la escalera	*stairwell*
la escoba	*broom*
el espejo	*mirror*
el estante	*shelf*
el fregadero	*sink*
el hogar	*home*
el horno	*oven*
el inodoro	*toilet*
el jardín	*garden*
el lavabo	*bathroom sink*
la lavadora	*washing machine*
el lavaplatos	*washer*
el mueble	*furniture*
la pared	*wall*
el piso	*floor; apartment*
los quehaceres	*chores*
el reproductor	*player (CD, DVD, etc.)*
la sala/el salón	*living room*
la secadora	*dryer*
la silla	*chair*
el sillón	*armchair*
el techo	*ceiling, roof*

el tocador	*dressing table, dresser*
el/la vecino/a	*neighbor*
la ventana	*window*

Verbos

barrer	*to sweep*
descansar	*to rest*
despertar	*to wake up*
guardar	*to put away*
lavar	*to wash*
limpiar	*to clean*

Otras palabras y expresiones

la alacena	*cupboard*
el acero inoxidable	*stainless steel*
adornar	*to decorate*
alcanzar	*to reach*
la argamasa	*mortar*
la baldosa	*tile*
la cafetera	*coffee maker*
capaz	*capable*
colgar	*to hang*
conocido/a	*well-known*
cuidadosamente	*carefully*
cumplir	*to turn (age)*
demasiado	*too much*
el desagüe	*drain*
drenar	*to drain*
la encimera	*counter top*
la fuente	*fountain*
la instalación fija	*fixture*
instalarse	*to settle in*
ladrillo	*brick*
loco/a	*crazy*
la madera	*wood*
mandar	*to send*
manejar	*to drive (a vehicle)*
el marco	*frame*
el mármol	*marble*
sencillo/a	*simple*
el tamaño	*size*
al azar	*in random order*
a menudo	*often*
de acuerdo a	*according to*

Cognados

Review the cognates in *Adelante* and the false cognates in *¡Atención!*. For a complete list of cognates, see Appendix 4 on page 605.

¿Se trabaja para vivir o se vive para trabajar?

In this Investigación you will learn:

▶ How to talk about lifestyles

▶ How to express commands to family and friends, and in formal situations

▶ How to express a series of actions based on a chronological order

▶ How views on time, work, family and leisure impact a culture's daily routine, behavior and philosophy of life

¿Cómo puedes hablar de una vida sana?

Puedes preguntar sobre diferentes aspectos de la vida, como el trabajo y los pasatiempos.	¿Cómo es tu trabajo? ¿Es tu trabajo físico o trabajas con tu mente? ¿Disfrutas de tu tiempo libre?
Puedes describir las obligaciones que tienes además de estudiar.	Tengo otras obligaciones además de estudiar. Tengo poco/mucho tiempo libre. En mi tiempo libre, me gusta jugar videojuegos y enviar mensajes de texto a mis amigos.
Puedes decirle a alguien lo que debe o no debe hacer para tener un equilibrio entre el trabajo y los otros aspectos de la vida.	Para tener una vida sana: Duerma 7-8 horas cada noche. Coma comida saludable. Haga ejercicio. Pase tiempo con su familia y sus amigos. No trabaje demasiado. Busque un pasatiempo favorito. No fume. No beba demasiado.

Adelante

¡Ya lo sabes! El trabajo y la calidad de vida

la ambición	ameno/a	celebrar
la calidad	cordial	contratar
la competencia	carismático/a	dedicarse a
la compañía	diplomático/a	forzar
el empleado	dócil	obligar
el pasatiempo	tenso/a	sacrificar
el salario		
tiempo completo/parcial		

6B.1 AUDIO SCRIPT: 1. la competencia, 2. ameno, 3. cordial, 4. diplomático, 5. el pasatiempo, 6. forzar, 7. tenso, 8. dócil. Answers may vary. Have students defend their answers.

6B.1 **¿Positivo o negativo?** Vas a escuchar una serie de palabras. Mientras escuchas las palabras, indica si tienen asociaciones positivas o negativas. Luego, verifica tus respuestas con la clase.

	Positivo	Negativo
1.	☐	☑
2.	☑	☐
3.	☑	☐
4.	☑	☐
5.	☑	☐
6.	☐	☑
7.	☐	☑
8.	☐	☑

6B.2 **Busca la palabra correcta.** Túrnate con un/a compañero/a para leer cada definición y para encontrar, en la lista a continuación, la palabra o expresión a la cual corresponde. Luego, comprueba tu trabajo con la clase.

a. tiempo completo   **e.** el empleado

b. ameno   **f.** obligar

c. celebrar   **g.** la ambición

d. contratar   **h.** la calidad

_c_   **1.** Este verbo se refiere a una acción que asociamos con las fiestas, el cumpleaños y los días feriados como la Navidad y el Día de Acción de Gracias.

_e_   **2.** Esta palabra se refiere a una persona que trabaja para una compañía.

_h_   **3.** Esta palabra se refiere al valor o finura *(refinement)* de un producto o un material.

_f_   **4.** Este verbo es un sinónimo del verbo *forzar*.

_d_   **5.** Este verbo se refiere a la acción de darle un trabajo a una persona.

_b_   **6.** Este adjetivo es lo contrario de *antipático*.

_a_   **7.** Esta expresión significa trabajar 40 horas o más a la semana.

_g_   **8.** Esta palabra se refiere al sentimiento de desear un trabajo más prestigioso con más responsabilidades y por más dinero.

6B.3 **¿Qué palabra es?** Con un/a compañero/a, escojan cuatro de las siguientes palabras, y escriban un enunciado verdadero y uno falso sobre cada uno de ustedes. Intercambien sus enunciados con los de otro grupo para adivinar *(guess)* cuáles de las cuatro oraciones sobre sus compañeros son falsas y cuáles son ciertas. Luego, reúnanse para comprobar sus respuestas.

la ambición	dócil	el salario
la calidad	carismático	tiempo parcial
la competencia	la compañía	contratar
dedicarse a	forzar	ameno

6B.3 TEACHING TIP: Ask students if they learned something new about their classmates based on their true and false statements. Poll the class to see what those things were.

6B.4 **Adivina la palabra.** Con un/a compañero/a túrnense para describir en español, o indicar con gestos o actuando, el significado de tantas *(as many)* palabras de *Adelante* como sea posible. Luego, digan el número de palabras que han adivinado.

6B.4 FOLLOW-UP: As a follow-up to this activity, ask students for the number of words they were able to guess so that you identify the pair or pairs of students with the highest number of guessed words. Keep these students in mind to provide reviews (in Spanish and/or through facial expressions, gestures, or acting) of previous vocabulary as a warm-up in future classes.

www **¡Conéctate!**

How dedicated and ambitious are you about learning Spanish? Are you interested in finding opportunities to practice your Spanish outside of class? Check out http://www.italki.com to network with people from around the world to find someone with whom you can practice. The objective is for give-and-take relationships to be developed. For instance, you would match up with a Spanish speaker that is learning English so that you could both help one another. See if you can find someone with similar interests and start practicing your Spanish.

¿Trabajar para vivir o vivir para trabajar?

Ma. Renée Cortés B.

Con los nuevos cambios dictados por la llegada de la modernidad, la calidad de vida del ser humano ha experimentado cambios inadvertidos (*unnoticed*). ¿Cuáles son los elementos necesarios para la buena calidad de vida? Lo que antes eran los elementos básicos, hoy parecen ser insuficientes. Las necesidades actuales (*current*) ya no son las mismas que antes; cada vez son más y la competencia es mayor. ¿Qué hacemos para seguir este ritmo? ¿A costa de qué? Parece paradójico que estemos buscando la "calidad de vida", sacrificando la vida que ya tenemos. ¿A qué llegamos? A un nuevo contexto global y a una nueva situación laboral que trae consecuencias físicas y psicológicas para el ser humano. Como explica el doctor Franz Siles, médico psiquiatra y psicoanalista, "gran parte de las enfermedades hoy tienen implicaciones psicológicas".

6B.5 Comprensión. Lee cada enunciado y determina si es cierto o falso según la lectura. Luego, compara tus respuestas con las de algunos de tus compañeros.

Cierto	Falso	
☑	☐	**1.** La modernidad ha cambiado la calidad de vida del ser humano.
☑	☐	**2.** Hoy en día tenemos que hacer más para tener los elementos básicos de la vida.
☐	☑	**3.** Los elementos básicos de la vida de antes son iguales a los de ahora.
☑	☐	**4.** Tenemos que saber hacer más en nuestro trabajo hoy en día que en el pasado.
☑	☐	**5.** Sacrificamos nuestra salud para tener la "calidad de vida" que queremos.

EXPRESIONES ÚTILES

ganarse la vida   *to earn a living*
Mucha gente **se gana la vida** trabajando de 8:00 a 5:00 de lunes a viernes.

realizar un sueño   *to fulfill a dream*
Muchos actores **realizan sus sueños** en la Ciudad de Nueva York y Los Ángeles.

echarse una siesta   *to take a nap*
Por la tarde es natural tener sueño y por eso **nos echamos una siesta.**

soñar despierto   *to day dream*
Cuando estamos en un lugar aburrido, **soñamos despiertos.**

estar de buen/mal humor   *to be in a good/bad mood*
Cuando nos gusta nuestro trabajo, parece que siempre **estamos de buen humor.**

TEACHING TIP: Have students scan the article briefly for an idea of what it is about. You may also direct them to the true/false questions after the reading to help them focus on main ideas. Then, give them 5 minutes to read it.

READING STRATEGY: In a previous chapter, the strategy of looking at titles and subtitles was shared. Based on the title, have students make predictions about what they are going to read.

6B.5 TEACHING TIP: As you go over the answers, probe further by asking their opinions about those statements. For instance: *¿Están de acuerdo? ¿Tenemos que saber hacer más en nuestro trabajo hoy en día que en el pasado?*

EXPRESIONES ÚTILES: As a follow-up to these expressions, ask students questions such as, *¿Cuándo no estás de buen humor? ¿Has realizado tus sueños ya? ¿Cómo te ganas la vida?* etc.

VÍVELO: CULTURA

La siesta

El término *siesta* viene del término latino "sexta hora", o mediodía, que se refiere a un período de descanso autorizado para los monjes medievales. Con el tiempo el término fue asociado con el descanso después de una comida a la mitad de la tarde en el que la gente en climas cálidos *(warm)* duerme durante el momento más caliente del día. También era una forma de dividir el día de trabajo para descansar y refrescarse antes de regresar a trabajar durante la tarde cuando la temperatura está más fresca. La siesta determinaba muchos aspectos de la vida diaria, especialmente las horas para los negocios: las oficinas y tiendas cerraban por dos o tres horas a mitad de la tarde y abrían otra vez más tarde. Comúnmente asociada con la cultura hispana y generalmente estereotipada, la siesta está desapareciendo *(disappearing)* en muchos países hispanos y particularmente en las grandes ciudades. Tres de los factores que contribuyen a la desaparición de la siesta son: 1) las largas distancias que los trabajadores tienen que cubrir para volver a la casa a comer y después regresar al trabajo; 2) la globalización y el enfoque multinacional de muchas empresas están forzando a las oficinas gubernamentales y a los negocios de diferentes países a sincronizar sus horas de trabajo; y 3) los padres están cada vez menos dispuestos *(willing)* a trabajar hasta altas horas de la tarde y prefieren pasar ese tiempo con su familia. La siesta, vista por algunos como una forma de mantener la buena salud y una vida balanceada, es ahora vista por otras personas como un obstáculo en el progreso económico y la vida familiar.

6B.6 La siesta. Escucha los enunciados siguientes sobre la siesta, e indica si son **ciertos** o **falsos** de acuerdo a lo que has leído arriba. Luego, comprueba tus respuestas con la clase.

	Cierto	Falso
1.	☑	☐
2.	☐	☑
3.	☐	☑
4.	☐	☑
5.	☑	☐

VÍVELO: CULTURA: Give students a time limit for reading the *Vívelo: Cultura* information, such as three minutes.

6B.6 AUDIO SCRIPT 1. La tradición de la siesta tiene sus orígenes en un aspecto de la vida religiosa. 2. La tradición de la siesta se asocia con climas fríos. 3. En las grandes ciudades es fácil regresar a casa para la siesta. 4. A causa de la globalización, la costumbre de la siesta se ha extendido por todo el mundo. 5. Algunos padres creen que la costumbre de la siesta afecta negativamente a sus familias.

Bien dicho

El sonido de la *p*

Awareness of the differences between the English and Spanish pronunciation of the letter **p** should go a long way in improving how you sound as a Spanish-speaker. Moreover, because this sound is easily achievable, the pronunciation of the Spanish **p** is worth the effort and practice.

The basic difference between the pronunciation of **p** in Spanish and English is that English speakers insert a tiny puff of air, called an aspiration, after the **p** at the beginning of a word and Spanish does not. To avoid/reduce the aspiration, press your lips more tightly together than you would when you pronounce **p** in English and then release them as you pronounce the following vowel or consonant. This will help reduce the amount of air that is released when you pronounce **p**. Another strategy may be to think of how you pronounce *p* when preceded by *s* in English *(e.g., spin, span, sports)* and apply that pronunciation to all cases of **p** in Spanish.

6B.7, 6B.8 TEACHING TIP: For both exercises in this section, you may want to distribute small pieces of paper to the students and invite them to hold the paper in front of their mouths to monitor the amount of aspiration. Explain to the students that if they pronounce *p* with aspiration, the paper will move whereas it will not move if there is no aspiration.

6B.8 SUGGESTION: You may want to introduce this activity by asking students if they know tongue twisters in English with *p* such as: "Peter Piper picked a peck of pickled peppers. If Peter Piper picked a peck of pickled peppers, where's the peck of pickled peppers Peter Piper picked?" or "Picky people pick Peter Pan peanut-butter; it's the peanut-butter picky people pick." You may want to encourage students to use the piece of paper to monitor their aspiration of *p*. A follow-up or an alternative to doing this activity in pairs would be to recite each tongue twister 3-4 times as a class, each time getting faster.

6B.7 **¡Atención a la *p*!** Escucha los siguientes cognados que empiezan con la letra *p*. Mientras vuelves a escuchar las palabras, repítelas, tratando de reducir/eliminar la aspiración de la *p* inicial.

1. público
2. perfecto
3. primero
4. pintor
5. profesional
6. protestar
7. participar
8. posible
9. pasatiempos
10. prometer
11. preocupado
12. progresivo
13. pacífico
14. precisamente

6B.8 **Trabalenguas con *p*.** Túrnate con un/a compañero/a para recitar los siguientes trabalenguas *(tongue twister)*, y concéntrate en reducir/eliminar la aspiración de la **p**. Dile a tu compañero/a cuando escuches la aspiración de la **p**. Al completar la actividad, intercambia las oraciones y repítelas. ¿Quién recitó el trabalenguas más rápidamente, con más fluidez?

1. Él puso el peso en el piso y de paso el piso del pozo pisó.
2. Pedro Picapiedras pica piedras. Pobre Pedro Picapiedras.
3. Pancha plancha con cuatro planchas. ¿Con cuántas planchas plancha Pancha?
4. Pepe Peña pela papas, pica piña, pita un pito; pica piña, pela papas Pepe Peña.
5. Peta pela una papa, una papa pela Peta. Peta ponla en la maleta, pon la papa, ponla Peta.
6. Porque puedo, puedes; porque puedes, puedo. Pero si no puedes, yo tampoco puedo.
7. Pedro Pérez Porrata, pintor puertorriqueño, pinta precisosos paisajes para personas pobres por pocas pesetas, pero pronto piensa partir para París.
8. Aviso al público de la República que el agua pública se va a cobrar para que el público de la República tenga agua pública para tomar.

Palabras clave 1 El bienestar

el bienestar	El bienestar de una persona depende del equilibrio entre la vida espiritual, física y mental de una persona.
pasarlo bien/mal	Cuando tenemos una buena experiencia, decimos que lo pasamos bien. Cuando la experiencia es mala, decimos que lo pasamos mal.
buscar un trabajo	Todos tenemos que buscar un trabajo para mantener a nuestra familia.
hacer una cita	Cuando queremos solicitar un trabajo, primero tenemos que hacer una cita con el dueño o gerente de la compañía.
jubilarse	Hoy en día, hay que tener por lo menos 65 años para jubilarse.
despedir	Los jefes despiden a los empleados que faltan mucho al trabajo *(miss work a lot)*.
renunciar a	En realidad, no podemos renunciar a nuestro trabajo sólo porque no nos gusta.
disfrutar de/ gozar de	Me gusta trabajar en el hospital y siempre gozo y disfruto de mis actividades.
hacer planes	Tenemos que hacer planes si queremos ir de vacaciones al extranjero *(abroad)*.
descansar	Es importante descansar después de trabajar ocho horas.
no hacer nada	Cuando estás enfermo, es necesario estar tranquilo y no hacer nada.
la empresa	Donald Trump tiene muchas empresas.
la solicitud	Las empresas siempre piden una solicitud completa para poder verificar las referencias de los solicitantes.
la entrevista	Es importante contestar las preguntas con sinceridad en una entrevista de trabajo.
el sueldo	El sueldo es el dinero que recibe el empleado por su trabajo.
el pasatiempo	El pasatiempo favorito de la mayoría de los estadounidenses es mirar la televisión.
el tiempo libre	En el tiempo libre, tratamos *(we try)* de visitar a nuestros amigos y a nuestra familia.
los ratos libres	En los ratos libres contestamos las llamadas que están en el contestador automático *(answering machine)*.
los quehaceres domésticos	Los quehaceres domésticos incluyen lavar los platos, lavar, secar y doblar *(fold)* la ropa y preparar y cocinar la comida.
el/la empleado/a doméstico/a	La empleada doméstica es una persona que trabaja para los dueños de una casa y hace los quehaceres domésticos.

6B.9 ¡Adivina! Con un/a compañero/a de clase, averigüen el significado de las palabras y expresiones que aparecen arriba. Luego, escriban cada palabra o expresión en español, al lado de su significado en inglés. Sigan el modelo.

hacer una cita	**a.** to make an appointment	el sueldo	**f.** the salary
la entrevista	**b.** the interview	la solicitud	**g.** the application
despedir	**c.** to fire someone	renunciar	**h.** to resign
la empresa	**d.** business/enterprise	buscar un trabajo	**i.** to look for a job
jubilarse	**e.** to retire	los solicitantes	**j.** the applicants

6B.9 STANDARDS: COMMUNICATION/ INTERPRETIVE MODE. An important skill for students to develop, and one supported by this activity, is the ability to make meaning based on the context. Remind students to pay attention to the context in which the words are used to figure out their meaning.

SUGGESTION: As students look at this list of vocabulary, see how many words they can make good guesses at. Let them know that the next exercise will provide them with an opportunity to get more comfortable with these words.

El mundo del trabajo

Es necesario trabajar para ganarse la vida; es decir, para tener casa, comida, ropa, transporte y otras cosas esenciales. De esta manera, uno no tiene que depender económicamente de otra persona. Para muchas personas, encontrar el trabajo perfecto significa realizar un sueño. Sin embargo, el proceso de **buscar un trabajo** puede ser largo y difícil. Primero, es necesario mandar una carta *(letter)* de presentación y tu currículum *(resumé)* a varias **empresas.** A veces, también es necesario completar una **solicitud. La solicitud** es un documento que pide información personal acerca de **los solicitantes.** También es posible **hacer una cita** y tener **una entrevista** con la persona que supervisa a los empleados. Durante **la entrevista** es posible hablar del horario y **el sueldo.** Si uno no va al trabajo, si llega tarde, si roba o si insulta a los clientes, **la empresa** lo va a **despedir.** Si uno no está contento(a) con su trabajo, puede **renunciar a** ese trabajo y buscar otro trabajo. Después de muchos años de trabajar, a los 65 ó 70 años, es normal **jubilarse;** o sea, dejar de trabajar.

El tiempo libre

El tiempo libre es un período de tiempo cuando no tenemos obligaciones. En los **ratos** (o momentos) **libres,** las personas no **tienen ganas** de hacer actividades como trabajar o estudiar. Tampoco tienen ganas de hacer los **quehaceres domésticos** como limpiar la casa o lavar la ropa. En cambio, las personas tienen ganas de hacer actividades divertidas. Muchas personas **disfrutan** (les gusta) participando en sus **pasatiempos** (actividades) favoritos como hacer deportes, leer, escuchar o tocar música, ir al cine, pintar, etc. Otras personas **gozan (disfrutan de) pasando tiempo** (estar) con su familia o sus amigos. Algunas personas prefieren **hacer planes** para salir con sus amigos. Por ejemplo, salen a cenar a un restaurante o a tomar una copa en un bar. Los novios y los esposos hacen **citas** en las que pueden **pasar tiempo** juntos como pareja. Otras personas **gozan de** la oportunidad de **descansar** y **relajarse.** O sea, de **no hacer nada** (no participar en ninguna actividad). Para estas personas, echar una siesta o **dedicar** tiempo para soñar despierto (pensar en cosas agradables) o meditar son las mejores formas de **pasar** sus **ratos libres.**

Todos deseamos tener una vida satisfactoria. Nadie quiere **pasarlo mal** (tener experiencias desagradables). No tener **tiempo libre** afecta negativamente a la condición física y emocional de la persona. El **tiempo libre** es esencial para estar de buen humor (estar contento) y mantener **el bienestar** (condición física y emocional positiva).

6B.10 ORIENTATION: Not all words can be guessed via context. We provide synonyms we thought students would know in Spanish to help convey the meaning of the word or expression when this is the case.

6B.10 TEACHING TIP: After going over the answers with students, have them reread the passage to see how much more they understood.

6B.10 **¡A adivinar otra vez!** Lee el texto sobre lo que hace la gente en su tiempo libre. Presta atención a las palabras en negrita y luego adivina los significados según el contexto. Luego, compara tus respuestas con las de otros compañeros.

_____ **a.** well-being

_____ **b.** to spend unpleasant time

_____ **c.** to feel like (doing something)

_____ **d.** housework

_____ **e.** enjoy

_____ **f.** free time

_____ **g.** to spend time

_____ **h.** to do nothing

_____ **i.** time free of responsibilities or obligations

VÍVELO: LENGUA

Expressing order: Ordinal numbers

Ordinal numbers, *first, second, third, fourth*, etc., are used to rank items in a list based on some type of measure, organize steps in terms of a specific sequence, or link information sequencially across paragraphs. The ordinal numbers *first* through *tenth* in Spanish are:

primero/a (primer)	**sexto/a**
segundo/a	**séptimo/a**
tercero/a (tercer)	**octavo/a**
cuarto/a	**noveno/a**
quinto/a	**décimo/a**

Ordinal numbers occur before the noun they modify.

La primera esposa de Marc Anthony se llama Dayanara Torres.
La segunda esposa de Marc Anthony es Jennifer López.

When **primero** and **tercero** modify a masculine singular noun, they are shortened to **primer** or **tercer.**

El primer presidente de EE.UU. se llama George Washington.
El tercer presidente se llama Thomas Jefferson.

6B.11 **El proceso de buscar trabajo.** Usando números ordinales, narra los enunciados en orden para reflejar la secuencia de buscar un nuevo trabajo. Escribe el número ordinal al lado de cada enunciado. Luego, comprueba tus respuestas con la clase.

primero	sexto
segundo	séptimo
tercero	octavo
cuarto	noveno
quinto	décimo

_____ **a.** Ser buen/a empleado/a.

_____ **b.** Escribir una carta de presentación.

_____ **c.** Contestar las preguntas durante la entrevista.

_____ **d.** Empezar a trabajar para la empresa.

_____ **e.** Buscar información acerca de la empresa.

_____ **f.** Completar la solicitud.

_____ **g.** Decidir para qué empresa quiere trabajar

_____ **h.** Hablar de los detalles del contrato.

_____ **i.** Preparar el currículum.

_____ **j.** Mandar el currículum y la carta de presentación.

6B.11 ANSWERS: Since some answers may vary, you may want students to read their statements to a partner to see if they agree. a. décimo, b. cuarto, c. séptimo, d. noveno, e. segundo, f. sexto, g. primero, h. octavo, i. tercero, j. quinto

6B.12 **¿Positivo o negativo?** Vas a escuchar varios enunciados. Indica si cada enunciado tiene una asociación positiva o negativa. Luego, comprueba tus respuestas con la clase.

	Positivo	Negativo		Positivo	Negativo
1.	☑	☐	**6.**	☑	☐
2.	☐	☑	**7.**	☐	☑
3.	☐	☑	**8.**	☑	☐
4.	☑	☐	**9.**	☑	☑
5.	☑	☑	**10.**	☐	☑

VÍVELO: LENGUA

Expressing preferences: *Repaso y expansión*

You have been using **gustar** with indirect object pronouns to indicate what you and others like/don't like or what you like/don't like to do.

Me gusta jugar al tenis.
¿Te gustan las películas románticas?
Le gusta el nuevo sofá.

To express what you and someone else together, or what a number of others like, use the phrases **nos gusta/gustan…** and **les gusta/gustan.**

A mi hermana y a mí **nos gusta** descansar después de correr por el parque. También **nos gusta** el parque por donde corremos. Además **nos gustan** los chicos que corren por ese parque. A ellos **les gusta** conversar con nosotras cuando paramos a tomar agua. Parece que **les gustan** las chicas atléticas.

Notice that once clarification of who **nos** or **les** refers to, for example, **a mi hermana y a mí, a ellos,** there is no need to repeat the **a**-phrase.

WILEY PLUS Go to *WileyPLUS* and review the tutorial for this grammar point.

6B.13 **¿Cierto o falso?** Indica si cada uno de los enunciados siguientes es cierto o falso. Luego, compara tus respuestas con las de tus compañeros de clase, hasta que encuentres a alguien con las respuestas más parecidas a las tuyas. Escribe qué tienen en común en tu **Retrato de la clase.**

Cierto Falso

☐ ☐ **1.** Cuando hace buen tiempo estoy de buen humor.

☐ ☐ **2.** Cuando estoy de vacaciones prefiero trabajar.

☐ ☐ **3.** Leer, escuchar música y jugar al tenis son ejemplos de pasatiempos.

☐ ☐ **4.** Cuando trabajo 70 horas a la semana disfruto de la vida.

☐ ☐ **5.** En muchas clases sueño despierto.

☐ ☐ **6.** Me encanta no hacer nada los fines de semana.

☐ ☐ **7.** A veces tengo ganas de llorar sin razón.

☐ ☐ **8.** Me gusta hacer los quehaceres domésticos.

Retrato de la clase: Mi compañero/a de clase _____ y yo estamos de buen humor cuando hace buen tiempo. A mi compañero/a de clase _____ y a mí no nos gusta trabajar cuando estamos de vacaciones. Pensamos que leer, escuchar música…

6B.14 ¿Obligación o tiempo libre?   Entrevista a un/a compañero/a para determinar sus percepciones sobre las siguientes actividades. Él/Ella tiene que decir si las siguientes actividades se consideran una obligación o una actividad para el tiempo libre.

> Modelo: E1: *Echarse una siesta, ¿es una obligación o es una actividad para el tiempo libre?*
> E2: *Es una actividad para el tiempo libre.*

	Obligación	Tiempo libre
1. echarse una siesta	☐	☐
2. pasar tiempo con la familia	☐	☐
3. lavar los platos	☐	☐
4. cenar en un restaurante	☐	☐
5. estudiar para un examen de química	☐	☐
6. hacer la tarea de matemáticas	☐	☐
7. tomar café con amigos	☐	☐
8. trabajar	☐	☐
9. ir al cine	☐	☐
10. limpiar el baño	☐	☐

6B.15 Los pasatiempos favoritos de los compañeros.   Escribe en la primera columna tres de tus pasatiempos o actividades de tiempo libre favoritos. Luego, entrevista a tres compañeros sobre sus pasatiempos o actividades de tiempo libre y escríbelos en las columnas indicadas. Determina con el resto de la clase cuáles son las actividades más populares e inusuales. Anota los resultados en el **Retrato de la clase.**

¿Cuáles son tus pasatiempos favoritos?

Yo	Compañero/a 1	Compañero/a 2	Compañero/a 3

Retrato de la clase: Los pasatiempos más populares de la clase son… Algunas actividades inusuales son…

6B.16 Un día perfecto.

Paso 1: Imagina que tienes un día sin obligaciones (por ejemplo, trabajo, clases, tareas). ¿Cómo pasas ese día? ¿Qué haces? Escribe un párrafo corto para describir tu "día perfecto". Sigue el modelo.

> Modelo: *Un día perfecto para mí consiste en* (consists of) *ir a la playa con amigos, comer y descansar. Un día perfecto también consiste en salir a desayunar a un café y luego ir de compras.*

Paso 2: Intercambia párrafos con un/a compañero/a y comparen sus "días perfectos". Escribe un breve resumen sobre lo que tienes en común con tu compañero/a en tu **Retrato de la clase.**

Retrato de la clase: Para nosotros (___ y yo) el día perfecto consiste en…

6B.14 TEACHING TIP: Before students interview a partner, go over how they would transform those phrases into questions. Ask students to model how they would go about doing that and make sure they are on the right track before they find a partner. Tally student responses to these items to determine unusual responses, i.e., some students might consider going to a movie more as an obligation than a choice. Point out that not all students have to conform to what is considered "normal." For some students, spending time with family might be considered an obligation. Similarly, some might consider exercising to be a leisure activity. Point out that *cita* can be either a date when talking about romantic partners, or an appointment as in item 12 when talking about the professor.

6B.15 INSTRUCTOR'S RESOURCES: WileyPLUS: You will find a reproducible chart for use with Activity 6B.15 in your Instructor's Resources.

6B.15 FOLLOW-UP: Students have been learning things about each other in this class. You may want to ask if they found out something unique or if they learned they had something in common with a classmate.

6B.16 TEACHING TIP: Remind students of the expressions *por la mañana/por la tarde/por la noche*. Call attention to the modeling of *consistir en*. Students may expect *de* to follow *consistir*.

6B.17 TEACHING TIP:
This activity will help
students compare their
cultural practices with
those they will read
about in *Vívelo: Cultura*
on page 290.

6B.17 Tus expectativas. PRE-READING: Un pasatiempo típico en varias culturas es salir de compras en el tiempo libre. Indica cuáles son las expectativas de la relación entre un/a cliente y un/a dependiente/a en tu cultura.

☐ **1.** El cliente siempre tiene la razón.

☐ **2.** Es importante atender al cliente inmediatamente.

☐ **3.** Para el/la dependiente/a, la venta de un producto es sumamente importante.

☐ **4.** La relación entre el/la dependiente/a de un gran almacén y sus clientes debe ser cálida y amena.

☐ **5.** En las ciudades grandes, los dependientes no suelen ser *(aren't usually)* cálidos, con los clientes, especialmente en los grandes almacenes.

VÍVELO: CULTURA: Con-
trast students' responses
in 6B.17 with information
in *Vívelo: Cultura*. Ask
students who have trav-
eled to Spanish-speaking
countries to relate their
personal experiences with
salespersons. How valid is
this description, based on
their experiences? Explore
the variety of factors that
can influence business
practices anywhere, such
as the size of the city,
the size of the business,
etc.

¡ATENCIÓN! Challenge
students who are false
beginners, in terms of
having had previous ex-
posure to Spanish before
this course, to make the
most of the sections
entitled *¡Atención!* While
it is important that all
students recognize that
these are false cognates,
our more advanced
students can be pushed
to incorporate them into
their repertoire.

VÍVELO: CULTURA

El vendedor y su cliente

Es verdad que los comportamientos *(behaviors)* en la casa o en el trabajo muestran los valores de una cultura. Ciertos valores sociales y conductas relacionadas con el trabajo y la diversión pueden parecer únicas de las grandes ciudades. El cliente no siempre tiene la razón. En estos casos la venta *(sale)* no siempre es la meta *(goal)* más importante. Si dos vendedores están hablando entre ellos y un cliente entra en el establecimiento, los vendedores continúan la conversación (hasta un punto razonable) y después atienden al cliente. Su conversación es más importante que el cliente. La impresión es que la interacción entre vendedores y clientes en las ciudades grandes es cortés, pero no cálida *(warm)*. Este tipo de interacción, sin embargo, puede ser común en las ciudades grandes de España o de Latinoamérica, al igual que en otras grandes ciudades como Toronto, la Ciudad de Nueva York o París. Es importante tener en cuenta la gran cantidad de factores que influyen en este tipo de conducta porque en las pequeñas ciudades o pueblos, la interacción puede ser relativamente cálida.

Claro que como en toda generalización, siempre hay excepciones. ¿Qué se considera una conducta apropiada en tu comunidad? ¿Hay información útil sobre tu comunidad que debe saber un visitante?

¡Atención!

6B.18 ANSWERS: 1.
La seda es una ~~fábrica~~
(tela) muy elegante. 2. El
~~currículum~~ (programa de
estudios or plan de estu-
dios) del Departamento
de Español incluye cursos
de literatura mexicana. 3.
Para encontrar un trabajo
bueno, es necesario tener
un ~~resumen~~ (currículum)
excelente. 4. (Correct as
written.)

6B.18 TEACHING TIP:
Have the sentences
from 6B.18 visible to all
students on the board,
overhead, etc. Invite volunteers to come up and
make changes to each
sentence, or not, so that
they make sense.

Currículum	does not mean *curriculum* in the sense of a list of courses taught at a school, college or university. It refers to a *curriculum vitae* or *resumé* that one prepares when looking for a job. A **resumen** in Spanish is a *summary*. *Curriculum* in the academic sense is **un plan de estudios** or **un programa de estudios** in Spanish.
	Cuando tienes una entrevista, no te olvides de llevar tu currículum. El crítico ha presentado un buen resumen de la película.
Fábrica	does not mean *fabric*. It refers to a *factory*. *Fabric* is la tela in Spanish.
	Mi tío trabaja en una fábrica de Ford cerca de Detroit. La tela de este vestido es muy bonita.

6B.18 Corregir el error. De las cuatro oraciones que aparecen abajo, una es correcta. Corrige el error en las otras oraciones, prestando mucha atención al uso correcto de las palabras **fábrica** y **currículum.** Luego, comprueba tus respuestas con la clase.

1. La seda es una fábrica muy elegante.

2. El currículum del departamento de español incluye cursos de literatura mexicana.

3. Para encontrar un trabajo bueno, es necesario tener un resumen excelente.

4. Estos zapatos tienen un defecto de fábrica.

Estructuras clave 1 Formal commands

WILEY PLUS
Go to *WileyPLUS* and review the tutorial for this grammar point.

WILEY PLUS

You will find PowerPoint presentations for use with *Estructuras clave* in *WileyPLUS*.

Beginning in *Capítulo 5* you have been following directions in Spanish to complete the activities in your text book. What have you noticed about these directions, in forms like **Lee el párrafo** or **Contesten las preguntas**? These are commands, or in Spanish, **mandatos.** They are the verb forms you use to tell someone to do something, in the case of affirmative commands, or not do something, in the case of negative commands. For example, when you were young and your parents said to you, "Clean your room" or "Don't run in the house", they were using commands. Similarly, when your instructor says to the class, "Open your books to page 150" or "Don't forget that the compositions are due tomorrow", he/she is also using commands.

For many English speakers, the idea of using commands with strangers, such as a server in a restaurant, may seem rude, but it is completely normal and acceptable to do so in Spanish when they are used with **por favor** and **gracias**. However, it is very important to bear in mind whether the situation is *informal,* such as talking to a child, a friend, or even your pet, or *formal,* such as a customer talking to a sales clerk or a doctor talking to a patient. There are also separate forms for singular (addressing one person) or plural (addressing more than one person).

Formal commands are used in cases where you would use the **usted** form to address an individual and where you would use the **ustedes** form to address a group of people. Both the affirmative and negative **usted** commands are formed as follows: For most verbs, you drop the final **−o** of the **yo** form and add **−e** if the verb is an **−ar** verb, or **−a** if the verb is an **−er** or **−ir** verb. (For the **ustedes** commands, the endings are **−en** and **−an**.) Note that the endings use the "opposite" vowel of the infinitive. In the case of **manejar** *(to drive),* for example, you drop the **−o** from **manejo,** add **−e** since it's an **−ar** verb, and end up with **maneje** (or **manejen**), as in the examples **Maneje (Manejen) con cuidado** and **No maneje (manejen) a una velocidad excesiva.** Look at these additional examples.

Descanse. Ha trabajado 12 horas hoy.	*Rest. You have worked for 12 hours today.*
No salga de la casa cuando hay tormentas.	*Don't leave the house when there are storms.*
Corra diariamente para estar en buena forma física.	*Run daily to be in good shape.*
No beba mucho alcohol.	*Don't drink too much alcohol.*

Verbs ending in **−gar, −car,** and **−zar** have the following spelling changes.

jugar	⟶ **Juegue** con sus hijos.	buscar	⟶	**Busque** la llave del carro.
sacar	⟶ **Saque** el libro de la mochila.	empezar	⟶	**Empiece** la tarea.

Some verbs have irregular **usted/ustedes** command forms.

dar	⟶ **dé/den**	¿El dinero? Déselo al dependiente.
decir	⟶ **diga/digan**	Diga "a, e, i, o, u".
estar	⟶ **esté/estén**	No esté furioso conmigo.
ir	⟶ **vaya/vayan**	Vayan al centro.
saber	⟶ **sepa/sepan**	Sepa la respuesta correcta.
ser	⟶ **sea/sean**	Sean niños bien educados.

Commands and object pronoun placement

Object pronouns are attached to the affirmative commands and placed before negative commands.

Este libro es bueno. **Léanlo.**	Estos platos están sucios. **No los toque.**
Tráigame la cuenta, por favor.	Este dibujo, **descríbaselo** a su compañero.
No me mientan.	

6B.19 **Adivina quién da el mandato.** Lee los enunciados siguientes y selecciona a la persona que más probablemente lo haya dicho. El primero está hecho como modelo. Luego, comprueba tus respuestas con un/a compañero/a.

a. El/la comandante del ejército

b. El/la gerente de un hotel

c. El/la político/a

d. El/la policía

e. El/la bombero/a

f. El/la instructor/a de

g. El/la médico/a

h. El/la vendedor/a de electrodomésticos

___f___ **1.** Cierren el libro, tenemos examen.

___g___ **2.** Saque la lengua y diga "Ahhh".

___h___ **3.** Compre la tele de plasma.

___a___ **4.** Protejan al presidente.

___d___ **5.** No conduzca rápido.

___b___ **6.** Limpien bien los cuartos.

___c___ **7.** Voten por mí.

___e___ **8.** Salgan de la casa.

6B.20 **Marisol Escobar viene a esta universidad.** Marisol Escobar es una joven de Panamá que viene a estudiar a tu universidad. En grupos de cuatro, preparen una serie de instrucciones para Marisol para asegurarse de que tenga éxito social y académico. Además, piensen en la ropa y otros accesorios que pueda necesitar para vivir cómodamente. Como aún no conocen a Marisol personalmente, usen "usted" para dirigirse a ella. Comparen y contrasten sus respuestas con las de otros grupos para ver si hay ideas comunes.

6B.21 **¿Cómo se hace la actividad?** Trabajando con un/a compañero/a de clase, escojan una de las actividades de la lista a continuación. Escriban una lista de instrucciones para explicar cómo hacer la actividad, pero no escriban el nombre de la actividad en su lista. Van a intercambiar su lista de instrucciones con otra pareja y la otra pareja va a adivinar qué actividad se describe. Usen mandatos de **ustedes** para escribir las instrucciones.

lavar la ropa
poner la mesa
buscar un trabajo
recibir visita en tu casa
mandar un paquete
preparar una tortilla española
preparar café
caminar al centro estudiantil
hacer un sándwich de jamón

VÍVELO: CULTURA

Los negocios en los países hispanos

La manera de hacer negocios es diferente en cada cultura y por eso es necesario recordar estas observaciones si quieres hacer negocios en un país hispano:

- Usa "usted" para hablar con las personas.

- Usa títulos y el apellido paterno (por ej. Sr. Gómez, Doctora Flores) para hablar con las personas.

- Las presentaciones deben ser formales, acompañadas de un breve apretón de manos *(handshake)*. Mantener contacto visual durante la presentación es crucial. Entre amigos o colegas cercanos los abrazos entre los hombres y los besos en la mejilla *(check)* entre las mujeres, o entre hombres y mujeres, son comunes.

Una papelería en Cuernavaca, México. Los negocios pequeños se encuentran frecuentemente en los vecindarios *(neighborhoods)* residenciales.

- El sentido del espacio personal entre los hispanos es muy diferente al de la cultura en Estados Unidos. Los hispanos tienden a pararse *(stand)* cerca de la otra persona y mantienen contacto visual constante mientras hablan entre ellos. Además, los hispanos tienden a tener más contacto físico cuando hablan, como una palmada *(pat)* en el brazo *(arm)* o en el hombro *(shoulder)*.

- En algunos países hispanos, hay menos énfasis en la puntualidad en comparación con la cultura de Estados Unidos. Para las citas de negocios es mejor llegar a tiempo; de cualquier manera, para eventos sociales el llegar 10 ó 15 minutos tarde no se considera de mala educación *(bad manners)*.

- Las conversaciones superficiales o sobre asuntos familiares son aspectos importantes de las citas de negocios. Es normal, en una reunión de negocios, comenzar con este tipo de charla antes de comenzar con la agenda de la reunión. Establecer una conexión personal entre los individuos es un elemento importante en cualquier relación de negocios.

- Aunque los almuerzos y las cenas son comunes en las relaciones de negocios, realmente durante la comida a veces no se habla de trabajo sino hasta el final; por ejemplo, cuando es el momento del postre o del café.

VÍVELO: CULTURA: As you go over these culturally-appropriate behaviors, see if students have had experience with any of these themes. Also, consider having students work in small groups to develop a skit to use for teaching cultural sensitivity to individuals planning on doing business in the Spanish-speaking world.

6B.22 Queremos abrir un negocio.

Paso 1: Trabajen en grupos de cuatro. Dos miembros del grupo representan unos comerciantes que quieren abrir un negocio nuevo y buscan un espacio para alquilar *(to rent)*. Los otros dos representan agentes de bienes raíces *(real estate)* que tienen varios espacios para ofrecer. Uno/a de los/las comerciantes conoce a uno/a de los/las agentes, pero los demás no se conocen.

Comerciantes: Piensen en qué tipo de negocio desean abrir y cuánto pueden pagar por mes.

Agentes: Piensen en qué tipos de espacios tienen para ofrecerles a sus clientes y a qué precio.

Paso 2: Simulen una reunión entre los/las comerciantes y los/las agentes de bienes raíces para hablar de las distintas posibilidades y tomar una decisión sobre el espacio para el nuevo negocio.

Go to *WileyPLUS* and review the tutorial for this grammar point.

You will find PowerPoint presentations for use with *Estructuras clave* in WileyPLUS.

LINE UP: Have your students line up across from you. Depending on the size of the class and the space you are using, you may have to line them up in several lines. Once they are lined up, you can give them orders like *Álex, ponte a la derecha de Xiong. René, ponte detrás de Silvana.* etc. After students get the hang of this activity, you may have one of them giving the orders. Or you could have them separate into groups of four to five students taking turns giving each other orders of where to stand.

TEACHING TIP: Provide students with a lot of input around these forms. Give them commands, such as *escribe, mira, ábrelo,* etc. They should perform the action as they hear the command.

NOTE: The affirmative and negative command forms for *vosotros* are not explicitly taught or practiced in this *Investigación;* however, instructors who wish to present and practice these command forms are encouraged to refer to the summary of *vosotros* command forms in Appendix X-ref.

Estructuras clave 2 Informal commands

In the previous *Estructuras clave* section, you learned about command forms that are used when addressing an individual formally as **usted,** or a group of individuals as **ustedes.** The same form is used in these instances whether the command is affirmative or negative. There are different command forms that are used when addressing an individual informally as **tú.** Again, think of the command forms you have seen in activity directions such as **lee las preguntas, escribe la palabra correcta,** etc.

Affirmative *tú* commands

An easy way to remember the **tú** affirmative command for most verbs is to use the **tú** form of the verb in present tense and drop the final **–s:**

	-ar	**-er**	**-ir**
Present tense (tú)	caminas	comes	escribes
Affirm. command (tú)	**camina**	**come**	**escribe**

Hija, recoge tus juguetes.	*Daughter, pick up your toys.*
Lava los platos.	*Wash the dishes.*
Llámame esta noche.	*Call me tonight.*
Escríbeme una carta.	*Write me a letter.*
Papi, léenos un cuento, por favor.	*Daddy, read us a story please.*

Some verbs have irregular affirmative **tú** commands.

venir	→ **Ven** conmigo a la fiesta.	hacer	→ **Haz** la tarea antes de salir.
decir	→ **Di** la verdad.	salir	→ **Sal** de mi cuarto.
ir	→ **Ve** al supermercado.	ser	→ **Sé** cortés.
poner	→ **Pon** la mesa.	tener	→ **Ten** cuidado.

Negative *tú* commands

The majority of negative **tú** commands are formed almost like the formal commands except that you will attach an **–s** to the end of the command. First drop the final **–o** from the **yo** form of the verb. Then add **–es** to verbs whose infinitives end in **–ar,** or **–as** to verbs whose infinitives end in **–er** or **–ir.** (Again, think of the "opposite" vowel.)

No hables durante la clase.	*Don't talk in class.*
No duermas durante la clase.	*Don't sleep during class.*
No pongas tus zapatos en la mesa.	*Don't put your shoes on the table.*

There are a few irregular negative **tú** commands.

dar	→ **No le des** este libro a Paco.
estar	→ **No estés** nervioso.
ir	→ **No vayas** a la casa de Alberto.
ser	→ **No seas** indiscreto.

There are also spelling changes with the negative **tú** commands of verbs ending in **–gar, –car** and **–zar** as shown in the following examples.

–gar	g → gu	**No pagues** demasiado por ese suéter.
–car	c → qu	**No saques** ese juguete, es hora de dormir.
–zar	z → c	**No almuerces** en la cafetería.

Object pronouns are placed between the word **no** and the verb in negative **tú** commands.

Estas copas son muy frágiles, **no las toques.**
No les prestes dinero a ellos.
Esta información, **no se la digas** a nadie.

6B.23 ¿Formal o informal? Vas a escuchar dos veces una serie de mandatos. La primera vez indica si el mandato es lógico o ilógico. Pon √ al lado del número si el mandato es lógico o pon una X al lado del número si es ilógico. La segunda vez, escucha e indica si el mandato es formal o informal. El primero está hecho como modelo. Luego, comprueba tus respuestas con la clase.

¿Lógico?		Informal	Formal	¿Lógico?		Informal	Formal
X	1.	☐	☑	X	5.	☐	☑
X	2.	☐	☑	✓	6.	☑	☐
✓	3.	☑	☐	X	7.	☐	☑
X	4.	☑	☐	X	8.	☑	☐

6B.24 Simón dice. Anota de seis a ocho mandatos con **tú.** Luego, en grupos de seis, túrnense diciendo un mandato a otro de los miembros del grupo, quien tiene que seguir ese mandato.

6B.25 ¿Lógico o ilógico? Con un/a compañero/a, túrnense para leer cada una de las situaciones de las que aparecen abajo e indicar si los mandatos asociados con esas situaciones son lógicos o ilógicos. Luego, comprueben sus respuestas con un/a compañero/a de clase.

	Lógico	Ilógico
Una madre a su hijo/a:		
1. No juegues en la calle.	☑	☐
2. Recoge tu ropa.	☑	☐
Una joven a su novio:		
3. No me traigas flores.	☐	☑
4. Invítame a bailar.	☑	☐
Un estudiante de español a una compañera de clase:		
5. No duermas en la clase.	☑	☐
6. Haz la tarea todos los días.	☑	☐
Un/a joven a un/a amigo/a que busca trabajo:		
7. Lleva un traje a la entrevista.	☑	☐
8. No escribas una carta de presentación.	☐	☑

6B.26 Consejos para buscar trabajo. Con dos compañeros, preparen una lista de consejos *(advice)* para ayudar a un/a amigo/a a encontrar su primer trabajo. En su lista incluyan cuatro sugerencias generales para una entrevista exitosa *(successful),* cuatro sugerencias relacionadas con cómo vestirse *(to dress)* y cuatro relacionadas con la conducta. Comparen su lista con las sugerencias del resto de la clase. ¿Cuáles son las sugerencias más comunes?

6B.23 AUDIO SCRIPT: 1. Camine sola por la noche. 2. Lleve mucho dinero en el carro. 3. Sé generoso. 4. Barre la alfombra. 5. Traigan a la clase sus muebles. 6. Pon las llaves siempre en el mismo lugar. 7. Pídales dinero a sus amigos. 8. Juega videojuegos todo el día.

6B.23 ALTERNATIVE DELIVERY: Show students the sentences, so that they may decide whether a sentence represents a formal or informal command (this is particularly helpful for visual learners).

6B.24 SUGGESTION: Have students sit and form a circle once they have their commands ready. Each student should offer one command to the student seated directly opposite to him/her, which that student in turn has to act out. Note: Groups should have at least five students in them. For more advanced students: Do not have students prepare their sentences ahead of time, but rather offer them on the spot.

6B.25, 6B.26 RECYCLING: These activities recycle previously studied material such as clothing vocabulary, leisure activities, days of the week, courses, times of day, etc.

6B.25 TEACHING TIP: As you go over the answers, ask students how they would go about making the affirmative commands negative and vice versa. You may even want them to change the statements marked *Ilógico* so that they make sense.

6B.26 SUGGESTION: Encourage students to think about their own experiences with job interviews. For the interview suggestions, encourage students to think of things that their friend should not do in addition to things that he/she should do (e.g. *No llegues tarde; Lleva un traje; Contesta las preguntas claramente; No comas durante la entrevista).*

INVESTIGACIÓN 6B • DOSCIENTOS NOVENTA Y TRES **293**

6B.27 INSTRUCTOR'S RESOURCES: Reproducible charts are available for use with Activity 6B.27 in your Instructor's Resources.

6B.27 PRE-CONVERSATION ACTIVITY: In order to ensure that students push themselves to use as much language as possible, have them prepare their schedule in Spanish before coming to class. While they will likely not have time to ask about each box on their partner's schedule, their goal should be to get a good grasp of what each other's schedules are like. Before having students begin their dialogues with a partner, go over possible questions they can ask of one another. Encourage students to ask follow-up and clarification questions.

VÍVELO: CULTURA: Ask students if they know small business owners or have small business owners in their family.

6B.27 **El bienestar.** Averigua el horario de un/a compañero/a de clase para que puedas darle un buen consejo. Primero, túrnate con un/a compañero/a en la descripción de sus horarios en una semana típica (de lunes a domingo). Asegúrense de mencionar sus horarios de clases, trabajo y otras actividades (compromisos familiares, reuniones, etcétera.). También hablen de cuánto tiempo libre tienen y cómo lo usan. Mientras tu compañero/a describe su horario, anota la información en la tabla que aparece abajo. Luego aconseja a tu compañero/a sobre cómo balancear aspectos de su vida, si el horario muestra que eso es necesario.

El horario de mi compañero/a _____

	lunes	martes	miércoles	jueves	viernes	sábado	domingo
Por la mañana							
Por la tarde							
Por la noche							

¿Cuántas horas libres tiene a la semana? ¿Qué hace en su tiempo libre? ¿Qué hace los martes por la noche?

VÍVELO: CULTURA
El trabajo y la vida a la vez

En Latinoamérica es muy común la existencia de negocios *(businesses)* pequeños y variados tales como panaderías, floristerías, zapaterías, etcétera. Sin embargo, el negocio más común y popular es la "tiendita". En la tiendita las personas pueden comprar pan, frutas, verduras, jabón *(soap)*, refrescos y todo tipo de producto de uso diario. Por lo general, la tiendita es un negocio de familia: una familia decide adaptar una sección de su casa (el garaje, por ejemplo) y establecer el negocio ahí. Esto es muy oportuno *(convenient)* pues literalmente trabajan donde viven y pueden pasar más tiempo en familia. También para los consumidores resulta muy práctico porque no necesitan subir a su carro para ir al supermercado, sólo tienen que caminar unos pocos metros para encontrar lo que necesitan. Las tiendas son un fenómeno muy positivo en Latinoamérica porque promueven la unidad entre los vecinos del barrio, quienes frecuentemente coinciden en la tiendita. También promueven la unidad familiar pues los dueños no tienen que salir de la casa para trabajar. Además, es un beneficio práctico para las personas que no tienen mucho tiempo para ir de compras y, finalmente, promueven el ejercicio pues la gente camina para encontrar una tiendita.

Una tienda de vestidos al lado de una residencia de familia en Puebla, México.

¡Conéctate!
Do you have any *tienditas*, or *bodegas*, in your neighborhood? These are not only a common sight in Latin America, but also in many large cities in the U.S. Search for images of *bodegas*. You may want to limit your search to New York City as they are ubiquitous there. How would you describe these *bodegas*? Do they seem to share anything in common?

6B.28 Voy a la tiendita.

Paso 1: Con un/a compañero/a de clase, revisen la lista de productos a continuación e indiquen si es lógico o ilógico encontrar esos productos en una tiendita.

	Lógico	Ilógico
1. una aspiradora	☐	☐
2. pan para hacer sándwiches	☐	☐
3. un bolígrafo	☐	☐
4. un televisor	☐	☐
5. café instantáneo	☐	☐
6. una escoba	☐	☐
7. un lavaplatos	☐	☐
8. unos caramelos *(candies)*	☐	☐
9. sal y azúcar	☐	☐
10. un boleto de lotería	☐	☐

Paso 2: Imaginen cada uno/a una tiendita cerca de la universidad que todo el mundo conoce y piensen en por lo menos tres cosas que necesiten de esa tiendita. Túrnense usando mandatos para pedirle a su compañero que les compre esas cosas en la tiendita. Sigan el modelo.

Modelo: E1: *Si vas a Cooper's cómprame una revista.*

E2: *¿Qué revista quieres?*

E1: *Cómprame Newsweek. No me compres Time.*

Enlaces

6B.29 Enlaces. Lee las oraciones siguientes para adivinar el significado de la frase **en eso.**

1. Muchos electrodomésticos nuevos se han inventado en Estados Unidos. **En eso,** los estadounidenses han tenido mucho éxito.

2. ¿Las relaciones familiares? **En eso** la cultura hispana enfatiza mucho la importancia de la familia.

3. Hay muchos factores que determinan la moda; sin embargo, **en eso,** los medios de comunicación tienen más influencia que otros factores.

En eso significa _____.

a. furthermore

b. in that respect

c. nevertheless

6B.29 ANSWERS: *En eso* means "In that (respect)". Try to be more conscientious about using expressions with *en eso* while drawing students' attention to how you use them. The more input they receive around specific language, the more likely they are to acquire it.

FUNCTIONAL OUTCOMES:
The central question that frames this *Investigación* is "*¿Cómo puedes hablar de una vida sana?*" Explore whether students can now address this question and how they would go about it. Have them review the chart on the first page of this *Investigación*.

6B.30 ANSWER: The first statement best represents the main idea of the paragraph. Remind students of some of the reading strategies they have practiced thus far (e.g. skimming, contextual clues, prior knowledge, titles).

6B.30 Resumir la idea principal.   Lee el siguiente fragmento de un artículo titulado "Trabajar para vivir". Luego, selecciona el enunciado a continuación que resuma mejor la idea principal de este párrafo. Compara tus respuestas con las de un/a compañero/a y luego con las del resto de la clase.

Trabajar para vivir

¿Vives para trabajar o trabajas para vivir? Pregúntaselo a cualquiera *(anyone)* y te va a decir sin pensarlo que trabaja para ganarse la vida o para realizar sus sueños. Es decir que trabaja para vivir. Por lo general, **en eso** los españoles están por delante de muchos. En cambio en otros países como Estados Unidos, Japón o China la gente da más importancia al trabajo. Para mucha gente en esos países, el trabajo es lo más importante en su vida.

☑ Attitudes about work in Spain are different from those in the US, Japan, and China.

☐ People in Spain are becoming as "workaholic" as people in the US, Japan, and China.

☐ People in Spain are struggling to find a balance between work and other aspects of their lives, just like people in the US, Japan, and China.

6B.31 **¿Tú vives para trabajar o trabajas para vivir?** ¿Es cierta para tus compañeros y para ti la idea principal de la lectura anterior? Selecciona 8 de las 16 preguntas a continuación y luego entrevista a un/a compañero/a. De acuerdo a sus respuestas, determina si tu compañero/a vive para trabajar o trabaja para vivir. Compara las respuestas de tu compañero/a con las de otros miembros de la clase. ¿Cuántos estudiantes viven para trabajar y cuántos trabajan para vivir? Anota tus resultados en tu **Retrato de la clase.**

1. ¿Con qué frecuencia comes comida rápida? ¿Cocinas?

2. ¿Comes solo/a o con otra(s) persona(s)? ¿Con quiénes?

3. ¿Comes en la mesa o en otro lugar, por ejemplo, en tu carro, en tu oficina, enfrente del televisor?

4. Aunque estés ocupado/a, ¿tomas tiempo para comer tranquilamente?

5. ¿Pasas mucho o poco tiempo preparándote por la mañana?

6. ¿Vas de compras sólo por necesidad o también para relajarte?

7. ¿Pasas mucho o poco tiempo decidiendo qué ropa comprar o ponerte?

8. Cuando vas de compras, ¿prefieres ir solo/a o con otra(s) persona(s)? ¿Con quiénes?

9. ¿Prefieres vivir solo/a o con otras personas? ¿Con quiénes?

10. ¿Con qué frecuencia se reúne tu familia en casa? ¿Para qué se reúnen?

11. ¿Tomas tiempo para limpiar tu casa/apartamento/cuarto regularmente? ¿Lavar la ropa? ¿Lavar los platos?

12. Según tu experiencia, ¿es buena idea trabajar desde la casa? Explica tu repuesta, por favor.

13. ¿Trabajas además de estudiar? ¿Dónde?

14. ¿Cuántas horas a la semana tienes clase? ¿Estudias? ¿Trabajas?

15. ¿Es más importante tener un trabajo que te guste o ganar mucho dinero?

16. ¿Es más importante pasar tiempo con la familia y los amigos o tener un trabajo prestigioso?

Retrato de la clase: La mayoría de la clase vive para trabajar/trabaja para vivir… Algunos estudiantes…

Estas chicas van de compras durante su hora de almuerzo. ¿Crees que viven para trabjar o que trabajan para vivir?

Perspectivas

6B.32 SUGGESTION: Encourage students to interview native Spanish speakers or bilingual speakers if possible. Remind them that the interviewees' perspectives could be influenced by the amount of time away from their native country or by whether they are first, second, or third generation Spanish speakers.

6B.32 **¿Y los hispanos?** ¿Tú crees que los latinoamericanos viven para trabajar o trabajan para vivir? Usando las preguntas de la Actividad 6B.31, entrevista a varias personas, preferiblemente bilingües o cuya *(whose)* lengua materna sea el español. De acuerdo a los resultados, escribe al menos 4 o más ideas que apoyen *(support)* tu opinión. Comparte tu opinión con la clase y anota las conclusiones en tu **Retrato de la clase.**

Retrato de la clase: Según la información de las entrevistas, creo que los latinoamericanos viven para trabajar/trabajan para vivir porque 1)… 2)… 3)…4)…

Vocabulario: Investigación B

Vocabulario esencial

Sustantivos

el bienestar	well-being
el día feriado	holiday
la empresa	company
la entrevista	interview
el/la jefe/a	boss
el pasatiempo	hobby
los ratos libres	free time
el/la solicitante	applicant
la solicitud	application
el sueldo	income
el tiempo libre	free time
el/la vendedor/a	sales representative
la venta	sale

Adjetivos

agradable	pleasant
ameno/a	enjoyable
antipático/a	unpleasant
dispuesto/a	willing

Verbos

buscar un trabajo	to look for a job
cobrar	to charge
comprar	to buy
dedicarse a	to dedicate oneself to something (esp. professionally)
descansar	to rest
despedir	to fire
disfrutar de/ gozar de	to enjoy
hacer una cita	make an appointment
hacer planes	make plans
jubilarse	to retire
pasarlo bien/ mal	to have a good/bad time
relajarse	to relax
renunciar	to resign, to quit
solicitar	to apply

Adverbios

demasiado	too much
pronto	soon

Otras palabras y expresiones

el apretón de manos	handshake
cálido/a	warm
la cancha	court, field (sports)
ciertos	certain
cómodamente	comfortably
el comportamiento	behavior
el currículum	resumé
inadvertido/a	unnoticed
la llamada	phone call
llorar	to cry
la mercancía	merchandise
la mitad	middle, half
el monje	monk
la palmada	pat
el peso	weight
pisar	to step on
la plancha	iron
planchar	to iron, to press
el pozo	well
resumir	to summarize
robar	to rob
sano/a	healthy
el ser humano	human being
la sinceridad	honesty
¿A costa de qué?	At what price?
al menos	at least
a tiempo completo	full time
a tiempo parcial	part time
de cualquier manera	in any case
de tantas… como	as many… as
echarse una siesta	take a nap
en el extranjero	abroad
estar de buen/ mal humor	to be in a good/bad mood
faltar al trabajo	miss work
ganarse la vida	to earn a living
hacer negocios	to do business
ir de compras	go shopping
lavar los platos	do the dishes
lavar la ropa	do the laundry
mandar un paquete	send a package
pararse cerca	to stand close to
realizar un sueño	to fulfill a dream
soñar despierto	to day dream
soler + infinitive	to usually (do something)

Cognados

Review the cognates in *Adelante* and the false cognates in *¡Atención!*. For a complete list of cognates, see Appendix 4 on page 605.

En vivo

¿Cómo es tu cuarto? Choose a room in your house or apartment or your dorm room. Describe the objects, furniture, décor, etc. and the types and location of furnishings in the room to your partner while he/she draws the room. Switch roles. When you have both finished describing your rooms, compare your partner's drawing with your descriptions to see how well they match. If you both chose the same room (e.g., your dorm rooms), what are the similarities and the differences between the two rooms? What do the rooms indicate about your health, work, and well being?

Los negocios en EE.UU. y en Latinoamérica. Reflect on the readings of this *Investigación* dealing with work and leisure. Take into account what you learned about common business practices and perspectives on balance in the Spanish-speaking world as well as what you know about your own culture. Imagine that a friend of yours, with little understanding of these cultural differences, is preparing for a business trip to Mexico. Send your friend an email in preparation for this business trip.

Paso 1: Draw a Venn Diagram like the one below comparing and contrasting cultural perspectives on work/leisure to organize your thoughts on this topic.

Perspectives and Practices on Work/Leisure

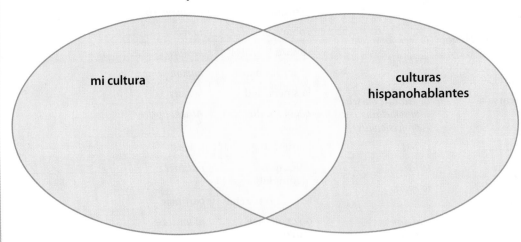

mi cultura   culturas hispanohablantes

Paso 2: Start your email by writing, **Querido/a…** and focus on four to five important things that they need to take into account. Sign it, **Atentamente,…**

Paso 3: Revise your email and make sure that you have done a good job preparing your friend for cultural perspectives for which he or she might not otherwise be prepared. Make any changes/additions necessary so that you have included the content you deem important.

Paso 4: Now, give your email a second revision. This time focus on the form and accuracy of your email, specifically on your use of informal commands. Make any corrections necessary.

Paso 5: Reread and be proud of your ability to convey these cultural perspectives to your friend.

En directo

INVESTIGACIÓN A: El patio andaluz

> **Antes de ver el video.** Responde a las siguientes preguntas: ¿Cuál es el lugar más importante en tu casa? ¿Por qué? ¿Para qué lo usas?

> **El video.** Indica si cada uno de los enunciados es **cierto** o **falso**. Reescribe los enunciados falsos para hacerlos ciertos. Comprueba tus respuestas con un/a compañero/a.

Vocabulario útil
restaurado *repaired*
arreglado *arranged*
hermoso *beautiful*

Cierto	Falso	
☐	☑	**1.** El patio ha sido un lugar muy importante en Andalucía desde el siglo XVI.
☑	☐	**2.** El patio tiene influencias árabes y es tan importante como otros cuartos.
☑	☐	**3.** El patio de la casa del doctor funciona como sala de espera.
☐	☑	**4.** La oficina del médico se encuentra en la planta principal.

> **Después de ver el video.** En parejas, respondan a las siguientes preguntas. Luego compartan sus respuestas con el resto de la clase: ¿Son similares los patios en Estados Unidos y en Andalucía? ¿Cuáles son las diferencias?

INVESTIGACIÓN B: ¿Para qué trabajamos?

> **Antes de ver el video.** Ordena del 1-6 (1 = **más importante**, 6 = menos **importante**) las siguientes ideas según tu opinión. Luego, compara tus respuestas con un compañero.

___ ganar un buen salario   ___ trabajar más de ocho horas

___ disfrutar de la familia   ___ echar una siesta

___ salir con los amigos   ___ practicar deportes

Vocabulario útil
ambiente *environment*
alberca/ *swimming pool*
piscina

> **El video.** Ordena las siguientes actividades sobre el tiempo libre según aparecen en el video.

  _4_ **a.** Dedícate a un pasatiempo.   _3_ **d.** Disfruta con la familia.

  _1_ **b.** Practica algún deporte.   _2_ **e.** Pásalo bien con los amigos.

> **Después de ver el video.** En parejas, responde a la siguiente pregunta: ¿Qué le sugieres a una persona que tiene mucho estrés a causa del trabajo? Hagan una lista de sugerencias usando mandatos informales, por ejemplo: Sal con los amigos y descansa más.

TEACHING TIP:
Information gap activities help develop students' interpersonal communication skills. Although they are not completely spontaneous, they do encourage the exchanging of information as well as the negotiation of meaning.

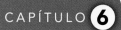 **Retrato de la clase Checklist**

You should have recorded information in your **Retrato de la clase** in conjunction with the following activities:

WILEY
PLUS

TESTING PROGRAM:
You will find a complete testing program for use with *¡Vívelo!* in *WileyPLUS*.

- [ ] **6A.12 ¿Cómo es la casa de tu compañero/a?**
- [ ] **6A.13 Lo más esencial**
- [ ] **6A.22 Más breves**
- [ ] **6A.29 Para ti la verdad es...**
- [ ] **6A.34 ¿Cómo refleja tu casa tu cultura?**

- [ ] **6B.13 ¿Cierto o falso?**
- [ ] **6B.15 Los pasatiempos favoritos de los compañeros**
- [ ] **6B.16 Un día perfecto**
- [ ] **6B.31 ¿Tú vives para trabajar o trabajas para vivir?**
- [ ] **6B.32 ¿Y los hispanos?**

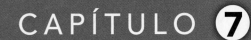

El arte y lo objetivo

¿Cómo se describe una obra de arte?

In this Investigación you will learn:

▶ How to describe the people and objects in a piece of art

▶ How to express reflexive and reciprocal actions

▶ About a variety of classical and contemporary Hispanic artists

▶ How to make comparisons among artists and their work

¿Cómo se puede describir una obra de arte?

You can describe the people and the scene in the work of art.	¿Quiénes son las personas? ¿Es hombre, mujer, niño? ¿Dónde están las personas? ¿En una plaza? ¿En un hospital? ¿En un hotel?
You can describe the objects in a work of art.	¿Qué hay en el cuadro (*painting*)? ¿Un autobús? ¿Una banana? ¿Un televisor?
You can describe what the people and objects are like.	¿Cómo se visten las personas? ¿Llevan ropa elegante? ¿Llevan ropa de colores oscuros o brillantes? ¿Qué apariencia tiene la persona en el cuadro? ¿Es rubia?
You can express what is going on in the work of art.	Muchos artistas se pintan. Estas pinturas son autorretratos. En algunos casos, los artistas que se conocen se pintan los unos a los otros. Por ejemplo, Diego Rivera pintó a Frida Kahlo y Frida pintó a Diego.

Adelante

¡Ya lo sabes! Para hablar de un cuadro

la apariencia	abstracto/a	captar
el/la artista	artificial	considerar
la catedral	brillante	observar
el cigarro	plástico/a	reflexionar
el color	real	representar
la expresión	sensual	
la figura	serio/a	
la forma		
la galería de arte		
la imagen		
el/la pintor/a		
las proporciones		
la realidad		
el torso		

7A.1 **¿A qué categoría pertenece?** En parejas, creen una tabla como la que aparece en la página 305 y escriban las palabras de *Adelante* en las categorías correspondientes según el modelo. Luego, comprueben sus respuestas con otros tres compañeros.

Las acciones	Las cosas/los conceptos	Los lugares	Las palabras descriptivas
representar	la apariencia	la catedral	artificial

7A.2 Definiciones. Escucha las definiciones y empareja cada definición con la palabra que corresponde según el modelo. Luego comprueba tus respuestas con la clase. **¡Ojo!** No se usan todas las palabras.

_b_ **1.**
_c_ **2.**
_d_ **3.**
_h_ **4.**
_i_ **5.**
_f_ **6.**
_a_ **7.**
_e_ **8.**

a. reflexionar
b. serio
c. la galería
d. el cigarro
e. la forma
f. el plástico
g. la imagen
h. observar
i. las proporciones
j. brillante

7A.3 Verifica el significado. Escoge una de las palabras de la lista de *Adelante* para completar cada una de las oraciones a continuación. Luego, comprueba tus respuestas con la clase.

1. El __torso__ es la parte central del cuerpo *(body)* humano.
2. El __color__ de la noche es negro.
3. El círculo, el triángulo y el rectángulo son ejemplos de __formas__ geométricas.
4. Westminster Abbey es una __catedral__.
5. Jennifer López es muy __sensual__.
6. Una persona __seria__ generalmente es responsable.
7. Los astrónomos __observan__ las estrellas para estudiar el universo.
8. Hay muy pocas cosas auténticas hoy en día porque hay muchas cosas __artificiales__.
9. Para ver y comprar diferentes tipos de obras *(works)* de arte, puedes ir a una __galería__.
10. El arte abstracto no __representa__ la realidad.

7A.4 ¡A adivinar! Túrnate con un/a compañero/a para definir una palabra de la lista de *Adelante*. Pueden usar oraciones en español, asociaciones, nombres o gestos, pero no pueden usar inglés. Cuenten las palabras que adivinan correctamente para ver qué pareja fue la más rápida y exitosa de la clase.

Modelo: E1: *Usamos esta palabra para describir a la famosa Marilyn Monroe.*
E2: *sensual*

7A.1 SUGGESTION: If you want to save time, you can adapt this activity into an aural one by writing the categories on the board and having students close their textbooks. Then, read the words aloud and students can indicate the appropriate category for each word.

7A.2 AUDIO SCRIPT: 1. Es lo opuesto de cómico. 2. Es un lugar donde se venden piezas originales de varias expresiones artísticas como pinturas, esculturas y artesanías. 3. Tabaco enrollado que tiene nicotina y se fuma. Es malo para la salud porque causa cáncer. 4. Es la acción de mirar con atención. 5. Es la relación de dimensión, peso o volumen entre dos objetos diferentes o entre partes de un objeto. 6. Es un material sintético que es fácil de modelar. 7. Es la acción de pensar o meditar sobre una cosa, 8. Es la apariencia exterior de un objeto.

7A.3 TEACHING TIP: Before going over the answers as a class, have students go over their answers with a partner. If they have different answers, have them explain why they came up with what they did. Then, go over the answers with the entire class.

7A.4 ORIENTATION: Circumlocution, or describing a word without stating it, is an excellent skill for students to begin developing at these early stages. Remind students that they may not use sentences that have been used in previous activities.

Fernando Botero

Fernando Botero es un pintor y escultor colombiano. Es famoso por los colores intensos de sus pinturas, por la suspensión del movimiento en sus imágenes y, especialmente, por las redondas (round) y corpulentas figuras que aparecen en sus pinturas. Generalmente él pinta encantadoras (pleasant) escenas de celebraciones y de la vida diaria. Esta pintura se titula Frank Lloyd con su familia en Paradise Island (1972), y es un ejemplo de cómo Botero combina los colores y representa figuras grandes y redondas hasta la obesidad, lo que comúnmente se interpreta como símbolo de una vida rica y abundante.

Frank Lloyd con su familia en Paradise Island (1972).

7A.5 **¿Quién es Fernando Botero?** Basándote en la lectura de arriba, escucha los enunciados sobre Fernando Botero para determinar si lo que dice cada uno es **cierto** o **falso.** Luego, corrige los enunciados falsos.

	Cierto	Falso	
1.	☐	☑	(de Colombia)
2.	☑	☐	
3.	☑	☐	
4.	☐	☑	(de celebraciones y de la vida diaria)

 ¡Conéctate!

Conduct a Google search of Fernando Botero for additional samples of his work. Is the description of his art an accurate one based on the artwork you found? What additional descriptions would you include for a more accurate portrayal of his artwork?

7A.6 **¡Qué divinos son los cuadros de Botero!**   Ahora, lee las siguientes descripciones del cuadro de Botero para decidir si cada enunciado es **cierto** o **falso**. Si es falso, tacha *(cross out)* o inserta "no" para que sea cierto. Compara y comprueba tus respuestas con las de un/a compañero/a.

	Cierto	Falso
1. Botero no usa *el color negro* en sus cuadros.	☐	☑
2. Las personas llevan *una expresión sensual*.	☐	☑
3. Hay muchas *formas abstractas* en el cuadro.	☐	☑
4. No hay *palmas* en el cuadro.	☐	☑
5. La niña tiene *un bebé* (una muñeca).	☑	☐
6. El hombre no tiene *un cigarro*.	☐	☑
7. La expresión de la mujer *es seria*.	☐	☑
8. El hombre *observa* a su esposa.	☐	☑
9. El hombre lleva *jeans*.	☐	☑
10. Las personas no *expresan* emoción.	☑	☐

7A.6 ANSWERS: 1. no usa, 2. *no* llevan, 3. *no* hay, 4. no hay, 6. no tiene, 7. *no* es seria, 8. *no* observa, 9. *no* lleva

7A.6 RECYCLING: Most of the vocabulary items in these sentences are recycled from previous chapters or are cognates. The purpose of the exercise is to ensure students examine the painting carefully. You may want to have students notice that the word for "doll" in this context is *muñeca*. In the context of the next *Palabras clave* section, it is presented and practiced as "wrist."

◠ Bien dicho

El sonido de la *t*

There are two things to remember about the pronunciation of **t** in Spanish. First, it is pronounced with the front part of the tongue held firmly against the bottom edge of the top teeth. This contrasts with its pronunciation in English where the front part of the tongue is held more loosely against the hard ridge immediately behind the top teeth. Pronouncing the Spanish **t** with your tongue in this position might lead to some misunderstanding because it could be interpreted as **r**. The second thing to remember is that, as we saw with **p** in *Investigación 6B*, there is no aspiration (puff of air) with **t** in Spanish. To avoid/reduce aspiration, your tongue should be more tense than when pronouncing the sound in English. Another strategy may be to think of how you pronounce **t** when preceded by **s** in English (e.g., start, store, step) and apply that pronunciation to all cases of **t** in Spanish.

7A.7 **Escucha e indica.**   Escucha las siguientes palabras. Indica qué palabra percibes.

1.	☐ foto	☑ foro
2.	☑ moto	☐ moro
3.	☑ flotes	☐ flores
4.	☐ mito	☑ miro
5.	☐ rato	☑ raro
6.	☑ nota	☐ Nora

7A.7 AUDIO SCRIPT: 1. foro, 2. moto, 3. flotes, 4. miro, 5. raro, 6. nota

7A.8 **Les toca a ustedes.**   Túrnate con un/a compañero/a para leer las siguientes oraciones. Intercambien papeles para que cada uno *(each one)* tenga la oportunidad de pronunciar todas las oraciones. Traten de *(Try to)* reducir o eliminar, tanto como les sea posible, la aspiración de la *t*.

1. El plástico es un material artificial muy útil.

2. Tito Puente también tocaba la trompeta.

3. Fernando Botero es un artista latinoamericano notable.

4. Es importante estirarse para no torcerse el tobillo.

5. El bigote, las pestañas y la frente son partes del rostro.

6. El señor Alberto Torres Treviño es alto y corpulento.

7. El deporte del fútbol consiste en patear el balón sin tocarlo con la mano.

8. El museo de arte se encuentra enfrente de la catedral.

7A.8 SUGGESTION: You may want to have students hold a piece of paper in front of their mouths to check for degree of aspiration.

Palabras clave 1 Las partes del cuerpo

Estas fotos son de los famosos artistas hispanos, Diego Rivera y Frida Kahlo, de México, Fernando Botero, de Colombia y Carmen Lomas Garza, de Estados Unidos.

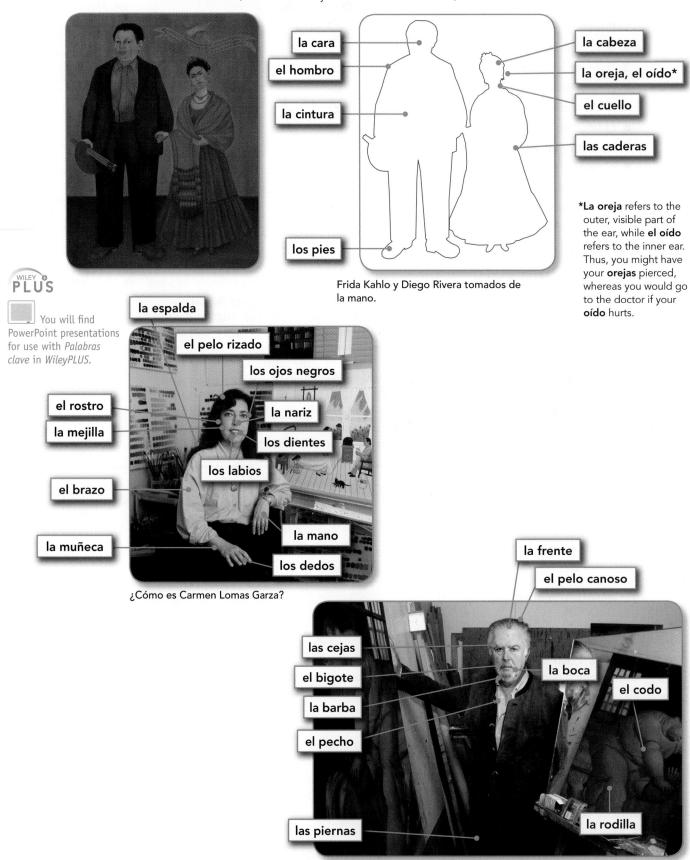

la cara
el hombro
la cintura
los pies

la cabeza
la oreja, el oído*
el cuello
las caderas

Frida Kahlo y Diego Rivera tomados de la mano.

*La oreja refers to the outer, visible part of the ear, while el oído refers to the inner ear. Thus, you might have your orejas pierced, whereas you would go to the doctor if your oído hurts.

la espalda
el pelo rizado
los ojos negros
el rostro
la mejilla
la nariz
los dientes
los labios
el brazo
la muñeca
la mano
los dedos

¿Cómo es Carmen Lomas Garza?

la frente
el pelo canoso
las cejas
el bigote
la barba
el pecho
la boca
el codo
la rodilla
las piernas

¿Cómo es Fernando Botero?

7A.9 ¡A confirmar!

Paso 1: Túrnate con un/a compañero/a para decir las palabras de la lista a continuación e indicar con una ✓ si están ilustradas en las fotos de los artistas. Pongan una X al lado de las palabras que no tienen ilustración.

El cuerpo

✓ la cabeza	✓ la cara	✓ el rostro	✓ la nariz
✓ las piernas	✓ los pies	✓ el bigote	✓ la barba
✓ el hombro	✓ los labios	✓ las manos	✓ la espalda
✓ los brazos	X las pestañas	✓ los ojos	✓ el pelo
✓ la muñeca	✓ la cintura	✓ la rodilla	✓ el cuello
X el corazón	✓ el codo	✓ las cejas	✓ la frente
✓ las caderas	✓ las orejas	✓ la mejilla	✓ los dientes

Paso 2: Miren cuidadosamente estas definiciones de las partes del cuerpo que no aparecen el las fotos de los artistas. Complétenlas con la parte del cuerpo correspondiente.

1. El _____ es un órgano importante en el pecho. Late *(it beats)* para hacer circular la sangre *(blood)*.

2. Las _____ son como pequeños pelos alrededor de los ojos, que sirven para protegerlos del polvo *(dust)*, entre otras cosas.

7A.10 Asociaciones.

Primero, lee la lista de las partes del cuerpo a continuación. Luego, vas a escuchar varias prendas de ropa o accesorios. Empareja cada prenda con la parte del cuerpo que corresponde lógicamente según el modelo.

_a_ 1.		**a.**	los ojos
_b_ 2.		**b.**	las piernas
_c_ 3.		**c.**	los pies
_f_ 4.		**d.**	la cintura
_g_ 5.		**e.**	las orejas
_d_ 6.		**f.**	el cuello
_e_ 7.		**g.**	los hombros
_h_ 8.		**h.**	los dedos de la mano

7A.11 Ver y responder.

En parejas, seleccionen la tarjeta A aquí o B en la página 310. Luego, léanse el uno al otro los enunciados de las tarjetas para completar la tabla sobre los cuadros de Diego Rivera, Frida Kahlo, Fernando Botero y Carmen Lomas Garza. Marquen sus respuestas con ✓ según el modelo en la página 310.

> **A**
>
> 2. Muestra *(Shows)* los dientes.
>
> 4. Muestra las piernas y rodillas más claramente.
>
> 6. Tiene una cintura grande.
>
> 8. Lleva un rebozo sobre los hombros.

7A.9 EXTENSION ACTIVITY: Encourage students to make flash cards. On one side, they can draw the body part and on the other, the word in Spanish. They can use these cards to review the vocabulary. You can also play *Señala la parte del cuerpo* by calling out body parts in Spanish and having students close their eyes and then point to the body part. This can serve as a warm-up at the beginning of a class too.

7A.9 TEACHING TIP: Have students focus their attention on linguistic cues in the sentences in *Paso 2* to help them associate the right words with their descriptions (1. el corazón, 2. las pestañas).

7A.10 AUDIO SCRIPT: 1. los lentes, 2. los pantalones, 3. los zapatos, 4. el collar, 5. el rebozo, 6. el cinturón, 7. los aretes/los pendientes, 8. los anillos

7A.10 RECYCLING: This activity recycles clothing vocabulary.

7A.11 INSTRUCTOR'S RESOURCES: You will find reproducible cards for Activity 7A.11 in your Instructor's Resources.

7A.11 TEACHING TIP: Before doing this activity, have students look over the photos of the artists to be described.

	Diego Rivera	Frida Kahlo	Fernando Botero	Carmen Lomas Garza
1.			✓	
2.				✓
3.			✓	
4.			✓	
5.				✓
6.	✓			
7.			✓	
8.		✓		

7A.12 TEACHING TIP: Make sure to explain that while several answers might be correct, one was the most popular among Mexican citizens surveyed. Before beginning activity 7A-12 you might want to survey the class in order to have the most popular answers to the question, then have students compare their answers to the most popular answer of the whole class.

7A.12 ¿Y tú qué dices? *Cien mexicanos dijeron (One Hundred Mexicans Said)* es un programa de televisión mexicano en el que el anfitrión *(host)* hace preguntas y los participantes tratan de adivinar las respuestas más populares según encuestas *(surveys)* hechas a mexicanos. En grupos de tres, un/a estudiante debe leer las preguntas y los otros dos deben responder. Luego, comprueben sus respuestas con las que les dé el/la profesor/a, para ver qué grupo adivinó correctamente.

1. ¿Cuál es la parte de tu cuerpo que menos te gusta?

☑ los pies　　　　☐ las orejas

☐ la nariz　　　　☐ las manos

2. ¿Qué característica física debe tener un extraterrestre?

☐ la nariz larga　　☐ unas antenas

☐ el pelo largo　　☑ los ojos grandes

3. Nombra una parte del cuerpo que tenemos en pares.

☐ los ojos　　　　☐ los labios

☑ las manos　　　☐ las orejas

4. Nombra la parte del cuerpo que necesitamos cubrir cuando hace frío.

☐ los hombros　　☑ la cabeza

☐ las manos　　　☐ los pies

5. Especifica una parte del cuerpo donde es común recibir un beso.

☐ el cuello　　　☑ la boca

☐ la mejilla　　　☐ la mano

¿Cuántas de tus respuestas son las mismas que las respuestas más populares entre los mexicanos?

Palabras clave 2 Características físicas

El cabello*

canoso

lacio

rubio

fino

suelto

negro

calvo

grueso

corto

largo

rizado

pelirrojo

castaño

*Note: **El cabello** refers specifically to the hair on someone's head; **el pelo** is a more general word for *hair*. **Pelirrojo/a** is the equivalent of *redhead* in English.

Otras características físicas

grande	Una cosa enorme o vasta es grande.
pequeño/a	Frida Kahlo no es grande. Es una mujer pequeña.
alto/a	Diego Rivera es alto.
bajo/a	Frida es baja.
anciano/a	Una persona anciana tiene muchos años.
joven	Una persona joven tiene pocos años.
gordo/a	Las personas corpulentas y obesas son gordas.
delgado/a	Una persona delgada no es gorda.
de estatura mediana	Una persona de estatura mediana no es ni alta ni baja.

Estados físicos

estar parado *(to be standing up)*	Frank Lloyd y su esposa están parados.
estar sentado *(to be sitting down)*	La bebé Wright está sentada.
estar acostado *(to be in lying down)*	Cuando dormimos estamos acostados.

7A.13 ¿Con qué o con quién asociamos estas características? Trabaja con un/a compañero/a. Seleccionen una de las tarjetas A o B. Mientras tu compañero/a lee el nombre o la descripción de una persona u objeto, empareja la persona u objeto con el adjetivo o la frase correspondiente. Comprueba tus respuestas con tu compañero/a.

A

Paso 1: Listen to the names or descriptions read by your partner and match each person or object to the appropriate adjective or phrase.

a	**1.** calvo		c	**5.** anciano
g	**2.** estar acostado		f	**6.** alta
h	**3.** el pelo largo		b	**7.** gordo
e	**4.** pequeño		d	**8.** estar paradas

Paso 2: Read these names or descriptions to your partner.

- **a.** una mujer de 50 años
- **b.** una silla
- **c.** *Little Orphan Annie*
- **d.** un elefante
- **e.** una mini-falda
- **f.** muchos escandinavos
- **g.** una gimnasta
- **h.** los lentes

B

Paso 1: Read these names or descriptions to your partner

- **a.** Homer Simpson
- **b.** Santa Claus
- **c.** un hombre de cien años
- **d.** estar de pie
- **e.** un insecto
- **f.** una jugadora de básquetbol
- **g.** la cama
- **h.** los hippies

Paso 2: Listen to the names or descriptions read by your partner and match each person or object to the appropriate adjective or phrase.

e	**1.** corta		a	**5.** madura
c	**2.** el pelo rizado		b	**6.** estar sentada
d	**3.** grande		g	**7.** baja
h	**4.** corto de vista		f	**8.** el pelo rubio

7A.14 ¿En quién o en qué piensas? En la tabla de abajo, completa la columna de "Yo", con una persona, personaje u objeto que asocies con el adjetivo o frase de la columna de la izquierda. Entrevista a dos compañeros y anota sus respuestas. Informa a la clase sobre las semejanzas y diferencias. Basándote en las respuestas, indica qué conclusiones generales pueden hacerse en tu **Retrato de la clase.**

Modelo: E1: *¿Con quién asocias el pelo rizado?*
E2: *Con Alicia Keys, Andie MacDowell y Nicole Kidman.*

	Yo	Compañero/a de clase 1	Compañero/a de clase 2
calvo			
pelo rubio			
pelo largo y suelto			
pelo lacio			

Retrato de la clase: La mayoría de la clase dice nombres de (actores, cantantes, figuras históricas, políticos, estudiantes, atletas) en sus respuestas. Muchos estudiantes nombran a ____, ____ y ____ en sus ejemplos.

EXPRESIONES ÚTILES

Para hablar de los cuadros

al fondo	in the background
en el primer plano	in the foreground
en la parte superior	in/at the top
en la parte inferior	in/at the bottom

7A.15 Los autorretratos de Juan O'Gorman.

Paso 1: Miren el cuadro a continuación. Luego, comenten sobre los colores, objetos y personas del cuadro.

> Modelo: *Hay un cuadro de Juan O'Gorman en el centro del cuadro.*

Paso 2: Con un/a compañero/a, lean la descripción del cuadro y completen cada oración con la palabra que tenga sentido *(makes sense)* según lo que vean en el cuadro. Luego, comprueben sus respuestas con la clase.

En la parte _____superior_____ (1. superior/inferior) del cuadro hay una luna y un sol. _____Encima_____ (2. Detrás/Encima) del hombro de O'Gorman hay un demonio rojo. En la esquina _____derecha_____ (3. izquierda/derecha) y en la parte _____inferior_____ (4. superior/ inferior/central) del cuadro, una mano con un pincel *(paintbrush)* pinta a O'Gorman sentado. _____Enfrente_____ (5. Enfrente/Detrás) del cuadro de O'Gorman aparece O'Gorman sentado en una silla. _____Al lado_____ (6. Al lado/Debajo/Encima) del O'Gorman sentado hay otro cuadro en el que vemos su reflejo. _____Enfrente_____ (7. Al fondo/Enfrente/Encima) del cuadro a la derecha hay un pájaro amarillo. En la esquina *(corner)* y _____en la parte inferior_____ (8. en la parte inferior/al fondo) del cuadro hay una raqueta de tenis.

O'Gorman pintó un mural gigantesco en un edificio de la Universidad Nacional Autónoma en la Ciudad de México.

7A.16 ¡Ahora tú eres el artista!

Paso 1: Vas a escuchar una descripción del retrato de una persona. En una hoja de papel, dibuja el retrato basándote en la descripción. Luego, comprueba que tu dibujo refleje la descripción comparándolo con el dibujo de un/a compañero/a. Clarifica cualquier diferencia con tu profesor/a.

Paso 2: Ahora, vas a diseñar un retrato. Una vez que lo hayas completado, descríbelo a un/a compañero/a, para que lo dibuje de acuerdo a tu descripción y haz tú un dibujo de la descripción de tu compañero/a. Luego, comparen sus dibujos para ver si reflejan las descripciones.

7A.16 AUDIO SCRIPT: PASO 1. La figura es de un hombre viejo de estatura alta. Está parado. Tiene pelo canoso y es calvo excepto en los lados donde tiene pelo rizado y largo. Tiene cejas gruesas, ojos grandes, labios pequeños y una nariz delgada. Tiene bigote canoso y una barba corta. El cuello del hombre es grueso.

7A.16 SUGGESTION: PASO 2. This would be an ideal task to require students to complete over the phone, each in their respective residence. They could bring their drawings and compare them at the beginning of class.

7A.15 TEACHING TIP: As students describe things and colors in the painting, write them on the board in Spanish.

7A.15 RECYCLING: This activity recycles expressing location.

7A.15 TEACHING TIP: Have students share their answers with a partner, explaining why they chose the answers they did, and clarifying any disagreements. Then, go over the answers as a large group.

Palabras clave 3 Una clase de arte

fruncir

arrodillarse

oler

agarrar

chupar

pegar

7A.17 ANSWERS:
Answers will vary. 1. los pies/las piernas, 2. las cejas, 3. la boca/los labios, 4. los pies/las piernas, 5. la nariz, 6. las manos, 7. los hombros, 8. los brazos, las manos, los pies

7A.17 EXTENSION ACTIVITY: This game is called *No mires.* Have students work with a partner. Establish who is person A and who is person B. Have person B close their eyes or turn their back to the board. On the board, write down three parts of the body (e.g. *los hombros, el estómago, las manos*). Person A needs to get person B to say those words by making statements like those in activity 7A.18 (e.g. *Es posible...*).

7A.17 ¿Con qué parte del cuerpo? ¿Qué parte del cuerpo se usa más con estos verbos? Con un/a compañero/a decidan qué partes del cuerpo les permiten ejecutar las siguientes acciones. Luego, comparen sus respuestas con las de otra pareja de estudiantes para ver posibilidades que no habían considerado.

1. Es posible patear con… *los pies / las piernas*

2. Es posible fruncir…

3. Es posible chupar con…

4. Es posible trotar con…

5. Es posible oler perfume con…

6. Es posible agarrar con…

7. Es posible encoger…

8. Es posible tirar con…

www **¡Conéctate!**
Check out gestures that could be used to express the meaning of verbs by googling American Sign Language. Share three that you find relevant with the class. They can try to guess the verb in Spanish.

patear · torcerse · empujar · rodear · estirar · tirar · encogerse de hombros · trotar

7A.18 Acción y reacción. Lee las oraciones de a–f. Luego, vas a escuchar la descripción de varias situaciones. Para cada situación, selecciona la reacción más lógica. Luego, comprueba tus respuestas con la clase.

7A.18 AUDIO SCRIPT:
1. Una estudiante sale para la clase de español. 2. No gana la lotería. 3. Patean la pelota. 4. No han sacado la basura esta semana. 5. Alguien empuja a una persona. 6. Los niños saltan en los muebles.

_c_ **1.**   **a.** Pueden torcerse el tobillo (ankle).

_f_ **2.**   **b.** Juegan al fútbol.

_b_ **3.**   **c.** Agarra su mochila con su libro y su cuaderno.

_d_ **4.**   **d.** El olor es horrible.

_e_ **5.**   **e.** Frunce las cejas.

_a_ **6.**   **f.** Se encoge de hombros.

7A.19 ¡A escribir y leer!   Escribe dos oraciones usando uno de los verbos a continuación. Una de las oraciones debe ser obviamente cierta y la otra obviamente falsa. Lee una de las oraciones a la clase para que digan **cierto** o **falso: rodear, empujar, estirar, trotar.**

¡Atención!

¡ATENCIÓN!: Ask students to identify the meaning of the false cognates as used in each sample sentence.

Capa	is not cap. It refers to a *cloak* or *cape*. It can also mean *layer,* as in the ozone layer, **la capa ozono.** A *cap* is **una gorra.**
	En el cuadro de Botero, el niño de Frank Lloyd no lleva una gorra blanca. Súperman y Batman usan capas. Las emisiones de dióxido de carbono causan muchos problemas en la capa de ozono.
Largo	is not large. It means *long* or *lengthy.* The word **alargado** means *elongated* as in **cara alargada** (*elongated face*).
	Pinocchio tiene una nariz muy larga. Las figuras que pinta El Greco son muy alargadas.
Anciano/a	is a synonym of **viejo/a,** which means *old.* The word *ancient* in Spanish is **antiguo,** or **anticuado.** In Spanish, **anciano** is the preferred term to refer to an elderly person.
	Los pintores siempre pintan a las abuelitas ancianas sentadas en una silla. Estas ruinas de la época romana son muy antiguas. Debido a (*due to*) la nueva tecnología, esta máquina está muy anticuada.
Actual	does not mean actual. It means *present, current* or *modern.* **Actualmente** is the corresponding adverb. Something *actual,* in the sense of *real,* in Spanish is **verdadero/a** or **real.** *Actually* in English is **en realidad** in Spanish.
	Actualmente, la definición de arte es mucho más amplia que en la Edad Media. Uno de los pintores actuales más famosos es Botero. En realidad, mi pintora favorita es abstracta y no le gusta ilustrar cosas verdaderas o reales.

7A.20 FOLLOW-UP: After going over the answers, ask the class questions like *¿Están a favor o en contra de la censura del arte que pueda ser ofensivo para otros? ¿Por qué?* Give students time to think of their responses. They should be able to begin defending their opinion on a very basic level.

7A.20 ¿Estás de acuerdo?   Lee las siguientes oraciones y completa los espacios en blanco con las palabras apropiadas de la lista. Luego, indica si estás de acuerdo con el enunciado o no. Comprueba tus respuestas con las de un/a compañero/a y luego con toda la clase. Averigua si hay enunciados con los que la mayoría de la clase no estuvo de acuerdo.

actualmente	largos	capa	realidad
verdadero	largas	verdadera	capas

¿Estás de acuerdo?

Sí	No	
☐	☐	**1.** En los cuadros del lejano Oeste *(Far West)* los vestidos de las mujeres siempre son _____.
☐	☐	**2.** En las fotos de Drácula, él siempre lleva una _____ larga y negra.
☐	☐	**3.** El _____ artista está en contra (*against*) de la censura de cualquier tipo de arte.
☐	☐	**4.** En _____, los vampiros no existen.
☐	☐	**5.** _____ hay muchas personas en el planeta y por eso existe tanta contaminación del agua y del aire.

Estructuras clave 1 Reflexive and reciprocal constructions

WILEY
PLUS
Go to *WileyPLUS* and review the tutorial for this grammar point.

WILEY
PLUS

You will find PowerPoint presentations for use with *Estructuras clave* in WileyPLUS.

TEACHING TIP: You may want to point out that the reflexive pronouns for all but the third person are the same as direct and indirect object pronouns.

Something that someone does to or for himself or herself is called a *reflexive* action (the verb is *reflected* back on the subject). Any action that one can logically do to or for one's self can be expressed with a reflexive construction. Reflexive actions in Spanish are signaled by the use of reflexive pronouns. Compare these examples:

Lorena se baña.	*Lorena takes a bath.* (i.e. *She bathes herself.*)
Lorena baña al niño.	*Lorena bathes the baby.*

In the first example, Lorena is both the subject and the object of the action. She performs the action on herself, and this reflexive situation is signaled by the pronoun **se**. In the second example, Lorena is the subject while the baby is the object of the action. We might represent the relationship between subject, verb, and object in these two sentences as follows:

Lorena se baña.	☺ ⟵
Lorena baña al niño.	☺ ⟶ ☺

Verbs that are most frequently used reflexively are often signaled in text books with the addition of **–se** to the infinitive. Note the reflexive pronoun corresponding to each subject in the following examples using **vestirse** (*to get dressed,* i.e. *to dress one's self*).

(Yo) **me** visto.	(Nosotros/as) **nos** vestimos.
(Tú) **te** vistes.	(Vosotros/as) **os** vestís.
(Él/Ella/Usted) **se** viste.	(Ellos/Ellas/Ustedes) **se** visten.

Position of reflexive pronouns

Placement of reflexive pronouns follows the same pattern you learned for placement of direct and indirect object pronouns. That is, reflexive pronouns are placed before a conjugated verb. When a verb phrase is comprised of a conjugated verb and an infinitive, the reflexive pronoun may be attached to the infinitive or may precede the conjugated verb.

Necesito levantar**me** temprano.	**Me** necesito levantar temprano.
Preferimos acostar**nos** antes de las 9:00.	**Nos** preferimos acostar antes de las 9:00.

When using a direct object pronoun with a reflexive verb, the reflexive pronoun goes before the direct object pronoun.

Quiero lavar**me la cara**.	Quiero lavár**mela.** / **Me la** quiero lavar.
Deseo poner**me el sombrero**.	Deseo ponér**melo.** / **Me lo** deseo poner.

Note that when both the reflexive pronoun and the object pronoun are attached to an infinitive a written accent is needed to maintain the original stress of the verb.

7A.21 Conexión con el infinitivo. En la tercera columna, escribe el infinitivo de los siguientes verbos en español y agrega *(add)* –**se** al final si la acción señala una acción reflexiva. El primero está hecho como modelo. Luego, comprueba tus respuestas con dos compañeros de clase.

	Infinitivo en inglés	Infinitivo en español (with –**se** attached to indicate verb is used reflexively)		Infinitivo en inglés	Infinitivo en español (with –**se** attached to indicate verb is used reflexively)
1. Se estira.	to stretch (oneself)	*estirarse*	6. Se pone la gorra.	to put (something) on (oneself)	ponerse
2. Se viste.	to get dressed	vestirse	7. Se sienta.	to sit (oneself) down	sentarse
3. Se afeita.	to shave (oneself)	afeitarse	8. Se levanta.	to get (oneself) up	levantarse
4. Se pinta.	to paint oneself	pintarse	9. Se ducha.	to take a shower (to shower oneself)	ducharse
5. Se rodea de libros.	to surround oneself	rodearse	10. Se arrodilla.	to kneel (oneself) down	arrodillarse

Reciprocal actions

When an action is reflected back on a plural subject, the situation may be reflexive, e.g. the subjects perform the action on *themselves,* or it may be what is called a *reciprocal* action, wherein the subjects perform the action on *each other.* Look at how we might graphically represent the relationship between subject, verb, and object in the following situations.

Reflexive	Reciprocal
Nos levantamos.	Nos saludamos.
We get up. (i.e. *We get ourselves up.*) ☺☺ ⟵	*We greet each other.* ☺ ⟷ ☺ ☺☺ ⟷ ☺☺
Ellos se lavan las manos. *They wash their hands.* ☺☺ ⟵	Ellos se hablan por teléfono. *They talk to each other on the phone.* ☺ ⟷ ☺ ☺☺ ⟷ ☺☺

Just as any action that one can logically do to or for *oneself* may be expressed with a *reflexive* construction, any action that two or more people can logically do to or for *each other* may be expressed with a *reciprocal* construction.

TEACHING TIP: Read this together as a class. After going over it, have students explain the main idea to a partner. Elicit some responses from the group to see how well they understood the concept. Let them know that the activities to come will help practice this concept.

Ask the class if they can figure out the linguistic pattern in the sentences and the change in meaning triggered. Hopefully the students will note the *se* before a plural verb indicates that the action occurs reciprocally (to each other).

Acciones ordinarias	Acciones recíprocas	Acciones ordinarias	Acciones recíprocas
agarrar El chico agarra la tarjeta postal.	Ellos se agarran de la mano porque son buenos amigos.	**patear** La chica patea la pelota.	Los chicos se patean cuando practican el karate.
empujar La chica empuja la puerta.	Ellos se empujan.	**besar** El chico besa a su madre.	El marido y su esposa se besan.
abrazar La niña abraza a la muñeca.	Los hermanos se abrazan.	**pintar** Él pinta a la chica.	Ellos se pintan.

7A.22 La relación entre los objetos. Indica la relación entre el sujeto, el verbo y el objeto en las siguientes oraciones con el símbolo ☺ ↔ ☺ si la oración es recíproca (dos o más individuos realizando la acción el uno al otro), o el símbolo ☺ → si el sujeto está realizando la acción a alguien o algo más (la oración tiene un objeto directo). Identifica las oraciones que no son ni recíprocas ni tienen objeto directo con el símbolo Ø. Luego, comprueba tus respuestas con la clase.

	☺ ↔ ☺	☺ →	Ø
1. Romeo mira a Julieta.	☐	☑	☐
2. Los artistas contemporáneos se conocen.	☑	☐	☐
3. Diego besa a Frida.	☐	☑	☐
4. Salvador Dalí llama a Gala.	☐	☑	☐
5. Botero saluda a O'Gorman.	☐	☑	☐
6. Frank Lloyd y su esposa no se abrazan.	☑	☐	☐
7. Los pintores se aprecian.	☑	☐	☐
8. Velázquez pinta muy bien.	☐	☐	☑

7A.23 Jugar con datos triviales. Indica, con un/a compañero/a, si los siguientes hechos son lógicos o ciertos, o ilógicos y probablemente falsos.

Lógico	Ilógico	
☑	☐	**1.** Casarse joven ya no es tan común como antes.
☑	☐	**2.** Hay muchos pintores famosos que se pintan en sus cuadros.
☑	☐	**3.** Salma Hayek y Jennifer López se llaman por teléfono.
☐	☑	**4.** Velázquez y Botero se conocen personalmente.
☑	☐	**5.** Al Gore se preocupa por la contaminación del mundo.
☑	☐	**6.** George W. y Jeb Bush se ayudan políticamente.

7A.24 Sopa de tareas.

Paso 1: Indica la relación entre sujeto, verbo y objeto en los siguientes dibujos con los símbolos: ☺ → si la acción es del sujeto hacia un objeto, ☺ ↔ ☺ si la acción es ejecutada recíprocamente por dos o más individuos unos a otros o ☺ ← si la acción es ejecutada por una persona hacia sí misma *(himself/herself).*

Paso 2: Empareja la oración con el dibujo correspondiente. El primero está hecho como modelo. Luego, comprueba tus respuestas con la clase.

☺ → _d_ **1.** Se baña.	☺ ↔ ☺ _e_ **5.** Se pintan.
☺ → _c_ **2.** Levanta al niño.	☺ ← _f_ **6.** Se afeita.
☺ ← _b_ **3.** Se levanta de la silla.	☺ → _g_ **7.** Afeita a su abuelo.
☺ → _a_ **4.** Baña al bebé.	☺ ↔ ☺ _h_ **8.** Se saludan.

a. b. c. d. e. f. g. h.

7A.25 Dictado y espectáculo. Escucha las oraciones y representa el significado de los verbos con el símbolo ☺ ← o ☺ ←→ ☺ para comprobar tu comprensión. Si el caso puede ser tanto recíproco como reflexivo, usa los dos símbolos. Luego, comparte tus dibujos con otros compañeros de clase.

1. _____ ☺ ← _____
2. _____ ☺ ←→ ☺ _____
3. _____ ☺ ←→ ☺ _____
4. _____ ☺ ← _____
5. _____ ☺ ← _____
6. _____ ☺ ← , ☺ ←→ ☺ _____
7. _____ ☺ ← _____
8. _____ ☺ ← _____

7A.25 AUDIO SCRIPT: 1. Se pone los zapatos. 2. Se miran. 3. Se saludan. 4. Se sienta. 5. Se levantan. 6. Se mira en el espejo. 7. Se pinta. 8. Se encogen de hombros.

7A.25 TEACHING TIP: Make salient to students that two interpretations can be used with a *se* before some plural verbs (reciprocally or two reflexive actions occurring simultaneously), but other verbs, such as *encogerse* are inherently reflexive and would be difficult to interpret as reciprocal actions. The context will determine which meaning is the appropriate one.

7A.26 ¿Qué haces?

Paso 1: Contesta las siguientes preguntas sobre ti mismo/a. Escoge la opción que te corresponda o da una respuesta original.

1. ¿Cuándo te vistes por la mañana?
   Me visto antes de desayunar. / Me visto después de desayunar.

2. ¿Te lavas el pelo diariamente?
   Sí, me lo lavo diariamente. / Me lo lavo cada tres días. / (¿Otro?)

3. ¿Te afeitas?
   Sí, me afeito la cara. / Sí, me afeito las piernas. / No, no me afeito nada.

4. ¿Te pones perfume?
   A veces me lo pongo. / Siempre me lo pongo. / Nunca me lo pongo.

5. ¿En que cuarto te quitas los zapatos?
   Me los quito en mi recámara. / Me los quito en el corredor. / (¿Otro?)

6. ¿A qué hora te acuestas por la noche?
   Me acuesto a las…

Paso 2: Ahora, usa las preguntas para entrevistar a un/a compañero/a de clase y apunta sus respuestas en el **Retrato de la clase.**

Retrato de la clase: Mi compañero de clase _____ se viste antes de desayunar, se lava el pelo diariamente, se afeita la cara, nunca se pone perfume, se quita los zapatos antes de entrar a la casa y se acuesta a las 11:00 de la noche.

Enlaces

through; by means of	**A través de** las expresiones de la cara, se revela la emoción verdadera de la persona.
in addition to	**Además de** ser escultor, da Vinci también pinta.
on the other hand	El famoso pintor español El Greco no es surrealista. **Por otro lado,** tampoco es realista.

7A.27 EXTENSION ACTIVITY: Based on what students have learned about the artists they have studied, have them write sentences using these new *Enlaces*.

7A.27 Enlaces. Con un/a compañero/a, conecten las ideas de las oraciones y los párrafos de abajo usando la expresión apropiada. Luego, comprueben tus respuestas con la clase.

1. _Además de_ pintar celebraciones, a Botero también le gusta pintar cosas de la vida cotidiana *(daily life)*.

2. _A través de_ sus pinturas, O'Gorman presenta las luchas sociales que son parte de la historia política mexicana.

3. A Botero le encanta pintar. _Por otro lado_, también se dedica a hacer esculturas.

7A.28 A otro contexto.

Paso 1: ¿Cuántos pintores conoces? En parejas, hagan una lista de los pintores estadounidenses que conozcan. Luego, compartan su lista con la clase, para ver cuántos artistas diferentes puede nombrar la clase. Ahora, hagan una lista de todos los actores de cine que conozcan y compartan esos nombres con la clase. ¿Cuál es la más larga? ¿Cómo explican la diferencia?

Posibles interpretaciones:

☐ Nos gusta más el arte que el cine.

☐ Pasamos más tiempo mirando películas que mirando arte.

☐ Nunca vamos a los museos.

☐ No hay suficientes opciones para estudiar arte en las escuelas públicas.

☐ Es necesario ir a una ciudad grande para visitar un buen museo.

☐ Otras posibilidades: _____

Paso 2: Pintores estadounidenses: ¿Jackson Pollock, Norman Rockwell o Georgia O'Keeffe? Después de revisar *(review)* las palabras de la tabla, lean en grupos de tres la descripción del pintor que aparece abajo. Si conocen el pintor cuyo *(whose)* trabajo se describe no lo digan todavía *(yet)*. Luego, busquen ejemplos de cuadros de Jackson Pollock, Norman Rockwell y Georgia O'Keeffe en la Internet para determinar qué artista corresponde a la descripción. ¿Cómo lo saben?

Vocabulario clave	
Antónimos (opuestos)	**Sinónimos (similares)**
realista ≠ idealista	diseñar = crear
normal ≠ espectacular	cotidiano = común
tradicional ≠ moderno	tradiciones = costumbres
auténtico ≠ irreal	obras = cuadros/pinturas

Pintor norteamericano: ¿Quién es?

Este artista norteamericano es, **además de** pintor, periodista *(journalist)* e ilustrador. Diseña imágenes idealizadas y populares de una sociedad norteamericana trabajadora y con valores tradicionales. **A través de** sus cuadros, todo lo cotidiano *(ordinary)* se idealiza. Sus obras crean un sentimiento nostálgico de la tradición y las costumbres populares de la primera mitad del siglo XX. **A través del** uso de colores suaves y de personajes típicamente comunes, presenta una realidad serena y pacífica. **Además** los capta haciendo una gran variedad de actividades. Se bañan, se afeitan, se abrazan, se miran en el espejo, van al trabajo, lloran *(they cry)*, bailan, almuerzan, estudian y practican deportes. Pinta personas ancianas y jóvenes, padres y madres, trabajadores y amas de casa *(homemakers)* y todos expresan en los rostros una variedad de emociones. Walt Disney y este pintor tienen mucho en común: los dos crean mundos de fantasía y ofrecen un escape de la realidad auténtica.

Perspectivas

7A.29 Carmen Lomas Garza.   Ahora vamos a entrar al mundo de una de las artistas chicanas (méxico-americanas) más conocidas en Estados Unidos: Carmen Lomas Garza.

Paso 1: Las palabras necesarias. Examinen con cuidado el cuadro a continuación de Carmen Lomas Garza y luego hagan una lluvia de ideas para obtener una lista de palabras que puedan usar para describirlo.

Paso 2: En tus propias palabras. En parejas, escriban varios párrafos que describan el cuadro. Además de cualquier información que encuentren relevante, deben incluir respuestas a las siguientes preguntas. Incluyan información falsa en uno de los párrafos (por ejemplo, *La gente está en una iglesia.*) para ver si la clase la puede identificar.

Una descripción de *La feria*, de Carmen Lomas Garza

1. ¿Dónde está la gente: en un funeral, en una demostración política?

2. ¿Quiénes participan en la escena: familiares, animales, niños, madres, novios, vendedores?

3. En términos generales, ¿Cómo se viste la gente en esta obra: con ropa formal, con trajes de baño?

4. ¿Qué hacen los niños: juegan, cantan, se miran, bailan, comen, beben, se hablan, uno se chupa el dedo, uno trota, uno empuja a otro?

5. ¿Qué emociones expresan las personas a través de gestos (de la cara o el cuerpo): algunos se agarran de la mano, se besan, pelean, una persona frunce los labios?

6. ¿Qué hace la gente parada?

7. ¿Qué hace la gente sentada?

8. ¿Qué han hecho los vendedores para prepararse para la feria: han preparado la comida, han practicado con sus instrumentos musicales?

9. ¿Qué van a hacer los vendedores después de la feria: van a cocinar más comida, van a ponerse ropa elegante, van a casa a descansar?

Carmen Lomas Garza's painting "La feria".

7A.29 TEACHING TIP: Encourage students to move beyond words and to use phrases to describe Lomas Garza's work. Write words and phrases on the board as students produce them during their brainstorming.

7A.29 TEACHING TIP: Have students read their description to the class so that the false information can be identified.

7A.30 TEACHING TIP: In order to provide the class with the best exposure to comprehensible input, you will want to make sure that their responses are well-written and polished. After students have written their first draft as a group, have them exchange their description with one or two other people. They should focus on the content by considering the following questions: 1. Is it interesting?, 2. Is it unique?, 3. Is it clear? After students have made changes to their original drafts, have them exchange their drafts one more time. This time they should focus on accuracy by considering the following grammatical points: 1. Subject/verb agreement, 2. Noun/adjective agreement. At this point, students prepare their final draft. You can expect them to be much better written than had they shared their original drafts.

7A.30 Piénsalo. Lee los siguientes enunciados e indica si estás de acuerdo o no. Si no estás de acuerdo, subraya *(underline)* la parte de la oración con la que no estás de acuerdo. Luego, comparte y apoya tu opinión con dos compañeros de clase. ¿Hay algún enunciado que particularmente provoque conversación o desacuerdo?

Sí   No

☐ ☐ **1.** Botero idealiza a sus personajes porque todos son corpulentos y eso indica que tienen una vida de abundancia.

☐ ☐ **2.** El arte de O'Keefe hace un comentario sobre la vida política y social de Estados Unidos.

☐ ☐ **3.** Todas las personas en el cuadro de Carmen Lomas Garza tienen la misma expresión neutral.

☐ ☐ **4.** Carmen Lomas Garza y Rockwell dan una imagen positiva de las culturas que representan en sus cuadros.

☐ ☐ **5.** No hay mucha variación en las características de las personas en los cuadros de Botero. En otras palabras, todos se parecen.

☐ ☐ **6.** Los pintores de países hispanos no tienen nada en común con los pintores de otros países.

☐ ☐ **7.** Las preocupaciones sociales, políticas, económicas y ecológicas varían de país a país, pero la condición humana (las emociones, las ideas, las necesidades, la espiritualidad, etcétera) es algo que tienen en común todos los artistas.

☐ ☐ **8.** Los personajes en las obras de Rockwell, Botero y Carmen Lomas Garza son muy expresivos.

☐ ☐ **9.** Sólo Norman Rockwell pinta a personas con rostros expresivos en sus cuadros.

☐ ☐ **10.** Botero y Lomas Garza presentan a la gente en diversas situaciones sociales como vacaciones, fiestas, ferias, cumpleaños y celebraciones culturales.

7A.31 ¿Qué tienen en común? ¿Qué otras características tienen en común los artistas y los cuadros de este capítulo? Escribe al menos dos cosas que dos o tres artistas tienen en común, que no estén incluidas en la actividad de arriba y comparte esa información con la clase. ¿Hay un consenso expresado por la clase sobre los cuadros? Informa sobre las observaciones generales de la clase en tu **Retrato de la clase.**

Retrato de la clase: En general, la clase está de acuerdo en que los artistas de este capítulo…

DICHOS

En boca cerrada no entran moscas	*A shut mouth catches no flies.*
Barriga llena, corazón contento	*The way to a man's heart is through his stomach*

Vocabulario: Investigación A

Vocabulario esencial

Sustantivos

la barba	*beard*
el bigote	*moustache*
la boca	*mouth*
el brazo	*arm*
el cabello...	*hair*
castaño	*brown hair*
corto	*short hair*
fino	*thin hair*
grueso/a	*thick hair*
lacio	*straight hair*
largo	*long hair*
negro	*black hair*
rizado	*curly hair*
suelto	*loose hair*
la cabeza	*head*
las caderas	*hips*
la cara	*face*
las cejas	*eyebrows*
la cintura	*waist*
el codo	*elbow*
el cuello	*neck*
los dedos	*fingers*
los dientes	*teeth*
la espalda	*back*
la frente	*forehead*
el hombro	*shoulder*
los labios	*lips*
la mano	*hand*
la mejilla	*cheek*
la muñeca	*wrist; doll*
la nariz	*nose*
obra de arte	*work of art*
el oído	*ear (inner)*
los ojos	*eyes*
la oreja	*ear (outer)*
el pecho	*chest*
el pelo	*hair*
las piernas	*legs*
las pestañas	*eyelashes*
los pies	*feet*
el retrato	*portrait*
la rodilla	*knee*
el rostro	*face*
el tobillo	*ankle*

Adjetivos

alto/a	*tall*
amplio/a	*wide, extensive*
anciona/a	*old*
bajo/a	*short*
calvo/a	*bald*
canoso/a	*gray haired*
cotidiano/a	*common; ordinary*
delgado/a	*slender*
gordo/a	*fat*
grande	*big*
joven	*young*
rubio/a	*blond*
pelirrojo	*red haired*
pequeño/a	*small*

Verbos

abrazar	*to hug*
acostarse	*to go to bed; to lie down*
afeitarse	*to shave oneself*
agarrar	*to grab*
arrodillarse	*to kneel down*
bañarse	*to bathe*
besar	*to kiss*
chupar	*to suck*
conocerse	*to know each other; to meet*
ducharse	*to shower oneself*
empujar	*to push*
estirar	*to stretch*
fruncir	*to frown*
levantarse	*to get up*
oler	*to smell*
patear	*to kick*
pintar	*to paint*
ponerse	*to put (something) on*
quitarse	*to take (something) off*
rodear	*to surround*
sentarse	*to sit down*
tirar	*to throw*
torcerse	*to twist (a part of the body)*
trotar	*to jog*
vestirse	*to get dressed*

Otras palabras y expresiones

el ama de casa	*home maker*
el/la anfitrión/a	*host*
el autorretrato	*self-portrait*
la censura	*censorship*
la contaminación	*pollution*
corto de vista	*short-sighted*
los datos	*facts*
encantador/a	*enchanting*
la esquina	*corner*
el pincel	*paintbrush*
el polvo	*dust*
la recámara	*bedroom (Mex.)*
redondo/a	*round*
revisar	*to review*
la sangre	*blood*
suave	*soft*
la tabla	*chart*
la tarjeta postal	*postcard*
todavía	*yet*
al fondo	*in the background*
debido a	*due to*
de estatura mediana	*of average height*
en el primer plano	*in the foreground*
en la parte inferior	*in/at the bottom*
en la parte superior	*in/at the top*
encogerse de hombros	*to shrug your shoulders*
estar acostado/a	*to be lying down*
estar en contra de	*to be against (philosophically)*
estar parado/a	*to be standing up*
estar sentado/a	*to be seated down*
tener sentido	*to make sense*

Cognados

Review the cognates in *Adelante* and the false cognates in *¡Atención!*. For a complete list of cognates, see Appendix 4 on page 605.

INVESTIGACIÓN 7B
¿Cómo se describe lo que ocurre en una obra de arte?

In this **Investigación** you will learn:

▶ How to describe a scene in a piece of art

▶ How to describe what is going on in a piece of art

▶ About characteristics of famous Hispanic artists

▶ How art can be interpreted

¿Cómo se puede describir lo que ocurre en una obra de arte?

You can ask what the scene portrays.	Es una escena panorámica. Es una celebración pero a través de la perspectiva de una persona. El tema es la soledad.
You can ask what and who is in the work.	La escena tiene lugar en la ciudad. La escena es un *collage* de grupos étnicos. Hay gente en un desfile (*parade*) en el centro de la ciudad.
You can ask what happens, what has happened, what is happening.	Los niños están corriendo por la playa. Los padres están hablando y bebiendo refrescos.

Adelante

¡Ya lo sabes! Para hablar de la escena

el desastre	la perspectiva	construir
el conflicto	la religión	detectar
el evento	la sinfonía	distinguir
la escena	la sociedad	documentar
los grupos étnicos	el tema	ilustrar
la interpretación		manifestar
la leyenda	clarificar	ocurrir
el panorama	contemplar	

7B.1 AUDIO SCRIPT:
1. notar, 2. el análisis, 3. manufacturar, 4. la comunidad, 5. dibujar, 6. la disputa, 7. explicar, 8. reflexionar, 9. la idea

7B.1 EXTENSION ACTIVITY: After completing activity 7B.1, in groups of three, have students take turns describing one of the words in the list while their partners say the word being described.

7B.1 **Buscar los sinónimos.** Vas a escuchar varias palabras. Empareja cada palabra que escuches con su sinónimo. El primero está hecho como modelo. Luego comprueba tus respuestas con la clase.

__7__ clarificar   __1__ detectar

__6__ el conflicto   __5__ ilustrar

__3__ construir   __2__ la interpretación

__4__ la sociedad   __8__ contemplar

__9__ el tema

7B.2 **Definiciones.** Con un/a compañero/a, empareja las palabras de abajo con sus correspondientes definiciones. Luego, comprueba tus respuestas con la clase.

a. la escena

b. el desastre

c. el evento

d. documentar

e. la leyenda

f. el panorama

g. la religión

h. la sinfonía

_a_ **1.** Se refiere a las circunstancias (tiempo, lugar) en que ocurre una situación.

_f_ **2.** La vista completa de una escena, un paisaje o un espectáculo.

_d_ **3.** Significa certificar o verificar algo con información específica.

_g_ **4.** Se asocia con la devoción, el dogma, la piedad y la espiritualidad.

_c_ **5.** Es algo que pasa o sucede.

_e_ **6.** Un cuento o un mito establecido para explicar algo o entretener al pueblo.

_h_ **7.** Se asocia con un concierto.

_b_ **8.** El resultado de una cosa mala como un huracán, un tornado o una inundación (_flood_).

7B.3 **¿Con qué?** Mientras escuchas cada frase, indica la parte del cuerpo que necesitas para realizar la acción. Puede haber más de una respuesta correcta. Compara tus respuestas con las de otros dos compañeros de clase.

1. _e_   **a.** las manos

2. _a/d/e_   **b.** los pies

3. _f_   **c.** los oídos

4. _c_   **d.** los ojos

5. _a/d/e_   **e.** el cerebro (_brain_)

6. _g_   **f.** el cuerpo completo

7. _e_   **g.** la nariz

8. _f/h/d_   **h.** las cejas

7B.3 AUDIO SCRIPT: ¿Con qué partes del cuerpo puedes... 1. contemplar una idea? 2. pintar un cuadro? 3. acostarse en la cama? 4. detectar tonos o notas musicales? 5. construir un marco (_frame_) para un cuadro, una mesa o una silla? 6. distinguir entre distintos perfumes? 7. considerar una opción o pensar en la solución de un problema? 8. manifestar una reacción negativa con una expresión?

¿Quién es John A. Swanson?

John August Swanson es de Los Ángeles, California. Su madre es mexicana y su padre es sueco; ambos influyeron en su arte. Swanson recuerda las leyendas que su madre le contaba de niño y las historias de su padre sobre sus recuerdos (*memories*) como inmigrante en Estados Unidos. Durante su juventud, Swanson estudió en escuelas católicas. La religión tiene una influencia obvia en su trabajo. Su arte refleja tanto los aspectos internos y espirituales del ser humano así como aspectos externos y sociales. Él se describe a sí mismo como un observador de eventos e ideas que después intenta recrear visualmente. Su arte se caracteriza también por sus colores brillantes y los detalles que ayudan a crear su muy particular visión de la vida interna y externa de los seres humanos.

7B.4 AUDIO SCRIPT:
1. John Swanson es de Estados Unidos. 2. El padre de Swanson es mexicano. 3. Los padres de John inmigraron a California. 4. A Swanson le gusta incluir muchos detalles en su arte. 5. Swanson expresa su espiritualidad a través de sus obras de arte.

7B.4 EXTENSION ACTIVITY: Have students study Swanson's painting for a minute. Then, have them do a three-minute freewrite about the painting. This consists of writing without stopping. If they do not know what to write, instead of stopping, they can write anything (e.g. *"no sé qué escribir, no sé qué escribir"*) until an idea comes to them. The objective is to create opportunities to develop their writing fluency (there is no need to go back and correct this, just as there is no need to correct all speech) and in doing so, to have students recycle previously-learned language.

7B.4 **Vas a escuchar varios enunciados sobre John Swanson.** Según lo que has leído sobre él, determina si cada enunciado es **cierto** o **falso.** Luego, confirma tus respuestas con la clase.

	Cierto	Falso
1.	☑	☐
2.	☐	☑
3.	☑	☐
4.	☑	☐
5.	☑	☐

🎧 Bien dicho

La ortografía y pronunciación del sonido /k/

The sound /k/ in Spanish is associated with the letter **c** before the vowels **a**, **o** and **u**, and any consonant. It is also associated with the letter combination **qu** before the vowels **e** and **i**, and with the letter **k** (very rare in Spanish, but found in cases such as **kilómetro**, **kilogramo** and **kínder**).

cantar	(kan-tár)	parque	(pár-ke)
cosas	(kó-sas)	equipo	(e-kí-po)
cura	(kú-ra)	quemar	(ke-már)
clarifica	(kla-ri-fí-ka)	química	(kí-mi-ka)
detectar	(de-tek-tár)		

Note that the **u** is silent in the combinations **que** and **qui**.

The basic difference between the pronunciation of the /k/ sound in Spanish and its English counterpart is that /k/ in Spanish is never aspirated. To avoid/reduce aspiration (or puff/spit of air), press the back of your tongue against the roof of your mouth more firmly than you would to pronounce the /k/ sound in English. Another strategy may be to think of how you pronounce /k/ when preceded by *s* in English (e.g., *score, skate, squirm*) and apply that pronunciation to all cases of /k/ in Spanish.

7B.5 ¿Cómo se escribe? Vas a escuchar una serie de palabras. Escucha e indica si se escriben con *c* o con *qu*.

	c	qu
1.	☑	☐
2.	☑	☐
3.	☐	☑
4.	☐	☑
5.	☑	☐
6.	☑	☐

7B.5 AUDIO SCRIPT: 1. costumbres, 2. criar, 3. equipaje, 4. quedarse, 5. campo, 6. rector

7B.6 ¡A pronunciar! Con un/a compañero/a, túrnense para pronunciar las siguientes oraciones. Cuando terminen, cambien de papel de modo que cada estudiante tenga la oportunidad de pronunciar todas las oraciones. Intenten reducir/eliminar, tanto como sea posible, la aspiración de /k/.

1. Ese compositor escribe música contemporánea.
2. El continente de África se compone de muchas culturas.
3. Esos conciertos se tocan para el público de aquí.
4. Alfonso Cuarón es un director de películas mexicano.
5. La carne se compra por kilos en aquel supermercado.
6. En esta comunidad se reciclan los periódicos.
7. Hay muchas computadoras caras en la biblioteca.
8. Después de considerarla, Marcos contestó la pregunta.

7B.6 SUGGESTIONS: You may want to have students use a piece of paper to check their degree of aspiration of /k/.

Palabras clave 1   Las diversiones y los intereses

las estrellas

al aire libre

la pareja

contarse

regalarse

tocar

la carta

el equipaje

La pareja de enamorados **se siente** bien porque están de vacaciones.
Después de cenar van a una fiesta y luego a **divertirse** en Puerto Rico.

Note: Infinitives given with **–se** attached to them indicate that the verb may be used to indicate reflexive actions and/or reciprocal actions. Some verbs change meaning slightly when they are used reflexively/reciprocally.

RECYCLING:
Much of the vocabulary in this *Palabras clave* is recycled from previous chapters.

7B.7   **Seguir las categorías.**   Con un/a compañero/a completen el mapa semántico en la página 331. Usen primero el vocabulario de *Palabras clave*, seguido de más palabras en español que quepan *(that fit)* dentro de esas categorías semánticas (como repaso). Luego, comparen sus mapas semánticos con los de otros grupos de la clase. Su profesor/a puede aclarar cualquier pregunta.

TEACHING TIP: Ask questions to focus students' attention on the meaning of these words. For example, *¿Los novios comen dentro del restaurante o comen al aire libre? ¿Cómo sabemos que la escena tiene lugar de noche? ¿Qué indicio hay de que los novios salen de vacaciones? ¿Qué hace la gente en la iglesia? Las noticias del día, ¿son buenas o malas? ¿Las gemelas son idénticas en actitud tanto como físicamente?*

7B.7 SUGGESTION: You may divide the class into groups so that every group has one of the semantic maps that they complete together on paper. Then, each group can supply the words that correspond to their group on the board so that all semantic maps are completed more quickly.

la iglesia

los enfermos

la gente

la pantalla

cuidarse

rezar

el periódico

la guerra

Las gemelas se parecen mucho pero tienen diferentes intereses. Una piensa en los demás *(others)* **mientras** que la otra piensa en sí misma *(herself)*.

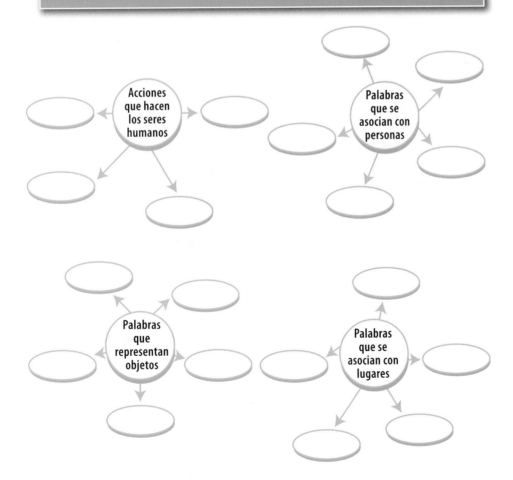

Acciones que hacen los seres humanos

Palabras que se asocian con personas

Palabras que representan objetos

Palabras que se asocian con lugares

7B.8 **¿Cuál no pertenece?** Indica la palabra que *no* pertenece a cada categoría. Luego, comprueba tus respuestas con la clase.

1. las cosas que pueden hacer dos personas:	contarse	divertirse	sentirse	cuidarse
2. las personas en un hospital:	las estrellas	los pacientes	la gente	los médicos
3. actividades al aire libre:	hacer deportes	ver las estrellas	visitar los enfermos	trabajar en el jardín
4. cosas o actividades que se asocian con la religión:	la iglesia	el padre	rezar	reírse
5. aspectos de la guerra:	la violencia	el conflicto	los cadáveres	el regalo
6. viajar a lugares exóticos:	el equipaje	el puerto	el avión	la casa
7. ejemplos de la compasión:	dar de comer a los menos afortunados	participar en una guerra	cuidar a los animales y la naturaleza	visitar a los enfermos
8. ejemplos de actividades familiares:	visitar a los abuelos	cenar juntos	leer un libro	limpiar la casa

7B. 9 **La perspectiva del artista.** En la escena de abajo del cuadro de Swanson, los estudiantes están leyendo biografías de personajes importantes. Vas a escuchar descripciones de los libros que leen. Empareja la descripción de cada libro con el nombre de la persona de quien se trata *(that it is about)*. Luego, comprueba tus respuestas con un/a compañero/a de clase.

Los estudiantes leen libros sobre...

	Anne Frank	Rosa Parks	William Shakespeare
1.	☐	☐	☑
2.	☑	☐	☐
3.	☐	☑	☐

7B.10 Swanson en detalle. A continuación, en la sección del cuadro de Swanson, los estudiantes leen sobre otros temas. Con un/a compañero/a examinen cuidadosamente las ilustraciones que rodean a los dos estudiantes de la escena. Luego, escuchen varios temas e indiquen si cada tema se ilustra en la escena o no. Después, comprueben sus respuestas con la clase.

	Sí	No
1.	☑	☐
2.	☑	☐
3.	☐	☑
4.	☑	☐
5.	☐	☑
6.	☐	☑

7B.10 PRE-LISTENING ACTIVITY: Have students describe to their partner (in Spanish) what they see in the painting. This will help them familiarize themselves with it so they are prepared to listen to the descriptions.

7B.10 AUDIO SCRIPT AND ANSWERS: 1. Cómo cuidar a los animales (Sí), 2. La celebración de Hanukah (Sí), 3. La ciencia y la tecnología (No), 4. Una variedad de instrumentos musicales (Sí), 5. Cómo cuidar a los enfermos (No), 6. Cómo construir un edificio (No)

WILEY
PLUS

7B.11 INSTRUCTOR'S RESOURCES: You will find reproducible cards for Activity 7B.11 in your Instructor's Resources.

7B.11 WAIT TIME: When you are reviewing these answers as a class, instead of calling on the first student that offers an answer, quietly count to four before calling on a student. If you offer students more time, you may notice that more of them, particularly the quieter ones, will volunteer themselves.

7B.11 FOLLOW-UP: Ask students which details from the Swanson painting they like most. Elicit responses from students. Ask them why they like the scenes they mentioned. (e.g. *¿Cuál es tu escena favorita? ¿Por qué?*)

7B.11 Pequeñas escenas. En parejas, examinen las escenas a–f del cuadro de Swanson. Seleccionen la tarjeta A o la tarjeta B, y túrnense para leerse el uno al otro las oraciones de las tarjetas y escribir la letra de la escena que corresponda con cada oración. Luego, confirmen sus respuestas con la clase.

A

1. __d__ Los estudiantes levantan la mano en la clase para hacer preguntas.
2. __f__ La familia reza antes de comer.
3. __b__ Los hijos visitan a su madre. Es su cumpleaños y por eso llevan flores y un pastel.

3. __e__ Los novios dan de comer a los animales domésticos.
2. __a__ El hombre es buen padre porque les lee libros a sus hijos.
1. __c__ El hermano da de comer a su hermanito mientras su madre lava los platos y su hermana barre.

B

7B.12 TEACHING TIP:
Encourage students to be as descriptive as possible. At this point, they should be able to describe a variety of aspects of the paintings. You can suggest that students write their descriptions as homework and then do the activity when the class meets again. The level of detail would probably be higher. Explain that while students should not use English, they don't need to try to translate brand names, titles, etc.

7B.12 **En detalle.** Con un/a compañero/a, examinen las escenas en miniatura rotuladas a–h en el cuadro de Swanson que aparece a continuación. Luego, túrnense para describirlas en detalle de manera que su compañero/a pueda identificarlas por la letra. ¿Qué escenas se describen con más detalle?

Sigan estas reglas:

• You cannot use English.

• Listen to the entire description before identifying the scene.

• If your partner cannot figure out the scene you are describing, provide more information, repeat information, rephrase information. If this doesn't work, you should choose a different scene.

• Keep a tally of the number of scenes your team correctly identified.

Modelo: E1: *La escena ocurre en el campo al aire libre. Tres personas plantan legumbres. La mujer tiene el pelo negro y lleva lentes. Su blusa es roja y su traje es marrón. Ella y un hombre están de rodillas. El hombre de rodillas lleva una gorra marrón y una camisa del mismo color. Su traje es morado. El hombre al fondo de la escena está parado. Lleva jeans y una camisa blanca.*

E2: *c*

a

b

c

d

e

f

g

h

VÍVELO: CULTURA

Pablo Picasso

Otro de los más grandes artistas del siglo XX es Pablo Picasso (1881-1973). Picasso nació en Málaga, España, en una familia bien acomodada. Su padre era profesor de dibujo, pero no se conoce mucho de su madre excepto que Picasso la respetó mucho. El arte de Picasso pasa por varios períodos distintos que se caracterizan según la técnica predominante. Por ejemplo, el período entre 1901 y 1904 se conoce como su período azul porque el color azul domina sus cuadros. Después de su período azul, sus obras se caracterizan por el color rosa (período rosa) y los temas de sus obras tienden a hacer referencia al mundo del zoológico y del circo con imágenes de máscaras, arlequines (*harlequins*) y payasos (*clowns*). Luego, es notable la influencia del arte africano en sus obras. Empieza a reducir la obra a un conjunto (*set*) de planos angulares, sin fondo (*depth*) ni perspectiva espacial llevándolo al cubismo. Entre 1907 y 1914 las figuras de sus obras se representan con formas geométricas, como cuadrados y triángulos. Durante este período Picasso deforma la realidad al descomponer los rostros (*faces*) y los cuerpos. En una obra, por ejemplo, se representa la mitad (*half*) de la cara de frente y la otra mitad de lado. Después de la Primera Guerra Mundial, su arte tiene toques del surrealismo. Picasso, horrorizado por el bombardeo del pueblo de Guernica, pinta una de sus obras más famosas, *Guernica*, en 1937. Al final de la Segunda Guerra Mundial sus cuadros son más optimistas. Picasso fue testigo (*witness*) de ambas guerras mundiales y de la Guerra Civil de España pero por ser pacifista nunca se alió (*sided*) a ningún lado político. En 1944, después de la Segunda Guerra Mundial, se incorporó al Partido Comunista Francés, en el que participó hasta su muerte en Francia en 1973.

7B.13 Comprensión. Escoge la opción que completa correctamente la oración.

1. Picasso nació en (Madrid/Málaga/Barcelona/Sevilla).
2. De 1901 a 1904 el color que más se asocia con los cuadros de Picasso es el (azul/verde/rojo/amarillo).
3. Durante el período rosado, los cuadros de Picasso frecuentemente hacen referencia a (la familia/el amor/los deportes/el circo).
4. Después del período rosado, se nota la influencia del arte (japonés/africano/mexicano/estadounidense) en las obras de Picasso.
5. El (impresionismo/romanticismo/cubismo/surrealismo) es el movimiento artístico que consiste en representar las figuras de formas geométricas y en deformar la realidad.
6. El cuadro *Guernica* lo pinta para protestar el bombardeo de un pueblo durante (la Primera Guerra Mundial/la Segunda Guerra Mundial/la Guerra Hispano-Estadounidense/la Guerra Civil Española).
7. Picasso era (pacifista/belicoso/radical/extremista).
8. Picasso muere en (España/Estados Unidos/Francia/Argentina).

7B.13 ANSWERS: 1. Málaga, 2. azul, 3. el circo, 4. africano, 5. cubismo, 6. la Guerra Civil Española (can be inferred from date of painting and by process of elimination), 7. pacifista, 8. Francia (can be inferred from his membership in French communist party)

¡Conéctate!

www

Google Pablo Picasso to find images of his artwork. Connect some of his paintings to the various periods that characterize his art. Share your findings with the class. Which of his periods is most popular with the class?

EXPRESIONES ÚTILES

Las muletillas *(fillers)*

Fillers are words or expressions, such as *I mean, like, uh, okay*, etc. that we use to fill in the gaps of our speech. Characteristic fillers in Spanish include:

a ver	*let's see*
así que	*so / so that*
este…	*uh… / um…*
pues	*well*

To express an afterthought or an unrelated topic as you would in English with *by the way*, or *incidentally*, in Spanish use **por cierto** or **a propósito**.

Por cierto, ¿cómo se llama?	*By the way, what is your name?*
A propósito, ¿cuándo abre la exhibición?	*Incidentally, when does the exhibit open?*

7B.14 ORIENTATION: The purpose of this activity is to get students to "negotiate meaning" with each other. In other words, students will make errors but the purpose is to use whatever language they have at hand or have internalized to express themselves. You may dedicate class time to this activity, or assign some or most of it as outside-of-class work. If your school has a computer lab, students may use a variety of software to chat online with each other. In this way you can have access to the processes students go through to communicate with each other. A follow-up to this activity would be to have students actually describe their work in a cohesive paragraph and then take one description and correct it with the class (on overhead or using a document camera or a smart board). In this way both communication and accuracy are attended to.

7B.14 **¡Sean los artistas!** En grupos de tres, van a crear su propia obra de arte para que la clase la interprete. Por ejemplo, podemos decir que Swanson valora el aprendizaje y la lectura. La atención de Picasso a las figuras y a las formas es tan importante como el tema de sus pinturas. Es importante tener una idea clara del propósito *(purpose)* de la obra de arte. También es importante que su obra exprese un mensaje. El objetivo de esta tarea es comunicarse y colaborar <u>en español</u>.

Paso 1: Deben tomar juntos, <u>en español</u>, las siguientes decisiones.

- Decidan el lugar de la escena. Por ejemplo, ¿es una escena al aire libre en el campo? ¿En un parque? ¿En el jardín de una casa? O, ¿es adentro de un edificio como una biblioteca, un hospital, una escuela o en un salón de clase?

- Decidan qué y quiénes van a aparecer en la obra. ¿Qué cosas hay en la obra? ¿Qué gente hay en la obra?

- Decidan qué hace la gente en la obra.

- Decidan cómo van a crear la obra. Por ejemplo, ¿van a usar un cartel *(poster board)* o una hoja de papel? ¿Van a dibujar todo o van a usar recortes (fotos o arte) de revistas o periódicos? ¿Van a usar la Internet?

- Decidan qué va a hacer cada miembro del grupo y para cuándo.

- Decidan cómo van a presentar la obra. ¿Van a describir la obra? ¿Van a hacer preguntas a la clase? ¿O sólo van a contestar preguntas?

Paso 2: Escriban algunas observaciones generales sobre el arte creado por sus compañeros de clase. ¿Qué semejanzas y diferencias notan en las escenas, personas y actividades representadas en las obras de arte? ¿Hay temas en común? ¿Qué notan sobre el medio y los colores escogidos? ¿Qué comentario(s) general(es) pueden hacer sobre la clase basándose en las obras creadas? Anoten sus observaciones en su **Retrato de la clase.**

Retrato de la clase: Las escenas son variadas/semejantes e incluyen… En general, las personas son/están…. En las obras las personas… Los temas incluyen… Las obras son originales/incorporan imágenes de otras fuentes (sources). Los colores son… La clase prefiere … A la clase le interesa(n)/no le interesa(n)…

VÍVELO: CULTURA

Diego Rivera

Diego Rivera (1886-1957) es posiblemente el pintor mexicano más famoso del siglo XX. Viajó por Europa por 15 años y cuando volvió a México en 1922 el gobierno lo contrató para pintar grandes murales en los edificios más importantes de México: el Palacio de Cortés en Cuernavaca, el Palacio Nacional y el Palacio de las Bellas Artes de la Ciudad de México. En estas pinturas Rivera encontró su propio (own) estilo con influencias de las culturas indígenas. Sus murales se asocian con la ideología de la Revolución Mexicana. Rivera se casó en cuatro ocasiones pero su más famosa esposa fue la pintora mexicana Frida Kahlo.

www ¡Conéctate!

Learn more about Diego Rivera by running a Google search. View his paintings and murals to gain insights into his artwork and technical style. Youtube also has numerous good quality shorts on Diego Rivera. What are the most interesting aspects of his life and work? Print (or project) your favorite Diego Rivera piece to share with your class.

VÍVELO: CULTURA: This is a brief introduction to Diego Rivera to encourage students to explore his life and work. Once students have gathered additional information about him, have them share their findings with the class. The historical and political aspects of his life and work are particulary significant because his murals initiated a popular sense of nationalism in Mexico, one that served the dominant political party, el Partido Revolucionario Institucional (PRI) for over 70 years, until 2000 when it was defeated by Vicente Fox of the Partido Acción Nacional (PAN).

¡Atención!

Espectáculo	means *show* in Spanish, without the negative connotation that spectacle often has in English.
	Vamos a ver un espectáculo en Broadway.
Desgracia	does not mean disgrace. In Spanish it means *misfortune, tragedy, mishap*.
	¡Qué desgracia! Casi toda su familia murió en el terremoto.
Edificar	does not only mean *to edify* as in to educate a person. It also means *to build*.
	Van a edificar un monumento en honor al ex presidente.

7B.15 **Un poco de todo.** Como repaso de cognados falsos ya conocidos y otros nuevos, empareja la palabra en A con su correspondiente definición en B. Luego, compara tus respuestas con las de un/a compañero/a de clase.

	A		B
h	**1.** apuntar	**a.**	una tragedia o un desastre
e	**2.** edificar	**b.**	acción de leer
i	**3.** divertirse	**c.**	un programa musical o teatral
a	**4.** desgracia	**d.**	relacionado con la familia
g	**5.** escolar	**e.**	construir una estructura
c	**6.** espectáculo	**f.**	los miembros de una familia
f	**7.** parientes	**g.**	relacionado con la escuela
d	**8.** familiar	**h.**	tomar notas o escribir un dato específico
b	**9.** lectura	**i.**	pasarlo bien, disfrutar

Estructuras clave 1 The present progressive

TEACHING TIP: Write the following sentences on the board and ask students to figure out how Spanish forms the progressive based on them. *Estoy mirando la televisión. Estás hablando muy rápidamente. Está viviendo aquí. Estamos hablando español en clase. Están corriendo al autobús.* Provide a hint: You have to use some form of one particular verb and attach certain endings to the second verb. After going over this description, have students describe the gist of it to their partner.

As you saw in *Capítulo 2,* the present tense in Spanish is used to convey what *happens,* what *is happening,* or, often with the addition of adverbs, what *will happen* at some future moment. Another way to express what *is happening*–in other words, an action in progress– is to use the *present progressive.* Look at the following examples.

Habla con su profesor. Está hablando con su profesor.	*She is speaking with her instructor.*
Hace la tarea. Está haciendo la tarea.	*He is doing his homework.*
Nos vestimos. Estamos vistiéndonos.	*We are getting dressed.*

The second sentence in each of these examples is in the present progressive. Progressive constructions are formed with **estar** + the *present participle* of the verb. The present participle is formed by attaching **–ando** to **–ar** verb stems, and **–iendo** to **–er/–ir** verb stems.

	hablar	**comer**	**escribir**
estoy estás está estáis estamos están	habl**ando**	com**iendo**	escrib**iendo**

There are some irregular present participles as well.

decir	**diciendo**	creer	**creyendo**
dormir	**durmiendo**	leer	**leyendo**
pedir	**pidiendo**	oír	**oyendo**

It is important to note that Spanish uses the present progressive much less frequently than English does. Since the simple present tense in Spanish easily conveys actions in progress, the present progressive is generally reserved for emphasizing the importance of the on-going nature of an action at the moment the speaker utters the sentence.

Tiene calor, pero está bebiendo agua para refrescarse.	*He's hot, but he is drinking water to cool off.*
En este momento, está escribiéndole una carta a su tía.	*Right now, she is writing a letter to her aunt.*
No puedo. Estoy hablando por teléfono.	*I can't, I am talking on the phone.*
No podemos salir ahora. Estamos comiendo.	*We can't leave now. We are eating.*

The simple present is usually used to describe a scene, unless the speaker is placing himself/herself inside the picture (time wise) to describe happenings, or wants to emphasize an action that is in progress while another action is occurring.

7B.16 TEACHING TIP: For more advanced students, encourage them to come up with their own true/false statements about the drawing. They should then share those sentences with a partner who will decide whether or not they are depicted.

7B.16 Busca y encuentra. En parejas, miren el dibujo de la página 341 e identifiquen con una ✓ lo que está pasando en la habitación cuando entra la profesora de la clase de teatro. Luego, comprueben sus respuestas con la clase.

Cuando entra la profesora...

☑ **1.** unos estudiantes están jugando al fútbol.

☑ **2.** un estudiante está rezando.

☑ **3.** unos estudiantes están bailando.

☐ **4.** unos estudiantes están comiendo.

☑ **5.** unos estudiantes están escribiendo.

☐ **6.** un estudiante está poniéndose unos pantalones.

☑ **7.** unos estudiantes están leyendo.

☐ **8.** unos estudiantes están bebiendo refrescos.

☑ **9.** unos estudiantes están pintando un mural.

☐ **10.** unos estudiantes están jugando béisbol.

☐ **11.** un estudiante está afeitándose la barba.

☑ **12.** un estudiante está lavándose las manos.

7B.17 **Usa tu imaginación.** Imagina lo que los siguientes individuos están haciendo en este momento. Selecciona a tres de la lista de abajo o piensa en otros nombres de personas conocidas. Luego, escribe un enunciado lógico para describir lo que cada individuo está haciendo en este momento. La clase adivina de quién se trata de acuerdo a la información que des.

> Modelo: E1: *Está besando a su esposa Michelle Obama.*
> Clase: *Barack Obama*

Oscar de la Hoya (boxeador)   Penélope Cruz (actriz)
Manny Ramírez (beisbolista)   Joseph Acaba (astronauta)
Isabel Allende (escritora)   Carlos Santana (músico)
Sandra Cisneros (escritora)   Edward James Olmos (actor)
Elizabeth Vargas (periodista)   Juan Pablo Montoya (corredor de autos)
Cameron Díaz (actriz)   Benicio del Toro (actor)

7B.17 ALTERNATIVE DELIVERY: Have students write their sentences as homework. As they come into class, collect their sentences. Then, read a selection of the sentences to the class (making any needed revisions) while they guess who the famous figure is.

7B.17 NOTE: In case these two figures are not known, you may inform students of who they are: *Joseph Acaba se convirtió en 2009 en el primer astronauta de NASA de descendencia puertorriqueña. Juan Pablo Montoya es colombiano y corredor de autos que en el año 2000 ganó las 500 millas de Indianápolis.*

www **¡Conéctate!**
How up-to-date are you on the news? Visit http://cnn.com/espanol and scroll down to the section with recent videos. Watch a couple of these short news summaries and write a few sentences expressing what was happening, and what still may be continuing to happen, in the news. Share these sentences with your class.

7B.18 La lectura es fundamental.   Lee el siguiente párrafo con un/a compañero/a. Mientras leen, cambien los verbos subrayados del presente del progresivo al presente simple. Luego, confirmen sus respuestas con dos compañeros de clase.

En la obra de Swanson, hay una serie de actividades humanas. En la sección principal de la obra, parece que el pintor quiere comunicar que es bueno leer libros. ¿Cuál es una posible interpretación de la serie de dibujos aparte de la sección principal?

En la primera escena, los niños ¹están tocando instrumentos mientras ²están visitando a un amigo en el hospital. Parece que tocan música para hacer sentir mejor a un amigo enfermo. En la segunda escena, los niños le ³están dando unas flores a una amiga que tiene que usar silla de ruedas *(wheelchair)*. En la siguiente escena, los jóvenes les dan de comer a sus mascotas *(pets)*. En la siguiente escena, la gente ⁴está participando en un acto de solidaridad contra las atrocidades que se cometen en las guerras. Todos ⁵están llevando velas *(candles)* porque ⁶están asistiendo a una manifestación en el centro de la ciudad. Van a pasar la noche en silencio y reflexión. En la siguiente escena, una pareja les ⁷está escribiendo cartas a los políticos, otra forma de manifestar su inconformidad.

7B.19 Interpretaciones.   Con un/a compañero/a indiquen la frase que usarían para traducir al inglés los verbos de 1–7 que escribieron en el presente simple. Discutan sus respuestas antes de verificarlas con la clase.

1. ☐ play instruments   ☑ are playing instruments
2. ☑ visit a friend   ☐ are visiting a friend
3. ☐ give flowers   ☑ are giving flowers
4. ☐ participate   ☑ are participating
5. ☐ carry candles   ☑ are carrying candles
6. ☐ attend a demonstration ☑ are attending a demonstration
7. ☐ write letters   ☑ are writing letters

7B.20 Lotería ¡Firma aquí!   Usando las preguntas de la tabla en la página 341, entrevista a tantos compañeros de clase como puedas para recoger sus firmas. Asegúrate de leer las reglas antes de empezar. Luego, comparte tus resultados con la clase y escribe cualquier observación interesante en tu **Retrato de la clase.**

> Modelo: E1: *¿Hablas inglés?*
> E2: *Sí, hablo inglés.*
> E1: *Firma aquí, por favor.*

Sigan estas reglas:

- You must ask the questions aloud; do not simply point to the question.

- If your classmate answers "Sí," you say "¡Firma aquí!" and (s)he will sign below the question (s)he just answered.

- When you have five signatures horizontally, vertically or diagonally, you say "¡Lotería!"

- You will report the results of your survey like this: (Nombre) va al cine frecuentemente, (Nombre) tiene clase todos los días, (Nombre) va a viajar a Europa, (Nombre) va a otra clase después de ésta, y (Nombre) sabe bailar salsa y merengue.

- Your instructor will question the students who signed your game card in order to verify the information.

- Note what you learned about your classmates in your **Retrato de la clase.**

Retrato de la clase: En general, mis compañeros de clase comen/van a comer a las 6:00 esta tarde, van al cine frecuentemente, estudian los fines de semana…

¿Vas al cine frecuentemente?	¿Tienes clase todos los días?	¿Vas a viajar a Europa alguna vez?	¿Vas a otra clase después de ésta?	¿Tienes clase esta tarde a las 4:00?
¿Vas al cine los fines de semana?	¿Estás hablando francés?	¿Hablas español con tu profesor?	¿Trabajas este fin de semana?	¿Vas a bailar hoy en la noche?
¿Vas al cine más tarde?	¿Vas a ir a las montañas este fin de semana?	¿Estás firmando con lápiz o pluma?	¿Vas a tomar un café después de la clase?	¿Tienes una computadora en casa?
Ahora mismo, ¿me estás escuchando?	¿Visitas a tu familia este fin de semana?	¿Vas a pintar una obra maestra en el futuro?	¿Estudiamos juntos más tarde?	¿Hablas inglés en la clase?
¿Estás hablando español ahora?	¿Estudias los fines de semana?	¿Escribes poemas?	¿Vas a viajar este verano?	¿Vas a cenar con tu familia mañana?

Enlaces

7B.21 **Enlaces.** Con un/a compañero/a, lean sobre el uso de estas expresiones en español. Luego, emparejen cada expresión en español con su equivalente en inglés. Comprueben sus respuestas con otra pareja de estudiantes.

a. A propósito Se usa para decir algo que no tiene ninguna relación con el discurso o para decir algo relacionado con el discurso, aunque no directamente; o para cambiar el tema *(topic)*.

b. Al fin y al cabo Se usa para resumir un argumento a modo de conclusión.

c. Por consiguiente Se usa para indicar que lo que se va a decir es consecuencia de la información presentada anteriormente.

<u>b</u> **1.** After all <u>c</u> **2.** As a result <u>a</u> **3.** By the way

7B.22 **¿Discurso completo?** Selecciona el enunciado más lógico para completar la conversación y las ideas a continuación. Luego, comparen sus respuestas con las de otros compañeros.

Opciones:

a. Por consiguiente, nunca tienen tiempo para estudiar y no aprueban *(pass)* sus clases.

b. A propósito, ¿has hecho la tarea de matemáticas? Vamos a comparar las respuestas.

c. Al fin y al cabo, es necesario para tener éxito en la universidad.

1. –¿Te gusta leer?
– Claro que sí. Me divierto mucho y aprendo muchas cosas. Para mí, es un escape.
– <u>c</u>

2. Tengo una amiga a quien le gusta mucho hablar, pero a mí no. Además, ella siempre habla de cosas que a ella le gusta hacer pero a mí no. Cuando no quiero escuchar más, le pregunto algo relacionado con nuestros estudios. Por ejemplo, <u>b</u>

3. Es verdad que hay muchos estudiantes sin padres ricos. Tienen que trabajar mucho para comprar sus libros, la gasolina, la comida o rentar un apartamento. <u>a</u>

7B.20 TEACHING TIP: 1) Prior to beginning this activity, you may want to ask questions similar to those they will be asking in this signature search, like *¿Con quién vas al cine?, ¿Vas a viajar este fin de semana?, ¿Adónde vas?* or *¿A qué clase vas después de ésta?* The reason for this is that students will sometimes answer 'yes' when they have no idea what the question is asking. Moreover, since signature searches are a recurring activity, holding students accountable for the information they learn about their fellow students will encourage them to listen more attentively to each other. 2) This is also a great activity to review students' names at the beginning of the semester and for creating a sense of community by making reference to the responses and asking such questions as *¿Cómo se llama la estudiante que va a viajar a Europa?* or *¿Cómo se llama el alumno que va a la clase de matemáticas después de ésta?*

7B.21 SUGGESTION: Encourage students to incorporate these transitional phrases into their daily vocabulary, stressing that it will help them express themselves better.

7B.22 EXTENSION ACTIVITY: Encourage more advanced students to take these initial dialogues a step further by actually role playing them. This is a good activity to do with your false beginners and can be done while the rest of the class is doing another activity or as something to prepare outside of class.

FUNCTIONAL OUTCOMES:
The central question that frames this *Investigación* is "*¿Cómo se puede describir lo que ocurre en una obra?*" Explore whether students can now address this question and how they would go about it. Have them review the chart on the first page of this *Investigación*.

As in *Investigación A* of this chapter, here in *Contextos y perspectivas* we move from the US point of reference to the Hispanic.

7B.23 TEACHING TIP:
Encourage students to read through the sentences before going back to the passage. It should still be fresh in their minds. This will help them to think about the broader meaning of the passage before trying to isolate the line or phrase they need to reference.

7B.23 EXTENSION ACTIVITY: Encourage your more advanced students to write a description of the painting.

7B.23 Antes de leer.

Paso 1: Mira el cuadro de Edward Hopper que aparece abajo y crea una lista de palabras en español que asocies inmediatamente con este cuadro. Comparte tus primeras impresiones con la clase. Mientras lees el artículo de abajo, piensa en las semejanzas entre tus primeras impresiones y lo que el artículo dice sobre Hopper y su estilo artístico.

EDWARD HOPPER
EL OTRO MAGO DEL SUSPENSO

El Semanal, Nº. 876, del 8 al 14 de agosto de 2004, págs. 56-60

NOCTÁMBULOS (NIGHTHAWKS) es una escena en una cafetería de la Ciudad de Nueva York. Es una de las imágenes pictóricas más célebres del siglo XX, un ícono visual a la altura de la Marilyn Monroe de Andy Warhol. Hopper pinta esta obra en 1942, pocas semanas después del ataque a Pearl Harbor que provoca la entrada
5 de Estados Unidos en la Segunda Guerra Mundial, pero en el cuadro de Hopper no hay nada que exprese violencia o alarma. Al contrario, los personajes de Hopper habitan un mundo personal que está distanciado de los sucesos de su época y que carece *(lack)* de crítica social. Además, sus personajes son siempre figuras vestidas como en la década de 1940. Como ocurre en las películas de Hitchcock, Hopper también crea una tensión
10 con imágenes rutinarias e inocentes, pero da la impresión de que pronto algo va a romper con *(break with)* la armonía de la escena. Y cuanto más se prolonga la espera, mayor es el suspenso.

¿Cómo crea la tensión? Primero, la crea con los personajes. Hopper es un *voyeur* que 'espía' a sus personajes sin ningún motivo particular. Lo hace por el
15 simple placer de captar detalles triviales de su existencia. Escoge a personas e individuos y los retrata en situaciones que causan incomodidad. Segundo, Hopper crea tensión a través de los escenarios. Hopper está siempre fuera de la escena, mirando a la gente a través de ventanas o espiándola desde una distancia cercana. Él es sólo un testigo silencioso de la soledad y la desesperación de los individuos
20 que retrata.

Por ejemplo, miremos con atención la escena en *Noctámbulos*. El mesero de la cafetería lava los platos y aparentemente habla con un hombre con sombrero y una mujer pelirroja. (**A propósito**, es interesante notar que la modelo en todos los cuadros de Hopper es su esposa Josephine). Hay una sensación de cordialidad.
25 El tercer hombre está de espaldas, **por consiguiente**, sin rostro. Este detalle y la oscuridad de las sombras ayudan a crear suspenso y falta de conexión con los personajes. Es decir, **a través de** los espacios oscuros y reducidos, y de personajes sin expresiones faciales y sin diálogo se evoca una sensación
30 de soledad.

"Nighthawks", a painting by Edward Hopper (1942)

Paso 2: ¿Cuánto has entendido? En grupos de tres, comprueben o rechacen los siguientes enunciados, al conectar los enunciados con la información del artículo que pruebe *(proves)* que son válidos o inválidos (hagan referencia a las líneas del artículo). Luego, comparen sus resultados con la clase.

Cierto	Falso	
☐	☑	**1.** Hopper pinta esta obra antes de la Segunda Guerra Mundial.
☐	☑	**2.** La presencia de la guerra es obvia en *Noctámbulos*.
☑	☐	**3.** Hopper se parece a Hitchcock porque los dos buscan crear tensión.
☑	☐	**4.** Hopper crea un sentido de tensión y suspenso por medio de las sombras y el silencio.
☐	☑	**5.** A Hopper le gusta observar a la gente para conocerla mejor.
☑	☐	**6.** Hopper crea la tensión de sus obras a través de sus técnicas artísticas.
☐	☑	**7.** El espectador de las obras de Hopper siente una conexión emocional con los personajes en la obra.

7B.24 ¡En español! Responde a la siguiente pregunta en español y luego comparte tus respuestas con la clase.

Según la lectura y tu opinión, ¿cómo crea Hopper un sentido de tensión en sus obras?

Perspectivas

7B.25 Cambio de escenas.

Paso 1: Examina la pintura de Picasso *Masacre en Corea* que aparece abajo y luego compárala con la de Hopper, indicando qué enunciado se refiere a Picasso, a Hopper, a ambos (selecciona los dos recuadros) o a ninguno (no selecciones ningún recuadro). Luego, escribe dos preguntas y léelas a la clase para que puedan contestarlas.

Hopper	Picasso	
☑	☐	**1.** La escena es muy tranquila.
☐	☑	**2.** La escena evoca sentimientos personales del pintor.
☐	☑	**3.** Su arte documenta actos de violencia contra la humanidad.
☐	☑	**4.** Los personajes son expresivos.
☑	☑	**5.** Utiliza colores oscuros como técnica artística.
☐	☑	**6.** Los asesinos son fríos e inhumanos.
☐	☑	**7.** Las víctimas son mujeres y niños.
☑	☑	**8.** La escena provoca tristeza.

Pregunta para la Clase 1. _____

Pregunta para la Clase 2. _____

Picasso's painting "Masacre en Corea" (1951)

7B.23 TEACHING TIP: When going over your students' first impressions, probe further by asking specific questions like, *¿El hombre y la mujer del restaurante son una pareja?* or *¿Qué hace el trabajador?*

7B.25 TEACHING TIP: Have students share their two questions in groups of three. Then, have each group identify one or two sentences that stood out to share with the class.

7B.25 SUGGESTION: We recommend you fill in any gaps in the students' statements by providing a corrected version of what they wrote. For example, if you read *"Picasso document la violencia del mundo y Hopper presents otros aspectes de las personas,"* you might correct the student's mistakes to read *Picasso documenta la violencia del mundo y Hopper presenta otros aspectos de las personas.*

7B.26 TEACHING TIP:
An alternative method of going over the answers would be to ask students to stand up in front of the room. In two extremes of the room hang signs reading *"Estoy de acuerdo."* and *"No estoy de acuerdo."* As you read the statements, invite students to move somewhere along the continuum between these two signs. This activity not only gets students moving around the room, but it also builds on their listening skills. It also provides a more engaging way of following up with relevant questions like: *¿Cómo celebra la comunidad las obras de Swanson?, ¿Por qué piensan que las obras de Picasso ofrecen un escape de la realidad?* Take advantage of this format to build in similar follow-up questions to push students' thinking.

7B.26 EXTENSION WRITING ACTIVITY: As a homework assignment, consider having students not only write whether they agree or disagree with the statements, but why.

7B.27 NOTE: The painting in this *Investigación* is not very representative of Swanson's work, but the paintings by Picasso and Hopper are fairly representative of their individual artistic styles.

7B.27 FOLLOW-UP:
After students have had a chance to share their opinions with their classmates, conduct an informal poll of how they felt about the three artists' paintings by asking them to raise their hands. At this point, you may want to elicit a few responses on each artist from the class.

Paso 2: Dos perspectivas. Entre 1930 y 1950, la violencia y la guerra dominaron el panorama mundial. Con otro/a estudiante, escriban uno o dos enunciados en español, para comparar cómo Picasso y Hopper se ocupan, de maneras distintas, de los sucesos mundiales. Luego, dénselos al profesor/a para que los lea a la clase y ver si hay consenso sobre el tema.

7B.26 Conexiones. ¿Qué tienen en común las pinturas de Picasso, Swanson, Hopper y Lomas Garza? Con un/a compañero/a lean los siguientes enunciados y marquen con una √ aquéllos con los que estén de acuerdo. Comparen sus respuestas con las de sus compañeros de clase.

☐ **1.** Los cuadros de Carmen Lomas Garza y John A. Swanson ofrecen perspectivas optimistas de la sociedad.

☐ **2.** Lomas celebra la familia y la comunidad. Swanson celebra los libros, el aprendizaje *(learning)* y la conciencia social.

☐ **3.** Las obras de Hopper también celebran la comunidad.

☐ **4.** A través de la obra de cada pintor, conocemos aspectos personales de ellos.

☐ **5.** En *Noctámbulos,* Hopper crea una escena que provoca sensaciones como la soledad y la falta de comunidad, pero las obras de Lomas Garza y Swanson inspiran sentimientos positivos.

☐ **6.** Swanson es el único pintor de los tres que incluye aspectos religiosos en su obra.

☐ **7.** Los personajes de los cuatro pintores no son expresivos. Es la escena lo que inspira emoción.

☐ **8.** Cada una de las obras de estos cuatro pintores inspiran emociones diferentes.

☐ **9.** Picasso y Hopper ofrecen un escape de la realidad.

☐ **10.** Las formas de los personajes de Picasso son simbólicas. Es decir, representan un concepto además de una persona.

7B.27 ¿Son representativas? Busca en la Internet otras pinturas de estos tres pintores para ver si las que aparecen en el capítulo son representativas de su trabajo. Marca con √ tu opinión y completa las oraciones. Luego compara tus opiniones con las de tus compañeros y den opiniones sobre el estilo de cada artista.

1. *The Classroom* ☐ es / ☑ no es representativa de las obras de Swanson porque…

2. *Noctámbulos* ☑ es / ☐ no es representativa de las obras de Hopper porque…

3. *Masacre en Corea* ☑ es / ☐ no es representativa de las obras de Picasso porque…

DICHOS

Mucho ojo, que la vista engaña.	*Appearances can be deceiving.*
Ojos que no ven, corazón que no siente.	*What you don't know won't hurt you*

Vocabulario: Investigación B

Vocabulario esencial

Sustantivos

el campo	countryside
la carta	letter
el cartel	poster
el desfile	parade
las diversiones	fun things to do
el equipaje	luggage
las estrellas	stars
la fuente	source
la gente	people
la guerra	war
la iglesia	church
los intereses	interests
la oscuridad	darkness
la pantalla	screen
la pareja	couple
los recuerdos	memories
la sombra	shadow
el suceso	event
el tema	topic
el testigo	witness

Verbos

contar	to tell
cuidarse	to take care of yourself/each other
divertirse	to have fun
regalar	to give (a gift)
tocar	to touch
aclarar	to clarify
aparecer	to appear
aprobar	to pass (a class, an exam)
componer	to compose; to repair
componerse de	to consist of
descomponerse	to break (down)
romper	to break (something)
sentirse	to feel
valorar	to value

Otras palabras y expresiones

el aprendizaje	learning
el cadáver	corpse
carecer	to lack
célebre	famous
el cerebro	brain
el/la compositor/a	composer
el conjunto	set
la incomodidad	discomfort
incorporarse a	to join
moreno/a	dark (complexion)
a propósito	incidentally
a ver	let's see
al aire libre	outdoors
así que	so/so that
este…	uh…/um…
hacer sentir mejor	to make (someone) feel better
por cierto…	by the way…
pues	so/well
sí mismo/a	himself/herself

Cognados

Review the cognates in *Adelante* and the false cognates in *¡Atención!*. For a complete list of cognates, see Appendix 4 on page 605.

¡VÍVELO!

En vivo

Entrevista sobre los artistas. In pairs, you will complete a chart that summarizes much of the information about the artists and art work in this chapter. Each student has information the other does not have. To obtain the information you need, you will have to ask for it in Spanish. Use the following as a guide.

1. ¿Cuál es la nacionalidad de ___?
2. ¿En qué fecha nació y en qué fecha murió? *(birth and death dates)*
3. ¿Cómo es el artista físicamente?
4. ¿Cómo se titula la obra de este artista mencionada en esta tabla?
5. ¿Cómo es la obra?
6. ¿Hay más información interesante?

A

Artistas	Nacionalidad	Fechas	Descripción física del artista	Nombre de su obra	Descripción de la obra	Varios
Botero	colombiano		Hombre maduro, tiene pelo gris y rizado, ojos grandes, bigote y barba.		Usa figuras corpulentas y pinta escenas de celebraciones.	
O'Gorman		1905-1982		Autorretrato		También fue arquitecto.
El Greco	español			El entierro del conde de Ordaz	Sus figuras son alargadas y sus temas son espirituales.	Nació en Grecia pero vivió toda su vida en España.
Dalí		1904-1989	hombre maduro, delgado y moreno con un bigote muy largo		Crea un mundo imaginario y surreal.	
Rockwell	estadounidense			Triple Self-Portrait		periodista e ilustrador
Swanson	estadounidense				Ofrece detalles minúsculos e incluye conceptos religiosos.	Su madre es mexicana y su padre sueco.
Picasso	español	N/A				
Hopper				Noctámbulos		

B

Artistas	Nacionalidad	Fechas	Descripción física del artista	Nombre de su obra	Descripción de la obra	Varios
Botero		1932		Frank Lloyd y su familia en Paradise Island		También es escultor.
O'Gorman	mexicano		Hombre delgado, joven, tiene pelo negro y lacio. Usa lentes y no tiene barba.			Pinta especialmente temas históricos.
El Greco		1541-1614	hombre con barba y bigote negros			
Dalí	español			La última cena		Gala es una mujer muy importante en la vida del pintor.
Rockwell		1894-1978	Hombre delgado y viejo. Tiene pelo gris y lleva lentes.		Pinta escenas de la vida diaria y personas comunes.	
Swanson			N/A	The Classroom		
Picasso			N/A			
Hopper	estadounidense		N/A		La falta de comunicación y la soledad predominan como temas en sus obras.	Su esposa Josephine aparece en muchas de sus obras.

Retrato de un/a artista. Write a brief review of a painter and/or his/her art and include the following information.

- Name of painter
- Country of origin, biographical dates (birth-death), recognitions, etc.
- Name of art piece(s)
- Description of artwork—colors, people, objects, actions, movement, relationships, spatial description
- Artist's style (in general terms)

En directo

INVESTIGACIÓN A: El arte y su temática

> **Antes de ver el video.** ¿Estás de acuerdo con las siguientes afirmaciones? ¿Por qué?
1. La característica más importante de un cuadro son los colores y las formas.
2. Es necesario que una obra de arte represente la realidad. Answers will vary.

> **El video.** Indica si cada uno de los enunciados es **cierto** o **falso**. Reescribe los enunciados falsos para hacerlos ciertos. Comprueba tus respuestas con un/a compañero/a.

Cierto	Falso	
☑	☐	**1.** Manuel Pardo es un artista cubano que vive y trabaja en Nueva York.
☐	☑	**2.** La figura de su padre ha influido mucho en su pintura.
☑	☐	**3.** La madre de Manuel aparece idealizada en sus cuadros.
☑	☐	**4.** Las obras de Manuel prueban que las apariencias engañan.

> **Después de ver el video.** En parejas, respondan a las siguientes preguntas: 1. ¿Qué significa la expresión "las apariencias engañan"? 2. ¿Están de acuerdo con esta expresión? ¿Por qué?

Vocabulario útil

soledad	*loneliness*
manga corta	*short sleeve*
pecas	*freckels*
nariz	*upturned*
respingada	*-nose*
maquillaje	*make-up*

INVESTIGACIÓN B: El arte: reflejo del artista

> **Antes de ver el video.** En parejas, contesten a la siguiente pregunta: ¿Crees que es necesario conocer a un artista para entender su obra? ¿Por qué? Answers will vary.

> **El video.** Escucha las opiniones de las personas en el video. Luego indica si estos enunciados sobre la mujer del cuadro son **cierto** o **falso**.

Cierto	Falso	
☐	☑	**1.** Parece que era una persona alegre.
☑	☐	**2.** Parece una mujer responsable que duda de la vida.
☑	☐	**3.** Todo el mundo la mira porque es atractiva.
☐	☑	**4.** Parece que tiene miedo.

> **Después de ver el video.** Escribe dos oraciones que describan la pintura de Manuel Pardo, según tu opinión. Luego, compara tu descripción con las de dos compañeros. ¿Son similares sus opiniones? ¿Qué diferencias hay?

Vocabulario útil

inquietud	*restlessness*
fortaleza	*fortitude*
venganza	*revenge*

CAPÍTULO **7**

WILEY **PLUS**

TESTING PROGRAM:
You will find a complete testing program for use with *¡Vívelo!* in *WileyPLUS*.

Retrato de la clase Checklist

You should have recorded information in your **Retrato de la clase** in conjunction with the following activities:

- ☐ **7A.14 ¿En quién o en qué piensas?**
- ☐ **7A.26 ¿Qué haces?**
- ☐ **7A.31 ¿Qué tienen en común?**

- ☐ **7B.14 ¡Sean los artistas!**
- ☐ **7B.20 ¡Lotería! Firma aquí.**

El arte y la interpretación

¿Qué emociones expresa y evoca el arte?

In this **Investigación** you will learn:

▶ How to express states of emotion

▶ How to express being in the past

▶ How to talk about general personality traits

¿Cómo se pueden describir las emociones que evoca o provoca una obra de arte?

You can express the emotions expressed on the faces of the characters.	Observa las expresiones de la gente en la obra. ¿Están ansiosos los personajes, nerviosos, tranquilos?
You can observe the scene depicted in the work.	¿Es una escena agradable (*pleasant*) o desagradable? ¿Inspira la escena tristeza u horror? ¿Inspira interés o indiferencia?
You can connect personal information about the painter of the work to inform your interpretation of the work.	¿Cuál es el estado del pintor cuando pinta la obra? ¿Qué motiva al artista a pintar la obra?

STANDARDS: CONNECTIONS. As you go over the objectives for this *Investigación,* remind students that learning a language is more than learning lists of vocabulary and grammar, but also about the cultures that go with the language. The National Standards speak to the value of making connections across curricular areas. As you teach Spanish, you are teaching art, history, geography, language, etc. In this particular case, the focus is on teaching Spanish through art.

SUGGESTION: Ask students to create their own facial expressions and gestures for these words. Then, have them share gestures with the class who will guess which word is being represented.

Adelante

¡Ya lo sabes! Las emociones y los sentimientos

agitado/a	horrorizado/a
calmado/a	impetuoso/a
controlado/a	inspirado/a
decidido/a	motivado/a
desconcertado/o	nervioso/a
desorganizado/a	obstinado/a
determinado/a	ordenado/a
equilibrado/a	reservado/a
estresado/a	preocupado/a
frustrado/a	satisfecho/a

8A.1 Opuestos y parejas.

Paso 1: Empareja las palabras de la primera columna con su significado opuesto en la segunda columna según el modelo.

_g_	**1.** flexible	**a.** condescendiente	
_h_	**2.** expresivo/a	**b.** extrovertido	
_e_	**3.** inteligente	**c.** controlado	
_b_	**4.** introvertido/a	**d.** ordenado	
_f_	**5.** agresivo/a	**e.** tonto (*unintelligent*)	
_d_	**6.** desorganizado/a	**f.** dócil	
_a_	**7.** respetuoso/a	**g.** obstinado	
_c_	**8.** impetuoso	**h.** reservado	

Paso 2: Escoge las cuatro palabras que te describan mejor y compártelas con la clase. Luego, busca a la persona que tenga el mayor número de palabras iguales a las tuyas y resume, en tu **Retrato de la clase,** en qué se parecen y en qué se diferencian.

Modelo: *En general, soy flexible, competitiva y decidida.*

Retrato de la clase: En general, mi compañero/a y yo somos ____, ____ y ____. En cambio, él/ella es ____ mientras que yo soy ____.

8A.2 De tendencias generales a estados temporales.
Responde a las situaciones a continuación. Luego compara tus respuestas con las de otros compañeros de clase.

1. Tú quieres mucho a tu novio/a pero un día pasas por la cafetería y lo/la ves besar a tu mejor amigo/a en una forma muy romántica.

Yo	Mi compañero/a de clase
a. Estoy motivado/a.	**a.** Está motivado/a.
b. Estoy agitado/a.	**b.** Está agitado/a.
c. Estoy descontrolado/a.	**c.** Está descontrolado/a.

2. Recibes una carta de invitación a una fiesta elegante pero no tienes vestidos o trajes adecuados y no tienes suficiente dinero para ir de compras.

Yo	Mi compañero/a de clase
a. Estoy estresado/a.	**a.** Está estresado/a.
b. Estoy horrorizado/a.	**b.** Está horroizado/a.
c. Estoy frustrado/a.	**c.** Está frustrado/a.

3. Recibes una F en tu clase de inglés y tienes que hablar con tu profesor sobre esta nota. Tocas la puerta y entras a su oficina.

Yo	Mi compañero/a de clase
a. Estoy tranquilo/a.	**a.** Está tranquilo/a.
b. Estoy desconcertado/a	**b.** Está desconcertado/a.
c. Estoy determinado/a.	**c.** Está determinado/a.

4. Tu mejor amigo quiere copiar tus respuestas en medio de un examen.

Yo	Mi compañero/a de clase
a. Estoy nervioso/a.	**a.** Está nervioso/a.
b. Estoy preocupado/a.	**b.** Está preocupado/a.
c. Estoy inspirado/a.	**c.** Está inspirado/a.

8A.1 EXTENSION ACTIVITY: The following are two activities that can be used to further practice these cognates: 1) Pairing Tool: Write these words on slips of paper. To pair students, randomly distribute the slips of paper. Students must find the person with the antonym. 2) *Mata-mosca:* Write these words so that they are spread across the board. Have the class form two lines in front of the board. Say one of the words and have students hit its antonym with a rolled up piece of paper. Make sure that you create opportunities where they hear and see this vocabulary several times in order for them to internalize it better.

8A.1 TEACHING TIP: Have students share the four words that best describe themselves and ask the class to take notes to arrive at some general statements about the class as a whole. Only do as many as you can afford to do with the amount of time you have in class. You could also have students guess the four words students chose for themselves and then compare notes to see how accurate they were.

8A.2 FOLLOW-UP: Answers will vary. Elicit responses from students to see how they answered. Conduct informal polls to see how they felt as a whole in the various situations and find out why. Ask students if the classmate they matched up with in Activity 8A.1 was the same classmate they found in Activity 8A.2. What might that mean?

EXTENSION ACTIVITY:
For a homework assign-
ment, invite students to
do some Internet research
on Goya. They should find
information on any of the
following topics: his family, his background, his
interests, etc. They can
also find an example of
one of his paintings. They
could write what they
learned in Spanish and
turn it in for a homework
grade. Students can also
share their individual
assignments with some
classmates. The objective
of doing this is to get
students to use vocabu-
lary/grammar they have
been exposed to while
moving into the unit on
the art.

8A.3 AUDIO SCRIPT: 1.
¿Cuál es la nacionalidad
de Goya? 2. ¿Por qué
se considera uno de los
pintores más famosos de
España? 3. ¿Cuándo pinta
sus "pinturas negras"? 4.
¿Cómo se llaman las pin-
turas de Goya que reflejan
que estaba desilusionado
y amargado?

8A.4 EXTENSION
ACTIVITY: Have students
go beyond stating how
they feel when look-
ing at the painting by
explaining why they feel
that way (e.g. *Me siento
horrorizado/a porque hay
cadáveres*).

¿Quién es Francisco de Goya?

Francisco de Goya (1746-1828), quien nació en Fuen-
detodos, Zaragoza, es uno de los más famosos pintores
españoles y es considerado "El padre del arte moderno".
Goya introdujo en su arte una nueva forma de expresión,
rompiendo *(breaking)* con los conceptos artísticos anteriores. Él fue *(was)* un pintor versátil cuya producción se extendió por sesenta años. La pintura que se muestra aquí
se titula El tiempo de la mujer y es representativa de sus
"pinturas negras" que reflejan el estado psicológico de
Goya en su vejez *(old age)*. El contraste entre las pinturas
de su juventud *(youth)* y sus "pinturas negras" muestra su
cambio de actitud hacia la vida. Las pinturas de su vejez
evocan emociones oscuras *(dark)*: Goya está amargado
(bitter) y desilusionado *(disappointed)* tanto con la gente
como con la sociedad. Los trabajos de su juventud, por
otra parte, evocan emociones más positivas aunque también representan una crítica social sobre las diferencias
entre la vida de los ricos y la de los pobres.

8A.3 **Goya.** Vas a escuchar varias preguntas sobre Goya. Selecciona la mejor respuesta a cada
pregunta según lo que has leído sobre el pintor. Luego, comprueba tus respuestas con la
clase.

1. **a.** Es argentino.
   b. Es ecuatoriano.
   c. Es español.

2. **a.** Su arte es surrealista.
   b. Su arte presenta nuevas técnicas artísticas.
   c. Su arte es típico de la tradición española.

3. **a.** en su adolescencia
   b. en los años antes de morir *(to die)*
   c. cuando se casa

4. **a.** las pinturas azules
   b. las pinturas negras
   c. los cuadros desesperados

8A.4 **¡Qué cara!** Mira las caras en el cuadro de Goya y marca con una ✓ las emociones que
el cuadro despierta *(awakens)* en ti. Luego, pregúntale a un/a compañero/a qué le hace
sentir la pintura y escríbelo en el espacio en blanco. Finalmente, averigua qué palabras
representan la reacción de la mayoría de tus compañeros hacia el cuadro. Apunta esa
información en tu **Retrato de la clase.**

Modelo: E1: *¿Qué te hace sentir esta pintura?*
E2: *Me siento agitada y desconcertada.*

Yo	Ante esta pintura, mi compañero/a se siente...
☐ ansioso/a	_____
☐ preocupado/a	*agitada*
☐ agitado/a	_____
☐ decidido/a	_____
☐ inspirado/a	*desconcertada*
☐ desconcertado/a	_____

☐ reservado/a   _____

☐ tranquilo/a   _____

☐ horrorizado/a   _____

☐ ¿otro?   _____

Retrato de la clase: La mayoría de los estudiantes de la clase se sienten _____, _____ y _____ ante la obra *El tiempo y las viejas* de Goya.

Bien dicho

La pronunciación y ortografía del sonido /b/

You have learned previously that the letters **b** and **v** both correspond to the /b/ sound in Spanish. However, the /b/ sound in Spanish is not pronounced the same in every context.

After a pause and after **m** or **n,** a **b** or a **v** in Spanish is pronounced by the upper and lower lips coming together with a hard sound similar to the /b/ sound in English.

> El hombre tiene hambre por costumbre.

In every other context, and especially between vowels, **b** and **v** are pronounced with a "softer" sound without the lower and upper lips touching. Instead, a small opening is left between the lips resulting in some friction. There is no real equivalent to this sound in English; however, a good rule of thumb is to pronounce **b** like you would in English, but without allowing your lips to touch.

> Mi burro baila la rumba siempre que come legumbres.

8A.5 **¿Sonido fuerte o sonido suave?** Vas a oír una serie de palabras y frases. Escucha y luego indica si oyes un sonido fuerte o un sonido suave. Comprueba tus respuestas con las de un/a compañero/a.

	Sonido fuerte	**Sonido suave**
1.	☑	☐
2.	☐	☑
3.	☑	☐
4.	☑	☐
5.	☐	☑
6.	☐	☑

8A.6 **Ahora tú.** En parejas, ayúdense a pronunciar las siguientes palabras y frases en español, de acuerdo con las reglas de arriba. Luego, la clase va a comprobar la pronunciación.

1. Rebeca es obstinada.

2. una observación desagradable

3. Beto se levanta temprano.

4. Botero y Rivera son artistas.

5. Los vamos a invitar.

6. un estilo abstracto y expresivo

7. Provocó una reacción violenta.

8. Los niños saben brincar bien.

8A.7 Asociaciones. En parejas, túrnense para leer las palabras de *Palabras clave* e indicar oralmente con qué categoría se asocia cada palabra. Si no se asocia con ninguna de las categorías, digan "ninguna".

Modelo: E1: *andar*

E2: *acciones físicas*

Categorías

Sentimientos alegres

Acciones físicas

Acciones invisibles

Emociones negativas

8A.8 ¿Qué acaba de pasar? En parejas, completen las siguientes oraciones con las respuestas más lógicas. Luego, comparen sus respuestas con las de otro/a compañero/a.

___b___ **1.** Diego Rivera está triste porque…

___e___ **2.** Goya está desilusionado porque…

___d___ **3.** Hopper se siente solo *(alone)* y aislado *(isolated)* porque…

___a___ **4.** Swanson está contento porque…

___c___ **5.** O'Gorman está muy alegre porque…

___f___ **6.** Botero tiene sueño porque…

a. acaba de donar muchos libros a una escuela.

b. acaba de morir Frida.

c. acaba de terminar el mural de la Universidad Nacional Autónoma de México.

d. acaban de bombardear el puerto de Pearl Harbor.

e. acaba de estallar *(break out)* una guerra entre España y Francia.

f. acaba de tomar algo para dormir.

8A.8 TEACHING TIP: Remind students that they need to use their knowledge about these artists (from *Capítulo 7*) to be able to answer the questions successfully.

8A.9 **¿Cómo están? o ¿Cómo se sienten?**   En grupos de tres, jueguen a un tipo de Pictionary en el cual cada miembro se turna para escoger una emoción al azar *(randomly)* y dibujar una cara que refleje esa emoción. Los otros estudiantes deben adivinar la emoción.

8A.10 **¿Cómo te sientes cuando...?**   Forma una pareja con un/a estudiante de tu clase de español que no conozcas bien. Escoge la Tarjeta **A** o **B** y lee las preguntas cuidadosamente. Selecciona cuatro preguntas para hacerle a tu compañero/a y escribe sus respuestas en tu **Retrato de la clase.** Usen el vocabulario de *Palabras clave*.

A
1. ¿Cómo te sientes cuando tienes que hablar con un policía?
2. ¿Cómo te sientes después de bañarte y tomar leche caliente?
3. ¿Cómo te sientes cuando una persona no asume sus responsabilidades en grupos?
4. ¿Cómo te sientes cuando conoces por primera vez a alguien que te gusta?
5. ¿Cómo te sientes cuando a un/a compañero/a de trabajo le gusta bromear y hablar sin parar *(non-stop)*?
6. ¿Cómo te sientes cuando tienes que ir a una fiesta y no conoces a nadie?
7. ¿Cómo te sientes cuando alguien te da un regalo?
8. ¿Cómo te sientes cuando bebes una bebida alcohólica (cerveza, vino, margarita)?

B
1. ¿Cómo te sientes cuando muere un pariente?
2. ¿Cómo te sientes cuando tienes muchas cosas que hacer?
3. ¿Cómo te sientes cuando estás muy, muy cansado/a?
4. ¿Cómo te sientes cuando te descuidas y no comes bien?
5. ¿Cómo te sientes cuando alguien dice algo bueno de ti enfrente de muchas personas?
6. ¿Cómo te sientes cuando un/a compañero/a de clase quiere copiar tus respuestas en un examen?
7. ¿Cómo te sientes cuando acabas de ver una película excelente?
8. ¿Cómo te sientes cuando estás en las montañas por la noche y puedes ver muchas estrellas?

Retrato de la clase: Mi compañero de clase _____ se siente muy nervioso/a cuando habla con un policía.

8A.11 *Un día en la vida de una niña.*   Mira el cuadro de Norman Rockwell en la página 357. Con un/a compañero/a, pongan las oraciones siguientes en orden cronológico según las imágenes. Después, comparen el orden de sus oraciones con el de otra pareja y luego con la clase.

   3   **a.** Se mira en un espejo.

  10   **b.** Johnny comparte un "hot dog" con ella.

   6   **c.** Se tira al agua.

   8   **d.** A ella no le gusta y le grita a Johnny.

   1   **e.** Por la mañana, Rebeca duerme.

   2   **f.** Se levanta.

   7   **g.** Johnny trata de hundir *(dunk)* a Rebeca en el agua.

   4   **h.** Mientras desayuna una banana, corre a su clase de natación.

___9___   **i.** Ella trata de hundir a Johnny.

___14___   **j.** Se despiden.

___11___   **k.** Anda en bicicleta con Johnny.

___13___   **l.** Miran la película.

___12___   **m.** Johnny la invita al cine.

___15___   **n.** Rebeca se ducha.

___18___   **o.** Johnny la acompaña a casa.

___16___   **p.** Rebeca se peina *(combs her hair)* para una fiesta de cumpleaños.

___19___   **q.** Johnny besa a Rebeca en la frente.

___22___   **r.** Rebeca duerme.

___20___   **s.** Rebeca escribe todo en su diario.

___21___   **t.** Rebeca reza.

___17___   **u.** Asisten a la fiesta.

___5___   **v.** Se pone un gorro de natación *(swimming).*

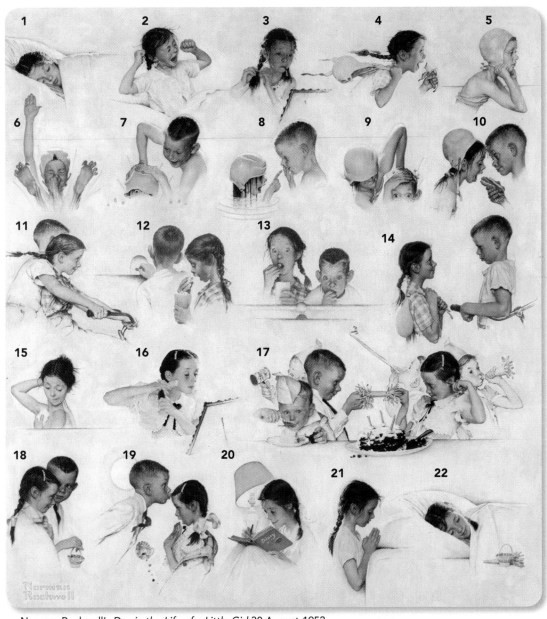

Norman Rockwell's *Day in the Life of a Little Girl* 30 August 1952

8A.12 TEACHING TIP: If you have a particularly large class, you may want to divide the class into more manageable groups for this activity (perhaps six people per group). You may want to have a student from each group read the entire enriched narrative to illustrate how much improved it is compared to the original.

8A.12 TEACHING TIP: Provide visual support by projecting the image of Rockwell's painting while students complete Activity 8A.12.

8A.12 Una narrativa más rica. Tu profesor/a dividirá la clase en dos grupos. Un grupo completará las oraciones de la 1 a la 11 con las frases a–k que aparecen a continuación. El otro grupo completará las oraciones de la 12 a la 22 con las frases l–v. Compara estas dos narrativas con la de la Actividad 8A.11. Como clase, comenten cuál es más personal y emotiva, y por qué.

Narrativa A

g **1.** Se mira en un espejo…

h **2.** Johnny comparte un "hot dog" con ella…

i **3.** Se tira al agua…

e **4.** A ella no le gusta y le grita a Johnny…

a **5.** Por la mañana, Rebeca duerme…

d **6.** Se levanta…

b **7.** Johnny trata de hundir a Rebeca en el agua…

k **8.** Mientras desayuna una banana, corre a su clase de natación…

j **9.** Ella trata de hundir a Johnny…

c **10.** Se despiden…

f **11.** Anda en bicicleta con Johnny…

a. con tranquilidad.

b. cuando ella sube *(comes up)*.

c. pero Johnny no está muy contento al despedirse de ella.

d. aunque todavía tiene mucho sueño.

e. pero a él no le molesta *(bothers)* la regañada *(scolding)*.

f. y es obvio por la expresión de Rebeca que ella se divierte.

g. pero tiene sueño y se nota en los ojos que se reflejan en el espejo.

h. porque es simpático y sabe que Rebeca tiene mucha hambre.

i. con los pies arriba, la nariz tapada *(blocked)* y el brazo levantado.

j. pero él está preparado, aunque todavía se sorprende un poco.

k. porque no quiere llegar tarde.

Narrativa B

o **12.** Miran la película…

n **13.** Johnny la invita al cine…

t **14.** Rebeca se ducha…

m **15.** Johnny la acompaña a casa…

u **16.** Rebeca se peina para la fiesta de cumpleaños…

r **17.** Johnny besa a Rebeca en la frente…

s **18.** Rebeca duerme…

l **19.** Rebeca escribe todo en su diario…

v **20.** Rebeca reza…

p **21.** Asisten a la fiesta…

q **22.** Se pone un gorro de natación *(swimming)*…

l. porque está ansiosa por escribir sobre su primer beso.

m. en silencio pero está decidido a actuar.

n. porque está enamorado de ella.

o. con mucha atención e interés.

p. y ambos se divierten mucho.

q. amarillo para protegerse el pelo.

r. y Rebeca está realmente sorprendida.

s. profundamente porque ha sido un día muy activo.

t. en preparación para la fiesta.

u. y está entusiasmada porque va con Johnny.

v. con devoción y seriedad.

¡Atención!

Sano	does not mean sane. It means *wholesome, healthy, sound*. To refer to someone who is sane in Spanish, use the words **sensato** or **cuerdo**. **Sensato** can also mean *sensible*.
	Un persona sana come bien y hace ejercicios con frecuencia.
	Las personas cuerdas no confunden lo real y lo irreal.
	Prefiero una compañera de casa sensata y responsable.
Simpático	does not mean sympathetic. It means *likeable, pleasant* or *friendly*. To refer to someone who is *sympathetic* or *understanding* in Spanish, use the words **compasivo** or **comprensivo**.
	Ese chico es muy simpático porque siempre me recoge el periódico de la calle.
	Los psicólogos son compasivos hacia los problemas de sus pacientes.
Sensible	does not mean sensible. It means *sensitive* as in highly susceptible or easily hurt.
	Estoy muy sensible porque acabo de perder mi trabajo.
Realizar	does not mean to become aware, like realize in English. It means *to make something happen* (such as a dream, a plan, a goal, or an activity). In other words, to make something a reality. To express the notion of *becoming aware* of something, Spanish uses the expression **darse cuenta**.
	Cenicienta (*Cinderella*) realizó su sueño al casarse con el príncipe.
	Hay jóvenes que no se dan cuenta del peligro del alcohol.

8A.13 En tu opinión. Entrevista a un/a compañero/a para averiguar su opinión sobre los siguientes temas. Luego, comparte con la clase la opinión de tu compañero/a para saber si la mayoría siente lo mismo. Escribe en tu **Retrato de la clase** cualquier generalización que se pueda hacer acerca de las respuestas de la clase. **¡Ojo!** Aquí también se reciclan cognados falsos de capítulos anteriores.

1. En tu opinión, ¿quién es más simpático, Arnold Schwarzenegger, Sylvester Stallone, Jackie Chan o Chris Rock?
2. ¿Qué música te irrita más, la ópera, la música *heavy metal*, la música *country* o el *jazz*?
3. ¿A quién has visto más furioso en la pantalla, al Increíble Hulk, al Terminador o a Darth Vader?
4. ¿Quién es más sensible, Oprah, el Papa Benedicto XVI, Rush Limbaugh o Diane Sawyer?
5. ¿Quién es más sano, Lebron James, Albert Pujols, Tiger Woods o Carlos Beltrán?

8A.13 TEACHING TIP: In order to maximize the effects of this activity, process students' answers as a class. Ask them what their opinions were and invite disagreements to occur. Make sure students are speaking Spanish throughout this activity.

www **¡Conéctate!**

Select an artistic movement that has been mentioned, such as *cubismo, surrealismo, realismo mágico,* or another one you may have heard in the past, such as *impresionismo, dadaísmo, neoclasicismo, modernismo, postmodernismo, romanticismo, rococó,* or *simbolismo* and google it to learn more about this artistic movement. Find a few images that reflect this artistic genre, include a brief description and share them with the class.

Estructuras clave The verbs *ser* and *estar*

DISCOVERY LEARNING: Before reading through *Estructuras clave* as a class, invite students to figure out for themselves when to use *ser* and *estar*. Encourage them to consider when each verb is used. Can they come up with their own explanation of how these verbs function? When students are encouraged to become language detectives, they can make sense of "grammar rules" on their own.

SER VS. ESTAR RHYME: The following rhyme may help students, particularly those with a strong musical intelligence: *How you feel and where you are always take the verb* estar; *What you're like and where you're from always take the other one.*

You have been using these Spanish equivalents of *to be* throughout your experience as a beginning Spanish speaker. What seems to characterize the ideas you express with **ser**? What seems to characterize the ideas you express with **estar**? In English we say "I am intelligent, responsible and creative" and "I am tired, sad, bored, etc.". We use *I am* in both sentences without differentiating between the type of descriptor that follows (intelligent/responsible/creative vs. tired/sad/bored). In Spanish, however, a distinction is made between the use of **ser** and **estar** depending on the types of descriptors that follow the verb.

Ser

So far we have used **ser** to describe people and things, as in **Es profesora** or **Pau Gasol es alto;** for talking about where someone is from, as in **Soy de Austin;** for expressing possession, as in **Es mi libro;** and for expressing what something is made of, as in **Es de madera. Ser** is used for descriptions of inherent nature or identity, meaning the way things and people are no matter what happens to them. The answer to the question "What's that person like?" involves talking about the inherent qualities that make him/her who he/she is. A person can be inherently happy and extroverted (**Ella es alegre y extrovertida**) or perhaps gloomy and introverted (**Él es sombrío e introvertido**).

Estar

You first used **estar** in greeting classmates and your instructor with the question **¿Cómo está/estás?** You have also used **estar** to talk about the location of people and things, as in **El libro está en la mesa,** and you have used it frequently to say whether you agree (**estoy de acuerdo**) or disagree (**no estoy de acuerdo**) with things. **Estar** is used to talk about the state of something, or someone's emotions at a given moment, and to talk about those states and emotions that are produced in response to an event or that are the resultant condition of an action. For example, someone feeling especially happy because they received a raise might say **Estoy feliz.** Someone feeling sad because their dog died might say **Estoy triste.** In talking about people, if you equate *to be* with **ser** and *to be feeling* with **estar,** you may find it easier to know when to use which verb.

Now let's take a closer look at this distinction in Spanish. The use of **ser** or **estar** may change the meaning of the statement slightly even when the same adjective is used.

Descriptor	Inherent qualities/Identity	Resultant condition or state
alegre (happy)	Soy alegre. Siempre sonrío. (I am happy by nature. I'm a happy person most of the time, in general. I'm always smiling.)	Estoy alegre porque mañana comienzan las vacaciones. (I am feeling happy because vacation starts tomorrow.)
guapo/a (good looking)	Salma Hayek es guapa. (Salma Hayek is good looking. She is a beautiful woman.)	Es la noche de los premios Oscar y Salma Hayek está muy guapa con su vestido de gala. (It's the night of the Oscars and Salma Hayek looks great in her gown.)
tranquilo/a (calm)	Soy tranquila la mayor parte del tiempo. (I'm calm most of the time. I'm a calm person by nature.)	No estoy muy tranquila en el trabajo porque mi jefe es un dictador. (I am not very calm at work because my boss is a dictator.)

Some adjectives change their meaning slightly depending on whether you use *ser* or *estar.*

Descriptor	Meaning when used with *ser*	Meaning when used with *estar*
listo/a (bright, clever; ready)	Soy lista. (I am, in general, a bright/clever person.)	Acabo de vestirme. Estoy lista. (I just finished getting dressed. I'm ready.)
vivo/a (alert, astute; alive)	Es muy viva. (She is an alert/astute person.)	La planta está viva porque la cuido bien. (The plant is alive because I take care of it well.)
aburrido/a (boring; bored)	Esta exhibición es aburrida. Vamos a otra galería. (This exhibit is boring. Let's go to another gallery.)	Si llevas a los niños a la exhibición van a estar aburridos. (If you bring the kids to the exhibit they're going to be bored.)
verde (green; unripe)	La casa es verde. Está al lado de una casa gris. (The house is green. It's next to a gray house.)	¡No comas ese melón! Está verde. (Don't eat that melon! It's not ripe.)

8A.14 **¿Ser o estar?** En parejas, determinen si en las oraciones de abajo se debe usar una forma de **ser** o de **estar.** Luego, conjuguen los verbos según el sujeto como en el modelo. Como clase, discutan sus selecciones.

1. El pintor colombiano, Fernando Botero _es listo_. Usa su pintura para expresarse.

   (a.) ser listo. **b.** estar listo.

2. Cuando un pintor tiene una idea original _está ansioso_ por empezar una obra nueva.

   a. ser ansioso **(b.)** estar ansioso

3. Una persona que _es viva_ tiende a ser observadora.

   (a.) ser viva **b.** estar viva

4. La terapeuta mira los dibujos que hacen los niños para determinar si _son alegres_.

   (a.) ser alegre **b.** estar alegre

5. Para hacer tostones *(plantain fritters)* hay que usar los plátanos cuando _están verdes_.

   a. ser verde **(b.)** estar verde

8A.14 TEACHING TIP: As students are going over their answers with a partner, remind them that they should explain why they arrived at their answers and to help each other understand the difference between *ser* and *estar.*

¡Conéctate!

Visit the famous *Museo del Prado* from the comfort of your computer. Open up the following website: http://www.museodelprado.es. Explore the website to see what masterpieces the museum has. Click on *PradoPlay* for interactive activities that will help you get to know the museum better. Make note of what you learned about the museum to share with your classmates.

8A.15 Escoger palabras. Mira las palabras que aparecen abajo y asegúrate de que conoces el significado de todas ellas. Luego, lee las siguientes oraciones y selecciona la palabra que complete mejor cada oración. Después, compara tus respuestas con las de otros dos compañeros de clase.

cansado/a
conservador/a
pesimista
avergonzado/a
embarazada
descuidado/a
triste
inteligente
responsable
enamorado/a
comprensivo/a

A. Identidad

1. Soy __responsable__. Siempre trato de hacer las tareas y nunca falto *(miss)* a clase.

2. Mi hermana es muy __comprensiva__. Ella escucha mis problemas y siempre trata de ayudar.

3. Hay personas que son muy __inteligentes__ pero no son maduras emocionalmente; por eso sus acciones a veces no son adecuadas.

4. Mis amigos son muy __conservadores__. Votan siempre por el candidato republicano.

B. Estado resultante

5. Estoy __triste__ porque no tengo dinero y no puedo ir al cine con mis amigos.

6. El médico me dice que voy a tener un hijo. ¡Estoy __embarazada__! ¡Qué alegría!

7. Estoy un poco __avergonzada__ porque he llegado tarde a mi primer día de trabajo.

8. Estoy tan __enamorada__ de mi novio. Nos vamos a casar el próximo año.

9. El profesor ha leído cien composiciones en dos días. Está muy __cansado__.

10. La casa de mi abuela es muy vieja. No la han pintado ni remodelado nunca. Está muy __descuidada__.

VÍVELO: LENGUA

Using past participles as adjectives

Past participles can function as adjectives and as such, they have to agree in number and gender with the nouns they modify, just like any adjective.

Son edificios restaurados.	*They are restored buildings.*
Es una reacción exagerada.	*It is an exaggerated reaction.*
Él está preocupado porque perdió su trabajo.	*He is worried because he lost his job.*

8A.16 ¿Cómo estabas? *(How were you feeling?)* Recuerda que **estar** se usa para expresar una condición que ocurre como consecuencia de algo que ha pasado anteriormente. Con un/a compañero/a emparejen lo que ocurre en la primera columna con el resultado lógico de la segunda columna según el modelo. Luego, comparen sus respuestas con las de otros/as compañeros/as.

8A.16 ANSWERS: Answers may vary and different reactions could be explored.

8A.16 TEACHING TIP: Call students' attention to the *estaba* form. This activity previews the use of the imperfect for descriptions in the past. Since the second part of the sentences are already written, this language becomes comprehensible input for students even though they haven't formally studied the imperfect tense yet.

Después de...,

_a_ **1.** brincar en el trampolín por dos horas

_c_ **2.** resbalarme *(to slip)* en la lluvia…

_b_ **3.** hablar con mi mejor amigo/a sobre un problema…

_h_ **4.** llegar tarde a mi primera cita…

_f_ **5.** conocer a Botero personalmente

_g_ **6.** apretar el botón muchas veces sin respuesta

_d_ **7.** volver del trabajo y luego ducharme…

_e_ **8.** consumir seis botellas de cerveza…

yo...

a. estaba *(I was)* cansado/a

b. estaba menos estresado/a.

c. estaba preocupado/a por mi traje nuevo.

d. estaba refrescado/a.

e. estaba borracho/a *(intoxicated).*

f. estaba inspirado/a.

g. estaba frustrado/a.

h. estaba avergonzado/a.

8A.17 Opina. Escribe un ejemplo de cada una de estas cosas o personas, según el modelo. Luego, comparte tus ejemplos con la clase para determinar las personas o cosas que más se repiten. Escribe tus resultados en tu **Retrato de la clase.**

1. artista conocido/a   *Picasso es un artista conocido.*

2. político dedicado/a

3. figura celebrada

4. libro censurado

5. extranjero/a *(foreigner)* admirado/a en Estados Unidos

6. celebridad triste

7. lengua ya no hablada

8. libro leído por muchas personas

Retrato de la clase: Para la mayoría, el artista más conocido es _____ (los artistas más conocidos son _____, _____ y _____). Según la clase, el libro más censurado es _____.

8A.18 Reciclaje. Contesta las siguientes preguntas. Luego, en grupos de tres, compartan sus respuestas a las siguientes preguntas y luego hagan lo mismo con el resto de la clase. Escriban cualquier observación general en el **Retrato de la clase.**

1. ¿Qué has celebrado recientemente?

2. ¿Adónde has viajado recientemente?

3. ¿Qué película has visto recientemente?

4. ¿Qué noticias has escuchado recientemente?

5. ¿Qué has hecho esta mañana?

Retrato de la clase: Muchos compañeros de clase han celebrado _____ recientemente. Algunos han viajado a _____.

8A.20 Antes de leer. Mientras lees en *Vívelo: Cultura* sobre Sonia Solanilla, una artista panameña cuyo trabajo presenta elementos del realismo mágico, examina su pintura para comprender las características de ese género literario y artístico. Haz una lista de las palabras o ideas que puedan caracterizarlo. Luego, comparte tus respuestas con la clase.

VÍVELO: CULTURA

Reflejos de la tierra, por Diana N. González

Sonia Solanilla Morales (1975-), nacida en Penonomé, provincia de Coclé, Panamá, a través de su plástica (sus obras de arte) y creatividad, reivindica la riqueza cultural panameña y su infinito amor hacia la naturaleza. Confiesa ser una mujer orgullosa (*proud*) de sus raíces (*roots*) y agradecida con la vida. Su talento se dejó ver desde niña y una vez finalizados sus estudios secundarios decide profesionalizarse. Estudió Arte y Decoración en la Facultad de Arquitectura Española en Madrid (1975) y en la Escuela Nacional de Artes Mateo Inurria en Córdoba, España (1982).

La adquisición de estos conocimientos la llevó a personalizar su obra pictórica con gran fuerza cromática y con un demostrado equilibrio entre el realismo de sus personajes y la fascinación de su contexto basado en lo cotidiano (*the day-to-day*). Para ella, su obra trasciende de lo estético para poner al descubierto (*uncover*) el misterio que habita en el interior de sus personajes.

"En mis creaciones podrán ver el retrato de gente común, la vegetación voluptuosa y mágica, el estilo colorista e intenso que reflejan la tierra". Su deseo es presentar al espectador un conjunto emotivo y técnicamente impecable, que "nos lleve a decir una vez más que el arte tiene sentido", asegura la artista. A través de sus imágenes, impregnadas de colores y paisajes, proyecta ángulos sobre la visión de la humanidad, basada en los sentimientos y las emociones. "Se traduce en un reflejo de nosotros mismos", a través de la percepción de su creadora.

Fine art photo of painting by Sonia Solanilla, La herencia.

En sus cuadros, Solanilla deja grabados sus sentimientos diarios, tristezas y alegrías. Está muy alerta a las expresiones cotidianas, a lo fantástico en la gente común, al profundo significado de cada gesto y a lo maravilloso de cada destello (*sparkle*) de luz y color.

8A.20 Opinión personal.

Paso 1: En parejas, lean el pasaje que aparece a continuación y escriban la traducción de los verbos subrayados según el modelo. Luego, comprueben sus respuestas con la clase. ¿Estás o no estás de acuerdo con el autor? ¿Por qué?

Para ser feliz en la vida, es importante ser realista. Nunca he pintado[1] un cuadro. Por eso estoy segura[2] de que no puedo pintar bien. No tengo la experiencia ni he demostrado[3] ningún talento como artista. Como soy lista, he reconocido[4] mis limitaciones *(shortcomings)* y mis habilidades. Gracias a ese reconocimiento, he escogido[5] una carrera donde puedo usar mi talento. Muchas personas no están dispuestas[6] *(willing)* a admitir su falta de talento en la música, la escritura, la pintura, etcétera, porque están contentas[7] con sólo hacer lo que les gusta. Yo soy[8] así. ¿Qué piensas tú? ¿Crees que el talento debe determinar la carrera o que es más importante disfrutar *(to enjoy)* de una carrera aunque no tengas talento para ella?

1. *I have never painted*
2. I feel/am sure.
3. nor have I demonstrated (neither have I demonstrated)
4. I have recognized
5. I have chosen
6. are willing/are not willing
7. they feel happy
8. I am

Paso 2: Entrevista a un/a compañero/a para ver si está de acuerdo o no con la posición de la autora. Hazle estas preguntas: ¿Qué piensas tú? ¿Crees que el talento debe determinar la carrera o que es más importante disfrutar de una carrera aunque no tengas talento para ella?

8A.20 STANDARDS: INTERPRETIVE MODE. The National Standards for Foreign Language Learning invite language professionals to look beyond the four traditional skills of language learning (reading, writing, listening, speaking) and undergo a paradigm shift by thinking of communication as the development of three modes (interpretive-*making sense of a message*, interpersonal-*spontaneous exchange of information*, presentational-*rehearsed and polished language*). Activity 8A-20 helps students develop their interpretive mode of communication. Through their response, as to whether or not they are in agreement with the author, they will be able to demonstrate their comprehension.

Enlaces

Las siguientes expresiones ayudan a relacionar las ideas de una oración con la otra parte de la oración, o las ideas de un párrafo con otra parte del párrafo.

ENLACES: Encourage students to use these expressions so that they are better able to string together sentences.

8A.21 Enlaces.
Según las definiciones y funciones que se describen a continuación, escoge la expresión en español que corresponde con cada expresión en inglés. Luego comprueba tus respuestas con la clase.

___b___ **1.** On the other hand

___a___ **2.** Customarily, in general practice

___c___ **3.** Since

a. Por lo común   Señala que algo ocurre con frecuencia o normalmente.

b. En contraste   Se usa esta expresión para indicar que el autor va a dar otra perspectiva que es contraria a la que acaba de dar.

c. Puesto que   Es otra forma de decir "porque" pero se usa para dar alguna justificación de algo que ya se ha mencionado.

8A.22 En contexto.
Escribe la expresión que mejor complete estas oraciones. Luego, comprueba tus respuestas con las de un/a compañero/a.

1. _Por lo común_, los amigos no se besan al saludarse en Estados Unidos.

2. _En contraste_ con Europa, no pagamos precios altos por la electricidad.

3. El precio que pagamos por la gasolina ha subido _puesto que_ el huracán Katrina destruyó muchas refinerías en el Golfo de México y en Luisiana.

8A.23 Antes de leer. Lee las siguientes preguntas antes de leer el artículo sobre Frida Kahlo.

1. What events in Frida's life led her to have a life of suffering?

2. When did Frida begin to paint seriously and for what purpose?

La pintora mexicana inolvidable

El nombre completo de Frida Kahlo fue Magdalena Carmen Frida Kahlo Calderón. Sus padres fueron Guillermo Kahlo, de origen judío-alemán y su madre Matilde Calderón, mexicana. **Por lo común** es reconocida como una de las pintoras mexicanas más importantes del siglo XX. Su arte es en gran medida *(to a great extent)* autobiográfico **puesto que** sus pinturas proyectan sus sufrimientos tanto físicos como emocionales.

A los seis años de edad sufre un ataque de poliomielitis que afecta su pierna derecha. Después, el año 1926 es muy trágico para Frida ya que sufre un accidente cuando el autobús en que viaja colisiona con un tranvía *(cable car)*. Ella sufre una fractura en tres diferentes áreas de la columna vertebral además de fracturarse tres costillas *(ribs)*, la clavícula, y la pierna y el pie derecho. Durante su vida los doctores le practican diversas cirugías y tiene que pasar meses completos recuperándose en cama, de hecho *(in fact)* muchos de sus mejores cuadros los pintó acostada.

Frida Kahlo se casa con el famoso pintor Diego Rivera

a la edad de 21 años cuando Diego tiene 42. Sin embargo, conoce a Diego cuando ella tiene 15 años y estudia en la escuela Nacional Preparatoria en donde observa a Rivera por primera vez mientras pinta su famoso mural "La Creación". Aunque Frida ama a Diego intensamente, su relación es muy problemática **puesto que** a Diego le gustan todas las mujeres y Frida constantemente sufre su infidelidad.

En 1953 tiene su primera y única exhibición individual en la Ciudad de México a la que asiste transportada en su cama porque a ella le es imposible caminar. Ese mismo año su pierna derecha es amputada. Finalmente muere en 1954 y sus cenizas *(ashes)* están en su casa del barrio de Coyoacán, que ahora es un museo, en la Ciudad de México.

En el año 1995 se publica un diario que Frida escribió en el periodo de 1944 a 1954. El diario contiene dibujos de Frida e ideas sobre el dolor, el amor, Diego, México y la pintura. En el año 2002 Salma Hayek interpreta el papel de la famosa pintora en la película *Frida*.

8A.24 Comprensión. En parejas, lean los siguientes enunciados sobre Frida y determinen si son ciertos o falsos. Hagan referencia a las líneas del artículo que prueben o no su validez. Compartan sus respuestas con la clase.

1. La obra de Frida Kahlo es muchas veces autobiográfica. cierto

2. Frida conoce a Diego Rivera cuando ella tiene 15 años. cierto

3. Diego Rivera es un esposo ejemplar y ellos viven una relación feliz. falso

4. Frida Kahlo solamente tiene una exhibición individual en toda su vida. cierto

5. Frida pinta muchas de sus obras sentada. falso

6. Los padres de Frida son mexicanos. falso

7. La pierna izquierda de Frida es amputada y sufre una fractura en el brazo derecho. falso

8A.25 ¿Cómo te sientes? Examina la fotografía y la pintura que aparece abajo y describe las emociones que inspiran esas dos imágenes. Comparte tus respuestas con la clase. ¿Cuáles son las emociones según la clase que más se asocian con la fotografía y la pintura? Escribe tus resultados en tu **Retrato de la clase.**

8A.25 FOLLOW-UP: Poll students to see how they felt about the picture and painting. Have them explain their reactions.

Modelo: La foto: *Cuando miro la foto estoy triste.*
El cuadro: *Al mirar el cuadro me siento horrorizado.*

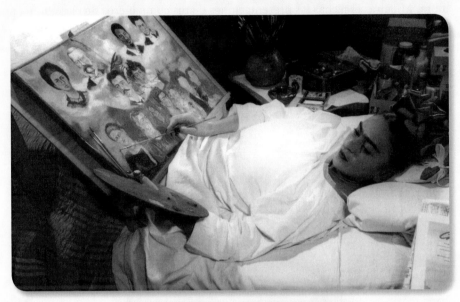

8A.26 *Frida* a la Hollywood. Busca y ve la película *Frida* en la que Salma Hayek hace el papel de Frida Kahlo. Algunos críticos han señalado que Hayek está demasiado *(too)* alegre en su papel y no representa el sufrimiento que hay detrás del carácter de Frida. Después de ver la película, escribe un párrafo de diez o más líneas en el que expliques por qué estás o no de acuerdo con esa opinión. Comparte tu opinión con la clase para comprobar si la mayoría está o no de acuerdo contigo.

Modelo: *Estoy de acuerdo/No estoy de acuerdo con que Salma Hayek está demasiado alegre. Creo que… También pienso que… Es obvio que… Además, creo que… Por eso pienso que… En conclusión/resumen, no estoy (o estoy) de acuerdo con los críticos que dicen que Salma Hayek no transmite el sufrimiento que hay detrás del personaje de Frida.*

Perspectivas

8A.27 La red. Tanto en el *Capítulo 7* como en esta *Investigación* has aprendido a describir obras de arte y muchos aspectos relacionados con varios artistas. Ahora, escoge uno de los artistas que aparecen abajo y busca en la Internet información personal sobre ese artista que pueda dar pistas *(clues)* sobre los aspectos emocionales y psicológicos de su obra. Mientras escuchas las presentaciones de tus compañeros de clase, toma apuntes de al menos ocho de estos pintores y usa esos apuntes para responder a las preguntas del ejercicio 8A.28.

8A.27 NOTE: Students may find the following website helpful when researching Latin American artists: http://lanic.utexas.edu/la/region/art/

8A.28 ANSWERS: Answers will vary. Encourage students to express their opinions, and for those that are especially advanced (false beginners and heritage learners), encourage them to defend their answers.

Diego Velásquez
Juan O'Gorman
Carmen Lomas-Garza
Francisco de Goya
El Greco
Robert A. Swanson
Edward Hopper
Jackson Pollock
Salvador Dalí
Norman Rockwell
Frida Kahlo
Pablo Picasso
Fernando Botero
Georgia O'Keefe
Diego Rivera
Otro: _____

8A.28 En mi opinión. Responde a las siguientes preguntas de acuerdo a los apuntes que tomaste en el ejercicio 8A.27. Escribe tus respuestas a continuación. Luego, busca a una persona de la clase que tenga pintores similares a los tuyos para trabajar juntos en la defensa de sus respuestas cuando compartan sus resultados con la clase.

De los pintores que hemos visto,…

1. ¿quién hace más transparentes las emociones de sus personajes?
2. ¿quién evoca sentimientos más profundos a través de a) la escena, b) el mensaje, o c) las técnicas artísticas de la obra?
3. ¿quién hace el comentario social más profundo?
4. ¿quién ha tenido la vida más interesante?
5. ¿quién ha sufrido más?
6. ¿quién tiene más complejos psicológicos?
7. ¿quién tiene el estilo artístico más original?
8. ¿a quién quieres conocer con más profundidad?
9. ¿quién ha realizado los sueños de su juventud?
10. ¿quién va a ser más reconocido por los sentimientos que inspira su arte en vez de por su estilo artístico?

Vocabulario: Investigación A

Vocabulario esencial

Sustantivos

la broma	*joke*
el conocimiento	*knowledge*
el dolor	*pain*
el hambre (f.)	*hunger*
el sufrimiento	*suffering*
la vejez	*old age*
sueño	*dream*

Adjetivos

aburrido/a	*bored; boring*
agradable	*pleasant*
alegre	*happy*
asustado/a	*scared*
cansado/a	*tired*
desilusionado/a	*disappointed*
embarazada	*pregnant*
enamorado/a	*in love; lover*
enojado/a	*upset, angry*
guapo/a	*good-looking*
inolvidable	*unforgettable*
listo/a	*smart, clever; ready*
preocupado/a	*worried*
solo/a	*alone, lonely*
temprano/a	*early*
tranquilo/a	*calm*
triste	*sad*
verde	*green; unripe*
vivo	*alert, astute; alive*

Verbos

andar	*to walk*
brincar	*to jump*
molestar	*to bother*
promover	*to promote*
subir	*to go up*

Otras palabras y expresiones

aislado/a	*isolated*
amargado/a	*bitter*
apretar	*to press; to tighten*
avergonzarse	*to feel ashamed*
borracho/a	*drunk*
descuidar	*to neglect*
el destello	*sparkle*
estallar	*to break out; to explode*
grabado/a	*engraved; recorded*
hundir	*to dunk; to sink*
las pistas	*clues*
regañar	*to scold*
resbalarse	*to slip*
tapado/a	*covered*
tirarse	*to throw oneself*
tonto/a	*not smart*

acabar de	*to have just done something*
andar en (bicicleta/carro)	*to ride (a bike/car)*
cosas que hacer	*things to do*
estar seguro/a	*to be sure*
la mayor parte del tiempo	*most of the time*
realizar un sueño	*to make a dream come true*
sin parar	*non-stop*
sin respuesta	*without an answer*
tener sueño	*to be sleepy*

Cognados

Review the cognates in *Adelante* and the false cognates in *¡Atención!*. For a complete list of cognates you've seen in this **Investigación**, see Appendix 4 on page 605.

¿Qué constituye una obra de arte?

In this **Investigación** you will learn:

▸ How to talk about diverse art forms

▸ How to describe a variety of artistic techniques

▸ How to talk about the purpose of art

▸ How to make an impersonal expression

▸ How to talk about what art is

¿Cómo se puede hablar de las diversas manifestaciones del arte visual?

You can talk about the medium the work represents.	Por ejemplo, ¿es una pintura, una escultura, una pieza de cerámica o una instalación? ¿Es un mural? ¿Es una foto? ¿Es arte digital?
You can locate the work within various contexts.	Por ejemplo, ¿es moderna, clásica o contemporánea? ¿Es abstracta o simbólica?
You can offer a general or personal interpretation of the work.	Esta obra provoca comentarios sociales y políticos. Esa obra sólo presenta imágenes estéticamente agradables.
You can offer a few criteria that define what art is and talk about the works according to those criteria.	El arte inolvidable tiene que inspirar emoción. Tiene que tener un mensaje.

Adelante

¡Ya lo sabes! La expresión artística

el desastre	el filme	convertir
el arte visual	el fresco	elevar
el arte digital	la fotografía	hipnotizar
el arte gráfico	la instalación	revelar
las artes musicales	el montaje	ofrecer
las artes decorativas	el mural	
la cerámica	el talento	
la cinematografía	el tatuaje	
el collage	el tema	
la escultura		
el graffiti		

8B.1 **Diversas expresiones artísticas.** En parejas, hagan una lluvia de ideas sobre las diversas expresiones artísticas y agreguen *(add)* otras si es posible. Usen el mapa semántico de la página 371. Luego, comparen sus mapas semánticos con los de otros compañeros.

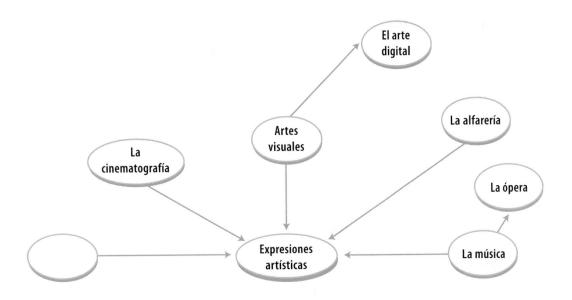

8B.1 TEACHING TIP: If students call out art forms not on the list, write the words in Spanish on the board, for example, *alfarería* = pottery (one of the earliest forms of art). Remember that while your students are brainstorming words they associate with the artwork, there are no wrong answers.

8B.2 Asociaciones. Selecciona la palabra que **no** pertenece a la categoría. Luego, comprueba tus respuestas con la clase.

1. Artes plásticas *(Non-performing arts)*
   a. arte de instalación
   b. arte escultural
   c. arte de metal
   d. arte teatral

2. Arte visual
   a. el karaoke
   b. el arte digital
   c. los frescos
   d. los murales

3. Movimientos artísticos
   a. el realismo
   b. el curiosismo
   c. el surrealismo
   d. el cubismo

4. Géneros literarios
   a. la poesía
   b. la novela
   c. la fotografía
   d. el cuento

5. Artes escénicas *(Performing arts)*
   a. la danza
   b. el teatro
   c. la ópera
   d. la arquitectura

6. Categorías temporales de arte
   a. moderno
   b. folclórico
   c. clásico
   d. contemporáneo

7. Artes musicales
   a. el jazz
   b. el graffiti
   c. la ópera
   d. la música clásica

8. Cinematografía
   a. el filme
   b. la película
   c. la cerámica
   d. el documental

8B.2 EXTENSION ACTIVITY: To further practice the cognates, have your students write sentences illustrating the meaning of the word but inserting a blank where the cognate word would be (as a homework assignment). For example, *Una ___ es arte físico y móvil. Muchas veces es de metal.* They can bring it to class and exchange their activities with a partner. They can complete each other's activities, review and correct them for further practice.

8B.3 ¿Es arte? Indica si estás de acuerdo o no con cada uno de los enunciados que aparecen abajo. Luego, compara tu perspectiva con la de un/a compañero/a y compártela con la clase. Apunta las opiniones compartidas en tu **Retrato de la clase.**

Sí   No

□   □   1. Una instalación es arte.

□   □   2. El arte digital es arte.

□   □   3. Una escultura de metal es arte.

□   □   4. Los murales en los edificios son arte.

□   □   5. El graffiti es una expresión artística.

□   □   6. El arte de la pintura tiene valor cultural.

□   □   7. Las artes literarias tienen valor en nuestra cultura.

□   □   8. La cinematografía es la forma de arte del futuro.

Retrato de la clase: Mi compañero de clase ____ dice que las instalaciones no le conmueven. No provocan emoción y por eso no son arte…

8B.3 TEACHING TIP: To tally students' responses to the 8 statements, ask them to raise their hand if they agreed or disagreed with each statement. Ask those who agreed with any of the statements to explain why. If they cannot express themselves in Spanish, let them know it is okay to express themselves in English. You, however, should ensure that you paraphrase in Spanish what the students say. In that way, they can express the criteria they are using to make judgments about art. You may want to note the various reasons they give, such as "It's not appealing" or "I can't relate to it", and then have them think about them, as in *Marcos dice que 'el arte te tiene que conmover'* y *Sofía dice que 'el arte tiene que complacerte'. Piénsenlo.*

8B.4 PASO 1: FOLLOW-UP. Explore with the class how many statements were not selected, which ones they were and why, and what students wrote down as other purposes that art serves. This activity is important "content" for this chapter and we will refer back to it.

8B.4 PASO 2: TEACHING TIP. Tally students' responses by asking for a show of hands of people who agree with each statement, i.e. *¿Quiénes están de acuerdo con que el arte sirve para provocar comentarios sociales?* Write the number of students who agree with that statement on the board, or use the chart provided in your Instructor's Resources to keep track of the counts.

8B.4 WILEY PLUS: INSTRUCTOR'S RESOURCES: A reproducible chart for tallying responses in Activity 8B.4 is available in your Instructor's Resources.

8B.5 TEACHING TIP: Have your students share their findings with a partner before sharing the answers as a large group.

8B.4. **Funciones del arte.**

Paso 1: De la lista a continuación, selecciona los enunciados que, en tu opinión, describen con precisión las funciones del arte. Compara tus respuestas con las de otros dos compañeros y escribe dos funciones más sobre el arte.

El arte sirve para…

☐ provocar comentarios sociales.

☐ señalar injusticias.

☐ inspirar emociones o sentimientos.

☐ hipnotizar a su audiencia para controlarla.

☐ provocar violencia.

☐ ofrecer diferentes perspectivas.

☐ crear formas de escape de la realidad.

☐ promover imágenes estéticamente agradables.

☐ explorar diversas formas de expresión.

☐ elevar la conciencia social de las masas.

☐ documentar un acontecimiento histórico.

☐ expresar los sentimientos del artista.

☐ describir o narrar una historia.

☐ instigar cambios sociales, políticos, espirituales.

☐ divertir a su público.

☐ otras posibilidades: _____

Paso 2: Comparte tus respuestas con la clase y escucha las respuestas de tus compañeros. Luego, escribe las funciones del arte más aceptadas en tu **Retrato de la clase.**

Retrato de la clase: Según la clase, el arte sirve principalmente para _____, _____ y _____.

8B.5 **Rompecabezas.** Después de leer la información sobre los artistas y sus piezas en *Imágenes y símbolos* en la página 373, empareja las descripciones de la columna **A** con el título de la pieza y el nombre del artista de la columna **B**. Comprueba tus respuestas con las de un/a compañero/a.

A	B
_c_ 1. La obra combina varios materiales como manuscritos antiguos, formas geográficas, mapas y templos precolombinos para hacer un collage fotográfico en blanco y negro.	a. *Heirs Come to Pass 3* Martina López
_a_ 2. La obra es un montaje digital de fotografías que simbolizan historias familiares anónimas.	b. *Transplant* Irene Pérez
_b_ 3. La obra usa símbolos para expresar la historia familiar de la artista. La planta, por ejemplo, simboliza la vida; la maleta representa la inmigración de su familia y las raíces (*roots*) son las raíces de la cultura de la artista profundamente plantadas en su país de origen.	c. *Totem Negro XVI* María Martínez-Cañas

Imágenes y símbolos

Martina López (estadounidense)
Heirs Come to Pass, 3 (1991) Mediante fotografías, Martina López coloca a las personas con ropas de la época victoriana en un paisaje *(landscape)* hostil. El título es un juego de palabras. De acuerdo con López *Heirs* son los niños que reciben la herencia y la acumulación de riqueza de sus ancestros. La palabra *heirs* es también homófono de la palabra *errors*... los errores que salpican *(speckle)* la historia familiar. Los herederos *(heirs)* heredan los errores así como los frutos de la vida de sus ancestros.

Irene Pérez (venezolana)
Transplant (1996) Esta escultura fue hecha para su exposición en el Nuevo Museo de Arte Moderno del centro de Austin, Texas. Está hecha con tierra, raíces *(roots)*, árbol, maleta *(suitcase)* y soporte de metal. "Representa generaciones de inmigrantes en mi familia, incluyéndome a mí misma, e ilustra el traslado *(move)* de nuestras raíces a nuestra nueva patria".

María Martínez-Cañas (cubana)
Totem Negro XVI (1992) Martínez-Cañas es una fotógrafa y en esta instalación usa manuscritos antiguos, mapas, estampillas, templos precolombinos y contornos *(environments)* geográficos para reflejar su lucha interior en relación con su herencia. "En los últimos años mi trabajo se relaciona con la búsqueda *(search)* de una identidad personal... la vida diaria de la cultura cubana antes de la revolución, las historias de mi familia, los recuerdos de Cuba, lugar donde nací pero del que no tengo memoria... Me enfrento con... una terrible sensación de encerramiento *(enclosure)*, separación y alienación. Siempre he sentido el deseo de pertenecer *(belong)* a un "lugar en particular"... A través de... un lenguaje visual de signos y símbolos.... expreso mi propio sentimiento de exilio".

All images provided by the Smithsonian American Art Museum, Washington, DC/Art Resource, NY

NOTE: The sense of alienation that Martínez-Cañas' work touches on reflects what many second-generation immigrants experience.

EXPRESIONES ÚTILES:
Ask students to share their thoughts on the works depicted in *Imágenes y símbolos* and to say what emotions the three art pieces provoke in them.

EXPRESIONES ÚTILES:
Without going into a lengthy grammatical explanation, point out the difference between *Me gusta la combinación de colores* (singular verb with singular subject) and *Me gustan los colores* (plural verb with plural subject). Or, ask students to tell you why *gusta* is used in one expression and *gustan* in the other. *Conmover* and *atraer* work like *gustar*.

VÍVELO: CULTURA: Ask students to write three statements that are either true or false based on the information about Dalí. Then have students read at least one of their sentences to the class for their response *(cierto/falso)*. Encourage students to google *La persistencia de la memoria* to verify the description of the painting.

EXPRESIONES ÚTILES

Me gusta/no me gusta…

...la combinación de colores.

...el diseño.

...el estilo.

Me gustan/no me gustan…

...los colores.

...las imágenes.

Me conmueve/no me conmueve. *It moves me/doesn't move me.*
No me atrae para nada. *It does not appeal to me in the least.*

VÍVELO: CULTURA
Salvador Dalí

Salvador Dalí (1904–1989) nació en Figueras, Cataluña, y es uno de los más importantes pintores españoles del siglo XX. Tanto su estilo artístico como su imagen personal llamaban la atención. Llevaba un bigote grande, parecido al de Velázquez, pelo largo y ropa excéntrica. El estilo de Dalí combina elementos estilísticos del cubismo, el dadaísmo y el surrealismo. En su conocida obra *La persistencia de la memoria,* se observan tres relojes doblados *(folded)*, uno encima de una mesa, otro colgando *(hanging)* de una rama *(branch)* y el tercero encima de una cosa en proceso de descomposición. El reloj blando *(soft)* es una imagen que se repite en otras de sus obras. Otra imagen que se repite en las obras de Dalí es la de su esposa, Gala, a quien amó hasta su muerte. Por último, la influencia freudiana es otra característica de sus obras.

DICHOS

Buenas y malas artes hay en todas partes. *There is good art and bad art everywhere.*

Cabeza grande, talento chico. *Big head, little talent.*

Fortuna te dé Dios, talento no. *May God give you luck, not talent.*

Al ciego no le aprovecha pintura, color, espejo ni figura. *Neither paint, color, mirrors nor shape are of any use to a blind person.*

Bien dicho

El sonido de la *d*

In Spanish, the letter **d** is pronounced in different ways depending on its environment. After a pause, and after **n**, **m**, or **l**, the /d/ sound in Spanish is a hard sound similar to the /d/ sound in the English words *dog, modem, daily,* and *chord*. Note that the hard /d/ sound is produced across word boundaries, such as when one word ends in an **n**, **m**, or **l** and the next word begins with a **d**, as in **tan diferente.**

dama	caldo
diferente	con datos

In every other environment, and especially between vowels, the /d/ is a soft sound pronounced with the tongue lightly positioned between the teeth. A close equivalent to this soft /d/ sound is the sound associated with the combination *th* in the English words *these, father, then, bother.* Note the slight vibration of the tongue between the teeth when you say these words in English. This sound is also produced across word boundaries as in the third example below where both "d" sounds are soft.

confiado	es de Denver
relajado	enamorado

8B.6 **¿Sonido fuerte o suave?** Escucha estas frases e indica si la **d** subrayada en cada una tiene un sonido fuerte o un sonido suave.

Fuerte	Suave	
☑	☐	**1.** el <u>d</u>rama trágico
☑	☐	**2.** un <u>d</u>irector español
☐	☑	**3.** jóvenes motiva<u>d</u>os
☐	☑	**4.** la realida<u>d</u> actual
☐	☑	**5.** Debes estu<u>d</u>iar arte.
☐	☑	**6.** la au<u>d</u>iencia

8B.7 **Ahora tú.** En parejas, ayúdense a pronunciar las siguientes frases. Teniendo en cuenta las reglas presentadas arriba y en la Investigación 8A. Presten atención a la pronunciación de la **d** y la **b.**

1. el medio ambiente
2. la humanidad
3. una película documental
4. una cámara digital
5. de piedra o madera
6. la danza moderna
7. Describan aquel dibujo.
8. un álbum de fotos

¡BIEN DICHO!: Point out to students that the *th* in *these, father, then,* and *bother* is not the same as the *th* sound in other English words like *thin, thimble,* and *with,* so that they have a good frame of reference.

8B.6 AUDIO SCRIPT: 1. el drama trágico, 2. un director español, 3. jóvenes motivados, 4. la realidad actual, 5. Debes estudiar arte. 6. la audiencia

8B.6 TEACHING TIP: Make sure that students have had ample opportunity to hear these phrases pronounced. Before moving on to the next phrase, check with students to see what they heard. To get a read on how students are doing, have them raise one finger to indicate "d fuerte" or two fingers to indicate "d suave." This way you can get a sense of how well they are doing processing this difference.

8B.7 SUGGESTION: You may want to model the pronunciation of the first couple examples for them. If you have them repeat a polysyllabic word after you, start with the last syllable and work your way to the beginning (e.g. –do, –pado, –cupado, preocupado).

Palabras clave 1 Otras expresiones artísticas

TEACHING TIP: To further develop students' acquisition of this vocabulary, read these statements and have the class say whether each is *cierto* or *falso*. 1. *En la clase de historia, estudiamos los eventos y las personas importantes del pasado.* 2. *Stephen Spielberg y George Lucas son cinesastas hispanos famosos.* 3. *Los cuentos de* Los hermanos Grimm *son cómicos.* 4. *El guión les indica a los actores qué tienen que decir y cómo deben decirlo.* 5. *Javier Bardem es un actor famoso que interpretó el papel de Anton Chigurh en la película* No Country for Old Men. 6. *Los estudiantes se mandan mensajes de texto durante la clase.* 7. *Percibimos sonidos con los oídos.* 8. *Los arquitectos diseñan casas y otros edificios.*

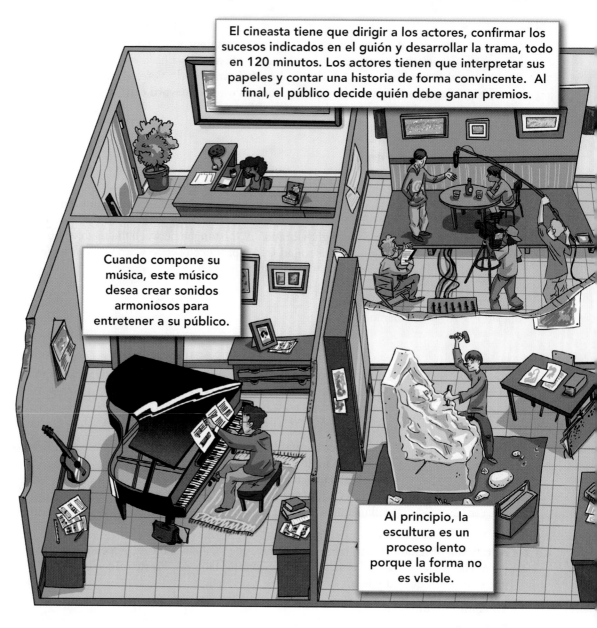

El cineasta tiene que dirigir a los actores, confirmar los sucesos indicados en el guión y desarrollar la trama, todo en 120 minutos. Los actores tienen que interpretar sus papeles y contar una historia de forma convincente. Al final, el público decide quién debe ganar premios.

Cuando compone su música, este músico desea crear sonidos armoniosos para entretener a su público.

Al principio, la escultura es un proceso lento porque la forma no es visible.

8B.8 ¿Quién hace arte? Selecciona la palabra que menos se asocia con el sujeto dado. Luego, indica con una ✓ los sujetos que consideres que son creadores de arte. Compara tus respuestas con las de un/a compañero/a.

☐ **1.** el/la cineasta
   a. la película
   b. el documental
   c. el filme
   d. el edificio ⬭

☐ **2.** el/la guionista *(script writer)*
   a. el teatro
   b. el bailarín ⬭ *(dancer)*
   c. la película
   d. el programa de televisión

☐ **3.** el cantante
   a. de rock
   b. de salsa
   c. de jazz
   d. de surrealismo ⬭

☐ **4.** el pintor
   a. la obra
   b. el mural
   c. el cine ⬭
   d. el fresco

La interpretación de un personaje depende de la habilidad del actor. Tiene que ser inolvidable para ganar el premio de "Mejor Actor".

Las artes gráficas tienen relación con las formas geométricas, el espacio, el diseño y el color.

El arte de instalación es normalmente duradero.

Los artistas cuentan con un modelo paciente porque modelar es muy aburrido y los modelos no ganan mucho dinero.

5. el compositor
   a. de música ópera
   b. de música clásica
   c. de música de orquesta
   d. de música fotográfica

6. el escritor
   a. la guitarra
   b. la novela
   c. el cuento
   d. la poesía

7. el/la arquitecto/a
   a. de edificios
   b. de centros comerciales
   c. de casas
   d. de lagos

8. los músicos
   a. violinistas
   b. guitarristas
   c. pianistas
   d. guionistas

9. los diseñadores
   a. de directores
   b. de videojuegos
   c. de tecnología innovadora
   d. de moda

10. los fotógrafos
   a. de canciones
   b. de escenas
   c. de paisajes
   d. de rostros (caras)

8B.8 FOLLOW-UP:
Explore which subjects students did not indicate as capable of creating art. Ask students *¿Crees que hay alguna diferencia entre arte y talento? Por ejemplo, un músico puede tener mucho talento pero no crear una obra de arte musical. Un diseñador de videojuegos puede diseñar un videojuego, pero ¿es un videojuego una expresión de arte?* The objective is to encourage students to think about these issues.

8B.9 ALTERNATE/ FOLLOW-UP: Have students turn in their responses to you. Then, randomly call out their responses to trigger a question, somewhat like how you play *Jeopardy*. For example, a group offers the title *Pan's Labyrinth* for item 2. You say *Pan's Labyrinth* and the class says *¿Qué película tiene una trama complicada?*

8B.9 **Nombra…** En grupos de tres, traten de dar un ejemplo por cada enunciado a continuación. Luego, averigüen cuáles fueron las respuestas más comunes de la clase. Escriban los resultados en su **Retrato de la clase.**

Nombren…

1. …un actor/actriz que ha hecho una interpretación inolvidable.
2. …una película con una trama complicada.
3. …un acontecimiento inolvidable.
4. …una novela con mensaje profundo.
5. …una persona que ha ganado un Óscar, un Grammy o un Emmy.
6. …una historia con un fin inesperado.
7. …una expresión de arte de baja calidad.
8. …un diseño original.
9. …un director talentoso.
10. …un filme duradero *(enduring,* as in *ever-popular).*
11. …una música o un cantante con sonido innovador.
12. …un papel difícil de interpretar.

Retrato de la clase: Según la clase, ____, ____ y ____ son películas con una trama complicada.

8B.10 TEACHING TIP: Walk around the room helping students with their sentences. This way you can ensure that the sentences that are read are clearly written.

8B.10 **Cierto o falso.** Escribe dos enunciados, uno cierto y otro falso, usando el vocabulario de *Palabras clave.* Comparte uno de los enunciados con la clase para que tus compañeros adivinen si el enunciado es el cierto o el falso.

VÍVELO: CULTURA
Cineastas hispanos

Guillermo del Toro, Pedro Almodóvar y Alejandro González Iñárritu son directores hispanos de fama internacional. Guillermo del Toro, nacido en México en 1964, ha dirigido o producido películas de terror y fantasía histórica desde *Hellboy, Blade II, El laberinto del fauno* (Pan's Labyrinth), *El orfanato* (The Orphanage), y *El espinazo del diablo* (The Devil's Backbone). A Guillermo del Toro le fascina la biología, el arte simbolista, el mundo fantástico y los temas oscuros. Otro elemento de sus películas es que sus protagonistas tienden a ser niños.

Pedro Almodóvar, nació en España en 1951. Es director, guionista y productor, y ha recibido dos premios Óscar en diversas categorías. Sus películas suelen *(tend to)* representar una realidad marginal y provocadora. Ejemplos de sus películas incluyen *La mala educación, ¿Qué he hecho yo para merecer esto?, Matador, La ley del deseo, Mujeres al borde de un ataque de nervios, ¡Átame!, Tacones lejanos, Kika, La flor de mi secreto, Carne trémula, Todo sobre mi madre, Hable con ella* y *Volver.* Sus películas han contado con la interpretación de artistas como Gael García Bernal, Antonio Banderas, Penélope Cruz y Javier Bardem.

Alejandro González Iñárritu nació en la Ciudad de México en 1963 y es director de cine. Dirigió la película *21 gramos* (21 Grams) (2003) con la interpretación de Naomi Watts, Sean Penn y Benicio del Toro. Por la película *Babel* ganó el premio de mejor director (Best Director) en el Festival de Cannes en 2006 y en 2007 ganó el premio Golden Globe de mejor película dramática. La película cuenta con las interpretaciones estelares de Gael García Bernal, Cate Blanchett y Brad Pitt.

EXPRESIONES ÚTILES

El cine

Es un clásico del cine.	It's a classic film./It's a film classic.
Ha tenido muy buena aceptación del público.	It has been well received by audiences.
Es un éxito de taquilla.	It's a box-office hit.
Es un fracaso de taquilla.	It's a box-office failure.
Ha recibido buena/mala crítica.	It has received good/bad reviews.

8B.11. ¿Has visto? Entrevista a tus compañeros de clase para saber si han visto alguna de estas películas. Cuando alguien contesta que sí ha visto la película debe escribir sus iniciales en tu tabla.

Modelo: E1: *¿Has visto El orfanato?*
E2: *Sí.*
E1: *Firma aquí, por favor. ¿Has visto Babel?*
E2: *No. No la he visto.*

El orfanato	El laberinto del fauno	21 gramos	Volver
Babel	Hellboy	Blade II	El espinazo del diablo
Vicky Cristina Barcelona	Mujeres al borde de un ataque de nervios	Spanglish	Hable con ella
Todo sobre mi madre	Como agua para chocolate	El amor en los tiempos del cólera	La casa de los espíritus

www **¡Conéctate!**
Learn more about these directors (or other Hispanic directors) online and/or watch at least one of their movies. Most video stores should have *Pan's Labyrinth, Volver, Babel,* and *21 Grams.* Check with your university library. Most will have many of these under foreign films. Share your thoughts about the director and the movie with the class.

EXPRESIONES ÚTILES: As a class, ask students to provide the names of movies that could be described with each of these phrases. For example, for *Es un éxito de taquilla* students might call out *The Dark Knight.*

8B.11 FOLLOW-UP: Survey the class for the movies with the highest number of signatures. This activity serves as a follow-up to *Vívelo: Cultura.* The last three movies are based on novels by Mexican novelist Laura Esquivel, Colombian novelist Gabriel García Márquez, and Chilean novelist Isabel Allende, respectively.

8B.11 RECYCLING: Call students' attention to the *modelo.* This activity recycles present perfect and direct object pronouns. Challenge students to tell you why *la* is the pronoun used in *No la he visto.* (It refers to *la película* titled *Babel.*) This may not be transparent to students until you point it out.

WILEY PLUS

INSTRUCTOR'S RESOURCES: You will find a reproducible chart for use with Activity 8B.11 in your Instructor's Resources.

¡Atención!

Disgustar	does not mean to disgust. To express to disgust in Spanish, use **dar asco**, **repugnar** or **indignar** the same way you use **gustar**. In Spanish **disgustar** means to *annoy* or to *displease*. In its reflexive form, **disgustarse** means *to get angry*. The related noun, **el disgusto**, means *unpleasantness*. Me disgusta la forma de hablar de individuos abusivos. El disgusto que causa una nota baja puede evitarse.
Cándido	does not mean candid as you might think. Instead, it means *innocent*, *ingenuous*, *naïve*. Use the words **franco** or **sincero** to express *candid*. Los niños de 4 años son siempre cándidos. Mis amigos son muy francos. Siempre me dicen lo que piensan.
Complaciente	does not mean complacent. In Spanish, it holds a very different meaning. It means **satisfying, pleasing, pleasurable**. The verb **complacer** means *to be pleasing* or *satisfying*, and the related noun is **la complacencia**. Me complace visitar los museos de Madrid, Washington D.C., Ciudad de Nueva York y París. Para muchos, sentarse a leer una buena novela es complaciente.
Relevante	does not mean relevant. In Spanish, use the word **pertinente** or **relacionado** for *relevant*. In Spanish, **relevante** means *outstanding*, *excellent*, *important* or *significant*. Cervantes es tan relevante en España y el mundo hispanohablante como lo es Shakespeare en el mundo angloparlante. La belleza no está relacionada con la inteligencia.

8B.12 SUGGESTION: For students who finish early, have them create their own sentences using at least three of the five words listed.

8B.12 Selecciona. Escoge una palabra de la lista para completar las oraciones. Uno de los espacios en blanco permanecerá vacío. Luego, comprueba tus respuestas con las de un/a compañero/a y después con la clase.

cándida   disgusto   disgusta   complacencia   relevantes

1. Las familias Bush y Kennedy son ____relevantes____ en la política de EE.UU.

2. La ___complacencia___ más grande de mi vida es estar con mis hijos.

3. La niña siempre lleva una expresión ____cándida____ y pura como una santa.

4. Me ____disgusta____ extremadamente la idea de no poder participar.

5. Después del ____disgusto____ entre mi padre y mi hermano, no los quiero ver.

8B.13 TEACHING TIP: Ask students if they know why there is an "A" before the name of their classmate sometimes and not others. No complex response need be given, merely that with the verb *gustar,* we would say *Le gusta(n)...* and the phrase *A + name* clarifies who *le* is.

8B.13 Entrevista. Entrevista a un/a compañero/a con el/la que no hayas tenido mucho contacto, usando las preguntas de abajo. Luego, comparte con la clase lo que hayas aprendido sobre él/ella. Anota en tu **Retrato de la clase** las respuestas más comunes a las siguientes preguntas.

1. ¿Qué te disgusta de la universidad?

2. ¿Conoces a alguna persona cándida? ¿Quién es?

3. ¿Quién es el político más relevante de tu país?

4. ¿Qué te complace cuando estás triste?

5. ¿Qué material de la clase de español es pertinente al mundo real?

Retrato de la clase: A (nombre) le disgusta ____ de la universidad. Conoce a una persona cándida. Se llama ____. Opina que el político más relevante de su país es ____. A (nombre) le complace ver escenas alegres cuando está triste. Para él/ella la material más pertinente de la clase de español es ____.

VÍVELO: CULTURA
Cantante de ópera

José Plácido Domingo Embil nació en España en 1941, pero cuando era pequeño se fue a vivir a México con su familia. Él es un cantante de ópera y director de orquesta. Es famoso por su voz de tenor, sonora y clara. Es un cantante muy versátil con una producción en español, inglés, italiano, francés, alemán y ruso. En el año 2008 la revista *BBC Music* seleccionó a Plácido Domingo como el mejor tenor en la historia gracias al voto de 16 críticos de ópera. También ha dirigido la Ópera Nacional de Washington y la Ópera de Los Ángeles. Además de su trabajo como cantante y director, Plácido Domingo es conocido por su labor humanitaria ya que ha ofrecido numerosos conciertos a beneficio de diferentes organizaciones benéficas. En la Ciudad de México existe una estatua de dos metros de altura y 660 libras de la figura del cantante como reconocimiento y homenaje a su generosidad.

Plácido Domingo

8B.14 **La decisión es tuya.** Selecciona los tres enunciados de la lista de a–o que aparece a continuación que mejor describan a cada artista. (Escribe las letras que corresponden a los enunciados en los recuadros a la izquierda del nombre del artista). Luego compara tus resultados con los de otros dos o cuatro compañeros.

☐	☐	☐	Martina López (artista)
☐	☐	☐	Irene Pérez (artista)
☐	☐	☐	María Martínez-Cañas (artista)
☐	☐	☐	Guillermo del Toro (director)
☐	☐	☐	Pedro Almodóvar (director)
☐	☐	☐	Alejandro González Iñárritu (director)
☐	☐	☐	Plácido Domingo (cantante)

a. Provoca comentarios sociales.

b. Critica injusticias.

c. Inspira emociones o sentimientos.

d. Ofrece distintas perspectivas.

e. Crea formas de escape de la realidad.

f. Promueve imágenes estéticamente agradables.

g. Explora diversas formas de expresión.

h. Eleva la conciencia social del público.

i. Expresa el interior del artista.

j. Describe o narra una historia.

k. Expresa la conciencia colectiva de un pueblo o de una comunidad.

l. Es portavoz *(spokesperson)* de realidades marginales.

m. Expresa ideas que atraen al público sin tener mensajes profundos.

n. Entretiene al público pero no por medio del *(through)* arte.

o. Otra: _____.

8B.14 EXTENSION ACTIVITY: Encourage students, in their conversations with their classmates, to make attempts to justify their choices. This is a more advanced linguistic function. However, you may have many false beginners that would be ready for such a challenge.

TEACHING TIP: Suggest to students that they look for examples of the impersonal or passive *se* in their communities. They should take pictures to bring in and/or find examples in advertisements to share with the class.

SUGGESTIONS: Challenge students to tell you one other use of *se* they have encountered. Write *Dalí le dedica el cuadro a Gala.* on the board. Then ask students *¿A quién le dedica el cuadro?* to elicit *Se lo dedica a Gala.* Students should recognize *se* as a replacement for *le* when an indirect and direct object pronoun are used together.

STANDARDS: COMMUNITY. This standard speaks to the importance of making the language relevant by connecting it to a community. Have your students find examples of how the *se* is used in these types of sentences within the community. By exploring communities with a significant Spanish-dominant population, they may come across signs that read *se vende...*, *se habla...*, *se alquila...*, etc. They can take pictures of these and share them with the class.

8B.15 FOLLOW-UP: Invite students to consider what kinds of similar signs, with text, they could make for places they frequent.

Estructuras clave 1

The impersonal and passive *se*

You have used the pronoun **se** in the context of reflexive constructions (as in **La profesora se pone los lentes**) and reciprocals (as in **Jorge y Ana se escriben cartas**). You have also seen **–se** attached to infinitives to signal that a verb is used reflexively, as in **vestirse** or **levantarse.**

Spanish also uses **se** + verb to indicate what are called *impersonal* subjects. In English, when the subject of a verb is unspecified, unknown, or intentionally deemphasized, we say *one, you, they,* as in *One never knows what will happen tomorrow, You can't win them all,* or *They say it's going to rain.* Spanish conveys this notion of impersonality with **se** and a third-person verb form, as in **Nunca se sabe lo que va a pasar mañana,** or **Se dice que va a llover.**

Whether to use a third-person singular verb form or a third-person plural verb form depends on whether the verb is being used with a singular noun, a phrase or clause (whole idea), or a plural noun.

Se da una película sobre Picasso en la tele.	*They're showing a film about Picasso on TV.*
Se habla mucho de la arquitectura verde.	*They talk a lot about green architecture.*
Se cree que la expresión artística es importante para el desarrollo infantil.	*They believe artistic expression is important in child development.*
Se ven las montañas en el fondo del cuadro.	*One sees the mountains in the background of the painting.*
Se venden fotos en la tienda del museo.	*They sell prints in the museum store.*

If the verb is being used with a singular noun, a phrase, or a clause, use a singular verb form. If the verb is being used with a plural noun, use a plural verb form.

The use of **se** + verb can also correspond to the use of the passive voice in English, and is often referred to as the *passive* **se.** For example, the last two sentences above are just as easily expressed in English as *The mountains are seen in the background* and *Prints are sold in the museum store.* A sign on a window that says **Se habla español** thus can be interpreted in English as *Spanish is spoken here* (passive) or *One speaks/They speak Spanish here* (impersonal).

8B.15 Símbolos. Empareja los letreros *(signs)* de la página 383 con sus significados. Luego, comprueba tus respuestas con las de un/a compañero/a.

___ **1.** Aquí se ofrece café caliente.

___ **2.** Aquí se vende gasolina.

___ **3.** Aquí no se estaciona.

___ **4.** Aquí no se fuma.

___ **5.** Se sale por aquí.

a
b
c

d
e

8B.16 **Normas culturales.** ¿Cuáles son algunas normas de comportamiento *(behavior)* sociales no verbales en los siguientes contextos? Usa el ***se* impersonal o pasivo** para escribir estas normas no verbales de comportamiento. Luego, comprueba tu trabajo con la clase.

> Modelo: en un restaurante
> *Se deja una propina.*

1. en una iglesia/templo/sinagoga

2. en una ceremonia matrimonial

3. en un funeral

4. en un museo

5. en la clase de español

8B.16 ANSWERS:
Answers will vary. Have students go over their responses in groups of three. Do they agree on the unspoken rules of behavior? This may spark an interesting discussion.

8B.17 **En tu opinión…** En parejas, entrevístense usando las preguntas a continuación. Anoten las respuestas de su compañero/a para compartirlas con la clase. ¿Pueden hacer alguna generalización sobre su clase de acuerdo a las respuestas?

1. ¿Qué se necesita para ser buen artista?

2. ¿Dónde se encuentra el arte que más te gusta: en un museo, en una galería?

3. ¿Dónde se escucha música hispana en tu ciudad?

4. ¿Crees que se debe estudiar el arte para ser buen artista?

5. ¿Se puede estudiar arte, música, fotografía o cinematografía en tu universidad?

8B.17 ALTERNATIVE DELIVERY. Instead of having students work with one partner, have them work with several classmates. You may want to have them mill around an open area in the classroom chatting informally with several classmates to elicit the same answers. After working on this for seven to eight minutes, you could process this as a class standing in a circle. This simple tweak adds an innovation to the class structure.

8B.18 **Se…** Empareja las expresiones con ***se* impersonal o pasivo** de la izquierda, con sus correspondientes asociaciones en la lista de la derecha. Luego, comprueba tus respuestas con la clase.

<u>e</u> **1.** Se debe lavar las manos.

<u>a/b/d</u> **2.** No se debe fumar.

<u>d</u> **3.** Se prohíben armas.

<u>c</u> **4.** Se habla español.

<u>a/b</u> **5.** Se acepta VISA.

a. En la gasolinera

b. En Macy's

c. En Puerto Rico

d. En el avión

e. En el baño

www **¡Conéctate!**
Search online for examples of images of the impersonal or passive *se.* Look for images using some of the following searches: **se habla, se vende, se alquila,** etc. Make a collage of the images to share with your classmates.

8B.19 ¡Que tenga sentido! En parejas, completen las siguientes oraciones para que tengan sentido. Al terminar, compartan sus oraciones con al menos dos parejas de compañeros. ¿Son semejantes o diferentes las oraciones finales?

1. Para crear arte digital, se requiere…

2. Para pintar una obra, se compra…

3. Para escaparse de la realidad se crea…

4. Para garantizar tener éxito como artista, se diseña…

5. Para diseñar una escultura de mármol *(marble)*, se necesita…

8B.20 Usos de se. ¿Cómo sabes qué función tiene **se** en una oración? Todo depende del contexto y del contenido. La situación y el significado generalmente determinan la función del **se.** Identifica qué indica el **se** en las siguientes oraciones. Luego, compara tus respuestas con las de un/a compañero/a y con las de la clase. Si necesitas aclaración de alguna respuesta, pregúntale a tu profesor/a.

Funciones:

a. Indicates reciprocity *(to each other)*

b. Indicates reflexivity *(to one's self)*

c. Indicates impersonal/passive statement *(one, "they" or "you" in a general sense)*

_b_ 1. Hay muchos pintores que **se** pintan a sí mismos en sus cuadros.

_a_ 2. Todos los personajes en los cuadros de Lomas Garza **se** parecen.

_c_ 3. **Se** necesita talento para ser pintor.

_c_ 4. **Se** dice que las personas talentosas son raras.

_c_ 5. No **se** debe cobrar tanto por los cuadros porque sólo la gente rica tiene dinero para comprarlos.

_c_ 6. Es difícil mantener el cabello cuando **se** tiene el pelo rizado y largo como lo tenía Diego Velázquez.

_a_ 7. Todas las estrellas en Hollywood **se** conocen.

_c_ 8. **Se** sabe que Pedro Almodóvar es uno de los mejores directores en el campo de la cinematografía.

8B.21 La publicidad. Examina la publicidad de la exhibición de arte que aparece a continuación. Luego, en grupos de tres diseñen un anuncio de cualquier detalle de un cuadro. Cada miembro del grupo debe hacer un comentario para la publicidad usando dos formas diferentes de **se** (un uso reflexivo/recíproco y otro impersonal/pasivo). En la parte de atrás, hagan una lista de los usos de **se,** como se muestra debajo del ejemplo de publicidad.

Modelo:

¡LAS OBRAS DE

DIEGO VELÁZQUEZ

SE EXHIBEN EN EL MUSEO DE GALAXIA!

¿Cuándo? 3 de agosto, 2015

¿Horas? **Se abre**[1] el museo a las 9:00 y **se cierra**[2] a las 18:00

¿Dónde? Calle 6, No. 351

¡Inspírese[3] con "Las Meninas!"
El cuadro más conocido del siglo XVII.
Diego Velázquez **se pinta**[4] en "Las Meninas" y también los Diegos **se miran**[5].

[1] abrirse - passive se (The museum is opened, but could say Someone (not specified) opens the museum) *se impersonal.*

[2] cerrarse - passive se (The museum is closed, but could argue Someone (not specified) closes the museum) *se impersonal.*

[3] inspirarse - reflexive (Inspire yourself)

[4] pintarse - reflexive (He paints himself)

[5] verse - reciprocals (The two Diegos look at each other.)

Estructuras clave 2

Comparisons of equality and inequality

Go to *WileyPLUS* and review the tutorial for this grammar point.

You will find PowerPoint presentations for use with *Estructuras clave* in *WileyPLUS*.

Equality

To talk about equality in terms of *quality*, Spanish uses **tan** + *adjective* + **como** *(as...as)*. **Tan** and **como** do not change forms, but the adjective must agree with what it is describing.

Esta galería es tan variada como esa.	*This gallery is as varied as that one.*
Dalí es tan conocido como Picasso.	*Dalí is as well known as Picasso.*
Swanson no es tan famoso como Hopper.	*Swanson is not as well known as Hopper.*

To talk about equality in terms of *quantity*, Spanish uses **tanto/–a/–os/–as** + noun + **como** *(as much/many…as)*. **Tanto** is an adjective and must agree with the noun it describes.

Javier Bardem no tiene tanto dinero como Paris Hilton.	*Javier Bardem does not have as much money as Paris Hilton.*
Sonia Solanilla no tiene tantos cuadros como Carmen Lomas Garza.	*Sonia Solanilla doesn't have as many paintings as Carmen Lomas Garza.*
No hay tantas galerías en Nashville como en la Ciudad de Nueva York.	*There aren't as many galleries in Nashville as (there are) in New York City.*

Inequality

To make comparisons of inequality in terms of quality, Spanish uses **más/menos** + *adjective* + **que** *(more/less…than)*, and to make comparsions of inequality in terms of quantity, **más/menos** + *noun* + **que** *(more/less/fewer…than)*.

Las pinturas son más interesantes que las fotografías.	*Paintings are more interesting than photos.*
El programa *Heroes* es más violento que el programa *Brothers and Sisters*.	*The program* Heroes *is more violent than the program* Brothers and Sisters.
El teatro tiene menos espectadores que el cine.	*The theater has fewer spectators than the cinema.*

To express *more than or fewer than* with numbers, use **más/menos de** + *number*.

El museo exhibe más de diez cuadros de Dalí.	*The museum is exhibiting more than ten Dalí paintings.*
Hay menos de cien obras en la galería.	*There are fewer than a hundred works in the gallery.*

8B.22 ¿Estás de acuerdo?

Paso 1: Lee los siguientes enunciados y escribe *Sí,* si estás de acuerdo o *No,* si no lo estás. Luego, busca a un/a compañero/a cuyas *(whose)* respuestas sean, en su mayoría, iguales a las tuyas. Trabaja con ese/a estudiante en el segundo paso en la página 386.

____ Mi clase de español es más interesante que mis otras clases.

____ Montar en bicicleta es más económico que manejar un auto.

____ Comer en casa es más barato *(inexpensive)* que comer en un restaurante.

____ Las películas son más entretenidas que los programas de televisión.

____ La música de Jay Z me gusta más que la música de Eminem.

____ Los libros son más interesantes que las revistas *(magazines)*.

____ Las fotos son más bonitas que los videos.

____ Hacer mi tarea es más divertido que pasar tiempo en Facebook.

____ El fútbol es más divertido que el béisbol.

____ Los tacos son menos populares que la pizza.

____ Mi profesor/a es más alto/a que yo.

Paso 2: Escriban tres enunciados en los que usen **más/menos que** cuando ambos/as estén de acuerdo, como por ejemplo: El programa *The Colbert Report* es más interesante que *American Idol*. Compartan sus enunciados con la clase y escriban cualquier resultado interesante en sus **Retratos de la clase.**

Retrato de la clase: En general, hacer la tarea no es más interesante que pasar tiempo en Facebook.

8B.23 ¿Cierto o falso?

Paso 1: Indica si cada uno de los siguientes enunciados es **cierto** o **falso.**

Cierto Falso

☐ ☐ **1.** Mis amigos son tan inteligentes como yo.

☐ ☐ **2.** El fútbol es tan popular en Brasil como el béisbol en la República Dominicana.

☐ ☐ **3.** El básquetbol es tan popular en Estados Unidos como el golf en México.

☐ ☐ **4.** Brad Pitt es tan guapo como Usher.

☐ ☐ **5.** La música de los Rolling Stones es tan popular como la música de Coldplay.

☐ ☐ **6.** Los deportes son tan populares en Estados Unidos como la política.

Paso 2: Escribe tus propios enunciados en una hoja aparte usando elementos de las tres columnas a continuación. Luego, lee al menos dos a la clase, que tratará de adivinar si para ti el enunciado es **cierto** o **falso.**

Ir al gimnasio	bonito/a	correr
Mi amigo	bailable	los partidos de básquetbol
La música salsa	divertido/a	mi profesor/a
Los deportes	saludable	la música alternativa
Las fiestas	talentoso/a	leer libros
	interesante	los juegos de mesa
	aburrido/a	mi amiga
	guapo/a	

Go to *WileyPLUS* and review the tutorial for this grammar point.

VÍVELO: LENGUA

Expressing superlatives

Superlatives express ideas such as *the biggest, the youngest, the tallest, the smartest, the most beautiful, the least expensive,* etc. Spanish uses the following construction:

el/la/los/las ___*(noun)* **más/menos** + *adjective.*

The noun may be omitted when it is understood through context or to avoid repetition. To indicate the field of comparison, such as *in the world, in the class, in my family,* etc. Spanish uses the preposition **de,** not **en.**

El país más grande del mundo es Rusia mientras que la Ciudad del Vaticano es el más pequeño.
La Miss EE.UU. y la Miss América son las mujeres más bonitas de este país.
El género literario menos estudiado de todos es el ensayo.

There are some irregular superlatives that do not use **más** or **menos:**

el/la mayor	los/las mayores	*the oldest* (people), *the greatest* (magnitude)
el/la menor	los/las menores	*the youngest* (people), *the least* (magnitude)
el/la mejor	los/las mejores	*the best*
el/la peor	los/las peores	*the worst*

Ricardo es el menor de su familia. Tiene tres hermanos mayores.
Las mejores películas del año son nominadas para los premios Óscar y las peores son nominadas para los premios Golden Raspberry.

8B.24 **Los superlativos artísticos.** Completa los espacios en blanco con la persona o el título que, en tu opinión, corresponda con la descripción. Comprueba con varios compañeros y con tu profesor/a, para ver quiénes tienen las opiniones más parecidas *(similar)* a las tuyas. Apunta la información en tu **Retrato de la clase.**

La actriz más inteligente   _____

El actor menos egoísta   _____

El/la director/a más talentoso/a   _____

La mejor película del año   _____

La peor novela que he leído   _____

El/la escritor/a más profundo/a   _____

La mejor canción de la primera década del 2000   _____

El peor género musical   _____

El programa de televisión menos interesante   _____

El/la pintor/a más famoso/a   _____

Retrato de la clase: La persona con opiniones artísticas más parecidas a las mías es _____ porque _____.

Enlaces

A veces es necesario hacer conexiones entre una cláusula y otra de una oración. Esto se hace con palabras como **quien, cuyo, y que,** entre otras.

8B.25 **Relaciones dentro de las oraciones.** Adivina lo que significa la palabra subrayada en las siguientes oraciones. Luego, comprueba tus respuestas con la clase.

who	whose	that

___who___ **1.** Hoy en día los descendientes de los peregrinos *(pilgrims)*, <u>quienes</u> inmigraron a Plymouth Rock en el siglo XVII, todavía viven allí.

___whose___ **2.** Muchos hispanos, <u>cuyos</u> padres heredaron *(inherited)* tierra en Texas bajo el gobierno mexicano, perdieron *(lost)* su tierra cuando Texas obtuvo su independencia en 1836.

___that/that___ **3.** Un mural es una obra de arte <u>que</u> expresa conceptos o ideas en forma de collage y <u>que</u> se hace en una pantalla o una pared *(wall)* dentro o fuera de un edificio.

8B.26 **Enlaces.** Empareja el significado según el contexto de la palabra subrayada y las palabras en inglés, abajo. Luego, comprueba tus respuestas con al menos otros dos compañeros de clase.

a. who   **b.** whose   **c.** that

___a___ **1.** El artista, quien nos puede inspirar, en muchos casos depende de fondos federales para poder trabajar.

___c___ **2.** Algunos políticos quieren eliminar de los programas escolares las asignaturas que fomentan la creatividad, como el arte.

___b___ **3.** El artista, cuyo arte nos puede inspirar, en muchos casos depende de fondos federales para poder trabajar.

8B.25 TEACHING TIP: Before doing this activity, ask students what the word *que* means. Encourage them to think of the many ways they have seen it used.

8B.26 TEACHING TIP: You may expand on answers by translating the antecedent and relative clause should you think it useful. 1. Art, which encourages creativity... 2. The artist, who can inspire us... 3. The artist, whose art can inspire us... 4. ...the classes that encourage creativity....

8B.26 EXTENSION ACTIVITY: If you have an advanced first-year class, have students create a sentence for both uses of the word *que,* the use of *quien/es* and *cuyo/a/os/as.* They should share their sentences with a partner. Have volunteers write some examples on the board.

8B.27 El muralismo. En parejas, lean lo siguiente sobre Judith Baca, una muralista estadounidense. Compartan su comprensión de la lectura sin traducir el texto palabra por palabra.

FUNCTIONAL OUTCOMES: The central question that frames this Investigación is *"¿Cómo se puede hablar de las diversas manifestaciones del arte visual?"* Explore whether students can now address this question and how they would go about it. Have them review the chart on the first page of this *Investigación*.

Judith Baca

Muralista chicana contemporánea

En la tradición de los grandes muralistas mexicanos, como Diego Rivera, José Clemente Orozco y David Alfaro Siqueiros, **quienes** crearon una conciencia nacional mexicana, el arte de Judith Baca se conoce como la expresión colectiva de los mexicoamericanos del suroeste de Estados Unidos. La gente mexicoamericana (o chicana), **cuyos** ancestros vivían en California, Nuevo México, Arizona, Colorado o Texas cuando esos estados pertenecían a México, o **que** inmigró a Estados Unidos para escapar de la violencia de la Revolución Mexicana, conserva aspectos culturales mexicanos, pero también ha absorbido aspectos de la cultura estadounidense. Judith Baca concibió la idea de *The World Wall* (El Mural Mundial) en colaboración con 45 artistas internacionales. Su meta fue elaborar una visión de un futuro sin miedo, sin guerra, sin discriminación, de paz y cooperación. El mural consiste en siete murales portátiles de 10 x 13 pies de largo. A continuación hay una descripción de cuatro de los siete murales.

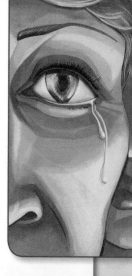

Triunfo de las manos: Este panel muestra la energía de las manos **cuya** fuerza puede triunfar frente a los esfuerzos destructivos para luego producir labores humanas positivas.

Resistencia sin violencia: Este panel presenta una visión de resistencia pacífica. Es a través de la unidad colectiva de los individuos **que** se puede contener la destrucción. Aquí se ve **que** la unidad colectiva de un pueblo, o sea, la conciencia colectiva de una comunidad, puede crear una transformación política, sicológica y social.

Triunfo del corazón: Este panel muestra una visión del origen de cualquier movimiento social hacia *(towards)* la paz. Es el individuo **quien** toma el primer paso hacia la acción.

Balance: Este es el panel central de los siete murales. Se basa en los conceptos de la tribu hopi y en la filosofía oriental del Yin y el Yang. Es un balance armónico donde el hombre llega por fin a respetar todas las formas de la vida.

8B.28 El muralismo. ¿Qué mensajes comunican estos paneles? Pon una ✓ al lado de los enunciados que crees que son ciertos, de acuerdo a las asunciones y mensajes expresados en estos murales, y agrega cualquier otro que no haya sido mencionado. Luego, comparte tus respuestas con la clase. ¿Hay algún enunciado que no fue apoyado por la mayoría de la clase?

☐ Es importante vivir en paz con el medio ambiente *(environment)*.

☐ No debemos permitir la guerra.

☐ Las transformaciones sociales, políticas e históricas mundiales se han producido porque una persona decidió separarse de las masas y pensar de una forma diferente.

☐ Tenemos que respetar la tierra, el ambiente natural, el aire y el ser humano porque todos se necesitan.

☐ La coexistencia en el mundo es mejor que la violencia.

☐ Debe respetarse a las personas humildes o algún día pueden unirse y rebelarse contra la desigualdad.

☐ Las máquinas controlan nuestras vidas.

☐ Las entidades impersonales controlan nuestras vidas.

☐ Otro: _____

Perspectivas

We return to the questions we asked at the beginning of this *Investigación:* What is art? What purpose does it serve and for whom?

8B.29 ¿Qué es arte? Como clase, averigüen cuántos creen que el graffiti de abajo se puede considerar arte. Luego, hagan una lista de los criterios que usaron.

8B.30 FOLLOW-UP: Can you discern any patterns in class based on students opinions? You may assign students to write a brief reflection over what they learned in this module that they did not know prior to it.

8B.30 De una cultura a otra. ¿Qué conclusiones puedes hacer sobre lo que se considera arte o lo que influencia esa opinión? Coloca una ✓ al lado de cada enunciado que consideres cierto. Luego, busca al menos otros dos compañeros de clase que hayan respondido como tú. Escribe tres enunciados más y compártelos con la clase.

☐ Una obra se aprecia más cuando no se conoce el contexto en el que el artista crea la obra.

☐ El arte debe hacernos pensar.

☐ El arte puede incluir comentarios sociales, pero sobre todo debe expresar los sentimientos del artista.

☐ Cuando veo una obra de arte, debo sentir sentimientos complacientes.

☐ Una obra de arte no sólo debe narrar una historia, también debe elevar la conciencia social del público.

☐ Todas las culturas tienen sus propias formas de arte que sólo se pueden apreciar si eres miembro de esa cultura.

☐ El verdadero arte transciende los idiomas puesto que el arte es un idioma; es el lenguaje de los sentimientos humanos.

☐ El verdadero arte tiene la capacidad de conmover a cualquier individuo puesto que los mensajes son universales.

☐ Las obras de arte de alto nivel *(level)* se concentran en temas universales, como la búsqueda *(search)* de identidad, las injusticias, los conflictos psicológicos o los sucesos históricos de una cultura o de la humanidad.

☐ Otro: _____

Vocabulario: Investigación B

Vocabulario esencial

Sustantivos

el actor/la actriz	actor
el arte de instalación	installation art
las artes gráficas	graphic arts
la belleza	beauty
el/la cineasta	cinematographer
el color	color
el diseño	design
la escultura	sculpture
el espacio	space
el guión	script
la historia	story
el homenaje	tribute
el medio ambiente	environment
el modelo	model
el papel	role
la patria	homeland
la paz	peace
la película	movie
el personaje	character
el premio	award
el público	audience
los sonidos	sounds
la trama	plot

Adjetivos

armonioso/a	harmonious
barato/a	cheap
duradero/a	lasting, durable
egoísta	selfish
inesperado/a	unexpected
mejor	better
peor	worse

Verbos

conmover	to move (emotionally)
enfrentar	to face, to confront
entretener	to entertain
evitar	to avoid
interpretar (un papel)	to act (in a role)
llamar la atención	to attract attention

Adverbios

hacia	towards
mediante	through

Otras palabras y expresiones

la alfarería	pottery
confiado/a	convinced; trusting
los contornos	environment, surroundings
la dama	lady
doblado/a	folded
la desigualdad	inequality
la estampilla	stamp
infantil	children's
el juego de mesa	board game
la norma	rule
oriental	eastern
el/la portavoz	spokesperson; speaker
precolombino	pre columbian
la rama	branch
la rompecabeza	puzzle
salpicar	to splash, splatter
el soporte	stand; support
tender a ser	to tend to be
el traslado	transfer
Me conmueve/ No me conmueve.	It moves me/doesn't move me.
No me atrae para nada.	It does not appeal to me in the least.

Cognados

Review the cognates in *Adelante* and the false cognates in *¡Atención!*. For a complete list of cognates you've seen in this **Investigación**, see Appendix 4 on page 605.

En vivo

Experiencias en la comunidad. Explore the community beyond the classroom: You will need to document five activities you participated in outside of class. These may include going to see a movie in Spanish, visiting an art gallery, attending a lecture on Hispanic art, literature, music, etc. volunteering with Spanish speakers, watching a TV program in Spanish five times (counts as one experience), going to a cultural event, etc. Use the following table as a model to keep track of your experiences. Then, share your top favorite experiences in groups of three. The class will vote on the most popular cultural experience.

You will need to document five times that you tapped into the Spanish-speaking community outside of your classroom. Take in as many cultural events as you can throughout the semester (e.g. movies, concerts, etc.).

	What?	Where?	Content Information	Comments:
1st				
2nd				
3rd				
4th				
5th				

TEACHING TIP: Have students anonymously post their descriptions. Classmates should guess to whom each description belongs.

La universidad Reflect on your college experience. Is college different from high school? What do you like most of all about college? What do you like least? What things are the same? What is there more of in college that there was not enough of in high school? What is there less of in college that there was plenty of in high school? What rules are the same in college as in high school? Is your college experience turning out to be a positive one?

Paso 1: Make a Venn Diagram (overlapping circles) to organize your thoughts in Spanish for this description. In the left circle include thoughts on your high school experience. In the right circle, include thoughts about your college experience. Include the similarities where the circles converge.

Paso 2: Once you have your Venn Diagram completed, you will have examples to make your comparisions.

Paso 3: Revise your description to ensure that you have included relevant details that will help you best compare your experiences.

Paso 4: Now that your content is solid, revise your writing focusing on form and accuracy. Make the necessary revisions and write your final draft.

Paso 5: Be proud of your final draft. It should be rich in detail and clear in form.

INVESTIGACIÓN A: El mural: arte con mensaje

> **Antes de ver el video.** Responde a las siguientes preguntas: ¿Hay murales en tu barrio o en otra ciudad cerca de donde vives? ¿Qué representan?

> **El video.** Indica si cada uno de los enunciados es **cierto** o **falso**. Reescribe los enunciados falsos para hacerlos ciertos. Comprueba tus respuestas con un/a compañero/a.

Cierto	Falsoz	
☐	☑	**1.** Los muralistas no tratan temas actuales.
☐	☑	**2.** La historia de Miami se creó hace 100 años con los anglosajones.
☑	☐	**3.** A Xavier Cortada le preocupa la destrucción de los manglares.
☑	☐	**4.** Cortada trata otros temas como la familia, la salud y los problemas sociales.

> **Después de ver el video.** En parejas, respondan a las siguientes preguntas. ¿Qué temas de los murales de Cortada les interesan más? ¿Por qué? Comparen sus respuestas con las de otra pareja.

Vocabulario útil

manglar	*mangrove swamp*
enfocar	*to focus*
cuna	*cradle*
semilla	*seed*
hundir	*to sink*

INVESTIGACIÓN B: Artesanías de Masaya

> **Antes de ver el video.** Indica cual de las siguientes afirmaciones están relacionadas con el concepto de "artesanía".

   ① Se realiza de forma manual.   **③** Muchos se usan como objetos decorativos.

   2. Se suele usar maquinaria moderna.   **④** Se producen individualmente.

> **El video.** Mira el video y ordena las fases del proceso de elaboración de la cerámica masaya.

   _2_ **a.** Con una espátula se remueven los restos de arcilla y se les aplica varias capas de arcilla líquida.

   _5_ **b.** La pieza de cerámica se pinta con pinturas hechas de óxidos, y se lleva al horno por aproximadamente 9 horas.

   _1_ **c.** Los pedazos de arcilla se moldean en el torno.

   _4_ **d.** Los relieves de los diseños son tallados con instrumentos filosos.

   _3_ **e.** Se deja secar por varios días, antes de pintarla.

> **Después de ver el video.** En el proceso de elaboración de la cerámica masaya, ¿cuál crees que es la fase más difícil? ¿Y la más fácil? Compara tus respuestas con las de un/a compañero/a.

Vocabulario útil

arraigado/a	*deep-rooted*
rasgos	*features*
arcilla	*clay*
relieve de los diseños	*raised designs*
tallar	*to carve*
texturas rugosas	*wrinkled textures*
instrumentos filosos	*sharped instruments*

TEACHING TIP:
Information gap activities help develop students' interpersonal communication skills. Although they are not completely spontaneous, they do encourage the exchanging of information as well as the negotiation of meaning.

Retrato de la clase Checklist

WILEY PLUS

TESTING PROGRAM:
You will find a complete testing program for use with *¡Vívelo!* in *WileyPLUS*.

You should have recorded information in your **Retrato de la clase** in conjunction with the following activities:

☐	8A.1	**Opuestos y parejas**
☐	8A.4	**¡Qué cara!**
☐	8A.10	**¿Cómo te sientes cuando…?**
☐	8A.13	**En tu opinión.**
☐	8A.17	**Opina.**
☐	8A.18	**Reciclaje.**
☐	8A.25	**¿Cómo te sientes?**
☐	8B.3	**¿Es arte?**
☐	8B.4	**Funciones del arte.**
☐	8B.9	**Nombra…**
☐	8B.13	**Entrevista.**
☐	8B.22	**¿Estás de acuerdo?**
☐	8B.24	**Los superlativos artísticos.**

Los días feriados

¿Cuáles son los días feriados y qué nos dicen de las culturas del mundo?

In this **Investigación** you will learn:

▶ How to express the names of holidays and describe the customs or traditions associated with the holidays

▶ About how some celebrations originated and what they have in common across cultures

▶ How a country's celebrations offer insights into its culture

▶ How to express habitual or repeated past actions

TEACHING TIP: In order to draw attention to the main theme of this chapter, start out by writing several important dates on the board (e.g. *4 de julio, 1 de abril, 14 de febrero,* etc.). Ask students what these dates mean to them to get their focus directed to the idea of *días feriados*.

¿Cómo se habla de los días feriados?

You can provide the name of a holiday and the date it is celebrated.	El Día de San Valentín se celebra el 14 de febrero en Estados Unidos.
You can describe the celebration.	Los novios se dan chocolates o regalos. Se dan cartas amorosas y se regalan flores.
You can describe the practices and customs of how you used to celebrate a particular holiday.	Se ponían las velas en un pastel y luego se encendían *(to light)* las velas y todos cantaban "Feliz cumpleaños".
You can draw conclusions about a country's culture based on its holidays.	La celebración nacional de la Inmaculada Concepción indica que hay una gran cantidad de católicos en Bolivia.

TEACHING TIP: Invite students to scan over the list of words in *Adelante*. Ask them to give you a percentage of words they recognized at first glance. Subsequent activities will help them take these words that they recognize and begin using them in context.

Adelante

¡Ya lo sabes! Días feriados y celebraciones

el amor	fabuloso
el carnaval	horroroso
la ceremonia	impresionante
la conmemoración	maravilloso
el Día de la Independencia (el 4 de julio)	
el Día de San Patricio (el 17 de marzo)	adornar
el Día de San Valentín (el 14 de febrero)	celebrar
el origen	simbolizar
el patriotismo	
Jánuca	
Ramadán	
el ritual	
Yom Kipur	

9A.1 **Los sinónimos o asociaciones.** Para cada palabra que escuches, busca la palabra asociada o el sinónimo de la lista a continuación. Luego, verifica tus respuestas con la clase.

a. el color verde

b. decorar

c. el ritual

d. fabuloso

e. un carnaval

f. la celebración

g. el Día de la Independencia

h. simbolizar

1. __a__   5. __e__

2. __b__   6. __g__

3. __c__   7. __d__

4. __h__   8. __f__

9A.1 AUDIO SCRIPT: 1. San Patricio, 2. adornar, 3. la ceremonia, 4. representar, 5. Mardi Gras, 6. el patriotismo, 7. maravilloso, 8. la fiesta

9A.1, 9A.2 TEACHING TIP: Consider making partner cards out of Activities 9A.1 and 9A.2. One person would receive a card that reads *el color verde* and they would need to partner with the student that had the card *San Patricio*. You will then be able to use these throughout the chapter, or later, to further practice this vocabulary.

9A.2 ALTERNATIVE STRATEGY: Have students complete this activity on their own and then compare their responses.

9A.2 **Crucigrama.** Con un/a compañero/a de clase, completen el crucigrama con las palabras que corresponden a las oraciones según la lista de palabras horizontales o verticales. Luego, comparen sus respuestas con las de otros grupos.

```
        1 H O 2 R R O R O S O
              I
3 I M P R E S I O N A N T E      4 O
              U         5 C      R
              A           A      I
          6 S           R      G
          7 I N D E P E N D E N C I 8 A
     9 Y  M             S  A      M
10 A D O R N A 11 R  B       A      O
   A      M  O  L       V      R
   M      K  L       A
   A      I  I       L
   D      P  Z
   12 J A N U C A
   N      R
```

Horizontal

horroroso impresionante Independencia Jánuca adornar

1. El adjetivo ____horroroso____ describe a algo que nos inspira mucho terror.

3. El adjetivo ____impresionante____ es un sinónimo de majestuoso, magnífico o poderoso (*powerful*).

7. El Día de la ____Independencia____ es un día que nos inspira mucho patriotismo.

10. El verbo decorar es un sinónimo del verbo ____adornar____.

12. Durante el ____Jánuca____ los judíos encienden velas (*candles*) durante las ocho noches del festival.

Vertical

Ramadán origen amor rituales Yom Kipur carnaval simboliza

2. El bautismo y la primera comunión son ____rituales____ importantes para los católicos.

4. El ____origen____ se refiere al lugar o al momento en que comienza algo.

5. Durante un ____carnaval____ la gente celebra mucho con procesiones y bailes en la calle.

6. La menorah ____simboliza____ las ocho noches de Jánuca.

8. El ____amor____ es una emoción positiva muy fuerte hacia otra persona.

9. El ____Yom Kipur____ es un día muy solemne para los judíos.

11. Durante el mes de ____Ramadán____ los musulmanes sólo comen por la noche.

www

¡Conéctate!
Three Kings' Day, or *el Día de los Reyes Magos*, is celebrated throughout the Spanish-speaking world. Beyond its religious significance, children also make wish lists for gifts, much like what children do for Christmas in the US Visit http://mujer.terra.es/muj/navidad/carta/carta.htm and with the help of a few clicks, you will be on your way to seeing what one of these letters might look like.

LISTENING
COMPREHENSION: Even
though students have
read similar descriptions
of these holidays, the
focus in 9A.3 is listening
comprehension. Have stu-
dents scan the names of
the holidays before they
listen to the descriptions
so they know what might
be described.

9A.3 AUDIO SCRIPT:
1. Una celebración
judía de ocho días que
normalmente ocurre en
diciembre, 2. El día que
las personas de un país
conmemoran su liberación
de otro país, 3. Una ce-
lebración musulmana que
dura aproximadamente un
mes, 4. El día religioso
más importante de los
judíos, 5. Una celebración
alegre de varios días,
como la de Mardi Gras, 6.
La fiesta que asociamos
con el amor

TEACHING TIP: As an
introduction to the
reading, write *Cuaresma*
on the board with the
English translation "Lent"
beside it. Then ask
students: *¿Quién sabe lo
que es la Cuaresma para
los cristianos?* As they
provide ideas, write them
on the board (if students
provide information in
English, restate and write
the information in simple
Spanish). Tell students
that they will be reading
about how indigenous
ceremonies influenced
and were influenced by
the Cristianity brought
to the New World by the
Spaniards. They should
also read about the
customs and practices
associated with the Car-
naval de Oruro.

READING STRATEGIES:
Remind students to scan
for cognates. They do not
need to understand every
word to get the gist of
the passage. They should
also take into account
what the context is.

9A.3 **¿Qué se celebra?** Escucha las descripciones de algunas celebraciones e indica a cuál se refieren. Luego, verifica tus respuestas con un/a compañero/a de clase.

a. el carnaval

b. el Día de la Independencia

c. Yom Kipur

d. el Día de San Valentín

e. Jánuca

f. Ramadán

1. __e__

2. __b__

3. __f__

4. __c__

5. __a__

6. __d__

El Carnaval de Oruro

La ciudad de Oruro, situada en los Andes de Bolivia, se llama la Capital Folclórica de Bolivia, principalmente debido al gran Carnaval de Oruro, el mayor evento cultural del año en Bolivia. El Carnaval de Oruro representa una combinación interesante de tradiciones indígenas y católicas, ya que tiene sus orígenes en el festival de Ito celebrado por los urus, un grupo indígena de la región, desde la época precolombina.

Durante la época colonial, el festival de Ito se incorporó al festival católico del carnaval, los dioses andinos se convirtieron en imágenes cristianas y se veneraron (were worshiped) como santos católicos.

Hoy en día, este carnaval comienza diez días antes de la Cuaresma (*Lent*). El festival incluye varias celebraciones basadas en la música, la danza y la artesanía tradicional. El elemento más notable del Carnaval de Oruro es una magnífica procesión de veinte horas que tiene lugar durante el tercer día. En esa procesión participan unos veinte mil bailarines y unos diez mil músicos que pasan por la ciudad por una ruta de cuatro

kilómetros. Los participantes se dividen en unos cincuenta grupos. Cada grupo lleva un traje o disfraz (*costume*) tradicional diferente y desfila (*parades*) al ritmo de un baile de gran importancia cultural e histórica.

El Carnaval de Oruro es muy conocido y atrae a muchos turistas de todo el mundo. En 2001, la organización de la UNESCO (United Nations Educational Scientific and Cultural Organization) reconoció la importancia cultural del Carnaval de Oruro al nombrarlo una obra maestra de la herencia oral e intangible de la humanidad.

TEACHING TIP: Have students go to http://youtube.com to watch any number of videos featuring this festival. This will offer context to students who may benefit from the video format.

STANDARDS: COMMUNICATION/INTERPRETIVE MODE. An important skill that students need to develop is their interpretive skill, or in other words, their ability to get the gist of a message. This reading and the subsequent activities
help students toward that goal of developing their interpretive skills.

9A.4 **El Carnaval de Oruro.**

Paso 1: Vas a escuchar varias oraciones. Indica si son ciertas o falsas de acuerdo a lo que has leído y corrige cualquier información falsa. Luego, verifica las respuestas con la clase.

	Cierto	Falso	
1.	☐	☑	Bolivia
2.	☐	☑	la Cuaresma/el festival católico de carnaval
3.	☑	☐	
4.	☑	☐	
5.	☑	☐	
6.	☐	☑	atrae a muchos turistas de todo el mundo; es reconocido por la UNESCO

Paso 2: Con un/a compañero/a de clase, contesten las siguientes preguntas en español usando el diagrama Venn para organizar la información. Luego, verifiquen sus respuestas con otro grupo.

1. ¿Con qué festival popular en EE.UU. podemos asociar el Carnaval de Oruro?

2. ¿Dónde ocurre este festival?

3. ¿Cuáles son los aspectos que tienen en común este festival y el Carnaval de Oruro?

Carnaval en EE.UU. **Aspectos en común** **Carnaval de Oruro**

Modelo: *Podemos asociar el Carnaval de Oruro con el festival de Mardi Gras en Nueva Orleáns. Los dos ocurren antes de la Cuaresma, los dos tienen procesiones durante varios días y los dos atraen a muchos turistas.*

9A.4 AUDIO SCRIPT: 1. La ciudad de Oruro está en Guatemala. 2. El Carnaval de Oruro se asocia con el Año Nuevo. 3. La parte más importante del Carnaval de Oruro es una gran procesión. 4. La procesión incluye muchas danzas tradicionales. 5. El Carnaval de Oruro se basa en un festival indígena. 6. El Carnaval de Oruro sólo tiene importancia para la gente de la ciudad.

WILEY
PLUS

9A.4 INSTRUCTOR'S RESOURCES: You will find a reproducible Venn Diagram for use with Activity 9A.4 in your Instructor's Resources.

VÍVELO: CULTURA

Las fiestas patronales

En diferentes regiones de España existe una tradición muy antigua en la que cada barrio (*neighborhood*) de la región tiene un Santo Patrón (*Patron Saint*). El día del Santo Patrón toda la comunidad lo celebra con una fiesta popular llamada fiesta patronal. En la región de Andalucía, al sur de España, son comunes las procesiones de gente que camina por las calles principales de la ciudad cargando (*carrying*) una imagen muy grande del Santo o de la Virgen que celebra su día. Estas procesiones son solemnes y siempre son organizadas por la Iglesia Católica. En otras regiones, sin embargo, las celebraciones de los santos tienen un tono más festivo, como en el caso de Barcelona, en donde las tradiciones han adquirido un sentido más contemporáneo y donde los orígenes religiosos de la tradición casi no se sienten.

Las celebraciones patronales son una tradición tan antigua que también se celebran en toda Latinoamérica debido a la influencia española. Uno de los efectos positivos de estas fiestas es que sirven para unir a los habitantes de distintas comunidades.

¿Existen fiestas populares en tu comunidad? ¿Qué actividades unen a las comunidades en tu país?

Decoraciones para una competencia en la Fiesta de Gracia (fiesta patronal de Barcelona, España)

🎧 Bien dicho

La pronunciación y ortografía del sonido /g/

In *Investigación 5B,* you learned that in Spanish the letter **g** before the vowels **e** and **i** and the letter **j** corresponds to a sound close to the *h* in English, although the sound is made in the back of the throat.

In Spanish, the letter **g** before the vowels **a**, **o**, and **i**, and before consonants, corresponds to a sound similar to the *g* of *got* in English. In Spanish, however, the /g/ sound is not pronounced the same in all contexts. After a pause, **m** or **n**, /g/ is pronounced with a hard sound like the *g* in the English words *got, gave,* and *gum.* In other contexts, the /g/ sound is pronounced more softly. The soft /g/ is similar to the way many English speakers pronounce the letter *g* in *sugar.*

Recall that in the combinations **que** and **qui**, the **u** is silent. In this same way, the **u** in the combinations **gue** and **gui** is silent. If the word is written with **ü**, then the **ü** is pronounced like *w* in English. Note the following contrasts:

guerra	[gé-rra]	güera *(blonde)*	[gwé-ra]
sigue	[sí-ge]	bilingüe	[bi-lín-gwe]
guitarra	[gi-tá-rra]	lingüística	[lin-gwís-ti-ka]
guía	[gí-a]	pingüino	[pin-gwí-no]

TEACHING TIP: Make sure that students have had ample opportunity to hear these words and phrases pronounced. Before moving on to the next sentence, verify their answers. To get a read on how students are doing, have them raise one finger to indicate hard *g* or two fingers to indicate soft *g*. This way you can get a sense of how well they are doing processing this difference.

9A.5 AUDIO SCRIPT: 1. organizada, 2. elegante, 3. San Gabriel, 4. antigua, 5. un gran libro, 6. Galo

9A.5 🎧 **¿Suave o fuerte?**   Escucha las palabras y frases e indica si escuchas una *g* fuerte o suave. Luego, verifica tu respuesta con la clase.

	g fuerte	*g* suave
1.	☐	☑
2.	☐	☑
3.	☑	☐
4.	☐	☑
5.	☑	☐
6.	☑	☐

9A.6 TEACHING TIP: You may want to model the pronunciation of the first couple of examples for students. If you have them repeat a polysyllabic word after you, start with the last syllable and work your way to the beginning (e.g. *–go, –bargo, –embargo, sin embargo*).

9A.6 MULTIPLE INTELLIGENCES: MUSICAL. After going through this exercise, you may want to have students pick one of the sentences and focus on perfecting it. Encourage them to add rhythm or a beat to what they are reading. After students have had a chance to practice, go around the room hearing students recite their line.

9A.6   **Ahora tú.**   En parejas, ayúdense a pronunciar las siguientes palabras y frases en español de acuerdo a las reglas que aparecen arriba. Luego, la clase verifica la pronunciación en grupo.

1. en lugar de
2. sin embargo
3. Los griegos ganaron la guerra.
4. unos regalos bien guardados
5. aquellos ingleses muy guapos
6. un gran gastrónomo gordo
7. gobernaban en Guatemala
8. A Agustín le gusta el guión.

9A.6 EXTENSION ACTIVITY: Have students create their own sentences focused on the pronunciation of the letter *g*. Offer students an extra homework point if they can tie it to the theme of *días festivos*.

Palabras clave Los días festivos religiosos, culturales o nacionales

1 de enero	Año Nuevo
6 de enero	el Día de Reyes/la Epifanía
31 de octubre	la Víspera de Todos los Santos*
1 y 2 de noviembre	el Día de los Muertos/de Todos los Santos
3ᵉʳ jueves de noviembre	el Día de Acción de Gracias
24 de diciembre	la Nochebuena
25 de diciembre	la Navidad
28 de diciembre	el Día de los Inocentes (es parecido a *April Fool's Day*)
31 de diciembre	la Nochevieja
la Pascua	la celebración de la resurrección de Jesucristo
la Semana Santa	la semana antes de la Pascua

*La Víspera de Todos los Santos *(All Saints' Eve)* se refiere a una celebración religiosa. No debe confundirse con Halloween, que hoy en día es una celebración secular.

Después de tres años de **compromiso**, Juana y Luis se casan porque **la boda es una costumbre** de sus **antepasados**.

Los padres y **los padrinos** del bebé participan en la ceremonia del bautismo.

Los jóvenes van a **desvelarse** después de la fiesta. **Festejan** su **amistad** y el **cumpleaños** de un compañero.

En las fiestas de Halloween, la gente lleva **una máscara** o **un disfraz** que **oculta** su identidad.

WILEY PLUS

You will find PowerPoint presentations for use with *Palabras clave* in WileyPLUS.

TEACHING TIP: Ask students to guess the corresponding English holiday based on the dates. Call attention to the note about *La Víspera de Todos los Santos* and Halloween. You may want to explain that the way in which people celebrate the contemporary, secular Halloween holiday has roots in the Celtic celebration of the end of the harvest season. Despite its Celtic roots, it is generally held that its name indeed derives from the Christian feast of All Saints' Day. "All Hallows' Eve" is another term for "All Saints' Eve". The two celebrations were aligned by popes in the early church. Students will make comparisons between *El Día de los Muertos* and Halloween in *Contextos y perspectivas* later in this *Investigación*.

TEACHING TIP: Model the relationship between "the refrigerator", "to refrigerate" and "refrigerated creme". Explore whether students can identify which is a noun, verb, and adjective. Then, encourage students to build on vocabulary they have learned. For example, if *simbolizar* means "to symbolize", what might *símbolo* mean? If *disfraz* means "costume", what might *disfrazarse* mean? If we can help students make these connections and develop strategies to do so, they will be better equipped to make meaning connections within word families.

9A.7 AUDIO SCRIPT: 1. Día en que los cristianos celebran el nacimiento de Jesucristo. 2. Día en que los cristianos conmemoran la resurrección de Jesucristo. 3. En Estados Unidos es el primero de abril. 4. El día en que un país conmemora su liberación de otro país. 5. En Estados Unidos se celebra el cuarto jueves de noviembre con una comida grande. 6. Se celebra el seis de enero y tradicionalmente los niños en los países hispanos reciben regalos ese día. 7. Se celebra el primero de enero. En Estados Unidos hay varios desfiles y partidos de fútbol americano. 8. Se celebra el treinta y uno de diciembre. Hay muchas fiestas y se canta la canción *"Auld Lang Syne"*.

9A.7 TEACHING TIP: You may elaborate or provide examples, such as *el desfile de Macy's* for item 1.

9A.8 TEACHING TIP: Suggest that students read the words on their card before they hear the statements to facilitate accessing the correct words.

9A.8 ANSWERS: A: 1. estar desvelado, 2. regalar, 3. las velas, 4. los antepasados, 5. la boda. **B:** 1. disfrazarse, 2. el regalo, 3. la amistad, 4. los padrinos, 5. darle gracias

9A.7 **¿Qué día festivo es?**   Escucha las definiciones e indica a qué día festivo se refiere.

_f_	**1.**	**a.**	el Año Nuevo
_h_	**2.**	**b.**	el Día de Acción de Gracias
_d_	**3.**	**c.**	el Día de la Independencia
_c_	**4.**	**d.**	el Día de los Inocentes
_b_	**5.**	**e.**	el Día de Reyes
_e_	**6.**	**f.**	la Navidad
_a_	**7.**	**g.**	la Nochevieja
_g_	**8.**	**h.**	la Pascua

9A.8 **¿Qué palabra corresponde?**   Escoge la tarjeta A o B y léele a un/a compañero/a de clase las definiciones y descripciones de la columna a la izquierda. Tu compañero/a te va a decir qué palabra defines o describes. Verifica tus respuestas con la clase.

> Modelo: E1: *Es algo que se pone sobre la cara que cambia su aparencia.*
> E2: *la máscara*

A	
Definiciones y descripciones para leerle a tu compañero/a:	**Palabras que corresponden a las definiciones y descripciones que va a leer tu compañero/a:**
1. Esta expresión describe el estado mental de una persona después de acostarse tarde.	los padrinos
2. Este verbo es un sinónimo de *dar*.	disfrazarse
3. Las luces que ponemos en un pastel de cumpleaños	el regalo
4. Los parientes muertos de varias generaciones atrás	darle gracias
5. La ceremonia en que dos personas se casan	la amistad

B	
Definiciones y descripciones para leerle a tu compañero/a:	**Palabras que corresponden a las definiciones y descripciones que va a leer tu compañero/a:**
1. Significa "ponerse ropa especial para una celebración"	los antepasados
2. Es algo que recibimos en la Navidad, en el cumpleaños u otra celebración.	estar desvelado
3. Una relación íntima no romántica	la boda
4. Son las personas más importantes para un/a niño/a en la ceremonia del bautismo católico (aparte de los padres).	las velas
5. Es lo que haces después de recibir un regalo de una persona.	regalar

9A.9 **Apunta el mensaje.** Escucha el mensaje que ha dejado un/a amigo/a en un contestatdor automático y escribe la información más importante. Luego verifica tu respuesta con otros compañeros de clase.

Para: Juan

De parte de: Irma

Mensaje: Invitación a quinceañera el sábado, 12 de abril en casa

de los padrinos, calle Los Almendros, 8:00 pm

9A.10 **Preparar una invitación.** Con un/a compañero/a, preparen y presenten un diálogo breve en el que una persona invita a la otra a un evento. Sigan la secuencia indicada y consulten las *Expresiones útiles*.

Estudiante A
• Saluda a tu compañero/a.
• Invita a tu compañero/a a un evento.
• Responde a las preguntas.
• Reacciona apropiadamente y despídete.

Estudiante B
• Responde al saludo.
• Pregunta los detalles (día, hora, etcétera).
• Acepta/Discúlpate de la invitación.
• Despídete.

EXPRESIONES ÚTILES

Las invitaciones

Las invitaciones son un aspecto importante de las celebraciones y de la vida normal. Las invitaciones son importantes cuando queremos que los familiares y los amigos nos acompañen al cine, a comer, a tomar un café, a un concierto o a una fiesta. Aquí hay una serie de expresiones útiles que se usan para invitar a alguien, para aceptar una invitación o para rechazar *(reject)* una invitación con cortesía cuando no puedes asistir. Cuando alguien te invita a comer, también implica que esa persona va a pagar la cuenta.

Para invitar:
¿Quisiera ir a...?
¿Quisieras ir a...?
¿Quisieran ir a...?

Would you like to go (to)...

Te/Le/Les invito a...
¿Te/Le/Les gustaría ir conmigo a...?

I'm inviting you to...
Would you like to go with me to...?

Para aceptar una invitación:
Por supuesto, me gustaría ir a comer/ir al cine/conocer a tus padres, etcétera.
Me encantaría...
Sería un placer...

Of course I'd like to go out to eat/go to the movies/meet your parents, etc.
I'd love to...
It would be a pleasure...

Para rechazar una invitación:
Lo siento, no puedo porque...
¡Qué pena! Ese día tengo otro compromiso.
Lo siento pero tengo que...
¡Qué lástima! A esa hora tengo una cita con el médico.

I'm sorry. I can't because...
What a shame! That day I have another engagement.
I'm sorry, but I have to...
What a shame! I have a doctor's appointment at that time.

9A.9 AUDIO SCRIPT: Hola Juan. Soy Irma. Quisiera invitarte a mi fiesta de quinceañera el próximo sábado, el 12 de abril, en la casa de mis padrinos. Ellos viven en la calle Los Almendros. La fiesta es a las ocho y vamos a celebrar toda la noche. Vienes, ¿no? Déjame saber. ¡Adiós!

9A.10 PREPARATION: Give students a time limit (perhaps four minutes) to prepare for this dialogue. Encourage them to do so without a script. They may just want to jot some notes as they prepare, but they should not depend on them when they present their dialogue. If students ask you for new words, hesitate from giving them new vocabulary since they already have enough new information to take into account. However, you may want to set a limit; for example, no more than one new word per pair with the agreement that they need to present the new words to the class before modeling their dialogue so that everyone understands.

9A.10 ALTERNATIVE DELIVERY: The interpersonal mode of the standard for communication focuses on spontaneous speech. You may want to randomly call on students to model a dialogue for the class without preparation. While they will have an idea of what the language functions are (e.g. making invitations), they will not know who they will be talking to and in what direction the conversation will go.

TEACHING TIP: Give students a few minutes to form groups and take turns inviting one another to hypothetical events (e.g. dinner, a party, etc.).

9A.11 ¿Cuál es tu día festivo favorito? Camina por la clase y pregúntales a diez compañeros cuál es su día festivo favorito y por qué. Crea una tabla como ésta con sus respuestas. Luego, repasa tus respuestas con la clase. ¿Cuál es el día festivo favorito más mencionado? Apunta las conclusiones en tu **Retrato de la clase.**

Nombre	Día festivo favorito	¿Por qué?

Retrato de la clase: Por lo general, el día festivo favorito de la clase es ___ porque...

9A.12 ¿Cómo celebran los días festivos? Describe un día festivo de tu cultura nativa siguiendo los siguientes pasos.

Paso 1: Contesta las siguientes preguntas usando el mapa semántico para organizar tus respuestas.

- ¿Cuál es el día festivo?
- ¿Cómo lo celebras?
- ¿Con quién(es) lo celebras?
- ¿Dónde lo celebras?
- ¿Qué comidas/bebidas especiales asocias con ese día festivo?
- ¿Qué actividades o costumbres asocias con ese día festivo?
- ¿Das regalos, tarjetas u otras cosas ese día? ¿A quién(es)?
- ¿Qué te gusta más/menos de ese día festivo?

Paso 2: Encuentra a un/a compañero/a de clase que describa el mismo día festivo y comparen sus apuntes.

Paso 3: Escribe en tu **Retrato de la clase** las semejanzas *(similarities)* y diferencias entre cómo tú y tu compañero/a de clase celebran el día festivo.

Retrato de la clase: Cuando ___ y yo celebramos ___ vamos a...

VÍVELO: CULTURA

El día del santo

Por siglos, una tradición hispana era nombrar a los hijos de acuerdo al día de su santo. Según las tradiciones católicas y ortodoxas, cada día del año está dedicado a un santo. La persona recibe el nombre del santo del día en que nació y así el día del santo es el mismo día que el cumpleaños. Hoy en día esta costumbre va desapareciendo. Sin embargo, el día del santo sigue siendo importante en muchos países. Por ejemplo, en pueblos católicos y ortodoxos, se celebra el día del santo además, o en lugar, del cumpleaños. La celebración del día del santo es similar al cumpleaños. La persona recibe las felicitaciones de sus familiares y amigos, puede haber una fiesta o comida especial y la persona puede recibir regalos.

Algunos nombres populares en Hispanoamérica de acuerdo al santo o la santa:

San Agustín	28 de agosto	Santa Elena	18 de agosto
San Antonio	17 de enero	San Fernando	30 de mayo
Santa Ana	26 de julio	San Francisco	4 de octubre
Santa Bárbara	4 de diciembre	Santa Isabel	4 de julio
San Carlos	3 de junio	San José	19 de marzo
San Cristóbal	10 de julio	San Juan	24 de junio
San Daniel	20 de marzo	Santa Mónica	27 de agosto

¡Atención!

Máscara does not mean mascara. As we learned in *Palabras clave*, it means mask. To express *mascara*, use **el rímel.**

Durante el robo, los ladrones *(thieves)* llevaban máscaras.
Carla se pinta las pestañas *(eye lashes)* con rímel violeta.

Ocultar does not mean occult. Instead, it means to *hide*. To express the idea of the *occult*, Spanish uses **lo oculto.**

Paco ocultó su cara con una máscara.
A mi amiga Sara le interesa lo oculto.

Ofrenda is not related to the verb to offend. To express to *offend*, use the verb **ofender.** Instead, **la ofrenda** means *offering*, in the sense of a gift, and is commonly used to refer to the money one gives during the collection at a religious service or to the offering given when requesting help from a divinity. To express *to offer*, use the verb **ofrecer.** The expression **estar en oferta** can be used to express the idea of a product being on sale.

Los parroquianos *(parishioners)* dejan una ofrenda generosa durante la ceremonia religiosa.
Muchas familias mexicanas ponen ofrendas en los altares en el Día de los Muertos.
María les ofrece bebidas a los invitados.
Los tenis más caros están de oferta esta semana.

Reunión does not mean reunion as in a social activity, like a high school reunion, or meeting someone again after a long time. Instead, it means *get together* or *meeting* as in an organized gathering, particularly in a professional context or in the context of a *family reunion*. To express the idea of *reunion*, use **reencuentro.**

Hoy tenemos una reunión con el cliente.
Voy a ver a Catarina mañana por primera vez en cinco años. Va a ser un reencuentro emocionante.
Tenemos una reunión familiar este domingo.

TEACHING TIP: Poll your students to see if any of them knows if their name corresponds to that of a saint. While some of your students may have a name that corresponds to a saint's name, many may not. Encourage students to find out when their saint's day falls. Remind them that in the Spanish-speaking world, this day can be as important as one's birthday.

TEACHING TIP: You may have students go to www.youtube.com to look for different interpretations of the birthday practices, such as of *Las mañanitas* in Mexico. Students can also visit http://gomexico.about.com/od/historyculture/qt/mananitas.htm where they can find a translation of the song and different activities and stories about topics like *La piñata, El día de la independencia,* etc.

9A.13 EXTENSION ACTIVITY: Encourage students to develop their own similar activities. This will help them draw even more attention to *los amigos falsos.*

9A.13 ¿Lógico o ilógico? Indica si los siguientes enunciados son lógicos o ilógicos y corrige los enunciados ilógicos. Luego, verifica las respuestas con la clase.

Lógico Ilógico

☐ ☑ **1.** La máscara es un cosmético para los ojos. el rímel

☑ ☐ **2.** Las ofrendas generalmente incluyen velas, flores, fotos y comida para recordar a la persona muerta.

☐ ☑ **3.** En esa tienda los precios son bajos. Siempre tienen muy buenos ofrecimientos. buenas ofertas

☐ ☑ **4.** Acabo de leer un artículo interesante acerca de la reunión de dos hermanos separados al nacer *(at birth).* del reencuentro

☑ ☐ **5.** No nos gustan las reuniones largas porque son aburridas.

9A.14 TEACHING TIP: Make sure to give students a chance to go over their answers with a partner. This way, they can clarify any issues they may have had.

9A.14 Completar la oración. Completa la oración con la palabra correspondiente de la lista. Luego, verifica tus respuestas con otros/as compañeros/as de clase.

máscara   oculto
oculta   oferta
ocultar   ofrenda
rímel

1. Cuando voy a la iglesia, dejo una ____ofrenda____ de $10.

2. Lo ____oculto____ se asocia con lo sobrenatural.

3. Queremos comprar esa casa. Vamos a hacerle una ____oferta____ al agente de bienes raíces *(real estate).*

4. Para hacer resaltar *(highlight)* los ojos, se pintan las pestañas con ____rímel____.

5. Los padres deben ____ocultar____ bien los regalos de Navidad para que los hijos no los encuentren.

PRE-READING ACTIVITY: Poll students before you read this passage to see if they know about the existence of Hispanic Heritage Month, and if so, when it is celebrated. Have students explore what celebrations occur in your community, city and university for Hispanic Heritage month.

VÍVELO: CULTURA

Celebración del Mes de la Herencia Hispana en EE.UU.

El Mes de la Herencia Hispana reconoce y celebra la rica influencia hispana en Estados Unidos. Del 15 de septiembre al 15 de octubre, una variedad de programas especiales, actos públicos, exhibiciones y sitios en la Internet celebran la herencia, la cultura, el espíritu y las extraordinarias contribuciones de los hispanos a Estado Unidos.

La celebración del Mes de la Herencia Hispana empezó a celebrarse a nivel nacional en 1968 con la promulgación de la Ley Pública 90-498, que autorizó una proclamación presidencial que declara la semana que incluye el 15 y el 16 de septiembre Semana de la Herencia Hispana. La semana se designó en estas fechas para coincidir con las celebraciones de la independencia de Costa Rica, El Salvador, Guatemala, Honduras y Nicaragua el 15 de septiembre y de México el 16 de septiembre.

Estructuras clave 1 The imperfect: Forms and functions

WILEY PLUS Go to *WileyPLUS* and review the tutorial for this grammar point.

WILEY PLUS You will find PowerPoint presentations for use with *Estructuras clave* in *WileyPLUS*.

In one of the activities in *Capítulo 8,* we used the imperfect form of **estar** to express states or conditions resulting from some past action:

Yo **estaba** cansado después de bailar y cantar toda la noche.	*I was tired after singing and dancing all night.*

The imperfect is also used to express habitual or repeated actions in the past:

Mi familia y yo siempre **visitábamos** a mis abuelos para celebrar la Navidad.	*My family and I always used to/would visit my grandparents to celebrate Christmas.*

In the context of a story narrated in the past, the imperfect is used to set the scene, describing the characters, the setting, and the existing state of affairs.

Era Carnaval y **eran** las doce de la noche. **Hacía** muy buen tiempo y **había** mucho alboroto ya que la gente **bailaba** y **cantaba** en la calle. Todos **llevaban** disfraces fabulosos y **estaban** contentos.	*It was Carnival and it was 12:00 at night. The weather was nice and there was a lot of commotion because people were dancing and singing in the street. Everyone was wearing fabulous costumes and everyone was happy.*

The forms of the imperfect are very easy to learn as there are only three verbs that are irregular and there are no verbs with stem-changes or spelling changes. There are two sets of endings in the imperfect: one set (based on **–aba**) for the **–ar** verbs and one set (based on **–ía**) for both **–er** and **–ir** verbs. Moreover, the **yo** form and the third-person singular forms of the verb are the same in all cases.

	–ar	**–er**	**–ir**
	celebrar	hacer	vivir
Yo	celebr**aba**	hac**ía**	viv**ía**
Tú	celebr**abas**	hac**ías**	viv**ías**
Él/ella/usted	celebr**aba**	hac**ía**	viv**ía**
Nosotros/as	celebr**ábamos**	hac**íamos**	viv**íamos**
Vosotros/as	celebr**abais**	hac**íais**	viv**íais**
Ellos/ellas/ustedes	celebr**aban**	hac**ían**	viv**ían**

Irregular verbs in the imperfect

There are only three irregular verbs in the imperfect: **ser**, **ir**, and **ver**. **Ser** in the imperfect is used for telling time in the past and describing how someone or something *used to be*. **Ir** is used to mean *would go* or *used to go,* or in the sense of on-going action, *was going.*

	Ser	**Ir**	**Ver**
Yo	**era**	**iba**	**veía**
Tú	**eras**	**ibas**	**veías**
Él/ella/usted	**era**	**iba**	**veía**
Nosotros/as	**éramos**	**íbamos**	**veíamos**
Vosotros/as	**erais**	**ibais**	**veías**
Ellos/ellas/ustedes	**eran**	**iban**	**veían**

De niño, él **era** muy inteligente. Leía mucho y le gustaba hacer rompecabezas. Además, **era** muy simpático. Siempre **iba** a visitar a su abuela los fines de semana.

LEARNING BY WRITING: Some of our students are more likely to retain information if they have already written it down. Encourage students to write down the gist of *Estructuras clave* in a section of their notes they can readily reference.

TEACHING TIP: Have students focus on the forms of *haber, hacer, bailar, cantar, llevar,* and *estar* in the example, and ask them how they would describe the imperfect forms.

9A.15 PRE-LISTENING STRATEGY: Before reading the statements about América Ferrera, ask students what they should be listening for to determine whether a statement is in the present or past. They may mention how the verb ends.

9A.15 AUDIO SCRIPT: 1. Protagoniza la telenovela *Ugly Betty*. 2. Estudia en la Universidad de Southern California. 3. Actuaba en la escuela y en el teatro comunitario. 4. Tiene una familia grande. 5. Vivía en un barrio con pocos hispanos. 6. Asistía a la Escuela Secundaria El Camino Real. 7. Sale con su novio, Ryan Piers Williams. 8. Trabajaba como mesera en un restaurante.

9A.16 TEACHING TIP: Remind students that if they do not know the individual(s) mentioned they should either try to find the answer through a process of elimination, or when they verify their answers with a partner. Were there any people students were unable to identify?

9A.17 TEACHING TIP: Allow students time to complete the signature search and then poll the class for results to see how many students used to do each activity. You can expand on items by asking follow-up questions such as: *¿Qué instrumento tocabas? ¿Qué deporte(s) jugabas? ¿De qué clubs eras miembro? ¿Dónde trabajabas?* Write on the board, *muchos, pocos, ningún, ninguno/a, nadie* for students to use as they summarize their findings.

9A.15 La vida de América Ferrera. Escucha las frases que describen la vida de la actriz hondureña-americana América Ferrera. Indica si las acciones son acciones habituales en el presente o en el pasado. Luego, verifica tus respuestas con la clase.

	En el presente	En el pasado
1.	☑	☐
2.	☑	☐
3.	☐	☑
4.	☑	☐
5.	☐	☑
6.	☐	☑
7.	☑	☐
8.	☐	☑

América Ferrera, actriz de *Ugly Betty* de la cadena ABC.

9A.16 Las profesiones de hispanos famosos del pasado. Con un/a compañero/a de clase, para cada persona o pareja famosa, indiquen cuál era su profesión. Luego, verifiquen las respuestas con otros compañeros de clase.

__a__	**1.** Diego Rivera y Frida Kahlo	**a.** pintábamos cuadros y murales
__e__	**2.** Robert Frost y Pablo Neruda	**b.** iba a muchas islas en el Caribe
__h__	**3.** Juan y Evita Perón	**c.** cantaba música tejana
__c__	**4.** Selena	**d.** éramos los reyes de España
__f__	**5.** Desi Arnaz	**e.** escribían poemas
__d__	**6.** Fernando e Isabel	**f.** estaba casado con Lucille Ball
__g__	**7.** César Chávez	**g.** ayudaba a los obreros agrícolas
__b__	**8.** Juan Ponce de León	**h.** gobernábamos en Argentina

9A.17 Las actividades de la escuela secundaria. Camina por la clase y pregúntales a tus compañeros si hacían estas actividades en la escuela secundaria. Si alguien contesta "Sí", pídele que firme en el espacio correspondiente. Después de repasar los resultados con la clase, apunta el número de estudiantes que hacía cada actividad en tu **Retrato de la clase**.

1. ¿Tocabas en una banda/orquesta? _____

2. ¿Cantabas en el coro? _____

3. ¿Caminabas a la escuela? _____

4. ¿Veías a tus amigos con frecuencia? _____

5. ¿Escribías para el periódico estudiantil? _____

6. ¿Actuabas en obras de teatro? _____

7. ¿Participabas en el equipo de debate? _____

8. ¿Eras miembro de algún club estudiantil? _____

9. ¿Trabajabas? _____

10. ¿Ibas a los partidos de fútbol americano? _____

Retrato de la clase: Por lo general, ___ compañeros de clase tocaban en una banda, ___ cantaban en el coro…

9A.18 Los jóvenes de hoy y los jóvenes de las décadas de 1960 y 1970. En grupos de cuatro personas, comparen la vida y las actividades de los niños y los jóvenes de hoy con las de los niños y los jóvenes del pasado (por ejemplo, cómo celebraban sus cumpleaños) y apunten la información en la tabla. Piensen en diferentes aspectos de la vida, como las fiestas, los días feriados, la ropa, la música, la tecnología, la comida, la rutina diaria, los pasatiempos, la política, los cambios culturales/sociales, etcétera. La información acerca de los jóvenes de hoy se debe expresar con el tiempo presente mientras que la información acerca de los jóvenes del pasado se debe expresar con el imperfecto.

Los niños/jóvenes de hoy	Los niños/jóvenes del pasado
Celebran sus cumpleaños en un restaurante.	Celebraban sus cumpleaños en sus casas.
Reciben regalos electrónicos o tecnológicos.	Recibían regalos más sencillos (simple).

9A.18 TEACHING TIP: Have students interview an older adult, such as a parent, grandparent, aunt, or uncle to find out what they used to do for fun when they were children. For example, what they did to celebrate birthdays, Christmas, specific holidays, etc. Compare students' responses by having them volunteer to read some of their sentences to the rest of the class.

Enlaces

9A.19 ¿Qué significan? Determina el significado de las palabras o frases subrayadas según el contexto de las oraciones. Escoge de las siguientes opciones. Luego, verifica tus respuestas con la clase.

a. at the same time
b. just like
c. above all

___c___ **1.** En el Día de los Muertos, se pueden ver ofrendas en muchos lugares públicos, <u>sobre todo</u> en los cementerios.

___a___ **2.** <u>Al mismo tiempo</u> que celebraban la cosecha *(harvest)*, los indígenas mexicas conmemoraban a los adultos muertos.

___b___ **3.** <u>Al igual que</u> en Estados Unidos, los mexicanos van al cementerio a limpiar y arreglar las tumbas de sus familiares en el aniversario de su muerte.

9A.19 TEACHING TIP: Remind students of the importance of incorporating these *enlaces* into their everyday speech.

9A.20 ¿Puedes conectar las ideas? Conecta las ideas empleando la expresión apropiada. Luego, verifica tus respuestas con la clase.

a. al igual que
b. al mismo tiempo
c. sobre todo

___c___ **1.** Se emplean muchas cosas para adornar las tumbas y los altares con ofrendas, pero _____ dulces y juguetes para los niños, y pan de muerto y cigarros o bebidas favoritas para los adultos.

___a___ **2.** _____ conmemoraban a los niños muertos, los indígenas mexicas conmemoraban a los adultos muertos el mes siguiente.

___b___ **3.** _____ que en México se celebra el Día de los Muertos, en Estados Unidos se celebra Halloween.

9A.20 EXTENSION ACTIVITY: Have students write their own sentences using this new vocabulary.

9A.21 El Día de los Muertos. Antes de leer el siguiente texto sobre el Día de los Muertos, una celebración mexicana, lee las siguientes descripciones de los cuatro párrafos para darte una idea general de la lectura. Luego al leer el texto, empareja el número del párrafo con la descripción que le corresponde.

El párrafo número...

_1_ explica la influencia indígena en el día feriado del Día de los Muertos.

_4_ explica lo que se hace en las visitas al cementerio.

_3_ explica el propósito de las ofrendas.

_2_ explica la influencia de la iglesia católica en el Día de los Muertos.

El Día de los Muertos

1 La celebración del Día de los Muertos es una de las más importantes y conocidas de México. Para muchas personas, es el día que más se asocia con la cultura mexicana o mexicoamericana. Durante la época precolombina, muchas culturas indígenas en Mesoamérica conmemoraban a los muertos, pero las celebraciones de los indígenas mexicas (los aztecas) fueron los antecedentes más directos del ritual contemporáneo. Durante lo que ahora es el mes de agosto, los mexicas celebraban el festival de Miccailhuitontli, en el que conmemoraban a los niños muertos. El mes siguiente celebraban Hueymiccaihuitl, en el que conmemoraban a los adultos muertos. Al mismo tiempo, celebraban la cosecha con el festival de Xocotl Huetzi. De esa manera, los mexicas combinaban la conmemoración de los muertos con la celebración de la cosecha *(harvest).*

2 Cuando llegaron los españoles en el siglo XVI, decidieron conservar algunos aspectos de estos festivales indígenas pero cambiaron otros para que coincidieran con las fiestas católicas de Todos los Santos *(All Saints' Day)* y el Día de los Difuntos *(All Souls' Day)* que se celebraban el primero y el dos de noviembre, respectivamente. Hoy en día, se puede ver cómo se combinaron los festivales mexicas y las fiestas católicas porque en muchos lugares, el primero de noviembre se conmemora a los niños muertos mientras que el dos de noviembre se conmemora a los adultos muertos.

3 Un aspecto muy importante del Día de los Muertos son las ofrendas que preparan las personas en sus casas. Las ofrendas se ponen en un pequeño altar que se construye para conmemorar a los muertos. Los altares muchas veces consisten en una serie de cajas *(boxes)* arregladas en diferentes niveles y cubiertas de telas *(cloth).* Para decorar los altares, las personas emplean ofrendas como flores, velas, fotos, decoraciones de papel y calacas o catrinas (figuras cómicas con forma de esqueletos). También se pone comida como pan de muerto, frutas, dulces *(sweets),* especialmente calaveras *(skulls)* de azúcar y otras comidas. En los altares para adultos se pueden incluir cigarros y alcohol, como tequila o mezcal. Para los niños, se incluyen juguetes *(toys).* Hoy en día, se pueden ver altares con ofrendas en muchos lugares públicos, tales como escuelas, oficinas y tiendas. Esto puede ser una manera de combatir la influencia de la fiesta estadounidense de Halloween, que ha influenciado la celebración del Día de los Muertos, sobre todo en las grandes ciudades.

4 Al igual que en el Día de la Conmemoración de Estados Unidos, las visitas al cementerio (o panteón) son una parte importante del Día de los Muertos. Las personas van al cementerio para limpiar, arreglar, pintar y decorar las tumbas de sus familiares. En algunos lugares, especialmente en zonas rurales, la visita al cementerio se convierte en una especie de reunión familiar que dura toda la noche. Las personas se reúnen en el cementerio para pasar tiempo juntos y con los espíritus de sus familiares. Se hace una especie de picnic y se cuentan relatos (*stories*) para recordar a los muertos. Esta alegre y respetuosa celebración es una manera de demostrar que la muerte no es una cosa triste ni temible (*frightening*), sino una parte normal del ciclo de la vida.

9A.22 ¿Qué comprendiste de la lectura? Depués de leer la información acerca del Día de los Muertos, con un/a compañero/a de clase completen las oraciones con la información correcta. Luego, consulten con otros compañeros para verificar las respuestas.

noviembre
la cosecha
ofrendas
Halloween
calavera
juguetes
Día de los Difuntos
contar relatos

1. Los mexicas combinaban la conmemoración de los muertos con otro festival que celebraba _____la cosecha_____.

2. Los españoles convirtieron los festivales mexicas en dos fiestas católicas: Todos los Santos y _____Día de los Difuntos_____, los cuales se celebran el uno y el dos de _____noviembre_____.

3. Las _____ofrendas_____ se ponen en un altar que se construye para conmemorar a los muertos.

4. Hay miedo (*fear*) de que el Día de los Muertos sea eclipsado por la fiesta de _____Halloween_____ debido a la influencia de la cultura estadounidense.

5. Los dulces que más se asocian con el Día de los Muertos tienen forma de _____calavera_____.

6. Muchas veces, se usan _____juguetes_____ para conmemorar a los niños.

9A.22 TEACHING TIP: Remind students to move on to the next sentence if they cannot find the right answer. They can always come back to previous sentences.

Perspectivas

9A.23 **Una comparación entre el Día de los Muertos y Halloween.** Busca información en la Internet o en otras fuentes acerca de los orígenes de la celebración de Halloween. Entonces, compara Halloween con el Día de los Muertos y apunta las semejanzas y diferencias en el cuadro. En la próxima clase, habla con tres compañeros para comparar la información que encontraron. Apunta las conclusiones de tu grupo para poder presentarlas a la clase.

9A. 23 EXTENSION ACTIVITY: Ask students to do research on Halloween as homework. In the following class, have groups of students compare their findings and then go over each group's conclusions as a class.

Halloween
diferencias

semejanzas

El Día de los Muertos
diferencias

En las fiestas de Halloween, la gente lleva **una máscara** o **un disfraz** que **oculta** su identidad.

DICHOS

Año nuevo, vida nueva.	*New year, new life.*
Entre Todos los Santos y Navidad, es invierno de verdad.	*Between All Saints Day and Christmas, it is truly winter.*
En Carnaval todo pasa, hasta los novios a las casas.	*Anything can happen during Carnival.*
Al bueno, regalo; al malo, palo.	*To the good person, a gift; to the bad person, a stick (a beating).*
A cada santo le llega su día de fiesta.	*Every saint will have his feast. (Every dog will have its day.)*

Vocabulario: Investigación A

Vocabulario esencial

Sustantivos

la amistad	friendship
el amor	love
los antepasados	ancestors
el barrio	neighborhood
los bienes raíces	real estate
la boda	wedding
la caja	box
el compromiso	engagement
la costumbre	custom
el cumpleaños	birthday
el disfraz	costume
la madrina	godmother
la máscara	mask
el padrino	godfather
el regalo	gift
las velas	candles
el Año Nuevo	New Year
el Día de Acción de Gracias	Thanksgiving Day
el Día de los Inocentes	Day of the Innocent
el Día de los Muertos	Day of the Dead
el Día de Reyes	Three King's Day
la Navidad	Chirstmas Day
la Nochebuena	Christmas Eve
la Nochevieja	New Year's Eve
la Pascua	Easter
la Semana Santa	Holy Week
la Víspera de Todos los Santos	All Saint's Eve

Verbos

adornar	to decorate
cargar	to carry
casarse (con)	to marry
desvelarse	to stay awake
festejar	to celebrate; to party
ocultar	to hide

Otras palabras y expresiones

el alboroto	commotion
la calavera	skull
la cosecha	harvest
de oferta	on sale
los dioses	gods
emocionante	exciting
el juguete	toy
el/la ladrón/a	thief
el miedo	fear
musulmán	muslim
nombrar	to name
la obra de teatro	play
el/la obrero/a agrícola	farm worker
el ofrecimiento	offering
la ofrenda	offering
la parroquia	parish
poderoso	powerful
la promulgación	enactment
el relato	story
resaltar	to highlight
el robo	robbery
temible	frightening

Expresiones útiles

por lo general	generally speaking
Para invitar:	
¿Quisiera ir a…? ¿Quisieras ir a…? ¿Quisieran ir a…?	Would you like to go (to)…
Te/Le/Les invito a…	I'm inviting you to…
¿Te/Le/Les gustaría ir conmigo a…?	Would you like to go with me to…?
Para aceptar una invitación:	
Por supuesto, me gustaría ir a comer/ir al cine/ conocer a tus padres, etcétera.	Of course I'd like to go out to eat/go to the movies/ meet your parents, etc.
Me encantaría…	I'd love to…
Sería un placer…	It would be a pleasure…
Para rechazar una invitación:	
Lo siento, no puedo porque…	I'm sorry. I can't because…
¡Qué pena! Ese día tengo otro compromiso.	What a shame! That day I have another engagement.
Lo siento pero tengo que…	I'm sorry, but I have to…
¡Qué lástima! A esa hora tengo una cita con el médico.	What a shame! I have a doctor's appointment at that time.

Cognados

Review the cognates in *Adelante* and the false cognates in *¡Atención!*. For a complete list of cognates, see Appendix 4 on page 605.

¿Por qué celebramos a los atletas?

In this **Investigación** you will learn:

▶ How to talk about a variety of sports

▶ About which sports are popular in the Spanish-speaking world

▶ How athletes arrive at their current positions

▶ How to narrate in the past tense

¿Cómo se puede hablar de los deportes y los atletas de una cultura?

You can talk about different aspects of sports.	El hockey patín es un deporte popular en Chile. Principalmente un deporte mental, el ajedrez, un juego de mesa entre dos personas, es uno de los deportes más populares del mundo. El fútbol americano es un deporte muy competitivo.
You can talk about who athletes are.	Archie Manning era un muy buen jugador de fútbol norteamericano en la década de 1970 y actualmente sus hijos Peyton y Eli son excelentes jugadores (players). Muhammed Ali es uno de los boxeadores más famosos de las Américas.
You can read about the events that brought fame to a person.	Pelé es venerado mundialmente y apreciado como héroe nacional en su país nativo de Brasil. Es el único futbolista que ha recibido tres medallas de oro en las Copas Mundiales. Dale Earnhardt ganó 76 carreras de auto antes de morir en 2001 durante la carrera de Daytona 500. Se le conocía como "el Intimidador" por su estilo agresivo de conducir.

Adelante

¡Ya lo sabes! Los deportes

el fútbol	el tenis
el fútbol americano	los atletas
el béisbol	la adversidad
el golf	el bate
el hockey	la dedicación
el automovilismo	el triunfo
el ciclismo	la raqueta
el voleibol	esquiar
el boxeo	hacer camping
el básquetbol	

9B.1 **¿Con qué deporte se asocia(n)?** Con un/a compañero/a de clase escriban los nombres de atletas que se asocian con cada deporte. Luego, comparen sus respuestas con la clase para determinar quiénes son los atletas más populares.

el básquetbol	el fútbol americano	el ciclismo	el fútbol
el béisbol	el golf	el hockey patín	el tenis

TEACHING TIP: Use the following statements as a true/false activity to determine from the outset how much your students know about sports and athletes. Most are meant to be true but you may change to make them false for variety: *1. El inglés David Beckam ahora juega al fútbol para el Galaxy de Los Ángeles, pero también continúa en el equipo nacional de Inglaterra. 2. Shaquille O'Neal y Michael Jordan juegan al básquetbol. 3. Lance Armstrong es un ciclista de Plano, Texas, que ganó el Tour de Francia siete años consecutivos, de 1999 a 2005. 4. Óscar de la Hoya y Mike Tyson son boxeadores que tienen buena y mala fama. 5. Dale Earnhardt es uno de los automovilistas más conocidos en el mundo. 6. El beisbolista dominicano Manny Ramírez juega para los Dodgers de Los Ángeles. 7. Payton Manning es el futbolista más conocido del nuevo milenio. 8. Andre Agassi se retiró del tenis profesional en 2006.*

9B.1 TEACHING TIP: When you go over the answers, ask students questions such as *¿Cuántos atletas tienen bajo la categoría de ciclismo?* and *¿En qué categoría tienen más/menos nombres de atletas conocidos?* You could also ask them questions about whether or not they mentioned athletes from the Spanish-speaking world (e.g. *¿Mencionaron atletas hispanohablantes?*).

9B.2 **Las asociaciones.** Escucha el deporte e indica con qué nombre se asocia. Luego, verifica tu respuesta con la clase. El primero está hecho como modelo.

<u>_1_</u> **a.** el campeón del peso *(weight)* welter
<u>_5_</u> **b.** el parque Fenway
<u>_9_</u> **c.** el Indy 500
<u>_4_</u> **d.** la Copa Mundial
<u>_2_</u> **e.** el Super Bowl
<u>_10_</u> **f.** la Copa Stanley
<u>_3_</u> **g.** la NBA
<u>_8_</u> **h.** Wimbledon
<u>_7_</u> **i.** el Circuito de la PGA
<u>_6_</u> **j.** el Tour de Francia

9B.2 AUDIO SCRIPT: 1. el boxeo, 2. el fútbol americano, 3. el básquetbol, 4. el fútbol, 5. el béisbol, 6. el ciclismo, 7. el golf, 8. el tenis, 9. el automovilismo, 10. el hockey

9B.2 TEACHING TIP: An alternate option is to ask students to write their answers on paper and then turn in their answers. Count the number of students who knew all the answers. It would be interesting to observe if there are differences based on gender, who the most informed are (with regard to sports), etc. Then, review answers with the class.

9B.3 ANSWERS: 1. Cierto, 2. Falso: No es necesario tener agua para jugar al golf., 3. Cierto, 4. Falso: NASCAR se asocia con el automovilismo., 5. Cierto, 6. Falso: El básquetbol es un deporte para las personas altas., 7. Cierto, 8. Falso: Muhammad Ali se asocia con el boxeo.

9B.3 TEACHING TIP: You could play/read one statement at a time and have the class respond after each one. In this way students can more easily correct false information.

9B.4 ANSWERS: 1. equiar, 2. Hacer camping, 3. voleibol, 4. raqueta, 5. adversidades, 6. hockey, 7. golf, 8. triunfo

9B.4 TEACHING TIP: Ask students to take turns reading a sentence to each other. The person who does not read attempts to guess the word and vice versa.

9B.3 **¿Cierto o falso?** Indica si estos enunciados son ciertos o falsos. Luego, con un/a compañero/a corrijan la información falsa.

Cierto	Falso	
☑	☐	**1.** La adversidad es sinónimo de problema, dificultad u obstáculo.
☐	☑	**2.** Es necesario tener agua para jugar al golf.
☑	☐	**3.** La Serie Mundial se asocia con el béisbol.
☐	☑	**4.** NASCAR se asocia con el ciclismo.
☑	☐	**5.** Esquiar sobre agua se asocia con el verano.
☐	☑	**6.** El básquetbol es un deporte para las personas bajas.
☑	☐	**7.** Para jugar al tenis se necesitan dos personas.
☐	☑	**8.** Muhammad Ali se asocia con el voleibol.

9B.4 **Completar las oraciones.** Busca la palabra o la expresión de la siguiente lista que complete cada oración. Verifica tus respuestas con un(-a) compañero(-a).

adversidades   golf   raqueta   triunfo
hacer camping   esquiar   hockey   voleibol

1. El estado de Colorado tiene montañas majestuosas y perfectas para _____ en el invierno.
2. _____ es un pasatiempo popular para las personas a quienes les gusta la naturaleza y el aire libre *(outdoors)*.
3. En el sur de California, el _____ se juega en la playa.
4. El tenista necesita una _____ para jugar.
5. La pobreza, la falta *(lack)* de educación y la discriminación son ejemplos de _____ que limitan las oportunidades de muchas personas.
6. El canadiense Wayne Gretzky jugaba al _____. Era entrenador *(coach)* y es codueño de los Coyotes de Phoenix (NHL).
7. Tiger Woods juega al _____ y gana probablemente más de 75 millones de dólares al año.
8. El equipo de fútbol de FC Barcelona celebró un _____ en la Liga de Campeones de la UEFA contra Manchester United en la final de 2009.

9B.5 **Cierto o falso.** Lee las siguientes declaraciones. Después de leer el siguiente texto, indica si las declaraciones son ciertas o falsas y corrige la información falsa. Luego, verifica tus respuestas con la clase.

Cierto Falso

☑ ☐ **1.** El fotógrafo es el que mejor captura el instante de un gol.

☐ ☑ **2.** La autora ofrece una perspectiva negativa del fútbol.

☑ ☐ **3.** El fútbol se asocia con el control del cuerpo y de las emociones.

☑ ☐ **4.** El gol es una metáfora para cosas que son incomprensibles.

☐ ☑ **5.** Marcar un gol no tiene ningún valor social.

El gol es la clave

El gol por Carmen Villoro

La palabra "gol" es breve como su existencia. Los comentaristas de la televisión la alargan *(lengthen)* queriendo prolongar la experiencia. Las cámaras lo repiten para ver si lo atrapan *(capture)*. Sólo los fotógrafos, pescadores del tiempo, logran capturar el instante: el balón *(ball)* que tensa la red *(net)*, el hombre que levanta la pierna como una invocación al cielo *(sky)*. Por eso la expresión de alegría es tan grande en jugadores y aficionados, porque los escasos *(scarce)* momentos del gol son como esos espacios de una sinfonía en que toda la orquesta nos sorprende y escuchamos el poderío de los timbales *(the power of the kettledrums)* para luego recuperar la melodía.

El fútbol es control: el pase y ritmo preciso, pero el gol es la clave. En el tiro de gracia *(coup de grâce)* se explota el espíritu del hombre, se escucha entonces el grito atrapado en la garganta *(throat)*.

El gol es la metáfora de lo imponderable. Su ausencia significa la derrota *(defeat)* y su presencia la gloria. Es el giro *(turn)* que marca la historia, el azar *(chance)* que escribe por nosotros, la calle equivocada *(wrong)* que se toma o el encuentro fortuito que define el resto de la vida. Por eso nos emocionamos, porque en el partido se juega, sin saberlo, el propio destino de una población. Cuando el jugador celebra su gol, asistimos a uno de esos momentos en que lo íntimo se funde con *(melds with)* lo social; es la dignidad de un pueblo que de pronto condensa su historia en un balón.

En tu cultura, ¿hay algo (deporte, rito, fiesta, etc.) que despierte sentimientos similares?

www **¡Conéctate!**

In the Caribbean **el béisbol,** or **la pelota,** as it is more commonly called, is the dominant sport. While the World Series is a completion of Major League Baseball in the U.S. and Canada, the World Baseball Classic is a tournament among the best baseball-playing countries' national teams. Check out http://wwww.worldbaseballclassic.com and click on *En español*. What countries have been most dominant? What countries from the Spanish-speaking world field strong teams? Were you surprised by anything you found on this website? Share your thoughts with the class.

Bien dicho

Las abreviaturas y la puntuación

In Spanish, as in English, abbreviations and acronyms are used frequently in writing as a way to save space and time. You have already seen a number of very common abbreviations throughout this textbook: *Ud./Uds. (usted/ustedes), Sr./Sra./Srta. (señor/señora/señorita), EE.UU. (Estados Unidos), D.F. (Distrito Federal,* used to refer to Mexico City). Other common abbreviations include: *Rep. (República), cap. (capítulo), pág./pg. (página), avda. (avenida), izq./izqda (izquierda), dcha. (derecha), 1.ª (primera), 3.ᵉʳ (tercer), p. ej. (por ejemplo)* and *Cía.* (Company).

Acronyms are words or abbreviations formed from the initial letters of the elements of a compound term: *ONU (Organización de Naciones Unidas), RAE (Real Academia Española), FARC (Fuerzas Armadas Revolucionarias de Colombia).*

Punctuation organizes discourse and allows us to avoid ambiguity in texts that could have different interpretations. The rules governing the use of the various punctuation marks in Spanish are similar to those in English. However, there are some important differences:

1. In a list of items, commas are not used before **y** *(and)* and **o** *(or).*
2. Periods have traditionally been used to separate hundreds, thousands, millions, etc. when writing out numerals in Spanish. Spaces may be used instead of periods for clarity when writing longer numbers. Like in the US, commas are used in some Latin American countries.
3. Both commas and periods are acceptable to separate whole numbers from the decimal portion (*5.75* or *5,75*).
4. Both periods and colons can be used to separate hours from minutes (*10:15* or *10.15*).
5. A colon is used after the salutation of any letter, including informal letters.
6. As you already know, questions and exclamations are introduced with inverted question and exclamation marks.

9B.6 **¿Qué significan las abreviaturas y los acrónimos?** Para los números 1–6, busca el significado de las abreviaturas en el siguiente sitio web de la Real Academia Española: http://buscon.rae.es/dpdI/ (haz clic en el enlace *Apéndices* y luego en el enlace *Apéndice 2: Las abreviaturas).* Para los números 7–12, busca los significados de los acrónimos en el sitio web http://www.acronyma.com/?language=es . ¿Puedes determinar los equivalentes en inglés?

1. JJ.OO.	**4.** n.º	**7.** OTAN	**10.** FMI
2. C.P.	**5.** P.D.	**8.** PSOE	**11.** SIDA
3. S.A.	**6.** Cdad.	**9.** UNAM	**12.** OEA

9B.7 **Una carta a un amigo.** Lee la carta siguiente y coloca los signos de puntuación apropiados donde sean necesarios. Verifica tus respuestas con un/a compañero/a. Luego, lee la carta en voz alta, usando la puntuación como guía de pronunciación.

Madrid 19 octubre de 2008

Querido Paco
Gracias por tu última carta Me alegro de tener noticias tuyas y de saber que todos están bien Esta semana estoy muy ocupado Tengo que hacer mucha tarea estudiar para un examen trabajar y asistir a la práctica de fútbol Viste (past tense of ver in the tú form) el partido entre Barça y Real Madrid Qué increíble Mi hermano que vive en Barcelona va a todos los partidos del Barça El Real Madrid es mi equipo favorito sin embargo Barça siempre juega bien y los partidos son emocionantes (exciting) Cuando vienes a visitarnos Queremos llevarte a conocer muchos lugares el Museo del Prado el Palacio Real el Parque del Retiro la Plaza Mayor y otros Vamos a pasarlo muy bien
Saludos
Jaime

WILEY PLUS
INSTRUCTOR'S RESOURCES: A reproducible copy of the letter showing the correct punctuation is available in your Instructor's Resources.

9B.6 ANSWERS: Juegos Olímpicos *(Olympic Games),* 2. Código postal *(ZIP Code/Postal Code),* 3. Sociedad Anónima *(Inc./Ltd.),* 4. número *(number),* 5. Posdata *(P.S.),* 6. Ciudad *(City),* 7. Organización del Tratado del Atlántico Norte *(NATO),* 8. Partido Socialista Obrero Español *(Spanish Socialist Workers Party),* 9. Universidad Nacional Autónoma de México *(National Autonomous University of Mexico),* 10. Fondo Monetario Internacional *(IMF),* 11. Síndrome de Inmunodeficiencia Adquirida *(AIDS),* 12. Organización de los Estados Americanos *(OAS).*

Palabras clave 1 Deportes y lugares donde se practican

TEACHING TIP: Point out that *baloncesto* is a synonym for *básquetbol*, which students saw in *Adelante* and have used up to now. Write the words *peligroso* (dangerous) and *seguro* (safe) on the board and as you call out the name of the sport in Spanish, ask them to respond as *peligroso* or *seguro*.

la caza/cazar

montar a caballo

patinar sobre hielo

la pista de patinaje

buceo/bucear

patinar en línea

la natación/nadar

la piscina

9B.8 **Asociaciones.** Con un/a compañero/a de clase, escriban los deportes que saben decir en español según dónde se juegan. Luego, comparen sus respuestas con otro grupo. Algunos pueden usarse en más de un lugar.

En una cancha	En una pista de patinaje	En un estadio deportivo	En el campo	En el agua

practicar/hacer surfing

el campo de béisbol

la cancha de voleibol

la pesca/pescar

el remo/remar

la pelota

el equipo de baloncesto

9B.9 **¿A qué deporte se refiere?** Escucha las definiciones e indica a qué deporte se refiere cada definción. Luego, verifica tus respuestas con la clase.

a. el béisbol

b. bucear

c. cazar

d. el fútbol

e. el golf

f. hacer surfing

g. andar en bicicleta

h. nadar

i. patinar

j. remar

k. el tenis

l. el voleibol

<u>j</u> **1.**

<u>a</u> **2.**

<u>d</u> **3.**

<u>k</u> **4.**

<u>h</u> **5.**

<u>c</u> **6.**

<u>i</u> **7.**

<u>b</u> **8.**

<u>g</u> **9.**

<u>f</u> **10.**

9B.9 AUDIO SCRIPT: 1. Se hace para poder navegar un bote pequeño o una canoa. 2. Es un deporte muy popular en el verano. Se juega en un estadio o un campo y cada equipo tiene nueve jugadores. 3. Es el deporte más popular de todo el mundo. Cuando se juega, no se puede usar las manos. 4. Este deporte se juega en una cancha con una raqueta. Puede haber dos o cuatro jugadores. 5. Es un deporte que se asocia con el agua. La persona usa los brazos y las piernas para moverse por el agua. 6. Es la acción de buscar animales y matarlos, a veces para poder comer la carne. 7. Es un deporte que asociamos con el hielo. También es una acción que se asocia con el hockey. 8. Este deporte consiste en nadar debajo del agua con tanques de oxígeno para ver animales acuáticos. 9. Es la acción de viajar en un vehículo que no requiere gasolina y es buen ejercicio físico. 10. Es un deporte acuático que se asocia con los estados de Hawai y California. La persona pasea en una tabla por encima del agua.

9B.10 ¡Ay caramba! En grupos de tres, jueguen *¡Ay caramba!* según las siguientes reglas.

Reglas:

- Roll a dice or draw a number from 1–6.
- Move the number of spaces indicated on the dice (from 1–6 only) and answer the question on the board.
- If you answer with the correct word or phrase, the next person gets a turn.
- If you answer incorrectly, move back two spaces, and the next person gets a turn.

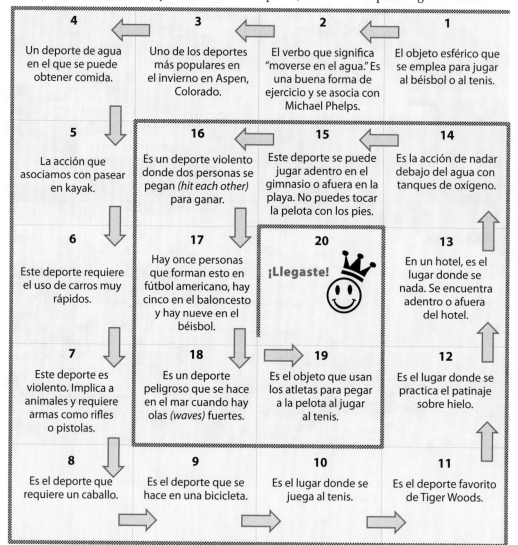

9B.11 Los deportes favoritos de los compañeros. Escribe tus deportes favoritos para practicar y para mirar. Entonces, habla con diez compañeros de clase para determinar qué deportes prefieren practicar y cuáles les gusta mirar. Apunta sus respuestas en una tabla como la de abajo. Recuerda: necesitas escribir los nombres de los deportes en español. Después de repasar la información con la clase, apunta las conclusiones en tu **Retrato de la clase**.

Modelo: E1: *¿Cuál es tu deporte favorito para practicar?*
E2: *La natación*

Nombre	Deporte favorito para practicar	Deporte favorito para mirar
Yo		

Retrato de la clase: El deporte favorito para practicar de la clase de español es ___ y para mirar es ___.

VÍVELO: CULTURA

Los deportes más populares en Estados Unidos y los países hispanos

País	Deporte(s)
Argentina	fútbol, rugby, básquetbol, hockey sobre hierba, hockey, tenis, automovilismo
Bolivia	fútbol
Chile	fútbol, tenis, hockey, básquetbol
Colombia	fútbol, béisbol, básquetbol
Costa Rica	fútbol
Cuba	béisbol, boxeo, voleibol, atletismo
Ecuador	fútbol, atletismo, básquetbol
El Salvador	fútbol, básquetbol, voleibol
España	fútbol, básquetbol, ciclismo, tenis, voleibol, rugby
Estados Unidos	béisbol, fútbol americano, básquetbol, hockey, automovilismo, fútbol, voleibol, lacrosse, golf, tenis, boxeo, atletismo, ciclismo, esquí, caza, pesca
Guatemala	fútbol, boxeo
Honduras	fútbol, béisbol, básquetbol
México	fútbol, boxeo, béisbol, golf, atletismo, ciclismo
Nicaragua	béisbol, fútbol, boxeo
Panamá	fútbol, básquetbol
Paraguay	fútbol
Perú	fútbol, tenis, voleibol, surf, básquetbol, natación
Puerto Rico	básquetbol, béisbol, voleibol, boxeo, fútbol, golf, surf, vela
Rep. Dominicana	béisbol, voleibol, básquetbol, fútbol, natación, atletismo
Uruguay	fútbol, básquetbol, rugby
Venezuela	béisbol, fútbol, boxeo, natación, tenis

Glosario deportivo: hockey sobre hierba *(field hockey)*, atletismo *(track and field)*, vela *(sailing)*

9B.12. Los deportes en el mundo hispanohablante. En grupos de tres, contesten las siguientes preguntas según la información en *Vívelo: Cultura.*

1. ¿Cuáles son los tres deportes más populares entre todos estos países?
2. ¿Cuáles son los cuatro países con la mayor variedad de deportes?
3. ¿Cuáles son los países que tienen solamente un deporte? ¿Cuál es el deporte?
4. ¿Qué información les sorprende?

TEACHING TIP: Brainstorm with the class the sports they know or think are popular in Spanish-speaking countries as a way of setting the stage for the information in the next *Vívelo: Cultura.*

STANDARDS: COMMUNITY. If students have access to an individual from one of the countries mentioned in the accompanying chart, have them interview that person to find out what sports they like as well as which are popular in their country.

9B.12 ANSWERS: 1. fútbol, béisbol, básquetbol, 2. Estados Unidos, Argentina, España, Puerto Rico, 3. Bolivia, Costa Rica, Paraguay, el fútbol 4. Sample answers: hockey en Chile y Argentina (el hockey se juega mucho en Estados Unidos y Canadá), rugby en Argentina, España, Uruguay (se asocia más con países como Gran Bretaña, Australia y Nueva Zelanda), surf en Perú (se practica mucho en los estados de Hawai y California)

9B.12 TEACHING TIP: After students have had ample time to go over their answers in groups of three, go over them quickly to make sure that they got them right. While you go over these answers, process this activity further by asking if they were surprised by any of the new information. Many students assume that *fútbol* is the most popular sport in the entire Spanish-speaking world. In the Spanish-speaking countries of the Caribbean this could not be further from the truth. As evidenced by the amount of Major League Baseball players from these countries, it is no surprise that *béisbol*, or *pelota* as it is often called, is the most popular sport.

VÍVELO: CULTURA

La corrida de toros no es tan popular como lo era en el pasado

La corrida de toros, o el toreo, es un espectáculo que consiste en lidiar un toro (to fight a bull) siguiendo una estricta serie de normas basadas en objetivos estéticos o artísticos. Las normas de la corrida de toros moderna se establecieron a finales del siglo XVIII y desde entonces la corrida de toros se convirtió en una tradición cultural muy imporante. La corrida de toros también recibe el nombre de "fiesta brava" pues la palabra *brava* hace referencia al valor que los toreros necesitan para lidiar al toro.

Aunque en el pasado las corridas de toros se celebraban en algunos países europeos, en el presente se asocian sobre todo con España y México, y en menor grado con países latinoamericanos como Colombia, Perú, Ecuador y Bolivia.

Hoy en día, sin embargo, la corrida de toros no es tan popular como lo era en el pasado. Por ejemplo, una encuesta Gallup al principio del nuevo milenio indicó que sólo el 31% de la población española se muestra interesada en las corridas de toros. Junto con esa falta de interés, especialmente entre la gente joven, hay fuerte oposición tanto de grupos que defienden los derechos de animales. Estos grupos protestan por la crueldad y el abuso que sufren los animales (toros y caballos) que participan en la corrida.

¿Te gustaría ir a una corrida de toros? ¿Por qué?

Graffiti en la Universidad Complutense de Madrid criticando las corridas de toros. ¿El torero contra el toro? o ¿El toro contra el torero?

9B.13 Cierto o falso. Después de leer el texto, escucha algunas frases y determina si son ciertas o falsas de acuerdo con la lectura. Compara tus respuestas con las de la clase.

	Cierto	Falso
1.	☑	☐
2.	☐	☑
3.	☐	☑
4.	☑	☐
5.	☑	☐
6.	☑	☐

¡Atención!

Balón	does not mean balloon, but rather *ball,* especially one that is inflated with air. To express *balloon* in Spanish, use **el globo.**
	Cuando se juega al fútbol, no se debe tocar el balón con las manos. En mi cumpleaños, mis amigos van a decorar mi casa con globos de muchos colores.
Casco	does not mean cast, but rather *helmet.* The word **yeso** means *cast* when referring to what the doctor puts on a broken arm or leg.
	Cuando uno monta en bicicleta, es importante llevar un casco. Tengo el brazo roto *(broken)* y el médico me ha puesto un yeso.
Partido	means game/match in the sense of an athletic competition. It also means *party* when referring to a political organization. To refer to a celebration, use the word **fiesta.**
	A María le encanta el hockey patín, así que asiste a los partidos de hockey patín con frecuencia. Mis padres votan por el partido republicano pero yo voto por el partido demócrata. ¡Vamos a organizar una fiesta para celebrar el fin del semestre!

9B.14 Completar las oraciones. Busca la palabra apropiada de la siguiente lista para completar las oraciones. Luego, verifica tus respuestas con las de otros compañeros de clase.

hacer camping   yeso
balón   partidos
fiesta   globos
cascos

1. El médico le pone un ____yeso____ al paciente cuando se le rompe un hueso *(break a bone).*
2. El payaso *(clown)* les regala ____globos____ a los niños.
3. En la ____fiesta____ de Año Nuevo vamos a cantar *"Auld Lang Syne".*
4. Los ____cascos____ de los jugadores de fútbol americano tienen el símbolo de su equipo.
5. En Estados Unidos realmente sólo existen dos ____partidos____ políticos: el demócrata y el republicano.
6. Otra palabra para *pelota* es ____balón____.

9B.14 TEACHING TIP: Before going over the answers as a class, have students work with a partner to make sure they arrived at the correct answer.

www **¡Conéctate!**
El fútbol is undoubtedly the most popular sport in the world. Check out http://es.fifa.com and find out what is currently happening in the soccer world. What big games or tournaments are being played? Who are some of the current stars? Share your answers with the class.

WILEY PLUS
Go to *WileyPLUS* and review the tutorial for this grammar point.

Estructuras clave 1 The preterit tense

WILEY PLUS

You will find PowerPoint presentations for use with *Estructuras clave* in *WileyPLUS*.

TEACHING TIP: Hopefully, in addition to the different verb forms, students will note that *él/ella/usted* take the same verb form, that the *nosotros/as* forms are similar to the present tense, and that the first- and third-person singular forms require accents.

TEACHING TIP: Point out the importance of the written accent to indicate past tense. Contrast the pronunciation of the present tense *hablo* (yo) and *habló* (él, ella, usted) to illustrate that the significance of the written accent mark can carry a change in meaning depending on how a word is pronounced. The accent indicates how a word should be pronounced and written to indicate one meaning over another.

In *Investigación 9A* you learned to express habitual, repeated or on-going actions, and actions in progress in the past by using the imperfect. In the context of a story, you used the imperfect to set the scene and describe the characters, the setting and the existing state of affairs.

There is an additional way to talk about the past in Spanish using what is called the preterit tense. As you will see here, and in greater detail in *Capítulo 10*, the preterit is used to express single, completed actions in the past, and within the context of a story, the preterit is used to narrate the main events of the plot.

> Ayer, el profesor **se levantó** tarde y **perdió** las llaves; por eso **llegó** tarde.
> *Yesterday the instructor got up late and lost his keys; that is why he was late.*

> El sábado pasado **lavé** ropa, **limpié** la cocina, **barrí** el patio y **pasé** la aspiradora.
> *Last Saturday, I washed clothes, cleaned the kitchen, swept the patio and vacuumed.*

Many verbs are regular in the preterit and there are no stem-changes with **–ar** or **–er** verbs. What are the patterns that you notice for the regular verbs whose preterit forms are shown below?

	bailar	**volver**	**asistir**
Yo	**bailé**	**volví**	**asistí**
Tú	**bailaste**	**volviste**	**asististe**
Él/ella/usted	**bailó**	**volvió**	**asistió**
Nosotros/as	**bailamos**	**volvimos**	**asistimos**
Vostros/as	**bailasteis**	**volvisteis**	**asististeis**
Ellos/ellas/ ustedes	**bailaron**	**volvieron**	**asistieron**

Note that there are two sets of endings: **–é, –aste, –ó, –amos, –asteis, –aron** for **–ar** verbs and **–í, –iste, –ió, –imos, –isteis, –ieron** for **–er** and **–ir** verbs. For **–ar** and **–ir** verbs, the **nosotros/as** form is identical in the present and preterit tenses (e.g., **bailamos** = *we dance/we danced;* **asistimos** = *we attend/we attended*). In those cases, context will help you determine whether the action is past or present. The verb **ver** is essentially a regular **–er** verb except that there are no accent marks on the **yo** and **él, ella, usted** forms: **vi, viste, vio, vimos visteis, vieron.**

9B.15 TEACHING TIP: As you prepare students for this activity, ask them to highlight the difference between the preterit and the imperfect. They should point out that the preterit refers to something that occurred in the past and the imperfect refers to ongoing past events. Play the audio twice. As students listen, remind them to focus on the meaning of the sentences the first time, and to listen for the verb in each sentence the second time.

9B.15 Acción singular o acción habitual. Escucha las oraciones e indica si la acción es singular (pretérito) o habitual (imperfecto).

	Acción singular	**Acción habitual**
1.	☐	☑
2.	☑	☐
3.	☐	☑
4.	☑	☐
5.	☐	☑
6.	☑	☐
7.	☑	☐
8.	☑	☐

9B.15 AUDIO SCRIPT: 1. Danica Patrick corría autos a la edad de 10 años. 2. Sasha Cohen apareció en dos películas: *Blades of Glory* y *Bratz: The Movie.* 3. Gabriela Sabatini y Arantxa Sánchez Vicario jugaban al tenis. 4. María Kirilenko, la tenista rusa, comenzó a jugar tenis a los 5 años. 5. De niña, Ana Ivanovic, la tenista serbia, practicaba en una piscina sin agua en Serbia. 6. Óscar de la Hoya perdió su título mundial en 2007. 7. George W. Bush firmó un documento que permitió a la canadiense Tanith Belbin representar a EE.UU. en patinaje sobre hielo. 8. Tanith Belbin y Ben Agosto recibieron una medalla de plata en los Juegos Olímpicos de Invierno de Turín.

9B.16 ¿Qué hicieron esos famosos? Con un/a compañero/a, necesitan completar la siguiente tabla. Ustedes tienen información diferente y por eso necesitan hacerse preguntas para encontrar toda la información.

A

¿Quién es?	¿Qué hizo?
1. Miguel Cotto	
2.	Nació en Caracas, Venezuela el 22 de abril de 1972 y es corredora de automóviles.
3. Manu Ginóbili	
4. Lorena Ochoa	
5.	Ciclista español que ganó el Tour de Francia cinco veces entre 1991 a 1995.
6.	Atleta de Nueva York que participó en el deporte de taekwondo y recibió dos medallas de oro.
7. Óscar de la Hoya	
8.	Futbolista hondureño que logró 32 goles en 103 partidos con los MetroStars/ Red Bulls antes de jugar para el Chivas USA.
9. Ellen Ochoa	
10.	Futbolista del Chicago Fire que nació en la Ciudad de México en 1973.

B

¿Quién es?	¿Qué hizo?
1.	Boxeador puertorriqueño que recibió el título de campeón de WBO Light Welterweight por dos años consecutivos, 2004-2006.
2. Milka Duno	
3.	Basquetbolista argentino de los Spurs de San Antonio. Ganó una medalla de oro en básquetbol en los Juegos Olímpicos de 2004.
4.	Golfista mexicana que ganó un millón de dólares por su triunfo en el ADT Championship de West Palm Beach.
5. Miguel Induráin	
6. Steven López	
7.	Generó $120 millones de dólares en televisión por su lucha contra Floyd Mayweather Jr.
8. Amado Guevara	
9.	Astronauta hispana de California que voló en el transbordador espacial cuatro veces.
10. Cuauhtémoc Blanco	

Expresiones de tiempo que se usan con el pretérito

These words and expressions refer to specified and limited times in the past and can often trigger the use of the preterit tense.

ayer	*yesterday*
anoche	*last night*
anteayer	*day before yesterday*
el sábado/lunes pasado	*last Saturday/Monday*
la semana pasada	*last week*
el mes/año pasado	*last month/year*
una vez	*once, one time*
el otro día	*the other day*
hace dos semanas	*two weeks ago*
hace diez años	*ten years ago*
de repente	*suddenly*

Ayer miré el partido de béisbol por televisión.
El verano pasado buceamos en el Caribe.
Me gradué de la escuela secundaria hace cinco años.

Why would we use these expressions with the preterit tense?

9B.17 **¿Quién de la clase...?**   Habla con los compañeros para determinar a quién de la clase corresponden las siguientes actividades. Necesitas hacerle una pregunta a cada persona y si la persona contesta "Sí", pídele que firme en el espacio indicado. Si la persona contesta "No" puedes hacerle una pregunta más antes de hablar con otra persona. **¡Ojo!** Para hacer las preguntas, tienes que cambiar los verbos a la forma de tú. Después de repasar las preguntas con la clase, apunta las generalizaciones en tu **Retrato de la clase**.

¿Quién de la clase...

1. recibió más de un mensaje de correo electrónico esta mañana? _____

2. asistió a un partido de tenis la semana pasada? _____

3. se rompió el brazo cuando era niño/a? _____

4. salió con sus amigos el sábado por la noche? _____

5. trabajó ayer? _____

6. se acostó tarde el viernes pasado? _____

7. comió en McDonald's recientemente? _____

8. vio una película el fin de semana pasado? _____

9. asistió a todas sus clases la semana pasada? _____

10. conoció a su mejor amigo/a en la escuela primaria? _____

Retrato de la clase: Por lo general, _____ compañeros de clase recibieron más de un mensaje de correo electrónico esta mañana....

9B.18 ¿Cuántos hay? Lee las oraciones e indica si son ciertas o falsas. Para cada oración, indica el número correcto.

Modelo: En un equipo de fútbol americano hay menos de diez jugadores.
Falso. Hay once.

	Cierto	Falso		¿Cuántos hay?
1.	☑	☐	En Estados Unidos hay más de cuarenta estados.	_____
2.	☐	☑	En esta clase hay menos de cinco estudiantes.	_____
3.	☐	☑	Tengo más de seis clases este semestre.	_____
4.	☑	☐	Hay menos de ocho continentes en el mundo.	_____
5.	☐	☑	Para formar un equipo de béisbol, se necesitan más de diez personas.	_____
6.	☑	☐	Una persona que nació en 1945 tiene menos de ochenta años.	_____

9B.18 ANSWERS: 1. Cierto (cincuenta), 2. Falso (likely response, number will vary), 3. Falso (likely response, number will vary), 4. Cierto (seis/siete), 5. Falso (nueve), 6. Cierto (number will vary)

9B.18 RECYCLING: Activity 9B.18 recycles comparisons with quantities, which students saw and practiced in *Investigación 8B*.

Estructuras clave 2 Preterit forms of *ser* and *ir*

Ser and **ir** have the same verb forms in the preterit. Context indicates which of the two meanings *(to be* or *to go)* is intended.

	Ser/Ir
yo	**fui**
tú	**fuiste**
él/ella/usted	**fue**
nosotros/as	**fuimos**
vosotros/as	**fuisteis**
ellos/ellas/ustedes	**fueron**

Fuimos a Atlanta a ver un partido de fútbol americano. (ir)
Antes de ser actor, Mickey Rourke fue un boxeador profesional. (ser)

Ser is used in the preterit to indicate that a situation has ended or changed. It can also be used to indicate a situation that lasted for a particular period of time.

Mi abuelo, quien murió el año pasado, fue actor de teatro durante muchos años.
Su primo fue abogado hasta que se fue a vivir a Rusia.

9B.19 ¿Ser o ir? Escucha las oraciones e indica si el significado del verbo se relaciona a ser o ir.

	ser	ir
1.	☑	☐
2.	☐	☑
3.	☑	☐
4.	☐	☑
5.	☐	☑

9B.19 AUDIO SCRIPT: 1. Babe Ruth y Lou Gehrig fueron peloteros famosos. 2. Mis amigos y yo fuimos al gimnasio para jugar al voleibol. 3. Mi abuelo fue un hombre excepcional. 4. ¿Fuiste al partido de básquetbol? 5. Fui al estadio para ver el partido de fútbol americano.

9B.20 **¿Pretérito o imperfecto?** Prestando atención al contexto, lee las oraciones e indica qué forma del verbo **ser** se necesita en cada caso: pretérito o imperfecto. Verifica tus repuestas con la clase.

1. La clase de hoy **fue/era** muy interesante. La profesora nos habló de la España musulmana.

2. **Fue/Era** un día frío de invierno. No quería salir de la casa, pero tenía que ir al trabajo. Me levanté y me puse ropa caliente.

3. Yo **fui/era** abogado, pero decidí cambiar de carrera. Ahora soy periodista.

4. Mis amigos y yo **fuimos/éramos** estudiantes dedicados en la escuela secundaria y todavía estudiamos mucho.

5. Los incas **fueron/eran** el grupo indígena más poderoso *(powerful)* de Sudamérica y hoy en día muchos de sus descendientes viven en la región andina.

6. Si ayer **fue/era** martes, ¿qué día es hoy?

7. Cuando **fuiste/eras** niño, ¿qué deportes practicabas?

8. Las lluvias **fueron/eran** torrenciales. Duraron solamente 10 minutos pero se inundó toda la ciudad.

9B.21 **Veinte preguntas.** Piensa en tus actividades durante las vacaciones más recientes y apunta seis cosas que hiciste *(you did)* durante ese tiempo. Entonces, busca a un/a compañero/a y hazle preguntas de tipo sí/no para determinar qué hizo él/ella durante las vacaciones. Compara tus respuestas con las respuestas de tu compañero/a. Escríbelas en tu **Retrato de la clase** y preséntalas a la clase. **¡Ojo!** Cuando le hagas las preguntas a tu compañero/a, usa la forma **tú** del pretérito.

Actividades que yo hice

_____
_____
_____
_____
_____

Actividades que mi compañero/a hizo

_____
_____
_____
_____
_____

Retrato de la clase: Mi compañero/a _____ y yo _____ durante nuestras vacaciones…

9B.22 **Adivina.** En grupos de tres, cada estudiante debe describir a un/a atleta famoso/a y el grupo va a adivinar su nombre. Hagan descripciones de por los menos tres atletas cada uno.

Modelo: E1: *Este atleta nadó en las Olimpiadas de Beijing en 2008. Ganó ocho medallas de oro.*

E2, E3: *Michael Phelps*

Enlaces

9B.23 **Enlaces.** Según el contexto de la oración, escoge el significado de las palabras a continuación. Escribe la letra que corresponde al significado apropiado al lado del número de la oración. Después compara tus respuestas con la clase.

> **a.** but rather **b.** consequently **c.** in light of

_b_ **1.** Una mala decisión, una indecisión o un momento equivocado puede cambiar por completo la vida. **Por consiguiente,** es importante ser maduro, tener buen juicio *(judgment)* y pensar las cosas bien antes de hacerlas.

_a_ **2.** Un atleta no sólo es un héroe social, **sino que** es la cara nacional dentro y fuera del país.

_c_ **3.** Encontraron al atleta entonado *(tipsy)* y con drogas en el carro. **A la luz de** esto, las compañías rechazaron la posibilidad de usarlo en sus anuncios televisivos.

9B.24 **¿Puedes conectar las ideas?** Conecta las ideas de las siguientes oraciones empleando la expresión apropiada. **¡Ojo!** Hay algunas expresiones que estudiaste en otros capítulos.

> a la luz de   sino que
> por consiguiente   además
> al mismo tiempo   a través de
> con fin de

1. ___Además___ de ser buenos atletas, Peyton Manning y su hermano Eli Manning tienen muchas virtudes personales.

2. Los atletas famosos pueden influenciar al público a favor de compañías como Reebok, Nike o Adidas. ___Por consiguiente___ las compañías les pagan a los atletas mucho dinero para promocionar sus productos.

3. Nadie pensó que Brett Favre jugaría *(would play)* para los Vikings de Minnesota. Pero, ___a la luz de___ su integración al equipo, los aficionados de los Vikings están muy contentos.

4. ___Al mismo tiempo___ que era entrenador de un equipo de béisbol, Pete Rose apostaba *(bet)* en los partidos.

5. ___Con el fin de___ ganar un campeonato de la NBA, los Celtics de Boston contrataron a Kevin Garnett y Ray Allen.

6. No es que no me guste el tenis, ___sino que___ lo juego muy mal.

7. ___A través de___ la dedicación al equipo, todos los jugadores empezaron a jugar mejor.

9B.24 TEACHING TIP: Before going over this exercise as a class, have students share their answers with a partner. As you ask students for their answers, consider having them hold up one finger to represent *a*, two to represent *b*, and three to represent *c*. This way, you can get a better sense of how well they understood these new words.

9B.24 TEACHING TIP: Have students go over their answers with a partner before you go over them as a class.

FUNCTIONAL OUTCOMES: The central question that frames this *Investigación* is *"¿Cómo se puede hablar de los deportes y los atletas de una cultura?"* Explore whether students can now address this question and how they would go about it. Have them review the chart on the first page of this *Investigación*.

9B.25 Los héroes deportivos.   Lee el siguiente artículo con el fin de comprender las ideas principales. Luego, con un compañero de clase, escriban un resumen del artículo de dos o tres oraciones.

HÉROES DE BARRIO

"El nacimiento del deporte responde a la conciencia que adquirió la burguesía a lo largo del siglo XIX por la necesidad de controlar las poblaciones para asegurar su productividad". –Michel Foucault

¿Los héroes deportivos existen para lograr el control y la cohesión social? Según Foucault, si el pueblo está contento, vive en un ambiente positivo y *además* tiene un héroe donde proyectar todos sus sueños e ideologías, trabajará mejor y *por consiguiente* será mucho más productivo. *Al mismo tiempo,* si todo el pueblo tiene una conexión afectiva hacia un atleta o un equipo determinado, va a existir una identificación cultural y una necesidad de formar parte de un grupo. *Por ejemplo,* si hay un grupo de aficionados *(fans)* del equipo de fútbol más importante de tu ciudad, las implicaciones son muy importantes. Puede influir a modestos trabajadores *con el fin* de que apoyen a su equipo con muchos sacrificios de tiempo y financieros.

¿Los héroes deportivos tienen imagen de prestigio social? Es posible convertirse en figura nacional como atleta. Si un atleta obtiene un triunfo muy importante las consecuencias pueden ser muy grandes. Estos atletas, o héroes, no solamente ganan un premio, *sino que* pueden influir en cómo se ven sus países en el mundo internacional. Por ejemplo, si un país en desarrollo *(developing)*, logra un triunfo muy grande, *a través* del atleta puede ganar mucho prestigio desde una perspectiva internacional.

9B.26 Implicaciones.   Indica si estás de acuerdo o no con las siguientes implicaciones del artículo. Luego, comparte tus respuestas con la clase para obtener una idea general de las perspectivas dominantes de la clase y escribe los resultados en tu **Retrato de la clase**.

1. Los atletas deben considerarse buenos modelos de conducta.
2. Es correcto usar un evento atlético para crear un sentimiento nacionalista.
3. Los deportes pueden disminuir divisiones socioeconómicas entre los aficionados.
4. Los deportes no tienen mucha influencia en la cultura de un país.
5. Es apropiado pagarles tanto dinero a los atletas.
6. El pueblo no quiere hacer sacrificios económicos por sus atletas favoritos.
7. Un triunfo a nivel internacional puede dar mucho prestigio a un país en desarollo.
8. Un atleta exitoso y popular puede unificar a una comunidad.

Retrato de la clase: En general, la clase cree que los atletas deben considerase buenos modelos de conducta, pero a veces no lo son…

Perspectivas

9B.27 **Más allá.** El siguiente artículo ofrece otra perspectiva sobre los deportes.

 Paso 1: En grupos de tres, lean el artículo y confirmen entre sí *(among each other)* su comprensión de las ideas principales.

SE VENDEN TALENTOS DEPORTIVOS

Contratar a jugadores extranjeros *(foreign)* es una práctica común entre los clubes profesionales, especialmente en las disciplinas deportivas como el básquetbol, el fútbol y el béisbol, entre otros deportes. Ahora los países ricos *(rich)* van un paso más allá de *(beyond)* la contratación de jugadores extranjeros *(foreign)*. Muchos atletas extranjeros de países en desarrollo *(development)* no sólo reciben contratos para jugar profesionalmente en estos nuevos países, sino que también reciben ciudadanías *(citizenship)* para jugar. Por ejemplo, el gran jugador "brasileño" Deco se convirtió en ciudadano portugués y ahora es una estrella en la selección (el equipo) de fútbol de su nuevo país.

Esta práctica es muy común en países desarrollados *(developed)*, o sea países más ricos, con atletas de países en desarrollo, o sea países más pobres. Esto afecta a países en desarrollo de una forma negativa y al espíritu de competencia deportivo. Los países en desarrollo pierden a sus atletas más competitivos debido a las ofertas financieras hechas por clubes de países desarrollados.

En la actualidad nos enfrentamos a una tendencia globalizada en la cual los países más ricos invierten *(invest)* recursos económicos astronómicos para obtener resultados deportivos. El objetivo de la inversión es atraer *(to attract)* a los mejores atletas del planeta hacia los países más poderosos *(powerful)*. Esto impacta la competitividad de países en desarrollo. En los Juegos Olímpicos sólo los países con dinero llegan a ser muy competitivos mientras que los países en desarrollo pierden interés en las Olimpiadas y eventos similares.

La compra de atletas es una nueva y peligrosa manifestación capaz *(capable)* de destruir la esencia misma del deporte y el propio ideal del Olimpismo.

Paso 2: El artículo de la página anterior habla de la comercialización de los atletas profesionales. No tienes que entender cada palabra para entender el mensaje principal. Al terminar de leer el artículo trabaja con un/a compañero/a para llenar la tabla con las razones del artículo y con las propias opiniones de ustedes sobre esta polémica.

Razones en contra de la comercialización de atletas	Razones a favor de la comercialización de atletas

Paso 3: Compartan sus respuestas con la clase para ver cómo piensa la mayor parte de sus compañeros. ¿Ha cambiado tu perspectiva sobre el papel de los deportes después de leer las dos lecturas anteriores y después de escuchar las perspectivas de la clase?

Retrato de la clase: En general, mis compañeros de clase están en contra/a favor de la comercialización de atletas porque…

Desde muy jóvenes, los niños juegan al fútbol en cualquier lugar. Aquí juegan en una plaza pequeña al lado de una iglesia.

Vocabulario: Investigación B

Vocabulario esencial

Sustantivos

el aficionado	*fan; amateur*
el ajedrez	*chess*
el atletismo	*track and field*
el buceo	*scuba diving*
el/la campeón/ona	*champion*
el campo de béisbol	*baseball field*
la cancha de voleibol	*volleyball court*
la caza	*hunting*
el equipo de baloncesto	*basketball team*
la natación	*swimming*
la pelota	*ball*
la pesca	*fishing*
la piscina	*pool*
la pista de patinaje	*skating rink*
el remo	*oar; rowing*

Adjetivos

deportivo/a	*sports-related*
equivocado/a	*wrong*
escaso/a	*scarce*
incomprensible	*unexplainable*
roto/a	*broken*

Verbos

bucear	*to dive*
cazar	*to hunt*
hacer camping	*to go camping*
nadar	*to swim*
patinar en línea	*inline skating*
patinar sobre hielo	*ice skating*
pescar	*to fish*
remar	*to row*

Adverbios

ayer	*yesterday*
anoche	*last night*
anteayer	*the day before yesterday*
el año/mes pasado	*last year/month*
la semana pasada	*last week*

Otras palabras y expresiones

la abreviatura	*abbreviation*
alargar	*to lengthen*
apostar	*to bet*
atrapar	*to capture*
la ausencia	*absence*
el automovilismo	*racecar driving*
el/la boxeador/a	*boxer*
el cielo	*sky*
la comercialización	*marketing*
la contratación	*hiring, contracting*
la corrida de toros	*bullfight*
entonado/a	*tipsy*
fundir	*to melt*
la garganta	*throat*
la hierba	*grass*
el hockey patín	*hockey on rollerblades*
lidiar	*to fight (bullfigthing)*
marcar	*to score*
el/la pescador/a	*fisher*
la polémica	*controversy*
la red	*net*
los timbales	*kettledrums, timps*
el tiro	*shot*
el toreo	*bull fighting*
el/la torero/a	*bullfighter*
el toro	*bull*

el transbordador espacial	*space shuttle*
el yeso	*cast*

en desarrollo	*developing*
en menor grado	*to a lesser degree*
entre sí	*among each other*
junto con	*together with*

Cognados

Review the cognates in *Adelante* and the false cognates in *¡Atención!*. For a complete list of cognates, see Appendix 4 on page 605.

En vivo

 Un día de fiesta nuevo. Trabajando en grupos de tres, inventen un día festivo nuevo. Usen las preguntas indicadas para guiar la discusión del grupo y apunten las respuestas. Van a presentar su nuevo día festivo a la clase y la clase va a votar para determinar cuál es el mejor nuevo día festivo.

- ¿Cómo se va a llamar el día festivo nuevo?

- ¿Qué se va a celebrar/conmemorar ese día?

- ¿Cuándo se va a celebrar? ¿Por cuánto tiempo?

- ¿Va a ser una fiesta religiosa; patriótica; familiar; deportiva?

- ¿Cómo se va a celebrar?

- ¿Va a haber comidas/bebidas especiales o competiciones deportivas que se asocien con ese día festivo? ¿Cuáles?

- ¿Va a haber actividades o costumbres que se asocien con ese día festivo? ¿Cuáles?

- ¿Se van a dar regalos, tarjetas u otras cosas ese día? ¿A quién(es)?

- ¿Por qué va a ser importante/especial ese día festivo?

- ¿Por qué se debe adoptar ese día festivo?

 El Día de los Muertos. Your task is to write an interpretation of a Day of the Dead altar. By studying the images, pictures and other features present on the altar, you will be able to learn a lot about the person to whom it is dedicated.

Paso 1: Identify an altar that you will use for your interpretation. There are many places you can begin looking (e.g. online, books, local galleries, etc.).

Paso 2: Make a copy of the image and write a description of it. Make sure to describe objects, food, scenes, emotions, etc. in the image. Ask yourself if your description captures the essence of the person being conmemorated.

Paso 3: Write your interpretation of who is being honored by the altar. Based on what you deduce about the person to whom the altar is dedicated, write three questions you would like to ask him/her.

Paso 4: Make any necessary revisions until you are satisfied with the content of your description and questions, then revise your work focusing on form and accuracy. Make the necessary corrections and prepare your final draft.

Paso 5: Feel proud of your increased awareness of perspectives on the celebration of the Day of the Dead.

En directo

INVESTIGACIÓN A: La feria de San Isidro

> **Antes de ver el video.** Responde a las siguientes preguntas y comparte tus respuestas con el resto de la clase: ¿Cuál es tu día feriado favorito? ¿Cuándo se celebra? ¿Qué se celebra? ¿Por qué es tu favorito?

> **El video.** Elige la opción correcta según el video.

1. La Feria de San Isidro es…

   a. una fiesta religiosa.   **b.** una fiesta pagana.   **c.** las dos son correctas.

2. ¿Cuándo es el día de San Isidro?

   a. el 2 de mayo.   **b.** el 5 de mayo.   **c.** el 15 de mayo.

3. La gente empieza el día yendo a…

   a. la iglesia de San Isidro.   **b.** procesiones.   **c.** la Plaza Mayor.

4. ¿Cuál es el traje tradicional de Madrid?

   a. el traje de flamenco   **b.** el traje de torero   **c.** el traje de chulapo

> **Después de ver el video.** Contesta las siguientes preguntas y comparte tus respuestas con el resto de la clase: ¿Es similar la Feria de San Isidro a alguna fiesta de tu país? ¿En qué sentido? ¿Conoces otras celebraciones hispanas? ¿Qué hacen las personas?

Vocabulario útil

patrón: *patron*
rosquilla: *doughnut*
oír misa: *to hear mass*

TEACHING TIP:
Information gap activities help develop students' interpersonal communication skills. Although they are not completely spontaneous, they do encourage the exchanging of information as well as the negotiation of meaning.

INVESTIGACIÓN B: El fútbol: Una pasión común

> **Antes de ver el video.** En parejas o grupos de tres, respondan a las siguientes preguntas. Luego, comparen sus respuestas con el resto de la clase: ¿Cuáles son sus deportes favoritos? ¿Cuál es el deporte más popular en su país? ¿Y en los países hispanos?

> **El video.** Completa las siguientes oraciones con la información correcta.

1. Al latino le apasiona el fútbol porque es parte de la __cultura__. Uno crece jugándolo.

2. He tratado de conocer más personas. He hecho más __amigos/as__.

3. A los hispanos les gusta el fútbol porque es __saludable__ y es __divertido__.

4. Me gustan casi todos los deportes pero en ninguno encuentro la __pasión__ que hay en el fútbol.

> **Después de ver el video.** Contesta las siguientes preguntas y luego compara tus respuestas con el resto de la clase: ¿Te gusta el fútbol? ¿Por qué? ¿Por qué crees que el fútbol es el deporte más popular del mundo?

Vocabulario útil

copa mundial: *world cup*
saludable: *healthy*
apasionar: *to make (someone) passionate about (something)*

Retrato de la clase Checklist

You should have recorded information in your **Retrato de la clase** in conjunction with the following activities:

- ☐ **9A.11 ¿Cuál es tu día festivo favorito?**
- ☐ **9A.12 ¿Cómo celebran los días festivos?**
- ☐ **9A.17 Las actividades de la escuela secundaria.**

- ☐ **9B.11 Los deportes favoritos de los compañeros.**
- ☐ **9B.17 ¿Quién de la clase...?**
- ☐ **9B.21 Veinte preguntas.**
- ☐ **9B.26 Implicaciones.**
- ☐ **9B.27 Más allá.**

Perspectivas distintas

PLUS

INVESTIGACIÓN **10A**	INVESTIGACIÓN **10B**

¿Quiénes fueron los mayas, los aztecas y los incas?

¿Existe una verdad objetiva?

ADELANTE

▶ ¡Ya lo sabes! Las civilizaciones indígenas

▶ Las grandes civilizaciones de las Américas

Bien dicho: El sonido de la *y*

ADELANTE

▶ ¡Ya lo sabes! Personas y sucesos históricos

▶ Simón Bolívar: El Libertador

Bien dicho: El sonido de la *ll*

PALABRAS CLAVE

▶ Antiguos imperios

PALABRAS CLAVE

▶ El reportaje de eventos

ESTRUCTURAS CLAVE

▶ More on the preterit: Functions and verbs with spelling changes

▶ More on the preterit: Functions and verbs with stem changes

ESTRUCTURAS CLAVE

▶ Irregular preterit verbs

▶ The imperfect and the preterit in contrast

VÍVELO: LENGUA

▶ Expressing *ago*

▶ Expressing time frames

VÍVELO: LENGUA

▶ Expressing different meanings with the same verb using the preterit or the imperfect

VÍVELO: CULTURA

▶ Los olmecas

▶ Las tribus indígenas del norte

▶ Las creencias de las tribus indígenas norteamericanas

CONTEXTOS Y PERSPECTIVAS

Los mayas, los aztecas y los incas

CONTEXTOS Y PERSPECTIVAS

Che: El mito y la realidad

¡VÍVELO!

En vivo:
Examinar el legado ambiguo
Un punto de vista distinto

En directo:
A: Ollantaytambo: cultura milenaria
B: ¿Existe una verdad objetiva?

¿Quiénes fueron los mayas, los aztecas y los incas?

In this **Investigación** you will learn:

▶ About the various contributions of indigenous peoples in the Americas

▶ About the great civilizations of Central and South America

▶ How to express actions in the past interrupted by other actions

▶ How to express the beginning or end of past events

¿Cómo se puede hablar de las antiguas civilizaciones de América Latina?

You can talk about the various achievements of the great indigenous civilizations.	Los mayas inventaron un sistema avanzado de matemáticas, geometría y astronomía.
You can describe each civilization.	Los incas crearon un imperio más grande que el imperio romano durante su esplendor. El calendario azteca es más antiguo que el calendario gregoriano. No sabemos cómo se desintegró la civilización de los mayas.
You can investigate the state of these civilizations today.	¿Qué idiomas indígenas se hablan en la actualidad? ¿Cómo se trata en la actualidad a los grupos indígenas en las Américas?
You can narrate the sequence of events that explain what happened to the great civilizations of the Americas.	Colón llegó a las islas del Caribe y luego exploró la región de Nicaragua y Panamá. Regresó a España desilusionado porque nunca descubrió las riquezas que quería.

LANGUAGE THROUGH CONTENT: As your students are developing their Spanish skills, they are doing so while they learn new content that will help them develop a more acute sense of the complexity of language. By making the connection between language and culture more vivid, they will be developing their intercultural communicative competence.

Adelante

¡Ya lo sabes! Las civilizaciones indígenas

TEACHING TIP: Have students provide the cognates from the list that belong to the word families of the following words: *preservar, repeler, medicar, fertilizar, sistematizar, alimentar, naturalización, higiénico, insecticidas, invasión, ocupación, aceptación, civilización, asimilación, extinción*

el acueducto	el imperio	abandonar
el adobe	la influenza	aceptar
la arquitectura	la malaria	armar
la barbacoa	la medicina herbal	asimilar
la bola	la preservación de	atacar
el cacao	alimentos	capturar
la canoa	los recursos naturales	civilizar
el censo	el repelente de insectos	conquistar
el champú	el sistema de	cultivar
el cólera	infraestructura	defender
la conservación del agua	la tuberculosis	descubrir
el detergente		extinguir
la ecología		invadir
el fertilizante		ocupar
la higiene personal		

10A.1 **¿A qué categorías pertenecen?** Con un/a compañero/a de clase escriban los cognados de la lista de la página anterior en las categorías apropiadas. Incluyan otras categorías si son necesarias. Luego, compartan sus mapas semánticos con otra pareja.

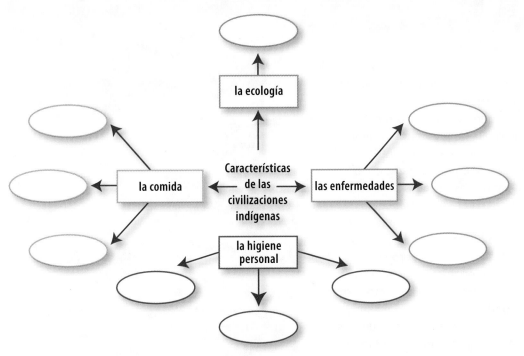

10A.2 **¿Qué palabra no corresponde?** Indica la palabra que no tiene nada en común con las demás según el modelo. Luego, verifica tus respuestas con otros compañeros de clase.

1. el chile	el frijol *(bean)*	el maíz	(la canoa)
2. el detergente	(el censo)	el champú	el repelente de insectos
3. (el tabaco)	el tomate	la papa	el chocolate
4. la tuberculosis	la malaria	(el fertilizante)	el cólera
5. la malaria	(el colador)	la tuberculosis	el cólera
6. invadir	atacar	(cultivar)	conquistar
7. (abandonar)	conservar	preservar	defender
8. la serpiente	la alpaca	el búfalo	(la bola)

10A.3 **Descripciones.** Escucha las descripciones y escribe el término correspondiente de la lista de cognados. Luego, verifica tus respuestas con la clase.

1. _____la canoa_____
2. _____el adobe_____
3. _____el acueducto_____
4. ___los recursos naturales___
5. _____el champú_____
6. ___la medicina herbal___
7. ___la preservación de alimentos___
8. _____el censo_____
9. ___el repelente de insectos___
10. _____el fertilizante_____

10A.4 **En parejas.** Túrnate con tu compañero/a para describir palabras de la lista de cognados. Una persona describe una palabra, sin decirla, mientras que la otra persona adivina la palabra descrita.

10A.1 TEACHING TIP: Encourage students to create additional categories and to insert additional words. For example, there are many more cognates under food than the three indicated in the semantic map above. This type of exercise recycles previously learned vocabulary.

10A.1 FOCUSED PRACTICE: Because the words on this list are cognates, you can thus expect your students to need less contact with them in context than if they were brand new words. However, be realistic in terms of what you expect students to have readily accessible in their own language production. Here are two strategies you could use to approach cognate vocabulary: 1. Have students make a list of items that they come in contact with on a daily basis. 2. Have students organize the vocabulary by themes. Remember to encourage students to build as many connections as possible to this vocabulary so that it does become more accessible for them.

10A.2 TEACHING TIP: Before going over answers as a class, have students share their answers with a classmate. Encourage them to explain to one another why they chose the answers they did so that they help each other understand their choices.

10A.3 AUDIO SCRIPT: 1. Se usa como forma de transporte en los ríos. 2. Se usa para construir casas. 3. Se usaba para transportar el agua. 4. Son cosas como el agua, los árboles, los metales y los minerales. 5. Se usa para lavarse el pelo. 6. Se usa para algunas enfermedades aunque los médicos prefieren recomendar algo farmacéutico. 7. Se usa para no tener hambre. 8. Se usa para contar el número de personas de un país. 9. Se usa para protegerse contra los insectos. 10. Se usa sobre la tierra para facilitar el cultivo de las plantas.

Las grandes civilizaciones de las Américas

Para entender las culturas latinoamericanas es importante comprender las diversas influencias formativas en las culturas de hoy. Una influencia muy importante es la indígena. Para entender mejor esta influencia es importante aprender sobre las civilizaciones más conocidas: la maya, la azteca y la inca. Estas civilizaciones no sólo fueron importantes imperios precolombinos (antes de Cristóbal Colón), sino que influyeron en el idioma, la religión y la cultura de las naciones latinoamericanas modernas. La producción agrícola, artesanal, artística y literaria de estos pueblos constituye un elemento fundamental del patrimonio (heritage) económico y cultural de sus respectivos países. Sus descendientes contemporáneos todavía son una parte significativa de varios países latinoamericanos, tales como México, Guatemala, Ecuador, Perú y Bolivia.

Por otro lado, es importante reconocer que aunque todavía existen poblaciones cuyos antepasados pertenecían (belonged) a las antiguas civilizaciones, la mayoría de las poblaciones fueron eliminadas por las enfermedades que llegaron con los españoles, como el cólera, la malaria, la tuberculosis y la influenza.

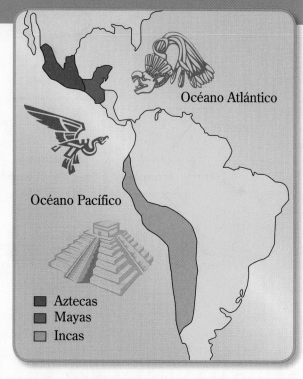

Océano Atlántico

Océano Pacífico

■ Aztecas
■ Mayas
□ Incas

10A.5 ANSWERS:
1. Falso (Sí, tuvieron gran impacto). 2. Falso (América Central) 5. Falso (América del Sur) 8. Falso (Todavía son parte de la población de ciertas regiones).

10A.5 TEACHING TIP:
Encourage students to determine whether the statements are true or false without referring back to the passage. After they have responded to the statements, have them go back to the passage and check their answers. How did they do?

10A.5 **Cierto o falso.** Indica si estas oraciones son ciertas o falsas. Luego, verifica tus respuestas con la clase.

Cierto Falso

☐ ☑ **1.** Los mayas, incas y aztecas no tuvieron un gran impacto en la formación de las culturas del Nuevo Mundo.

☐ ☑ **2.** Los mayas fueron muy importantes en Perú.

☑ ☐ **3.** La civilización azteca fue muy dominante en lo que hoy es México.

☑ ☐ **4.** Las religiones indígenas influyeron en las tradiciones religiosas actuales.

☐ ☑ **5.** Los incas tuvieron un imperio muy extenso en América Central.

☑ ☐ **6.** Los españoles trajeron enfermedades mortales para los indígenas.

☑ ☐ **7.** Las civilizaciones indígenas elaboraron formas de arte, artesanía y literatura.

☐ ☑ **8.** La conquista de los pueblos indígenas causó su extinción completa.

EXPRESIONES ÚTILES

Reacciones expresivas

¡Qué lástima!/¡Qué pena! *(What a shame/pity!)*
  ¡Qué lástima! María no puede venir a la fiesta.
  ¡Qué pena! No puedo ir al cine contigo porque tengo que trabajar.

¡Qué horror! *(How horrible/awful!)*
  ¡Qué horror! Muchos indígenas sufrieron de enfermedades traídas por los europeos.

¡Qué desafortunado! *(How unfortunate!)*
  ¡Qué desafortunado! Han desaparecido muchas tradiciones antiguas.

¡Qué triste! *(How sad!)*
  ¡Qué triste! Han cancelado la excursión a causa de la lluvia.

¡Qué afortunado!/¡Qué suerte! *(How fortunate!/ What luck!)*
  ¡Qué afortunados! Los Gómez han ganado la lotería.
  ¡Qué suerte! Los zapatos que quería están en oferta ahora.

¡Qué chévere! *(How cool!)*
  ¡Qué chévere! Este jardín es hermoso.

¡Qué alegría! *(How great/wonderful!)*
  ¡Qué alegría! Las vacaciones comienzan mañana.

10A.6 **Situaciones.** Responde con la expresión más apropiada para cada una de las situaciones siguientes.

1. Escuchas en las noticias que hay una epidemia de cólera en tu universidad.

2. Descubres que tus padres han perdido su casa por un huracán.

3. Tu mejor amigo te dice que se casa en el verano.

4. Encuentras dinero inesperadamente en uno de tus libros.

5. Tu mejor amigo/a admite que es alcohólico/a.

10A.6 ANSWERS:
Answers will vary.

VÍVELO: CULTURA

Los olmecas

La civilización que los mexicas llamaban olmeca, una de las más antiguas de América, se desarrolló en la costa del Golfo de México entre los años 1200 y 400 antes de Cristo aproximadamente. Se extendió hasta el Valle Central de México, Guatemala y El Salvador. La astronomía, la arquitectura y el arte de esta antigua cultura influyeron tanto a los mayas como a los aztecas. De los olmecas son famosas las esculturas en piedra de cabezas monumentales, las pequeñas esculturas en piedra y en jade azul, la escritura jeroglífica y los sistemas de irrigación de las ciudades que mantenían la producción agrícola. El juego de la pelota y el culto al jaguar-niño eran dos de las características simbólicas de esta antigua civilización.

Es importante entender que antes de las tres grandes civilizaciones, la azteca, la inca y la maya, había muchas otras civilizaciones que contribuyeron a su desarrollo.

VÍVELO: CULTURA: The objective of this *Vívelo: Cultura* is to show students that although the Aztecs, Incas, and Mayas are the main groups that are often talked about, there were other great civilizations that came before them.

HOMEWORK ACTIVITY: Encourage students to go online to research other pre-Columbian civilizations. Have them include an image along with a short description of when the civilization existed and some major points about them.

10A.7 **Cierto o falso.** Escucha las oraciones e indica si son ciertas o falsas. Luego, verifica tus respuestas con un/a compañero/a de clase.

	Cierto	Falso
1.	☑	☐
2.	☑	☐
3.	☐	☑
4.	☑	☐
5.	☑	☐

VÍVELO: CULTURA

Las tribus indígenas del norte

Había una gran variedad de pueblos indígenas en América del Norte, algunos sedentarios y otros nómadas. La lista a continuación enumera algunas tribus e identifica la región donde se encontraban. ¿Cuáles de ellas reconoces?

los shoshones	Región de la Gran Cuenca
los inuits	Región Ártica
los shawnis	Región Nordeste
los crees	Región Subártica
los sioux	Región de las Grandes Llanuras
los comanches	Región de las Grandes Llanuras
los crows	Región de las Grandes Llanuras
los wichitas	Región de las Grandes Llanuras
los seminolas	Región Sudeste
los cheroquíes	Región Sudeste
los chickasaws	Región Sudeste
los cheyenes	Región de la Gran Cuenca
los spokanes	Región de la Gran Meseta
los apaches	Región Sudoeste
los hopis	Región Sudoeste
los navajos	Región Sudoeste
los zunis	Región Sudoeste
los zacatecas	Región Sudoeste
los senecas	Región Nordeste
los mohicanos	Región Nordeste

www ¡Conéctate!

North America, like Central and South America, has a rich history of Native American societies. Do you know what group lived where you live today? Despite a treacherous history against Native American cultures, many tribes continue the traditions of their ancestors. Visit http://www.nativeculturelinks.com to learn more about their rich histories. Identify three groups that you would like to learn more about. Find out where they were primarily based and where they are today. Learn more about general characteristics of these groups to share with your classmates.

Bien dicho

El sonido de la y

In most varieties of Spanish, the sound associated with the letter **y,** whose symbol is /y/, corresponds closely to the sound associated with the *y* in the English words *you, yes, yellow* or *yo-yo*. Note the tension of your tongue on the roof of your mouth when you pronounce the *y* in these English words as opposed to the "ee" (/i/) sound of the *y* in words like *easy* or *haywire*. Spanish pronunciation is closer to the tenser /y/ sound in English. For example, **mayo** should be pronounced [má-yo] rather than [mái-o], and **leyó** should be pronounced [le-yó] rather than [lei-ó].

In Spanish, the combination **hi** before the vowels **e** or **a** also corresponds to the /y/ sound, for example in words like **hielo** [yé-lo] (ice) and **hiato** [yá-to] *(pause).*

There are many dialectal variations in the pronunciation of **y** in Spanish. One very prominent variant occurs in Argentina, Uruguay and parts of Chile. In this region, called the **Cono Sur,** or Southern Cone, **y** is frequently pronounced like the *s* in *measure* and *treasure*, or like the combination *sh* in *shoe* and *ship*. In other regions, such as Mexico, **y** is often pronounced like the *j* in *June* and *jar*.

10A.8 **¿Cómo se escribe?** Escucha las palabras pronunciadas e indica si se escriben con la letra **i** por una parte o con **y** o **hi** por otra parte. Luego, verifica tus respuestas con la clase.

	i	y o hi
1.	☑	☐
2.	☐	☑
3.	☐	☑
4.	☐	☑
5.	☑	☐
6.	☑	☐

10A.8 AUDIO SCRIPT:
1. vienen 2. yerno 3. hierro 4. creyó 5. leía 6. caliente

10A.9 **Ahora les toca.**   Con un/a compañero/a, túrnense para pronunciar las oraciones siguientes prestando atención a la pronunciación estándar de las letras **y** o **hi**. Repitan el ejercicio pronunciando las oraciones que no articularon la primera vez.

1. Ayer Yolanda comió yogur de papaya.

2. Hay muchas ruinas mayas en Yucatán.

3. Los reyes construyeron un palacio feo.

4. ¿Los tíos tuyos son uruguayos o paraguayos?

5. Vaya a comprar joyas para la novia suya.

6. Mi pobre hermano mayor se cayó en el hielo.

7. Mi yerno contribuyó mucho a ese proyecto.

8. El Sr. Yáñez leyó la carta y luego la destruyó.

10A.9 TEACHING TIP: Students can be encouraged to investigate regional variations in the pronunciation of *y/hi*. Ask them if a standard exists, and if so, who decides what is considered the "standard". This same debate exists in the many varieties of English. Ask students how many of them think they speak standard English. Then ask them how many people in England would agree that what we speak in the U.S. is standard English.

Palabras clave Antiguos imperios

el águila

el dios del Sol

las esculturas de piedra

la cosecha

el entendimiento

contar

10A.10 TEACHING TIP: Encourage students to explain to their partners how they arrived at their answers, especially if they have different answers. The purpose of having students share their answers with one another is that it makes them more accountable and it gives them an extra layer of support as they expand their vocabulary.

10A.10 PARTNER CARDS: On slips of paper, you could write down each word from both columns in activity 10A.10. Save them for future partnering activities. Randomly pass them out when you want students to work with a partner. If a student had the sheet reading *"el siglo,"* they would need to find the student with the slip reading *"cien años."* This will not only encourage further practice of the vocabulary but it will also provide students with a chance to physically move around the classroom, something that is important to helping students stay focused.

10A.10 Conceptos similares. Empareja el nuevo vocabulario con conceptos similares. Luego, compara tus respuestas con un/a compañero/a.

_g_ **1.** avanzar	**a.** dominación/monarquía
_d_ **2.** mundial	**b.** hierbas
_e_ **3.** contar	**c.** dolor
_c_ **4.** sensación física	**d.** internacional
_h_ **5.** temperatura alta	**e.** enumerar
_a_ **6.** imperio	**f.** piedra
_j_ **7.** extenderse	**g.** desarrollar
_f_ **8.** recurso natural	**h.** fiebre
_i_ **9.** el siglo	**i.** cien años
_b_ **10.** plantas medicinales	**j.** aumentar

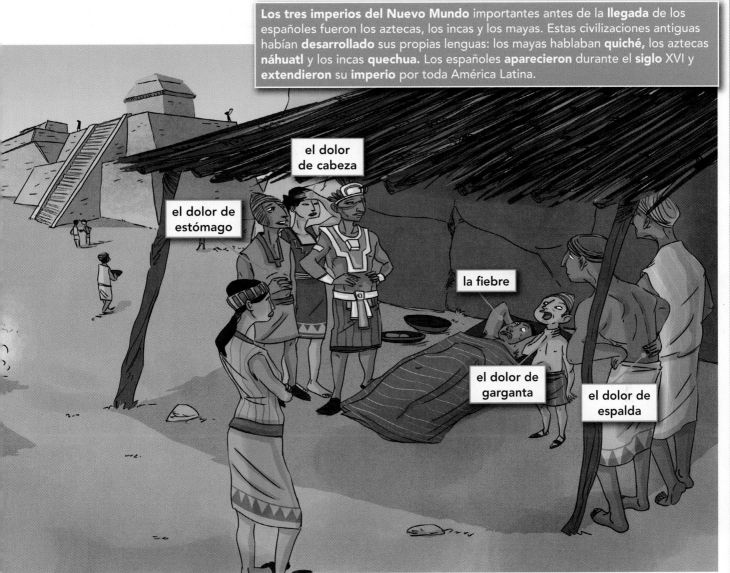

Los tres imperios del Nuevo Mundo importantes antes de la llegada de los españoles fueron los aztecas, los incas y los mayas. Estas civilizaciones antiguas habían desarrollado sus propias lenguas: los mayas hablaban quiché, los aztecas náhuatl y los incas quechua. Los españoles aparecieron durante el siglo XVI y extendieron su imperio por toda América Latina.

el dolor de cabeza

el dolor de estómago

la fiebre

el dolor de garganta

el dolor de espalda

10A.11 ¿Es lógico? Lee los enunciados a continuación y decide si son lógicos o ilógicos. Si son ilógicos, corrígelos para que sean lógicos. Luego verifica tus respuestas con la clase.

Lógico Ilógico

☑ ☐ **1.** Cuando tienes fiebre a veces se recomienda tomar una aspirina.
☐ ☑ **2.** Cuando tienes dolor de garganta, es bueno salir al aire frío.
☑ ☐ **3.** El campesino (*peasant*) depende de una buena cosecha cada año.
☑ ☐ **4.** Para los dolores de espalda, es importante acostarse.
☐ ☑ **5.** Es bueno beber cerveza cuando tienes dolor de estómago.
☑ ☐ **6.** Para evitar los mosquitos, se recomienda repelente de insectos.

10A.11 TEACHING TIP: The purpose of this activity is to expose students to more comprehensible input while practicing new vocabulary. Invite a variety of possible corrections of illogical statements.

10A.12 TEACHING
TIP: As you correct this exercise, invite students to volunteer reading one line at a time. While you are going over it, feel free to probe further by asking questions such as, *¿En qué año llegaron los europeos a las Américas?* Also, offer students a moment to discuss the last two questions in small groups. The purpose of this activity is to further familiarize students with the new vocabulary while offering them more language around this topic.

10A.12 ¿Descubrimiento o conquista? Usa las palabras nuevas para completar este párrafo. Cuando lo termines, compara tus respuestas con las de dos compañeros y contesta la pregunta al final.

Mundo   siglos
entendimiento   desarrollaban
desarrolladas   imperio

Cuando se habla de las Américas típicamente se refiere a estos países como parte del Nuevo [1] _____Mundo_____. Pero la verdad es que "nuevo" depende de la perspectiva. Dicen que los europeos descubrieron las Américas hace más de cinco [2] _____siglos_____. Esa teoría refleja una ignorancia de la historia de las culturas indígenas que llevaban *(had lived for)* miles de años en las Américas. Por ejemplo, el _____imperio_____ incaico era más grande que el imperio romano en su época, antes de que llegaran los españoles. Había culturas y sociedades muy [4] _____desarrolladas_____. Por ejemplo, los mayas tenían un [5] _____entendimiento_____ increíble de las matemáticas. No solamente las entendían sino que también las [6] _____desarrollaban_____. En fin, ¿era descubrimiento o conquista? ¿Qué opinas tú?

VÍVELO: CULTURA

Las creencias de las tribus indígenas norteamericanas

Según la perspectiva de las tribus indígenas norteamericanas, la vida era cíclica. El pasado y el presente estaban siempre cerca *(close by)*. Así se transformaban todas las culturas en un presente eterno, renovándose y rehaciendo su identidad cultural con cada historia. Muchos grupos eran nómadas, o sea, se mudaban según las estaciones del año y la búsqueda *(search)* de alimentos. Sus mitologías y religiones reflejaban un sentido de búsqueda que los llevaba fuera *(out of)* de su ambiente conocido a lugares y territorios nuevos y desconocidos.

La mayoría de las tribus norteamericanas fueron eliminadas, con excepción de las regiones más al norte y del Ártico. Varios gobiernos estadounidenses trataron de imponerles *(impose)* una cultura occidental y convertirlos al cristianismo. Los indígenas firmaban la venta *(sales)* de sus tierras sólo porque los jefes de las tribus no concebían posible la venta de algo que no se podía llevar — la tierra, el agua, el aire, el viento y todo lo demás que hay en el planeta.

Reserva indígena, suroeste de EE.UU.

¿Sabes cuántas reservas indígenas existen en la actualidad? Haz una investigación para ver cuántas existen en Estados Unidos, el vasto territorio que una vez les perteneció.

¡Atención!

Reclamar	means *to claim, to demand* or *to lodge (a complaint)*. **Reclamar** does not mean *to reclaim*. To express the idea of *to reclaim*, use the verb **recuperar**, as in *to recuperate*.
	El servicio en el hotel era terrible. Le reclamé a la administradora y nos dio un desayuno gratis.
	Muchos grupos indígenas recuperaron parte de las tierras que habían perdido.
Asistir (a)	means *to attend*. **Asistir** does not usually mean *to assist* or *to help*. To express the idea of *to help*, use the verb **ayudar**.
	Me gustaría asistir al próximo concierto de Maná.
	Mi profesora siempre me ayuda cuando no entiendo algo.
Atender (e-ie)	means *to take care of, to provide service*. It does not mean *to attend*.
	Cuando regreso a mi casa durante las vacaciones mi mamá me atiende muy bien.

10A.13 Sé honesto. Con un/a compañero/a de clase, túrnense haciendo preguntas de la tabla y contestando honestamente. Si tu compañero/a responde "sí," puedes poner una "X" en esa caja. Escribe lo que aprendas sobre tu compañero/a en tu **Retrato de la clase.**

10A.13 PARTNERING STUDENTS: A unique and effective way of partnering students is by having students find their partner using the cards you may have prepared from activity 10A.10. Once students are with a partner, have them establish who will go first. You can either have students do this activity on a shared board, or have them each use their own board so that they have more options of questions available to them.

¿Asistes a muchos conciertos?	Si recibes servicio malo, ¿reclamas?	¿Los profesores siempre deben atender a sus estudiantes?	¿Asistes a todas tus clases?
¿Atiendes a personas enfermas?	¿Te gusta ayudar a tus amigos con sus tareas?	¿Ayudas a tu familia mucho?	¿Siempre recuperas las cosas que prestas a tus amigos?

Retrato de la clase: Mi compañero/a de clase _____ asiste a muchos conciertos. Mi compañero/a de clase nunca/siempre reclama cuando recibe servicio malo....

10A.14 ¿Cuáles son más importantes? Lee las oraciones siguientes y selecciona las dos más importantes en tu opinión. También selecciona las dos menos importantes. Después compara tus selecciones con las de un/a compañero/a de clase. ¿Son similares o diferentes sus respuestas?

10A.14 ALTERNATIVE DELIVERY: Give more students the added challenge of developing their own sentences using the vocabulary from the *Atención* section to do the same activity.

- Es importante reclamar cuando existen injusticias sociales.
- Es importante ofrecer tus servicios para ayudar a otras personas.
- Me gustaría asistir a un concierto de Eminem.
- Si tu hamburguesa de Burger King no está caliente es necesario reclamar tu dinero o que te den *(that the give you)* otra hamburguesa.
- Es importante atender a nuestros invitados cuando hacemos fiestas.
- Los padres siempre deben atender a sus hijos.
- Los estudiantes siempre deben asistir a clase de español.

Estructuras clave 1 More on the preterit: Functions and verbs with spelling changes

PLUS
Go to *WileyPLUS* and review the tutorial for this grammar point.

PLUS
You will find PowerPoint presentations for use with *Estructuras clave* in *WileyPLUS*.

TEACHING TIP: This is a good time to review the pronunciation of *c* and *g* before *i* or *e* as opposed to other vowels.

You learned in *Capítulo 9* that there are patterns to the way in which regular verbs end in the preterit depending on whether or not they are **–ar, –er,** or **–ir** verbs.

bailar		comer		vivir	
bail**é**	bail**amos**	com**í**	com**imos**	viv**í**	viv**imos**
bail**aste**	bail**asteis**	com**iste**	com**isteis**	viv**iste**	viv**isteis**
bail**ó**	bail**aron**	com**ió**	com**ieron**	viv**ió**	viv**ieron**

You learned that the preterit is used to express completed actions in the past and to relate a past condition during a defined time period.

> La semana pasada fuimos al museo de antropología.
> Vimos cosas interesantes durante la visita.

The preterit is also used when expressing the beginning or end of a past event.

> Comenzó a estudiar lingüística cuando fue a la universidad.
> Terminó su maestría después de que su bebé nació.

Verbs with spelling changes in the preterit

While the majority of verbs you use will follow the patterns shown above, there are a few more variations that you will learn in this *Investigación* to help you express yourself on a broader level. These variations deal with slight spelling changes in some verbs.

Still considered regular verbs, there are some verbs ending in **–car, –gar,** and **–zar** that change spelling in the first person singular (the **yo** form). For instance:

bus**car**		lle**gar**		comen**zar**	
bus**qué**	buscamos	lle**gué**	llegamos	comen**cé**	comenzamos
buscaste	buscasteis	llegaste	llegasteis	comenzaste	comenzasteis
buscó	buscaron	llegó	llegaron	comenzó	comenzaron

The reason they change their spelling is to maintain the pronunciation of the consonant in the stem. Here are some other commonly used **–car, –gar,** and **–zar** verbs you already know that fall in this category.

almorzar *(to eat lunch)*	jugar *(to play)*	realizar *(to achieve)*
dedicar *(to dedicate)*	organizar *(to organize)*	sacar *(to take out)*
educar *(to educate)*	pagar *(to pay)*	significar *(to mean)*
empezar *(to begin)*	pescar *(to catch, to fish)*	tocar *(to touch, to play*
explicar *(to explain)*	publicar *(to publish)*	[music])*

10A.15 Respuestas personales.

Paso 1: Contesta las preguntas siguientes según tu opinión personal. Puedes escoger más de una respuesta.

1. ¿Por qué empezaste a estudiar español?

☐ Empecé a estudiar español porque muchas personas lo hablan en Estados Unidos y quiero comunicarme con ellas.

☐ Empecé porque es necesario tener dos semestres de un idioma para graduarse.

☐ Empecé porque tengo familia o amigos que hablan español.

☐ Otras razones: _____

2. ¿Cuándo llegaste a clase hoy?

☐ Llegué más o menos quince minutos antes de la clase.

☐ Llegué menos de quince minutos antes de la clase.

☐ Llegué tarde a clase hoy.

☐ Llegué _____.

3. ¿Dedicaste tiempo a ayudar a alguna causa este año?

☐ Dediqué tiempo a *Habitat for Humanity*.

☐ Dediqué tiempo a *Big Brothers, Big Sisters*.

☐ No dediqué tiempo a ninguna organización.

☐ Dediqué tiempo a _____.

4. ¿Practicaste algún deporte durante el fin de semana?

☐ Sí, jugué al fútbol.

☐ Sí, jugué al béisbol.

☐ No, no practiqué ningún deporte.

☐ Sí, jugué a _____.

5. ¿Organizaste algún evento el año pasado?

☐ Sí, organicé una fiesta para _____.

☐ Sí, organicé un comité para _____.

☐ No, no organicé ningún evento el año pasado.

☐ Sí, organicé _____.

6. ¿Buscaste un apartamento durante el verano?

☐ No, no busqué un apartamento durante el verano.

☐ Sí, busqué un apartamento.

☐ No, busqué una casa.

☐ No, busqué _____.

Paso 2: Usando el diagrama de Venn, compara tus respuestas con las respuestas de un/a compañero/a de clase. ¿Son similares? ¿Son diferentes? Luego, prepárate para presentar tus conclusiones a tus compañeros. Incluye información interesante en tu **Retrato de la clase.**

Yo — Lo que tenemos en común — Mi compañero/a de clase

Retrato de la clase: Mi compañero/a de clase y yo empezamos a estudiar español porque es necesario tener dos semestres de un idioma para graduarse.

10A.15 TEACHING TIP: PASO 2. As students prepare to fill in their Venn diagrams, encourage them to pay attention to the ending of the verbs depending on who is being talked about. For instance, when comparing and contrasting answers, they will need to use the *nosotros* form. When speaking about themselves, they will use the *yo* form, and when they speak about their partner, they will use the *él/ella* form.

10A.15 TEACHING TIP: PASO 2. Here are some ways that you might consider when you have students share their Venn diagrams with their classmates: 1. Form groups of four to six. Each student shares their Venn diagram. 2. You could randomly ask questions such as *¿Quién tiene mucho en común con su amigo/a?* or *¿Qué diferencias existen entre tus repuestas y las de tu compañero/a?* 3. Have students stand and move about the room to share their Venn diagrams. They should share them with one other person at a time. Give students two minutes to share their diagrams before asking them to move to another person. The idea is to provide students with the opportunity to take this information a step further and share it with others.

B	
La tribu	**La contribución**
1.	un sistema de símbolos para representar letras o números, es decir un código
2. Los cheyenes, pawnis, kiowas, crows, comanches, arapahos, kiowas, dakotas, lakotas y nakotas	
3.	los zapatos para la nieve
4. Las culturas de las tribus árticas y subárticas	
5.	un aparato para amplificar la voz (megaphone)
6. Las culturas de América del Norte, la región ártica y subártica	los kayaks
7.	los insecticidas
8. Las tribus de América del Norte, el noroeste y *Great Plains*	
9.	la medicina para un dolor de cabeza
10. Los iroqueses y los hurones	
11.	los diuréticos
12. Los iroqueses y los algonquinos	
13.	las papitas (potato chips)
14. Los chippewas y las tribus en la región de los Grandes Lagos	

A	
La tribu	**La contribución**
1. Los choctaws	
2.	el idioma de gestos llamado *Sign Language*
3. Las culturas de las tribus del ártico, subártico y noroeste	
4.	las chaquetas con gorro llamadas parkas
5. Los iroqueses y los chippewas	
6.	los kayaks
7. Varias tribus del *Great Basin, Plateau* y la costa del noroeste	
8.	la ropa de *fringe*
9. Los zunis	
10.	la interpretación de los sueños
11. Los ho-chunks, dakotas, natchez y blackfeet	
12.	la idea de dos camas, una sobre la otra (bunkbeds)
13. La mayoría de las tribus del norte	
14.	las palomitas de caramelo (caramel popcorn)

10A.16 Las contribuciones. Las tribus norteamericanas contribuyeron al idioma y a la cultura estadounidense. Con un/a compañero/a, completen la tabla a continuación que ofrece varias contribuciones de las tribus norteamericanas. Ustedes tienen información diferente. Necesitan hacerse preguntas empleando los verbos a continuación para encontrar toda la información.

inventar
originar
empezar
construir
diseñar
crear
introducir
desarrollar

Modelo: E1: *¿Quiénes crearon un sistema de símbolos para representar letras o números?*
E2: *Los choctaws*

10A.16 INSTRUCTOR'S RESOURCES: Filled out cards are available in your Instructor's Resources for distribution as an answer key.

10A.16 INFORMATION/GAP ACTIVITY: This activity is an excellent way of helping students gain skills as they work toward developing their interpersonal communication skills.

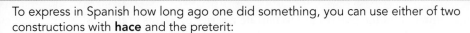

VÍVELO: LENGUA

Expressing *ago*

To express in Spanish how long ago one did something, you can use either of two constructions with **hace** and the preterit:

hace + time + **que** + preterit verb
preterit verb + **hace** + time

Hace un año que vi a mi hermano
en Argentina.

*I saw my brother one year ago in
Argentina.*

Vi a mi hermano en Argentina hace un año.

Hace tres semanas que él vino a verme.   *He came to see me three weeks ago.*
Vino a verme hace tres semanas.

To ask how long ago something took place, use **¿Cuánto tiempo hace que** +
preterit?

— ¿Cuánto tiempo hace que se mudó
a Argentina?

— *How long ago did he move to
Argentina?*

— Hace tres años.

— *Three years ago.*

VÍVELO: LENGUA:
Remind students of the use of *hace* + time + *que* + present tense to talk about how long an action or condition has been on-going. Point out the difference in the use of the present versus use of the preterit with these *hace* time expressions. With use of the present, the focus is on the *duration of time* from the moment the action began, whereas with the use of the preterit, the focus is on *distance in time* from the moment the action occurred. Write *Hace tres años que se mudó a Argentina* and *Hace tres años que vive en Argentina* on the board and have students explain the difference in meaning as a function of the verb tense used.

10A.17 La última vez.   Entrevista a un/a compañero/a de clase para saber la última vez que hizo las actividades siguientes. Emplea una de las construcciones con **hace** y el pretérito en las respuestas. Escribe las respuestas de tu compañero/a de clase en tu **Retrato de la clase**. **¡Ojo!** Tienes que cambiar los verbos a la forma de tú para entrevistar a tu compañero/a.

> Modelo: E1:   *¿Cuándo fue la última vez que almorzaste con tu familia?*
> E2:   *Hace dos semanas que almorcé con mi familia.* o *Almorcé con mi familia hace dos semanas.*

¿Cuándo fue...

1. la última vez que visitó el campo?

2. la última vez que usó repelente de insectos?

3. la última vez que comió maíz?

4. la última vez que plantó algo?

5. la última vez que pescó en el río?

6. la última vez que jugó a las cartas?

7. la última vez que organizó una fiesta?

8. la última vez que sufrió un dolor de garganta?

Retrato de la clase: Hace ___ semanas/años que mi compañero/a fue al campo...

DICHOS

Con las glorias se olvidan las penas.	*With glories, sorrows are forgotten.*
Cuando joven, de ilusiones; cuando viejo, de recuerdos.	*A young man has dreams; an old man has memories.*
La verdad, como el aceite, siempre sale a flote.	*Truth, like oil, always floats to the top.*

Estructuras clave 2 More on the preterit: Functions and verbs with stem changes

Additional functions of the preterit are to narrate a series of events in the past, such as the events that advance the plot of a story, and to describe an action that interrupts an on-going action in the past.

Abrió los ojos, se levantó, vio al león y corrió por la selva.	*He opened his eyes, got up, saw the lion, and ran through the jungle.*
Cuando corría por la selva, se cayó.	*While he was running through the jungle, he fell.*

Verbs with stem changes in the preterit

Some verbs have stems that change in the **él/ella/usted** and the **ellos/ellas/ustedes** forms. In these cases a **y** is placed between two vowels. Notice where the accent falls on these verbs.

leer *(to read)*		caerse *(to fall)*		creer *(to believe)*	
leí	leímos	me caí	nos caímos	creí	creímos
leíste	leísteis	te caíste	os caísteis	creíste	creísteis
leyó	leyeron	se cayó	se cayeron	creyó	creyeron

destruir *(to destroy)*		oír *(to hear)*		incluir *(to include)*	
destruí	destruimos	oí	oímos	incluí	incluimos
destruiste	destruisteis	oíste	oísteis	incluiste	incluisteis
destruyó	destruyeron	oyó	oyeron	incluyó	incluyeron

Stem-changing **–ar** and **–er** verbs in the present do not change their stems in the preterit. However, stem-changing **–ir** verbs do experience changes in the stems, but differently than they do in the present tense. Look at the following chart to see how **preferir** and **dormir** change in the present and in the preterit. In the preterit, they change in the **él/ella/usted** and the **ellos/ellas/ustedes** forms.

preferir *(to prefer)*				dormir *(to sleep)*			
Present (e ⟶ ie)		Present (e ⟶ i)		Present (o ⟶ ue)		Present (o ⟶ u)	
prefiero	preferimos	preferí	preferimos	duermo	dormimos	dormí	dormimos
prefieres	preferís	preferiste	preferisteis	duermes	dormís	dormiste	dormisteis
prefiere	prefieren	prefirió	prefirieron	duerme	duermen	durmió	durmieron

Other examples of **e ⟶ i** stem-changing verbs in the preterit are the following.

pedir	pedí, pediste, pidió, pedimos, pedisteis, pidieron
repetir	repetí, repetiste, repitió, repetimos, repetisteis, repitieron
seguir	seguí, seguiste, siguió, seguimos, seguisteis, siguieron
sentir	sentí, sentiste, sintió, sentimos, sentisteis, sintieron
servir	serví, serviste, sirvió, servimos, servisteis, sirvieron

Morir *(to die)* follows the same pattern as **dormir** in the preterit.

morir	morí, moriste, murió, morimos, moristeis, murieron

10A.18 Cada acción causa una reacción. Escucha las acciones 1–5 e indica la reacción más probable de las oraciones a–e. Luego, comparte tus respuestas con un/a compañero/a de clase.

_4_ **a.** Los españoles empezaron a importar esclavos de África.

_2_ **b.** Facilitaron la llegada a la Ciudad de México y la conquista de los aztecas.

_5_ **c.** La población indígena no resistió las enfermedades y muchos murieron.

_1_ **d.** Murió un hombre común desconocido.

_3_ **e.** Se dio cuenta de *(He realized)* su error muy tarde.

10A.18 AUDIO SCRIPT:
1. Cristobal Colón nunca realizó su sueño de encontrar riquezas en el Nuevo Mundo. 2. Algunos pueblos indígenas ayudaron a Hernán Cortés. 3. Moctezuma creyó que los españoles eran dioses. 4. Los reyes españoles empezaron a proteger al pueblo indígena en el Caribe. 5. Los españoles trajeron muchas enfermedades al Nuevo Mundo.

www ¡Conéctate!

Google the following names to learn their role in the colonization of Central and South America: Bartolomé de las Casas, Francisco Pizarro, Hernán Cortés, La Malinche, Ponce de León, Bernal Díaz del Castillo, Atahualpa, Moctezuma. Briefly share your findings with the class.

10A.19 Mi familia y el fin de semana. Lee el párrafo siguiente sobre una familia. Complétalo usando el verbo correcto y su forma correcta. Luego verifica tus respuestas con varios compañeros de clase y decide con ellos si fue un fin de semana divertido o aburrido.

1. Yo _dediqué_ (comenzar/leer/dedicar) tiempo a estar con mi familia este fin de semana y lo pasamos muy bien.

2. Mi mamá _durmió_ (dormir/jugar/buscar) hasta las nueve de la mañana porque estaba muy cansada.

3. Mi papá nos _sirvió_ (seguir/almorzar/servir) un desayuno muy rico a las diez de la mañana.

4. Para desayunar, mi papá _preparó_ (preparar/repetir/creer) café, huevos revueltos y pan tostado.

5. Después del desayuno, nosotros caminamos al parque y yo _jugué_ (sacar/jugar/educar) con mi perrita. Yo tiraba su pelota de tenis mientras que ella la buscaba.

6. Mi perrita _destruyó_ (servir/destruir/morir) su pelota de tenis y ahora necesita una pelota nueva.

7. Por la noche, nosotros invitamos a muchos amigos a casa y les _servimos_ (servir/publicar/colocar) comida que preparamos por la tarde.

8. El domingo por la mañana nosotros no _dormimos_ (dormir/llegar/organizar) hasta tarde porque teníamos muchos planes.

9. Nuestros primos que viven lejos nos iban a visitar. Ellos _llegaron_ (educar/creer/llegar) a las nueve y media de la mañana.

10. Nosotros _dedicamos_ (organizar/dedicar/almorzar) el día a estar juntos y lo pasamos muy bien. Nuestros primos regresaron a casa por la noche.

10A.19 TEACHING TIP: Have students skim the sentences first to get an idea of the context. They should then go through and choose the verb that best fits each sentence. After that, they can make the changes depending on what the subject of the verb is.

10A.19 EXTENSION ACTIVITY: Have students do a five-minute freewrite about their weekend. The rules for a freewrite are to write without stopping for the time allotted. Afterwards, they can go back and make changes if necessary. If they do not know what to write during the freewrite, they simply write *no sé que escribir, no sé qué escribir…* until an idea comes to them.

10A.20 Los amigos de la clase. Conversa con tus compañeros de clase para ver qué oraciones coinciden con ellos. Si contestan una pregunta afirmativamente, deben firmar en el cuadro correspondiente en la página 454. No puedes tener más de tres firmas de la misma persona. **¡Ojo!** Debes usar la forma de **tú** de los verbos para hacerles preguntas a tus compañeros. Después de repasar las preguntas con la clase, apunta la información en tu **Retrato de la clase.**

¿Pidió muchas pizzas por teléfono? ___	¿Leyó el periódico esta mañana? ___	¿Creyó que no iba a hacer calor hoy? ___	¿Distribuyó un email a todos sus amigos? ___
¿Oyó un chisme (*rumor*) muy interesante? ___	¿Incluyó orégano en una receta que preparó recientemente? ___	¿Se cayó (*fell*) de su bicicleta cuando era niño/a? ___	¿No durmió lo suficiente anoche? ___
¿Se sintió bien cuando su candidato ganó las elecciones? ___	¿Repitió un chiste (*joke*) que oyó? ___	¿Leyó una revista la semana pasada? ___	¿Se cayó mientras caminaba a la escuela el año pasado? ___
¿Creyó que había examen hoy? ___	¿Durmió durante una clase este semestre? ___	¿No repitió un chisme que oyó? ___	¿No siguió una receta (*recipe*) y la comida era deliciosa? ___

Retrato de la clase: En general, pocos/muchos compañeros de clase leyeron el periódico esta mañana…

VÍVELO: LENGUA

Expressing time frames

Just as there are words, such as **a menudo** (*often*) and **siempre** (*always*), that tend to be used in the past with the imperfect, there are words that frame time in the past and are consequently often used to trigger the preterit. If a specific amount of time is indeed framed in the past, it indicates that the action began and/ or was completed, and as such, the verb will be a preterit verb. For example, **por fin** means *finally*, as in "We finally got on the train." Can you explain why the other words/phrases below would also usually trigger a preterit verb in Spanish?

por fin	⟶	Por fin nos subimos al tren.
más tarde	⟶	Más tarde llegaron mis abuelos.
finalmente	⟶	Finalmente terminó la guerra contra los apache.
pronto	⟶	Muy pronto se declaró líder del Nuevo Mundo.

10A.21 Machu Picchu.

Paso 1: Lee la siguiente descripción de la primera vez que un niño fue a Machu Picchu. Subraya con una línea todos los ejemplos del imperfecto y subraya con dos líneas los ejemplos en el pretérito. Luego, compara tus respuestas con las de un/a compañero/a de clase.

Cuando era niño mi familia y yo viajábamos a menudo por Latinoamérica en los veranos. Mis padres eran muy generosos y siempre nos atendían a mi hermano menor y a mí. Yo era muy pequeño y curioso. A finales de un verano, llegamos a Machu Picchu. Era el mes de julio y hacía fresco porque allí era invierno. Llegamos en tren desde Cuzco y más tarde subimos la montaña en autobús para visitar esta ciudadela. Pronto llegamos a las ruinas. Había muchas personas de todo el mundo. Era como una reunión mundial. Mi familia y yo caminamos muchas horas ese día. Observamos las magníficas estructuras arquitectónicas que construyeron los incas. Nunca me voy a olvidar de ese día.

Paso 2: Escucha las oraciones e indica si son ciertas o falsas. Luego, verifica tus respuestas con la clase.

	Cierto	Falso
1.	☑	☐
2.	☐	☑
3.	☐	☑
4.	☐	☑

Paso 3: Ahora, cuéntale a tu compañero/a cómo eran las vacaciones u otras actividades con tu familia cuando eras niño/a y cuéntale una experiencia específica.

10A.22 Carta al pueblo español. Imagínate que es el año 1540, has estado mucho tiempo en las Américas y has conocido las culturas indígenas. España, entre otros países europeos, está pensando seguir la conquista y colonización del continente. Tú tienes la oportunidad de escribirles una carta a los reyes españoles de lo que ha ocurrido en el Nuevo Mundo. Incluye en tu carta cosas como los desarrollos, las tradiciones, etcétera.

Enlaces

10A.23 Enlaces. Según el contexto de la oración, escoge el significado de las palabras a continuación. Escribe la letra que corresponde al significado correcto. Luego, verifica tus respuestas con la clase.

a. still, however, nonetheless
b. through, across
c. with respect to, regarding

_____ a **1.** Comí mucho y no tengo hambre. **Sin embargo** me encanta el chocolate y si me ofreces chocolate, me lo voy a comer.

_____ c **2.** Casi todos los futbolistas del equipo argentino van a jugar en los partidos preliminares para la Copa Mundial. **En cuanto a** Carlos Tévez, no se sabe si va a poder regresar de Inglaterra.

_____ b **3.** Si caminas **a través del** bosque llegarás a la casita al lado del lago.

10A.24 Completa las oraciones. Usa las expresiones para completar estas oraciones. Luego, verifica tus respuestas con un/a compañero/a de clase.

sin embargo
a través de
en cuanto a

1. Mi papá trabaja en dos lugares más de sesenta horas a la semana. _Sin embargo_ nuestra familia no tiene seguro *(insurance)* médico.

2. _En cuanto a_ la posibilidad de viajar a Nicaragua este verano, todavía no sé si voy a poder hacerlo.

3. Existe mucha información sobre la cultura azteca pero _en cuanto a_ la civilización maya no sabemos mucho.

4. _A través del_ (el) tiempo nos olvidamos de los problemas.

5. No voy a poder ir a clase mañana. _Sin embargo_ tengo que completar la tarea y mandársela a la profesora por correo electrónico.

10A.21 PASO 2: AUDIO SCRIPT AND ANSWERS. 1. De niño, el narrador iba a menudo con su familia a Latinoamérica. (cierto), 2. El narrador era hijo único. (falso, tenía un hermano menor), 3. El narrador cuenta su viaje a Venezuela. (falso, Machu Picchu está en Perú, Cuzco está en Perú.), 4. Machu Picchu está en un valle. (falso, está en las montañas).

10A.22 TEACHING TIP: Have students read over the instructions for this activity with a partner. To ensure understanding, ask them to tell you in their own words what their task is. Once you are sure that students understand the task at hand, remind them that their goal should be to write a convincing letter.

10A.23 TEACHING TIP: Before going over this exercise as a class, have students share their answers with a partner. As you ask students for their answers, consider having them hold up one finger to represent A, two to represent B, and three to represent C. This way, you can get a better sense of how well they understood these new words.

10A.23 SUGGESTION: Encourage students to use these expressions so that they are better able to string sentences together.

10A.24 TEACHING TIP: Have students go over their answers with a partner before you review them as a class.

10A.25 **Los mayas, incas y aztecas.** En grupos pequeños, lean el ensayo que les asigna su instructor/a sobre los mayas, los aztecas o los incas. Después de leer el texto, escriban las ideas principales en dos o tres oraciones y hagan una lista de los logros *(achievements)* principales de esa civilización. Luego, formen grupos nuevos. Estos grupos deben incluir a personas que representen los tres grupos originales. Cada persona tiene que presentar las ideas principales de su texto al resto del grupo.

Las civilizaciones indígenas más famosas: Los mayas, los aztecas y los incas

Los mayas

La civilización maya se extendía desde lo que hoy es el occidente (el oeste) de Honduras y El Salvador hasta la península de Yucatán en México. Cuando llegaron los españoles a principios del siglo XVI, las ciudades mayas ya estaban abandonadas y la mayoría de la población vivía en zonas rurales. **Sin embargo**, la cultura maya tuvo una particular influencia en la construcción de la identidad nacional de México.

Los mayas estaban muy avanzados tecnológicamente, comparados con las sociedades europeas de la misma época. Tenían un alto grado de conocimiento matemático y científico. El calendario maya era uno de los más precisos de aquella época. El sistema matemático estaba basado en 20 símbolos, incluido el cero. Hicieron grandes avances en astronomía y crearon lugares de observación que demostraban un entendimiento muy desarrollado. También tenían un sistema de escritura con jeroglíficos.

No se sabe por qué ni cómo desaparecieron los mayas de sus ciudades principales. Esta desaparición produjo controvertidas teorías en los últimos siglos. Aunque "desaparecieron", hoy en día los descendientes de los mayas todavía viven en esas regiones y mantienen no solamente los idiomas sino también muchas de las costumbres culturales.

Los aztecas

Al valle central de México, alrededor del lago Texcoco, llegó a partir del siglo XIII un grupo de culturas que hablaban diferentes variantes del idioma náhuatl. Venían de una región norteña llamada Aztlán (en lo que hoy es parte de EE.UU.), y fundaron su capital en el centro de un lago porque allí, según cuenta la leyenda, encontraron la señal indicada por los dioses: un águila devorando a una serpiente sobre un nopal *(cactus)*. La ciudad, fundada hacia 1325, se llamaba Tenochtitlán, y para 1428 formó una triple alianza con otras dos ciudades – Texcoco y Tlacopán – consolidando lo que ahora llamamos el gran imperio azteca. Para 1519, cuando llegaron los españoles, Tenochtitlán era una de las ciudades más imponentes del mundo, con cerca de 250,000 habitantes. Situada estratégicamente en una isla del lago Texcoco, la capital estaba conectada con tierra firme por medio de una serie de puentes *(bridges)*, los cuales permitían una defensa y control más eficientes de un imperio que tenía frecuentes guerras.

10A.25 TEACHING TIP: Have students use the chart below to keep track of things that their classmates share from each part of the reading.

10A.25 NOTE: This is a good time to revisit students' KWL chart in order to pay close attention to the last column, "What I learned."

Sus manifestaciones artísticas (1259-1521 d.C) se encuentran entre las más importantes de Mesoamérica antes de la llegada de los europeos. El arte es un lenguaje utilizado por la sociedad para transmitir su visión del mundo, que a su vez refuerza su propia identidad. El arte azteca puede ser violento y rudo pero deja ver una complejidad intelectual y una sensibilidad que nos hablan de su enorme riqueza simbólica. **En cuanto al** desarrollo científico, el pueblo se destacó *(stood out)* en medicina y farmacopea. También estaban avanzados en astronomía, la base de su calendario, herencia de la cultura maya.

En cuanto a la religión, uno de los aspectos más característicos era la práctica de sacrificios. Los aztecas tenían varios dioses. Sacrificaban el corazón de animales o humanos como ofrenda a la divinidad Huitzilopochtli, el dios de la guerra. La divinidad más importante, sin embargo, era Quetzalcóatl. Quetzalcóatl era el dios del viento, de la vida, de la fertilidad, inventor del maíz y de la agricultura, creador del calendario solar y organizador de los ritos religiosos y no le gustaban los sacrificios humanos. Cuando llegaron los españoles encontraron a los aztecas en un momento de esplendor aunque con algunas dificultades. Moctezuma II, el rey azteca, creyó que los extraños visitantes que llegaron en 1519 eran en realidad Quetzalcóatl, quien volvería según una antigua profecía.

Los incas

La civilización inca se desarrolló aproximadamente en el siglo XV, basada en la herencia de varias culturas anteriores. Hacia 1470, los incas habían conquistado un vasto territorio y habían incorporado muchas culturas vecinas. El imperio se llamaba Tahuantinsuyo y ocupaba desde lo que hoy es el sur de Colombia hasta el norte de Chile, con unos diez millones de habitantes. Este imperio llegó a ser más vasto que el imperio romano. La capital imperial era Cusco, que significa "el ombligo *(belly button)* del mundo." La lengua oficial era el quechua. La base de la estructura social era un grupo de familias que trabajaban como comunidad y se llamaba el *ayllú.* Un tercio *(one third)* de la cosecha era para el rey (el Inca), otra porción para la institución religiosa y la tercera parte se distribuía entre las familias de cada ayllú según sus necesidades.

Una de las bases del éxito imperial incaico fue la eficiente construcción de casi 18,000 millas de caminos y puentes *(bridges)* que unían la capital con las diversas zonas. Los *chasquis* eran mensajeros cuya misión consistía en llevar órdenes del Inca y noticias a todas las regiones del imperio. Corrían largas distancias y tenían un sistema de relevos *(relays)* en el que se pasaban los *quipus,* que eran instrumentos compuestos de nudos *(knots)* de distintos colores y formas para llevar la contabilidad y documentar las noticias. El sabio, llamado *amauta,* tenía la misión de conservar y presentar la tradición histórica del imperio en días especiales.

Las dos divinidades importantes eran el Inti o Viracocha (el sol), que fertilizaba con sus rayos a su esposa Pacha Mama (la tierra). Un saludo común de los incas, que revela su código ético, era: "Ama sua, ama llulla, ama quella", que significa "no robes, no mientas, no seas perezoso" *(Don't rob, don't lie, don't be lazy).* Algunos años antes de que llegaran los europeos en 1532, el último emperador, llamado Huayna Cápac, había muerto sin designar a su sucesor. Por eso, sus dos hijos, Huáscar y Atahualpa, gobernaban cada uno la mitad del imperio y estaban en guerra para unificar otra vez el Tahuantinsuyo. Finalmente Atahualpa triunfó sobre su hermano y se proclamó rey, o Inca. Poco después llegaron Pizarro y sus soldados españoles.

Mayas	Aztecas	Incas

10A.26 Civilizaciones y sus contribuciones. Decide a qué grupo corresponden las frases siguientes de acuerdo a la información que leíste sobre los mayas, aztecas e incas. Escribe la letra, o letras, que corresponden a la descripción. Luego, comparte tu respuesta con la clase. Prepárate para defender tus respuestas frente a la clase.

Mayas	Aztecas	Incas	
☐	☐	☑	**1.** Hicieron miles de kilómetros de caminos.
☑	☐	☐	**2.** Sus ciudades fueron abandonadas antes de la llegada de los españoles.
☐	☐	☑	**3.** Su idioma principal era el quechua.
☐	☐	☑	**4.** Dijeron que robar, mentir y ser perezoso era malo.
☐	☑	☐	**5.** Su idioma principal era el náhuatl.
☑	☑	☐	**6.** Estaban muy avanzados en astronomía.
☐	☑	☐	**7.** Su rey se llamaba Moctezuma II.
☑	☑	☐	**8.** Desarrollaron un calendario muy preciso.

Perspectivas

10A.27 La historia de los indígenas. Lee las oraciones siguientes e indica si estás o no de acuerdo con ellas. Luego, en grupos de tres, conversen sobre sus razones para estar o no de acuerdo con las declaraciones.

Declaraciones	De acuerdo	No de acuerdo	¿Por qué?
Todos los grupos indígenas de las Américas se enfrentaron (faced) al mismo destino con la llegada de los ingleses o los españoles: extinción, eliminación, aislamiento, genocidio y destrucción cultural.			
Los ingleses masacraron a las tribus indígenas mientras que los españoles permitieron que coexistieran con ellos aunque no eran iguales.			
La intervención de la Iglesia católica influyó en cómo los españoles trataban a los indígenas.			
Los aztecas y los incas conquistaron tribus para expandir sus imperios mientras que los grupos indígenas norteamericanos eran más nómadas y estaban menos enfocados en extender sus dominios.			
Las contribuciones de las civilizaciones azteca, inca y maya eran más significativas que las contribuciones de las civilizaciones indígenas norteamericanas.			
La influencia cultural de los grupos indígenas influyó en la tolerancia, o intolerancia, de los colonos europeos hacia esos grupos.			
Los países latinoamericanos reconocen y celebran sus raíces (roots) indígenas más que Estados Unidos.			
El inglés y el español tienen palabras indígenas en su vocabulario.			
Hoy en día no existe la discriminación y el racismo hacia el indígena en las Américas.			
Muchas ciudades y estados en Estados Unidos tienen nombres indígenas.			

10A.27 TEACHING TIP: You may want to assign the first part of this task (students individually deciding if they agree, or not, with these statements) as homework to be done outside of class. This way, you could even suggest students do some research to back up their reasoning. Once students are in groups, they should share their reasons for their choices. As you process this with the class, you can ask for a show of hands to see how students feel about each statement, such as *Levanta la mano si estás de acuerdo con la declaración que dice...* From there you can follow up to get some of their reasons.

Vocabulario: Investigación A

Vocabulario esencial

Sustantivos

el camino	*path*
el/la campesino/a	*peasant*
el chisme	*rumor, gossip*
la cosecha	*harvest*
el dolor de cabeza	*headache*
el dolor de espalda	*backache*
el dolor de estómago	*stomach ache*
el dolor de garganta	*sore throat*
el entendimiento	*understanding*
la escultura (de piedra)	*(stone) sculpture*
la fiebre	*fever*
el imperio	*empire*
el/la jefe/a	*chief*
la llegada	*arrival*
el nudo	*knot*
el puente	*bridge*
el siglo	*century*
el soldado	*soldier*

Adjetivos y adverbios

controvertido/a	*controversial*
feo/a	*ugly*
finalmente	*finally*
gratis	*free*
más tarde	*later*
por fin	*finally*
solamente	*only*

Verbos

aparecer	*to appear*
contar	*to count*
cultivar	*to grow*
desarrollar	*to develop*
extender	*to extend*
recuperar	*to recover*

Otras palabras y expresiones

el águila	*eagle*
artesanal	*handmade*
la ciudadela	*citadel*
el código	*code*
el culto	*worship*
la divinidad	*deity, god*
la escritura	*writing*
los huevos revueltos	*scrambled eggs*
la manifestación artística	*artistic expression*
el nopal	*cactus*
el ombligo	*belly button*
las palomitas	*popcorn*
las papitas	*potato chips*
el patrimonio	*heritage*
reforzar	*reinforce*
rehacer	*to redo*
relevo	*relay*
renovar	*to renew*
las riquezas	*riches*
rudo	*rough, rude*
sabio/a	*wise*
el tercio	*a third*
a principios	*at the beginning*
última vez	*last time*

¡Qué lástima!	*What a shame!*
¡Qué pena!	*What a pity!*
¡Qué horror!	*How horrible/ awful!*
¡Qué desafortunado!	*How unfortunate!*
¡Qué triste!	*How sad!*
¡Qué afortunado/ suerte!	*How fortunate/ What luck!*
¡Qué chévere!	*How cool!*
¡Qué alegría!	*How great/ wonderful!*

Cognados

Review the cognates in *Adelante* and the false cognates in *¡Atención!*. For a complete list of cognates, see Appendix 4 on page 605.

¿Existe una verdad objetiva?

In this **Investigación** you will learn:

▶ To recount historical events in the past

▶ To describe past events and their corresponding actions

▶ About famous historical figures of Latin America

▶ About how historical events and figures are perceived within and across cultures

▶ About how historical events and figures change over time within cultures

TEACHING TIP: Explore what students know in terms of important dates and wars. This introduces the topic of history and reviews how to express dates and years in Spanish. In Spanish, you can provide dates and see if students can associate the correct events to those dates, such as 1492, 1776, 1918 (end of WWI), 1939 (beginning of WWII), etc.

TEACHING TIP: Draw students' attention to the relationship between the cognates and their word families. Most of the time the context of a sentence will indicate the part of speech. Then, read each of the following words and have students find a synonym or antonym from the list for each: *opresión (liberación), democrático (autoritario), realista (idealista), deplorar (venerar), prohibir (permitir), conquistar (invadir)*. All are antonyms except the last one. If, after having read them, there are students that are still unsure, provide them with the written word. We can help our students that are stronger visual learners by providing them with the visual word.

10B.1 TEACHING TIP: Have students review their answers with a partner before you go over them as a class. Students might find that more than one answer could be appropriate. Encourage them to narrow the possibilities down so that just one fits.

¿Cómo se puede hablar del pasado y de la historia?

You can ask about or explain historical events.	¿Quién fue un dictador de España y por cuánto tiempo gobernó? ¿Cuál fue la Guerra Sucia en Argentina y cuándo ocurrió?
You can explore the events in a person's life.	¿Cuándo nació? ¿Quiénes fueron sus padres? ¿Dónde vivió cuando era joven? ¿Qué hizo? ¿Cuándo murió?
You can offer a rich narrative of a past event.	La Guerra Sucia se refiere a las prácticas violentas y crueles por parte de la dictadura militar que gobernó Argentina entre los años 1976 y 1983. El macartismo *(McCarthyism)* también fue una forma de persecución política impulsada a comienzos de la década de 1950 por Joseph R. McCarthy.

Adelante

¡Ya lo sabes!   Personas y sucesos históricos

la dictadura (el dictador, dictar)
la liberación (el libertador, libertad, liberar)
la opresión (el opresor, oprimir)
el rebelde (la rebeldía, rebelarse)

autoritario/a (la autoridad)
carismático/a
democrático/a (la democracia)
histórico/a (el historiador, la historia)
idealista (ideal, idealizar)
influyente (la influencia, influir)
prohibido/a (prohibir)
visionario/a (la visión, visual)
venerado/a (venerar)

atacar (el atacante)
gobernar (el gobernador, gobernado, el gobierno)
invadir (la invasión, invadido)
inventar (el inventor, la invención)
permitir (el permiso, permitido)
revelar (la revelación)
votar (la votación, el voto)

10B.1 **¡A emparejar!**   Con un/a compañero/a de clase, emperejen los nombres de la columna A con las asociaciones correctas de la columna B. Luego verifiquen sus respuestas con otra pareja de compañeros de clase.

A	B
_f_ **1.** Adolph Hitler	**a.** inventor
_d_ **2.** El Álamo	**b.** votar por
_a_ **3.** Alexander Graham Bell	**c.** prohibida
_b_ **4.** el mejor candidato	**d.** atacado
_e_ **5.** Martin Luther King	**e.** carismático
_c_ **6.** la eutanasia	**f.** dictador

10B.2 Crucigrama. Con un/a compañero/a, completen las oraciones siguientes con la palabra más lógica de la lista de cognados y escríbanlas en el crucigrama. Conjuguen los verbos si es necesario. Luego, conprueben sus respuestas con la clase.

Horizontales

1. El comunista Fidel Castro _____ Cuba por más de 49 años. gobernó

5. La persona que no acepta las normas de la sociedad es un _____. rebelde

6. Una persona _____ normalmente también es optimista. idealista

9. La _____ de los esclavos era una meta de los Yankees en la Guerra Civil de Estados Unidos. liberación

11. Santa Anna llegó a _____ El Álamo en 1836. atacar

13. Un dictador tiende a ser _____. autoritario

14. La Segunda Guerra Mundial (WWII) ocurrió a causa de la _____ por parte de los nazis. opresión

15. Santa Anna decidió _____ a Stephen F. Austin la colonización de Texas. permitir

16. Hoy en día, Bolívar es _____ pero cuando vivía era un personaje polémico. venerado

Verticales

2. Era necesario _____ de forma violenta contra la esclavitud como lo hizo Nat Turner en Virgina en 1831. rebelarse

3. Un individuo tiene que _____ su espíritu fuerte para empezar la lucha contra los abusos sociales, como hizo Rosa Parks cuando decidió no sentarse al fondo del autobús. revelar

4. Un gobierno _____ permite la elección de un presidente. democrático

6. Los personajes _____ normalmente son carismáticos. influyentes

7. Simón Bolívar fue un _____. visionario

8. La _____ de Francisco Franco empezó al mismo tiempo que la Segunda Guerra Mundial. dictadura

10. Es importante _____ para tener una democracia auténtica. votar

12. Con la Internet es fácil investigar varias perpsectivas sobre un mismo evento _____. histórico

EXPRESIONES ÚTILES:
The reading below models usage of most of these words. For additional practice, ask students to write (draft) the order in which they completed actions this morning using the *Expresiones útiles*. Then, have them write the sentences on a blank page in random order and exchange their sentences with a partner for the purpose of guessing the order of actions. Compare each other's responses to the first draft.

PRE-READING ACTIVITY: Divide your class into groups of three and have each group create a three-columned KWL chart with the headings, What we know/ What we are going to learn/ What we learned. This will help tap into students' prior knowledge, encourage them to preview the reading and then highlight what they learned after reading the text about Simón Bolívar. Elicit information from students to include on a larger three column chart either on the board or screen for the entire class to view.

TEACHING TIP: Divide your class into groups of four. Assign one of the four paragraphs in this article to each group member. Then, ask students to share what they learned from their paragraph with the other members of the group so that the content of the entire article is covered more quickly. Then, do Activity 10B.4. As a follow-up, assign students to reread the entire article at home and ask students to write questions about the content to bring to the next class session and use them as a warm-up.

EXPRESIONES ÚTILES

Orden de acciones en una narrativa

When recounting events in the past, the following words and expressions will facilitate the cohesion of a narrative because they signal an order of events.

primero	Primero llegué a la casa a las 5:30.
luego	Luego, cené sola.
entonces	Entonces lavé los platos.
por último/ finalmente	Por último, escuché un ruido (noise) fuerte y corrí a la ventana a ver la causa.
mientras	Hablé con mis vecinos mientras esperábamos a la policía.
antes de	Antes de salir de la casa, recogí el celular.
después de	Después de ver el carro contra el árbol, llamé a la policía.

The last two are typically used with an infinitive.

Simón Bolívar: El Libertador

1 Simón Bolívar, conocido como "El Libertador", nació en Caracas, Venezuela, el 24 de julio de 1783 de padres aristócratas. Después de la muerte de sus padres, Bolívar vivió con sus tíos hasta los 15 años, cuando lo mandaron a España para continuar sus estudios. Allí conoció a su esposa. Se casaron en 1802 y volvieron a Venezuela, pero ella murió un año después, en 1803. Durante otro viaje a Europa, en 1805, Bolívar juró (swore) dedicarse a la liberación de Suramérica.

2 En 1810, Venezuela declaró su independencia y Bolívar fue a Inglaterra como diplomático. Volvió a Venezuela ese mismo año, pero en 1812 tuvo que escapar a Cartagena de Indias (hoy Colombia) después de la derrota (defeat) del líder venezolano Francisco de Miranda, ante los españoles. Allí, Bolívar escribió el Manifiesto de Cartagena, en el que pidió la cooperación de otras colonias en la lucha (fight) por la independencia de Venezuela.

3 En 1813, el ejército (army) de Bolívar invadió Venezuela y comenzó una serie de batallas, llamada la Campaña Admirable, para liberar Venezuela. Fue entonces cuando Bolívar recibió formalmente el título de El Libertador. Debido a varios conflictos, Bolívar se vio obligado a exiliarse otra vez. Primero fue a Jamaica, donde escribió la Carta de Jamaica, en la que describió su visión del futuro de Latinoamérica. Luego fue a Haití y con la ayuda del presidente haitiano Alexandre Petión, regresó a Venezuela una vez más para continuar la lucha.

4 Después de una serie de batallas que duraron desde 1818 hasta 1824, los ejércitos de Bolívar, Antonio José de Sucre y José de San Martín liberaron todo el continente suramericano. Bolívar fue presidente de la Gran Colombia (federación de los actuales países de Colombia, Venezuela, Ecuador y Panamá) desde 1821 hasta 1830. También fue presidente de Perú (1824-1825) y Bolivia (1825-1826). De hecho, Bolivia recibió su nombre en honor a Bolívar. En 1826, Bolívar organizó el Congreso de Panamá, el primer congreso hemisférico, para poner en práctica su visión de un continente unido. Sin embargo, debido a la oposición a sus tendencias autoritarias (por ejemplo, abogaba (he advocated) por tener un presidente poderoso elegido de por vida) y a conflictos entre y dentro de los nuevos países, esa visión no se realizó. Bolívar murió de tuberculosis el 17 de diciembre de 1830 en Santa Marta, Colombia. Cuando murió, Bolívar era detestado por muchos a causa de su forma autoritaria de gobernar y por los muchos conflictos que eso provocó. Sin embargo, hoy en día es venerado como uno de los héroes hispanos más importantes y admirados.

10B.3 **¿Qué aprendieron sobre Simón Bolívar?** En grupos de tres, lean las oraciones siguientes e indiquen si son ciertas o falsas. Entonces, corrijan la información falsa y verifiquen sus respuestas con la clase. ¿Hay figuras similares a Bolívar en la historia de Estados Unidos? ¿Quiénes son? ¿Por qué son semejantes a Bolívar?

Cierto	Falso		
☐	☑	**1.**	La familia de Bolívar era muy pobre.
☐	☑	**2.**	Bolívar y su esposa tuvieron muchos hijos.
☑	☐	**3.**	Bolívar conoció España e Inglaterra.
☑	☐	**4.**	Bolívar volvió a su país para luchar por la liberación de Venezuela.
☑	☐	**5.**	Después de luchar por algunos años, Bolívar salió exiliado de Venezuela.
☑	☐	**6.**	Bolívar quería ver Latinoamérica como un continente unido.
☐	☑	**7.**	Cuando Bolívar murió era muy popular entre la gente.
☐	☑	**8.**	La percepción acerca de Bolívar no ha cambiado desde su muerte.

Bien dicho

El sonido de la *ll*

In most varieties of Spanish, the letter **ll** and the letter **y** are associated with exactly the same sound. As you learned in *Investigación 10A*, this sound, represented by the symbol /y/, corresponds closely to the sound associated with the letter *y* in many English words. In order to avoid mispronunciations that mark a strong non-native accent in Spanish, be especially careful when pronouncing Spanish words that are written like English words or names with ll. For example, contrast the Spanish words **ella, bella, amarillo, vainilla, collar** and **llama** with the English words *Ella, Bella, Amarillo, vanilla, collar* and *llama*.

In *Investigación 10A* you learned about two specific regional variations in the pronunciation of **y.** These same variants would also apply to the pronunciation of **ll** in those regions. In other regions, principally the Andes, **y** is associated with the sound /y/ while **ll** is associated with a different sound, namely a sound similar to the combination "lli" in the English words such as *million, scallion* and *medallion*. This allows speakers in these regions to differentiate between words/phrases such as **se cayó** *(he/she fell down)* and **se calló** *(he/she was quiet)*.

10B.4 **¿Qué palabra escuchas?** Escucha las palabras pronunciadas e indica cuál de las dos palabras oíste. Luego, verifica tus respuestas con la clase.

	Español	Inglés
1.	☐ guerrilla	☑ guerrilla
2.	☑ valle	☐ valley
3.	☐ calloso	☑ callous
4.	☐ mallete	☑ mallet
5.	☑ villa	☐ villa
6.	☑ brillo	☐ Brillo (as in Brillo pad)

10B.5 **Ahora les toca.** Con un/a compañero/a, túrnense para pronunciar las oraciones siguientes prestando atención a la pronunciación estándar de la letra **ll**. Repitan el ejercicio pronunciando las oraciones que no articularon la primera vez.

1. Siempre llevo las llaves en el bolsillo.

2. Guillermo vive en aquella calle de Sevilla.

3. Los grillos chirrían y los pollos cloquean.

4. Llovió mucho allá en Amarillo anoche.

5. Las estrellas son bellas y brillantes.

6. Ellos se callaron cuando llegó el maestro.

7. El general llamó al batallón a la batalla.

8. Hallaron unas sillas en aquel pabellón.

10B.3 ANSWERS: Possible answers to open-ended question: George Washington, Thomas Jefferson, Abraham Lincoln

10B.3 TEACHING TIP: Remind students that not all students may understand why a statement is true or false at the same time. Ask students to refer back to the language in the reading that supports their answers. In this way, you ensure that all students in the group learn from each other and enhance language and reading skills.

10B.3 FOLLOW-UP ACTIVITY. Follow-up by asking students which countries formed the nation of la Gran Colombia. (Colombia, Venezuela, Ecuador and Panama).

SUGGESTION: You may want to include the fact that after la Gran Colombia was dissolved in 1830, Panama remained a part of Colombia. It was not until 1903, with the support of the US military, that Panama became its own country.

10B.4 AUDIO SCRIPT: 1. guerrilla (English) 2. valle 3. callous 4. mallet 5. villa (Spanish) 6. brillo (Spanish)

10B.5 STANDARDS: COMMUNITY. As noted in previous *Investigaciones*, students can be encouraged to seek out Spanish speakers to investigate regional variations in the pronunciation of *ll*. Students can seek out informants from among the institution's international students if there are a limited number of Spanish speakers in the community.

Palabras clave 1 El reportaje de eventos

TEACHING TIP: Use gestures and TPR to convey or confirm the meaning of as many new vocabulary words as possible. These can be helpful because they provide associations that are key to long-term retention.

ORIENTATION: The following three activities provide various forms of comprehensible input as it is essential to language learning. Students need to be exposed to a lot of language in context, either in written or spoken form, in order to internalize it.

La ONU **propone** sustituir el petróleo por energías más ecológicas **demostrando** así una preocupación por el medio ambiente *(environment)*.

¿Asesino o héroe? Ernesto "Che" Guevara es un **mártir** para los revolucionarios en todo el mundo.

La artista famosa **funda** una organización para **batallar** la pobreza.

Clinton **apoyó** a Obama en las elecciones. McCain **se opuso** a Obama y dijo que era un candidato **débil**.

10B.6 **¡A emparejar!** Termina las frases 1–8 con la frases más lógicas de a–h. Luego, verifica tus respuestas con un/a compañero/a de clase.

a **1.** Abraham Lincoln

d **2.** Para los franceses, Juana de Arco

b **3.** Cristóbal Colón

c **4.** El dinero

e **5.** Sigmund Freud

f **6.** Los prisioneros de guerra

a. quiso terminar con la **esclavitud** en Estados Unidos.

b. demostró que el mundo no era plano.

c. puede **esclavizar** el alma si no es moderada por la conciencia.

d. es una **mártir.**

e. propuso el complejo de Edipo.

f. no desean **recordar** sus experiencias.

No **se acordó de** la medicina que tomó para sus alergias. Es **peligroso** conducir un carro después de tomar algunas medicinas.

Hoy **recordamos la muerte** de esta mujer humilde que **eligió** una vida dedicada a ayudar a los otros.

Las negociaciones **tienen éxito** y los adversarios firman el tratado.

Bartolomé de las Casas luchó contra la **esclavitud** de los indígenas.

10B.7 **Asociaciones.** Escoge la opción que no se asocie con la palabra principal. Luego, verifica tu respuesta con un/a compañero/a de clase.

10B.7 TEACHING TIP: Have students go over their answers with a partner before you check the answers as a class.

___d___ **1.** la memoria

a. recordar **b.** olvidarse **c.** acordarse **d.** demostrar

___b___ **2.** la opresión

a. la dictadura **b.** el voto **c.** la monarquía **d.** la autoridad absoluta

___c___ **3.** oponerse a

a. la guerra **b.** la batalla **c.** la paz **d.** la esclavitud

___d___ **4.** establecer

a. fundar **b.** proponer **c.** descubrir **d.** morir

___c___ **5.** para tener éxito es necesario

a. ser eficaz **b.** ser persistente **c.** olvidarse de fechas **d.** no ser débil
   (effective)

10B.8 **¿De acuerdo o no?** Escucha los comentarios e indica si estás o no de acuerdo con ellos. Como clase, comenten las oraciones con las cuales no estuvo de acuerdo la mayoría de la clase.

	Sí	No
1.	☑	☐
2.	☑	☐
3.	☐	☑
4.	☐	☑
5.	☑	☐
6.	☑	☐

10B.9 **¡Adivina!** Con un/a compañero/a de clase, escriban la palabra de la lista que complete mejor el sentido de cada una de las siguientes oraciones.

fundar   demostró   se acuerdan   eligió
fundaron   apoyó   paz   muerte

1. En 2008 la gente de Estados Unidos ___eligió___ a un nuevo presidente.
2. Bill Gates y sus amigos ___fundaron___ Microsoft en la década de 1970.
3. Benito Juárez ___demostró___ que era posible tener un presidente indígena en México.
4. Es importante ___fundar___ organizaciones que ayuden a los desafortunados de un desastre natural.
5. La ___paz___ no llegó hasta 1945, tres años después del bombardeo de Pearl Harbor.
6. Muchos españoles no ___se acuerdan___ de cómo era la vida bajo el dictador Francisco Franco.
7. Hillary Clinton ___apoyó___ la candidatura de Barack Obama para la presidencia de Estados Unidos.
8. La ___muerte___ del dictador español Francisco Franco terminó con su gobierno autoritario.

10B.10 **¿Qué caracteriza a los héroes?**

Paso 1: Con tu compañero/a, decidan cuáles son las características de un héroe o una heroína y enumeren las características indicadas por orden de importancia. Luego, escriban un resumen de sus características en un párrafo corto.

Característica	¿Caracteriza a un héroe o a una heroína?	Orden de importancia
ser rico		
tener poder político		
desear ayudar a la gente		
poder inspirar a otros		
ser valiente		
ser humilde		
ser fuerte físicamente		
tener un talento especial		
saber luchar		
estar listo/a para sacrificarse por una causa		
ser honesto/a		
¿otra cosa? ¿cuál es?		

Paso 2: Presenten sus resultados a la clase. Luego, la clase tiene que identificar los aspectos comunes de las descripciones.

Paso 3: Apunten las conclusiones de la clase acerca de qué caracteriza a los héroes en su **Retrato de la clase.**

Retrato de la clase: Para nuestra clase, las características más importantes de los héroes son: … Las características que no se asocian con los héroes incluyen: …

¡Atención!

Historia	means *history* in Spanish, but it can also mean *story* or *tale*.
	La historia de las varias regiones de España es interesante y nos ayuda a entender los eventos actuales.
	Las historias de amor de las telenovelas son exageradas.
Memoria	means *memory* when referring to the mental function, as in "to learn by memory," but a *memory* in Spanish is **un recuerdo**.
	Los recuerdos de mi infancia son tristes.
	Para aprender un idioma extranjero, es necesario aprender la conjugación de los verbos de memoria.
Oprimir	means *to press* as in "to press the key on the keyboard," but in Spanish it also means *to oppress*.
	Oprime el botón para abrir el garaje.
	Los nazis oprimieron a los judíos en Alemania.
Militar	as a noun means *soldier* in Spanish and as an adjective means *related to the military*. To refer to the *military* in Spanish the word **ejército** is used.
	Los militares están preparados para sacrificarse por su país.
	El soldado tuvo *(had)* un funeral con honores militares.
	En 1948 el presidente de Costa Rica, José Figueres Ferrer, eliminó el ejército.

10B.11 La palabra apropiada. Escribe la palabra correcta según el contexto de la oración. Luego, verifica tus respuestas con un/a compañero/a de clase.

1. La ____historia____ del tratamiento de los indios en el Nuevo Mundo es muy triste.

2. Para apagar *(turn off)* la computadora, ____oprime____ el botón por tres segundos.

3. Tengo buenos ____recuerdos____ de mi infancia.

4. Los niños deben aprender de ____memoria____ los números de teléfono de sus padres.

5. Cada país latinoamericano, excepto Costa Rica, tiene su propio ____ejército____ para defender su nación contra agresores y ataques extranjeros.

6. Durante la colonización, los españoles ____oprimieron____ a los grupos indígenas.

10B.11 TEACHING TIP: Have students go over their answers with a partner before doing so as a large group.

Estructuras clave 1 Irregular preterit verbs

WILEY PLUS
Go to *WileyPLUS* and review the tutorial for this grammar point.

WILEY PLUS
You will find PowerPoint presentations for use with *Estructuras clave* in *WileyPLUS*.

In *Investigación 9B,* you were introduced to regular verbs in the preterit tense. In *Investigación 10A,* you were introduced to verbs that have spelling changes or stem-changes in the preterit tense. In this *Investigación,* you will be introduced to the other irregular verbs in the preterit tense. These verbs are all irregular because their stems/roots are different from the infinitive. These verbs can be divided into three main categories: verbs that have an **i**-stem, a **u**-stem, or a **j**-stem.

i-stem		u-stem		j-stem	
hacer	**hic*-**	andar	**anduv-**	conducir	**conduj-**
querer	**quis-**	estar	**estuv-**	decir	**dij-**
venir	**vin-**	poder	**pud-**	producir	**produj-**
		poner	**pus-**	traducir	**traduj-**
		saber	**sup-**	traer	**traj-**
		tener	**tuv-**		

*To maintain the correct pronunciation, the **él/ella/usted** form of **hacer** is written **hizo.**

The preterit endings for all **i**-stem and **u**-stem verbs are identical.

	andar	querer
yo	anduve	quise
tú	anduviste	quisiste
él/ella/usted	anduvo	quiso
nosotros/as	anduvimos	quisimos
vosotros/as	anduvisteis	quisisteis
ellos/ellas/ustedes	anduvieron	quisieron

What do you notice about the **yo** and **él/ella/usted** forms as compared to other verbs you have learned and used in the preterit? There are no written accents on the endings of these forms, and stress falls on the next-to-last syllable.

The endings for the **j**-stem verbs are similar except for the **ellos/ellas/ustedes** forms, where the initial **i** in the ending is omitted. As with the **i**-stem and **u**-stem verbs, there are no written accents on any of the forms.

	decir
yo	dije
tú	dijiste
él/ella/usted	dijo
nosotros/as	dijimos
vosotros/as	dijisteis
ellos/ellas/ustedes	dijeron

The verb **dar** is also irregular in the preterit. Here again, there are no written accents on any of the forms.

	dar
yo	di
tú	diste
él/ella/usted	dio
nosotros/as	dimos
vosotros/as	disteis
ellos/ellas/ustedes	dieron

TEACHING TIP: Ask students to recall the preterit forms shared by *ir* and *ser*. Point out that there are no accent marks needed on those forms either.

ALTERNATIVE STRATEGY: You may want to assign this *Estructuras clave* to be read outside of class. Ask students to write down four key points and two questions. The purpose of having them do this is to encourage them to read this information and begin to process it. You should remind them to refer back to it periodically as it will serve as an excellent reference.

One last irregular preterit is the preterit equivalent of **hay,** which is **hubo.** Remember, this is an invariable expression that can have a singular meaning *(there was)* or a plural meaning *(there were).*

Ayer no hubo clase porque la profesora no pudo venir.

El viernes pasado hubo una fiesta en la casa de Pedro.

Hubo muchas personas en la fiesta.

10B.12 La Presidenta de Chile. Escucha las oraciones sobre la vida de la presidenta de Chile, Michelle Bachelet. Indica si las oraciones están en el presente o en el pretérito. Luego, verifica tus respuestas con otros compañeros de clase y después con toda la clase.

	Presente	Pretérito
1.	☑	☐
2.	☐	☑
3.	☐	☑
4.	☑	☐
5.	☑	☐
6.	☐	☑
7.	☐	☑
8.	☑	☐

10B.12 PRE-LISTENING ACTIVITY: Ask students if they knew about Bachelet. If so, tap into some of their prior knowledge by asking them to share what they know.

10B.12 AUDIO SCRIPT: 1. Habla cinco idiomas. 2. Quiso estudiar sociología o economía. 3. Hizo estudios de estrategia y ciencias militares. 4. Pertenece al Partido Socialista de Chile. 5. Es cirujana y pediatra. 6. Fue a vivir a Australia y a Alemania del Este. 7. Estuvo en prisión bajo el gobierno de Augusto Pinochet. 8. Espera mejorar relaciones con otros países suramericanos.

10B.13 Un sondeo. Primero indica si las siguientes actividades son aplicables o no a ti. Escribe Sí o No en el espacio apropiado. Luego, habla con otros compañeros de clase para determinar si ellos hicieron o no las actividades. ¿Cuántos hicieron o no hicieron las actividades? Apunta los resultados en tu **Retrato de la clase.**

	Yo				
¿Hiciste la tarea para hoy?					
¿Fuiste al cine el sábado pasado?					
¿Anduviste ayer en bicicleta?					
¿Condujiste tu carro hoy a la universidad?					
¿Estuviste enfermo/a la semana pasada?					
¿Tuviste un examen esta mañana?					
¿Trajiste tu libro hoy a clase?					
¿Leíste un periódico antes de clase?					
¿Dormiste menos de siete horas anoche?					
¿Almorzaste una ensalada ayer?					

10B.13 TEACHING TIP: Encourage students to use *tú* forms of the verbs when asking questions. As an alternative, after students have a chance to poll four classmates, you can poll the entire class and ask students to record the results from the class in their *Retrato de la clase.* In polling the class, you will be able to incorporate the *ustedes* forms, e.g., *¿Cuántos/as de ustedes hicieron la tarea para hoy? ¿Quiénes trajeron sus libros hoy a clase?* You can also ask follow up questions, e.g., if students went to the movies, you can ask what they saw. If students didn't drive, you can ask how they got to campus, etc.

Retrato de la clase: Cuatro compañeros de clase hicieron la tarea para hoy. Nadie fue al cine. Dos anduvieron en bicicleta ayer. Todos condujeron su carro…

10B.14 Hispanos eminentes. Con un/a compañero/a, completa la tabla a continuación que ofrece información acerca de las acciones de algunos hispanos eminentes. Ustedes tienen información diferente. Deben hacerse preguntas para determinar el nombre de la persona o lo que él/ella hizo.

Preguntas útiles

¿Qué hizo ____?
¿Quién ____?
¿Cómo se llama la persona que ____?
¿Cómo se escribe el nombre?

A			
Jaime Escalante inspiró la película *Stand and Deliver*.	César Chávez _____ _____	_____ incorporó temas feministas en su poesía.	la Reina Isabel I de Castilla ayudó a Colón a conseguir lo que necesitaba para su viaje de 1492.
Gaspar Marcano hizo investigaciones sobre la sangre, la lepra y el cáncer.	_____ luchó por los derechos humanos en Guatemala.	Nora Gúnera de Melgar quiso ser presidenta de Honduras dos veces.	Juan Seguín _____
Jorge Isaacs escribió la novela romántica *María*	Charytín Goyco _____	_____ compuso la canción "La malagueña"	Rita Moreno ganó el premio Óscar por su actuación en *West Side Story*.
Nora Astorga _____	Vasco Núñez de Balboa vio el océano Pacífico desde Panamá.	_____ murió en defensa de los derechos humanos.	Galo Plaza Lasso estuvo a cargo de la Organización de los Estados Americanos.

B			
_____ ayudó a Colón a conseguir lo que necesitaba para su viaje de 1492.	Juana de Ibarbourou incorporó temas feministas en su poesía.	César Chávez fue un líder mexicano-americano, cofundador de una organización agrícola en California en la década de 1960.	_____ inspiró la película *Stand and Deliver*.
Juan Seguín se opuso al gobierno de Santa Anna en Texas.	_____ quiso ser presidenta de Honduras dos veces.	Rigoberta Menchú luchó por los derechos humanos en Guatemala.	Gaspar Marcano _____
Rita Moreno _____	Ernesto Lecuona compuso la canción "La malagueña".	Charytín Goyco salió en un programa de televisión.	_____ escribió la novela romántica *María*
_____ Galo Plaza Lasso	Óscar Romero murió defendiendo los derechos humanos.	_____ Vasco Núñez de Balboa	Nora Astorga se hizo embajadora nicaragüense a las Naciones Unidas.

10B.15 Querido diario. Con dos compañeros/as, piensen en una persona famosa del presente. Escriban un párrafo que describa lo que hizo ayer esa persona (según se imaginan ustedes). Sin mencionar el nombre de la persona, lean a la clase la descripción de lo que hizo para que adivinen entre todos a qué persona famosa corresponde.

Estructuras clave 2 The imperfect and the preterit in contrast

Go to *WileyPLUS* and review the tutorial for this grammar point.

You will find PowerPoint presentations for use with *Estructuras clave* in *WileyPLUS*.

TEACHING TIP: As you read through these explanations with students, encourage them to begin paying attention to whether the preterit or imperfect are being used in examples they read or hear.

You have learned to talk about events in the past using both the imperfect and the preterit. You learned that the imperfect is used to talk about usual or repeated actions in the past, to express on-going situations or actions in progress in the past, to relate the duration of an event in the past and to describe past conditions, such as time, weather, emotional states, age, and location. In order to talk about single, completed actions, the beginning or the end of actions, or to express completed past conditions in the past, you learned to use the preterit tense. In terms of telling a story, this would play out with the imperfect helping set the scene through description and on-going background actions/conditions. The preterit would be used to narrate the main events of the story as those would reflect completed events in the past.

The preterit is used to:

• Express a single, completed action/event/state in the past

> Ayer hice ejercicio en el gimnasio.
> ¿Cuándo llegaron ustedes?
> Nosotros fuimos al cine el sábado.
> Carlos estuvo triste ayer, pero hoy está contento. *(Indicates an end to his sad mood.)*

• Express an action/event/state with a specific time period

> Ellos vivieron en España por quince años.
> Anoche estudiamos matemáticas por cuatro horas.

• Mark the beginning point of some actions/events

> De repente, nevó. *(It began to snow.)*
> La niña corrió hacia el carro. *(She began to run/took off running towards the car.)*
> Yo me puse enferma. *(I got/became sick.)*

• As a result of its association with completed actions/events, the preterit is used to narrate the main actions or events of a story and to indicate an action/event that interrupts another action/event in progress.

> Dormía cuando sonó el teléfono. *(I was sleeping when the phone rang.)*
> Algunos estudiantes entraron mientras hablaba la profesora. *(Some students came in while the professor was talking.)*

The imperfect is used to:

• Express repeated or usual actions/events in the past (often equivalent to *used to*)

> Mis hermanos y yo jugábamos al fútbol todos los días.
> ¿Tocabas en la banda en la escuela secundaria?
> Ella siempre se levantaba a las ocho.
> Mis padres viajaban frecuentemente a Guatemala.

• Express an on-going or pre-existing action/event/state (often equivalent to *was/were…-ing*)

> Manejábamos por el centro. (on-going, *were driving*)
> Yo miraba la televisión. (on-going, *was watching*)
> Ellos estaban preocupados. (on-going state, no end indicated)
> Dormía cuando sonó el teléfono. *(I was sleeping when the phone rang.)*
> Algunos estudiantes entraron mientras hablaba la profesora. *(Some students came in while the professor was talking.)*

Note and analyze the use of the preterit and imperfect in the following familiar story. What can you determine about the use of the preterit or imperfect in each case?

> Cuando yo **era** niña, mi abuela **vivía** cerca de nosotros y yo la **visitaba** frecuentemente. Un día, **ocurrió** algo raro mientras **caminaba** por el bosque. Un lobo *(wolf)* feroz se me **acercó** *(approached/came up to me)* y me **pidió** toda la comida que **tenía** en mi cesto *(basket)*. Afortunadamente, cuando le **contesté** que no, él se **fue** corriendo. Más tarde, cuando **llegué** a la casa de mi abuela, **vi** que algo **estaba** mal. Cuando le **dije** a mi abuela: "Ay, abuelita, ¡qué dientes más grandes tienes!". El lobo me **respondió**: "¡Son para comerte mejor!". Un leñador *(woodcutter)* que **pasaba** cerca de la casa **oyó** el ruido, **entró** a la casa y **mató** al lobo. ¡Mi héroe!

10B.16 Vamos a conocer a Evita Perón. Escucha las siguientes oraciones acerca de la vida de Evita Perón e indica si el verbo de cada oración se asocia con la narración o con la descripción. Luego, verifica tus respuestas con la clase.

	Narración	Descripción
1.	☑	☐
2.	☐	☑
3.	☐	☑
4.	☑	☐
5.	☐	☑
6.	☑	☐
7.	☑	☐
8.	☐	☑
9.	☑	☐
10.	☑	☐

10B.17 El Mago de Oz. Con un/a compañero/a de clase lean el siguiente cuento e indiquen la forma correcta (pretérito o imperfecto) para cada verbo. Luego, verifiquen sus respuestas con otras parejas.

Érase una vez *(Once upon a time)* una chica que **se llamó/se llamaba** Dorothy. Ella **vivió/vivía** en Kansas y **tuvo/tenía** un perro, Toto. Un día, un tornado **se llevó/se llevaba** la casa de Dorothy a la tierra de los Munchkins. Para volver a casa, Dorothy y Toto **necesitaron/necesitaban** visitar al Mago *(wizard)* de Oz en la Ciudad de Esmeralda. **Empezaron/Empezaban** a caminar por el Camino de Ladrillo Amarillo. Mientras **caminaron/caminaban,** se **encontraron/encontraban** con un espantapájaros *(scarecrow)*, un hombre de hojalata *(tin)* y un león cobarde. Ellos **decidieron/decidían** acompañar a Dorothy y a Toto. Durante el viaje la bruja *(witch)* del Oeste **persiguió/perseguía** al grupo porque **creyó/creía** que Dorothy **mató/mataba** a su hermana. Por fin, todos **llegaron/llegaban** a la Ciudad de Esmeralda y Dorothy **pudo/podía** hablar con el mago. Al final, Dorothy **volvió/volvía** a casa después de taconear *(click heels)* tres veces los zapatos de rubí y decir "No hay lugar como el hogar".

www **¡Conéctate!**
Stories are a wonderful way of maintaining traditions and preserving cultures. The website http://www.miscositas.com/cuentos.html has many traditional Latin American folktales accompanied in an electronic storybook format. Pick two stories to read. Share the main message, or moral, with your classmates.

10B.18 **Un informe policíaco.** Un/a compañero/a y tú vieron un accidente de carro y ahora tienen que contestar las preguntas del policía. Al responder, piensen en la diferencia entre pretérito e imperfecto. Además, deben completar la oración con información original. Escriban el informe en una hoja aparte. ¡Sean creativos! Comparen su uso de los verbos con otra pareja. Luego, la clase va a escuchar cada informe para determinar cuál es el más lógico, el más cómico, el más original, etc.

> Modelo: ¿A qué hora ocurrió el accidente?
> *El accidente ocurrió a las 11:00 ayer/anoche/el lunes pasado.*

1. ¿Dónde estaban ustedes dos?

2. ¿Qué hacían?

3. ¿Qué tiempo hacía?

4. ¿Qué vieron con sus propios ojos?

5. ¿Cómo iban los carros? (rápido, lento…)?

6. ¿Qué hizo el carro rojo? ¿Y el carro azul?

7. Después del accidente, ¿qué hicieron los conductores?

8. ¿Cómo era el conductor del carro rojo?

10B.19 TEACHING TIP: Encourage students to use the many words they have learned in this text in the *Enlaces* section. These will help them make stronger connections between their ideas. In preparing to read their *informes* to the class, have them prepare a frame-by-frame illustration of the main points of the incident to share with the class for visual support.

VÍVELO: LENGUA

Expressing different meanings with the same verb using the preterit or the imperfect

	Pretérito	Imperfecto
conocer	*to meet for first time* Juan conoció a María en una fiesta.	*to be acquainted with* Juan conocía a María en la escuela primaria.
saber	*to find out/discover/learn* Supimos que ellos iban a casarse anoche.	*to know* Ya sabíamos que ellos iban a casarse. No nos sorprende.
querer	*to try to* Quise terminar la tarea antes de ver la película.	*to want to* Quería terminar la tarea, pero no la entendí bien.
no querer	*to refuse to* El niño no quiso acostarse y empezó a llorar.	*to not want to* El niño no quería acostarse porque no estaba cansado.
poder	*to succeed in, to manage to* ¿Pudiste hablar ayer con Mariana?	*to have the ability to* ¿Podías andar en bicleta a los seis años?
no poder	*to fail in, to not manage to* No pudimos encontrar las llaves. Están perdidas.	*to not have the ability to* No podíamos cocinar porque no había comida.

VÍVELO LENGUA: Encourage students to make note of these meaning changes in their notebooks. Often, when we write something down, we are more inclined to remember it later.

10B.19 ¿Qué recuerdas? Con un/a compañero/a de clase, contesten las preguntas 1–6 con las respuestas correctas a–f y escriban la letra de la respuesta al lado de la pregunta. Luego, verifiquen sus respuestas con la clase.

___d___ **1.** ¿Cuándo conoció Eva Perón a Juan Perón?

___a___ **2.** ¿Pudo Eva Perón tener un puesto político oficial?

___c___ **3.** ¿Tuvo Eva Perón la adoración de los argentinos?

___b___ **4.** ¿Conocía bien Evita la ciudad de Buenos Aires?

___f___ **5.** ¿Quiso Evita ser vicepresidenta de Argentina?

___e___ **6.** ¿Cuándo supo Evita que tenía cáncer?

a. No, porque descubrió que tenía cáncer.

b. Sí, porque vivió allí por muchos años.

c. Es muy probable que sí.

d. Lo conoció dos años antes de su campaña presidencial.

e. Lo supo un año antes de morir.

f. Sí, porque le gustaba la política.

10B.20 NOTE: José Martí is considered to be the father of Cuba. Regardless of modern day political affiliations, most Cubans consider him to be a great hero. The rest of the world, unknowingly perhaps, is already familiar with one of his famous poems *"Versos sencillos"* that was made famous by the song *"Guantanamera"*.

10B.20 TEACHING TIP: Remind students that whether they know the answers or not, they should be able to find them based on the possibilities shared. Through this activity, however, they will also be gaining this knowledge.

10B.20 TEACHING TIP: Challenge students to explain why they chose either the preterit or the imperfect for items 4 and 5.

10B.20 ¿Quién fue José Martí? Las oraciones siguientes presentan algunos de los hechos importantes de la vida del poeta cubano, José Martí. Con un/a compañero/a de clase, completen cada oración con el pretérito o el imperfecto del verbo más lógico de la lista.

trabajar	morir
nacer	deportar
mandar	casarse
dedicarse	tener

1. ___Nació___ el 28 de enero de 1853 en La Habana.

2. Las autoridades españolas lo ___mandaron___ a la prisión a los 16 años por traición y luego lo ___deportaron___ a España.

3. ___Se casó,___ con Carmen Zayas-Bazán en 1877 y ___tuvieron___ un hijo, José Francisco, en 1878.

4. En Estados Unidos, Martí ___trabajó___ como periodista, traductor, poeta y diplomático en la ciudad de Nueva York.

5. También ___se dedicó___ a continuar la lucha por la independencia de Cuba.

6. ___Murió___ durante una batalla en Cuba el 19 de mayo de 1895.

10B.21 **La historia de Texas.** Con un/a compañero/a de clase, lean el párrafo a continuación y escojan la palabra correcta según el contexto de la oración.

Stephen F. Austin **tuvo/tenía** permiso para ir a Texas con 300 colonialistas anglosajones. Austin **fue/iba** a Texas porque **quiso/quería** fundar una colonia en Texas. Sin embargo, Austin no **pudo/podía** fundar la colonia porque México **ganó/ganaba** su independencia de España en 1821. Esto **causó/causaba** muchos problemas para Austin porque México no **quiso/quería** reconocer su colonia. A su vez Austin **supo/sabía** cómo **funcionó/funcionaba** la política mexicana y **pudo/podía** entrar en esa política para iniciar cambios que le **favorecieron/favorecían.** Pero esto no **fue/era** suficiente. Los colonialistas de Austin **quisieron/querían** ser estado y de igual manera México no **quiso/quería** darles ese estatus. Aunque líderes de Texas y México, como Austin y Santa Anna, se **conocieron/conocían** bastante bien, no **supieron/sabían** cómo evitar la violencia. Texas **se rebeló/se rebelaba** contra México en 1835 y **obtuvo/obtenía** su independencia en 1836.

www ¡Conéctate!

What historical figure do you hold in high esteem? What characteristics about this individual do you appreciate? Google the name or research the life of that individual for specific facts about the person's life and accomplishments. Then, share what you learned with your classmates for them to guess the name of the historical figure. How many of your classmates selected politicians, inventors, religious figures, educators, etc.?

Enlaces

10B.22 **¿Qué significan?** Determina el significado de las frases subrayadas según el contexto de las oraciones. Escoge entre las siguientes opciones. Luego, verifica tus respuestas con la clase.

a. likewise   **b.** in turn   **c.** instead of

__c__ **1.** En lugar de venerar al Che, se le debe criticar por la tortura, los asesinatos y las atrocidades que cometió.

__b__ **2.** A su vez, la intransigencia del Che era reiterada por la violencia.

__a__ **3.** Che Guevara quería cambiar el mundo después de leer las obras de Karl Marx y Sigmund Freud. De igual manera, encontró su vocación durante una serie de viajes que hizo por Latinoamérica.

10B.23 **¿Puedes conectar las ideas?** Conecta las ideas de las oraciones siguientes empleando la expresión correcta. Luego, verifica tus respuestas con un/a compañero/a de clase.

a. a su vez   **b.** de igual manera   **c.** en lugar de

__b__ 1. El Che destestaba a la gente rica, pero _____ ignoraba totalmente cómo vivía la gente pobre.

__c__ 2. _____ aceptar un mito, se debe estudiar el personaje a fondo.

__a__ 3. No debemos olvidar otros aspectos menos conocidos, pero _____ más reales, de la vida y el carácter del Che Guevara.

10B.21 ANSWERS: tuvo, fue, quería, pudo, ganó, causó, quiso, sabía, funcionaba, pudo, favorecieron/favorecían, era, querían, quiso, conocían, sabían, se rebeló, obtuvo

10B.21 TEACHING TIP: Through the context of these sentences, students will learn more about the history regarding the connection between Texas and Mexico. Have students form groups of three in which they will go over their answers to this exercise. They should explain/justify the choices they made. This will help draw their attention to some of the specifics about the preterit/imperfect as well as the verbs that change mearning depending on which form of the past tense is being used.

CONÉCTATE: To maximize your students' efforts, have them write a three- to five-sentence description of the person they chose without using that person's name (e.g., *Esta persona...*) Collect all of the students' descriptions and, on a separate list, the names of all the individuals described. Assign each description a number and post all of them around the room. Write the names of all the people researched on the board. Give students time to walk around the room, read the descriptions, and decide who is being described.

10B.22 TEACHING TIP: Beyond familiarizing students with new ways of connecting their ideas, this activity serves as a good pre-reading activity for *10B.24 La imagen del Che Guevara.*

10B.23 TEACHING TIP: Have students go over their answers with a partner. When you go over them as a class, ask students to hold up one finger for a, two fingers for b, and three for c.

10B.24 La imagen del Che Guevara.   Antes de leer el artículo acerca del Che Guevara, piensa en lo que sabes de él y coméntalo con un/a compañero/a. Después de leer el artículo, contesta la pregunta: ¿Corresponde el artículo a tu opinión original?

Che: El mito y la realidad

1 Puro símbolo de moda o símbolo de una ideología, la imagen del revolucionario argentino Ernesto "Che" Guevara se reproduce en camisetas, gorras, tazas, carteles (*posters*) y otros objetos asociados con la cultura *pop*. El Che, figura emblemática de la década de 1960, es visto como un héroe, el símbolo de todas las luchas por todas las libertades. Se ha convertido en un verdadero mito. Sin embargo, ¿dónde está la realidad, el hombre detrás del mito?

2 Ernesto Guevara nació en 1928 en Argentina de una familia más bien liberal que ayudaba a los exiliados de la Guerra Civil Española. De joven hacía deportes, aunque sufría de asma, y leía mucho. Leer a autores como Alfred Adler, Sigmund Freud y Karl Marx lo inclinó a querer cambiar el mundo, un mundo que él consideraba injusto con los más débiles (*weak*). **De igual manera,** encontró su vocación durante una serie de viajes que hizo por Latinoamérica después de estudiar medicina, viajes que se relatan en la película *Diarios de motocicleta*. De allí comenzó su aventura revolucionaria.

3 En 1959, se convirtió en uno de los principales líderes de la revolución cubana. Fidel Castro supo utilizar eficazmente la personalidad carismática e idealista del Che para llevar a cabo (*to carry out*) sus fines (*ends*) revolucionarios. Más tarde, participó en una revolución en el Congo. En 1967, el Che murió en Bolivia, luchando contra el ejército boliviano y, según muchas personas, la CIA estadounidense. Se convirtió entonces en un mártir revolucionario en todo el mundo. Sin embargo, esta visión heroica no debe hacernos olvidar otros aspectos menos conocidos, pero **a su vez** más reales, de la vida y carácter del Che Guevara.

4 El Che Guevara era un hombre intransigente y exigente (*demanding*) consigo mismo y con los demás. Detestaba a la gente rica, pero de igual manera ignoraba totalmente cómo vivía la gente pobre. Trató, sin éxito, de regular varios aspectos de la vida personal de los cubanos. **En lugar de** iniciar reformas agrarias, dejó una desorganización enorme y una reducción espectacular de las cosechas del azúcar. Incluso recomendó a sus hombres robar los bancos. **A su vez,** la intransigencia del Che era reiterada por la violencia. Participaba en el sistema de represión del régimen cubano. Parece que el Che no tenía ningún escrúpulo en detener arbitrariamente a muchos, condenar a muchos a trabajos forzosos y ejecutar a muchos que se oponían al régimen cubano. En fin, muchos sufrieron porque el Che no conocía la clemencia, su justicia era rápida y cruel. Vistos desde esta perspectiva, la figura del Che y sus ideales de liberación e igualdad toman una dimensión muy diferente. El caso del Che nos demuestra que los seres humanos, incluso los "héroes", son muy complicados. Es peligroso idealizar a una persona, cualquiera que sea (*whoever he/she may be*), sin examinar más detenidamente su vida y sus acciones. Además de admirar las cualidades positivas de nuestros héroes, es necesario reconocer sus cualidades negativas. De esta manera, llegamos a conocerlos y a comprenderlos mejor.

10B.25 **¿Qué comprendiste de la lectura?** Indica si las oraciones siguientes son ciertas o falsas. Corrige la información falsa. Verifica tus respuestas con un/a compañero/a.

Cierto	Falso	
☑	☐	**1.** La figura del Che se asocia con la década de 1960.
☐	☑	**2.** El Che era cubano.
☑	☐	**3.** Al joven Che le molestaba mucho la injusticia.
☐	☑	**4.** El Che hizo una serie de viajes por Europa.
☑	☐	**5.** La personalidad del Che impresionó a Fidel Castro.
☑	☐	**6.** El Che participó en una revolución en África.
☐	☑	**7.** El Che murió en un accidente.
☑	☐	**8.** El Che no sabía cómo vivían los pobres.
☐	☑	**9.** El Che decidió no participar en la violencia del régimen cubano.
☑	☐	**10.** La historia verdadera del Che es polifacética *(many-sided)*.

¿Creen ustedes que el Che corresponde a la definición de lo que es un héroe? ¿Por qué sí o por qué no? Compartan sus conclusiones con la clase.

10B.25 ANSWERS:
Cierto: 1, 3, 5, 6, 8, 10; Falso: 2 (argentino), 4 (Latinoamérica), 7 (violentamente/ luchando contra el ejército boliviano), 8 (ignoraba cómo vivía la gente pobre), 9 (participaba en el sistema de represión del régimen cubano).

10B.25 STANDARDS: COMMUNICATION, INTERPRETIVE MODE. Encourage students to answer these questions without referring back to the reading to see how much they retained. Once they have done that, let students go over the answers referencing the reading. How much were they able to retain?

Ernesto "Che" Guevara

Perspectivas

10B.26 PRE-READING ACTIVITY: Have students read the myths in 10B.27 so that they can approach the reading with more focus and clarity. Tell them that one of their tasks will be to find evidence to refute those myths. Encourage students to make notes on the reading as they go through it.

10B.27 ANSWERS: l. Los antiguos griegos indicaron que la Tierra era redonda y muchas personas de la época de Colón aceptaban esa idea. Durante el Renacimiento, las ideas de los griegos reemplazaron la visión medieval del mundo. 2. Parece que los vikingos y posiblemente un marinero chino llegaron a las Américas antes que Colón. 3. Colón nunca pensó que había encontrado un continente "nuevo". Creía que había llegado a Japón y a China. 4. La primera persona en emplear el nombre fue un cartógrafo alemán, Martin Waldseemüller 5. Era un mal administrador. Hay testimonios que indican que era cruel, codicioso e intolerante. Lo arrestaron y lo regresaron a España. 6. Muchas personas, especialmente los grupos indígenas, dicen que Colón inició la conquista de los indígenas y la destrucción de sus culturas y civilizaciones. También dicen que introdujo la esclavitud y muchas enfermedades que mataron a muchos indígenas. En Venezuela no celebran el Día de la Raza el 12 de octubre sino el Día de la Resistencia Indígena.

10B.26 Anticipando la lectura. Antes de leer este artículo acerca de Cristóbal Colón, lee el título y advina cuál de las oraciones representa mejor la idea principal del artículo. Después de leer el artículo indica si tu primera respuesta es correcta o no.

a. No se conoce bien la figura de Cristóbal Colón porque muchos aspectos de su vida son misteriosos.

b. Hay aspectos de la personalidad y acciones de Cristóbal Colón que no corresponden con la visión heroica tradicional que se tenía de él.

c. Las críticas a Cristóbal Colón no son justas porque no se reconocen las consecuencias positivas de su llegada a las Américas.

El verdadero Cristóbal Colón

¿Quién es el verdadero Cristóbal Colón? Muchos lo admiran como un hombre valiente y visionario porque fue el primer europeo en encontrar lo que hoy son las Américas. Sin embargo, mucho de lo que se apende sobre Colón en las escuelas no es cierto. Por ejemplo, no fue el único en reconocer que la Tierra era redonda (*round*). Los antiguos griegos ya habían indicado que la Tierra era esférica. Durante la época de Colón, gracias al Renacimiento (*Renaissance*), las ideas de los geógrafos griegos reemplazaron la visión medieval del mundo. Ni las personas cultas (*educated*) ni los marineros creían por aquel entonces que la Tierra era plana (*flat*). Por otra parte, investigaciones recientes han indicado que Colón no fue la primera persona de otro continente en llegar a las Américas. En Terranova (en Canadá), se ha encontrado evidencia de que los vikingos llegaron y establecieron colonias allí por el año 1000. Otra teoría propone que Zheng He, un marinero chino, navegó por la costa occidental (*western*) de lo que hoy es Estados Unidos unos 70 años antes de la llegada de Colón a las Antillas. Además, Colón mismo (*himself*) nunca pensó que había encontrado un continente "nuevo". Hasta su muerte en 1506, creía que había llegado a Japón y a China. El cartógrafo alemán Martin Waldseemüller fue la primera persona en reconocer que Colón había llegado a un continente desconocido por los europeos y fue también la primera persona en emplear el nombre "América" en un mapa producido en el año 1507.

Más allá de estos mitos, muchas personas, especialmente los grupos indígenas, critican a Colón por ser quien inició la conquista de los indígenas americanos y la destrucción de sus culturas y civilizaciones. Lo critican también por ser la persona que introdujo la esclavitud a las Américas y por haber introducido enfermedades que mataron a muchos indígenas. También es criticado por ser mal administrador cuando los reyes españoles lo nombraron gobernador del territorio que había explorado. Lo pintan como una persona cruel, codiciosa (*greedy*) e intolerante. De hecho, fue arrestado y regresado a España como prisionero en 1500. Durante su juicio (*trial*), el testimonio de varias personas (en documentos encontrados en 2005), confirmó esta visión extremadamente negativa de Colón. Debido a esas críticas sobre Colón, en 2003, el gobierno de Venezuela declaró que el 12 de octubre se celebraría el Día de la Resistencia Indígena en lugar del Día de la Raza. Así que la verdadera historia de Cristóbal Colón no es tan heroica como se creía y va a seguir siendo (*will continue to be*) una figura muy polémica para muchas personas.

10B.27 Analizar la historia de Cristóbal Colón. Con un/a compañero/a busquen información citada en la lectura para desacreditar los siguientes mitos acerca de Colón. Apunten la información para luego comentarla con la clase.

1. Colón era una de las pocas personas que creían que la Tierra era redonda.

2. Colón fue la primera persona de otro continente en llegar a las Américas.

3. Colón sabía que había llegado a un continente desconocido por los europeos.

4. Colón fue la primera persona en emplear el nombre *América*.

5. Colón era un administrador benévolo y competente.

6. Colón es admirado por todos los habitantes de las Américas.

Vocabulario: Investigación B

Vocabulario esencial

Sustantivos

la actuación	*performance*
el bolsillo	*pocket*
la campaña	*campaign*
el cesto	*basket*
el comienzo	*start*
los derechos humanos	*human rigths*
la esclavitud	*slavery*
la muerte	*death*
el reportaje	*report*
el viaje	*journey*

Adjetivos

débil	*weak*
desconocido/a	*unknown*
peligroso/a	*dangerous*

Verbos

acercarse a	*to approach; to get closer*
acordarse de	*to remember*
apoyar	*to support*
batallar	*to battle*
demostrar	*to demonstrate; to prove*
elegir	*to choose, to elect*
oponerse	*to oppose*
proponer	*to propose*
recordar	*to remember*
tener éxito	*to be succesful*

Otras palabras y expresiones

abogar	*to advocate*
al fondo	*in the back; at the bottom*
la bruja	*witch*
chirriar	*to chirp; to squeak*
cloquear	*to cluck*
el cobarde	*coward*
codicioso/a	*greedy*
la derrota	*defeat*
detestado/a	*hated*

eficaz	*effective*
encarcelar	*to imprison*
el espantapájaros	*scarecrow*
exiliarse	*to go into exile*
fundar	*to found*
la hojalata	*tin*
intransigente	*stubborn*
el juicio	*trial*
jurar	*to swear*
el legado	*legacy*
el/la leñador/a	*woodcutter*
el lobo	*wolf*
luego	*then; after*
mientras	*while; during*
el mito	*myth*
el petróleo	*oil*
plano/a	*flat*
la poesía	*poetry*
polémico/a	*controversial*
polifacético/a	*many-sided*
el puesto político	*political position*
tres en raya	*tic-tac-toe*

de memoria	*by heart*
Érase una vez…	*Once upon a time…*

Cognados

Review the cognates in *Adelante* and the false cognates in *¡Atención!*. For a complete list of cognates, see Appendix 4 on page 605.

En vivo

TEACHING TIP: Allow students time to complete the chart. Go over student responses and record them on a blackboard or overhead transparency. Encourage students to not rely on the same well-known names used so far.

 Examinar el legado ambiguo. Tanto Che Guevara como Cristóbal Colón son figuras con un legado *(legacy)* muy ambiguo. Muchas personas creen que hicieron cosas muy heroicas (luchar por los pobres, viajar a un continente que no conocían los europeos e iniciar la combinación de culturas que hoy enriquece a Latinoamérica) mientras que otras personas creen que hicieron muchas cosas destructivas (encarcelar y ejecutar a muchas personas, iniciar la conquista de los indígenas en las Américas y la destrucción de sus culturas). Con un grupo de compañeros, piensen en figuras generalmente conocidas y apunten los aspectos positivos y negativos de su legado. Sigan el ejemplo del general George Custer. Luego, compartan sus resultados con otros grupos de la clase para ver si hay figuras que aparecieron en la mayoría de las listas.

Nombre	Aspectos positivos	Aspectos negativos
Gen. George Custer	Luchó para proteger a las familias pioneras.	Ayudó a obligar a los indígenas a segregarse en reservas y participó en la destrucción de sus culturas.

TEACHING TIP: The website http://www.homemadejam.org/re-thinking-columbus.html may be a helpful resource to students.

 Un punto de vista distinto. Imagine that you are a member of an indigenous group in the Americas. Your group's perspective on Cristóbal Colón and the "discovery of the Americas" is not the same as the one presented in typical social studies textbooks. Consider that a younger sibling or child of yours is attending a school that is about to celebrate Columbus Day. Take into account what you have learned in this chapter and write a letter to the school that your sibling or child is attending, asking them to reconsider how they celebrate Columbus Day. In order to make your case, write your version of history and how you think the day could be celebrated instead.

Paso 1: Organize your thoughts by doing the following: decide what group you will represent, make a list of the main historical points you would like to highlight, and make a note of an alternative type of celebration.

Paso 2: Now that you have taken your notes, write the first draft of your letter.

Paso 3: Revise your written product to ensure that it is rich in content. Ask yourself whether or not you made a compelling case for the school to rethink Columbus Day. Make any changes and rewrite it.

Paso 4: Now that your content is solid, revise your draft focusing on form and accuracy. Make the necessary revisions and write your final draft.

Paso 5: Be proud of your final draft. It should be rich in details and clear in form.

En directo

INVESTIGACIÓN A: Ollantaytambo: cultura milenaria

> **Antes de ver el video.** Contesta esta pregunta y comparte tu respuesta con el resto de la clase: ¿Crees que es necesario proteger a los grupos indígenas? ¿Por qué?

> **El video.** Completa las siguientes oraciones con la información del video.

1. Ollantaytambo está ubicado en el Valle Sagrado de los ___incas___.
2. Entre los siglos XIV y XVI era una ___fortaleza___ y un centro ___religioso___.
3. A los turistas les fascina ver que la ___tradición___ sigue ___viva___.
4. Conocer otras culturas actuales y antiguas nos permite ser más ___tolerantes___.

> **Después de ver el video.** Contesta esta pregunta con un/a compañero/a y luego con el resto de la clase: ¿Qué se puede aprender de las culturas indígenas o antiguas?

Vocabulario útil

esfuerzo	*effort*
fortaleza	*fortress*
reinado	*reign*
ladera	*hillside*
testigo	*witness*

INVESTIGACIÓN B: ¿Existe una verdad objetiva?

> **Antes de ver el video.** Indica si estás de acuerdo o no con las siguientes afirmaciones. Luego compara tus respuestas con las del resto de la clase. ¿Tienen todos la misma opinión?

1. No estoy a favor de la pena de muerte porque va en contra de los derechos humanos.

2. Creo que deberían de existir leyes más estrictas para regular la inmigración.

> **El video.** Mira el video y completa cada oración con su parte correspondiente.

___b___ **1.** No estoy de acuerdo con la pena de muerte…

___a___ **2.** Creo que sí debe haber leyes para regular la inmigración…

___d___ **3.** Yo creo que deben existir leyes que regulen la inmigración…

___c___ **4.** Estoy a favor de la pena de muerte, ¿por qué?...

a. pero siempre y cuando estas leyes respeten los derechos de las personas.

b. porque va en contra de los derechos humanos, del derecho humano a la vida.

c. porque considero "ojo por ojo, diente por diente".

d. todo país tiene derecho a regular sus fronteras, y todo debe tener un orden.

> **Después de ver el video.** ¿Estás a favor o en contra de la pena de muerte? ¿Crees que se debe regular la inmigración? Escribe dos oraciones para fundamentar tu opinión. Luego comparte tus argumentos con los del resto de la clase.

Vocabulario útil

pena de muerte	*death penalty*
ojo por ojo, diente por diente	*eye for an eye, a tooth for a tooth* (proverb)
castigar	*to punish*
frontera	*border*

Retrato de la clase Checklist

You should have recorded information in your **Retrato de la clase** in conjunction with the following activities:

WILEY
PLUS

TESTING PROGRAM:
You will find a complete testing program for use with *¡Vívelo!* in *WileyPLUS*.

☐	**10A.13**	**Sé honesto.**
☐	**10A.15**	**Respuestas personales.**
☐	**10A.17**	**La última vez.**
☐	**10A.20**	**Los amigos de la clase.**
☐	**10B.10**	**¿Qué carateriza a los héroes?**
☐	**10B.13**	**Un sondeo.**

Los avances tecnológicos

WILEY PLUS

INVESTIGACIÓN 11A
¿Cuál es la relación entre el transporte y la tecnología?

ADELANTE
- ¡Ya lo sabes!: Los medios de transporte
- La revolución inalámbrica en el transporte de Latinoamérica

Bien dicho: La letra *r*

PALABRAS CLAVE
- Los medios de transporte y la infraestructura
- ¿Qué sucede en el centro?

ESTRUCTURAS CLAVE
- The future tense
- The conditional

VÍVELO: LENGUA
- Expressing probability in the present
- Expressing courtesy
- Expressing probability in the past

VÍVELO: CULTURA
- El reloj de 24 horas

CONTEXTOS Y PERSPECTIVAS
Todos contra los biocombustibles

INVESTIGACIÓN 11B
¿Cómo influye la tecnología en una cultura?

ADELANTE
- ¡Ya lo sabes!: Las telecomunicaciones
- ¿Vida real o Segunda Vida?

Bien dicho: La letra *rr*

PALABRAS CLAVE
- La tecnología en casa

ESTRUCTURAS CLAVE
- The present subjunctive

VÍVELO: LENGUA
- Making formal commands (Review)

VÍVELO: CULTURA
- El uso de la Internet por hispanohablantes en diferentes países

CONTEXTOS Y PERSPECTIVAS
Las consecuencias de la tecnología

¡VÍVELO!

En vivo:
Un viaje
¿Cómo va a evolucionar la tecnología?

En directo:
A: El metro: transporte ecológico
B: La tecnología une a las familias

¿Cuál es la relación entre el transporte y la tecnología?

In this **Investigación** you will learn:

▶ How to talk about means of transportation

▶ How to describe travel arrangements

▶ How to express future possibilities

▶ How to express probability

¿Cómo se puede hablar de la relación entre el transporte y la tecnología?

You can inquire about the various means of transportation.	¿Qué formas de transporte existen hoy en día? ¿Hay un metro en tu ciudad natal? ¿Hay un aeropuerto en tu ciudad?
You can investigate the most popular means of transportation, most common forms of transportation.	¿Con qué frecuencia andas en bicicleta? ¿Manejas tu carro? ¿Tomas el autobús?
You can ask about vacations, travel patterns, travel preferences in the past, present and future.	¿Te gusta viajar? ¿Prefieres viajar solo/a, con tu familia o con amigos? ¿Adónde has viajado? ¿Harás un viaje durante las próximas vacaciones?
You can talk about and speculate about changes related to transportation in the future.	En el futuro no tendremos carros privados. Usaremos más el transporte público. Se inventarán nuevos tipos de combustible *(fuel).*
You can express what you would do as a result of new means of transportation or changing patterns of transportation in the future.	¿Qué harías para reducir la contaminación? ¿Comprarías un vehículo híbrido? ¿Manejarías un carro eléctrico? ¿Qué cambios recomendarías para tener medios de transporte más ecológicos?

Adelante

¡Ya lo sabes! Los medios de transporte

el aeropuerto	la motocicleta	abordar
el autobús	el motor	evolucionar
la capacidad	el pasajero	facilitar
la contaminación del aire	el pasaporte	modificar
la distancia	la plataforma	mover(se) (o → ue)
la energía eléctrica	el taxi	reservar
la estación de trenes	el transporte público	transformar(se)
la gasolina	el tren	
la máquina	el vehículo híbrido	
el metro	el vehículo eléctrico	

11A.1 ¡A escoger! Lee la oración y selecciona la opción más lógica según el modelo. Luego, verifica tu respuesta con un/a compañero/a de clase y después con toda la clase.

1. Siempre hay que esperar un poco antes de _____ el avión.

  a. romper   (**b.**) abordar   **c.** modificar

2. Los carros han _____ mucho en los últimos 50 años. Los carros del presente corren más rápido que los carros de la década de 1950.

  a. sacado   **b.** aburrido   (**c.**) evolucionado

3. La expansión del metro de Madrid en la década de 1970 _____ el movimiento de personas por toda la ciudad.

  a. prohibió   (**b.**) facilitó   **c.** diseñó

4. Han _____ los motores de los carros y ahora contaminan menos.

  (**a.**) modificado   **b.** bebido   **c.** escapado

5. A las cinco de la tarde, el tráfico en la ciudad _____ muy lentamente porque todos se van a casa.

  a. se peina   **b.** se acuesta   (**c.**) se mueve

6. En un restaurante elegante es costumbre llamar para _____ una mesa.

  a. cocinar   (**b.**) reservar   **c.** abordar

11A.2 ¿Qué palabra es? Escucha las definiciones e indica qué palabra corresponde a cada definición. Luego, verifica tus respuestas con la clase. **¡Ojo!** No se usan todas las palabras.

a. reservar   **f.** el metro
b. la capacidad   **g.** moverse
c. la plataforma   **h.** modificar
d. la distancia   **i.** los pasajeros
e. la electricidad   **j.** el pasaporte

1. __g__

2. __j__

3. __c__

4. __f__

5. __i__

6. __h__

VÍVELO: CULTURA

El reloj de 24 horas

En Estados Unidos, el reloj de 24 horas se asocia principalmente con contextos militares, pero en los países hispanos, se usa el reloj de 24 horas en horarios oficiales para diferenciar entre las horas de la mañana y las horas de la tarde o de la noche. El reloj de 24 horas se usa en los horarios relacionados con el transporte (autobús, tren, avión), los horarios de televisión y cine, los horarios comerciales y los horarios de eventos públicos (conciertos, bailes, actos culturales).

¿Cuál es el equivalente de... ?

18:00 horas   6:00 p.m.   13:15 horas   1:15 p.m.
20:30 horas   8:30 p.m.   17:25 horas   5:25 p.m.
23:05 horas   11:05 p.m.   22:20 horas   10:20 p.m.

11A.1 ADDITIONAL PRACTICE: Engage students in conversation using these words with questions such as: *¿Es necesario reservar una mesa en McDonalds? ¿Dónde es necesario reservar una mesa? ¿Con cuánto tiempo es necesario llegar al aeropuerto antes de abordar el avión? ¿Debemos modificar nuestros carros porque no habrá suficiente gasolina en el futuro?* Again, these questions require only one or two word responses and will be expanded on more fully later.

11A.2 AUDIO SCRIPT: 1. Un verbo que significa ir de un lugar a otro. 2. El documento que necesitamos cuando vamos a otro país. 3. La parte de la estación donde llegan y salen los trenes. 4. Un tren subterráneo en una ciudad grande. 5. Las personas que viajan en tren o autobús. 6. Un verbo que es sinónimo de transformar.

11A.2 TEACHING TIP: Allow students a moment to look over the list of words before listening to definitions.

VÍVELO: CULTURA: Have each student write down five different times, in military time (e.g. 13:15, 22:30, etc.). In pairs, have each student state their times (e.g. *Es la una y cuarto de la tarde, Son las diez y media de la noche,* etc.). Their partners then need to write these down in military time.

PRE-READING ACTIVITY:
To prepare students for this reading, bring a cell phone to class. Hold it up and ask students questions like, *¿El teléfono celular impacta la vida? ¿Qué impacto tiene el teléfono celular?* and *¿Somos más eficientes gracias al teléfono celular?* Ask students to talk to their partners for one to two minutes about this topic. When they are done, ask for general responses from the class. Then have students take a look at this article and let them know that they will read about the role that this type of technology plays in the transportation field in Latin America.

CULTURAL NOTE: The
socioeconomics of a country play a significant role in the type of public transportation available. Forms of transportation can vary from Mercedes Benz taxis with GPS units to small rickety buses overfilled with people.

11A.3 TEACHING TIP:
Have students focus on key words and not worry about understanding every word. Read each sentence twice before moving on to the next sentence.

La revolución inalámbrica en el transporte de Latinoamérica

El taxi

Las computadoras de mano, hasta ahora elegantes organizadores electrónicos llenos de números telefónicos y fechas de reuniones, pasan de los bolsillos (*pockets*) de los trajes a las manos de taxistas y conductores de autobús en Latinoamérica y han transformado su trabajo. Esa expansión del uso de la tecnología inalámbrica (*wireless*) al campo de transporte les permite trabajar más rápida y eficientemente. Por ejemplo, antes los taxistas procesaban toda la información acerca de pasajeros (*passengers*) y tarifas (*fares*) a mano y pasaban los recibos a la compañía personalmente. Ahora, todo esto se hace automáticamente por computadora.

El autobús

De manera semejante, los conductores de autobús usan teléfonos celulares y aparatos satelitales de posicionamiento global para transmitir una gran cantidad de información a la oficina central. Los conductores están en contacto constante con la oficina central y se puede comunicar información acerca del número de pasajeros, la posición exacta del autobús y la condición de las llantas (*tires*) u otros elementos mecánicos del autobús. Los despachadores también pueden determinar si las puertas del autobús están cerradas o

abiertas, si el conductor se desvía (*deviates*) de su ruta, si el conductor va a exceso de velocidad y si se sigue el programa de mantenimiento. Y claro, los conductores pueden comunicarse inmediatamente con la oficina central si hay problemas mecánicos u otro tipo de emergencia. Aunque los aparatos y las aplicaciones son diferentes en cada caso, está claro que la tecnología inalámbrica ha tenido gran impacto en el funcionamiento de los sistemas de transporte en Latinoamérica y en las actividades diarias de sus empleados.

11A.3 **Comprensión.** Lee el artículo e indica si las frases se refieren a los taxistas o a los conductores de autobús. Verifica tus respuestas con la clase.

Taxistas	Conductores de autobús	
☑	☐	**1.** Procesan automáticamente información acerca de las tarifas.
☐	☑	**2.** Usan aparatos satelitales de posicionamiento global.
☑	☐	**3.** Transmiten automáticamente los recibos a la compañía.
☐	☑	**4.** Pueden comunicarse rápidamente con la oficina central.
☐	☑	**5.** Los despachadores pueden determinar si manejan con exceso de velocidad.
☑	☐	**6.** Usan computadoras de mano.

Bien dicho

La letra *r*

TEACHING TIP: Let students know that this is a tough pronunciation point for many non-native speakers and that they should do the best they can.

The letter **r** in Spanish is not pronounced like the English *r*. Rather than folding your tongue towards the back of your mouth as you do when pronouncing *r* in English, the Spanish **r** is produced when the front part of the tongue briefly touches the hard ridge behind your top teeth. This pronunciation is called a "single flap" or "tap". The sound produced is similar to the sound associated with *d, dd, t,* and *tt* in the English words *rider, middle, photo,* and *butter.* Recall that when you pronounce **d** and **t** in Spanish, the tip of your tongue touches the bottom edge of your top teeth. This slight difference in the position of the tongue is enough to distinguish **d/t** from **r** in Spanish. Listen to the Spanish **r** in the following words.

pera	María	tropa
coro	favor	director
adorar	grande	hora

The "single flap" pronunciation is associated with **r** *except* when **r** begins the word or follows an **l, n,** or **s.** As you will see in **Investigación 11B,** a different pronunciation is associated with the **r** in these contexts.

11A.4 **Escucha e indica.** Escucha las palabras e indica qué palabra oíste en cada caso.

1. cada — cara
2. todo — toro
3. mudo — muro
4. comprada — comprara — comprará
5. oíd — oír
6. ida — ira
7. padecer — parecer
8. mirada — mirara — mirará
9. lodo — loro
10. sed — ser

11A.4 AUDIO SCRIPT AND ANSWERS: 1. cada, 2. toro, 3. muro, 4. comprará, 5. oíd, 6. ida, 7. parecer, 8. mirara, 9. loro, 10. sed

11A.5 **¡A practicar!** Con un/a compañero/a, pronuncien por turnos las oraciones. Al terminar, repitan el ejercicio pronunciando las oraciones que su compañero/a pronunció la primera vez. Presten atención a la pronunciación de **r.**

1. Alberto siempre prefiere viajar en primera clase.
2. El drama de la vida nos prepara para enfrentarnos a todo.
3. Para viajar a Uruguay, es necesario tener pasaporte.
4. Muchas personas dependen de aparatos inalámbricos.
5. Aquellos cruceros podrán navegar por el mar Caribe.
6. Favor de abordar ese tren en la plataforma catorce.
7. Se transmitió la información por medios electrónicos.
8. Hubo mucho tráfico a esa hora, por eso llegué tarde.

Palabras clave 1 Los medios de transporte y la infraestructura

TEACHING TIPS: Direct students' attention to the drawings containing the new vocabulary. Ask students about what types of transportation are most common on a daily basis (*¿Qué formas de transporte son más comunes en el día a día?*), and during holidays (*¿Qué formas de transporte son más comunes en vacaciones?*). You can also ask questions like, *¿Cómo se llama la forma de transporte por agua?* or *¿Por dónde tienes que pasar antes de abordar un avión?* Keep as many of these new vocabulary words in mind as you ask students questions. If you have a large class, you may want to ask questions and give students twenty seconds to answer, but to a partner. This way, more students will be able to participate.

11A.6 TEACHING TIP: Encourage students to read the vocabulary words first and provide their own definitions before reading the descriptions.

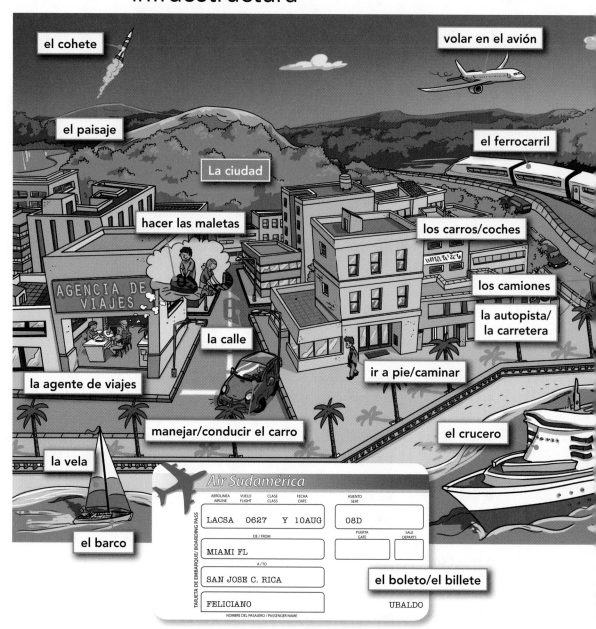

el cohete

volar en el avión

el paisaje

el ferrocarril

La ciudad

hacer las maletas

los carros/coches

AGENCIA DE VIAJES

los camiones

la autopista/ la carretera

la calle

ir a pie/caminar

la agente de viajes

el crucero

manejar/conducir el carro

la vela

el barco

Air Sudamérica

AEROLÍNEA AIRLINE	VUELO FLIGHT	CLASE CLASS	FECHA DATE	ASIENTO SEAT
LACSA	0627	Y	10AUG	08D

DE / FROM — MIAMI FL

PUERTA GATE — SALE DEPARTS

A / TO — SAN JOSE C. RICA

el boleto/el billete

FELICIANO — UBALDO

NOMBRE DEL PASAJERO / PASSENGER NAME

TARJETA DE EMBARQUE / BOARDING PASS

11A.6 Identificar las palabras correctas. Lee las oraciones a continuación e indica qué palabras corresponden a cada definición. Luego, verifica tu respuesta con un/a compañero/a de clase. Una de las palabras no se usa.

a. el ferrocarril   **c.** el boleto   **e.** el cohete   **g.** el vehículo eléctrico

b. la autopista   **d.** el paisaje   **f.** la aduana

___f___ **1.** El lugar en el aeropuerto donde se inspeccionan las maletas de los pasajeros que llegan de otros países

___e___ **2.** El vehículo que asociamos con los astronautas

___b___ **3.** Un tipo de calle donde se puede manejar muy rápido

___c___ **4.** El documento que indica que hemos pagado por viajar en avión, tren o autobús

___a___ **5.** El aspecto de la infraestructura que se asocia con los trenes

___g___ **6.** Un vehículo que no usa gasolina

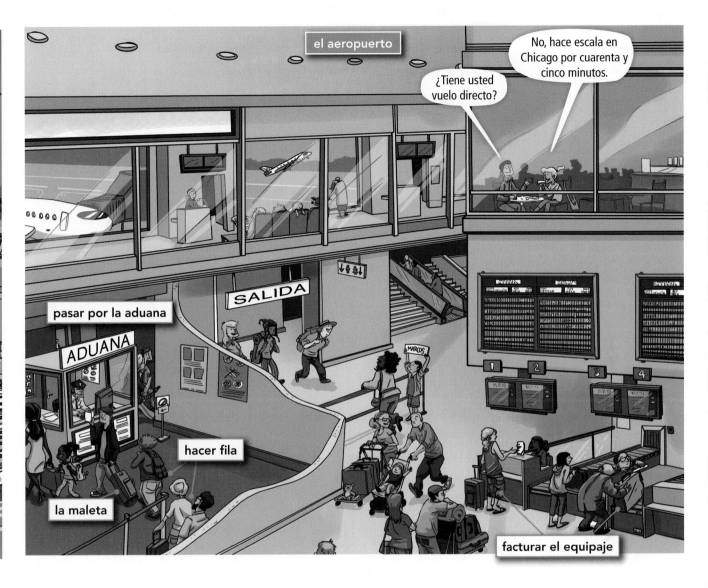

el aeropuerto

¿Tiene usted vuelo directo?

No, hace escala en Chicago por cuarenta y cinco minutos.

pasar por la aduana

SALIDA

ADUANA

hacer fila

la maleta

facturar el equipaje

11A.7 **Definiciones.** Lee las siguientes palabras y expresiones. Luego, escucha las definiciones e indica qué palabra o expresión corresponde a cada definición. Escribe el número de la oración al lado de la respuesta. Luego, verifica tus respuestas con la clase.

_5_ hacer escala

_6_ hacer fila

_4_ ir a pie

_1_ facturar las maletas

_2_ hacer la maleta

_3_ volar

11A.7 AUDIO SCRIPT: 1. La expresión que significa dejar las maletas con un empleado de la aerolínea antes de abordar el avión, 2. La expresión que significa poner la ropa en la maleta antes de un viaje, 3. El verbo que asociamos con los aviones, 4. Una expresión que es sinónimo de caminar, 5. La expresión que significa esperar en el aeropuerto entre dos vuelos, 6. La expresión que significa esperar su turno en una línea con otras personas.

www **¡Conéctate!**

Check out prices to Latin America. Visit http://lan.com and click on a country to begin a search (e.g. U.S.A. español). Pick the closest departure city to yours and the city in Latin America you would like to visit. Identify the best itinerary for you based on dates, price and times. Notice that times are shared in a 24-hour clock. Share your itinerary with your class.

11A.8 **Planear un viaje.** Con un/a compañero/a, pongan en orden las oraciones siguientes para indicar la secuencia lógica de un viaje internacional. Usen los números 1–9. Luego, comparen su secuencia con la secuencia de otros grupos. ¿Son iguales o diferentes?

_____ abordar el avión   _____ ir al aeropuerto

_____ hacer las maletas   _____ bajar del avión

_____ obtener el pasaporte   _____ facturar el equipaje

_____ pasar por la aduana   _____ comprar los boletos de ida y vuelta

_____ hablar con un/a agente de viajes

11A.9 **¿Quién de la clase?** Recorre la clase haciéndoles preguntas a tus compañeros sobre su experiencia con los viajes. Si una persona contesta "Sí", debe escribir su nombre en la línea al lado de la pregunta. Puedes hacerle solamente dos preguntas seguidas *(in a row)* a la misma persona. Comparte tus resultados con la clase y escribe un resumen de la información en tu **Retrato de la clase. ¡Ojo!** Tienes que cambiar el verbo a la forma de *tú* cuando hablas con tus compañeros.

1. Ha viajado en un barco de vela. _____

2. Ha viajado en un crucero. _____

3. Ha tomado el metro en otra ciudad. _____

4. Ha hecho un viaje largo en autobús. _____

5. Ha planeado un viaje con un agente de viajes. _____

6. Ha volado a Europa. _____

7. Ha pasado por la aduana. _____

8. Ha viajado en primera clase. _____

9. Ha manejado un vehículo híbrido. _____

10. Tiene vehículo. _____

Retrato de la clase: _____ personas de la clase han viajado en un barco de vela. _____ personas han viajado en un crucero _____ han tomado el metro en otra ciudad.

11A.10 **Un sondeo sobre los medios de transporte.** Habla con diez compañeros para determinar sus medios de transporte preferidos y los medios de transporte que menos les gustan. Escribe sus nombres y apunta respuestas en las columnas apropiadas. Luego, resume la información en tu **Retrato de la clase.**

Nombre	Medio de transporte preferido	Medio de transporte que menos le gusta
Yo		

Retrato de la clase: En esta clase, el medio de transporte más popular es_____. En segundo lugar está el _____. En tercer lugar está el _____.

11A.11 **¿Con qué frecuencia?**   Indica con qué frecuencia haces las siguientes actividades relacionadas con el transporte. Luego, en grupos de cuatro o cinco analicen los resultados de su grupo y compártanlos con la clase. ¿Se pueden hacer generalizaciones según los resultados? Apúntalos en tu **Retrato de la clase.**

	Todos los días	Varias veces al mes	De vez en cuando	Una o dos veces al año	Nunca
Montas en bicicleta					
Manejas un carro					
Manejas una motocicleta					
Viajas a distancias lejanas (far)					
Vas a lugares a pie					
Tomas el autobús					
Tomas el metro					
Viajas en tren					
Vuelas en avión					

Retrato de la clase: La mayor parte de la clase maneja su carro todos los días, monta en bicicleta una o dos veces al año…

11A.12 **Un viaje pasado.**   Escribe un párrafo que describa un viaje que hicisite en el pasado. ¿Cuándo fue? ¿Cuál fue el propósito *(purpose)* del viaje? ¿Adónde fuiste? ¿Con quién fuiste? ¿Cómo viajaste? ¿Qué hiciste durante ese viaje? Luego, intercambia tu párrafo con un/a compañero/a de clase. Comparte la descripción del viaje de tu compañero/a con el resto de la clase. Por último, apunta información interesante sobre los viajes de tus compañeros en tu **Retrato de la clase.** Usa algunas de estas preguntas como guía.

• ¿Quién viajó más lejos?

• ¿Quién usó más medios de transporte?

• ¿Quién viajó a un lugar exótico?

• ¿Cuántos viajaron con intención de relajarse?

• ¿Cuántos viajaron por negocio/trabajo?

• ¿Cuántos viajaron con amigos?

• ¿Cuántos viajaron con la famila?

Retrato de la clase: Mi compañero de clase ___ viajó más lejos que todos. Fue a ___ . Mis compañeros de clase ___ y ___ usaron varios medios de transporte, pero sólo ___ viajó a un lugar exótico.

WILEY PLUS

11A.11 INSTRUCTOR'S RESOURCES: You will find a reproducible chart for use with Activity 11A.11 in your Instructor's Resources.

11A.11 TEACHING TIP: Tally results and comment on most commonly/least commonly used forms of transportation. What forms of transportation are used every day/never?

11A.12 TEACHING TIP: Remind students to use preterit. Also remind them of sequential expressions such as *luego, entonces, después,* etc.

11A.12 TEACHING TIP: The *modelos* in the *Retrato de la clase* are merely samples of possible answers and are not meant to be used as an exact template for students to copy. Remind them to report their own findings and make their own conclusions.

Palabras clave 2 ¿Qué sucede en el centro?

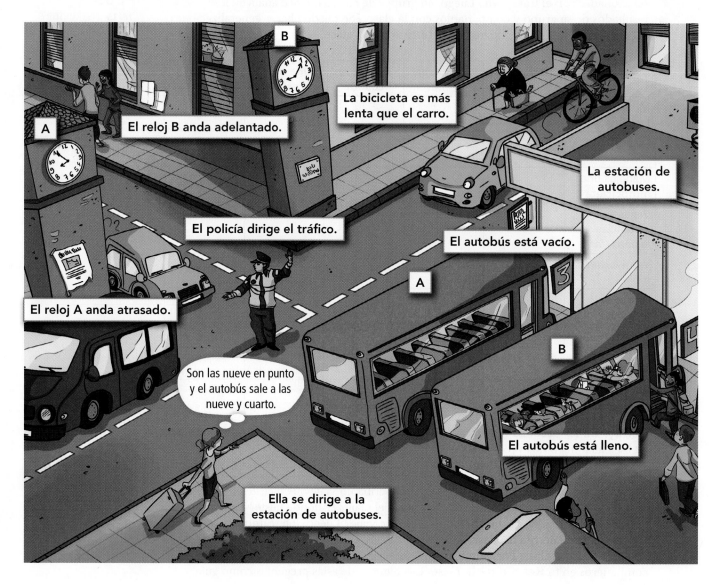

El reloj B anda adelantado.

La bicicleta es más lenta que el carro.

La estación de autobuses.

El policía dirige el tráfico.

El autobús está vacío.

El reloj A anda atrasado.

Son las nueve en punto y el autobús sale a las nueve y cuarto.

El autobús está lleno.

Ella se dirige a la estación de autobuses.

11A.13 TEACHING TIP:
Many of the expressions in *Palabras clave* recycle individual words students have learned in other contexts but which used in the context of transportation can take on a specific meaning.

11A.13 TEACHING TIP:
Have students share their answers with a partner before going over them as a class.

11A.13 Busca la palabra correcta. Con un/a compañero/a de clase, emparejen las definiciones con las palabras correctas. Luego, verifiquen las respuestas con sus compañeros de clase.

a. adelantado   **d.** cansar   **g.** la estación   **j.** recorrer
b. alcanzar   **e.** demorar   **h.** los ingresos   **k.** vacío
c. aprovecharse   **f.** la desventaja   **i.** lleno   **l.** la ventaja

___f___ **1.** Esta palabra se refiere a un aspecto negativo de algo.

___d___ **2.** Este verbo es un sinónimo de fatigar.

___c___ **3.** Este verbo significa beneficiarse de algo.

___e___ **4.** Este verbo significa tardar o retrasarse.

___g___ **5.** Esta palabra se refiere al edificio adonde vamos para tomar un autobús.

___k___ **6.** Este adjetivo describe un vaso que no contiene nada en ese momento.

___h___ **7.** Esta palabra se refiere al dinero que gana una persona o una compañía.

___b___ **8.** Este verbo significa extender el brazo y la mano para poder tocar algo.

11A.13 PARTNERING CARDS: Write down the vocabulary words above as well as the definitions on different slips of paper. Randomly pass them out and have students find their matching vocabulary word or definition.

Sustantivos

la ventaja	Cuando viajas a Uruguay, es una ventaja poder hablar español.
la desventaja	Ser pobre siempre es una desventaja.
el promedio	El promedio de las notas de un examen es la suma de las notas de todos los estudiantes dividida por el número de estudiantes.
los ingresos	Los ingresos de una familia son la combinación de los salarios de las personas que trabajan.
las cifras	Las cifras son los números presentados estadísticamente en cantidades como porcentajes, litros, millas, etc.

Verbos

alcanzar	Soy muy baja, por eso no puedo alcanzar los libros en ese estante.
aprovechar	Si desea aprovechar los precios razonables, debe comprar los boletos catorce días antes del viaje.
cansarle a uno	Los viajes largos nos cansan más que los cortos.
demorar(se)	A causa de lluvias fuertes o tormentas, los aviones se demoran y llegamos tarde a nuestros destinos.
llevar a	La invención del motor llevó a la invención del automóvil.
recorrer	Si vas a viajar a una ciudad grande o desconocida, es recomendable recorrer la ciudad a través de Google Earth.
tener lugar	La inauguración de los presidentes siempre tiene lugar en Washington D.C.

11A.14 ¿Cuál es la opción correcta?   Lee las oraciones siguientes e indica cuál de las dos opciones en negrita *(bold type)* es la mejor para completar la oración. Luego, verifica tus respuestas con un/a compañero/a.

1. Los agentes **recorrieron/demoraron** el barrio donde iba a hablar el presidente.

2. Cada 10 años el censo presenta **ingresos/cifras** acerca de la población estadounidense.

3. Si entro a la clase después de que ha empezado, llego **adelantado/atrasado.**

4. En Estados Unidos, los metros y los autobuses de las grandes ciudades normalmente están **llenos/vacíos** a las cinco de la tarde.

5. La tortuga *(turtle)* es un animal **lento/rápido.**

6. Jesús López Cobos **alcanza/dirige** la Orquesta Sinfónica de Madrid.

7. La reunión de los presidentes centroamericanos **llevó a/tuvo lugar en** Managua, Nicaragua.

8. En la sociedad estadounidense actual, tener un título universitario es una **ventaja/ desventaja** cuando se busca trabajo.

11A.15 ¿Cierto o falso?   Con un/a compañero/a de clase escriban por lo menos dos oraciones, una cierta y la otra falsa. Luego, léanlas a la clase para que la clase adivine cuál es la oración cierta y cuál es la falsa.

TEACHING TIP: Write the following words on the board: to reach, to delay, advantage, disadvantage, to tire, to lead to, to travel, to take advantage of, to take place, average, income, figures. Ask students to match up the Spanish words with their English equivalents based on the descriptions of new words in *Palabras clave.*

FOLLOW-UP EXERCISE: Give students the following words and ask them to indicate a synonym or antonym for each: *desventaja (ventaja), salario (ingresos), números (cifras), llegar a tiempo/ ser puntual (demorar), explorar (recorrer)*

11A.14 ANSWERS: 1. recorrieron, 2. cifras, 3. atrasado, 4. llenos, 5. lento, 6. dirige, 7. tuvo lugar en, 8. ventaja

11A.14 EXTENSION ACTIVITY: Have students write two additional sentences using these as a model.

¡Atención!

¡ATENCIÓN!: Encourage students to focus on the words that they think they will need the most. They should make a point of writing these down and reviewing them, so as to remember them for the long term.

Vagón	does not mean wagon like a child's toy or a vehicle pulled by horses. It means *railway car,* like the vehicles that make up a train. To express *wagon* in Spanish, use the word **carro** or **carrito. Carro** is also a synonym for **automóvil** or **coche.** Este tren es muy largo. Tiene cien vagones. Cuando era niña, llevaba mis juguetes en mi carro rojo. José maneja su carro a la universidad cada día.
Suceder	does not mean to succeed as when you receive good grades or earn a lot of money. In this case, use the expression **tener éxito. Suceder** is a synonym for **ocurrir, tener lugar,** or **pasar. Suceder** is also a synonym for **heredar** in the sense of inheriting a position, title, or power. Marcos ha tenido mucho éxito en su carrera. ¿Qué sucedió en la fiesta? Pues, todos se divirtieron mucho. Felipe, el Príncipe de Asturias, va a suceder al rey Juan Carlos I.
Mover(se)	as was pointed out before, means **ir de un lugar a otro.** When someone buys a new house or goes to live in a different apartment, use the verb **mudarse** as the equivalent of *to move* in English. El tráfico se mueve muy lentamente a las cinco de la tarde. Cuando tenía 10 años, mi familia se mudó de El Paso a Dallas.
Comodidad	does not mean commodity in the commercial sense. In this sense, use **producto, artículo,** or **mercancía. Comodidad** means *comfort, convenience,* or *amenity* in English. El petróleo es un producto esencial en el mundo de hoy. Para viajar con mucha comodidad, es mejor viajar en primera clase.
Maleta	means *suitcase.* To express *mallet,* use the word **mazo.** Cuando vamos de viaje, ponemos la ropa en una maleta. El carpintero desmanteló los muebles con un mazo.

11A.16 ANSWERS: No está bien: 1. (vagones), 4. (tener éxito), 5. (mudarme)

11A.16 TEACHING TIP: Remind students that they cannot always rely on direct translation. For instance, while the verb *mover* does mean to move, it is often confused for moving from one home to another. Students should pay attention to context more than the direct translations.

11A.17 TEACHING TIP: Before students read the sentences, encourage them to read through the list of possible vocabulary words.

11A.16 ¿Está bien?   Indica si en las siguientes oraciones se usan correctamente los cognados y corrige los errores en las oraciones con errores. Luego, verifica tus respuestas con un/a compañero/a de clase.

	Está bien.	No está bien.
1. ¡Cuántos carros tiene ese tren! Es interminable.	☐	☑
2. Los primeros trenes tenían motores a vapor *(steam).*	☑	☐
3. Cuando viajamos, ponemos la ropa en una maleta.	☑	☐
4. Si estudias mucho, vas a suceder en esta clase.	☐	☑
5. Después de graduarme, voy a moverme a Seattle.	☐	☑
6. En los cruceros, hay muchas comodidades.	☑	☐

11A.17 Completa las oraciones.   De la lista siguiente, escoge la palabra o expresión correcta para completar las oraciones. Luego verifica tus respuestas con la clase.

carros	mover	productos	vagón
maletas	mudar	suceder	

1. Este pueblo es muy tranquilo. Nada va a _____ suceder _____.

2. El oro y los diamantes son _____ productos _____ muy valiosos.

3. Antes de hacer un viaje es necesario hacer las _____ maletas _____.

4. Quiero _____ mover _____ esta mesa al otro lado del cuarto.

5. A los niños les gusta jugar con _____ carros _____ de control remoto.

Estructuras clave 1 The future tense

To talk about the future in Spanish, you learned to use the construction **ir + a** + *infinitive* (e.g., **voy a comer**). That construction often implies a near future and is generally used in informal conversation. There is also a future tense in Spanish that is used in more formal situations and written language. This future tense, generally translated as *will + verb*, is formed by adding the appropriate endings to the infinitive. These endings signal that the verb carries the meaning *will*, as in *will buy, will sell,* or *will ask for.* The endings are the same for **–ar, –er,** and **–ir** verbs.

WILEY
PLUS

You will find PowerPoint presentations for use with *Estructuras clave* in *WileyPLUS*.

TEACHING TIPS: As you read through this description with students, write down the endings that verbs take *(–é, –ás, –á, –emos, –éis, –án).* Ask students questions such as *¿Adónde viajarás este verano? ¿Querrás ir a Sudamérica después de graduarte?* or *¿Irás a una fiesta este fin de semana?*

	will buy	
Yo	comprar**é**	
Tú	comprar**ás**	
Él/Ella/Usted	comprar**á**	un boleto a Buenos Aires.
Nosotros/as	comprar**emos**	
Vosotoros/as	comprar**éis**	
Ellos/Ellas/Ustedes	comprar**án**	

	will sell	
Yo	vender**é**	
Tú	vender**ás**	
Él/Ella/Usted	vender**á**	una motocicleta.
Nosotros/as	vender**emos**	
Vosotros/as	vender**éis**	
Ellos/Ellas/Ustedes	vender**án**	

	will ask for	
Yo	pedir**é**	
Tú	pedir**ás**	
Él/Ella/Usted	pedir**á**	un taxi.
Nosotros/as	pedir**emos**	
Vosotros/as	pedir**éis**	
Ellos/Ellas/Ustedes	pedir**án**	

There are twelve verbs that have irregular stems in the future. The endings are the same as for the regular verbs in the future.

caber:	**cabr-**	poder:	**podr-**	salir:	**saldr-**
decir:	**dir-**	poner:	**pondr-**	tener:	**tendr-**
haber:	**habr-**	querer:	**querr-**	valer:	**valdr-**
hacer:	**har-**	saber:	**sabr-**	venir:	**vendr-**

La noche antes del viaje, **haré** las maletas.	*The night before the trip, I'll pack the suitcases.*
En el aeropuerto, **tendrás** que hacer fila.	*In the airport, you'll have to wait in line.*
El vuelo para Lima **saldrá** a las seis y media de la tarde.	*The flight to Lima will leave (depart) at 6:30 pm.*
Vosotros **vendréis** en tren.	*You'll come by train.*
Nosotras **pondremos** nuestros pasaportes en un lugar seguro.	*We'll put our passports in a safe place.*
Las jóvenes **querrán** montar en bicicleta.	*The kids will want to ride bikes.*

The future for **hay** *(there is/there are)* is **habrá** *(there will be).*

Habrá un vuelo a Santo Domingo por la mañana.
Habrá muchos carros en la autopista a las ocho de la mañana.

11A.18 ANSWERS:
Pasado: 1, 3, 4, 8; Futuro: 2, 5, 6, 7; 1 is false (los hermanos Wright) and 3 is true. Answers for 2 and 4-8 will vary depending on students' experiences/beliefs.

11A.18 Pasado o futuro. Lee las siguientes oraciones e indica si representan acciones en el pasado o en el futuro. Luego, indica si las acciones pasadas ocurrieron de verdad *(really)* y si las acciones futuras ocurrirán según piensas tú. Por último, comparte tus respuestas con un compañero de clase.

	Pasado	Futuro		Sí	No
1.	☑	☐		☐	☑
2.	☐	☑		☐	☐
3.	☑	☐		☑	☐
4.	☑	☐		☐	☐
5.	☐	☑		☐	☐
6.	☐	☑		☐	☐
7.	☐	☑		☐	☐
8.	☑	☐		☐	☐

1. Henry Ford inventó el primer avión.

2. Los astronautas volarán al planeta Marte.

3. Se construyeron muchas autopistas en la ciudad de Dallas.

4. Hoy yo llegué a la universidad en autobús.

5. Yo compraré un carro eléctrico.

6. El tren será una forma de transporte popular porque contamina menos.

7. Debido a Internet, no existirán las agencias de viajes.

8. Mi familia y yo hicimos un viaje al Gran Cañón.

11A.19 ANSWERS:
Answers may vary, but the most likely responses are: Probable: 3, 4, 6, 8; Improbable: 1, 2, 5, 7

11A.19 NOTE: While many students may have answered *improbable* for number 7, remind them that today in the European Union passports are not needed to travel from one country to another.

11A.19 El transporte del futuro. Lee las predicciones acerca del transporte del futuro e indica si crees que son lógicas o ilógicas. Explica tus respuestas a la clase.

	Probable	Improbable
1. La gente volará a la luna en su cohete personal.	☐	☐
2. Se eliminarán los barcos.	☐	☐
3. Se inventarán carros que no contaminen.	☐	☐
4. Más gente usará transporte público.	☐	☐
5. Todos tendremos cohetes privados.	☐	☐
6. Habrá más vehículos híbridos.	☐	☐
7. No necesitaremos pasaportes para viajar al extranjero.	☐	☐
8. Iremos menos a las agencias de viajes.	☐	☐

11A.20 RECYCLING:
This task recycles interrogatives in addition to illustrating the use of the future tense and providing current information about the world energy crisis. Walk around the room to help students write meaningful questions to ask the class. Remind them that they must provide the answers to their own questions. Then have them ask each other questions orally as a class.

11A.20 ¡Qué cara está la gasolina! En grupos de tres, lean el artículo sobre el precio de la gasolina de la página 497. Luego, subrayen todos los verbos del futuro y comparen sus listas. Por último, escriban cinco preguntas sobre el artículo para presentar a la clase que verifiquen la comprensión de las ideas principales.

¿Galón de gasolina a $7?

Frenará 10 millones de autos en el 2010

TORONTO, Canadá – El precio del barril de petróleo crudo costará más de $200 y el galón de gasolina regular $7 para el 2010, lo que hará que unos 10 millones de automóviles dejen de circular en las calles y carreteras de Estados Unidos, según un estudio de la firma canadiense de análisis de mercados CIBC World Markets.

Se venderán menos autos

"Para el 2012 habrá 10 millones de vehículos menos en las carreteras estadounidenses de los que hay hoy en día", aseguró Jeff Rubin, jefe economista de CIBC World Markets. "Y los que más sufrirán, serán los estadounidenses con ingresos *(incomes)* inferiores a los $25 mil". Una ventaja de la gasolina cara *(expensive)* es que hay menos tráfico. Por otra parte, Rubin aseguró, la crisis energética en los próximos años "empequeñecerá *(will reduce)* todos los ajustes *(adjustments)* previos" hechos por la industria automotriz y los productores de petróleo, incluida la Organización de Países Exportadores de Petróleo (OPEC).

"Con los hábitos de manejo, llenar el tanque del auto pasará del equivalente del 7% a 20% de los ingresos de una familia típica, un aumento que hará que muchos empiecen a tomar el autobús", explicó Rubin.

Con todos estos cambios, el futuro del transporte en Estados Unidos se acercará *(will approach)* a la realidad europea, según CIBC World Markets. Mientras que 90% de los estadounidenses utilizan el auto para ir a trabajar, y 60% de los hogares tiene dos o más vehículos, en Gran Bretaña las cifras son de 60% y 25%, respectivamente.

Además, los estadounidenses "conducen sus autos más. Hacen cuatro viajes al día mientras que los británicos hacen la mitad. Y por último, 30% de los británicos no tienen incluso un auto. En Estados Unidos menos de 10% de los hogares no poseen un vehículo", dijo Rubin.

El precio medio de la gasolina regular en Estados Unidos ha aumentado casi 100% en los últimos cuatro años. ¿Adónde llevarán los caros precios de la gasolina a la industria automotriz y los ciudadanos del mundo?

11A.21 El vehículo del futuro.   En grupos de cuatro personas, inventen un vehículo nuevo para el futuro. Las preguntas a continuación les facilitarán la discusión. Dibujen su vehículo. Luego, presentarán su vehículo a la clase y la clase votará para determinar cuál es el vehículo más probable/más fantástico.

1. ¿Cómo se llamará el vehículo?

2. ¿Cómo será el vehículo? ¿Grande, pequeño, etc.?

3. ¿De qué material estará construído el vehículo?

4. ¿Tendrá ruedas *(wheels)*? ¿Cuántas?

5. ¿Viajará por tierra? ¿Por aire? ¿Por agua? ¿Por el espacio?

6. ¿Cuántos pasajeros podrán viajar en este vehículo?

7. ¿El vehículo necesitará gasolina? ¿Otro tipo de combustible *(fuel)*?

8. ¿El vehículo servirá para viajes cortos, viajes largos o los dos?

9. ¿Qué tecnología/comodidades se incorporarán en el vehículo? (p.ej., GPS, Internet, sillones, DVD, etc.)

PRE-READING STRATEGY: Have students react to the question in the title *¿Galón de gasolina a $7?* by writing a list of consequences that come to mind. Have several ideas shared with the class to get them prepared for what they are about to read. The second part of the title includes the verb *frenar*. Remind them what it means through gestures and description *(es sinónimo de parar)*.

TEACHING TIP: Read silently through the passage as a class. Stop periodically to ask clarification questions. At the end, have students work in groups to answer the question that concludes the passage *¿Adónde llevará este aumento del precio de la gasolina a la industria automotriz y a los ciudadanos del mundo?*

11A.21 TEACHING TIP: Allow students sufficient time to design their vehicles, walking around to provide assistance as needed. Provide paper and colored pencils and markers for students to draw their vehicles. Encourage groups to incorporate future-tense verbs into their discussion/presentation. Ask each group to present its vehicle and then the class can vote for the most likely/most fantastic vehicles.

11A.22 TEACHING TIP: Instruct students to not make their cards visible to their partners. They should take several minutes to complete the information gap activity before figuring out who will be, and who will not be, participating in the concert.

WILEY
PLUS

11A.22 INSTRUCTOR'S RESOURCES: Reproducible cards are available for use with Activity 11A.22 in your Instructor's Resources.

11A.22 ¿Qué harán esos famosos? En algunos meses, habrá un concierto en Lima, Perú, para promover el desarollo de medios de transporte más limpios. Trabaja con un/a compañero/a y completa el siguiente cuadro para determinar qué harán algunos hispanos famosos durante esas fechas. Cada uno/a de ustedes tiene sólo una parte de la información. Necesitan hacerse preguntas para determinar quiénes participarán y no participarán en el concierto.

Modelo: E1: *¿Qué hará Shakira?*
E2: *Llevará un vestido fabuloso.*
Conclusión lógica: Shakira participará en el concierto.

A	
Shakira	
Paulina Rubio	cantará con Enrique Iglesias.
Luis Miguel	
Pablo Montero	comprará un traje nuevo para el concierto.
Thalía	
Chayanne	irá a Machu Picchu cuando esté en Perú.
Enrique Iglesias	
Ricky Martin	
Marc Anthony	estará haciendo una película en Europa.
Chenoa (María Laura Corradini Falomir)	tendrá un concierto importante en Nueva York ese mismo día.
El Puma (José Luis Rodríguez)	

B	
Shakira	llevará un vestido fabuloso.
Paulina Rubio	
Luis Miguel	volará a Lima el día antes del concierto.
Pablo Montero	
Thalía	no querrá dejar a su bebé que ha empezado a caminar.
Chayanne	
Enrique Iglesias	escribirá una nueva canción para el concierto.
Ricky Martin	saldrá ese día para África con oficiales de las Naciones Unidas.
Marc Anthony	
Chenoa (María Laura Corradini Falomir)	
El Puma (José Luis Rodríguez)	su hija se casa el día del concierto

¿Quiénes participarán en el concierto?	¿Quiénes no participarán en el concierto?
Shakira	Thalía
Paulina Rubio	Ricky Martin
Luis Miguel	Chenoa
Pablo Montero	El Puma
Chayanne	Marc Anthony
Enrique Iglesias	

VÍVELO: LENGUA

Expressing probability in the present

In addition to expressing future actions, things that *will* happen, the future tense can also be used to express *probability* or *conjecture* in the present. Notice the variety of expressions in English that correspond to this use of the Spanish future tense.

¿No llegan todavía? Habrá mucho tráfico.	*They haven't arrived yet? There must be a lot of traffic.*
¿A qué hora saldrá el avión?	*I wonder what time the plane is leaving?*
¿Dónde estará la estación de trenes?	*I wonder where the train station is?*
Vosotros tendréis muchas maletas.	*You all probably have a lot of luggage.*
Es un viaje largo. Ellos querrán viajar en primera clase.	*It's a long trip. They probably want to travel in first class.*

11A.23 ¿Cómo respondes tú? De la lista a–f, indica cuál es la respuesta lógica para cada situación de 1–6, teniendo en cuenta que se usa el futuro para expresar probabilidad en el presente.

_b_ **1.** Alguien te dice que Juan sólo durmió cuatro horas anoche.

_d_ **2.** Alguien te pregunta qué hora es, pero no tienes reloj.

_a_ **3.** Un compañero de clase comenta que sus vecinos no tienen carro.

_f_ **4.** Una amiga te pregunta el precio de un vuelo de Bilbao a Málaga y le das el precio aproximado.

_e_ **5.** Tu mamá menciona que a tu prima le interesa estudiar la cultura inca.

_c_ **6.** Un turista te pregunta dónde se encuentra la estación de tren, pero no conoces bien la ciudad.

a. Tomarán el autobús al trabajo.

b. Hoy tendrá mucho sueño.

c. Estará cerca de la plaza central.

d. Serán las cuatro más o menos.

e. Querrá viajar al Perú.

f. Costará menos de 300€.

¡Conéctate!

The city of Medellín, Colombia has a unique form of transportation in their Metro Cable, a gondola type of train that crosses across the city above homes and buildings. Visit the Internet to find pictures and videos of this mode of transportation by running a search with the following key words: Metro Cable and Medellín. Open up the website http://www.metrodemedellin.gov.co/ to learn more details about the Metro Cable to fully appreciate what it has offered the city of Medellín. Share your impressions with your class.

Estructuras clave 2 The conditional

TEACHING TIP: Point out that context or the use of the appropriate subject pronouns should clear up any ambiguity between first- and third-person conditional forms.

TEACHING TIP: As you read through this description with students, write down the endings that verbs take (*–ía, –ías, –ía, –íamos, –íais, –ían*). Ask students questions such as *¿Montarías en una motocicleta? ¿Correrías un maratón?* or *¿Participarías en American Idol?*

Compare the nature of the action in the following questions, considering the action from the perspective of the speaker (the person asking the question):

What will you do to cut fuel consumption in the future?
What would you do to cut fuel consumption in the future?

In the first question, the person asking seems to take for granted that the person asked *will do* something to cut fuel consumption. In the second question, the action is more hypothetical; the person asking isn't taking for granted that the person asked is going to cut fuel consumption. Instead, the person asking the question wonders what the other *would do* if conditions were such that he/she were going to cut fuel consumption.

To talk about hypothetical actions happening under some condition, Spanish uses a verb form called, appropriately enough, the conditional. The conditional, generally translated as *would + verb,* is formed like the future tense by adding appropriate personal endings to the infinitive. As with the future, the endings are the same for **–ar, –er,** and **–ir** verbs. Note that the **yo** and the **él/ella/usted** forms are identical.

Yo	viajar**ía**		
Tú	viajar**ías**		
Él/Ella/Usted	viajar**ía**	por barco.	(___ *would travel by boat*).
Nosotros/as	viajar**íamos**		
Vosotros/as	viajar**íais**		
Ellos/Ellas/Ustedes	viajar**ían**		

Yo	recorrer**ía**		
Tú	recorrer**ías**		
Él/Ella/Usted	recorrer**ía**	la ciudad en autobús.	(___ *would tour the city*
Nosotros/as	recorrer**íamos**		*by bus*).
Vosotros/as	recorrer**íais**		
Ellos/Ellas/Ustedes	recorrer**ían**		

Yo	ir**ía**		
Tú	ir**ías**		
Él/Ella/Usted	ir**ía**	al aeropuerto.	(___ *would go to the*
Nosotros/as	ir**íamos**		*airport*).
Vosotros/as	ir**íais**		
Ellos/Ellas/Ustedes	ir**ían**		

Verbs that have irregular stems in the future have the same irregular stems in the conditional. The endings are the same as for the regular verbs.

caber:	**cabr-**	poder:	**podr-**	salir:	**saldr-**
decir:	**dir-**	poner:	**pondr-**	tener:	**tendr-**
haber:	**habr-**	querer:	**querr-**	valer:	**valdr-**
hacer:	**har-**	saber:	**sabr-**	venir:	**vendr-**

Con un millón de dólares…	*With a million dollars…*
yo **haría** un viaje a Australia.	*I would take a trip to Australia.*
tú **podrías** ayudar a mucha gente.	*you would be able to help many people.*
ellos **tendrían** un avión privado.	*they would have a private airplane.*

The conditional for **hay** is **habría.**

> En una ciudad grande, **habría** metro.
> Durante las vacaciones, **habría** muchos pasajeros en la estación de tren.

> *In a big city, there would be a subway.*
> *During vacation days, there would be many passengers at the train station.*

As noted, the usual English translation for the conditional is *would* + *verb* (what ever action the verb expresses) and it is mainly used to express hypothetical or probable/possible actions.

> Para ahorrar *(save)* dinero, ellos viajar**ían** en clase turista.
> Para pagar menos, yo comprar**ía** un billete de ida y vuelta.
> Ese avión tendr**ía** que hacer una escala en Chicago para escapar la tormenta.
> ¿Adónde ir**ías** en tus vacaciones ideales?

¡Ojo! In situations where you use *would* in English as an equivalent to *used to* to refer to habitual action in the past, remember to use the imperfect tense.

> Yo mont**aba** en bicicleta.
> Nosotros vol**ábamos** frecuentemente.
> Roberto ven**ía** a cenar todos los viernes.
> Ellos recorr**ían** la ciudad a pie todos los días.

11A.24 **Completar las oraciones.** Con un/a compañero/a de clase, indiquen cuál de estas es la frase más lógica para completar las oraciones. Luego, verifiquen sus respuestas con la clase.

a. hablarías con un agente de viajes.
b. harían un viaje en crucero.
c. irías al aeropuerto.
d. montaría en bicicleta.
e. necesitaría un pasaporte.
f. podríamos mirar el paisaje *(landscape)*.
g. tomarían el metro.
h. preferiría viajar en tren.

_e_ **1.** Para visitar un país extranjero, mi primo…

_g_ **2.** Para recorrer la Ciudad de Nueva York o Madrid, los turistas…

_a_ **3.** Para planear un viaje, tú…

_h_ **4.** En lugar de volar, yo…

_b_ **5.** Para visitar las islas del Caribe, mis padres…

_d_ **6.** Para hacer ejercicio, yo…

_c_ **7.** Para abordar un avión, tú…

_f_ **8.** Durante un viaje en carro, nosotros…

11A.25 **Las vacaciones de ensueño.** Entrevista a un/a compañero/a para determinar cómo serían sus vacaciones ideales. Luego, describe las vacaciones de tu compañero/a a la clase y escojan entre todos las vacaciones preferidas. Será necesario cambiar los verbos de las preguntas a la forma tú cuando hablas con tu compañero/a.

- ¿Adónde iría?
- ¿Por cuánto tiempo estaría allí?
- ¿Con quién pasaría las vacaciones?
- ¿Cómo viajaría a su lugar preferido?
- ¿Dónde se quedaría? (p.ej., un hotel, un apartamento, etc.)
- ¿Qué documentos necesitaría?
- ¿Qué ropa/zapatos/accesorios llevaría?
- ¿Qué haría durante las vacaciones?

11A.24 TEACHING TIP: Have students read a–h first so that they know what their options are as they read sentences 1–8.

11A.24 EXTENSION ACTIVITY: Have students write down five questions regarding whether or not their classmates would do something somewhat unusual (e.g. *¿Saldrías en un "reality show"?*). Then have students form groups of four. They should take turns asking each other their questions. When they are finished, they should share meaningful information with the class. If students need encouragement to share their statements, ask specific questions such as *¿Qué haría Jimmy?* or *¿Qué no haría Toron?*

11A.25 TEACHING TIP: Before students find a partner, ask them how they would change the questions to fit the *tú* form. Once students understand what changes need to be made, give them several minutes to interview a partner regarding their ideal vacations.

11A.25 EXTENSION ACTIVITY: When they have finished, you may want to assign their descriptions as homework. Have students write their partner's dream vacation without actually using their name in the description. For the next class, collect students' descriptions and tape them along the perimeter of the classroom. You should put a number on each description. Give the class several minutes to walk around the room to read the descriptions in order to figure out who is being described. On a sheet of paper, students should write their guesses next to the numbers. Afterwards, go over their answers.

Expressing courtesy

Because the conditional is used to express hypothetical or possible actions, it represents a more indirect means of communication than the present or the future. For that reason, the conditional can be used to make requests, recommendations, and invitations in a more courteous and formal manner. As you compare the following examples, note that a similar construction exists in English.

¿Puede pasarme el pan?	*Can you pass me the bread?*
¿Podría pasarme el pan?	*Would/Could you pass me the bread?*
¿Quieres ir al cine?	*Do you want to go to the movies?*
¿Te gustaría ir al cine?	*Would you like to go to the movies?*
Debemos visitar a tus padres.	*We must visit your parents.*
Deberíamos visitar a tus padres.	*We ought to/should visit your parents.*

11A.26 Situaciones. Escoge la forma de cortesía que corresponde a cada situación.

a. ¿Podría usted escribirme una carta de recomendación para la Facultad de Medicina?

b. Deberías hablar con la profesora de química si tienes problemas en la clase.

c. Perdón, ¿cerraría la ventana, por favor? Es que tengo frío.

d. ¿Les gustaría acompañarme al concierto de John Legend?

e. ¿Me darían $100 para comprar libros?

f. ¿Me traería una hamburguesa y una cerveza, por favor?

___f___ **1.** Hablas con un/a camarero/a en el restaurante.

___a___ **2.** Necesitas una carta de recomendación de un/a profesor/a.

___b___ **3.** Hablas con un amigo que no tiene buenas notas.

___d___ **4.** Quieres invitar a unos amigos a un concierto.

___e___ **5.** Hablas con tus padres cuando necesitas dinero rápidamente.

___c___ **6.** Hablas con una señora al lado de la ventana cuando tienes frío.

Expressing probability in the past

Just as the future tense can be used to express probability or conjecture in the present, the conditional can be used to express probability or conjecture in the past. Context will determine the meaning intended by the speaker.

¿A qué hora llegarían ellos?	*I wonder what time they arrived?*
¿Cuánto costaría esa bicicleta?	*I wonder how much that bike cost?*
El viaje duraría cinco horas.	*The trip probably took five hours.*
Tú estarías cansado después del viaje.	*You were probably tired after the trip.*

11A.27 ¿Probabilidad en el presente o el pasado? Con un/a compañero/a de clase, lean las siguientes oraciones e indiquen si expresan probabilidad en el presente o en el pasado.

> Modelo: Está lloviendo y de repente las luces de tu casa se apagan. Le comentas a tu compañero de casa: "Será la tormenta." o "¿Sería que no pagué la electridad?"
> *Será indica probabilidad en el presente.* (It must be the storm.)
> *Sería indica probabilidad en el pasado.* (Could it be that I didn't pay the electric bill?).

1. Estás en una fiesta el 31 de diciembre y de repente escuchas muchos gritos de felicidad y concluyes: "Será el Año Nuevo".

2. Acabas de llegar al aeropuerto y no sabes si puedes llegar a la estación de autobús a tiempo. Te preguntas: "¿Habrá otro autobús más tarde, por si acaso *(just in case)*?".

3. Tu amiga compró una computadora usada. Tú piensas: "No tendría suficiente dinero para comprar una computadora nueva".

4. Una noticia de la televisión dice que se vendieron muchos vehículos híbridos el año pasado. Tú concluyes: "La gente estaría preocupada por el precio de la gasolina".

5. Hay mucha congestión en el centro de la ciudad y tu conductor de taxi comenta: "Será el desfile de San Patricio".

11A.27 ANSWERS:
Probabilidad en el presente: 1, 2, 5; Probabilidad en el pasado: 3, 4

11A.27 TEACHING TIP: This is a difficult task. Before students decide whether the sentences express probability in the present or the past, have them read the sentences for clues as to whether they refer to the present or the past. Make sure to review the answers with the class.

Enlaces

11A.28 Enlaces. Determina el significado de las palabras o frases en negrita según el contexto de las oraciones. Escoge entre las siguientes opciones. Luego verifica tus respuestas con la clase.

a. *as*

b. *from*

c. *therefore*

1. __a__ La crisis económica de Estados Unidos tiene **como** víctima a los países pobres.

2. __c__ **Por lo tanto,** la organización humanitaria Oxfam pidió que la pobreza y la crisis de alimentos sean *(be)* temas prioritarios.

3. __b__ Los biocarburantes, obtenidos **a partir de** materias primas *(raw material)* vegetales, han causado fuertes subidas en los precios.

11A.29 ¿Puedes conectar las ideas? Conecta las ideas de las oraciones y los párrafos siguientes empleando la expresión correcta. Luego, verifica tus respuestas con un/a compañero/a de clase.

a. a partir de

b. como

c. por lo tanto

__b__ **1.** Los biocombustibles pueden sustituir el petróleo _____ fuente de energía.

__a__ **2.** _____ ahora, el costo de la comida seguirá subiendo y dañará *(will hurt)* el crecimiento económico mundial.

__c__ **3.** Los precios de los productos de consumo masivo han subido muchísimo, _____ ha habido violentas protestas en Haití.

11A.28 CULTURAL NOTE: In reference to the first sentence, you may want to share the popular saying in Latin America that states that when Uncle Sam gets the sniffles, Mexico catches a cold and the rest of Latin America gets pneumonia.

11A.29 TEACHING TIP: After completing this activity, have students go over their answers with a partner. When you do go over them as a class, have students hold up one finger to represent "a," two for "b" and three for "c." This way you will be able to get a sense of how well they understood the new words without putting students on the spot.

11A.29 EXTENSION ACTIVITY: Have students write three sentences, modeled after those in the previous two activities. When they finish, they should exchange their sentences with a partner and complete it.

11A.30 De la gasolina a los biocombustibles. Previamente leíste un artículo sobre la subida del precio de la gasolina. Ahora, leerás cómo la solución podría ser desastrosa también en "Todos contra los biocombustibles". Después de leer el artículo, indica con un/a compañero/a de clase si las oraciones a continuación son ciertas o falsas. Busquen información en el artículo que justifique sus respuestas.

Cierto	Falso	
☐	☑	**1.** La producción de biocombustibles afecta a los países pobres de una manera positiva.
☐	☑	**2.** El costo de la comida ha bajado debido a la producción de biocombustibles.
☑	☐	**3.** Los biocombustibles están hechos de plantas u otras materias vegetales.
☑	☐	**4.** Según varias organizaciones internacionales, el costo de la comida se considera un problema grave.
☑	☐	**5.** Los problemas económicos actuales se originaron en Estados Unidos.
☐	☑	**6.** Todos están a favor de la producción de biocombustibles.
☑	☐	**7.** Los países pobres pueden verse afectados negativamente por los cambios del clima.
☐	☑	**8.** La producción de biocombustibles no tiene ninguna consecuencia negativa.

Todos **contra** los biocombustibles

La energía del futuro

Se habla mucho en las noticias de la fabricación de biocombustibles como la fuente de energía del futuro. Sin embargo, la sustitución de petróleo por biocombustibles puede generar otros problemas. Según varios informes de la organización humanitaria Oxfam, el aumento del uso de biocombustibles podría tener consecuencias negativas para los países más pobres del planeta.

En primer lugar, los biocarburantes, obtenidos a partir de materias primas vegetales, elevan los precios de los alimentos. Por ejemplo, muchos biocombustibles se realizan con el cultivo del maíz, el arroz, el trigo, la caña de azúcar y el aceite de palma. De hecho, los precios de alimentos básicos como el trigo, el maíz y el arroz ya han aumentado en los últimos meses y el Banco Mundial alertó recientemente que el aumento de los precios podría hundir (plunge) aún más en la pobreza a 100 millones de habitantes en países con ingresos bajos. Esto puede provocar una escasez (scarcity) de alimentos para algunos de los países más pobres.

En segundo lugar, los altos precios de los alimentos y la escasez de alimentos hacen vulnerables a los países en vías de desarrollo. El auge (increase) de la producción de biocombustibles provocaría la explotación de estas poblaciones por parte de sus gobiernos y compañías internacionales, arrebatándoles (seizing) sus tierras y desplazando (displacing) a sus comunidades.

Los informes de Oxfam nos hacen reflexionar. ¿Es aceptable que la gente más pobre del planeta tenga que pagar por las emisiones altas o sea quien mantenga el estilo de vida de la gente que vive en países más desarrollados?

Perspectivas

11A.31 **¡Reacciona!**   En grupos de tres, determinen si están de acuerdo o no con las siguientes declaraciones. Luego, analicen sus respuestas como clase.

¿Estamos de acuerdo?

Sí   No

☐ ☐ **1.** Cualquier avance tecnológico será inútil *(useless)* si no encontramos formas limpias y seguras de producir energía.

☐ ☐ **2.** Hay un efecto dominó global con respecto a la solución de la crisis de energía. Lo que puede ser una solución para un país puede dañar a otro.

☐ ☐ **3.** Los países pobres del mundo están a la merced de *(at the mercy of)* los países ricos.

☐ ☐ **4.** El descubrimiento de fuentes de energía nuevas yace *(lies)* en los recursos inexplorados que se pueden encontrar en países pobres.

☐ ☐ **5.** Los estadounidenses tendrán que cambiar su modo de vida basado en la conveniencia para ser como la gente de otros países desarrollados.

☐ ☐ **6.** La energía nuclear será la solución de los problemas de energía del futuro.

☐ ☐ **7.** Explorar el océano en busca de petróleo sería la mejor solución para la crisis de energía.

☐ ☐ **8.** Los países en vías de desarrollo han contribuido a la crisis de energía tanto como los países desarrollados.

☐ ☐ **9.** La necesidad de encontrar nuevas fuentes de energía debe predominar sobre la protección del medio ambiente.

☐ ☐ **10.** La economía global quedará completamente destruida si no encontramos nuevas fuentes de energía.

Basándose en las respuestas, ¿tienen ustedes una perspectiva optimista o pesimista sobre la energía del futuro?

☐ optimista   ☐ pesimista

¿Qué piensa la clase en general?

11A.31 TEACHING TIP: Consider having students complete this activity on their own as homework. Once they have completed it, they can share their responses in groups of three and pursue further discussion. After groups have had ample time to talk about their responses, elicit responses from the class. A unique way of doing this would be to write *Estamos de acuerdo* on one side of the board and *No estamos de acuerdo* on the other side. Read each statement and have students physically move closer to the side that best represents their opinion. You may want to pause once in awhile and probe deeper into their responses.

Vocabulario: Investigación A

Vocabulario esencial

Sustantivos

el aeropuerto	airport
el boleto/ billete	ticket
el/la agente de viajes	travel agent
el avión	airplane
la autopista	highway
el barco	boat
la bicicleta	bicycle
la calle	street
el camión	truck
el carro/coche	car
la carretera	road
las cifras	numbers; figures
la ciudad	city
el cohete	rocket
el crucero	cruise ship
la desventaja	disadvantage
la estación de autobuses	bus station
el ferrocarril	train
el ingreso	income
la maleta	bag/luggage
el paisaje	landscape
el promedio	average
el tráfico	traffic
la vela	sail
la ventaja	advantage
el vuelo (de ida y vuelta)	(round trip) flight

Adjetivos

caro/a	expensive
corto/a	short
lento/a	slow
lleno/a	full
vacío/a	empty

Verbos

alcanzar	to reach
andar adelantado	to be fast
andar atrasado	to be slow
aprovechar	to take advantage of
caminar	to walk
cansarle a uno	to tire one
demorar(se)	to delay; to become delayed
dirigir(se)	to direct; to head for
facturar el equipaje	to check in luggage
hacer fila	to wait in line
hacer escala	to have a layover
hacer las maletas	to pack the bags
ir a pie	to go by foot
llevar a	to take to; to lead to
manejar/ conducir el carro	to drive the car
montar en bicicleta	to ride a bike
pasar por aduana	to go through customs
tener lugar	to take place
tener sueño	to be sleepy
volar	to fly

Otras palabras y expresiones

ajuste	adjustment
arrebatar	to seize
biocombustible	biofuel
caña de azúcar	sugar cane
combustible	fuel
crudo/a	raw
dañar	to damage
desplazar	to diplace
desviar	to deviate
escasez	scarcity
fatigar	to tire
felicidad	happiness
inalámbrico/a	wireless
inútil	useless
lejano	far
llantas	tires
materia prima	raw material
mirada	look
muro	wall
padecer	to suffer (an illness)
peinarse	to comb your hair
propósito	purpose
recibo	receipt
recorrer	to cover, travel
retrasarse	to run late
rueda	wheel
sondeo	survey
tarifa	fee
vapor	steam

Cognados

Review the cognates in *Adelante* and the false cognates in *¡Atención!*. For a complete list of cognates, see Appendix 4 on page 605.

¿Cómo influye la tecnología en una cultura?

TEACHING TIP: Invite students to take out any electronics they may have brought to class (e.g. cell phone, iPod, laptop, PDA, etc.). Use these items as a vehicle to speak about technology. Ask questions like *¿Quiénes tienen un celular? ¿Prefieren hablar por celular o mandar mensajes de texto? ¿Cuántas canciones tienen en su iPod? ¿Les gusta escuchar podcasts o prefieren escuchar música en sus iPods?* These items will help focus their attention on the themes for the *Investigación.* As students answer questions, make sure to follow up on their responses with questions such as, *¿Quién es la persona que manda muchos mensajes de texto? ¿Quién/es tiene/n un iPod? ¿Cómo se llama la persona que trajo su computadora portátil a clase?* Spend five minutes on these questions before directing their attention to the goals for the *Investigación.*

PRACTICING VOCABULARY: Pair students for this activity. Let them know that you will be giving them categories and they will have 30-45 seconds to add words from the list to their categories. The following are some categories that you may want to offer students: *Lo uso todos los días./Lo uso cada dos o tres días./Lo uso cada semana./Lo uso cada mes./No lo uso nunca.* When they have filled in their categories, ask them how many words/ items they had under each category.

In this **Investigación** you will learn:

▶ How to talk about various forms of technology

▶ To talk about the influence of technology on society

▶ To express personal opinions regarding technology

¿Cómo se puede hablar del impacto de la tecnología en los individuos y en la sociedad?

You can talk about the technology that you use.	Para mirar la televisión, ¿tienes cable o satélite? ¿Miras películas por cable o con un aparato de DVD? ¿Escuchas música en un tocacompactos o prefieres usar un reproductor de MP3?
You can talk about the influence of technology in your personal life.	¿Con qué frecuencia consultas la Internet? ¿Usas la Internet para tus estudios? ¿para comprar cosas? ¿Tienes tu propia página web? ¿Tienes una página en *MySpace* o en *Facebook*?
You can express your opinion about the use or abuse of technology.	¿Prefieres que tus amigos te hablen por teléfono o que te manden un mensaje de texto? ¿Te gusta que te regalen los aparatos más modernos? ¿Es bueno o malo que los niños pasen tanto tiempo expuestos a la nueva tecnología?

Adelante

¡Ya lo sabes! Las telecomunicaciones

el aparato/reproductor de DVD	el (reproductor) MP3
la batería	el satélite
el cable	el sistema de posicionamiento global (GPS)
el ciberespacio	el teléfono celular/el móvil
la computadora (portátil)	el tocacompactos
el control remoto/el telemando	el universo virtual
el correo electrónico	el videojuego
el disco compacto	
la fotocopiadora	ajustar
el impacto	consumir
la Internet	contactar
la máquina de fax	funcionar
la página web	mandar mensajes de texto
la realidad virtual	navegar por la Internet

11B.1 ¿Dónde se usa? Escucha las palabras e indica dónde se usan principalmente los aparatos/medios mencionados. Luego, verifica tus respuestas con un/a compañero/a de clase.

	En la casa	En la oficina	En todas partes
1.	☑	☐	☐
2.	☐	☑	☐
3.	☐	☐	☑
4.	☐	☐	☑
5.	☐	☐	☑
6.	☐	☑	☐
7.	☐	☐	☑
8.	☐	☐	☑

11B.2 ¿Cuál es la definición? Lee las palabras en la lista a–l. Luego, con un compañero de clase, lean las siguientes definiciones e indiquen qué palabra o expresión corresponde a la definición. ¡Ojo! No todas las palabras se usan. Verifiquen sus respuestas con la clase.

a. ajustar **e.** el control remoto **i.** el mensaje de texto
b. el satélite **f.** funcionar **j.** la página web
c. el cable **g.** el impacto **k.** el tocacompactos
d. contactar **h.** el MP3 **l.** el videojuego

_b_ **1.** El aparato que nos permite recibir programas de televisión de todas partes del mundo

_e_ **2.** Un aparato pequeño que usamos para cambiar los canales de la televisión

_g_ **3.** La palabra que significa una influencia importante o grande

_j_ **4.** Un documento en la Internet que tiene información específica

_d_ **5.** Un verbo que es sinónimo de *comunicar*

_i_ **6.** Una forma de comunicarse por escrito usando el teléfono celular

_a_ **7.** Sinónimo del verbo *cambiar*

_h_ **8.** Un aparato portátil que usamos para escuchar música que descargamos *(we download)* de la Internet

11B.3 ¿Para qué se usan? Escucha la función de varios aparatos o medios de comunicación y luego indica cuál o cuáles de la lista corresponde/n a esa función. Puedes usar las opciones más de una vez y puede haber uno o varios aparatos/medios que correspondan a la función. Luego, verifica tus respuestas con otros compañeros de clase.

a. el aparato de DVD **e.** el GPS **i.** el tocacompactos
b. la computadora portátil **f.** el MP3 **j.** el universo virtual
c. el satélite **g.** el control remoto **k.** la realidad virtual
d. el correo electrónico **h.** el mensaje de texto

1. _f_ _i_ _b_ _a_   **5.** _h_ ___ ___
2. _d_ ___ ___   **6.** _g_ ___ ___
3. _a_ _b_ ___   **7.** _b_ ___ ___
4. _c_ ___ ___   **8.** _e_ ___ ___

11B.3 TEACHING TIP: Ask questions like *¿Para qué se usa el aparato de DVD? ¿Para qué se usa el MP3?*, etc. Elicit answers from various students before having them do the activity.

TEACHING TIP: Use these words in as many real contextual situations as possible so that your students become comfortable with them. Although they are cognates, students will need to hear and have opportunities to use them before they can be expected to manipulate them with ease. Ask them questions such as, *¿Hay sido muy grande el impacto del celular? ¿Debemos limitar nuestro consumo de electricidad? ¿Cómo les gusta contactar a sus amigos, a sus profesores, a su familia?* As students share their answers, follow up with questions related to these answers. Make sure to use these words as often as possible in your question and answer sequences to provide students with the necessary input.

11B.1 AUDIO SCRIPT: 1. El aparato de DVD, 2. la fotocopiadora, 3. el MP3, 4. la computadora portátil, 5. el cable, 6. la máquina de fax, 7. el celular, 8. el videojuego portátil

11B.2 TEACHING TIP: Have students read through the vocabulary words (a–l) in pairs and offer each other definitions before reading the definitions provided (1–8).

11B.3 AUDIO SCRIPT: 1. Para escuchar música se usa... 2. Para comunicarse por escrito en la computadora se usa... 3. Para ver películas en DVD se usa... 4. Para que funcione el GPS en el carro se necesita... 5. Para comunicarse por celular sin hablar se usa... 6. Para cambiar el canal sin tocar el televisor se usa... 7. Para tomar apuntes en clase se usa... 8. Para llegar a un nuevo lugar sin perderse se usa...

11B.4 TEACHING TIP:
Have students prepare
their descriptions outside
of class. You may want to
encourage them to write
these on a notecard.
On the flipslide, they
should provide an image
representing the *aparato*
being described. To
maximize students' work,
invite them to stand up
and walk around the room
sharing their descriptions
with various classmates.

**11B.5 PRE-READING
ACTIVITY:** Write *Segunda
Vida* on the board. In
groups of three, have
students write down all
the ideas they associate
with *Second Life*. If some
students are unfamiliar
with *Second Life* it is
quite possible that some-
one else in the group will
be familiar with it. Have
students share their ideas
before beginning the
reading.

**11B.5 POST-READING
COMPREHENSION:** Ask
students to raise their
hand if they have an
avatar. Ask those students
to explain to the rest of
the class what an avatar
is in Spanish. Then, have
the class address the following questions 1) ¿Qué
es Second Life? 2) ¿Cuáles
son algunos aspectos
positivos de la realidad
virtual? 3) ¿Cuáles son
algunos peligros para el
usuario de la realidad
virtual?

11B.4   **¿Qué aparato es?**   Del vocabulario presentado en esta *Investigación,* escoge cuatro aparatos y prepara una breve descripción de cada uno. Trabaja con varios compañeros. Túrnense para leer las descripciones en voz alta mientras que los demás adivinan qué aparato es.

11B.5   **Universos virtuales.**   Con un/a compañero/a de clase, lee el artículo siguiente sobre los universos virtuales y específicamente *Second Life* de Linden Labs. Después de leer el artículo, escriban cinco preguntas sobre las ideas priniciplales para hacérselas a la clase.

¿Vida real o Segunda Vida?

Más de 170.000 personas llevan ya una segunda vida en la Internet Un nuevo fenómeno irrumpe *(is breaking out)* con fuerza en la Internet: la vida en los universos virtuales. En vez de crear sitios web, como la Internet, los arquitectos virtuales del Metaverso crean espacios virtuales 3D que pueden imitar con mucho realismo el mundo físico, o ser tan diferentes del "mundo real" como lo permita la imaginación de sus creadores. Ya hay más de 170,000 habitantes en un mundo digital creado por el proyecto Segunda Vida de Linden Labs.

Pienso que podemos asumir que antes de 2015, la tecnología de la realidad virtual (VR) permitirá experiencias completamente realistas en la práctica. Luego habrá realidad VR de inmersión completa con estímulo directo al cerebro *(brain)*: virtualidad real tan buena como el universo físico. Y, por supuesto, conservando la posibilidad para los usuarios *(users)* de hacer cosas que serían imposibles en la realidad física, por ejemplo volar *(to fly)* sobre las islas del Caribe como un pájaro *(bird)* o caminar en Marte sin traje espacial.

Esto será fenomenal, pero también generará frustración en los usuarios que pueden entonces pensar que la vida verdadera no es tan buena como vida virtual. ¿Hay peligro de que la gente se olvide del mundo verdadero y se escape a la realidad virtual?

No lo creo. Lo que creo que sucederá es que los mundos verdaderos y virtuales se combinarán, y que todos utilizaremos al Metaverso como parte de nuestra vida diaria. Más y más gente trabajará en mundos virtuales. En vez de horas de frustración en las congestiones de tráfico para llegar al trabajo, algunas personas harán negocios en una oficina virtual, quizás situada en el otro lado del mundo.

Ciencia ficción, todavía, pero ya a punto de convertirse en rutina, tal como podemos ver con los primeros pasos de *Second Life.* La tecnología VR se está desarrollando rápidamente y pronto veremos algunos progresos prometedores.

Bien dicho

La letra *rr*

The pronunciation associated with the letter **rr** in Spanish is a very difficult sound for many non-native speakers of Spanish to acquire. The double **rr** or "trill" is produced when the front part of the tongue touches the hard ridge behind the top teeth 2-5 times in rapid succession. Place your tongue rather loosely in that position and then push air against your tongue very forcefully. It may help to visualize shuffling a deck of cards or the spokes of a bicycle wheel or a plastic bag caught in the closed window of a moving car. It may also help to think about the sound that children make when imitating motors. The trill sound is always associated with the letter **rr** and is also produced when an **r** occurs at the beginning of a word or after an **l, n,** or **s,** as in the words **alrededor, enriquecer,** or **Israel.**

It is especially important to distinguish between the flap sound of the **r** and trill sound of the **rr** when they appear between vowels because this is where that distinction produces a difference in the meaning of the words. Compare the following:

pero *(but)*	**perro** *(dog)*
caro *(expensive)*	**carro** *(car)*
ahora *(now)*	**ahorra** *(he/she saves [money])*
cura *(m. priest, f. cure)*	**curra** *(he/she works* [Spain, colloquial]*)*

11B.6 Escucha e indica. Escucha las palabras y marca la casilla que corresponde al sonido que escuchas. Luego, verfica las respuestas con la clase.

	Flap (r)	Trill (rr)		Flap (r)	Trill (rr)
1.	☐	☑	4.	☐	☑
2.	☑	☐	5.	☑	☐
3.	☐	☑	6.	☑	☐

11B.7 ¡A practicar! Con un/a compañero/a, túrnense para pronunciar las oraciones. Luego, cambien de papel para tener la oportunidad de pronunciar todas las oraciones. Presten atención a la pronunciación de /r/ o /rr/.

1. Para cocinar hamburguesas necesitamos una parrilla.
2. Es necesario cerrar la puerta de arriba porque hace frío.
3. Roberto me regaló un reloj de oro cuando me gradué.
4. Las carreteras y los ferrocarriles son parte de la infraestructura.
5. Los programas de telerrealidad son muy populares recientemente.
6. Si uno quiere corregir errores, es preferible borrarlos primero.
7. Se ha perdido el control remoto del reproductor de DVD.
8. Enrique recorrió rápidamente la ruta que pasa por Torreón.

www ¡Conéctate!

Podcasts are a tremendous way of developing your listening skills in Spanish. While many news agencies post their podcasts on their websites, an even easier way of accessing a great variety of podcasts is through http://itunes.com. Download this program and click on "iTunes Latino." You will see a list of podcasts related to "Latino" topics. If you use this program to listen to music and podcasts, consider adding some of these podcasts to your list of uploads. Share a list of three podcasts that interest you with your classmates. If you own an iPod, iTouch or iPhone, you can physically show your class your new uploads.

TEACHING TIP: Let students know that this is a tough pronunciation point for many non-native speakers and that they should do the best they can.

11B.6 AUDIO SCRIPT: 1. carro 2. caro 3. rápido 4. ahorra 5. ahora 6. trabajo

11B.6 TEACHING TIP: By focusing on recognition, students have an opportunity to become more comfortable with the "r" and "rr" sounds. This will help as they become more conscientious about modeling more accurate pronunciation.

11B.7 TEACHING TIP: A popular tongue twister that you can practice with students is the following: *"Erre con erre cigarro, erre con erre barril, rápido corren los carros cargados de azúcar, sobre los rieles del ferrocarril."* There are several versions of this *trabalenguas.* Write this one or another you know on the board and practice it with students.

CONÉCTATE: If you have an iPod, upload some of these podcasts to share with your students as well.

Palabras clave 1 La tecnología en casa

VOCABULARY PRACTICE: Direct students' attention to the drawing containing the new vocabulary. Make sure to provide students with as much comprehensible input as possible, that is, language a little bit above their level. Provoke as much dialogue based on these drawings as possible so as to expose students to the new vocabulary in a way that invites them to begin using it.

TEACHING TIP: Provide as much input around these verbs as possible. Begin by telling them a story (fictitious or not) about yourself, such as: *Acabo de conseguir cable para mi casa. Espero poder grabar muchos programas en TiVo.* And immediately follow up with questions for them, such as: *¿Ustedes graban programas de la televisión?* Make sure to offer these comprehension checks to ensure that students are indeed understanding the new vocabulary.

afuera

Descarga su música favorita de iTunes.

adentro

Envía mensajes a sus familiares por correo electrónico.

el usuario

la impresora

el timbre (del teléfono)

acabar	Ay, esta película es interminable. ¿Cuándo se acaba?
acabar de	Mis padres están contentos porque acaban de comprar un aparato de DVD nuevo.
andar bien	La fotocopiadora nueva anda bien. No hemos tenido ningún problema con ella.
andar mal	La computadora anda mal. Es necesario repararla.
avisar	La semana pasada pedimos servicio de satélite y nos van a avisar cuando puedan venir a instalarlo.
borrar	Después de escuchar los mensajes en el contestador automático, yo los borro.
descargar	Sólo descarga música que ha comprado.
dejar	No tengo mi celular hoy porque lo dejé en la casa de mi novio.
dejar que	Para limitar el acceso a la Internet, la señora Pacheco sólo deja que sus hijos pasen una hora a diario en la computadora.
esperar	Tenemos muchas ganas de comprar una computadora nueva. Esperamos comprarla el próximo mes.
grabar	Si no vas a estar en casa, puedes grabar tus programas favoritos en videocasete o en TiVo.
hacer falta	Nuestra máquina de fax es muy antigua. Hace falta comprar una nueva.
soltar (o → ue)	Cuando Alberto soltó el control remoto, cayó al piso y se rompió.
sonar (o → ue)	Cuando suena mi celular toca mi canción favorita en vez del *(instead of)* timbre normal.

TEACHING TIP: Write the following English verbs on 3 x 5 cards of a certain color: to record, to leave, to allow, to inform, to hope, to end/terminate/finish, to erase, to work well, to work poorly/not to work, to have just done (something). On another set of cards of a different color, write the corresponding Spanish infinitives from *Palabras clave*. Distribute the English words to half the class and the Spanish words to the other half of the class. Tell students to pair up for the next activity based on one's Spanish word matching up with the other's English equivalent.

11B.8 **¿Cierto o falso?** Con un/a compañero/a de clase, lean los enunciados siguientes. Luego, indiquen si son ciertos o falsos. Si es falso, corrijan la información. Verifiquen sus respuestas con la clase.

Cierto	Falso	
☑	☐	**1.** Es necesario avisar a nuestros jefes cuando estamos enfermos.
☐	☑	**2.** Es posible grabar programas en la fotocopiadora.
☑	☐	**3.** Una persona que no quiere trabajar es perezosa.
☐	☑	**4.** Una actividad fácil requiere mucho esfuerzo.
☑	☐	**5.** Si la impresora hace sonidos anormales, anda mal.
☐	☑	**6.** Borramos el videocasete antes de ver la película o el programa.
☑	☐	**7.** Los aparatos portátiles, como un MP3 o un tocacompactos normalmente necesitan baterías para funcionar.
☐	☑	**8.** Para charlar con otra persona, es necesario tener una impresora.

11B.8 EXTENSION ACTIVITY: Following these examples, have students write three sentences to share with their partner.

11B.8 ANSWERS: Cierto: 1, 3, 5, 7; Falso: 2 (en el aparato de DVD/ la videocasetera), 4 (requiere poco esfuerzo), 6 (después de ver la película o el programa), 8 (un teléfono)

11B.9 PREPARATION: In preparation for this activity, have students develop short descriptions, or definitions, of the words (a–i) with a partner.

11B.9 AUDIO SCRIPT: 1. El opuesto de adentro. 2. Este verbo es sinónimo de hablar. 3. El sonido que se oye cuando suena el teléfono. 4. Esta expresión indica que alguien no tiene algo que necesita. 5. Este verbo significa permitir. 6. La cosa que hace funcionar las computadoras portátiles y los celulares sin electricidad.

11B.10 TEACHING TIP: On the board, write *verb, noun,* and *adjective.* Have students read through the paragraph and make note of which one each space calls for. Then, have them read through it again and identify the words from the bank to best complete the paragraph.

11B.11 TEACHING TIP: Allow students to complete task and tally results and go over reasons for choices.

11B.12 TEACHING TIP: On the board or an overhead transparency, make a table in which you write down what students share. After they have shared several things, have them read the article in groups. As they read, they should make note of additional pros and cons mentioned in the article as well as those mentioned by the class.

11B.9 **¿Cuál es la palabra?**   Escucha las definiciones e indica cuál es la palabra que corresponde a la definición. Luego, verifica tus respuestas con la clase.

a. hacer falta   **d.** el timbre   **g.** soltar
b. la batería   **e.** dejar   **h.** esperar
c. charlar   **f.** después   **i.** afuera

___i___ **1.**   ___d___ **3.**   ___e___ **5.**

___c___ **2.**   ___a___ **4.**   ___b___ **6.**

11B.10 **Completa los párrafos.**   Con un/a compañero/a, estudien los párrafos a continuación y llenen los espacios con las palabras o expresiones de la lista. Presten mucha atención al contexto. Luego, verifiquen sus respuestas con otros compañeros de clase.

anda	con poco esfuerzo	hacen falta
perezosos	borra	batería
charlar	dejan	suena
usuarios		

Cuando 1) _____suena_____ el teléfono, lo contesto y saludo a la persona que me llama. Después de 2) _____charlar_____ por un rato, nos despedimos.

La tecnología moderna puede ser muy complicada y algunos 3) _____usuarios_____ se confunden cuando intentan instalar un aparato nuevo. En mi opinión, 4) _____hacen falta_____ aparatos más sencillos *(simple)* que se puedan conectar y programar 5) ____con poco esfuerzo____.

Parece que la computadora portátil no 6) _____anda_____ bien. Creo que 7) _____anda_____ mal porque la 8) _____batería_____ va a acabarse dentro de poco. Es necesario terminar el documento rápido antes de que se apague la computadora.

11B.11 **¿Cuál es el más importante?**   Habla con dos compañeros y ordenen de 1–6 los aparatos siguientes según su importancia o utilidad. Expliquen sus respuestas y apunten las razones. Comparen su lista con la de otros tres grupos. ¿Son semejantes o diferentes? Apunta las conclusiones en tu **Retrato de la clase.**

_____ el satélite   La razón:

_____ el teléfono celular   La razón:

_____ la computadora portátil   La razón:

_____ el tocacompactos   La razón:

_____ el aparato de DVD   La razón:

_____ el control remoto   La razón:

_____ los universos virtuales   La razón:

_____ otro:_____   La razón:

Retrato de la clase: Según la clase, _____, _____ y _____ son los aparatos más útiles porque…. _____ es el menos útil porque…

11B.12 **Las ventajas y desventajas de la tecnología.**   En grupos de tres, escriban una lista de las ventajas y desventajas del uso de la tecnología. Luego, compartan su lista con la clase y apunten los resultados en su **Retrato de la clase.** Al leer el siguiente artículo, decidan si las ideas mencionadas por la clase corresponden o no con la información del artículo.

Retrato de la clase: Según la clase, _____, _____ y _____ son ventajas de la tecnología mientras que _____, _____ y _____ son desventajas de la tecnología. En general, las ideas mencionadas por la clase corresponden/no corresponden a la información del artículo.

Tecnochicos: ¿Qué significa crecer con las nuevas tecnologías?

Un estudio reciente indica que buena parte de los adolescentes pasan más de seis horas diarias expuestos a las nuevas tecnologías: celulares, mensajes de texto, Internet, videojuegos, reproductores de MP3 y el programa de Linden Labs, La Segunda Vida. Y que el tiempo de exposición a ellas sigue aumentando en relación directa al grado de sofisticación que alcanzan los aparatos. A la luz del fenómeno, padres, profesores y especialistas se preguntan si es bueno poner límites al uso de los nuevos aparatos. Y crecen (grow) las advertencias (warnings) sobre los problemas asociados con su abuso, tales como la obesidad infantil, determinados problemas neurológicos o la tendencia al aislamiento (isolation).

Para Cecilia, una madre de Buenos Aires, el problema es bien concreto. Entiende que cada día le es más difícil captar la atención de su hijo Pedro (12), siempre dispersa entre los videojuegos, Internet y el moderno aparato donde reproduce archivos de MP3. A veces hasta se sorprende de ver a su hijo chateando con compañeros con los que se verá en unas pocas horas. ¿Es para preocuparse o es solamente una nueva forma de relacionarse con la tecnología que tienen los chicos?

Por una parte, unos neurólogos argentinos indican que la necesidad de procesar demasiada información puede llevar a déficits de atención, los cuales pueden causar ansiedad, estrés y depresión. El abuso de videojuegos, por ejemplo, puede afectar también las relaciones con amigos y familiares. Por otra parte, pueden facilitar la rapidez en la lectura, ver imágenes en espacios tridimensionales y seguir varias situaciones a la vez. También pueden estimular los procesos de pensamiento, la habilidad para tomar decisiones y la creatividad.

Para la psicóloga argentina María Stoika "todos estos nuevos elementos son muy útiles siempre y cuando se los sepa utilizar. Si se los usa de una forma abusiva las consecuencias pueden ser absolutamente negativas para la salud física, psíquica, emocional y afectiva". La especialista cree que los padres tienen que tener un rol muy activo en la elección de los medios que utilicen los hijos y en su control. En todo caso, el secreto es lograr un equilibrio entre el uso de celulares, computadoras y videojuegos, y la actividad física y el encuentro real con los amigos y la familia.

A pesar de ser un chico con apenas 12 años, su gran pasión es la tecnología. Se devora las revistas que hablan de lo último en este campo y su preferida es "PC magazine", porque según él, ahí aprende sobre lo que está de moda, el precio de los productos y sobre todo las funciones que tienen los artículos.

11B.13 **¿Qué comprendiste de la lectura?** Después de leer el artículo que aparece arriba, "Tecnochicos: ¿Qué significa crecer con las nuevas tecnologías?", indica si estos enunciados son ciertos o falsos. Después, corrige los enunciados falsos. Luego, verifica tus respuestas con la clase.

11B.13 ANSWERS: Cierto: 2, 3, 6. Falso: 1. más de seis horas diarias, 4. pueden facilitar la rapidez en la lectura, 5. pueden estimular la creatividad

	Cierto	Falso			Cierto	Falso
1.	☐	☑		4.	☐	☑
2.	☑	☐		5.	☐	☑
3.	☑	☐		6.	☑	☐

1. Los adolescentes pasan solamente tres horas diarias expuestos a las nuevas tecnologías.
2. El tiempo de exposición a las nuevas tecnologías aumenta en relación directa con su grado de sofisticación.
3. El abuso de las nuevas tecnologías puede llevar a problemas físicos, como la obesidad.
4. Los videojuegos no afectan la habilidad de leer.
5. Los videojuegos no son creativos.
6. Los videojuegos pueden desarrollar la capacidad para ver imágenes tridimensionales.

VÍVELO: CULTURA

El uso de la Internet por hispanohablantes en diferentes países

País	Número de usuarios	% de la población	Aumento del uso (2000-2008)
Argentina	20.000.000	49,4%	700,0%
Bolivia	1.000.000	10,5%	733,3%
Chile	8.368.719	50,9%	376,2%
Colombia	13.745.000	30,5%	1.465,6%
Costa Rica	1.500.000	35,7%	500.0%
Cuba	1.310.000	11,5%	2.083,3%
Ecuador	1.759.500	12,3%	877,5%
El Salvador	763.000	10,8%	1.087,0%
España	27.028.934	66,8%	114,1%
Guatemala	1.320.000	10,2%	1.930,8%
Honduras	424.200	5,6%	960,5%
México	23.874.500	21,7%	780,2%
Nicaragua	155.000	2,7%	210,0%
Panamá	745.300	22,5%	1.556,2%
Paraguay	530.000	7,8%	2.551,0%
Perú	7.636.400	26,2%	205,5%
Puerto Rico	1.000.000	25,3%	400,0%
República Dominicana	3.000.000	31,6%	5.354,5%
Uruguay	1.100.000	31,6%	197,3%
Venezuela	6.723.616	25,5%	607,7%

11B.14 El uso de la Internet en los países hispanohablantes. Mira el cuadro de *Vívelo: Cultura* y contesta las preguntas. Luego, compara tus respuestas con las de otros estudiantes de la clase.

1. ¿Qué país tiene el mayor/menor número de usuarios de la Internet?
2. ¿En qué país representan los usarios de la Internet el mayor/menor porcentaje (%) de la población?
3. ¿En qué país ha aumentado más/menos el número de usarios de la Internet?
4. ¿A qué conclusiones generales puedes llegar según los datos?

¡Atención!

Alterar	means *to alter* as in **cambiar,** but it also means to evoke negative emotions as *to upset, to anger, to disturb, to irritate.* El abuso de videojuegos puede alterar la personalidad de algunos niños. Marcos está alterado porque alguien le robó el MP3.
Cargar	means *to charge* as when one puts energy into a battery. It also means *to charge* in the sense of using one's credit card. In other contexts it means *to carry* (a load) as when one carries something heavy. To express *to charge* in the sense of selling something at a specific price, use the verb **cobrar.** Después de usar el teléfono celular, es necesario cargar la batería. — ¿Cuánto te cobraron por ese tocacompactos? — Pagué 100 dólares. Tendré que cargar la computadora nueva a mi tarjeta de crédito. Los estudiantes siempre cargan muchas cosas en su mochila.
Marcar	means *to mark* as when indicating something or putting a mark or sign next to it. It also means *to score* when referring to points in a game. When it refers to the telephone, it means *to dial.* En caso de emergencia, en Estados Unidos se marca el 911. El equipo América de Cali marcó cuatro goles en el partido contra el Real Cartagena. Deben marcar la respuesta correcta con una X.
Pulsar	means *to throb, beat, pulsate.* In the context of the telephone or computer, it means *to press, to tap.* In addition, it can be a synonym for **tocar** when referring to musical instruments. Cuando usas el cajero automático, es necesario pulsar los números de tu contraseña (*password*). Carlos Santana pulsó las cuerdas de su guitarra para ajustarlas. Se creó un cuestionario para pulsar las opinones del público.

11B.15 Completa la oración. Completa cada oración con la palabra correcta de la lista que aparece a continuación. Luego, verifica tus respuestas con la clase.

alterar	marcar
alterado	pulsó
carga	pulsar
cobrar	

1. Paco nunca paga con cheque. Él siempre ___carga___ todo a su tarjeta Visa.

2. Si programas tu teléfono celular, no tienes que ___marcar___ el número entero sino ___pulsar___ un sólo botón.

3. La pianista ___pulsó___ las teclas (*keys*) del piano antes de comenzar a tocar.

4. El secretario está ___alterado___ hoy porque la impresora no anda bien.

5. ¿Sabes cuánto piensan ___cobrar___ por el nuevo iPhone?

¡ATENCIÓN!: Ask students questions around the verbs *cargar* and *alterar,* such as *¿Cargan las baterías de sus celulares todos los días?, ¿Se alteran cuando no tienen sus celulares a la mano?* Draw attention to the meanings associated with these words so that students get a better feel for their usage.

11B.15 TEACHING TIP: Before going over this exercise as a class, ask students to share their answers with a partner. They should make sure that they are in agreement. This means that they will have to explain to one another why they chose the words they did. This interaction will help them better understand these words.

11B.16 ¿Está bien dicho? Indica si los siguientes enunciados están bien dichos o no y corrige los errores. Luego, verifica las respuestas con la clase.

Sí	No	
☐	☑	**1.** En esa tienda cargan mucho por arreglar computadoras portátiles.
☑	☐	**2.** Cuando usas el cajero automático (ATM), es necesario marcar los números de tu contraseña.
☑	☐	**3.** La mochila de Anita pesa (weighs) mucho porque ella carga muchos libros.
☑	☐	**4.** La Internet ha alterado mucho la manera de buscar información.
☐	☑	**5.** Los padres están alterados cuando los hijos sacan buenas notas.

VÍVELO: LENGUA

Making formal commands (Review)

You learned how to construct formal commands in *Capítulo 6*. The ability to identify the meaning that corresponds to each irregular command form is crucial for comprehension of advanced structures in Spanish. For example, **haga** comes from the verb **hacer** which means *to make* or *to do*. Do you remember the infinitive or the meaning of these command forms: **tenga, vaya, ponga, vuelva, salga** and **acuéstese?** If you do, you may have little problem understanding the meaning of verbs in the Spanish subjunctive, a sophisticated grammar structure.

haga	make/do	Sr. Smith, haga la tarea.
tenga	have	Tengan un buen fin de semana.
vaya	go	Vaya a preguntarle al médico.
ponga	put	No ponga el vaso ahí.
vuelva	return	No vuelva a llamar.
salga	leave	Salga de aquí, señor.
acuéstese	go to bed	Acuéstese en su cama ahora mismo.

DICHOS

Rápido como tren expreso.
Para todo hay remedio, menos para la muerte.

Lo más nuevo y completo pronto se torna obsoleto.
Compra lo que no te hace falta y no tendrás lo que te haga falta.

Fast as an express train.
Everything can be fixed, except death.

The newest and most complete things soon become obsolete.
Buy what you don't need and soon you won't have what you need.

Estructuras clave 1 The present subjunctive

WILEY PLUS
Go to *WileyPLUS* and review the tutorial for this grammar point.

The Spanish subjunctive is a structure that typically presents challenges for native English speakers, and one you will surely study more in depth as you continue your Spanish studies beyond the beginning stage. Our primary goal with the subjunctive in *¡Vívelo!* is to help you become familiar with subjunctive forms so that you can better understand the Spanish you hear and read.

The forms of the present subjunctive are the same forms you have used to make formal commands, so they're not really "new" to you. The important thing to remember in order to understand what's being said or what you read is the meaning behind the verbs. For example, in **Quiero que ellas vengan a mi fiesta**, the verb after the **que** stems from **venir**. (It is the same as the affirmative formal command form for *to come*, as in *"Come here."*) If you understand that the verb stems from the infinitive **venir** meaning *to come*, then you will gain succesful comprehension of the sentence, *"I want them to come to my party."* A more literal translation would be *I want that they come to my party*.

To test this strategy, see if you can select the best responses to the following questions. Remember, focus on the meaning of the verbs.

What would a teacher say to his/her students?
    a. No es necesario que ustedes hagan su tarea.
    b. Prefiero que ustedes no escuchen música en sus aparatos MP3 en la clase.
    c. Quiero que todos se copien de sus compañeros en el examen.
    d. Es importante que ustedes miren mucha televisión.

If you selected (b), you are correct! Note the verbs after the **que** in each sentence: **hagan, escuchen, copien** and **miren.** Did you recognize the meaning of each of these verbs?

Infinitive		Meaning
hagan	hacer	*make/ do*
escuchen	escuchar	*listen*
copien	copiar	*copy*
miren	mirar	*look/ watch*

Now, reread the sentences once more with this information in mind. Did your comprehension improve or did you understand just as much the first time around?

Try another example. Which of the following sentences best describes your ideal home?
    a. Yo quiero una casa que tenga 100 cuartos.
    b. Prefiero un hogar que tenga vista al mar.
    c. Deseo un apartamento que esté situado en el centro de una ciudad grande, como Nueva York, San Francisco, Chicago o París.
    d. Prefiero una casa que esté en las montañas.

If you were able to process the meaning of these sentences, then you are able to recognize and understand the subjunctive in Spanish.

The subjunctive verb usually occurs in a dependent clause introduced by **que,** which corresponds to *that* in English and functions to connect two clauses, an independent (or main) clause and a subordinate (or dependent) clause. Remember, if you know the meaning of the verbs, you should be able to process the meaning of a sentence. Identify the meaning of each of the verbs in bold type below. Then read each sentence and confirm its meaning with a classmate.

> Bill Gates **espera** que la compañía Apple no **invente** más tecnología académica.
> Linden Labs **duda** que los universos virtuales **desaparezcan.**
> Es posible que la vida real **sea** más aburrida que la vida virtual.
> Deseamos que la tecnología no **dependa** de la electricidad en el futuro.

WILEY PLUS
You will find PowerPoint presentations for use with *Estructuras clave* in *WileyPLUS*.

Most first and second year textbooks attempt to teach students how and when to produce the subjunctive, but in reality students need a great deal of proficiency to successfully produce the subjunctive. Instead of spending time learning the grammatical concepts behind the subjunctive use, this book will focus on comprehension of the subjunctive, a much more realistic goal at this early level. Increasing comprehension will lead to more language development, which will increase language proficiency. Again, the goal is not for students to produce the subjunctive spontaneously, but to gain a measure of comfort with it. This will indeed help them as they become reintroduced to the concept in subsequent courses.

11B.17 TEACHING TIP: Remind students that the present tense can function to describe future action, depending on the context. This is the case in both the indicative and the subjunctive. In the context of these sentences, some imply future action. Make sure students correctly understand the sentences. Here they are loosely translated: Bill Gates hopes that Apple will not invent additional academic technology. / Linden Labs doubts that virtual realities will disappear. / It is possible that real life is more boring than virtual realities. / We hope that technology will not depend on electricity in the future.

11B.17 TEACHING TIP:
Have students share their
answers. As they share
them, point out that they
are using the subjunctive.
Follow up with state-
ments that they should
complete, such as: *Prefiero una casa que tenga...,
Deseo un apartamento
que esté en...* Their task
is to understand the
subjunctive phrase and
finish the sentences ac-
cording to their personal
opinions. Remind them
that they have already
taken the first step with
the subjunctive, and
that is recognition of it
(Standards: Communica-
tion/Interpretive Mode).

11B.17 TEACHING TIP:
Follow up by asking
students why these
sentences were *lógico* or
ilógico.

11B.18 TEACHING TIP:
Take advantage of all of
the input offered through
these response possi-
bilities through follow-up
questions such as: *¿Por
qué es bueno que digas
la verdad? ¿Por qué es
malo querer a un hombre
que use drogas?* etc. Draw
attention to the form of
the subjunctive in your
questions.

11B.17 **¿Lógico o ilógico?** En grupos de tres, lean las siguientes declaraciones e indiquen si son lógicas o ilógicas. Luego, verifiquen sus respuestas con la clase.

Lógico Ilógico

☐ ☑ **1.** A los profesores les gusta que los estudiantes **manden** mensajes de texto durante la clase.

☑ ☐ **2.** Es posible que **haya** un cibercafé en el centro estudiantil de esta universidad.

☐ ☑ **3.** No es necesario que **carguemos** la batería del celular frecuentemente.

☐ ☑ **4.** Es probable que **compres** una videocasetera para ver películas en casa.

☑ ☐ **5.** No me sorprende que los estudiantes **escuchen** música en MP3 cuando caminan a clase.

☑ ☐ **6.** Te alegras de que tus amigos te **escriban** por correo electrónico.

☐ ☑ **7.** Los médicos recomiendan que los niños **jueguen** videojuegos seis horas diarias.

☑ ☐ **8.** Los padres prefieren que sus hijos **tengan** buenas relaciones con amigos y familiares.

11B.18 **¿Qué dicen estas personas?** Para cada situación, indica cuál es la opción más lógica. Luego, verifica tus respuestas con las de otros compañeros/as de para determinar cuáles son las respuestas más populares.

1. ¿Qué le dice un padre a su hija de 16 años?
   a. Recomiendo que hables por teléfono celular cuando manejas.
   b. Te pido que vuelvas a casa a las tres de la mañana.
   (c.) Es necesario que vayas a la escuela todos los días.
   d. Me alegro de que salgas con un hombre de 26 años.

2. ¿Qué le dice una médica a una mujer que va a tener un bebé?
   a. Es bueno que usted fume.
   (b.) Me opongo a que usted beba alcohol.
   c. No es importante que usted haga ejercicio.
   d. No recomiendo que usted coma frutas y vegetales.

3. ¿Qué le dice un agente de viajes a una pareja que va a Uruguay?
   (a.) Sugiero que ustedes obtengan el pasaporte lo más pronto posible.
   b. Es lógico que lleven mucho dinero en efectivo *(cash)*.
   c. Espero que ustedes no saquen muchas fotos.
   d. Insisto en que ustedes no recorran la ciudad de Montevideo.

4. ¿Qué le dice una pareja a unos vecinos *(neighbors)* nuevos?
   a. Aconsejamos que ustedes organicen muchas fiestas ruidosas *(noisy)*.
   (b.) Deseamos que vengan a cenar la semana próxima.
   c. No permitimos que sus hijos jueguen con los nuestros.
   d. Es ridículo que ustedes cuiden *(take care of)* el jardín de su casa.

5. ¿Qué le dice una mujer a una empleada de Match.com?
   a. Busco un hombre que sea feo *(ugly)*.
   b. Quiero un hombre que use drogas.
   c. Espero encontrar un hombre que esté casado.
   (d.) Deseo conocer a un hombre que tenga un trabajo estable.

6. ¿Qué le dice un cliente a un mesero en un restaurante?
   a. No es importante que usted sirva pronto la comida.
   b. No quiero que usted me traiga un vaso de agua.
   (c.) Recomiéndeme un plato que a usted le guste.
   d. Es ridículo que usted limpie la mesa.

7. ¿Qué le dice un empleado de una agencia de colocación *(placement)* a un estudiante universitario que se prepara para su primera entrevista?

a. Está bien que usted mienta *(lie)* acerca de su experiencia y habilidades.

b. Sugiero que usted no haga ninguna pregunta.

c. Es mejor que usted llegue tarde a la entrevista.

(d.) Aconsejo que se ponga un traje para la entrevista.

8. ¿Qué le dice una abuela a su nieto de 5 años?

(a.) Es bueno que tú digas la verdad.

b. Insisto en que tú interrumpas a los adultos cuando hablan.

c. Me gusta que mires películas que tengan mucha violencia.

d. Espero que duermas solamente seis horas cada noche.

11B.19 Busca la cláusula lógica. Busca la cláusula dependiente que mejor complete cada oración. Luego, verifica tus respuestas con un/a compañero/a de clase.

___e___ **1.** Es importante que…

___b___ **2.** El cable no anda bien. Espero que…

___c___ **3.** Los músicos se oponen a que…

___d___ **4.** La profesora insiste en que…

___a___ **5.** Para su cumpleaños, muchos adolescentes piden que…

___f___ **6.** Preferimos que la vida virtual…

a. … sus padres les compren un teléfono celular.

b. … un empleado de la compañía venga a repararlo pronto.

c. … el público grabe música sin pagar.

d. … no traigamos los MP3 a clase.

e. … los niños no pasen muchas horas en la computadora.

f. … no refleje la realidad.

11B.19 TEACHING TIP: Let students know that although some clauses could have more than one answer, ultimately each phrase (a-f) will fit with one of the beginning sentences.

Enlaces

11B.20 Enlaces. Determina el significado de las palabras o frases en negrita de acuerdo al contexto de las oraciones. Escoge de las siguientes opciones. Luego, verifica tus respuestas con la clase.

a. consequently   **b.** it so happens/ turns out that   **c.** on the other hand

___a___ **1.** Para muchas personas, la Internet es su única fuente de información. **Por consiguiente**, no reciben información de diferentes perspectivas.

___c___ **2.** El correo electrónico puede ser una forma de comunicación impersonal. **Por otra parte**, uno se puede comunicar más rápidamente por correo electrónico.

___b___ **3. Resulta que** una de las consecuencias de la tecnología es que la gente tiene que trabajar más.

11B.21 ¿Puedes conectar las ideas? Conecta las ideas en las oraciones y párrafos siguientes empleando la expresión apropiada. Luego, verifica tus respuestas con otro compañero de clase.

a. por consiguiente   **b.** por otra parte   **c.** resulta que

___c___ **1.** _____ el deseo de obtener la tecnología más moderna fomenta *(encourages)* el materialismo.

___a___ **2.** Debido a la tecnología, la vida hoy en día es más sedentaria. _____ la obesidad es una gran preocupación.

___b___ **3.** Muchas personas creen que la tecnología simplifica la vida, pero _____ hay personas que creen que la tecnología complica la vida.

11B.20 TEACHING TIP: Have students share their answers with a partner before going over them as a class. When you do go over them as a class, have students hold up one finger to represent "a," two for "b" and three for "c." This way you will be able to get a sense of how well they understood the new words without putting students on the spot.

11B.21 EXTENSION ACTIVITY: Have students write three sentences, modeled after those in the previous two activities. Once they finish, they should exchange their sentences with a partner and complete it.

FUNCTIONAL OUTCOMES:
The central question that frames this *Investigación* is *"¿Cómo se puede hablar del impacto de la tecnología en los individuos y en la sociedad?"* Explore whether students can now address this question and how they would go about it. Have them review the chart on the first page of this *Investigación*.

NOTE: In this *Investigación*, we move from students' personal experience with techology in *Contextos* into the exploration of a Hispanic perspective in *Perspectivas*.

11B.22 TEACHING TIP:
You could have students either read or complete this activity on their own. Another possibility would be to read each sentence and add more input. While you are doing this, you will get a better sense of students' comprehension, and be giving them time to choose an answer. Possible additional input to a sentence like *"La tecnología me hace más materialista."* might be *"Siempre quiero cosas nuevas y busco en la Internet qué cosas hay para comprar."* To get the final results from a class, ask them how many scored a five or higher on *"Estoy de acuerdo,"* a ten or higher, fifteen. Do the same for the *"No estoy de acuerdo"* column. In this way students will get a better sense of where their classmates stand as they fill in the results in their *Retrato de la clase*.

11B.22 **La tecnología en mi vida.** Indica las maneras en que la tecnología afecta tu vida personal en el cuadro siguiente. Después, habla con un/a compañero/a y comparen sus respuestas. Por último, comenten entre todos si la tecnología les afecta más o menos y escribe el resultado en tu **Retrato de la clase.**

Las consecuencias de la tecnología	Estoy de acuerdo	No estoy de acuerdo
1. Me siento ansioso/a cuando no puedo comunicarme por teléfono celular o correo electrónico.		
2. Les mando mensajes electrónicos a mis parientes o amigos en lugar de hablar con ellos.		
3. La tecnología me obliga a trabajar más.		
4. Aprender a usar la nueva tecnología es difícil.		
5. No puedo dejar el teléfono celular apagado (*turned off*).		
6. Siento la necesidad de leer el correo electrónico varias veces al día.		
7. Estoy aburrido/a cuando no puedo mirar la televisión o jugar videojuegos.		
8. Miro la televisión o juego videojuegos en lugar de estudiar o leer.		
9. Mi única fuente de información es la Internet.		
10. La tecnología afecta negativamente mis relaciones personales.		
11. Saber usar la tecnología más nueva es una manera de impresionar a mis parientes y a mis amigos.		
12. La tecnología me hace más materialista.		
13. Saber usar la tecnología más moderna será importante para mi futuro trabajo.		
14. Tengo que comprar muchos aparatos para obtener funciones diferentes.		
15. Debido a la tecnología mi vida es más sedentaria.		
Suma el total de puntos en cada columna:	/15	/15

Retrato de la clase: En general, la tecnología: ☐ Me afecta   ☐ No me afecta

Perspectivas

11B.23 **La tecnología en la cultura hispana.** En la sección de *Contextos*, averiguaste cómo la tecnología afecta tu vida y la de tus compañeros personalmente. Ahora, vamos a ver cómo la tecnología impacta a las culturas hispanohablantes. Las caricaturas (*cartoons*) son de Maitena, autora argentina. Con un compañero, miren las caricaturas siguientes y lean los comentarios que las acompañan. Según los comentarios, escriban la letra de la caricatura/s que corresponde/n a las consecuencias de la tecnología indicadas en la lista. Si no hay caricatura que corresponda a la consecuencia indicada, márquenlo con una X en lugar de una letra. ¡Ojo! Es posible que haya más de una caricatura que corresponda a la consecuencia indicada y es posible que una caricatura pueda corresponder a más de una consecuencia.

a.

b.

c.

d.

CULTURAL NOTE: Quickly review with students that in some parts of Latin America *vos* is used as the informal second person instead of *tú*. Have them take another look at the *Vívelo: Cultura* on page 12 in the *Investigación preliminar*. Point out that *vos* has its own set of verb forms. Given the reminder that *vos* replaces *tú*, students should be able to comprehend its use in the Maitena cartoons without detailed explanation. However, if students are interested, you can tell them that the *vos* forms are easy to recognize in that they resemble the *vosotros* forms, but without the *i* in the personal endings for –ar and –er verbs. The *vos* and *vosotros* forms for –ir verbs are identical. For example: *vosotros habláis/vos hablás, vosotros coméis/vos comés, vosotros decís/vos decís*. How *vos* is used varies by region, and in some places exists alongside both *tú* and *usted* as yet a third level of formality. In Argentina, where *vos* replaces *tú* altogether, *vos* forms are generally used in the present indicative and in the affirmative imperative (which simply drops the final –s of the present indicative, e.g. *vos escuchás → escuchá, vos comés → comé, vos decís → decí*). In other tenses and moods, the *tú* verb form is generally used with the *vos* pronoun, e.g. *Quiero que vos me escuches. Vos* is used as a subject pronoun and as a prepositional pronoun; *te* is used as the corresponding object/reflexive pronoun, e.g. *(Vos) tenés que levantarte temprano porque vienen a buscarte tus amigos para jugar al fútbol.*

11B.23 TEACHING TIP:
Before students match the cartoons to a description, have them write short descriptions with a partner of the main idea shared in each cartoon. Answers may vary. Encourage students to defend their answers.

11B.23 EXTENSION ACTIVITY: Have students develop their own cartoon following these as a model. Their cartoon should include some sort of commentary about the use of technology. Answers may vary. Encourage students to defend their answers.

Las consecuencias de la tecnología	Caricaturas
1. La gente se siente ansiosa cuando no puede comunicarse por teléfono celular o por correo electrónico.	
2. La tecnología obliga a la gente a trabajar más.	
3. Aprender a usar la tecnología nueva es difícil.	
4. La gente no puede dejar el teléfono celular apagado.	
5. La realidad de la juventud es totalmente distinta a la de sus padres o abuelos.	
6. Los videojuegos han reemplazado a los deportes y otras actividades en la vida de los jóvenes.	
7. Los jóvenes piensan que todas las personas están al día con la tecnología.	
8. La gente se siente perdida sin acceso a la tecnología.	
9. Se depende mucho de la tecnología pero puede provocar estrés en los que no tienen mucho conocimiento tecnológico.	
10. La gente tiene que tener muchos aparatos para funciones diferentes.	

Al comparar las consecuencias de la tecnología en tu vida personal, la vida de tu compañero/a y la cultura española, ¿cuál es la conclusión más lógica? ¿Por qué? Comparen su respuesta y su explicación con tres o cuatro grupos.

☐ Las consecuencias de la tecnología son distintas en culturas diferentes.

☐ Las consecuencias de la tecnología son parecidas en culturas diferentes.

☐ Las consecuencias de la tecnología son más personales que socioculturales.

¡Conéctate!

Google YouTube, then search for videos in Spanish on your favorite technological device or tools. Try to listen for the similarities in what things are called. For example, **realidad virtual** refers to virtual reality, **interfaz** refers to interface. See how much you can learn about topics you have some knowledge. You may also want to explore what videos in Spanish are available on topics of interest to you. Then share your findings with the class. In what ways is YouTube useful for learning Spanish and learning about the Spanish-speaking world?

Vocabulario: Investigación B

Vocabulario esencial

Sustantivos

la advertencia	*warning*
el aparato	*device*
el correo electrónico	*email*
la impresora	*printer*
los mensajes	*messages*
el timbre	*ring; doorbell*
el usuario	*user*

Verbos

acabar	*to end, finish*
ahorrar	*to save*
andar bien/mal	*to do well/bad*
avisar	*to inform*
borrar	*to erase*
charlar	*to chat, to talk*
dejar	*to leave; to allow*
descargar	*to download; to unload*
esforzarse	*to make an effort*
enviar	*to send*
esperar	*to wait*
estudiar	*to study*
grabar	*to record*
hacer falta	*to be needed; to be missing*
saludar	*to greet*
soltar	*to let go of*
sonar	*to ring; to sound*

Adverbios

adentro	*inside, indoors*
afuera	*outside, outdoors*
acabar de	*to have just to (do something)*
alrededor	*around*

Otras palabras y expresiones

el/la adolescente	*teenager*
afectivo/a	*emotional*
el aislamiento	*isolation*
anticuado/a	*old-fashioned*
la colocación	*placement*
la contraseña	*password*
enriquecer	*to enrich*
el esfuerzo	*effort*
expuesto/a	*exposed*
irrumpir	*to break out; to burst in*
obligar	*to force some one to do something*
pasar	*to spend (time)*
perezoso/a	*lazy*
prometedor/a	*promising*
el reproductor de DVD/MP3	*DVD/MP3 player*
ruidoso/a	*noisy*
la tecla	*key (on a key board)*
el tocacompactos	*CD player*
el videojuego	*videogame*

a la luz	*in light of*
dinero en efectivo	*cash*
mandar mensajes de texto	*to send text messages*
navegar por la Internet	*navegate the Internet*
prestar tención	*pay attention*

Cognados

Review the cognates in *Adelante* and the false cognates in *¡Atención!*. For a complete list of cognates, see Appendix 4 on page 605.

En vivo

 Un viaje. Con un/a compañero/a de clase preparen un diálogo para presentar a la clase o a su profesor/a usando la siguiente situación como guía.

Situación: Tu compañero/a y tú van a pasar el verano estudiando español en Antigua, Guatemala. Hay muchos cibercafés en Antigua pero el lugar donde se van a quedar también tiene conexión inalámbrica *(wireless)* a la Internet. Es importante saber si los celulares estadounidenses funcionan en Guatemala.

Expectativa: Conversa con tu compañero/a sobre qué cosas electrónicas deberían llevar al viaje. Tienen que ponerse de acuerdo sobre qué cosas llevar y qué cosas dejar en casa. Si quieren llevar algo que su compañero/a no quiere llevar, deben tratar de convencerlo/la sobre la importancia de ese objeto.

¿Cómo va a evolucionar la tecnología?

As a society, we continually see technological advances that change the way we are able to communicate with one another. Consider the growth you have seen in your lifetime as you reflect on where these advances may take us in the next five years. Write a prediction of where you perceive these advances taking us in the next decade. Consider issues such as the capabilities of the Internet, new cell phone technology, etc. You may want to include your opinion of whether these would be positive changes or not.

Paso 1: Consider how quickly technology evolves. Brainstorm a list of predictions you have regarding how technology around communication will be impacted. What advances will take place? Did you consider changes in the Internet and cell phone use?

Paso 2: Now that you have a list of predictions, organize them into a paragraph synthesizing your views.

Paso 3: Revise your written product to ensure that it is rich in content. Ask yourself whether or not your paragraph is clear in describing your prediction. If it is not, make the necessary changes to strengthen it.

Paso 4: Now that your content is solid, revise your draft focusing on form and accuracy. Make the necessary revisions and write your final draft.

Paso 5: Be proud of your final draft. It should be rich in detail and clear in form.

WILEY **PLUS**

INSTRUCTOR'S RESOURCES: You will find a rubric for evaluating students' dialogues in your Instructor's Resources.

SUGGESTION: Have students share their predictions in groups of four to five students. They should pick one plausible prediction to share with the class.

TEACHING TIP: To reach and motivate your more advanced students, challenge them to include their own opinion of whether these are positive advances or not.

En directo

INVESTIGACIÓN A: El metro: transporte ecológico

> **Antes de ver el video.** Contesta estas preguntas con un/a compañero/a. Luego, compartan sus respuestas con el resto de la clase. ¿Cuál es el medio de transporte más rápido en una ciudad? ¿y el más cómodo? ¿y el más barato?

> **El video.** Completa las siguientes oraciones con la información del video. Luego comprueba tus respuestas con la clase.

1. Hoy, más de cuatro millones de personas __tomarán el metro__. ¿Adónde irán?
2. Un viaje relativamente corto en __autobús__ o automóvil, puede __demorar__ una hora.
3. El mismo viaje en __taxi__, te __costaría__ el triple o más.
4. El uso del metro es una alternativa más __ecológica__. Emite menos contaminantes que los __automóviles__ y buses.

Answers: will vary

> **Después de ver el video.** Contesta la siguiente pregunta y luego compara tu respuesta con el resto de la clase. ¿Cuáles crees que son las principales ventajas y desventajas de cada uno de estos medios de transporte: el taxi, el autobús, el metro?

Vocabulario útil
pasajero/a: *passenger*
eficaz: *efficient*
cualquier
 parte: *anywhere*
destino: *destination*

INVESTIGACIÓN B: La tecnología une a las familias

> **Antes de ver el video.** Contesta las siguientes preguntas y después comparte tus respuestas con el resto de la clase: ¿Qué aparatos tecnológicos usas? ¿Y programas de computadora? ¿Para qué los usas?

> **El video.** Indica si cada uno de los enunciados es **cierto** o **falso.** Reescribe los enunciados falsos para hacerlos ciertos. Comprueba tus respuestas con un/a compañero/a.

Cierto	Falso	
☐	☑	**1.** Skype sólo incorpora audio e imagen.
☐	☑	**2.** Los protagonistas del video viven en España.
☑	☐	**3.** El hombre tiene que entregar un trabajo al día siguiente.
☐	☑	**4.** La mujer trabaja desde casa para ganar más dinero.
☑	☐	**5.** La familia piensa que la tecnología los une.

> **Después de ver el video.** En parejas o grupos de tres, contesten las siguientes preguntas. Luego, compartan sus respuestas con el resto de la clase. ¿Cuáles son los aspectos positivos de la tecnología? ¿Y los negativos?

Vocabulario útil
gratuitamente: *for free*
yayos: *grandparents*

TEACHING TIP:
Information gap activities help develop students' interpersonal communication skills. Although they are not completely spontaneous, they do encourage the exchanging of information as well as the negotiation of meaning.

WILEY
PLUS

TESTING PROGRAM:
You will find a complete testing program for use with *¡Vívelo!* in *WileyPLUS*.

 **Retrato de la clase Checklist**

You should have recorded information in your **Retrato de la clase** in conjunction with the following activities:

☐	**11A.9**	**¿Quién de la clase?**
☐	**11A.10**	**Un sondeo sobre los medios de transporte.**
☐	**11A.11**	**¿Con qué frecuencia?**
☐	**11A.12**	**Un viaje pasado.**
☐	**11B.11**	**¿Cuál es el más importante?**
☐	**11B.12**	**Las ventajas y desventajas de la tecnología.**
☐	**11B.22**	**La tecnología en mi vida.**

Perspectivas globales

WILEY **PLUS**

INVESTIGACIÓN 12A	**INVESTIGACIÓN 12B**
¿Facilita la tecnología el manejo de dinero?	¿Qué es la occidentalización?

ADELANTE

- ¡Ya lo sabes! El dinero
- El cajero automático cumple 40 años

Bien dicho: El sonido de la *c* y la *z* en España

ADELANTE

- ¡Ya lo sabes! El acceso y la conectividad
- ¿Qué es la occidentalización?

Bien dicho: Repaso de las vocales y la acentuación

PALABRAS CLAVE

- El manejo de dinero

PALABRAS CLAVE

- Conjunciones de tiempo, propósito y causa

ESTRUCTURAS CLAVE

- Making form-meaning connections
- The imperfect subjunctive

ESTRUCTURAS CLAVE

- The subjunctive or indicative in adverb clauses
- The subjunctive or indicative in adjective clauses

VÍVELO: LENGUA

- Talking about verbs

VÍVELO: LENGUA

- Using conjunctions and prepositions

VÍVELO: CULTURA

- Las monedas de los países hispanohablantes

VÍVELO: CULTURA

- La Internet y los pueblos indígenas de Latinoamérica
- Los zapatistas y el uso de la Internet como arma

CONTEXTOS Y PERSPECTIVAS

El dinero y la seguridad

CONTEXTOS Y PERSPECTIVAS

¿Cuánto sabes de otras culturas?

¡VÍVELO!

En vivo:
Debate sobre la tecnología
Conexión obligada

En directo:
A: Tecnología y dinero
B: Unidos por la globalización

¿Facilita la tecnología el manejo de dinero?

In this **Investigación,** you will learn:

▶ How to talk about money management

▶ What to say to purchase items

▶ To connect forms with the meanings inherent in their use

▶ To recognize a hypothetical situation

¿Cómo se puede hablar de la relación entre el dinero y la tecnología?

You can talk about how you manage your money.	¿Ahorras o gastas tu dinero? ¿Usas el cajero automático con frecuencia? ¿Cuántas tarjetas de crédito tienes? Si tuvieras mucho dinero, ¿lo invertirías o comprarías un coche?
You can address ways you will make money or want to make money in the future.	¿Tienes un trabajo? ¿Cuántas horas trabajas a la semana? ¿Qué tipo de trabajo buscarás cuando te gradúes? ¿Cuál sería tu trabajo ideal?
You can speculate on what you would do hypothetically with your money.	Si fueras dueño/a de una empresa, ¿a quiénes contratarías? Si heredaras *(inherit)* $1.000.000, ¿dejarías de trabajar? ¿Qué harías si ganaras la lotería?

Adelante

¡Ya lo sabes! El dinero

el banco	el interés
el cheque	la seguridad
el cliente/la clienta	la tarjeta de crédito
las cooperativas de crédito	la tarjeta de débito
el crédito	
el crimen	depositar
el/la criminal	contratar
la economía	obtener
la estabilidad	robar
el fraude	

12A.1 ¿Cierto o falso? Lee los siguientes enunciados e indica si son ciertos o falsos. Corrige los enunciados falsos y compara tus respuestas con la clase.

Cierto	Falso	
☑	☐	**1. La tarjeta de débito** no es una forma de crédito. Funciona como dinero en efectivo *(cash)*.
☑	☐	**2.** Tomar la identidad de otra persona es un ejemplo de **fraude**.
☑	☐	**3.** Emplear es sinónimo de **contratar**.
☐	☑	**4. Robar** es el sinónimo de dar.
☑	☐	**5.** Los bancos ganan dinero a través del **interés**.
☐	☑	**6. Obtener** es sinónimo de perder.

12A.2 Completa la frase. Completa la frase con la palabra más lógica.

crimen	estabilidad	cooperativas de crédito	cheques
economía	clientes	banco	crédito

1. Depositamos nuestro dinero en el _____banco_____.

2. Escribimos _____cheques_____ cuando no tenemos dinero en efectivo.

3. Es muy importante tener buen _____crédito_____ para poder comprar una casa.

4. Robar es un tipo de _____crimen_____ muy común.

5. Los bancos quieren tener muchos _____clientes_____.

6. Hay competencia *(competition)* entre los bancos y las _cooperativas de crédito_.

7. La _____economía_____ de Estados Unidos se basa en el capitalismo.

8. La _____estabilidad_____ política de un país es importante para su economía.

12A.3 Definiciones. Escucha las definiciones e indica cuál es la palabra que corresponde a cada definición. Luego, verifica tus respuestas con la clase.

a. el cliente	**e.** interés	**1.** _f_	**5.** _c_
b. el criminal	**f.** seguridad	**2.** _b_	**6.** _d_
c. robar	**g.** depositar	**3.** _g_	**7.** _e_
d. la tarjeta de crédito	**h.** crédito	**4.** _h_	**8.** _a_

12A.4 Adivina la palabra. Con un/a compañero/a de clase, describe, dibuja, usa gestos, asociaciones o cualquier forma de comunicación (excepto la traducción) para que tu compañero/a pueda identificar los cognados de *Adelante*. Puedes ofrecer la primera letra o la última letra de la palabra al final de tu definición.

> Modelo: E1: *Es un verbo que significa "tomar algo sin permiso" y empieza con la letra "r".*
> E2: *robar*

EXPRESIONES ÚTILES

¡De compras!

Cuando entras a un negocio, en las conversaciones muchas veces se usan muchas expresiones fijas. Mucho depende del tipo de negocio, pero por lo general las siguientes expresiones son útiles.

¿En qué puedo servirle?	How may I help you?
¿Cuánto cuesta(n)?	How much does it/do they cost?
Es/Son barato(-a, -os, -as).	It is/They are inexpensive.
Es/Son caro(-a, -os, -as).	It is/They are expensive.
Es/Son de buena calidad.	It is/They are of good quality.
¿Está(n) en venta/rebajado(a)?	Is it/Are they on sale?
¿Hay descuento?	Is there a discount?
Me lo/la/los/las llevo.	I'll take it/them.
¿Cómo desea pagar?	How would you like to pay for it/ them?
en efectivo	in cash
con cheque/tarjeta de crédito	with a check/credit card

12A.3 AUDIO SCRIPT:
1. Es la palabra que se asocia con la estabilidad. 2. Una persona que comete un acto ilegal. 3. El acto de poner dinero en el banco. 4. Cuando no tienes dinero puedes pedir esto de un negocio. 5. Obtener algo sin el permiso del dueño. 6. Una cosa plástica con números que funciona como dinero. 7. El dinero que tienen que pagar los consumidores a los bancos cuando compran cosas con tarjetas de crédito. 8. Es sinónimo de "consumidor".

12A.3 TEACHING TIP:
Before having students listen to the descriptions, give them two minutes to read the words from a–h so that when they hear the definition, they are familiar with the list of options.

12A.4 TEACHING TIP:
Give students a set amount of time (perhaps three minutes per person) to do this activity. Have groups keep track of how many words they got correct. After the time is up, poll the class to see how well they did. Circumlocution, or describing a word without saying it, is an excellent skill for students to continue developing. Encourage students to attempt descriptions before relying on drawings, gestures or other associations.

EXPRESIONES ÚTILES:
Have students use items they brought to class (e.g. items in their backpacks, coats, etc.). In groups of three, have them take turns with one person being the shopkeeper while the other two inquire about items/prices/etc. using this vocabulary.

12A.5 ¡A negociar! Las siguientes oraciones forman un diálogo que tiene lugar en un gran almacén *(department store)*. Léelas e indica la secuencia correcta del diálogo con los números 1–8. Después de completar diálogo, léelo en voz alta con un/a compañero/a.

   _6_   Ay, ¡qué bien! Me lo llevo ahora.

   _4_   Me gusta mucho este refrigerador negro porque no es muy grande. ¿Cuánto cuesta?

   _1_   Buenas tardes, ¿en qué puedo servirle?

   _8_   Con tarjeta de crédito.

   _3_   Muy bien. Tenemos varios refrigeradores. Pase por aquí.

   _5_   Pues, hoy está en venta/rebajado. Cuesta ciento cincuenta euros.

   _2_   Busco un refrigerador pequeño para mi cuarto.

   _7_   Muy bien. ¿Cómo desea pagar?

El cajero automático cumple 40 años

PRE-READING ACTIVITY:
Direct students' attention to the picture of the *cajero automático*. Poll the class to see what they think of the pros and cons of this technology with questions like, *¿Cuáles son las ventajas de los cajeros automáticos?* and *¿Y las desventajas?*. An additional question might be, *¿Para qué otras cosas se puede usar un cajero automático además de retirar dinero?* Students may not have enough language skills to fully answer these questions, but they serve the purpose of getting students to think about some of the topics they are about to read.

TEACHING TIP: Give students five minutes or so to read the passage silently. Then, ask students to reconstruct what they understood from the passage. Some students will have understood some things and others different things. If they offer information in English, make sure to provide the information in Spanish. Write the main ideas on the board as students articulate them.

El cajero automático fue inventado hace aproximadamente 40 años por John Shepherd-Barron de la compañía De La Rue. Se instaló en Barclays Bank en Enfield, al norte de Londres. Desde entonces este aparato se ha convertido en un elemento esencial de la vida moderna. La gente puede tener acceso a su dinero a toda hora, sin tener que guardarlo *(save it)* en la casa o depender del horario del banco.

Hoy en día, un total de 1,3 millones de cajeros automáticos se encuentran por todo el mundo. Se calcula que cada siete minutos se instala un cajero automático nuevo en alguna parte del mundo. El país con más cajeros automáticos es Japón, seguido por España en segundo lugar. Son convenientes para los usuarios y representan un ahorro para el banco porque tienen que contratar a menos empleados para atender a los clientes. El 60% de los usos de esos aparatos es para sacar dinero, pero también se puede depositar dinero, pagar facturas *(bills)*, recargar *(recharge)* teléfonos celulares de prepago e incluso comprar entradas *(tickets)* para algún evento. La tecnología relacionada con los cajeros automáticos ha evolucionado mucho durante las últimas cuatro décadas, especialmente en cuanto a la seguridad, que representa el problema más importante de los cajeros automáticos. Se buscan constantemente nuevas maneras de proteger tanto a los usuarios como a los bancos.

12A.6 Comprensión. Escucha las oraciones e indica si son ciertas o falsas según lo que leíste en el artículo. Corrige las oraciones falsas y luego verifica tus respuestas con la clase.

	Cierto	Falso
1.	☑	☐
2.	☑	☐
3.	☐	☑
4.	☐	☑
5.	☑	☐
6.	☑	☐

Bien dicho

El sonido de la c y la z en España

In some regions of Spain, mainly in the central and north central parts of the country, the letter **c** followed by the vowels **e** and **i** and the letter **z** corresponds to the Spanish sound represented by the symbol /θ/. This sound is very similar to the sound associated with the combination *th* in the English words *then, they, mother* and *earth*. On the other hand, as noted in Investigación 5A, the letter **s** corresponds to the sound /s/. The contrast between /s/ and /θ/ allows speakers in these regions of Spain to distinguish between words such as **casa/caza** *(hunt)* and **sumo** *(I add up)*/**zumo** *(juice)*.

12A.7 ¿Qué palabra oíste? Escucha las palabras y subraya la palabra que oíste en cada caso. Luego, verifica las respuestas con la clase.

1. cierra *(saw)* — sierra *(mountain range)*
2. vez — ves
3. ciento — siento
4. meza *(from* mecer = *to rock)* — mesa
5. cocer *(to cook)* — coser *(to sew)*
6. haz — has

12A.8 ¡A practicar! Con un/a compañero/a, imaginen que van a visitar Madrid y quieren practicar el sonido /θ/. Alternándose, pronuncien las siguientes oraciones. Cuando terminen el ejercicio, intercambien papeles y repitan las oraciones para que los dos tengan la oportunidad de pronunciarlas todas.

1. Los avances tecnológicos facilitan el manejo de dinero.
2. Isabel Pérez solicitó trabajo en una empresa internacional.
3. La condición financiera de este país es una preocupación.
4. Es muy eficaz y conveniente utilizar el cajero automático.
5. En generaciones anteriores se pagaban las cosas a plazos.
6. Las ciudades en el desierto dependen de la tecnología para obtener agua.

www ¡Conéctate!
Visit http://www.bancopopular.com, the website for a bank in the US, Puerto Rico and the U.S. Virgin Islands. Check out their website in Spanish. What services do they have that interest you? List them. Share them with your classmates. Are there any services available that you did not know about?

12A.6 AUDIO SCRIPT: 1. El cajero automático fue inventado por John Shepherd-Barron. 2. El primer cajero automático se instaló en Inglaterra. 3. Cada hora, se instala un cajero automático nuevo en el mundo. 4. El país con más cajeros automáticos es Estados Unidos. 5. En algunos cajeros automáticos es posible comprar entradas para algún evento. 6. El problema más grave de los cajeros automáticos es la seguridad.

12A.6 ANSWERS: Cierto: 1, 2, 5, 6; Falso: 3 (cada 7 minutos); 4 (Japón)

TEACHING TIP: You may want to bring excerpts from songs, television programs or films to illustrate the use of /θ/, particularly if you are not a speaker of Castilian Spanish.

12A.7 AUDIO SCRIPT: [Peninsular accent] 1. cierra, 2. ves, 3. ciento, 4. meza, 5. coser, 6. has

12A.7 TEACHING TIP: To supplement this activity, you may want to have students listen again to the excerpts you have provided and ask them to raise one finger when they hear /θ/ and two fingers when they hear /s/.

12A.8 ALTERNATIVE ACTIVITY: Unless students learn Spanish with a native Castilian speaker or in Spain, chances are they will not be using the /θ/ in their pronunciation. Consequently, you may opt to read these statements to your students randomizing the pronunciation of the /s/ and /θ/, and having them circle the times you used the /θ/ instead of the /s/.

Palabras clave 1 El manejo de dinero

ABRIR CUENTAS · PRÉSTAMOS

FINANZAS

INGRESOS · GASTOS

Sueldo $1400

Cheque de papá $50

Electricidad $95
Celular $47,50
Pago del carro $230

Aquí tiene la libreta de cheques y la tarjeta de débito para usar con su nueva cuenta corriente. ¿También desea abrir una cuenta de ahorros?

Queremos pedir un préstamo para comprar un carro. El problema es que no queremos endeudarnos demasiado.

Para manejar el dinero es importante hacer un presupuesto.

Sí, por favor. Pero dígame, ¿cuánto es el saldo mínimo que hay que mantener?

¿Tienen una cuenta bancaria o una tarjeta de crédito con nuestro banco? Cobramos intereses más bajos si ya son clientes del banco.

De acuerdo. Ahora tengo responsabilidades y no puedo gastar dinero en cosas frívolas. Es más, quisiera invertir unos mil dólares en una cuenta que pague buenos intereses.

Expresiones

llevarse bien/mal	Me llevo bien con mis amigos porque tenemos mucho en común. Sin embargo, no me llevo bien con personas negativas y que pueden ser crueles.
debido a	Debido a preocupaciones relacionadas con la seguridad, la tecnología de los cajeros automáticos ha evolucionado mucho.
pagar a plazos	No tengo el dinero suficiente para comprar el carro con un solo pago, entonces pido un préstamo para pagar un poco cada mes por 48 meses. Es decir, pago a plazos.

El cajero debe **comprobar** la identidad de los clientes.

el cajero

la guardia

LADRÓN

la contraseña

gerente de la sucursal

Abuela, ¿por qué no tienes una tarjeta de débito? Allí hay un **cajero automático.** Es muy **útil** para sacar dinero rápidamente.

CAJA 1   CAJA 2   CAJA 3   CERRADO

12A.9 Algo está de más. Estudia cada grupo de palabras o expresiones e indica qué palabra no se asocia lógicamente con las otras. Explica por qué. Compara tus respuestas con las de un/a compañero/a.

1. el dinero   la contraseña   la tarjeta de crédito   el cheque
2. el ladrón   la cárcel   la cuenta   el delito
3. los impuestos   las facturas   los préstamos   las sucursales
4. ahorrar   gastar   invertir   depositar
5. la factura   pedir préstamo   contraseña   endeudarse
6. el cajero   el gerente de la sucursal la guardia   la cárcel
7. cometer   hacer   financiar   ejecutar
8. útil   inestable   competente   seguro

12A.9 EXTENSION ACTIVITY: Have students develop on the spot their own exercise modeled after 12A.9 to share with a partner. Any vocabulary word is game. This will serve as a review of previous vocabulary and reveal the type of words they have retained. Once students have their exercises ready, they should exchange them with a student, complete them and then go over them.

12A.9 ANSWERS: 1. la contraseña (no es una forma de pagar), 2. la cuenta (no se asocia con el crimen/los criminales), 3. las sucursales (no son cosas que tenemos que pagar), 4. gastar (no nos ayuda a ganar dinero), 5. contraseña (no se asocia con los préstamos/las deudas), 6. la cárcel (no se asocia con puestos en un banco), 7. financiar (no se asocia con la acción de poner en práctica algo, 8. inestable (no es una característica positiva como las demás palabras)

12A.10 PARTNERING CARDS: You can turn this exercise into a partnering activity by writing down the vocabulary (a–m) and the definitions (1–10) on strips of paper. Make sure you have the correct amount for your class and then randomly distribute them, instructing students to find the person with the matching slip. Or, to save time but still encourage student-to-student interactions, form pairs of students and tell them to take turns reading a sentence for the other to select the answer and vice versa.

12A.10 Las definiciones. Lee las definiciones e indica cuál es la palabra o expresión que corresponde a cada definición según el modelo. Luego, verifica tus respuestas con un/a compañero/a de clase. **¡Ojo!** No se usan todas las palabras.

a. cobrar	**e.** la cuenta de ahorros	**i.** el/la gerente
b. comprobar	**f.** pedir un préstamo	**j.** útil
c. la contraseña	**g.** los impuestos	**k.** tener prisa
d. la cuenta corriente	**h.** el presupuesto	**l.** pagar a plazos

___C___ **1.** Es el número que necesitamos para usar el cajero automático.

___l___ **2.** Es cuando se paga una factura mensualmente por partes.

___i___ **3.** Es la persona principal en una entrevista de empleo en un banco.

___d___ **4.** Es la cuenta bancaria que asociamos con los cheques.

___k___ **5.** Es cuando una persona no tiene tiempo y por eso trata de salir o llegar a un lugar rápidamente.

___g___ **6.** Es el dinero que se paga al gobierno anualmente.

___j___ **7.** Es el adjetivo que describe una cosa práctica.

___f___ **8.** Es cuando vas al banco o a una cooperativa para obtener dinero que pagarás luego.

12A.11 TEACHING TIP: Before going over answers as a class, have students work with a partner to explain their responses to them. This is an opportunity for them to gain insight they might not have had when doing the exercise on their own.

12A.11 Las finanzas de Luis y Susana. Lee el párrafo siguiente y escoge las palabras o expresiones correctas para completar las oraciones. Luego, verifica tus respuestas con algunos compañeros de clase.

Luis y Susana generalmente (1. (manejan)/comprueban) bien su dinero. Los dos tienen buenos trabajos y cada semana, ellos (2. (depositan)/desperdician) una parte de su salario en su (3. tarjeta de crédito/(cuenta de ahorros)) porque piensan comprar una casa algún día. Además, ellos pagan puntualmente (4. (las facturas)/las contraseñas). Hoy, Luis y Susana van al banco para (5. pagar a plazos/(pedir un préstamo)) porque necesitan comprar un carro nuevo. Es muy conveniente porque hay (6. (una sucursal)/un puesto) de su banco cerca de su casa. Cuando lleguen al banco, van a hablar con (7. el cliente/ (el gerente)). Él les va a hacer una serie de preguntas para determinar si el banco debe (8. gastarles/(prestarles)) el dinero a Luis y a Susana. Como son muy responsables con su dinero, es probable que Luis y Susana reciban el dinero que piden y puedan comprar el carro pronto.

12A.12 TEACHING TIP: Allow students ample time to survey classmates and tally scores. Ask individual students to report on their findings. Discuss as a class whether or not the class as a whole manages their money well or poorly and why that might be.

WILEY PLUS

12A.12 INSTRUCTOR'S RESOURCES: You will find a reproducible chart for Activity 12A.12 in your Instructor's Resources.

12A.12 ¿Cómo maneja la clase el dinero? Contesta las siguientes preguntas y habla con por lo menos la mitad de la clase para determinar cuántos dicen "sí" y cuántos dicen "no". En general, ¿ustedes manejan el dinero bien o mal? ¿Por qué? Apunta tus conclusiones en tu **Retrato de la clase.**

	Yo	La clase	
		Sí	No
¿Tienes cuenta de ahorros?			
¿Tienes cuenta corriente?			
¿Tienes muchas tarjetas de crédito?			
¿Usas el cajero automático frecuentemente?			
¿Pagas las facturas puntualmente?			
¿Te molesta endeudarte?			
¿Intentas ahorrar dinero cada mes?			

Retrato de la clase: Por lo general, mis compañeros de clase tienen una cuenta de ahorros y una cuenta corriente. Les molesta endeudarse e intentan ahorrar dinero.

VÍVELO: CULTURA

Las monedas de los países hispanohablantes

Argentina	peso	Honduras	lempira
Bolivia	boliviano	México	peso
Chile	peso	Nicaragua	córdoba
Colombia	peso	Panamá	balboa
Costa Rica	colón	Paraguay	guaraní
Cuba	peso	Perú	nuevo sol
Ecuador	sucre	Puerto Rico	dólar
El Salvador	colón	República Domincana	peso
España	euro	Uruguay	peso
Guatemala	quetzal	Venezuela	bolívar

VÍVELO: CULTURA: Ask students if they know the currency of any Spanish-speaking countries. Write those they know on the board. Then, have them compare it to the information in *Vívelo: Cultura*.

 ¡Conéctate!

¿A cuánto está el dólar? Find out what the exchange rate for the US dollar is. Type "exchange rate" into an Internet search and start looking to see what the rate is. Write down the exchange rate for five different Spanish-speaking countries. What would your monthly budget be in those different currencies? Take this a step further by looking at different websites from those countries to see what prices are for things you typically consume. What did you find? Share your thoughts with the class.

12A.13 El presupuesto. Con un/a compañero/a de clase, preparen un presupuesto mensual. Ustedes son compañeros/as de cuarto y cada uno/a de ustedes recibe $2,000 al mes, así que tienen $4,000 en total. Comenten cuánto dinero van a gastar en las cosas que aparecen en la tabla y la cantidad que cada uno/a va a pagar. ¿Cuáles son los gastos individuales? ¿Cuáles son los gastos que van a compartir? Comparen su presupuesto con el presupuesto de otros grupos. ¿Qué tienen en común?

Categoría	Yo	Mi compañero/a
La vivienda (el apartamento, la casa)		
La comida		
La ropa		
El transporte		
Las facturas (electricidad, agua, etc.)		
Los gastos universitarios (libros, matrícula (tuition), etc.)		
El ocio (cine, restaurantes, conciertos, deportes, videojuegos, CDs, etc.)		
Suministros (supplies) (jabón, champú, detergente, plumas, papel, etc.)		
Pagos a plazos (préstamos)		
La cuenta de ahorros		
Varios		
Total	/$2,000	/$2,000

12A.13 TEACHING TIP: Give students time to complete their budget. Ask each group to present their budget. Note which group will spend the most/least on each item. Ask which are the individual/shared expenses. If groups have empty categories, ask them to explain why. If they have miscellaneous expenses, ask them to explain what they are including in that category. When students compared budgets, were budgets similar/different in terms of priorities? Amounts? Selection of individual/shared expenses? Amount each roommate contributed to shared expenses? What are advantages/disadvantages to preparing a budget such as this one? How many students prepare similar budgets for themselves?

12A.13 INSTRUCTOR'S RESOURCES: You will find a reproducible chart for Activity 12A.13 in your Instructor's Resources.

¡Atención!

¡ATENCIÓN!: Directing students' attention to the false cognates and their descriptions adds more comprehensible input so that they can hear these words in context. This is especially important with these words since their meanings are more easily misunderstood. Therefore, more contextual practice is important.

Meter	does not mean meter, but is rather a synonym for the verb **poner**. To express *meter* in Spanish, use the word **metro**.
	Carlos metió la tarjeta de crédito en su cartera. El banco está a cien metros de la estación de trenes.
Invertir	means *to invest* in the financial sense. It also means *to invert* (to reverse, turn inside out or upside down).
	Nosotros invertimos mucho dinero en la empresa de Susana. Mi imagen en el espejo siempre está invertida.
Renunciar	means *to renounce* but it also means *to resign* when referring to the decision to leave a job.
	Marcos renunció a su trabajo porque no se llevaba bien con el gerente. El criminal renunció al derecho de tener abogado.
Guardar	means *to guard* as in to defend or protect. It also means *to keep* or *to put away*. The verb **vigilar** means *to guard* as when one watches someone to keep track of what they are doing.
	La policía vigilaba al criminal. No es buena idea guardar mucho dinero en tu casa. Después de lavar y secar la ropa, la guardo.
Solicitar	means *to ask for* or *to request* in the sense of **pedir**. It also means *to apply for* when referring to looking for a job. **La solicitud** refers to the document that one fills out when looking for a job.
	Pienso solicitar un trabajo en esa compañía. Cuando vayas a la entrevista, trae la solicitud. Hay muchas organizaciones que solicitan dinero del público.
Patrón	does not mean patron or customer. It means *the boss*. It also means *pattern*. To express *patron* or *customer* in Spanish, use the word **el cliente/la clienta**.
	El patrón pide que los empleados trabajen horas extra. El empleado contestó las preguntas de la clienta. Los criminales generalmente tienen un patrón de conducta. Es importante tener un patrón para coser un vestido.

12A.14 TEACHING TIP: Encourage students to read the sentences without looking at the word bank. They should try to fill in the blanks on their own in order to anticipate what might appear in the word bank. Then, have them access the word bank for more exact answers. To encourage student-to-student interactions, make sure to tell students that they have to verify their answers orally.

12A.14 Completar las oraciones. Completa las oraciones con la palabra apropiada de la lista. Luego, verifica tus respuestas con la clase.

clientes	metros	renunciar	invertir
vigilar	patrón	meter	solicitar

1. Tienes que ___meter___ el libro en tu mochila.

2. A Teresa no le gusta su trabajo, por eso va a ___renunciar___.

3. El camarero les sirvió café a los ___clientes___.

4. Roberto es ingeniero. Quiere ___solicitar___ un trabajo en General Electric.

5. Estoy feliz porque mi ___patrón___ me aumentó el salario/sueldo.

6. No pienso ___invertir___ en esa empresa porque sus productos no son útiles.

7. Los guardias deben ___vigilar___ a los clientes sospechosos para evitar problemas.

8. La fábrica *(factory)* donde trabajo está a unos doscientos ___metros___ de mi casa.

DICHOS

El amor, como el dinero, no se puede ocultar.	*Love, like money, cannot be hidden.*
Tiene más dinero que pelos en la cabeza.	*He/She has more money than hairs on his/her head.*
Salud, amor y pesetas, y tiempo para gozarlos. (brindis tradicional)	*Health, love, and money, and time to enjoy them.*
Nada sacar y mucho meter, segura receta para enriquecer.	*Taking nothing out and putting a lot in, a guaranteed recipe to getting rich.*
El poder no es dicha plena, porque a veces envenena.	*Power isn't complete happiness, because sometimes it is poisonous.*
La pobreza no es vicio; pero es un inconveniente.	*Poverty is not a vice, but it is an inconvenience.*

VÍVELO: LENGUA

Talking about verbs

There are various terms related to the verbs in Spanish that you should be able to distinguish.

Tense indicates when the situation described by a sentence occurs in relation to when the sentence is written or uttered. The most common divisions of tense are present, past and future.

> Hablo español.
> Hablé con la profesora ayer.
> Hablaré con mi novio esta noche.

Aspect allows us to represent the various parts of a situation, mainly its beginning, its middle, or its end. In Spanish, the contrast between the preterit and the imperfect is based on aspect.

> Llovió a las ocho. (beginning of the action *llover*)
> Caminé al café. (end of the action *caminar*).
> Caminaba al café cuando vi a Juan. (middle of the action *caminar*)

The **indicative mode** (or **mood**) is used to make factual or objective statements and to express strong belief or affirmation.

> Estudiamos español este semestre.
> Creo que la tecnología facilita la vida.
> Ellos saben que María maneja bien su dinero.

The **subjunctive mode** (or **mood**) is used when expressing wishes, commands, requests, suggestions, doubt, emotion, and judgment, or when describing situations that are hypothetical or contrary to fact.

> Recomiendo que ustedes repasen el vocabulario para el examen.
> Es necesario que te levantes temprano.
> Buscamos una secretaria que sea bilingüe. (a hypothetical secretary)

VÍVELO: LENGUA: This information serves to sensitize students to grammatical terminology they may have seen or will see in the future. However, there is no need to pause on these grammatical points. You could use the sentences in the ¡*Atención!* section as examples and ask them to find the two sentences that use the subjunctive verb forms and the present or past (imperfect or preterit)

Estructuras clave 1 Making Form-Meaning Connections

WILEY PLUS

You will find PowerPoint presentations to use with *Estructuras clave* in *WileyPLUS*.

To make form/meaning connections, you must be aware of the verb endings that change the meaning of the verbs because the natural tendency, when processing a second language, is to pay closer attention to words with the most communicative value in a sentence, such as nouns and verb meaning. Moreover, just because you have been introduced to the various verb tenses/ aspects that appear below does not mean that you have memorized every verb and its conjugation. Connecting the verb form to the meaning it represents is one way to be a strategic language learner. You have seen the information in the chart below, but not all of it at once. Remember that the context and usage of a verb will contribute in significant ways to its meaning. Review the chart, keeping in mind that due to lack of space not all uses are indicated in the first left-hand column.

Tense / Aspect / Mode	Forms/endings for –ar verbs	Forms/endings for –er verbs	Forms/endings for –ir verbs	Examples
Present To indicate present or routine actions, an action in progress, or a future action	-o -as -a -áis -amos -an	-o -es -e -éis -emos -en	-o -es -e -ís -imos -en	Ahora se peina el pelo. Mañana comemos paella. Siempre comen pollo.
Present Progressive (-ing) To indicate an action in progress	estar (estoy, estás, está,estamos, estáis, están) + verb stem + ando	estar + verb stem + iendo	estar + verb stem + iendo	Está lloviendo.
Present Perfect To indicate an action that *has occurred* from the speaker's present perspective	haber (he, has, ha, habéis, hemos, han) + verb stem +ado	haber + verb stem + ido	haber + verb stem + ido	He enviado 100 mensajes de texto hoy.
Future (will ____) To make predictions about what *will happen* in the future or to make promises	Verb infinitive + -é -ás -á -éis -amos -án	Verb infinitive + -é -ás -á -éis -amos -án	Verb infinitive + -é -ás -á -éis -amos -án	Llegará mañana a las 3:00.
Ir + a + finitive (going to ____) Future from present perspective	voy a vas a van a vais a vamos a van a			Vamos a viajar a España en el verano.
Future from past perspective	iba a ibas a iba a ibais a íbamos a iban a			Íbamos a comer allí.

Present Subjunctive Often used in a dependent clause with **que** to express actions that *may occur*	verb stem + -e -es -e -éis -emos -en	verb stem + -a -as -a -áis -amos -an	verb stem + -a -as -a -áis -amos -an	Quiero que tú le escribas un correo electrónico.
Preterite To indicate actions that *began* or *happened* during a defined time period in the past	-é -aste -ó -asteis -amos -aron	-í -iste -ió -isteis -imos -ieron	-í -iste -ió -isteis -imos -ieron	Bebí mucho anoche.
Imperfect To refer to time, weather conditions, and other descriptive elements of a narrative in the past, and to describe actions that one *used to do* habitually	-aba -abas -aba -ais -ábamos -aban	-ía -ías -ía -íais -íamos -ían	-ía -ías -ía -íais -íamos -ían	En el verano siempre comíamos helado y caminábamos por la playa.
Past Perfect To refer to an action that *had occurred* prior to another past action or to the speaker's past perspective	haber (había, habías, había, habíais, habíamos, habían) + verb stem +ado	haber + verb stem +ido	haber + verb stem +ido	Anoche, a las 8:00 ya había comprado las entradas para el cine.
Conditional To express a conditional statement about what someone *would* do	Verb infinitive + -ía -ías -ía -íais -íamos -ían	Verb infinitive + -ía -ías -ía -íais -íamos -ían	Verb infinitive + -ía -ías -ía -íais -íamos -ían	Con $400,000 compraríamos una casa.
Formal Commands	-e -en	-a -an	-a -an	Hable con la patrona.
Negative	No hable	No coma	No escriba	No fume.
Informal Commands	-a -ad	-e -ed	-e -id	Camina más rápido.
Negative	No hables	No comas	No escribas	No inviertas dinero en fraudes.
Nosotros/as Commands	-emos	-amos	-amos	Salgamos temprano para evitar el tráfico.

WILEY PLUS

You will find PowerPoint presentations for use with *Estructuras clave* in *WileyPLUS*.

Although you were introduced to these verb forms separately, in reality, when we communicate, we often move in and out of different tenses/aspects. For example, note the various verbs in the paragraph below. Read the passage the first time focusing on the general idea of the passage. Then, focus on the verbs that are in bold for a meaning that is more precise in terms of time elements.

> **Tengo** un MacBook pero dentro de dos meses **compraré** un MacBook Pro porque me **han dicho** que son más rápidos. **He usado** los productos Apple desde que se **inventaron**. **Escribí** mi tésis en el primer modelo de la computadora Macintosh. Nunca **había usado** una computadora antes de escribir la tésis. La pantalla de esas computadoras **era** mucho más pequeña. **Creo** que **hay** más variedad hoy en día puesto que **existen** pantallas muy grandes y otras muy pequeñas pero no **he visto** una que **tenga** la pantalla tan pequeña como el primer modelo.

12A.15 ANSWERS: 1. Mañana, voy a salir/saldré con mis amigos., 2.Anoche tuve una discusión..., 3. Comí/ Había comido antes de las 5:00., 4. ...hablo/estoy hablando con...

12A.15 Enfócate en los usos. Indica los verbos que usarías para hacer una declaración lógica. En todos los casos, hay más de una respuesta correcta.

1. Mañana _____ con mis amigos.

- ☐ voy a salir
- ☐ salí
- ☐ saldré
- ☐ saldría
- ☐ había salido
- ☐ he salido
- ☐ salía

2. Anoche _____ una discusión sobre las desventajas y ventajas de la tecnología.

- ☐ voy a tener
- ☐ tuve
- ☐ tendría
- ☐ tenía
- ☐ había tenido
- ☐ he tenido
- ☐ tendré

3. _____ antes de las 5:00 y por eso no tenía hambre anoche.

- ☐ comí
- ☐ comeré
- ☐ comería
- ☐ comía
- ☐ voy a comer
- ☐ he comido
- ☐ había comido

4. No puedo ir a la puerta porque _____ con el médico por teléfono.

- ☐ hablé
- ☐ hablaba
- ☐ hablo
- ☐ he hablado
- ☐ había hablado
- ☐ voy a hablar
- ☐ hablaría
- ☐ estoy hablando

12A.16 AUDIO SCRIPT: 1. La economía será problemática. 2. Debemos aprender de nuestros errores. 3. Por nuestra dependencia de Wall Street tuvimos problemas. 4. Personalmente he perdido mucho dinero. 5. Algunos amigos míos habían comprado una casa 6. Perdieron su trabajo y luego perdieron la casa. 7. No tendrán otra oportunidad de tener una casa. 8. Por eso, creo que voy a continuar con mis ahorros.

12A.16 EXTENSION ACTIVITY: Have students listen to the statements again and say whether they agree or not, or whether the statement reflects their prsonal experience.

12A.16 ¿Pasado, presente, futuro? Escucha las oraciones e indica si se refieren al pasado, presente o futuro según la forma del verbo.

	Pasado	Presente	Futuro
1.	☐	☐	☑
2.	☐	☑	☐
3.	☑	☐	☐
4.	☑	☐	☐
5.	☑	☐	☐
6.	☑	☐	☐
7.	☐	☐	☑
8.	☐	☐	☑

Estructuras clave 2 The imperfect subjunctive

In this section, you will learn strategies to help you correctly process Spanish sentences that use the imperfect subjunctive like *"If I were the President, I would focus on the conservation of energy."*.

The forms of the imperfect subjunctive are easy to recognize. They share the same root as third-person plural (**ellos, ellas, ustedes**) forms of the preterit, for example, **tuvieron, hablaron, escribieron, pusieron,** but add the personal endings shown below. Any spelling changes, stem changes, and irregular stems that occur in the **ellos/ellas/ustedes** form of the verb in the preterit will occur in all forms of the imperfect subjunctive.

	Depositar	Obtener	Invertir
3rd-person plural preterit form:	deposit**aron**	obtuvi**eron**	invirti**eron**
Yo	depositara	obtuviera	invirtiera
Tú	depositaras	obtuvieras	invirtieras
Él/Ella/Usted	depositara	obtuviera	invirtiera
Nosotros/as	depositáramos	obtuviéramos	invirtiéramos
Vosotros/as	depositarais	obtuvierais	invirtierais
Ellos/Ellas/Ustedes	depositaran	obtuvieran	invirtieran

The endings are the same for **–ar**, **–er**, and **–ir** verbs. Note that the **yo** form and the **él/ella/usted** forms are identical. In addition, note that the **nosotros/as** form has an additional accent due to a change in where the stress of the word falls.

Just as recognizing the formal command form facilitates decoding the verb meaning behind the present subjunctive form, the third-person plural form of the preterit will help you unravel the meaning behind the imperfect subjunctive verb. The most important objective at this point is to accurately process complex sentences to avoid miscommunications.

Hypotheses and Contrary-to-fact situations

Compare the construction of this Spanish sentence and its English equivalent.

> **Si fuera el Presidente, me enfocaría en la conservación de energía.**
> *If I were the President, I would focus on the conservation of energy.*

Notice that both sentences are comprised of a dependent clause, *If I were the President*/**Si fuera el Presidente,** and a main clause, *I would focus on the conservation of energy*/**me enfocaría en la conservación de energía.** Contrary-to-fact hypothetical statements in English and Spanish follow similar patterns, using a past tense verb –the imperfect subjunctive– in the *if*, or **si** clause and the conditional in the main clause. (Recall that **si** means *if*.)

Cover up the English translations of the contrary-to-fact statements on page 544 and try to process the meaning of the Spanish sentence. Then, check yourself by reading the English interpretation. In processing the sentences for meaning you will need to identify the meaning of the verb and the subject, as expressed in the verb form. For example, in the first statement, **tuviéramos** stems from the verb **tener** *(to have)* and the subject is nosotros. Together, the main elements of each clause are decoded, *"we had"* for **tuviéramos** and *"we would travel"* for **viajaríamos.**

WILEY PLUS
Go to *WileyPLUS* and review the tutorial for this grammar point.

WILEY PLUS

You will find PowerPoint presentations to use with *Estructuras clave* in *WileyPLUS*.

TEACHING TIP: Write a few preterit verbs on the board as a review and introduction to *Estructuras clave 2*. To make sure that students know the meaning of the verbs, ask them to write a true or false sentence with the verbs and read their sentences to the class, such as *Las hijas del Presidente se graduaron de la universidad el año pasado.* The class will decide if the sentences are true or false. (Encourage use of third person plural in these true/false statements.)

TEACHING TIP: Point out that the order of the clauses may vary (*"I would focus on the conservation of energy if I were the President"* and *"Me enfocaría en la conservación de energía si fuera el Presidente".*).

Si tuviéramos mucho dinero, **viajaríamos** por todo el mundo. (pero somos pobres, no tenemos mucho dinero)	*If we had a lot of money, we would travel around the world.*
Si yo **ganara** la lotería, **compraría** una casa nueva. (pero no es muy probable que gane la lotería)	*If I won (were to win) the lottery, I would buy a new house.*
Si Juan **fuera** el dueño de la empresa, **trabajaría** para él. (pero Juan no es el dueño de la empresa, es un empleado normal)	*If Juan were the owner of the company, I would work for him.*
¿Estarías emocionada **si** Bill Gates te **ofreciera** un trabajo? (pero no es muy probable que Bill Gates te ofrezca un trabajo personalmente)	*Would you be excited if Bill Gates offered (were to offer) you a job?*
¿Qué harían ustedes **si vieran** a un ladrón en el banco? (pero no es muy probable que vean a un ladrón cuando estén en el banco)	*What would you all do if you saw (were to see) a robber in the bank?*

12A.17 ANSWERS:
Ocurrió: 1, 3, 4, 7;
No ocurrió: 2, 5, 6, 8

WILEY ⊕
PLUS

12A.17 INSTRUCTOR'S RESOURCES: You will find a reproducible chart for Activity 12A.17 in your Instructor's Resources.

12A.17 ¿Ocurrió o no ocurrió? Lee las oraciones 1–8 e indica si la acción ocurrió (pretérito) o no ocurrió (imperfecto de subjuntivo). Luego, indica si la oración te corresponde o no. Compara tus respuestas con algunos estudiantes de la clase para encontrar a la persona con respuestas más semejantes a las tuyas.

	¿Ocurrió?		¿Te corresponde?	
	Sí	**No**	**Sí**	**No**
1. Yo abrí una cuenta de ahorros cuando llegué a la universidad.				
2. Si recibiera un aumento de salario, compraría un coche nuevo.				
3. Mis padres me prestaron dinero el mes pasado.				
4. Ya pagué las facturas de este mes.				
5. Si no fuera estudiante, ahorraría más dinero.				
6. Si me robaran la tarjeta de crédito, llamaría a la policía.				
7. Obtuve un préstamo para asistir a la universidad.				
8. Si me ofrecieran un trabajo en Latinoamérica, lo aceptaría.				

12A.18 Lógico o ilógico.   Lee las siguientes oraciones e indica si son lógicas o ilógicas. Explica/corrige los casos ilógicos. Luego, verifica tus respuestas con tus compañeros de clase.

Lógico   **Ilógico**

☐ ☑ **1.** Si el cajero automático estuviera roto *(broken)*, llamaría a la policía.

☑ ☐ **2.** Si un amigo usara mi tarjeta de crédito sin mi permiso, ya no sería mi amigo.

☐ ☑ **3.** Si compraras un disco compacto, lo pagarías a plazos.

☐ ☑ **4.** Si fuéramos agricultores *(farmers)*, viviríamos en la ciudad.

☑ ☐ **5.** Si un amigo necesitara dinero para una operación, se lo prestaría.

☐ ☑ **6.** Si quisieras depositar dinero, irías al hospital.

☑ ☐ **7.** Si olvidaran su contraseña, crearían una contraseña nueva.

☑ ☐ **8.** Si tuviéramos problemas con otro empleado, hablaríamos con nuestra gerente.

12A.19 El juego de *Survivor*.   Habla con diez compañeros/as de clase para determinar qué harían ellos si ganaran el premio de $1.000.000 en el programa de *Survivor*. En tu **Retrato de la clase** apunta los resultados (en términos generales) de la clase.

Modelo: E1: *¿Qué harías con el dinero si ganaras el juego de "Survivor"?*
E2: *Compraría una casa en la playa.*

Compañero/a	Lo que haría si ganara el juego de *Survivor*

Enlaces

12A.20 Enlaces.   Determina el significado de las palabras en negrita según el contexto de las oraciones. Selecciona entre las siguientes opciones. Luego, verifica tus respuestas con la clase.

a. above all/especially   **b.** since/from the time that   **c.** since/because

___c___ **1.** Las huellas digitales *(fingerprints)* representan una forma muy segura de determinar la identidad de un individuo **ya que** es difícil falsificarlas.

___a___ **2.** El robo de identidad es una gran preocupación, **sobre todo** en países industrializados como Estados Unidos y Japón.

___b___ **3. Desde que** abrimos nuestra primera cuenta, debemos tomar medidas *(measures)* para proteger nuestro dinero.

12A.21 ¿Puedes conectar las ideas?   Usa las expresiones para conectar las ideas de estas frases. Luego, verifica tus respuestas con un compañero de clase.

desde que   sobre todo   ya que

1. Es necesario proteger los números de las cuentas bancarias, ___sobre todo___ cuando usamos el cajero automático o compramos algo por la Internet.

2. ___Desde que___ un feto empieza a desarrollarse, la distribución de las venas de la mano nunca cambia. Por eso, examinar esas venas es una buena manera de determinar la identidad de un individuo.

3. Los sistemas biométricos son muy sofisticados ___ya que___ dependen de una tecnología avanzada.

12A.18 ANSWERS: Lógico: 2, 5, 7, 8. Ilógico: 1 (informaría al banco), 3 (lo pagarías inmediatamente), 4 (en el campo), 6 (al banco)

12A.18 EXTENSION ACTIVITY: Challenge more advanced students to use this exercise as a model for developing three sentences of their own which they can later exchange with a classmate.

12A.19 TEACHING TIP: Allow ample time for students to poll classmates. Ask students to report classmates' responses, commenting on repeated or similar responses. Ask follow-up questions as appropriate. For example if John says *"Amy compraría un carro."* ask Amy *¿Qué tipo de carro comprarías? ¿Por qué?*

WILEY
PLUS
12A.19 INSTRUCTOR'S RESOURCES: You will find a reproducible chart for Activity 12A.19 in your Instructor's Resources.

12A.20 TEACHING TIP: Have students share their answers with a partner before going over them as a class. When you do go over them as a class, have students hold up one finger to represent "a", two for "b", and three for "c." This way you will be able to get a sense of how well they understood the new words without putting students on the spot.

12A.22 Nuevas formas de proteger el dinero. Lee los artículos acerca del uso de la biometría *(biometrics)* para proteger el dinero y la identidad. Luego, contesta las preguntas, indicando la opción correcta. Finalmente, verifica tus respuestas con la clase.

1. Según el primer artículo, la biometría más avanzada consiste en ___a___.
   a. leer el iris del ojo y las huellas digitales
   b. analizar el ADN
   c. examinar los dientes
   d. comparar la forma de la oreja

2. Según el segundo artículo, la biometría más avanzada consiste en ___c___.
   a. leer el iris del ojo y las huellas digitales *(fingerprints)*
   b. analizar el ADN
   c. examinar las venas de la mano
   d. comparar firmas

3. Después de leer los dos artículos, ___d___ será la mejor forma de proteger la identidad.
   a. leer el iris del ojo y las huellas digitales
   b. analizar el ADN
   c. comparar las características de la cara
   d. examinar las venas de la mano

La nueva tecnología protegerá tu dinero
Nuevos sistemas para acceder a tus cuentas

- Un nuevo sistema de seguridad será pronto implementado gracias a los avances tecnológicos; será algo así como lo que vemos en películas de acción como *Misión Imposible*.

- Esta nueva revolución tecnológica se llama biometría. Es más rápida y segura, pues le permite al dueño de la cuenta bancaria ser reconocido a través de su voz *(voice)*, firma o huellas digitales.

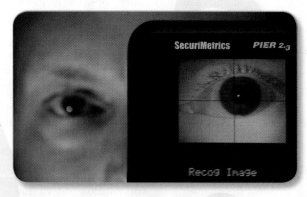

- Los sistemas biométricos literalmente leen la información guardada en el iris del ojo. Pueden examinar las facciones y contornos del rostro, y las líneas de los dedos.

- Podrás acceder a tus cuentas de forma biométrica en todos los bancos y cooperativas de crédito, tiendas, centros comerciales, estaciones de gasolina y supermercados de toda la nación.

- Eso quiere decir que tendrás que llevar una tarjeta plástica menos en tu bolsillo o billetera, y que las empresas que manejan los cajeros automáticos se ahorrarán millones de dólares.

Tus venas ayudarán a proteger tu dinero
Una identificación bancaria más segura

Un patrón único debajo de la piel

Los ladrones informáticos lo tienen cada día más difícil. **Sobre todo** en Japón, donde más de 16,000 oficinas bancarias y 16,400 cajeros automáticos cuentan con un nuevo sistema de identificación de lectura biométrica por el patrón de las venas de la palma de la mano que, al estar dos o tres milímetros por debajo de la epidermis, resulta un sistema infalsificable y mucho más eficaz que las huellas digitales o el iris ocular. Las investigaciones demuestran que el patrón de las venas es único para cada individuo, incluso en el caso de gemelos idénticos, y que éste permanece inalterable **desde que** el individuo se encuentra en el útero materno hasta su muerte. Asumir una falsa identidad falsificando las venas es extremadamente difícil, **ya que** la sangre tiene que estar fluyendo para registrar la imagen o patrón.

12A.23 El dinero y la tecnología. Indica si estás o no de acuerdo con las siguientes oraciones. Luego encuentra a un/a compañero/a de clase que tenga respuestas como las tuyas. Comparen sus respuestas con las del resto de la clase y apunten los resultados.

¿Estás de acuerdo?

Sí	No	
☐	☐	**1.** Es necesario modernizar la tecnología constantemente para poder proteger el acceso a nuestro dinero.
☐	☐	**2.** La seguridad de nuestros ahorros dependerá cada vez más de la biometría y otras formas de tecnología.
☐	☐	**3.** En el futuro, tendremos que inventar otras maneras para proteger nuestras cuentas bancarias.
☐	☐	**4.** Estoy seguro de que se inventará una tecnología completamente impenetrable para proteger nuestras identidades contra los fraudes.
☐	☐	**5.** Yo me preocupo por la seguridad de mis tarjetas de crédito.
☐	☐	**6.** En el futuro, no habrá dinero físico.
☐	☐	**7.** En general, tomo medidas para proteger mi identidad, mis cuentas bancarias y mis tarjetas de crédito.
☐	☐	**8.** La tecnología facilita el acceso al dinero en el banco.
☐	☐	**9.** En el futuro, no habrá bancos en edificios físicos.
☐	☐	**10.** Debido a la tecnología, existen más oportunidades para cometer fraude financiero.

12A.23 FOLLOW-UP:
Poll the class to see how many students agree/disagree with each statement. Then ask students to work with the person whose responses were most similar to their own to complete the following activity.

12A.24 FOLLOW-UP: Go over conclusions with the class, discussing any disagreements among the groups. The items themselves serve as the *modelo* for what and how students are to record information in the *Retrato de la clase.*

12A.24 ¿Qué piensa la clase acerca del dinero y la tecnología? Con un/a compañero/a, lean las siguientes oraciones e indiquen las conclusiones generales de la clase, según las respuestas de la actividad anterior. Escriban las conclusiones en su **Retrato de la clase.**

1. La clase piensa que el sistema bancario ha cambiado mucho/poco debido a la tecnología.

2. La clase se preocupa mucho/poco por la seguridad del dinero.

3. La clase piensa que la tecnología facilita la seguridad del dinero/el fraude financiero.

4. La clase piensa que en el futuro los bancos y el dinero serán iguales/diferentes.

5. La clase piensa que la tecnología es útil/inútil para proteger el dinero.

6. La clase piensa que es probable/improbable que la tecnología cambie cómo manejamos el dinero.

Perspectivas

12A.25 Los factores que influyen en el acceso a la tecnología. En grupos de cuatro, indiquen si los siguientes factores influyen en el acceso a la tecnología en diferentes países del mundo. Luego, apunten también los cinco factores que ustedes consideran los más importantes y por qué.

12A.25 TEACHING TIP: Allow students ample time to complete the chart. Discuss as a class how the factors affect access to technology (e.g., how can a war affect access to technology, how the type of economy affects access to technology). Go over each group's choices orally for the five most important factors and the reasons for the choices, pointing out similarities and differences.

12A.25 INSTRUCTOR'S RESOURCES: You will find a reproducible chart for Activity 12A.25 in your Instructor's Resources.

Factor	Influye en el acceso a la tecnología de un país	No influye en el acceso a la tecnología de un país	Los cinco factores más importantes (en orden de 1 a 5 según su importancia)
La geografía (urbano vs. rural)			
El nivel de desarrollo económico			
La forma de gobierno (democrático vs. totalitario)			
La estabilidad política			
La infraestructura (carreteras, ferrocarriles, puertos, etc.)			
El grupo socioeconómico			
El nivel escolar o de instrucción formal			
La población del país			
La movilidad de la población			
El grado de nacionalismo			
La guerra (si hay guerra o no)			
Los tipos/el número de recursos nacionales			
La tolerancia cultural (abierta vs. tradicional)			

Vocabulario esencial

Sustantivos

el/la cajero/a	*teller*
el cajero automático	*automated teller machine*
la cárcel	*jail*
la cartera	*wallet*
la cuenta bancaria	*bank account*
la cuenta corriente	*checking account*
la cuenta de ahorros	*savings account*
el delito	*crime*
la factura	*bill*
el gerente	*manager*
la guardia	*guard*
los impuestos	*taxes*
el ladrón	*thief*
el préstamo	*loan*
el presupuesto	*budget*
el saldo	*balance*
la sucursal	*branch (of a bank, business, etc.)*
la tarjeta de débito	*debit card*
la tarjeta de crédito	*credit card*

Adjetivos y adverbios

mensual	*monthly*
puntualmente	*on time*

Verbos

cobrar	*to charge*
comprobar	*to check*
depositar	*to deposit*
gastar	*to spend*
influir	*to influence*
invertir	*to invest*
manejar	*to manage*
obtener	*to obtain*
pagar a plazos	*to pay in installments*
pagar en efectivo	*to pay in cash*

Otras palabras y expresiones

la contraseña	*password*
endeudarse	*to get into debt*
enfocarse	*to focus*
la entrada	*ticket*
las facciones	*features*
el gran almacén	*department store*
la huella digital	*fingerprint*
la medida	*measure*
recargar	*to recharge*
los suministros	*supplies*
la traducción	*translation*
abrir cuentas	*to open accounts*
debido a	*due to*
llevarse bien/mal	*to get along/not get along*

Cognados

Review the cognates in *Adelante* and the false cognates in *¡Atención!*. For a complete list of cognates, see Appendix 4 on page 605.

INVESTIGACIÓN 12B
¿Qué es la occidentalización?

In this **Investigación,** you will learn:

▶ How to process complex Spanish propositions

▶ How to think critically about globalization

¿Cómo se puede hablar del impacto de la occidentalización en las culturas del mundo?

You can investigate what is meant by westernization of world cultures.	¿Qué es la occidentalización? ¿Cuáles son las ventajas de los medios de comunicación, el medio principal de la occidentalización? ¿Cuáles son las desventajas?
You can talk about various means of communication that unite the world.	¿Tienes acceso a la tecnología inalámbrica? ¿Cuántos aparatos portátiles tienes? ¿Crees que el video digital es un buen medio para las películas y programas de televisión? ¿Cuál es la mejor forma de difundir información?
You can speculate about the purposes and consequences of the various means of communication.	¿Usas audífonos (headphones) para que otras personas no oigan tu música? ¿Te gusta comunicarte por mensajería instantánea cuando tus amigos están en línea? ¿Es necesario controlar el costo de la conexión a la Internet a fin de que todos tengan acceso?

PREPARATION ACTIVITY: Invite students to scan through the two columns highlighting the goals for this *Investigación*. Remind them that there are many cognates that will help them make meaning. Ask them what they think they will be able to do by the end of the chapter.

Adelante

¡Ya lo sabes! El acceso y la conectividad

PRACTICING VOCABULARY: Since these words are cognates, students will have an easier time understanding them. However, in order to make these words a part of their active vocabulary, students need contextual exposure and the chance to manipulate them.

el acceso	el proceso
la banda	el punto de vista
la barrera	el obstáculo
la conectividad	la rapidez
la difusión de información	la sociedad equitativa
la diseminación de culturas	las transmisiones satelitales
el espacio	el video digital
la expansión tecnológica	
el imperialismo	generar
las líneas telefónicas	percibir
las nuevas fronteras	permitir
	reconfigurar

12B.1 PASO 1: TEACHING TIP. Encourage students to read through the sentences without referencing the word bank. They should jot down a word/idea/note of what should go in the blank. Then, have them reread the sentences to find the right match.

12B.1 La palabra apropiada.

Paso 1: Escribe la palabra que corresponde a las oraciones 1–10. Luego, comparte tus respuestas con un/a compañero/a de clase.

1. El uso de la Internet ha aumentado notablemente en los últimos años y esta ____expansión tecnológica____ no se limita a los países más avanzados.

2. Muchas personas creen que la globalización representa una nueva forma de ____imperialismo____ porque permite que los países ricos dominen a los países pobres.

3. La evolución de la Internet ha sido un ____proceso____ relativamente rápido que se ha acelerado recientemente.

4. Los comentarios de los economistas acerca de la globalización pueden ____generar____ mucha discusión y controversia.

5. Si no existiera la _____difusión_____ de información, sabríamos muy poco sobre las elecciones políticas o los acontecimientos mundiales *(world events)*.

6. La _____conectividad_____ a la Internet es cada día más rápida.

7. El _____punto de vista_____ de los republicanos es distinto del de los demócratas.

8. La mayoría de los medios de telecomunicación reciben información de satélites que están en el _____espacio_____.

9. Las _____líneas telefónicas_____ facilitan trabajar desde la casa porque proveen conexión a las máquinas fax, a la Internet y a nuevos sistemas de telecomunicaciones.

10. En la actualidad *(Nowadays)*, es muy difícil tener un negocio sin _____acceso_____ a la Internet.

Paso 2: Ahora, escojan las tres oraciones más significativas para ustedes y compártanlas con la clase para ver cuáles son las más comunes.

12B.2 ¡Adivina! Con dos compañeros de clase, traten de describir diferentes cognados de la sección *Adelante*, sin nombrarlos, para que sus compañeros puedan adivinar la palabra. Recuerden usar expresiones como "Es el opuesto de la palabra…", "Es sinónimo de..", "Se asocia con…". ¿Cuántas palabras o frases pudieron adivinar?

12B.1 PASO 2: FOLLOW-UP. Explore what the top three most significant propositions in 12B.1 are for the majority of the class. Keep them in mind as the class continues to explore their points of view on technology.

12B.2 TEACHING TIP: Tell students to keep track of the number of words/ phrases that they guess correctly. In addition, tell students they have only five minutes (or however long you deem appropriate) to do this activity. At the end, check with groups to see how many they got right.

VÍVELO: LENGUA

Using conjunctions and prepositions

Conjunctions are expressions that connect two clauses. They include the connector **que** and are followed by a conjugated verb, as in **Va a venir después de que le inviten** *(He will come after they invite him)*. When the connector **que** is not included, these phrases do not function as conjunctions but rather as prepositions (or prepositional phrases), and they are followed by the infinitive, as in **Después de comprar el iPod, descargó muchas canciones de iTunes** *(After buying the iPod, he downloaded many songs from iTunes)*. The infinitive after the preposition usually corresponds to the –ing form of the verb in English; however, it can also correspond to the infinitive (i.e., *to + verb*) or to a conjugated verb.

antes de + infinitive
Antes de ir al aeropuerto, ella preparó sus maletas.
Before going to the airport, she packed her suitcase.

sin + infinitive
Sin saber la respuesta, él contestó la pregunta correctamente.
Without knowing the answer, he responded correctly.

hasta + infinitive
Ella manejó hasta llegar a Washington D.C.
She drove until she arrived in/she got to Washington D.C.

para + infinitive
Para encontrar información acerca de otras culturas, puedes consultar la Internet.
In order to find out information about other cultures, you can consult the Internet.

12B.3 **Contesta lógicamente.**   En grupos de tres lean todas las opciones de 1–6 que aparecen a continuación y aclaren cualquier duda sobre estructuras o vocabulario entre ustedes *(among yourselves)*. Luego, trabajando solo/a, escucha las preguntas y escoge la respuesta más apropiada para ti. Después comparte tus respuestas con tus compañeros.

1.
a. Subo el volumen.
b. Apago la computadora.
c. Conecto la computadora.
d. La limpio.

2.
a. Me conecto a la *Internet*.
b. Me pongo los audífonos.
c. Me duermo.
d. Me miro en el espejo.

3.
a. Salgo con mis amigos.
b. Bebo un vaso de leche.
c. Miro la televisión.
d. Subo el volumen.

4.
a. Hablan de sus profesores.
b. Bailan el reguetón.
c. Beben cervezas.
d. Escuchan música rap.

5.
a. Voy a bailar.
b. Preparo la comida.
c. Leo los comentarios de mis amigos.
d. Descanso.

6.
a. para mandar y recibir correo electrónico
b. para lavar la ropa
c. para hacer ejercicio
d. para poner gasolina en mi carro

¿Qué es la occidentalización?

La occidentalización es percibida como un proceso de globalización. En este punto, todos están de acuerdo. La occidentalización ha contribuido al desarrollo del mundo a través del transporte, el comercio, la migración, la difusión de culturas distintas y la diseminación de los conocimientos científicos y tecnológicos más avanzados. La occidentalización también es la globalización de nuevos sistemas de telecomunicaciones como las transmisiones satelitales, la banda ancha para la red *(network)*, la radio y la Internet. El impacto de las nuevas telecomunicaciones ha llevado a la tecnología inalámbrica, la mensajería instantánea, el video digital y al aprendizaje *(learning)* a distancia, entre otros.

Dios bendiga a América, 1940 por Philip Reisman.

Hay, sin embargo, varias definiciones y puntos de vista sobre la occidentalización. Por una parte, la dominación occidental a veces se percibe como la continuación del imperialismo occidental. En esta visión, el capitalismo contemporáneo, conducido principalmente por Estados Unidos y Europa, establece reglas del comercio y de los negocios que no sirven a los intereses de los países pobres del mundo que no tienen acceso a la tecnología moderna. Los antiglobalizadores se oponen a las políticas que sostienen un libre mercado porque piensan que generan pobreza, desigualdad (inequality), conflictos sociales, destrucción cultural y daños (harm) ecológicos. Para ellos, el sistema de capitalismo occidental conduce a (leads to): una cultura consumidora y materialista, la sustitución de comidas regionales por comida instantánea genérica, el consumo de mini-aparatos de telecomunicaciones, y la imposición de productos culturales como el cine y la música sobre todas las culturas del mundo.

La globalización, consecuencia de las nuevas telecomunicaciones, también lleva a una interdependencia y conectividad entre las culturas, el comercio y los mercados del mundo. Esa interdependencia no permite la dominación total de un solo poder económico, pero ¿puede permitir la eliminación de las diferencias culturales del mundo?

12B.4 **¿Cuánto comprendes de la occidentalización?** Lee las oraciones y escoge la respuesta(s) correcta(s) según la información de la lectura. Luego, verifica tus respuestas con la clase.

1. En términos generales, es aceptable decir que la occidentalización representa la (democratización/globalización) del mundo.

2. Según una definición, la occidentalización se percibe como la continuación del (imperialismo/militarismo/racismo) occidental.

3. El capitalismo contemporáneo no se asocia con (Europa/Asia/Estados Unidos).

4. Los antiglobalizadores se oponen a las políticas que sostienen (el desarrollo económico/el libre mercado/la agricultura industrial) porque piensan que genera pobreza, desigualdad, conflictos sociales, destrucción cultural y daños ecológicos.

5. La influencia de la occidentalización en cuanto al transporte, el comercio, la migración, la difusión de culturas distintas y la diseminación de conocimientos tecnológicos y científicos ha sido (negativa/positiva/tanto positiva como negativa).

6. En resumen, los antiglobalizadores creen que el capitalismo lleva a _____. (Indica todas las opciones correctas según la lectura).

   a. una cultura consumidora
   b. mayor migración de regiones rurales a las ciudades
   c. la sustitución de comidas regionales
   d. un cine universal
   e. la eliminación de negocios pequeños o familiares
   f. mayor uso de mini-aparatos de telecomunicaciones

12B.4 ANSWERS: 1. la globalización; 2. del imperialismo occidental; 3. Asia; 4. el libre mercado; 5. positiva; 6. a, c, d, f

12B.4 TEACHING TIP: Encourage students to first complete this activity without referencing the reading. Once they have finished, have them go back over it, this time making reference to what they read. Did their answers change? How was the first time different from the second time? As you go over the answers with students, make statements like, *El capitalismo contemporáneo se asocia con Asia, ¿no?* to spark discussion. Ask questions that invite students to give longer answers, such as *¿Qué ejemplos de la globalización occidental conocen?*

12B.4 EXTENSION ACTIVITY: Brainstorm with students additional examples of ways to measure the effects of globalization on mass communities via technology, such as the number and the diversity of foreign languages on a given topic found on a) YouTube, b) Google searches, c) translations provided in Wikipedia, d) video games, etc. To include a variety of sources of data, allow students to explore these venues in addition to or as opposed to just popular movies. The point is to raise students' awareness about the topic of globalization and how it is propelled through technology.

Bien dicho

Repaso de las vocales y la acentuación

In *Investigaciones* 4A and 4B, you learned about the pronunciation of the vowels in Spanish, but several concepts merit review and practice. First, there are five principal vowel sounds in Spanish: [a] (ah), [e] (eh), [i] (ee) , [o] (oh), and [u] (ooh). Second, these vowels are much shorter and crisper than their English counterparts. Third, there is no glide at the end of the vowel as there often is in English (e.g, *say, to* versus Spanish **se, tú**). Fourth, diphthongs are never pronounced as two vowels, but rather as a single sound. If the **i** or the **u** of a vowel pair has a written accent mark, no diphthong is formed. Fifth, in the combinations **gue-, gui-, que-, qui-**, the **u** is silent: **guerra** [gé-rra], **equipo** [e-kí-po], but in the combinations **-güe** and **-güi** the letter **ü** corresponds to [w]: **bilingüe** [bi-líŋ-gwe], **pingüino** [piŋ-gwí-no]. Finally, unstressed vowels in Spanish are never pronounced with the "schwa" [ə] as they are in English.

As you have also seen previously, written accent marks in Spanish are used in cases where the stress of the word does not fall where it would naturally fall. Words ending in a vowel, **-n**, or **-s** whose accent falls on the last syllable require a written accent: **café** (ca-FE), **alemán** (a-le-MAN), **japonés** (ja-po-NES). Words ending in a consonant other than **-n** or **-s** whose accent falls on the next-to-last syllable also require a written accent: **lápiz** (LA-piz), **revólver** (re-VOL-ver), **cárcel** (CAR-cel). Words whose stress falls on a syllable other than one of the last two syllables always require a written accent mark: **máquina** (MA-qui-na), **Latinoamérica** (La-ti-no-a-ME-ri-ca), **tráigamelo** (TRAI-ga-me-lo). As mentioned above, written accent marks are also used over an **i** or **u** to indicate that there is no diphthong. Compare, for example, **día** [dI-a] and **diario** [dyA-ryo].

There are some words in Spanish that are spelled and pronounced the same way but have different meanings (homonyms) based on whether they use a written accent mark or not. A number of one-syllable words have written accent marks to distinguish them from a second one-syllable word that is spelled and pronounced the same, but which has a different meaning or function. Some of these include the following:

mi (possessive) Mi coche es rojo.	**mí** (prepositional pronoun) A mí me gusta bailar salsa.
tu (possessive) ¿Cuál es tu color favorito?	**tú** (subject pronoun) ¿De dónde eres tú?
el (definite article) El vestido de Carmen es corto.	**él** (subject pronoun) ¿Cuántos años tiene él?
te (object/reflexive pronoun) ¿A qué hora te levantaste hoy?	**té** (beverage) Los ingleses beben mucho té.
se (reflexive pronoun) María se ducha después de correr.	**sé** (yo form of **saber,** command of **ser**) No sé esquiar en el agua. Durante la entrevista, sé cortés.
de (preposition) El anillo de Marcos es de oro.	**dé** (command of **dar**) Nunca dé su contraseña a otra persona.
si (conditional conjunction) Si ganara la lotería, no trabajaría.	**sí** (affirmative adverb) —¿Te gustaría ir al cine? —Sí. ¿Qué película quieres ver?
mas (rarely used synonym of **pero**) Deseo acompañarte, mas no puedo ir.	**más** (comparative/quantitative adverb) Debes hacer más ejercicio. Carlota es más alta que Susana.

Words such as **qué, cuándo, dónde, cuál(es)** and **quién(es)** have a written accent mark when they begin either a direct or an indirect question, but not when they function as conjunctions or relative pronouns.

> Sara le explicó a Daniel dónde está la biblioteca.
> ¿Me puedes decir cuándo es la fiesta?
>
> Marco me dijo que viene a la fiesta.
> Voy a tu casa cuando tenga tiempo

12B.5 ¿Lleva acento escrito o no? Escucha las palabras y subraya *(underline)* la vocal o el diptongo que se enfatiza. Luego, pon un acento escrito en la palabra cuando sea necesario. Verifica tus respuestas con la clase y después practica la pronunciación de las palabras con un/a compañero/a, prestando atención a las vocales.

1. [kon-tem-po-ra-ne-o]   contemporaneo   contemporáneo
2. [de-si-gwal-dad]   desigualdad   desigualdad
3. [di-fu-syon]   difusion   difusión
4. [na-ve-ge]   navegue   navegué
5. [ra-pi-des]   rapidez   rapidez
6. [i-ma-xen]   imagen   imagen
7. [te-le-fo-ni-ka]   telefonica   telefónica
8. [kon-su-mi-do-ra]   consumidora   consumidora

12B.6 Pongan los acentos y eliminen la "schwa". Con un/a compañero/a, pongan los acentos escritos cuando sean necesarios. Luego, alternándose, pronuncien las siguientes oraciones, eliminando la vocal "schwa", especialmente en los cognados. Repitan el ejercicio pronunciando las oraciones que no pronunciaron la primera vez.

1. Para los jovenes de esta generacion, la tecnologia es una gran necesidad.
2. La mensajeria instantanea es un medio de comunicacion bastante comun.
3. Los daños ecologicos y la erosion cultural son desventajas de la globalizacion.
4. Maria compro una computadora que permite acceso inalambrico a la Internet.
5. Los portatiles seran mas pequeños y economicos algun dia.
6. Las comunidades indigenas combatiran la pobreza y la marginacion politica.
7. Prefeririamos ver la television digital por medio de transmision satelite.
8. La diseminacion de informacion y conocimientos cientificos en linea es rapida.

12B.7 El significado correcto. Lee las siguientes oraciones e indica cuál es la opción correcta para completar cada oración. Luego, verifica tus respuestas con un/a compañero/a de clase.

1. Por la noche, preferimos beber (te/té) en lugar de café.
2. Ellos son (de/dé) Costa Rica y viven en San José.
3. Antonio y su novia (se/sé) mandan muchos mensajes de texto.
4. Esta semana, he trabajado (mas/más) de 40 horas. ¡Estoy cansada!
5. –¿Cómo está (tu/tú) mamá? –Está muy bien, gracias.
6. (Si/Sí) tuviera tiempo libre, lo pasaría con mis amigos.
7. ¿Ustedes creen (que/qué) es necesario aprender español?
8. –¿(Quien/Quién) trajo esa ensalada tan deliciosa? –La trajo Francisco.

Palabras clave 1 Conjunciones de tiempo, propósito y causa

SUGGESTION: Review with students the conjunctions they learned in *Investigación 11B: antes de que, sin que, para que, a condición de que, con tal de que, en caso de que.*

LEARNING STRATEGIES: Subsequent activities will provide more focused practice around this vocabulary. It is important at this point to have students make a concerted effort to pay attention to the meaning of these conjunctions. These items are typically introduced in text books in the context of grammar explanations. In presenting and practicing them here as vocabulary, our intention is that students become comfortable with their *meaning* before seeing them used in upcoming *Estructuras clave* sections, so that their focus there can be on structure and the use of indicative versus subjunctive without the distraction of figuring out the meaning of individual conjunctions.

RECYCLING: Vocabulary associated with new technologies is recycled here in *Palabras* clave and throughout the chapter.

The following expressions (called conjunctions) are useful when conveying a sequence of actions and are used with the subjunctive.

antes (de) que *(before)*

Vamos a comprar una computadora antes de que aumenten los precios.

cuando *(when)*

Cuando me pagan siempre voy inmediatamente al banco a depositar el cheque.

después de que *(after)*

Al Gore dio discursos acerca de la ecología mundial después de que hizo su documental.

hasta que *(until)*

Siempre uso mi teléfono celular hasta que la batería se queda sin carga.

tan pronto como *(as soon as)*

Yo leo las noticias en la Internet tan pronto como llego a mi casa.

en cuanto *(as soon as)*

Respondió al mensaje en cuanto lo recibió.

a fin de que *(in order to)*

El primer ministro de Canadá quiere hablar con los presidentes de todos los países sudamericanos a fin de que se eliminen las barreras al comercio libre.

puesto que *(because/since)*

En las ciudades grandes hay más acceso a la tecnología puesto que existe la infraestructura tecnológica.

Conjunciones de condición

sin que *(without)*

Un iPod no va a funcionar sin que tenga la batería cargada.

para que *(so that)*

Los estudiantes compran celulares para que puedan enviar mensajes a sus amigos fácilmente.

a menos que *(unless)*

Los precios de los celulares son razaonables a menos que tengan muchos accesorios y conexión a la Internet.

con tal (de) que *(provided that)*

Pueden enviar mensajes en clase con tal de que no abusen de este privilegio.

en caso de que *(in case)*

Me voy a llevar la computadora portátil en caso de que tenga que trabajar.

Sustantivos y verbos

las reglas

Los padres deben implementar reglas para limitar el tiempo que sus hijos pasan en la Internet.

el daño

Muchos médicos indican que el uso constante de audífonos puede causar un daño irremediable a los oídos.

dañar

Algunos activistas se oponen a la globalización porque piensan que puede dañar las economías de los países pobres.

12B.8 Categorías de conjunciones. Categoriza las siguientes conjunciones según su función.

a fin de que   para que   cuando
tan pronto como   puesto que   antes de que
en caso de que   con tal de que   después de que
sin que   a menos que   a condición de que
en cuanto   hasta que

Conjunciones de...			
.... tiempo	.... condición	.... propósito	.... causa

12B.8 ANSWERS: Conjunciones de tiempo: tan pronto como, cuando, hasta que, después de que, en cuanto, antes de que; Conjunciones de condición: sin que, con tal de que, en caso de que, a menos que, a condición de que; Conjunciones de propósito: para que, a fin de que, con tal de que; Conjunciones de causa: puesto que

12B.9 Actitudes y experiencias acerca de la tecnología. Indica si las siguientes declaraciones son ciertas o falsas para ti. Luego, entrevista a un compañero de clase para ver si tienen mucho o poco en común. Comparte tus resultados con la clase.

Cierto   Falso

☐   ☐   **1.** Uso audífonos cuando escucho música.

☐   ☐   **2.** Tengo acceso a tecnología inalámbrica para poder hacer las tareas de mis clases.

☐   ☐   **3.** Puedo usar mi tarjeta de crédito en línea con tal de que el sitio ofrezca una garantía de alta seguridad.

☐   ☐   **4.** Paso más de dos horas diarias en línea puesto que soy adicto/a a los videojuegos.

☐   ☐   **5.** No me opongo a los videojuegos a menos que sean muy violentos.

☐   ☐   **6.** Mis padres tenían muchas reglas acerca del uso de la Internet para que no compráramos cosas en línea.

☐   ☐   **7.** Puedo aprender a usar la tecnología con gran facilidad con tal de que haya un manual de instrucciones.

☐   ☐   **8.** Siempre llevo mi celular conmigo en caso de que mi familia me necesite.

12B.9 TEACHING TIP: Guide students through the process of changing these statements to questions. You may want to model the first one with them before having them do the rest on their own. If you would like to also have students make a distinction between *tú* and *usted*, pick an identifying feature (wearing flip flops, glasses, shorts, etc.) among a third of your students and have those individuals be with whom *usted* is used. Allow students time to complete the survey. Encourage students to elaborate on their responses to spur class discussion. Tally the number of true and false statements for 1 through 8. Explore false statements because they may be the most interesting. Then, attempt some generalizations based on the data, such as *La mayoría de los estudiantes tiene conexión inalámbrica para hacer las tareas de sus clases.*

12B.10 Oraciones lógicas. Con un/a compañero/a de clase, emparejen las frases de la izquierda con las frases más lógicas de la derecha.

_e_ **1.** Voy al concierto el sábado por la noche

_f_ **2.** Asistimos a la universidad

_b_ **3.** Traeré el celular a la fiesta

_c_ **4.** Siempre uso el cajero automático

_d_ **5.** Mi hermana nunca sale de casa

_a_ **6.** Yo trabajo en la computadora

a. con tal de que tú envíes el fax.

b. en caso de que necesite llamar un taxi.

c. antes (de) que se me acabe el dinero.

d. sin que haya grabado sus programas favoritos en el TiVo.

e. a menos que me llamen para trabajar.

f. para que podamos encontrar un buen trabajo después de graduarnos.

12B.11 TEACHING TIP: Point out to students that the statements in 1–8 can be used to support their perspectives if they were to have a debate on the topic of globalization. In this way, you underscore the entire idea behind each statement and not just the correct meaning of the adverbial conjunction.

12B.11 ¿Cuál es la conclusión lógica? En grupos de tres, escojan la conclusión lógica para las siguientes oraciones. Luego, verifiquen sus respuestas con la clase.

1. Muchos recursos *(resources)* naturales se van a acabar a menos que…

   (a.) empecemos a protegerlos.
   b. aumentemos el desperdicio *(waste)*.

2. El acceso a la tecnología inalámbrica se debe expandir a fin de…

   (a.) proveer educación a regiones rurales.
   b. animar el uso de videojuegos violentos.

3. La globalización no avanzará sin que…

   (a.) todos países tengan acceso a las nuevas tecnologías
   b. todo el mundo ignore la tecnología.

4. La globalización puede ser positiva con tal de que…

   (a.) se puedan preservar las culturas regionales.
   b. se eliminen las culturas regionales.

5. Se eliminará la pobreza después de que…

   (a.) todos tengan los mismos derechos.
   b. las empresas controlen la economía del país.

6. Tendremos que depender de la Internet hasta que…

   (a.) se invente un sistema mejor.
   b. todas las computadoras sean obsoletas.

7. Es necesario que los países del mundo cooperen para que…

   a. podamos aprovecharnos de ellos.
   (b.) todos podamos vivir en paz.

8. El gobierno podrá implementar muchos programas a condición de que…

   a. no tenga el dinero.
   (b.) tenga el apoyo de sus ciudadanos *(citizens)*.

¡Atención!

Recurso	means *resource* as in raw material or financial asset. It also means *source*, which is where one finds information. To express recourse in Spanish, use *remedio*, *opción*, or *alternativa*.
	El petróleo es un recurso natural esencial para la economía mundial. La Internet es un buen recurso para encontrar información de muchos tipos. Ya no tienes opción. No hay otra solución.
La red	doesn't refer to the color. It means net or network. It is also a synonym for the Internet.
	La red es un sinómino de la Internet. Esta compañía tiene una red de distribución internacional. Los pescadores usan una red para pescar.
Grabar	doesn't mean to grab, but rather *to tape, to record.* The verb recordar means *to remember.* To express *to grab* in Spanish, use the verb agarrar.
	Marcos graba sus programas favoritos en TiVo. ¿Recuerdas que hoy hay examen en la clase de español? Antes de salir, siempre agarro las llaves y el celular.
Captar	means to attract, to catch, to captivate. To express *to capture, to arrest* or *to detain* in Spanish, use capturar, arrestar o detener.
	Este sitio web captó mi atención porque las fotos son muy bonitas. Los policías capturaron al ladrón cuando salió del banco.
Sostener	means *to support* as in to hold up. It also means *to hold* or *to maintain* when one expresses and defends an opinion. On the other hand, it can mean *to sustain* as when one offers moral or emotional support.
	Las columnas sostienen el techo del edificio. El sociólogo sostiene que la globalización puede eliminar diferencias culturales. El amor de sus hijos sostiene a María.

¡ATENCIÓN!: As you present this vocabulary, remember that students need to hear or see the word in context multiple times before it becomes a part of their active vocabulary. Additionally, this vocabulary needs to be put in various contexts so that students do not mistake them for their false cognates. When you present the vocabulary, make sure to make it relevant and engaging as much as possible, for example: *Recurso. La selva del Amazonas tiene muchos recursos naturales, ¿no? ¿Qué recurso es más importante: el agua o el petróleo? ¿Qué recursos ofrece nuestra universidad para buscar trabajo?* The idea is to get students interacting with the vocabulary on a receptive level before expecting them to produce it. Note that their answers do not need to include the new words, but they do need to understand them.

12B.12 ¿Lógico o ilógico? Indica si lo que dicen las oraciones es lógico o ilógico. Corrige las oraciones ilógicas. Luego compara tus respuestas con la clase.

12B.12 ANSWERS: Lógico: 2, 4, 5; Ilógico: 1 (rojo); 3 (grabar); 6 (agarré)

12B.12 TEACHING TIP: Before going over the answers as a class, have students share their answers with a partner.

Lógico	Ilógico	
☐	☑	**1.** Mi color favorito es la red.
☑	☐	**2.** La películas que tienen éxito en las taquillas *(box office)* son las que captan la atención del público.
☐	☑	**3.** A mí me gusta recordar música en mi MP3.
☑	☐	**4.** Los pobres no tienen muchos recursos económicos.
☑	☐	**5.** El cinturón sirve para sostener los pantalones.
☐	☑	**6.** Durante las escenas de miedo de la película, grabé la mano de mi amigo/a.

Estructuras clave 1 The subjunctive or indicative in adverb clauses

Clauses that describe the conditions, the purpose, the cause, or the timing of an action are called adverb (or adverbial) clauses. Conditional and purpose clauses, introduced with conjunctions like **con tal de que** and **para que,** use subjunctive, and causal clauses, introduced with conjunctions like **puesto que,** use indicative.

Causal clauses

Puesto que estudias mucho, recibirás buenas notas.	*Since you study a lot, you'll get good grades.*
Algunos se oponen a globalización porque les parece una forma de imperialismo.	*Some people are opposed to globalization because it seems like a form of imperialism to them.*

Purpose and condition clauses

Ellos ahorran una parte de su sueldo para que no tengan que pedir un préstamo.	*They are saving part of their salary so that they don't have to get a loan.*
La globalización puede ser un cosa beneficiosa con tal de que promueva el desarrollo económico de países en vías de desarrollo y no sólo de países desarrollados.	*Globalization can be a beneficial thing as long as it promotes economic growth in developing countries as well as developed countries.*

Conjunctions of time function to either indicate a habitual or past action, or to indicate a future action. Time clauses are the only adverb clauses that use either the indicative or the subjunctive. What is it about time clauses that dictates the use of subjunctive or indicative? If the clause describes an action or event that has not yet materialized, the verb is in the subjunctive, but if it refers to a habitual or past action, the verb is in the indicative. Look at the following examples.

Paco se acostó después de que **terminó** la película. (indicative) *Paco went to bed after the movie ended.*	Past action: We know that the action occurred.
Paco va a acostarse después de que **termine** la película. (subjunctive) *Paco will go to bed after the movie ends.*	Future action: We don't know when the movie will end, or if something else might happen to change Paco's plans.
Ellos siempre sirven la comida en cuanto **llegan** los invitados. (indicative) *They always serve the meal as soon as the guests arrive.*	Habitual, routine action: We know that they follow a predictable pattern.
Ellos servirán la comida en cuanto **lleguen** los invitados. (subjunctive) *They will serve the meal as soon as the guests arrive.*	Future action: We do not know when or if the guests will arrive.

12B.13 ¿Qué haré?　Lee las siguientes oraciones e indica la respuesta que te corresponda.

　　1. En cuanto compre una computadora nueva…
　　　　a. donaré mi computadora a una organización caritativa *(charitable)*.
　　　　b. llevaré mi computadora vieja a reciclar.
　　　　c. tiraré mi computadora vieja a la basura.
　　　　d. le regalaré mi computadora vieja a un/a amigo/a.

2. Cuando me gradúe de la universidad…
   a. buscaré un trabajo que pague bien.
   b. participaré en el Cuerpo de Paz *(Peace Corps)*.
   c. comenzaré estudios de posgrado *(graduate studies)*.
   d. viajaré.

3. Estudiaré esta noche a menos que…
   a. necesite trabajar.
   b. haya una fiesta.
   c. mis amigos quieran salir.
   d. pueda ver mi programa favorito en la televisión.

4. Visitaré a mi familia tan pronto como…
   a. tenga un fin de semana libre.
   b. mis padres me inviten a la casa.
   c. lleguen las próximas vacaciones.
   d. mi familia y yo celebremos una ocasión especial.

5. Después de que terminen mis clases hoy…
   a. haré ejercicio.
   b. iré al trabajo.
   c. estudiaré.
   d. jugaré videojuegos.

6. Es importante estudiar español para que…
   a. podamos comunicarnos con hispanohablantes.
   b. tengamos mejores trabajos.
   c. podamos escuchar música y ver películas en español.
   d. entendamos más acerca de la cultura hispana.

12B.14 Opiniones acerca de la tecnología. Lee las siguientes oraciones y decide si estás, o no, de acuerdo con ellas. Luego, compara tus respuestas con las de tus compañeros de clase en grupos de tres o de cuatro y escribe los resultados en el **Retrato de la clase.**

¿Con cuáles de las siguientes oraciones acerca del desarrollo tecnológico estás de acuerdo y por qué?

	¿Estás de acuerdo?		
	Sí	No	¿Por qué?
1. Las reglas que controlan la creatividad de inventores son malas.			
2. La invención de la bomba atómica ha causado y podrá causar, muchos daños.			
3. Los satélites son importantes para el desarrollo de la comunicación.			
4. La adicción a la Internet puede causar daños psicológicos.			
5. Deberíamos tener reglas más estrictas para el uso de la Internet.			
6. A veces los desarrollos tecnológicos dañan el medio ambiente.			

Retrato de la clase: La mayor parte de la clase piensa que…

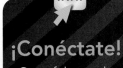

12B.13 FOLLOW-UP: Answers will vary. Go over responses orally as a class and explore the most unusual responses.

www

¡Conéctate!

One of the results of globalization is the flow of information across borders due to the Internet. This technology has opened doors which have helped us gain access to various cultural perspectives throughout this course. In order to learn about the different perspectives that exist on globalization in Spanish-speaking cultures, run the search **"globalización"** at http://youtube.com to view a variety of videos on this topic. Some of the videos have running text that may require you to frequently pause in order to get a strong grasp of the messages shared. What did you learn? Were there any new ideas introduced that you had not thought of before? Share your thoughts with the class.

VÍVELO: CULTURA

La Internet y los pueblos indígenas de Latinoamérica

En el mundo actual ya es común la presencia de las nuevas tecnologías de la información y comunicación que prometen desarrollar y modernizar a la humanidad. Sin embargo, los indígenas de Latinoamérica no han podido aprovechar completamente esas promesas debido a *(due to)* la marginación y el abandono en que viven. Algunas de las diversas barreras u obstáculos que les impiden el acceso a la Internet incluyen: la falta *(lack)* de experiencia en el uso de las computadoras, la falta de electricidad y líneas telefónicas en muchas comunidades indígenas, la falta de tarjetas de crédito que se necesitan para acceder a algunos sitios de la red y el hecho de que la información en la red está en inglés u otras lenguas que los indígenas no han tenido la oportunidad de estudiar y aprender.

Sin embargo, una vez superados estos obstáculos, los indígenas latinoamericanos han podido aprovechar la Internet en diversos campos como la educación, la telemedicina y el comercio electrónico. Además, el acceso a la Internet permite que las comunidades indígenas se comuniquen entre sí, facilitando así la cooperación y solidaridad. Por otra parte, el acceso a la Internet también permite que las comunidades indígenas presenten ellas mismas su cultura y sus preocupaciones al resto del mundo.

La Internet, bien empleada, puede servir para construir una sociedad equitativa, participativa y solidaria. Para alcanzar esta meta *(goal)*, se requiere más que el simple acceso a la Internet. Es necesario también aprender a usar la Internet para resolver problemas sociales concretos. La experiencia de los indígenas latinoamericanos nos ha demostrado que esto es posible.

12B.15 Comprensión.   Vas a escuchar varias oraciones sobre el uso de la Internet entre las poblaciones indígenas de Latinoamérica. Indica si son ciertas o falsas según lo que leíste en *Vívelo: Cultura*. Luego, verifiquen las respuestas como clase.

	Cierto	Falso			Cierto	Falso
1.	☐	☑		**4.**	☐	☑
2.	☑	☐		**5.**	☑	☐
3.	☑	☐		**6.**	☐	☑

12B.16 La Internet y los Zapatistas   Lee *Vívelo: Cultura* en la página 563 y contesta las siguientes preguntas. Después, comparte tus respuestas con un/a compañero/a de clase.

1. ¿Cómo ayudó la Internet al movimiento zapatista?

2. ¿Qué representa la foto de la pintura?

3. ¿Qué otros usos, fuera de los más comunes, hay para la Internet?

Los zapatistas y el uso de la Internet como arma

Del artículo "Fuera de la óptica indígena: Zapatistas y videoastas autónomos" de Alexandra Halkin

Los medios de comunicación siempre fueron parte del "arsenal" zapatista; de hecho, en los días que siguieron inmediatamente al levantamiento *(uprising)*, los zapatistas (vía partidarios simpatizantes) usaron la Internet para trasmitir su causa al mundo. Este uso estratégico de los medios de comunicación fue para hacer un llamado a la sociedad civil internacional para unirse a ellos en la construcción de un nuevo mundo. Este uso de la Internet generó mucho interés internacional y escrutinio global al que, frecuentemente, se le da el crédito de haber forzado al gobierno mexicano a una tregua *(truce)* y a una negociación con los zapatistas.

PRE-READING ACTIVITY: Have students skim, scan and get a general sense about the article entitled *Los zapatistas y el uso de la Internet como arma*. Direct their attention to the drawing as well. *EZLN* stands for *Ejército Zapatista de la Liberación Nacional* and the masked satellite emblematizes the masks that the Zapatistas wear to demonstrate their solidarity, be unrecognized and make a statement about their struggle.

Estructuras clave 2   The subjunctive or indicative in adjective clauses

 Go to *WileyPLUS* and review the tutorial for this grammar point.

As you saw with adverbial clauses, two sentences can be almost identical in word order but the propositions can be entirely different based on whether the verb is in the indicative or the subjunctive. The same is true with adjective clauses.

When the intention of the speaker is to describe a hypothetical (still inexistent) person, place, or object, the subjunctive will be used in the descriptive clause introduced by **que** (called an adjective or adjectival clause because it describes something in the main clause). If the clause introduced by **que** describes something that exists, the indicative is used. Look at the following examples.

Tengo un televisor que tiene dos pantallas.	*I have a television with two screens.*
Tenía un televisor que tenía dos pantallas.	*I used to have a television that had two screens.*
Quiero un televisor que tenga dos pantallas.	*I want a television that has two screens.*

The difference between the three sentences is that the television sets in the first two exist (or existed) and are simply being described by the adjective clause, while the television set in the last sentence is a hypothetical one (not yet acquired).

A general rule of thumb is that when an action is hypothesized or a person, object, or place being described is hypothetical, unknown, or unspecified, the verb in the adjective clause will be in the subjunctive.

You will find PowerPoint presentations for use with *Estructuras clave* in *WileyPLUS*.

ORIENTATION: If students can gain significant comfort with their receptive skills in understanding the subjunctive, they will greatly extend their Spanish. With time, and much practice, they will begin using the subjunctive appropriately themselves. However, it is premature to expect the vast majority of beginning students to use the subjunctive spontaneously with any significant degree of accuracy.

12B.17 ¿Subjuntivo o indicativo?   Read the following sentences and match them with their logical endings, keeping in mind that when the verb in one of the clauses is in the subjunctive, chances are that something is being hypothesized (either an action or a person, place, or thing).

___h___ **1.** Queremos comprar una máquina de fax que…

___d___ **2.** Es necesario tener una fotocopiadora que…

___b___ **3.** Es importante apoyar programas de desarrollo que…

___e___ **4.** Muchas personas prefieren votar por candidatos que…

___a___ **5.** Mis tíos desean encontrar una cámara digital que…

___c___ **6.** La universidad espera construir más edificios donde…

___f___ **7.** Se deben inventar modos de producción industrial que…

___g___ **8.** Muchos padres piden nuevos aparatos que…

a. …saque fotos con buena resolución.

b. …no dañen las economías de los países latinoamericanos.

c. …haya conexiones inalámbricas.

d. …haga copias rápidamente.

e. …se opongan a aumentar los impuestos.

f. …consuman menos recursos naturales.

g. …impidan que sus hijos vean contenido inapropiado.

h. …envíe documentos a color.

12B.18 SUGGESTION: Add a friendly element of competition to this activity by having the various groups of students compete against each other. These are some guidelines: 1) Ask each group to agree on an answer. (The benefit is that students will need to explain things to one another and justify their reasoning. Often, when students take on the role of the teacher, more learning takes place.) 2) Go over each sentence individually. Check one person's answer (from each group) to see if they earned a point or not. 3) The group with the most points wins.

12B.18 Lo real y lo hipotético.   En grupos de tres, lean los siguientes enunciados e indiquen si describen algo o alguien real o hipotético. También indiquen si son lógicos o ilógicos.

	Algo/ alguien real	Algo/ alguien hipotético	Lógico	Ilógico
1. Mis abuelos tienen muchos amigos que escuchan música con MP3.	✓			✓
2. El DVD es un aparato que usamos para ver películas.	✓		✓	
3. El cliente busca un contestador automático que se conecte al teléfono celular.		✓		✓
4. La democracia es una forma de gobierno que le permite votar a la gente.	✓		✓	
5. Queremos vivir en una ciudad grande donde haya poco tráfico.		✓		✓
6. Ellos van a comprar una fotocopiadora que haga copias a color.		✓	✓	
7. Hay muchos políticos que se oponen a eliminar la pobreza.	✓			✓
8. Si tu amigo/a es aficionado/a al golf, puedes regalarle videojuegos que simulen partidos al golf.		✓	✓	

12B.19 ¿Qué opinan? Usa le segunda columna para completar las oraciones de acuerdo a tus gustos. Luego, encuentra a un/a compañero/a de clase que tenga las respuestas más parecidas a las tuyas y escribe sus respuestas en la tercera columna y luego en tu **Retrato de la clase.** Sigue el modelo.

	Yo	Mi compañero/a de clase
Vivo en una ciudad que es…	*grande*	*muy grande*
Quiero vivir en una ciudad que sea…		
Tengo amigos que son…		
Quiero tener amigos que sean…		
Tengo un celular que puede…		
Deseo tener un celular que pueda …		
Tengo un trabajo que es…		
Deseo encontrar un trabajo que sea…		

Retrato de la clase: Mi compañero/a y yo queremos vivir en una ciudad que sea pequeña con un centro comercial pequeño.

Enlaces

12B.20 Enlaces Determina el significado de las palabras o frases en negrita según el contexto de las oraciones. Escoge de las siguientes opciones. Luego, verifica tus respuestas con la clase.

a. in fact

b. on this point

c. that is to say

___b___ **1. En este punto,** todos estamos de acuerdo.

___a___ **2. De hecho,** hay muchas personas que se oponen a la occidentalización.

___c___ **3.** La occidentalización, **mejor dicho** la globalización, se percibe como la continuación del imperialismo occidental.

12B.21 ¿Puedes conectar las ideas? Conecta las ideas en las oraciones y párrafos siguientes empleando la expresión apropiada. Luego, verifica tus respuestas con tus compañeros de clase.

a. de hecho

b. en este punto

c. mejor dicho

___c___ **1.** Los antiglobalizadores, _____ las personas que se oponen a la occidentalización, piensan que el capitalismo occidental lleva a una cultura consumidora y materialista.

___b___ **2.** _____ tú y yo no estamos de acuerdo. Yo soy antigloblista y tú crees que la globalización trae muchos beneficios a la sociedad.

___a___ **3.** La occidentalización no influye en todas las culturas y sociedades. _____ las estadísticas indican que en los países pobres hay pocas personas que tienen acceso a teléfonos celulares, correo electrónico y computadoras.

The next two tasks will offer immediate experience with forms of globalization at a personal level. You will conduct two surveys, one in your class and another out of class. The surveys attempt to gauge exposure to other cultures through technology.

12B.22 ¿Cuánto sabes de otras culturas? Primero, indica si has hecho estas actividades. Luego, hazles preguntas a cuatro compañeros para determinar si ellos/as han hecho las mismas actividades. Escribe los nombres de tus compañeros en la columna apropiada. Luego, analiza las respuestas y apunta nueva información en tu **Retrato de la clase**. ¡Ojo! No olvides cambiar la forma de los verbos de *yo* a *tú* cuando le hagas preguntas a tus compañeros.

	Yo	___	___	___	___
He visto películas extranjeras.					
He hablado en *Second Life* con personas de otros países o en otros idiomas.					
He mandado correos electrónicos a personas de otros países.					
He llamado por teléfono a personas de otros países.					
He comprado música de iTunes en otros idiomas.					
He escuchado música de otros países.					
Me he comunicado por mensajería instantánea con amigos que han estado de viaje en otros países.					
He visitado otros países y he mandado correos electrónicos desde países extranjeros.					
He visto programas de televisión de otros países a través de satélite.					
He llamado a personas de otros países por Skype.					

Retrato de la clase: La mayor parte de la clase ha visto películas de otros países, ha…

12B.23 Comparando los conocimientos culturales. Hazles las siguientes preguntas de la página 567 a cinco personas que no sean de Estados Unidos (por ejemplo, estudiantes internacionales en tu universidad) para determinar cuánto saben ellos de la cultura estadounidense. ¿A qué conclusión general llegas? ¿Por qué?

	Yo	___	___	___	___
Había visto películas extranjeras en su país nativo.					
En su país nativo, había hablado en *Second Life* con personas de otros países o en otros idiomas.					
En su país nativo, había mandado correos electrónicos a personas de otros países.					
En su país nativo, había llamado por teléfono a personas de otros países.					
En su país nativo, había comprado música de iTunes en otros idiomas.					
En su país nativo, había escuchado música de otros países.					
En su país nativo, se había comunicado por mensajería instantánea con amigos que han estado de viaje en otros países.					
En su país nativo, había visitado otros países y había mandado correos electrónicos desde países extranjeros.					
En su país nativo, había visto programas de televisión de otros países a través de satélite.					
En su país nativo, había llamado a personas de otros países por Skype.					

Conclusiones generales:

a. Los resultados indican que la tecnología provee acceso a otras culturas.

b. Los resultados indican que no hay mucho acceso a otras culturas a través de la tecnología.

c. Los resultados indican que la mayoría de los estudiantes no usan tecnología.

d. Los resultados indican que la mayoría de los extranjeros no usan tecnología en sus países nativos.

e. ¿Hay otras conclusiones?

Perspectivas

12B.24 La globalización: Cuestión de punto de vista. Lee el texto de la página 568 para entender la definición de globalización según los índices que utilizó el informe AT Kearney. Luego, contesta las preguntas que siguen según la tabla de datos sobre el nivel de globalización en los países hispanohablantes.

12B.23 TEACHING TIP: Call students' attention to the construction of the questions in the interviews. The past perfect is used here as a review. The interviews with individuals from other countries will most likely need to be conducted outside of class. If possible, it might be best to assign the interviews with individuals from other countries over a weekend in order to allow students time to complete the interviews. The questions are in Spanish for class discussion purposes, but students may have to ask the questions in English if the interviewee does not speak Spanish. Encourage students to ask their interviewees to expand on their responses. For example, students can ask interviewees to indicate which foreign movies they have seen, with whom they have spoken in *Second Life,* to whom they had sent emails and to which countries, etc. Students' findings and conclusions should be discussed orally during the following class meeting.

WILEY PLUS

12B.23 INSTRUCTOR'S RESOURCES: You will find a reproducible chart for Activity 12B.23 in your Instructor's Resources.

El nivel de globalización en varios países hispanohablantes

Cada año, la consultora AT Kearney, junto con la revista *Foreign Policy*, prepara un índice en el cual se analiza el nivel de globalización de 72 países del mundo. Este índice incluye varios países de habla española. La lista a continuación compara la posición que ocupan estos países en los índices de 2006 y 2007.

El índice se construye sobre la base de 12 variables divididas en cuatro grandes grupos: integración económica, contactos personales, compromiso político con la comunidad internacional y conectividad tecnológica.

En 2007 Singapur vuelve a ocupar el primer puesto en el índice de globalización por tercera vez. En segundo lugar se sitúa Hong Kong, seguido de Holanda, Suiza e Irlanda. Estados Unidos está en séptimo lugar, después de estar en tercer lugar en 2006. España también perdió cuatro puestos para clasificarse en el puesto 29.

Panamá, en el puesto 30, ocupa la primera posición entre los países latinoamericanos. Costa Rica, que se incluye en el índice por primera vez en 2007, ocupa el puesto 39. El tercer país latinoamericano en el índice es Chile, que ocupa el puesto 43.

Venezuela ocupa uno de los últimos puestos en el índice (68), con una caída de nueve puestos respecto a la edición anterior.

En el cuadro a continuación podemos ver la clasificación en el índice de globalización de los países hispanohablantes que aparecen en él.

Valoración de los países hispanohablantes en el índice de globalización:

País	2007	2006
Estados Unidos	7	3
España	29	25
Panamá	30	21
Costa Rica	39	ND
Chile	43	34
México	49	42
Colombia	50	54
Argentina	54	43
Perú	58	50
Venezuela	68	59

Puede ser llamativo el hecho de que todos los países latinoamericanos, con la excepción de Panamá, estén en la segunda mitad del índice. También es notable la reducción general del nivel de globalización en casi todos los países hispanohablantes.

1. En general, ¿el nivel de globalización subió o bajó en los países hispanohablantes?

2. ¿En qué país subió el nivel? ¿Cuántos puestos *(places)* subió?

3. ¿En qué países bajó? ¿En qué país bajó más?

4. ¿En qué región del mundo hispanohablante hay menos globalización?

5. ¿Hay alguna(s) conclusiones que te sorprendan?

Vocabulario: Investigación B

Vocabulario esencial

Sustantivos

el/la ciudadano/a	*citizen*
el desperdicio	*waste*
el daño	*harm, damage*
el/la invitado/a	*guest*
las reglas	*rules*

Conjunciones

a fin de que	*in order to*
a menos que	*unless*
antes (de) que	*before*
con tal (de) que	*provided that*
cuando	*when*
después de que	*after*
en caso de que	*in case*
en cuanto	*as soon as*
hasta que	*until*
para que	*so that*
puesto que	*because/since*
sin que	*without*
tan pronto como	*as soon as*

Otras palabras y expresiones

los audífonos	*headphones*
caritativo/a	*charitable*
dañar	*to harm, to hurt*
el dispositivo	*mechanism, device*
en línea	*online*
el levantamiento	*uprising*
la occidentalización	*westernization*
refutar	*to rebut*
solidario/a	*supportive*
superar	*to overcome*
la taquilla	*box office*
la tregua	*truce*
el/la videoasta	*one who makes videos*

Cognados

Review the cognates in *Adelante* and the false cognates in *¡Atención!*. For a complete list of cognates, see Appendix 4 on page 605.

En vivo

 Debate sobre la tecnología. La clase se dividirá en dos grupos. Un grupo presentará los aspectos positivos de la tecnología y el otro grupo presentará los aspectos negativos de la tecnología. Los dos grupos se dividirán otra vez para formar dos grupos más pequeños: cada grupo presentará los argumentos iniciales y el otro presentará los argumentos que refutan *(rebut)* los argumentos iniciales del grupo opuesto. Al final, tendrán la oportunidad de resumir *(summarize)* los argumentos a favor y en contra de la tecnología y la clase votará para determinar cuáles fueron los argumentos más convincentes.

Aspectos positivos	Aspectos negativos

 ¿Qué será? As you continue reflecting on the pros and cons of technology, consider how technological innovations will continue to shape our world in the future. What will technology enable people to do in the future that cannot be done today? How will these changes influence you at a personal level and will it continue influencing world cultures? With this in mind, write a brief column that explores the way we will live life daily and globally. Lastly, indicate whether you would prefer the technology of today or the future.

Paso 1: Think about the daily uses of technology today and how these may change in the future. Then think about what effects these changes may have on both a personal level and a global level, i.e. how will these innovations contribute to globalization.

Paso 2: Write your first draft.

Paso 3: Revise your column to ensure that you have provided a convincing column. Ask yourself whether or not you would be impressed by your argument. If it needs more detail, make the necessary changes to strengthen it.

Paso 4: Now that your content is solid, review the column focusing on form and accuracy. Make the necessary revisions and write the final draft of your column.

En directo

INVESTIGACIÓN A: Tecnología y dinero

> **Antes de ver el video.**   Contesta las siguientes preguntas y luego compara tus respuestas con las del resto de la clase. ¿Usas la Internet para administrar tus finanzas? ¿Para qué casos? ¿Crees que es un medio seguro?

> **El video.**   Completa cada oración con la información del video.

1. Soy de Puerto Rico, mi mamá vive en Puerto Rico… ayudamos a mi mamá _____ _____.

2. La persona puede ir por la Internet o puede venir aquí, llenar un formulario de estos y _____ _____.

3. Utilizo la Internet para administrar mi dinero, por ejemplo para pasar dinero de una _____ _____ a otra.

4. Si se presentara una situación de _____ _____ _____ probablemente lo denunciaría a la policía.

> **Después de ver el video.**   Contesta las siguientes preguntas y luego compara tus respuestas con las del resto de la clase. ¿Le recomendarías a la gente que utilizara la Internet para hacer finanzas o compras? ¿Por qué? Answers will vary.

Vocabulario útil
acortar: *to shorten*
suplantar: *to supplant*
denunciar a la policia:
   to report to the police

ANSWERS: 1. enviándole dinero, 2. pagar efectivo, 3. cuenta bancaria, 4. robo de identidad.

INVESTIGACIÓN B: Unidos por la globalización

> **Antes de ver el video.**   Contesta las siguientes preguntas con un/a compañero/a y luego compartan sus respuestas con el resto de la clase: ¿Qué es la globalización? ¿Piensan que es un fenómeno positivo o negativo? ¿Por qué?

> **El video.**   Indica si cada uno de los enunciados es cierto o falso. Reescribe los enunciados falsos para hacerlos ciertos. Comprueba tus respuestas con un/a compañero/a.

Cierto	Falso	
☑	☐	**1.** NOVICA es una compañía que usa la globalización para conectar artesanos de áreas remotas con clientes con más poder económico.
☐	☑	**2.** La mayoría de los productos se venden por Internet a través de intermediarios.
☑	☐	**3.** Uno de los beneficios para el consumidor es que puede poner su propio precio y el sistema es completamente transparente.
☑	☐	**4.** El artesano puede conocer quién está comprando el producto por medio de la página web.

Vocabulario útil
aumentar   *to increase*
aislado   *isolated*
embajador   *ambassador*

> **Después de ver el video.**   Contesta las siguientes preguntas y comparte tus respuestas con el resto de la clase: ¿En qué ayuda la globalización a la compañía NOVICA? ¿Y a los artesanos de América Latina, Asia y África? ¿Cuál es la función de la tecnología y la Internet en la relación entre la compañía, los artesanos y el consumidor?

Retrato de la clase Checklist

You should have recorded information in your **Retrato de la clase** in conjunction with the following activities:

☐ **12A.12** **¿Cómo maneja la clase el dinero?**

☐ **12A.19** **El juego de *Survivor.***

☐ **12A.24** **¿Qué piensa la clase acerca del dinero y la tecnología?**

☐ **12B.14** **Opiniones acerca de la tecnología.**

☐ **12B.19** **¿Qué opinan?**

☐ **12B.22** **¿Cuánto sabes de otras culturas?**

Regular Verbs: Simple Tenses

Infinitive Present Participle Past Participle	Indicative					Subjunctive		Imperative (commands)
	Present	Imperfect	Preterit	Future	Conditional	Present	Imperfect	
hablar *to speak* hablando hablado	hablo hablas habla hablamos habláis hablan	hablaba hablabas hablaba hablábamos hablabais hablaban	hablé hablaste habló hablamos hablasteis hablaron	hablaré hablarás hablará hablaremos hablaréis hablarán	hablaría hablarías hablaría hablaríamos hablaríais hablarían	hable hables hable hablemos habléis hablen	hablara hablaras hablara habláramos hablarais hablaran	habla/ no hables hable hablemos hablad/ no habléis hablen
comer *to eat* comiendo comido	como comes come comemos coméis comen	comía comías comía comíamos comíais comían	comí comiste comió comimos comisteis comieron	comeré comerás comerá comeremos comeréis comerán	comería comerías comería comeríamos comeríais comerían	coma comas coma comamos comáis coman	comiera comieras comiera comiéramos comierais comieran	come/ no comas coma comamos comed/ no comáis coman
vivir *to live* viviendo vivido	vivo vives vive vivimos vivís viven	vivía vivías vivía vivíamos vivíais vivían	viví viviste vivió vivimos vivisteis vivieron	viviré vivirás vivirá viviremos viviréis vivirán	viviría vivirías viviría viviríamos viviríais vivirían	viva vivas viva vivamos viváis vivan	viviera vivieras viviera viviéramos vivierais vivieran	vive/ no vivas viva vivamos vivid/ no viváis

Indicative						Subjunctive		
Present Perfect		Past Perfect		Future Perfect		Conditional Perfect		
he has ha hemos habéis han	hablado comido vivido	había habías había habíamos habíais habían	hablado comido vivido	habré habrás habrá habremos habréis habrán	hablado comido vivido	hanbría habrías habría habríamos habríais habrían	hablado comido vivido	

Subjunctive			
Present Perfect		Past Perfect	
haya hayas haya hayamos hayáis hayan	hablado comido vivido	hubiera hubieras hubiera hubiéramos hubierais hubieran	hablado comido vivido

Stem-changing -ar and -er Verbs: e → ie; o → ue

Infinitive / Present Participle / Past Participle	Indicative					Subjunctive		Imperative (commands)
	Present	Imperfect	Preterit	Future	Conditional	Present	Imperfect	
pensar (ie) *to think* / pensando / pensado	**pienso** **piensas** **piensa** pensamos pensáis **piensan**	pensaba pensabas pensaba pensábamos pensabais pensaban	pensé pensaste pensó pensamos pensasteis pensaron	pensaré pensarás pensará pensaremos pensaréis pensarán	pensaría pensarías pensaría pensaríamos pensaríais pensarían	**piense** **pienses** **piense** pensemos penséis **piensen**	pensara pensaras pensara pensáramos pensarais pensaran	piensa/ no pienses piense pensemos pensad/ no penséis piensen
volver (ue) *to return* / volviendo / vuelto (irreg.)	**vuelvo** **vuelves** **vuelve** volvemos volvéis **vuelven**	volvía volvías volvía volvíamos volvíais volvían	volví volviste volvió volvimos volvisteis volvieron	volveré volverás volverá volveremos volveréis volverán	volvería volverías volvería volveríamos volveríais volverían	**vuelva** **vuelvas** **vuelva** volvamos volváis **vuelvan**	volviera volvieras volviera volviéramos volvierais volvieran	vuelve/ no vuelvas vuelva volvamos volved/ no volváis vuelvan

Other verbs of this type are:

e → ie: cerrar, despertarse, empezar, entender, nevar, pensar, perder, preferir, querer, recomendar, regar, sentarse

o → ue: acordarse de, acostarse, almorzar, costar, encontrar, jugar, mostrar, poder, recordar, resolver, sonar, volar, volver

Stem-changing -ir Verbs: e → ie, i; e → i, i; e → ue, u

Infinitive / Present Participle / Past Participle	Indicative					Subjunctive		Imperative (commands)
	Present	Imperfect	Preterit	Future	Conditional	Present	Imperfect	
sentir (ie, i) *to feel, to regret* / **sintiendo** / sentido	**siento** **sientes** **siente** sentimos sentís **sienten**	sentía sentías sentía sentíamos sentíais sentían	sentí sentiste **sintió** sentimos sentisteis **sintieron**	sentiré sentirás sentirá sentiremos sentiréis sentirán	sentiría sentirías sentiría sentiríamos sentiríais sentirían	**sienta** **sientas** **sienta** **sintamos** **sintáis** **sientan**	sintiera sintieras sintiera sintiéramos sintierais sintieran	**siente**/ no **sientas** **sienta** **sintamos** sentid/ no **sintáis** **sientan**
pedir (i, i) *to ask (for)* / **pidiendo** / pedido	**pido** **pides** **pide** pedimos pedís **piden**	pedía pedías pedía pedíamos pedíais pedían	pedí pediste **pidió** pedimos pedisteis **pidieron**	pediré pedirás pedirá pediremos pediréis pedirán	pediría pedirías pediría pediríamos pediríais pedirían	**pida** **pidas** **pida** **pidamos** **pidáis** pidan	pidiera pidieras pidiera pidiéramos pidierais pidieran	**pide**/ no **pidas** **pida** **pidamos** pedid/ no **pidáis** **pidan**

Stem-changing *-ir* Verbs: e → ie, i; e → i, i; e → ue, u (continued)

Infinitive Present Participle Past Participle	Indicative					Subjunctive		Imperative (commands)
	Present	Imperfect	Preterit	Future	Conditional	Present	Imperfect	
dormir (ue, u) *to sleep* **durmiendo** dormido	**duermo** **duermes** **duerme** dormimos dormís **duermen**	dormía dormías dormía dormíamos dormíais dormían	dormí dormiste **durmió** dormimos dormisteis **durmieron**	dormiré dormirás dormirá dormiremos dormiréis dormirán	dormiría dormirías dormiría dormiríamos dormiríais dormirían	**duerma** **duermas** **duerma** durmamos durmáis **duerman**	**durmiera** **durmieras** **durmiera** **durmiéramos** **durmierais** **durmieran**	**duerme**/ no **duermas** **duerma** **durmamos** dormid/ no **durmáis** **duerman**

Other verbs of this type are:

e → ie, i: divertirse, invertir, preferir, sentirse, sugerir

e → i, i: conseguir, despedirse de, reírse, repetir, seguir, servir, vestirse

o → ue, u: morir(se)

Verbs with Spelling Changes

Infinitive Present Participle Past Participle	Indicative					Subjunctive		Imperative (commmands)
	Present	Imperfect	Preterit	Future	Conditional	Present	Imperfect	

1. c → qu: tocar (model); buscar, explicar, pescar, sacar

| tocar *to play (musical instr.),* *to touch* tocando tocado | toco tocas toca tocamos tocáis tocan | tocaba tocabas tocaba tocábamos tocabais tocaban | toqué tocaste tocó tocamos tocasteis tocaron | tocaré tocarás tocará tocaremos tocaréis tocarán | tocaría tocarías tocaría tocaríamos tocaríais tocarían | **toque** **toques** **toque** **toquemos** **toquéis** **toquen** | tocara tocaras tocara tocáramos tocarais tocaran | toca/ no **toques** **toque** **toquemos** tocad/ no **toquéis** **toquen** |

2. z → c: abrazar; Also almorzar, cruzar, empezar (ie)

| abrazar *to hug* abrazando abrazado | abrazo abrazas abraza abrazamos abrazáis abrazan | abrazaba abrazabas abrazaba abrazábamos abrazabais abrazaban | **abracé** abrazaste abrazó abrazamos abrazasteis abrazaron | abrazaré abrazarás abrazará abrazaremos abrazaréis abrazarán | abrazaría abrazarías abrazaría abrazaríamos abrazaríais abrazarían | **abrace** **abraces** **abrace** **abracemos** **abracéis** **abracen** | abrazara abrazaras abrazara abrazáramos abrazarais abrazaran | abraza/ no **abraces** **abrace** **abracemos** abrazad/ no **abracéis** **abracen** |

3. g → gu: pagar *to pay (for)*; Also apagar, jugar (ue), llegar

	Present	Imperfect	Preterite	Future	Conditional	Present Subjunctive	Imperfect Subjunctive	Commands
pagar *to pay (for)*	pago	pagaba	**pagué**	pagaré	pagaría	**pague**	pagara	
pagando	pagas	pagabas	pagaste	pagarás	pagarías	**pagues**	pagaras	paga/ no **pagues**
pagado	paga	pagaba	pagó	pagará	pagaría	**pague**	pagara	**pague**
	pagamos	pagábamos	pagamos	pagaremos	pagaríamos	**paguemos**	pagáramos	**paguemos**
	pagáis	pagabais	pagasteis	pagaréis	pagaríais	**paguéis**	pagarais	pagad/ no **paguéis**
	pagan	pagaban	pagaron	pagarán	pagarían	**paguen**	pagaran	**paguen**

4. gu → g: seguir (i, i); Also conseguir

	Present	Imperfect	Preterite	Future	Conditional	Present Subjunctive	Imperfect Subjunctive	Commands
seguir (i, i) *to follow*	**sigo**	seguía	seguí	seguiré	seguiría	**siga**	siguiera	
siguiendo	sigues	seguías	seguiste	seguirás	seguirías	**sigas**	siguieras	sigue/ no **sigas**
seguido	sigue	seguía	siguió	seguirá	seguiría	**siga**	siguiera	**siga**
	seguimos	seguíamos	seguimos	seguiremos	seguiríamos	**sigamos**	siguiéramos	**sigamos**
	seguís	seguíais	seguisteis	seguiréis	seguiríais	**sigáis**	siguierais	seguid/ no **sigáis**
	siguen	seguían	siguieron	seguirán	seguirían	**sigan**	siguieran	**sigan**

5. g → j: recoger *to pick up*; Also escoger, proteger

	Present	Imperfect	Preterite	Future	Conditional	Present Subjunctive	Imperfect Subjunctive	Commands
recoger *to pick up*	**recojo**	recogía	recogí	recogeré	recogería	**recoja**	recogiera	
recogiendo	recoges	recogías	recogiste	recogerás	recogerías	**recojas**	recogieras	recoge/ no **recojas**
recogido	recoge	recogía	recogió	recogerá	recogería	**recoja**	recogiera	**recoja**
	recogemos	recogíamos	recogimos	recogeremos	recogeríamos	**recojamos**	recogiéramos	**recojamos**
	recogéis	recogíais	recogisteis	recogeréis	recogeríais	**recojáis**	recogierais	recoged/ no **recojáis**
	recogen	recogían	recogieron	recogerán	recogerían	**recojan**	recogieran	**recojan**

6. i → y: leer *to read*; Also caer, oír. Verbs with additional i → y changes (see below): **construir**; Also destruir

	Present	Imperfect	Preterite	Future	Conditional	Present Subjunctive	Imperfect Subjunctive	Commands
leer *to read*	leo	leía	leí	leeré	leería	lea	**leyera**	
leyendo	lees	leías	leíste	leerás	leerías	leas	**leyeras**	lee/ no leas
leído	lee	leía	leyó	leerá	leería	lea	**leyera**	lea
	leemos	leíamos	leímos	leeremos	leeríamos	leamos	**leyéramos**	leamos
	leéis	leíais	leísteis	leeréis	leeríais	leáis	**leyerais**	leed/ no leáis
	leen	leían	**leyeron**	leerán	leerían	lean	**leyeran**	lean
construir *to construct, to build*	**construyo**	construía	construí	construiré	construiría	**construya**	**construyera**	
construyendo	**construyes**	construías	construiste	construirás	construirías	**construyas**	**construyeras**	**construye**/ no **construyas**
construido	**construye**	construía	**construyó**	construirá	construiría	**construya**	**construyera**	**construyas**
	construimos	construíamos	construimos	construiremos	construiríamos	**construyamos**	**construyéramos**	**construyamos**
	construís	construíais	construisteis	construiréis	construiríais	**construyáis**	**construyerais**	construid/ no **construyáis**
	construyen	construían	**construyeron**	construirán	construirían	**construyan**	**construyeran**	**construya**

Irregular Verbs

Infinitive / Present Participle / Past Participle	Present	Imperfect	Preterit	Future	Conditional	Subjunctive Present	Subjunctive Imperfect	Imperative (commands)
caer *to fall* / **cayendo** / caído	**caigo** / caes / cae / caemos / caéis / caen	caía / caías / caía / caíamos / caíais / caían	caí / caíste / **cayó** / caímos / caísteis / **cayeron**	caeré / caerás / caerá / caeremos / caeréis / caerán	caería / caerías / caería / caeríamos / caeríais / caerían	caiga / caigas / caiga / caigamos / caigáis / caigan	cayera / cayeras / cayera / cayéramos / cayerais / cayeran	cae/ no caigas / caiga / caigamos / caed/ no caigáis / caigan
conocer *to know, to be acquainted with* / conociendo / conocido	conozco / conoces / conoce / conocemos / conocéis / conocen	conocía / conocías / conocía / conocíamos / conocíais / conocían	conocí / conociste / conoció / conocimos / conocisteis / conocieron	conoceré / conocerás / conocerá / conoceremos / conoceréis / conocerán	conocería / conocerías / conocería / conoceríamos / conoceríais / conocerían	conozca / conozcas / conozca / conozcamos / conozcáis / conozcan	conociera / conocieras / conociera / conociéramos / conocierais / conocieran	conoce/ no conozcas / conozca / conozcamos / conoced/ no conozcáis / conozcan
conducir *to drive* / conduciendo / conducido	**conduzco** / conduces / conduce / conducimos / conducís / conducen	conducía / conducías / conducía / conducíamos / conducíais / conducían	**conduje** / **condujiste** / **condujo** / **condujimos** / **condujisteis** / **condujeron**	conduciré / conducirás / conducirá / conduciremos / conduciréis / conducirán	conduciría / conducirías / conduciría / conduciríamos / conduciríais / conducirían	conduzca / conduzcas / conduzca / conduzcamos / conduzcáis / conduzcan	condujera / condujeras / condujera / condujéramos / condujerais / condujeran	conduce/ no conduzcas / conduzca / conduzcamos / conducid/ no conduzcáis / conduzcan
dar *to give* / dando / dado	**doy** / das / da / damos / dais / dan	daba / dabas / daba / dábamos / dabais / daban	**di** / **diste** / **dio** / **dimos** / disteis / dieron	daré / darás / dará / daremos / daréis / darán	daría / darías / daría / daríamos / daríais / darían	**dé** / des / **dé** / **demos** / deis / den	diera / dieras / diera / diéramos / dierais / dieran	da/ no des / dé / demos / dad/ no déis / den
decir *to say, to tell* / **diciendo** / dicho	**digo** / **dices** / **dice** / decimos / decís / **dicen**	decía / decías / decía / decíamos / decíais / decían	dije / dijiste / dijo / dijimos / dijisteis / **dijeron**	**diré** / **dirás** / **dirá** / **diremos** / **diréis** / **dirán**	**diría** / **dirías** / **diría** / **diríamos** / **diríais** / **dirían**	diga / digas / diga / digamos / digáis / digan	dijera / dijeras / dijera / dijéramos / dijerais / dijeran	di/ no digas / diga / digamos / decid/ no digáis / digan

Irregular Verbs (continued)

estar *to be* estando estado	**estoy** **estás** **está** **estamos** **estáis** **están**	estaba estabas estaba estábamos estabais estaban	**estuve** **estuviste** **estuvo** **estuvimos** **estuvisteis** **estuvieron**	estaré estarás estará estaremos estaréis estarán	estaría estarías estaría estaríamos estaríais estarían	**esté** **estés** **esté** **estemos** **estéis** **estén**	estuviera estuvieras estuviera estuviéramos estuvierais estuvieran	estés/ no estés esté estemos estad/ no estéis estén
haber *to have* habiendo habido	**he** **has** **ha** **hemos** **habéis** han	había habías había habíamos habíais habían	**hube** **hubiste** **hubo** **hubimos** **hubisteis** **hubieron**	**habré** **habrás** **habrá** **habremos** **habréis** **habrán**	**habría** **habrías** **habría** **habríamos** **habríais** **habrían**	**haya** **hayas** **haya** **hayamos** **hayáis** **hayan**	hubiera hubieras hubiera hubiéramos hubierais hubieran	
hacer *to do, to make* haciendo **hecho**	**hago** haces hace hacemos hacéis hacen	hacía hacías hacía hacíamos hacíais hacían	**hice** **hiciste** **hizo** **hicimos** **hicisteis** **hicieron**	**haré** **harás** **hará** **haremos** **haréis** **harán**	**haría** **harías** **haría** **haríamos** **haríais** **harían**	haga hagas haga hagamos hagáis hagan	hiciera hicieras hiciera hiciéramos hicierais hicieran	**haz**/ no hagas haga hagamos haced/ no hagáis
ir *to go* yendo ido	**voy** **vas** **va** **vamos** **vais** **van**	**iba** **ibas** **iba** **íbamos** **ibais** **iban**	**fui** **fuiste** **fue** **fuimos** **fuisteis** **fueron**	iré irás irá iremos iréis irán	iría irías iría iríamos iríais irían	**vaya** **vayas** **vaya** **vayamos** **vayáis** **vayan**	fuera fueras fuera fuéramos fuerais fueran	**ve**/ no vayas vaya vayamos id/ no vayáis vayan
oír *to hear* **oyendo** **oído**	**oigo** **oyes** **oye** **oímos** oís **oyen**	oía oías oía oíamos oíais oían	oí **oíste** **oyó** **oímos** **oísteis** **oyeron**	oiré oirás oirá oiremos oiréis oirán	oiría oirías oiría oiríamos oiríais oirían	oiga oigas oiga oigamos oigáis oigan	oyera oyeras oyera oyéramos oyerais oyeran	oye/ no oigas oiga oigamos oíd/ no oigáis oigan

Infinitive Present Participle Past Participle	Indicative Present	Imperfect	Preterit	Future	Conditional	Subjunctive Present	Imperfect	Imperative (commands)
poder (ue) *to be able, can* poniendo podido	puedo puedes puede podemos podéis pueden	podía podías podía podíamos podíais podían	pude pudiste pudo pudimos pudisteis pudieron	podré podrás podrá podremos podréis podrán	podría podrías podría podríamos podríais podrían	pueda puedas pueda podamos podáis puedan	pudiera pudieras pudiera pudiéramos pudierais pudieran	
poner *to put, to place* poniendo **puesto**	**pongo** pones pone ponemos ponéis ponen	ponía ponías ponía poníamos poníais ponían	puse pusiste puso pusimos pusisteis pusieron	pondré pondrás pondrá pondremos pondréis pondrán	pondría pondrías pondría pondríamos pondríais pondrían	ponga pongas ponga pongamos pongáis pongan	pusiera pusieras pusiera pusiéramos pusierais pusieran	**pon**/ no pongas ponga pongamos poned/ no pongáis pongan
querer (ie) *to wish, to want, to love* queriendo querido	quiero quieres quiere queremos queréis quieren	quería querías quería queríamos queríais querían	quise quisiste quiso quisimos quisisteis quisieron	querré querrás querrá querremos querréis querrán	querría querrías querría querríamos querríais querrían	quiera quieras quiera queramos queráis quieran	quisiera quisieras quisiera quisiéramos quisierais quisieran	quiere/ no quieras quiera queramos quered/ no queráis quieran
saber *to know* sabiendo sabido	sé sabes sabe sabemos sabéis saben	sabía sabías sabía sabíamos sabíais sabían	supe supiste supo supimos supisteis supieron	sabré sabrás sabrá sabremos sabréis sabrán	sabría sabrías sabría sabríamos sabríais sabrían	sepa sepas sepa sepamos sepáis sepan	supiera supieras supiera supiéramos supierais supieran	sabe/ no sepas sepa sepamos sabed/ no sepáis sepan
salir *to leave, to go out* saliendo salido	salgo sales sale salimos salís salen	salía salías salía salíamos salíais salían	salí saliste salió salimos salisteis salieron	saldré saldrás saldrá saldremos saldréis saldrán	saldría saldrías saldría saldríamos saldríais saldrían	salga salgas salga salgamos salgáis salgan	saliera salieras saliera saliéramos salierais salieran	sal/ no salgas salga salgamos salid/ no salgáis

Irregular Verbs (continued)

Infinitive	Present	Imperfect	Preterite	Future	Conditional	Present Subjunctive	Imperfect Subjunctive	Commands
ser *to be* siendo sido	soy eres es somos sois son	era eras era éramos erais eran	fui fuiste fue fuimos fuisteis fueron	seré serás será seremos seréis serán	sería serías sería seríamos seríais serían	sea seas sea seamos seáis sean	fuera fueras fuera fuéramos fuerais fueran	sé/ no seas sea seamos sed/ no seáis sean
tener *to have* teniendo tenido	tengo tienes tiene tenemos tenéis tienen	tenía tenías tenía teníamos teníais tenían	tuve tuviste tuvo tuvimos tuvisteis tuvieron	tendré tendrás tendrá tendremos tendréis tendrán	tendría tendrías tendría tendríamos tendríais tendrían	tenga tengas tenga tengamos tengáis tengan	tuviera tuvieras tuviera tuviéramos tuviérais tuvieran	ten/ no tengas tenga tengamos tened/ no tengáis tengan
traer *to bring* trayendo traído	traigo traes trae traemos traéis traen	traía traías traía traíamos traíais traían	traje trajiste trajo trajimos trajisteis trajeron	traeré traerás traerá traeremos traeréis traerán	traería traerías traería traeríamos traeríais traerían	traiga traigas traiga traigamos traigáis traigan	trajera trajeras trajera trajéramos trajerais trajeran	trae/ no traigas traiga traigamos traed/ no traigáis traigan
venir *to come* viniendo venido (also **prevenir**)	vengo vienes viene venimos venís vienen	venía venías venía veníamos veníais venían	vine viniste vino vinimos vinisteis vinieron	vendré vendrás vendrá vendremos vendréis vendrán	vendría vendrías vendría vendríamos vendríais vendrían	venga vengas venga vengamos vengáis vengan	viniera vinieras viniera viniéramos vinierais vinieran	ven/ no vengas venga vengamos venid/ no vengáis vengan
ver *to see* viendo visto	veo ves ve vemos veis ven	veía veías veía veíamos veíais veían	vi viste vio vimos visteis vieron	veré verás verá veremos veréis verán	vería verías vería veríamos veríais verían	vea veas vea veamos veáis vean	viera vieras viera viéramos vierais vieran	ve / no veas vea veamos ved/ no veáis vean

GLOSARIO: ESPAÑOL-INGLÉS

A

a   to   Pre
a continuación   following   4B
a cuadros   checkered/plaid   5B
a fin de que   in order to   12B
a la derecha de   to the right of   3A
a la izquierda de   to the left of   3A
a la luz   in light of   11B
a la vez   at the same time;
   at a time   3A
a menos que   unless   12B
a menudo   often   5A
a partir de   from; starting from   11A
a menudo   often   6A
a pesar de   in spite of   1B
a principios   at the beginning   10A
a propósito   incidentally   7B
a punto   about to   3A
a rayas   striped   5B
a su vez   in turn   10B
a través de   through   3B
a veces   sometimes   3A
a ver   let's see   7B
abertura   f   opening   5B
abierto/a   open   4B
abogado/a   m/f   lawyer   2B
abogar   to advocate   10B
abrazar   to hug   5A
abrelata   m   can opener   5A
abrigo   coat   5B
abril   April   3A
abrir   to open   1B
abrir cuentas   to open
   accounts   12A
abuelo/a   m/f   grandfather/
   grandmother   2B
aburrido/a   bored; boring   8A
acabar   to end, finish   11B
acabar de   + infinitive   just +
   verb   5A
aceite   m   oil   4B
aceituna   f   olive   4A
acercarse   to approach; to get
   closer   10B
acero inoxidable   m   stainless
   steel   6A
aclarar   to clarify   7B
acontecimiento   m   event   3B
acordarse   to remember   10B
acostado/a   lying down   7A
acostarse   to go to bed; to lie
   down   7A
actor   m   actor   8B
actuación   f   performance   10B
actual   current   3A
actualización   f   update   3A
adelgazar   to lose, weight   5B
además   also, in addition   2A
adentro   indoors; inside   5B
adiós   goodbye   Pre
adivinar   to guess   3B
administración de
   empresas   f   business   2A

adolescente   m/f   teenager   4A
adornar   to decorate   6A
adquirir   to acquire   4B
advertencia   f   warning   11B
aeropuerto   m   airport   11A
afectivo/a   emotional   11B
afeitarse   to shave oneself   7A
aficionado/a   m/f   fan   1A
afilador   m   sharpener   6A
afuera   outdoors; outside   5B
agarrar   to grab   3B
agente de viajes   m/f   travel
   agent   11A
agosto   August   3A
agradable   pleasant   6B
agradecer   to appreciate   5B
agricultor/a   m/f   farmer   4B
agua   f   water   3A
aguacate   m   avocado   5A
águila   f   eagle   10A
ahora   now   4A
ahora mismo   right now   4A
ahorrar   to save   11B
aislado/a   isolated   8A
aislamiento   m   isolation   11B
ajuste   m   adjustment   11A
al aire libre   outdoors   5A
al azar   in random order   6A
al contrario   on the contrary   3B
al extranjero/en el
   extranjero   abroad   6B
al fin y al cabo   after all   7B
al fondo   in the background; at the
   bottom   7A
al igual que   just like; just as   9A
al lado de   next to   3A
al menos   at least   6B
al mismo tiempo   at the same
   time   9A
alacena   f   cupboard   6A
alboroto   m   commotion   9A
alcalde/sa   m/f   mayor   4A
alcanzar   to reach   6A
alegre   happy   8A
alemán   German   2A
alfarería   f   pottery   8B
alfombra   f   carpet   5B
algodón   m   cotton   5B
alguno/a   some, any   4A
alimento   m   food   5A
alma   f   soul   3B
almacén   m   store   4B
almorzar   to have lunch   2A
almuerzo   m   lunch   5A
alrededor   around   11B
alterar   to upset, disturb; to alter
   11B
alto/a   tall   1B
alumno/a   m/f   student   1B
ama de casa   f   homemaker   7A
amanecer   dawn   4A
amante   m/f   lover   5B
amar   to love   2B

amargado/a   bitter   8A
amarillo   yellow   5B
ambos   both   1B
ameno/a   enjoyable   6B
amigo/a   m/f   friend   1A
amistad   f   friendship   9A
amor   m   love   1A
amplio/a   wide, extense   7A
ancho/a   wide   5B
anciano   old   7A
andar   to walk   8A
andar adelantado   to be fast   11A
andar atrasado   to be slow   11A
andar bien/mal   to do well/bad   11B
andar en bicicleta   to go bike
   riding   1A
andino   Andean   9A
anfitrión/a   m/f   host   7A
angustia   distress, anxiety   2A
anillo   m   ring   1A
añadir   to add   5A
año   m   year   1B
año Nuevo   m   New Year   9A
ante tal + noun   in the face of   4B
anteojos   m pl   glasses   5B
antepasados   m pl   ancestors   9A
anterior   previous   3B
antes   before   1B
antes (de) que   before   12B
anticuado/a   old-fashioned   11B
antiguo/a   old   5A
antipático/a   unpleasant   6B
apagar   turn off   1B
aparato   m   device   5A
aparecer   to appear   7B
apellido   m   last name   Pre
aperitivo   m   appetizer   5A
apio   m   celery   5A
apoyar   to support   4A
apretado/a   tight fitting   5B
aprender   to learn   1B
aprendizaje   m   learning   7B
apretar   to press; to tighten   8A
apretón de manos   m
   handshake   6B
aprobación   f   approval   5B
aprobar   to pass (a class, an
   exam)   7B
aprovechar   to take advantage
   of   11A
aquí   here   1A
árbol   m   tree   3A
arete   m   earring   5B
argamasa   m   mortar   6A
armario   m   closet   6A
armonioso/a   harmonious   8B
arrebatar   to seize   11A
arriba de   above   3A
arrocera   f   rice maker   6A
arrodillarse   to kneel down   7A
arroz   m   rice   5A
arte de instalación   m   installation
   art   8B

artes gráficas *f pl* graphic arts 8B
artesanal handmade 10A
asegurarse to make sure 5B
asesino/a *m/f* murderer 4B
asesor/a *m/f* advisor 5B
así que so/ so that 7B
asiento *m* seat 1B
asignatura *f* academic subject 2A
asistir to attend 1B
aspiradora *f* vacuum cleaner 6A
asunto *m* issue 3B
asustado/a scared 8A
ataque de nervios *m* nervous breakdown 8B
atentamente sincerely yours (in a letter) 6B
atento careful; considerate; courteous 3B
atraer to attract 8B
audífonos *m pl* headphones 12B
auge *m* increase 11A
aumentar to grow 3A
aunque even though 1B
autobús *m* bus 4B
autopista *f* highway 11A
autorretrato self-portrait 7A
avanzar to advance 4B
avergonzarse to feel ashamed 8A
averiguar to find out 5B
avión *m* airplane 4B
avisar to inform 11B
ayuda *f* help 2B
ayudar to help 2B
azúcar *m* sugar 5A
azul blue 5B
azul marino navy blue 5B

B

bacalao *m* cod fish 5A
bachillerato *m* high school; secondary school 1B
bailar to dance 1A
bailarín/a *m/f* dancer 6A
baile dance 4A
bajo/a short 7A
baldosa *f* tile 6A
balón *m* ball 5B
bañarse to bathe 7A
bañera *f* bathtub 6A
baño *m* bathroom 6A
barato/a cheap 8B
barba *f* beard 7A
barco *m* boat 11A
barrer to sweep 6A
barrigón/a big bellied 2B
barrio *m* neighborhood 9A
base de datos *f* database 2A
base laboral *f* work base 3B
basura *f* garbage 3B
batallar to battle 10B
batir to beat, to whisk 5A
baúl *m* chest 4B
bebé *m/f* baby 3A
beber to drink 2B
bebida *f* drink 4A

beca *f* scholarship 3B
béisbol *m* baseball 1A
belleza *f* beauty 8B
besar to kiss 7A
beso *m* kiss 7A
biblioteca *f* library 1B
bicicleta *f* bycicle 2B
bien educado well mannered 1B
bienes raíces *m pl* real estate 9A
bienestar well-being 6B
bienvenido/a welcome 1B
bigotes *m pl* moustache 7A
biocombustible *m* biofuel 11A
bisnieto/a *m* great grandchild 2B
bistec *m* beef steak 5A
bizco cross-eyed 5B
blanco white 5A
blando/a soft 5A
boca *f* mouth 4B
boda *f* wedding 2B
bodega *f* corner store 4B
boleto/billete *m* ticket 11A
bolsillo *m* pocket 10B
bombero/a *m/f* firefigther 4B
bonito/a pretty 3A
bordado/a embroidered 5B
borde edge 8B
borracho/a drunk 8A
borrar to erase 11B
bosque *m* forest 3A
botón *m* button 1B
botones *m* bellhop 4B
brazo *m* arm 6B
breve brief 2B
brincar to jump 8A
brindis *m* toast 5A
broma *f* joke 8A
brujo/a *m/f* witch 10B
buen gusto *m* good taste 5B
buen provecho enjoy your meal 5A
buenas noches good night Pre
buenas notas good grades 4B
buenas tardes good afternoon Pre
bueno/a good 1B
buenos días good morning, good day Pre
buenos modales *m pl* good manners 2B
bufanda *f* scarf 5B
burro *m* donkey 1A
buscar un trabajo to look for a job 6B
búsqueda *f* search 3A

C

caballo *m* horse 3A
cabello *m* hair 7A
cabeza *f* head 7A
cada each 3A
cadáver *m* corpse 7B
cadena *f* chain 4B
cadera *f* hip 7A
cafetera *f* coffee maker 6A
caja *f* cash register 5B
caja *f* box 9A

cajero automático *m* automated teller machine 12A
cajero/a *m/f* teller 12A
calamar *m* squid 5A
calavera *f* skull 9A
calcetines *m pl* socks 5B
caldo *m* broth 8B
calentar to heat up 5A
cálido/a warm 6B
calientaplatos *m* plate warmer 6A
caliente hot 5A
calle *f* street 4B
calvo bald 7A
calzado *m* footwear 5B
cama *f* bed 6A
camarero/a *m/f* waiter/ waitress 4B
camarón *m* shrimp 5A
cambiar to change 1B
cambio *m* change 5A
caminar to walk 1A
camino *m* path 10A
camión *m* truck 11A
camisa *f* shirt 5B
camiseta *f* t-shirt 5B
campaña *f* campaign 10B
campeonato *m* championship 4A
campesino/a *m/f* peasant 10A
campo *m* field 2A
campo *m* countryside 7B
caña de azúcar *f* sugar cane 11A
cancha *f* court, field (sports) 6B
canción *f* song 2A
cándido/a innocent; naïve 8B
canoso/a gray haired 7A
cansado/a tired 8A
cansarle a uno to tire one 11A
cantante *m/f* singer 3B
cantar to sing 1A
capa *f* cloak, cape; layer 7A
capaz capable 6A
cara *f* face 7A
caramelo *m* candy; caramel 5B
cárcel *f* jail 12A
carecer to lack 7B
cargar to carry 9A; to charge (e.g. battery) 11B
cariño *m* affection 2B
caritativo/a charitable 12B
carne *f* meat 5A
carnicería *f* butcher shop 4B
carnicero/a *m/f* butcher 4B
caro/a expensive 4A
carpeta *m* binder 1B
carrera *f* career; course of study 1B
carrete de hilo *m* spool of thread 5B
carretera *f* road 3A
carro/coche *m* car 11A
carta *f* letter 2B
cartel *m* poster 7B
cartera *f* wallet 12A
cartera/bolsa *f* handbag 5B
cartero/a *m/f* letter carrier 4B
casa *f* house 1A

casado/a married 2B
casarse to marry 9A
casco *m* helmet 9B
cebolla *f* onion 5A
cejas *f pl* eyebrows 7A
célebre famous 7B
cena *f* dinner 5A
cenar to have dinner 5A
censura *f* censorship 7A
centro comercial *m* shopping mall 4B
cerca close 4A
cercano close 2B
cereal *m* cereal 5A
cerebro *m* brain 7B
cerrar to close 1B
cerveza *f* beer 5A
cesto *m* basket 10B
chaqueta *f* jacket 5B
charlar to chat, to talk 11B
chau/chao goodbye Pre
chico/a *m/f* guy/gal 2B
chirriar to chirp; to squeak 10B
chisme *m* rumor, gossip 10A
chorizo *m* sausage 4B
chubasco *m* heavy shower 3A
chuleta de puerco/cerdo *f* pork chop 5A
chupar to suck 7A
ciencias sociales *f pl* social science 1B
ciertos certain 6B
cifras *f pl* numbers 11A
cilantro *m* coriander 5A
cine *m* cinema 4A
cineasta *m/f* cinematographer 8B
cintura *f* waist 7A
cinturón *m* belt 5B
cirujano/ *m/f* surgeon 4B
ciudad *f* city 2A
ciudadanía *f* citizenship 4A
ciudadano/a *m/f* citizen 12B
ciudadela *f* citadel 10A
claro/a clear 5A
cláusula *f* clause 11B
cliente *m/f* client 5A
cloquear to cluck 10B
clóset *m* closet 6A
cobarde *m* coward 10B
cobrar to charge 6B
coche *m* car 3A
cochecito *m* stroller 4A
cocina *f* kitchen; stove 5A
cocinar to cook 1A
cocinero/a *m/f* cook 4B
codicioso/a greedy 10B
código *m* code 10A
codo *m* elbow 7A
cohete *m* rocket 11A
colegio *m* high school 1B
colgar to hang 6A
collar *m* necklace 4B
colocación *f* placement 11B
colocar to place 5A
coloquio *m* debate 2A
color color 8B

comandante del ejército *m/f* army major 6B
combatir to fight 1B
combustible *m* fuel 11A
comedor *m* dining room 6A
comenzar to start 2A
comer to eat 1A
comida *f* food 3B
comida casera *f* home-cooked food 5A
comida rápida *f* fast food 5A
comienzo *m* start 10B
cómo how, what (interrog) Pre
como like, as 1B
cómodamente comfortably 6B
comodidad *f* comfort 11A
cómodo/a comfortable 6A
compañero/a de clase *m/f* classmate 1B
compañero/a de cuarto *m/f* roommate 2B
compartir to share 1B
complaciente satisfying, pleasing; pleasurable 8B
componer to compose; to repair 7B
componerse to consist of 7B
comportamiento *m* behavior 6B
compositor/a *m/f* composer 7B
comprar to buy 3A
comprobar to verify 5A
comprometido/a engaged, commited 2B
compromiso *m* engagement; commitment, obligation 3B
computación *f* computer science 2A
computadora *f* computer 1A
con base en based on 1B
con este fin to this end 5B
con frecuencia frequently 2A
con permiso excuse me 5A
con tal (de) que provided that 12B
condimentos *m pl* condiments 5A
conducir to drive 4A
confiado/a convinced; trusting 8B
confitería *f* cake shop 4B
congelar to freeze 5A
congreso *m* conference 5A
conjunto *m* set 7B
conmigo with me 2A
conmover to move (emotionally) 8B
conocer to know (be familiar with) 1A
conocido/a well-known 6B
conocimiento *m* knowledge 8A
conseguir to obtain 4A
consejo *m* advice 5B
construir to build 3B
consultorio *m* (doctor's) office 3B
contabilidad *f* accounting 2A
contador/a *m/f* accountant 4B
contaminación *f* pollution 7A
contar to count 10A
contarse to tell each other 7B
contento happy 4A

contestador automático *m* answering machine 3B
contestar to answer 1B
contorno *m* environment, surroundings 8B
contra against 3B
contraseña *f* password 11B
contribuir to contribute 4B
controvertido/a controversial 10A
conveniente appropriate; suitable 4B
convertirse to become 3B
copa *f* glass of wine 5A
corazón *m* heart 4A
corbata *f* tie 5B
corona *f* crown 2B
corredor *m* hallway 6A
corredor de autos *m* racecar driver 7B
correo *m* mail 4B
correo electrónico *m* email 11B
correr to run, to go running 1A
cortapatatas *m* potato slicer 6A
cortar to cut 5A
corte *f* court (of law) 4B
cortina *f* curtain 6A
corto/a short 11A
corto/a de vista short-sighted 7A
cosa *f* thing 1A
cosecha *f* harvest 9A
cosmético *m* make-up 9A
costumbre *f* custom 5A
cotidiano/a common; ordinary 7A
crecer to grow 3A
creer to believe 4A
crucero *m* cruise ship 11A
crucigrama *m* crossword puzzle 10B
crudo/a raw 5A
cuaderno *m* notebook 1B
cuadro *m* painting 6A
cuál/es which (interrog) Pre
cuando when 12B
cuándo when (interrog) 2A
cuánto/a/os/as how much/many Pre
cuarto *m* room 6A
cuarto/a fourth 6B
cubierto/a covered 4B
cubiertos *m pl* utensils, silverware 5A
cubrir to cover 3B
cuchara *f* spoon 5A
cuchillo *m* knife 5A
cuello *m* neck 5B
cuenta *f* check 5A
cuenta bancaria *f* bank account 12A
cuenta corriente *f* checking account 12A
cuenta de ahorros *f* savings account 12A
cuento *m* story 1A
cuero *m* leather 4B
cuerpo *m* body 5B

cuestionamiento *m* questioning 3B
cuestionar to question 3B
cuidado *m* caution 1A
cuidadosamente carefully 6A
cuidar to take care of 2B
cuidarse to take care of yourself/ each other 7B
culpabilidad *f* guilt 4B
cultivar to grow 5A
culto *m* worship 10A
cumpleaños *m* birthday 2B
cumplido *m* compliment 5B
cumplir to turn (age) 6A
cuñado/a *m/f* brother/sister-in-law 2B
currículum *m* resumé 6B
cuyo/a whose 6B

D

dado *m* die 1B
dama *f* lady 8B
dañar to damage; to hurt/ harm 11A
daño *m* harm, damage 12B
dar to give 4B
datos *m pl* facts, data 7A
de from; of Pre
de acuerdo a according to 6A
de dónde from where (interrog) Pre
de esta manera in this way 3B
de estatura mediana average height 7A
de hecho in fact 3B
de igual manera likewise 10B
de la misma manera in the same way 4A
de memoria by heart 10B
de moda in style 5B
de oferta on sale 9A
de vez en cuando once in a while 3B
debajo de below 3A
deber to owe 5B
deber + *infinitive* should + infinitive 4A
deberes *m pl* homework 4A
debido a due to 7A
débil weak 10B
decepción *f* disappointment 3B
décimo tenth 6B
declaración *f* statement 3B
dedicarse a to dedicate oneself to something (esp. professionally) 6B
dedo *m* finger 7A
dejar to leave 5A
dejar de + *infinitive* to stop (doing something) 4B
dejar la propina to leave a tip 5A
dejar que to allow 11B
deleitarse to enjoy 5A
deletrear to spell 1A
delgado/a slender 5B
delito *m* crime 4B
demasiado too; too much 6A

demorar(se) to delay; to become delayed 11A
demostrar to demonstrate; to prove 10B
dentro de inside 5B
dependiente/a *m/f* clerk 4B
deporte *m* sport 1A
deportivo sports related 1A
depositar to deposit 12A
derecho *m* law; right 2A
derechos humanos *m pl* human rigths 10B
derretir to melt 5A
derrota *f* defeat 10B
desagüe *m* drain 6A
desarrollar to develop 10A
desarrollo infantil *m* child development 2A
desayuno *m* breakfast 5A
descalificar disqualify 3B
descansar to rest 4A
descarga eléctrica *f* electric discharge 3A
descargar to download; to unload 11B
descomponer to break up 7B
desconocido/a unknown 10B
descuidar to neglect 8A
desde from, since 6A
desear to wish 2A
desempeñar to perform (a task or job) 4B
desempleo *m* unemployment 2B
desfile *m* parade 7B
desfile de modas *m* fashion show 5B
desgracia *f* misfortune, tragedy 7B
desigualdad *f* inequality 8B
desilusionado/a disappointed 8A
desmantelar to disassemble 11A
despacho *m* office, study 6A
despedir a to dismiss, to fire 4B
desperdicio *m* waste 12B
despertador *m* alarm clock 4B
despertar to wake up 6A
desplazar to diplace 11A
desproporcionado out of proportion 3A
después after 1B
después de que after 12B
destello *m* sparkle 8A
destruir to destroy 1A
desvelarse to stay awake 9A
desventaja *f* disadvantage 4A
desviar to deviate 11A
detenidamente slowly 5B
detestado/a hated 10B
detrás behind 7A
día feriado *m* holiday 6B
diablo *m* devil 1A
diario *m* daily newspaper 4B
diario/a daily 6B
días de la semana *m pl* days of the week 2A
dibujar to draw 1A

dibujo *m* drawing 5B
diciembre December 3A
dictadura *f* dictatorship 3A
dientes *m pl* teeth 7A
diferir to differ, be different; to defer 3B
difunto/a *m/f* dead person; deceased 2B
dinero *m* money 3B
dios/a *m/f* god/goddess 9A
director/a de cine *m/f* movie director 2A
dirigir(se) to direct; to head for 11A
disco *m* record; disc 4A
discurso *m* speech; discourse 3B
diseñador/a *m/f* designer 5B
diseñar design 4B
diseño *m* design 8B
disfraz *m* costume 9A
disfrutar de/gozar de to enjoy 6B
disgustar to annoy; displease 8B
disparo *m* shot 4A
dispositivo *m* mechanism, device 12B
dispuesto/a willing 6B
distinto/a different 3A
diversión *f* fun 4A
divertir to entertain 4A
divertirse to have fun 7B
divinidad *f* deity, god 10A
divorciado/a divorced 2B
doblado/a folded 8B
doblar to fold 6B
documental *f* documentary 1A
dolor *m* pain 8A
dolor de cabeza *m* headache 10A
dolor de espalda *m* backache 10A
dolor de estómago *m* stomach ache 10A
dolor de garganta *m* sore throat 10A
domingo Sunday 2A
dónde where (interrog) Pre
dormir to sleep 4A
dormitorio *m* bedroom 1B
dramáticamente drastically 3B
drenar to drain 6A
ducha *f* shower 6A
ducharse to shower oneself 7A
dueño/a *m/f* owner 4B
dulce sweet 5A
duradero/a lasting, durable 8B
durar to last 1B

E

echarse una siesta take a nap 6B
edad age Pre
edad *f* age 2B
edificar build; build up 7B
edificio *m* building 1B
educativo educational 1B
efectivo cash (money) 11B
efecto effect 4A
eficaz effective 10B

egoísta selfish 8B
ejemplo *m* example 1B
ejercicio *m* exercise 5B
electrodomésticos *m pl* appliances 6A
elegir to choose 3B
elegir to choose, to elect 10B
embarazada pregnant 8A
embarrar to spread on something 5A
emocionante exciting 9A
emparejar to match 1B
empequeñecer to reduce; to shrink 11A
empezar to start 2A
empresa company 2A
empujar to push 4A
en in; on Pre
en cambio on the other hand 1B
en caso de que in case 12B
en contraste on the other hand 8A
en cuanto as soon as 12B
en cuanto a regarding; with respect to 3A
en efectivo in cash 12A
en eso in that respect 6B
en este punto on this point 12B
en la actualidad currently 3B
en línea online 12B
en lugar de instead of 10B
en negrita bold type 11A
en otras palabras in other words 4A
en realidad actually 3B
en tropel in a rush 3A
enamorado/a in love; lover 8A
enamorarse to fall in love 1B
enano/a *m/f* dwarf 1A
encantado/a delighted to meet you Pre
encantador/a enchanting 7A
encarcelar to imprison 10B
encargarse to be in charge of 5A
encender to turn on 9A
encerramiento *m* enclosure 8B
encima on top of 3A
encimera *f* counter top 6A
encogerse de hombros to shrug your shoulders 7A
encontrar to find 4A
encuesta *f* survey 3B
endeudarse to get into debt 12A
enero January 3A
enfatizar to emphasize 4A
enfermedad *f* illness 4B
enfermera nurse 2A
enfermería *f* nursing 2A
enfermero/a *m/f* nurse 4B
enfermo/a sick 4B
enfocarse to focus 12A
enfoque *m* focus 6B
enfrentar to face, to confront 8B
enfrente in front 7A
engordar to gain weight 5B
enojado/a upset, angry 8A
enriquecer to enrich 11B

ensalada *f* salad 4A
ensanchar to widen 5B
ensayo *m* rehearsal; essay 4A
enseñar to teach 4B
entender to understand 3B
entendimiento *m* understanding 10A
entonces then 10B
entrada *f* ticket 12A
entre between 6A
entregar to hand in 5B
entrenador/a *m/f* trainer 4A
entretener to entertain 8B
entretenimiento *m* entertainment 4A
entrevista *f* interview 2A
enunciado *m* statement 6A
enviar to send 11B
equipaje *m* luggage 7B
equipo *m* team 4A
Érase una vez... Once upon a time... 10B
es decir that is to say 1A
es más moreover; in addition 3A
escalera *f* stairwell 6A
escasez *f* scarcity 11A
esclavitud *f* slavery 10B
escoba *f* broom 6A
escoger to choose 2A
escribir to write 1A
escritor/a *m/f* writer 2B
escritorio *m* desk 1B
escritura writing 10A
escuchar to listen to, to hear 1A
escuela preparatoria *f* high school 1B
escuela primaria *f* elementary school 1B
escuela secundaria *f* junior high 1B
escuela técnica *f* vocational school 1B
escultura *f* sculpture 8B
esencialmente essentially 2A
esforzarse to make an effort 11B
esfuerzo *m* effort 11B
espacio *m* space 1A
espalda *f* back 7A
espantapájaros *m* scarecrow 10B
especialización specialty 2A
espectáculo *m* show 4B
espejo *m* mirror 6A
espera wait 7B
esperar to wait 11B
esposo/a *m/f* husband/wife 2B
esquina *f* corner 7A
estación *f* season 3A
estación de autobuses *f* bus station 11A
estado *m* state 2B
estadounidense U.S. citizen 1A
estallar to break out; to explode 8A
estampado *m* print 5B
estampilla *f* stamp 8B
estante *m* shelf 6A
estar to be 2A

estar de buen/mal humor to be in a good/bad mood 6B
estar en contra de to be against 7A
estar enamorado/a to be in love 2B
estar seguro/a to be sure 8A
estatura *f* height 5B
este... uh.../um... 7B
estirar to stretch 7A
Estoy de acuerdo. I agree. 3A
estrecho/a narrow 5B
estrella *f* star 7A
estudiante *m/f* student 1B
estudiar to study 11B
evitar to avoid 8B
examen *m* test 2A
exigente demanding 2A
exiliarse to go into exile 10B
éxito *m* success 1B
explicación *f* explanation 3B
expuesto/a exposed 11B
expulsar de to expel from 3B
extender to extend 10A
extranjero/a *m/f* foreigner 3B

F

fábrica *f* factory 6B
facciones *f pl* features 12A
fácil easy 4A
factura *f* bill 12A
facturar (el equipaje) to check in (luggage) 11A
facultad *f* university school or college 1B
falda *f* skirt 5B
falla *f* fault 3A
falta *f* lack of 3B
faltar al trabajo miss work 6B
familia anfitriona *f* host family 2A
familiar family related 2B
fatigar to tire 11A
fauno *m* fawn (mythological) 1A
febrero February 3A
fecha *f* date 1B
felicidad *f* happiness 11A
feliz *happy* 4A
feo/a ugly 10A
feria *f* fair 7A
ferrocarril *m* railroad 11A
festejar to celebrate; to party 9A
fiebre *f* fever 10A
fiesta *f* party 2B
fin de semana *m* weekend 3A
finalmente finally 10A
fino high quality 5B
fino/a fine, thin (hair) 7A
finura *f* refinement 6B
firma *f* signature 2A
firmar to sign 1A
flor *f* flower 4A
florecer to flourish 3B
floristería *f* flower shop 6B
fondo *m* bottom; depth 7B
forastero/a *m/f* foreigner 3B

franela *f* flannel 5B
fregadero *m* sink 6A
freír to fry 5A
frente *f* forehead 7A
fresa *f* strawberry 5A
frijoles *m pl* beans 5A
frijoles verdes *m pl* green beans 5A
frío *m* cold 3B
fruncir to frown 7A
fruta *f* fruit 5A
fuente *f* fountain 6A
fuente *f* source 7B
fuerte strong 3A
fuerza *f* strength, power 3A
fuerzas armadas *f pl* armed forces 2A
fumar to smoke 4A
funcionamiento *m* operation 11A
fundar to found 3B
fútbol *m* soccer 1A

G

gabinete *m* cabinet (gov) 6A
gafas *f pl* eyeglasses, sunglasses 5B
galleta *f* cookie 5A
ganar to win; to earn 4A
ganarse la vida to earn a living 6B
garbanzo *m* chick pea 5A
gastar to spend 12A
gasto *m* expense 2B
gemelo/a *m/f* twin 3B
genial great 1B
gente *f* people 1A
geografía *f* geography 3A
gerente *m/f* manager 4B
gerente de la sucursal *m/f* branch manager 12A
gesto *m* gesture 1A
gitano/a *m/f* gypsy 5B
gobierno *m* government 3B
gordo/a fat 7A
gorra *f* cap 5B
grabación *f* filming 5A
grabado/a engraved; recorded 8A
grabadora *f* recorder 1B
grabar to record 11B
gracioso/a funny 5B
gramática *f* grammar 1B
gran big, great 3A
gran almacén *m* department store 12A
grande big 1B
granos enteros *m pl* whole grains 5A
grasa *f* fat 5A
gratis free 10A
gris gray 5B
gritar to scream 4A
grito *m* scream 11A
grueso/a thick 7A
guante *m* glove 5B
guapo/a good-looking 8A
guardar to keep 3B

guardar to put away 6A
guardia *m/f* guard 12A
gubernamental government (adj.) 6B
guerra *f* war 3A
guerrillero/a *m/f* guerilla fighter 4B
guía *m/f* guide 4B
guía universitaria *f* university directory 2A
guión *m* script 4A
guisantes *m pl* peas 5A
gusto *m* liking, taste 6A

H

habitación *f* room 4B
habitante *m/f* inhabitant 3A
hablar to speak, to talk 1A
hacer to do 4B
hacer escala to make a stop (at an airport) 11A
hacer falta to need 11B
hacer fila to wait in line 11A
hacer la tarea to do homework 1B
hacer las maletas to pack the bags 11A
hacer negocios to do business 6B
hacer planes make plans 6B
hacer preguntas ask questions 1B
hacer una cita make an appointment 6B
hacia towards 8B
hambre *f* hunger 8A
hamburguesa *f* hamburger 1A
harina *f* flour 5A
hasta until 6A
hasta luego see you later Pre
hasta mañana see you tomorrow Pre
hasta pronto see you soon Pre
hay there is/there are 1B
hay que + *infinitive* to have to 4A
helado *m* ice cream 5A
heredar to inherit 3B
heredero/a *m/f* heir 2B
herencia *f* heritage 3B
hermanastro/a *m/f* stepbrother/stepsister 2B
hermano/a *m/f* brother/sister 2B
herramienta *f* tool 4B
hervir to boil 5A
hielo *m* ice 5A
hijastro/a *m/f* stepchild 2B
hijo/a *m/f* son/daughter 2B
hijo/a del medio *m/f* middle child 2B
hijo/a único/a *m/f* only child 2B
himno nacional *m* national anthem 3A
hispanohablante *m/f* Spanish-speaker 3B
historia *f* story; history 5B
hogar *m* home 4B
hoja de maíz *f* corn husk 5A
hoja de papel *f* sheet of paper 1B
hojalata *f* tin 10B

hola hi Pre
hombre *m* man 1A
hombro *m* shoulder 6B
homenaje *m* tribute 8B
honestidad *f* decency, decorum; modesty 4B
hora *f* time 2A
hora del día *f* time of day 2A
horario *m* schedule 2A
hornear to bake 5A
horno *m* oven 5A
horno (de) microondas *m* microwave oven 5A
horrorizado/a horrified 7B
hoy today 1B
huelga *f* worker's strike 3B
huella digital *f* fingerprint 12A
hueso *m* bone 6A
huevo *m* egg 5A
huevos revueltos *m pl* scrambled eggs 10A
humilde humble 6A
hundir to dunk; to sink 8A
huracán *m* hurricane 3A

I

ida y vuelta roundtrip 11A
idioma *m* language 2A
idiomas extranjeros *m pl* foreign languages 2A
iglesia *f* church 2B
igualmente likewise Pre
imperio *m* empire 10A
impermeable *m* raincoat 5B
implicar to entail 1B
impresora *f* printer 11B
impuestos *m pl* taxes 12A
inadvertido/a unnoticed 6B
inalámbrico/a wireless 11A
inclusive including 3B
incluso even 4B
incomodidad *f* discomfort 7B
incorporarse to join 7B
inculcar instill 2B
indígena indigenous; Native American 3B
indocumentado/a illegal 3B
inesperado/a unexpected 8B
infanta *f* princess 2B
infantil children's 8B
influir to influence 12A
informática *f* computer science 2A
ingeniería *f* engineering 2A
ingreso *m* income 11A
inodoro *m* toilet 6A
inolvidable unforgettable 8A
instalación fija *f* fixture 6A
instalarse to settle in 6A
intercambiar to exchange 6A
intercambio *m* exchange 2A
intereses *m pl* interests 7B
interminable never-ending 11A
interpretar to act 8B

intransigente stubborn 10B
introducir to introduce, insert 1A
inundación *f* flooding 3A
inútil useless 11A
invertir to invest 12A
investigador/a *m/f* researcher 5A
invierno *m* summer 3A
invitado/a *m/f* guest 12B
involucrar to involve 3B
ir to go 4A
ir a pie to go by foot 11A
ir de compras to go shopping 4A
irrumpir to break out; to burst in 11B
izquierda *f* left 5A
izquierdista/derechista left-wing/right-wing 7B

J

jabón *m* soap 6B
jalar to pull 3B
jamás never 3B
jamón *m* ham 4A
jardín *m* garden 6A
jardinería *f* gardening 6A
jarra de agua *f* pitcher of water 5A
jefe/a *m/f* boss; chief 6B
joven *m/f* young person 1B
joven young 7A
joya *f* jewel 4B
joyero/a *m/f* jeweler 5B
jubilado/a retired 4B
jubilarse to retire 6B
judío/a Jewish 3B
juego de mesa *m* borad game 8B
Juegos Olímpicos *m pl* Olympic Games 3A
jueves Thursday 2A
jugador/a *m/f* player 5A
jugar to play (sports, games) 1A
jugo *m* juice 5A
juguete *m* toy 9A
juicio *m* trail 4B
julio July 3A
junio June 3A
junto con along with 2B
juntos together 6A
jurar to swear 10B
juventud *f* youth 4A

L

labio *m* lip 5B
lacio/a straight (hair) 7A
ladrillo *m* brick 6A
ladrón/a *m/f* thief 9A
lago *m* lake 3A
lana *f* wool 5B
lápiz *m* pencil 1B
lápiz labial *m* lipstick 4A
largo/a long 5A
lata *f* can 5A
latir to beat 7A
lavabo *m* bathroom sink 6A
lavadora *f* washing machine 6A

lavaplatos *m* washer 6A
lavar to wash 4B
lazos *m pl* ties 4A
leal loyal 4B
leche *f* milk 5A
lechuga *f* lettuce 4A
lectura *f* reading 2B
leer to read 1B
legado *m* legacy 10B
legumbres *f pl* legumes 5A
lejano/a faraway, far 11A
leña *f* wood (for a fire) 5B
leñador/a *m/f* woodcutter 10B
lengua *f* language 2A
lengua *f* tongue 6B
lentes *m pl* eyeglasses 5B
lento/a slow 5A
lepra *f* leprosy 10B
letra *f* letter 1B
letras *f pl* liberal arts 4B
levantamiento *m* uprising 12B
levantar la mano raise your hand 1B
levantar pesas to lift weights 1A
levantarse to get up 7A
ley *f* law 4A
libro *m* book 1B
licencia de manejar *f* driver's license 2B
licenciatura *f* bachelor's degree 1B
liga *f* league 5A
ligero light 5A
limitación *f* shortcoming 8A
limpiar to clean 6A
liso/a smooth, even 5B
listo/a (with estar) ready; (with ser) clever, smart 5A
llamada *f* phone call 6B
llamar to call 1A
llamar la atención to attract attention 8B
llanos *m pl* Plains 3A
llanta *f* tire 11A
llanuras *f pl* plains 3A
llave *f* key 4A
llegada *f* arrival 10A
llegar to arrive 1B
lleno full 11A
llevar to wear; to take; to carry 5B
llevar a to take to, to lead to 11A
llevarse bien/mal to get along/not get along 12A
llorar to cry 4A, 6B
llover to rain 3A
lluvia *f* rain 3A
lo siento. I'm sorry. 1B
lobo *m* wolf 10B
loco/a crazy 6A
lodo *m* mud 11A
lograr to achieve 5B
loro *m* parrot 11A
luchar to fight for something 3B
luego then; after 10B
lugar *m* place 1B
lugar de nacimiento *m* place of

birth 2B
lujo *m* luxury 5B
lujoso/a luxurious 4A
luna moon 7A
lunes Monday 2A
luz *f* light 1B

M

madera *f* wood 6A
madrastra *f* stepmother 2B
madre *f* mother 2B
madrina *f* godmother 2B
maestría *f* master's degree 1B
maestro/a *m/f* teacher 4B
mago/a *m/f* magician 1A
maíz *m* corn 3B
mal poorly, not well Pre
malentendido *m* misunderstanding 1B
maleta *f* suitcase 4B
malévolo/a malicious 4B
malo/a bad 1B
mañana tomorrow 1B
mañana *f* morning 2A
mandar to order, to command 4B
mandar to send 6A
mandato *m* command 6B
manejar to drive (a vehicle) 1A
manejar to manage 12A
manejo *m* handling 6A
manera *f* way 2A
manga *f* sleeve 5B
manifestación artística *f* artistic expression 10A
mano *f* hand 4B
mano de obra *f* workers; workforce 3B
manta *f* shawl 5B
mantel *m* tablecloth 5A
mantener to maintain 3B
mantequilla *f* butter 5A
manzana *f* apple 5A
mapa *m* map 1B
mar *m* sea 1A
marca *f* brand 1B
marcador *m* marker 1B
marcar to dial (telephone); to mark 11B
marco *m* frame 6A
maremoto *m* seaquake 3A
marido *m* husband 2B
mariscos *m pl* seafood 5A
mármol *m* marble 6A
marrón brown 5B
martes Tuesday 2A
marzo March 3A
más more 8B
más allá beyond 1A
más de/más que more than 2A
más tarde later 10A
masa *f* dough 5A
masa de agua *f* body of water 3A
máscara *f* mask 7B
mascota *f* pet 1A
materia *f* school subject 2A

materia prima *f* raw material 11A
matrimonio *m* marriage 2B
mayo May 3A
mayor older 2B
me llamo … my name is … Pre
medianoche *f* midnight 2A
mediante through 2B
medias *f pl* pantyhose 5B
médico/a *m/f* doctor 6B
medida *f* measure 12A
medio
  ambiente *m* environment 8B
medio hermano/a *m/f* half brother/
  half sister 2B
mediodía *m* noon 2A
mejilla *f* cheek 7A
mejor better; best 2A
mejor dicho better said; that is to
  say 12B
memoria *f* memory (mental
  function) 10B
menor younger; youngest 2B
menos de/menos que less/fewer
  than 2A
mensaje *m* message 11B
mensual monthly 12A
mente *f* mind 4B
mentir to lie 4B
mercadeo *m* marketing 2A
mercancía *f* merchandise 6B
merienda *f* afternoon snack 5A
mes del año *m* month of the
  year 3A
mesa *f* table 1B
meseta *f* plateau 3A
meta *f* goal 4A
meter to put, place inside 12A
mezcla *f* mix, blend 3B
mezclar to mix 4A
microondas *m* microwave 5A
miedo *m* fear 9A
miel *f* honey 5A
miembro/a *m/f* member 2B
mientras (que) while 3B
miércoles Wednesday 2A
militar military (adj);
  m soldier 10B
mini-falda *f* mini-skirt 7A
mirada *f* look 11A
mirar to watch, to look at 1A
mismo/a same 5A
mitad *f* half 3A
mito *m* myth 10B
mochila *f* backpack 1B
moda *f* fashion 6B
modelo *m/f* model 8B
molestar to bother 8A
molinillo *m* grinder 6A
monje *m* monk 6B
montaña *f* mountain 3A
montar en bicicleta to ride a
  bike 11A
monte *m* woodlands 3A
morado/a purple 5B
moreno dark 7B
morir to die 7B

moverse to move (motion) 11A
mucho gusto nice to meet you Pre
mudarse to move (from one place to
  another) 2B
mueble *m* piece of furniture 6A
muerte *f* death 7B
muerto/a dead 2B
mujer *f* woman 1B
mundial world (adj.) 3A
mundo *m* world 1B
muñeca *f* wrist 7A
muñeca *f* doll 7A
muro *m* wall 11A
música *f* music 1A
musulmán muslim 9A

N

nacer to be born 1A
nada nothing 4A
nadar to swim 1A
nadie no one, nobody 2B
náhuatl *m* nahuatl (indigenous
  language/culture) 10A
naranja *f* orange 5A
nariz *f* nose 7A
natación *f* swimming 8A
naturaleza *f* nature 2A
navegar por la Internet navegate
  the Internet 11B
Navidad *f* Christmas 4A
necesidad *f* need 5B
necesitar to need 1B
negocio *m* business 2A
negro/a black 2B
nieto/a *m/f* grandson/
  grandaugther 2B
nieve *f* snow 5B
ninguno/a none 4A
niño/a *m/f* boy/girl; child 2B
nivel *m* level 3A
noche *f* night 2A
Nochebuena *f* Christmas Eve 9A
Nochevieja *f* New Year's Eve 9A
nombrar to name 9A
nombre *m* name 1A
nopal *m* cactus 10A
norma *f* rule 8B
nota *f* note; grade 1A
noticia, noticias *f, f pl* news 2B
noticiero *m* newscast 4B
notorio/a well-known, noted 4B
novedades *f pl* news 6A
noveno/a ninth 6B
noviembre November 3A
novio/a *m/f* boyfriend/
  girlfriend 3B
novio/novia *m/f* groom/bride 5B
nube *f* cloud 3A
nudo *m* knot 10A
nuera *f* daugther-in-law 2B
número *m* number 3A
nunca never 3B

O

o sea in other words 1A

obligar to force someone to do
  something 11B
obra (de teatro) *f* play 7B
obra de arte *f* work of art 7A
obra maestra *f* masterpiece 4A
obrero/a *m/f* worker, laborer 4B
obtener to obtain 12A
occidentalización *f*
  westernization 12B
ocio *m* leisure 4A
octavo/a eigth 6B
octubre October 3A
ocultar to hide 9A
ocuparse to see to; to take care
  of 7B
oficina *f* office 1B
oficio *m* trade 4A
ofrecimiento *m* offering 9A
ofrenda *f* offering 9A
oído *m* ear (inner) 7A
oír to hear 4B
ojo *m* eye 7A
ola *f* wave 3A
oler to smell 7A
olla *f* pot 5A
olla al vapor *f* steam cooker 6A
ombligo *m* belly button 10A
operación *f* surgery 4B
oponerse to oppose 10B
oprimir to press (e.g. a button); to
  oppress 10B
opuesto/a opposite 3A
oración *f* sentence 5A
oreja *f* ear (outer) 5B
orgullosamente proudly 3B
oriental eastern 8B
oro *m* gold 5B
oscuridad *f* darkness 7B
oscuro/a dark 5B
otoño *m* autumn 3A
otro/a *m/f* another 3A

P

pacífico peaceful 3B
padecer to suffer (an illness) 11A
padrastro *m* stepfather 2B
padre *m* father 1A
padre *m* priest 7B
padrino *m* godfather 2B
pagar to pay 5A
pagar a plazos to pay in
  installments 12A
página *f* page 1B
país *m* country Pre
paisaje *m* landscape 6A
pájaro *m* bird 3A
palabra *f* word 1B
palmada *f* pat 6B
palmera *f* palm tree 3A
palomitas *f pl* popcorn 10A
pan *m* bread 4A
pan tostado *m* toast 5A
panadería *f* bakery 6B
panecillo *m* sweet roll 5A
panorama *m* overview 3A

pantalla *f* screen 1B
papa *f* potato 5A
papas fritas *f pl* french fries 5A
papel *m* paper; role 6A
papelería *f* stationery store 6B
papitas *f pl* potato chips 10A
para que so that 12B
parado/a standing up 7A
paraguas *m* umbrella 5B
pararse to stand 6B
parecer to appear to be 3B
pared *f* wall 6A
pareja *f* couple 2B
pariente *m* relative 2B
parque *m* park 1A
parrilla *f* grill 5A
parroquia *f* parish 9A
partido *m* game, match 3B
partido político *m* political party 3A
partir to leave; to cut 6B
pasado *m* past 9A
pasar to spend (time) 11B
pasar a ser to become 3B
pasar por la aduana to go through customs 11A
pasar tiempo to spend time 6B
pasarlo bien/mal to have a good/ bad time 6B
pasatiempo *m* hobby 6B
Pascua *f* Easter 9A
paso *m* step 1A
pastel *m* cake 5A
pastelería *m* bakery 4B
pasto *m* pasture 3A
patear to kick 7A
patria *f* heartland 8B
patrimonio *m* heritage 10A
patrón *m* pattern 3A
payaso *m* clown 7B
paz *f* peace 8B
pecho *m* chest 7A
pedir to ask for 4A
pegar to hit 3B
peinarse to comb your hair 11A
pelar to peel 5A
pelear to fight 3B
película *f* movie 1B
peligroso/a dangerous 5A
peligroso/a dangerous 10B
pelirrojo/a redheaded 7A
pelo *m* hair 3B
pelota *f* ball 3B
peluquería *f* barber shop/ hairdressing salon 4B
peluquero/a *m/f* barber/ hairdresser 4B
pendiente *m* ear ring; pendant 5B
pensar to think 3B
peor worse; worst 8B
pequeño/a small 1B
perder to lose 4A
perdido/a lost 2B
perdón excuse me/I'm sorry 5A
peregrinos *m pl* pilgrims 7B

perezoso/a lazy 4B
perfil *m* profile 3A
periódico *m* newspaper 2A
periodismo *m* journalism 2A
periodista *m/f* journalist 7A
permitir to allow 1B
personaje *m* character 1B
pertenecer to belong 1B
pertenencia *f* sense of belonging 5B
pescado *m* fish 5A
peso *m* weight 6B
pestañas *f pl* eyelashes 7A
petróleo *m* oil 10B
picante spicy 3B
picar to cut 6B
piedra *f* stone 1A
piel *f* skin; leather 5B
pierna *f* leg 5B
pies *m pl* feet 7A
pimienta *f* pepper 5A
piña *f* pineapple 6B
pincel *m* paintbrush 7A
pino *m* pine tree 3A
pintarse to paint oneself 7A
pintor/a *m/f* painter 6B
piropo *m* flirtatious comment 5B
pisar to step on 6B
piso *m* floor; apartment 6A
pista *f* path; clue 8A
pitar to whistle 6B
pito *m* whistle 6B
pizarra *f* blackboard/ whiteboard 1B
plancha *f* iron 6B
planchar *f* to iron, to press 6B
plano/a flat 10B
planta *f* plant; floor, story (of a building) 6A
plátano *m* plaintain 5A
plato *m* dish 1A
plato principal *m* entreé 5A
playa *f* beach 3A
plaza *f* square 4A
pluma *f* pen 1B
población *f* population 3A
pobre poor 2B
pobreza *f* poverty 1B
poder *m* power 4A; to be able to 4A
poder adquisitivo *m* buying power 3B
poderoso powerful 9A
poesía *f* poetry 10B
polémico/a controversial 10B
polifacético/a many-sided 10B
pollo *m* chicken 5A
polvo *m* dust 7A
poner to put 4B
poner en orden to put in order 4B
poner la mesa to set the table 5A
ponerse to put something on 7A
por ciento percent 3B
por cierto by the way 2B
por consiguiente as a result 7B
por ejemplo for example 3B

por esa razón for that reason 4A
por eso for that reason; that's why 4A
por favor please 1B
por fin finally 10A
por lo común ordinarily; customarily 8A
por lo tanto therefore 11A
por otra parte on the other hand 11B
por otro lado on the other hand 7A
porque because 2B
portavoz *m/f* speaker 8B
posicionamiento *m* positioning 11A
postre *m* dessert 5A
potable drinkable 3A
pozo *m* well 6B
precio *m* price 3B
precolombino pre columbian 8B
pregunta *f* question 1B
premio *m* award 1B
prenda *f* garment 5B
preocupado/a worried 8A
preposición *f* preposition 3A
presión *f* pressure 3A
préstamo *m* loan 12A
prestar to lend 5B
prestar atención pay attention 4A
presupuesto *m* budget 12A
primavera *f* spring 3A
primero/a (primer) first 2A
primo/a *m/f* cousin 2B
primogénito/a *m/f* first child 2B
príncipe *m* prince 2B
probar to taste 4B
proceder to come from 3B
producir to produce 4B
profundidad *f* depth 8A
programa de concursos *m* TV game show 7A
promedio *m* average 2A
prometedor promising 11B
promocionar to promote 3A
promover to promote 1B
promulgación *f* enactment 9A
pronombre *m* pronoun 3A
pronóstico *m* forecast 3A
pronto soon 6B
propina *f* tip 4B
propio/a own 2A
proponer to propose 10B
propósito *m* purpose 11A
proveer provide 2B
próximo next 4A
proyector *m* projector 1B
prueba *f* test 1B
publicidad *f* advertising 2A
público *m* audience 8B
pueblo *m* town; people 3B
puente *m* bridge 10A
puerta *f* door 1B
puerto *m* port 7B
pues so/well 7B
puesto político *m* political position 10B

puesto que   since   8A; because   12B
pulsar   to press (a button); to tap   11B
punto   *m*   point   4A
punto de rocío   *m*   dew point   3A
punto de vista   *m*   point of view   4A
puntualmente   on time   12A

Q

que   that   1A
qué   what (interrog)   Pre
quechua   *m*   Quechua (indigenous language/culture)   10A
quehaceres   *m pl*   chores   6A
quemar   to burn   7B
querer   to want   4A
queso   *m*   cheese   4A
quiché   *m pl*   Quiché (indigenous language/culture)   10A
quien/es   who   8B
quién/es   who (interrog)   1A
químico/a   *chemical*   1B; *m/pl*   chemist   4B
quinto/a   fifth   6B
quitarse   to take off   7A

R

raíz   *f*   root   3B
rama   *f*   branch   8B
rápido   fast   2B
rasgos   *m pl*   traits   5A
ratos libres   *m pl*   free time   6B
razonable   reasonable   4B
real   royal   2B
realizar   to do, to complete   2A
realizar (un sueño)   to fulfill (a dream)   6B
rebanada   *f*   slice   5A
recámara   *f*   room   7A
recargar   to recharge   12A
receta   *f*   recipe   5A
rechazar   reject   3B
rechazo   *m*   rejection   3B
recibo   *m*   receipt   11A
recipiente   *m*   container   5A
recoger   to pick up   5A
reconocer   recognize   3B
recordar   to remember   2B, 10B
recorrer   to cover, travel   11A
recorte   *m*   cut-out, clipping   7B
recuerdos   *m pl*   memories   7B
recuperar   to recover   10A
recurso   *m*   resource   12B
red   *f*   net; network   12B
redondo/a   round   7A
reemplazar   to replace   5A
reflexionar   to reflect   3A
reforzar   reinforce   10A
refresco   *m*   softdrink   6B
refutar   to rebut   12B
regalar   to give as a present   5B
regalo   *m*   gift   5B
regañar   to scold   8A

régimen   *m*   diet   2A
reglas   *f pl*   rules   2B
regresar   to return   5A
regreso   *m*   return   6A
reguetón   *m*   reggaeton   4A
regular   so-so, okay   Pre
rehacer   to redo   10A
reír   to laugh   4A
reivindicar   to restore   8A
relajante   relaxing   6A
relajarse   to relax   6A
relámpago   *m*   lightning   3A
relato   *m*   story   9A
relevante   important   3A
relevo   *m*   relay   10A
reloj   *m*   clock/watch   1B
renovar   to renew   10A
renunciar   to resign, to quit   6B
repaso   *m*   review   6B
repetir   to repeat   4A
Repita, por favor.   Repeat, please.   1B
reportaje   *m*   report   10B
reproductor   *m*   player (CD, DVD, etc.)   6A
resaltar   to highlight   9A
resbalarse   to slip   8A
residencia estudiatil   *f*   student dorm   1B
resolver   to solve   3B
resplandor   *m*   brightness   3A
respuesta   *f*   answer   2A
restaurante   *m*   restaurant   5A
resulta que   it (just) so happens that; it turns out   11B
resumen   *m*   summary   1A
resumir   to summarize   6B
retomar   to take up again   6A
retrasarse   to run late   11A
retrato   *m*   portrait   7A
reunión   *f*   meeting   4B
reunir   to gather   2B
revisar   review   7A
revista   *f*   magazine   4B
rey   *m*   king   3B
rezar   to pray   4B
riesgo   *m*   risk   3A
rímel   *m*   eyeliner   9A
río   *m*   river   3A
riquezas   *f pl*   riches   10A
risa   *f*   laughter   5A
rizado   curly (hair)   7A
robar   to rob   6B
robo   *m*   robbery   9A
rodeado/a   surrounded   6A
rodear   to surround   4A
rodilla   knee   7A
rojo/a   red   5B
rompecabezas   *m*   puzzle   8B
romper   to break   7B
ropa   *f*   clothes   5B
rosa   pink   5B
rostro   *m*   face   7A
rubio/a   blond   7A
rudo   rough, rude   10A
rueda   *f*   wheel   11A

ruido   *m*   noise   4A
ruidoso/a   noisy   11B
rutinario/a   ordinary   7B

S

sábado   Saturday   2A
saber   to know   3A
sabio/a   wise   10A
sabor   *m*   taste   4B
sacar   to take out   5A
saco   *m*   sports jacket   5B
sala   *f*   living room   6A
salchicha   *f*   sausage   5A
saldo   *m*   balance   12A
salir   go out; to leave   3A
salón   *m*   room   6A
salón de clase   *m*   classroom   1B
salpicar   to splash   8B
salsa   *f*   sauce   5A
saltar   to jump   3B
salud   *f*   health   2B
saludable   healthy   5A
saludar   to greet   1B
salvaje   wild   3A
sandwichera   *f*   sandwich maker   6A
sangre   *f*   blood   7A
sano/a   healthy   6B
sartén   *m/f*   pan   5A
secadora   *f*   dryer   6A
secar   to dry   6B
sed   *f*   thirst   11A
seda   *f*   silk   6B
seguir   to follow   4A
según   according to   2A
según parece   apparently   5A
segundo/a   second   6B
selva   *f*   jungle   3A
Semana Santa   *f*   Holy Week   9A
semanal   *weekly*   4B
semejanza   *f*   similarity   5B
señal de protesta   *f*   sign of protest   3B
señalar   to point something out   1B
sencillo/a   simple; single   6A
sensible   sensitive   8A
sentado/a   sitting down   7A
sentarse   to sit down   7A
sentido   *m*   sense   1A
sentido de humor   *m*   sense of humor   4A
sentimiento   *m*   feeling   3B
sentirse   to feel   7B
septiembre   September   3A
séptimo/a   seventh   6B
ser   to be   1A
ser humano   *m*   human being   6B
servicio de mesa   *m*   tableware   5A
servilleta   *f*   napkin   5A
sexto/a   sixth   6B
sí mismo/a   himself/herself   7B
siempre   always   3B
sierra   *f*   mountain range, saw   12A
siglo   *m*   century   3B
significado   *m*   meaning   6A
significar   to mean   1B

siguiente following 3A
silla *f* chair 1B
silla de ruedas *f* wheelchair 7B
sillón *m* armchair 6A
simpático/a nice 8A
sin without 6A
sin embargo however 4B
sin parar non-stop 8A
sin que without 12B
sinceridad *f* honesty 6B
sino que but rather 2B
sobre on top of 3A
sobre todo above all, over 9A
sobrevivir to survive 2B
sobrino/a *m/f* nephew/niece 2B
sol *m* sun 5B
solamente only 3A
soldado *m* soldier 10A
soler + *infinitive* to tend to/usually do something 6B
solicitante *m/f* applicant 6B
solicitar to apply (job) 6B
solicitud *f* application 6B
solidario/a supportive 12B
solo/a alone, lonely 8A
soltar to let go of 11B
soltero/a not married 2B
sombra *f* shadow 7B
sombrero *m* hat 5B
sonar to ring; to sound 11B
soñar despierto to day dream 6B
sondeo *m* survey 11A
sonido *m* sound 8B
sonreír to smile 4A
sonrisa *f* smile 4B
sopa *f* soup 4B
soporte *m* stand; support; bracket 8B
sortija *f* ring 5B
sostener to support; to hold 4A
suave soft 7A
subida *f* surge 3A
subir to go up 8A
subrayar to underline 5B
suceder to take place; occur 11A
suceso *m* event 3A
suegro/a *m/f* father/mother-in-law 2B
sueldo *m* salary 6B
suelto/a loose 7A
suelto/a loose fitting 5B
suficiente enough 3A
sufrimiento *m* suffering 8A
sugerencia *f* suggestion 6B
suministros *m pl* supplies 12A
superar to overcome 12B
surgir to emerge, arise; appear 3A

T

tabla *f* chart 7A
tachar to cross out 6A
tal como such as 3B
talla *f* size 5B
taller workshop 4B
tamaño *m* size 2B

también also 1A
tampoco neither 2A
tan as 8B
tan pronto como as soon as 12B
tanto/a/os/as as much/many 8B
tanto...como both 6A
tapado/a covered 8A
taquilla *f* box office 12B
tarde *f* afternoon 2A
tarde late 4A
tarea *f* homework 3B
tarifa *f* fee 11A
tarjeta *f* card 5B
tarjeta de crédito *f* credit card 12A
tarjeta de débito *f* debit card 12A
tarjeta postal *f* postcard 7A
tarta *f* cake; pie 5A
tasa *f* rate 5A
taxista *m/f* taxi driver 4B
taza *f* cup 5A
techo *m* ceiling 6A
tecla *f* key 11B
tectónico/a tectonic (geol.) 3A
tejido *m* fabric, knitting 5B
tela *f* cloth; fabric 5A
teléfono *m* telephone Pre
telenovela *f* soap opera 1B
televisión *f* television 1A
televisor *m* television set 1A
tema *m* topic 7B
temible frightening 9A
temporada *f* season 4B
temprano/a early 8A
tender a ser to tend to be 8B
tenedor *m* fork 5A
tener to have 1B
tener éxito to succeed 4A
tener lugar to take place 11A
tener que must, to have to 2A
tener sentido to make sense 7A
tener sueño to be sleepy 8A
Tengo ... años. I am ... years old. Pre
Tengo una pregunta. I have a question. 1B
tenis *m* tennis 1A
tenista *m/f* tennis player 4A
terapeuta *m/f* therapist 8A
tercero/a (tercer) third 6B
tercio *m* a third 10A
terminar to finish 1B
término *m* term 2B
terremoto *m* earthquake 3A
testigo *m* witness 7B
tiempo completo *m* full time 6B
tiempo libre *m* free time 2B
tiempo parcial *m* half time 6B
tierra *f* land; ground 3A
timbre *m* ring; doorbell 11B
tímido/a shy 4A
tío/a *m/f* uncle/aunt 2B
tirar to throw (away) 3B
tirarse to throw oneself 8A

titulado/a titled 6B
título *m* title 4B
título universitario *m* college degree 4B
tiza *f* chalk 1B
tobillo *m* ankle 7A
tocacompactos *m* CD player 11B
tocador *m* dressing table, dresser 6A
tocar to play (an instrument), to touch 1A
tocino *m* bacon 5A
todavía still; yet 1B
todo/a all 1B
tomar to drink (a beverage); to take 1A
tomar apuntes take notes 1B
tomate *m* tomato 5A
tonto/a not smart 8A
toque *m* touch 5B
torcerse to twist (part of the body) 7A
tormenta *f* storm 3A
tornado *m* tornado 3A
torre *f* tower 4A
tortilla española *f* Spanish omelet 6B
trabajar to work 1B
trabajo *m* job; work 3A
trabajo social *m* social work 2A
trabalenguas *m* tongue twister 6B
traducción *f* translation 12A
traducir translate 4B
traer to bring 4A
tráfico *m* traffic 11A
traje *m* suit 5B
traje de baño *m* bathing suit 5B
traje espacial *m* space suit 11B
trama *f* plot 8B
tranquilamente calmly 6B
tranquilo/a calm; quiet 2B
transbordador espacial *m* space shuttle 4B
traslado *m* transfer 8B
tratamiento *m* treatment 4B
tratar to try 3B
tregua *f* truce 12B
tres en raya tic-tac-toe 10B
triste sad 3B
tristeza *f* sadness 7B
trotar to jog 7A
trozo *m* piece 5A
truco *m* trick 5B
trueno *m* thunder 3A
turnarse to take turns 5B

U

ubicar to locate 3B
última vez *f* last time 10A
último/a last 1B
unido/a united; close 2B
universidad *f* university 1B
untar to spread on something 5A
usuario *m* user 11B

útil   helpful   1B
uva   *f*   grape   5A

V

vaca   *f*   cow   1A
vacío   empty   11A
vagón   *m*   car (of a train)   11A
valor   *m*   value   1B
valorar   to value   7B
vapor   *m*   steam   11A
vaquero/a   *m*   cowboy/cowgirl   3A
vaso   *m*   glass   5A
vecindad   *f*   neighborhood   4B
vecino/a   *m/f*   neighbor   6A
vejez   *f*   old age   8A
vela   *f*   candle   9A; sail   11A
vendedor   *m/f*   sales representative   6B
vender   to sell   1A
venenoso   poisonous   3A
venir   to come   4B
venta   *f*   sale   6B
ventaja   *f*   advantage   3B
ventana   *f*   window   1B
ver   to see   4B
verano   *m*   summer   3A
verdad   *f*   thruth   3A
verdadero/a   true   3B
verde   green   5A; unripe   8A
verduras   *f pl*   vegetables   4B
vestido   *m*   dress   5A
vestido de novia   *m*   wedding dress   5B
vestirse   to get dressed   1A
vez   *f*   time (instance)   7B
viajar   to travel   3A
viaje   *m*   journey, trip   10B
vida   *f*   life   1B
videoasta   *m/f*   video maker   12B
videojuego   *m*   video game   1A
viejo/a   old   5A
viento   *m*   wind   3A
viernes   Friday   2A
vino blanco/tinto   *m*   white/red wine   5A
visitar   to visit   1A
Víspera de Todos los Santos   *f*   All Saint's Eve   9A
visto/a   seen   6B
viudo/a   widowed   2B
vivir   to live   1A
vivo   alert, astute; alive   8A
vocal   *f*   vowel   4A
volar   to fly   4B
voluminoso/a   bulky   5B
volver   to return   3B
voz   *f*   voice   4A
vuelo   *m*   flight   11A

Y

ya que   since (because)   12A
yacer   to lie   11A
yerno   *m*   son-in-law   2B

Z

zanahoria   *f*   carrot   5A
zapatería   *f*   shoe shop/store   4B
zapatero/a   *m/f*   shoe seller or repairer   4B
zapato   *m*   shoe   5A
zapatos de tacón   *m pl*   high heels   5B
zoológico   *m*   zoo   7B

GLOSARIO: INGLÉS–ESPAÑOL

A

about to a punto de 3A
above arriba de 3A
above all sobre todo 9A
abroad al extranjero/en el extranjero 6B
according to según 2A
accountant contador/a m/f 4B
accounting contabilidad f 2A
achieve lograr 5B
acquire adquirir 4B
act interpretar 8B
actor actor m 8B
actually en realidad 3B
add añadir 5A
adjustment ajuste m 11A
advance avanzar 4B
advantage ventaja f 3B
advertising publicidad f 2A
advice consejo m 5B
advisor asesor/a m/f 5B
advocate abogar 10B
affection cariño m 2B
after después 1B
after all al fin y al cabo 7B
afternoon tarde f 2A
afternoon snack merienda f 5A
against contra 3B
age edad f Pre
airplane avión m 4B
airport aeropuerto m 11A
alarm clock despertador m 4B
alert vivo 8A
alive vivo 8A
all todo/a 1B
All Saint's Eve Víspera de Todos los Santos f 9A
allow dejar que 11B; permitir 1B
alone solo/a 8A
along with junto con 2B
also también 1A; además 2A
alter alterar 11B
always siempre 3B
ancestors antepasados m pl 9A
Andean andino 9A
angry enojado/a 8A
ankle tobillo m 7A
annoy disgustar 8B
another otro/a m/f 3A
answer respuesta f 2A; contestar 1B
answering machine contestador automático m 3B
apartment piso m 6A
apparently según parece 5A
appear aparecer 7B
appear to be parecer 3B
appetizer aperitivo m 5A
apple manzana f 5A
appliances electrodomésticos m pl 6A
applicant solicitante m/f 6B
application solicitud f 6B
apply (for job) solicitar 6B
appreciate agradecer 5B
approach; get closer acercarse 10B
appropriate conveniente 4B
approval aprobación f 5B
April abril 3A
arise surgir 3A
arm brazo m 6B
armchair sillón m 6A
armed forces fuerzas armadas f pl 2A
around alrededor 11B
arrival llegada f 10A
arrive llegar 1B
artistic expression manifestación artística f 10A
as como 1B; tan 8B
as a result por consiguiente 7B
as much/many tanto/a/os/as 8B
as soon as en cuanto; tan pronto como 12B
ask for pedir 4A
ask questions hacer preguntas 1B
astute vivo 8A
at a time a la vez 3A
at least al menos 6B
at the beginning a principios 10A
at the same time a la vez 3A; al mismo tiempo 9A
attend asistir 1B
attract atraer 8B
attract attention llamar la atención 8B
audience público m 8B
August agosto 3A
aunt tía f 2B
automated teller machine cajero automático m 12A
autumn otoño m 3A
average promedio m 2A
average height de estatura mediana 7A
avocado aguacate m 5A
avoid evitar 8B
award premio m 1B

B

baby bebé m/f 3A
bachelor's degree licenciatura f 1B
back espalda f 7A
backache dolor de espalda m 10A
backpack mochila f 1B
bacon tocino m 5A
bad malo/a 1B
bake hornear 5A
bakery panadería f 6B; pastelería f 4B
balance saldo m 12A
bald calvo 7A
ball balón m 5B; pelota f 3B
bank account cuenta bancaria f 12A
barber peluquero/a m/f 4B
barber shop peluquería f 4B
baseball béisbol m 1A
based on con base en 1B
basket cesto m 10B
bathe bañarse 7A
bathing suit traje de baño m 5B
bathroom baño m 6A
bathroom sink lavabo m 6A
bathtub bañera f 6A
battle batallar 10B
be estar 2A; ser 1A
be able to poder 4A
be against estar en contra de 7A
be born nacer 1A
be fast (clock) andar adelantado 11A
be in a good/bad mood estar de buen/mal humor 6B
be in charge of encargarse 5A
be in love estar enamorado/a 2B
be sleepy tener sueño 8A
be slow andar atrasado 11A
be sure estar seguro/a 8A
beach playa f 3A
beans frijoles m pl 5A
beard barba f 7A
beat latir 7A; (as in whisk) batir 5A
beauty belleza f 8B
because porque 2B
become convertirse 3B; pasar a ser 3B
bed cama f 6A
bedroom dormitorio m 1B
beef steak bistec m 5A
beer cerveza f 5A
before antes 1B; antes (de) que 12B
behavior comportamiento m 6B
behind detrás 7A
believe creer 4A
bellhop botones m 4B
belly button ombligo m 10A
belong pertenecer 1B
belonging (sense of) pertenencia f 5B
below debajo de 3A
belt cinturón m 5B
better said mejor dicho 12B
better; best mejor 2A
between entre 6A
beyond más allá 1A
bicycle bicicleta f 2B
big grande 1B
big bellied barrigón/a 2B
bill factura f 12A
binder carpeta m 1B

biofuel biocombustible *m* 11A
bird pájaro *m* 3A
birthday cumpleaños *m* 2B
bitter amargado/a 8A
black negro/a 2B
blackboard/
  whiteboard pizarra *f* 1B
blend mezclar 4A; *mezcla* *f* 3B
blond rubio/a 7A
blood sangre *f* 7A
blue azul 5B
board game juego de mesa *m* 8B
boat barco *m* 11A
body cuerpo *m* 5B
body of water masa de agua *f* 3A
boil hervir 5A
bold type en negrita 11A
bone hueso *m* 6A
book libro *m* 1B
bored aburrido/a 8A
boring aburrido/a 8A
boss jefe/a *m/f* 6B
both ambos 1B
both...and... tanto...como... 6A
bother molestar 8A
bottom fondo *m* 7B
box caja *f* 9A
box office taquilla *f* 12B
boy niño; chico *m* 2B
boyfriend novio *m* 3B
bracket soporte *m* 8B
brain cerebro *m* 7B
branch rama *f* 8B;
  sucursal *f* 12A
branch manager gerente de la
  sucursal *m/f* 12A
brand marca *f* 1B
bread pan *m* 4A
break romper 7B
break out; burst in irrumpir 11B
break out; explode estallar 8A
break up descomponer 7B
breakfast desayuno *m* 5A
brick ladrillo *m* 6A
bride novia *f* 5B
bridge puente *m* 10A
brief breve 2B
brightness resplandor *m* 3A
bring traer 4A
broom escoba *f* 6A
broth caldo *m* 8B
brother/ hermano *m* 2B
brother-in-law cuñado *m* 2B
brown marrón 5B
budget presupuesto *m* 12A
build construir 3B; edificar 7B
building edificio *m* 1B
bulky voluminoso/a 5B
burn quemar 7B
bus autobús *m* 4B
bus station estación de
  autobuses *f* 11A
business administración de
  empresas *f* 2A; negocio *m* 2A

but rather sino que 2B
butcher carnicero/a *m/f* 4B
butcher shop carnicería *f* 4B
butter mantequilla *f* 5A
button botón *m* 1B
buy comprar 3A
buying power poder
  adquisitivo *m* 3B
by heart de memoria 10B
by the way a propósito 1A; por
  cierto 2B

C

cabinet (gov) gabinete *m* 6A
cactus nopal *m* 10A
cake pastel *m* 5A; tarta *f* 5A
cake shop confitería *f* 4B
call llamar 1A
calm tranquilo/a 2B
calmly tranquilamente 6B
campaign campaña *f* 10B
can lata *f* 5A
can opener abrelata *m* 5A
candle vela *f* 9A
candy; caramel caramelo *m* 5B
cap gorra *f* 5B
capable capaz 6A
cape capa *f* 7A
car carro, coche *m* 3A
car (of a train) vagón *m* 11A
card tarjeta *f* 5B
career carrera *f* 1B
careful; considerate;
  courteous atento/a 3B
carefully cuidadosamente 6A
carpet alfombra *f* 5B
carrot zanahoria *f* 5A
carry cargar 9A; llevar 5B
cash (money) efectivo 11B
cash register caja *f* 5B
caution cuidado *m* 1A
CD player tocacompactos *m* 11B
ceiling techo *m* 6A
celebrate; party festejar 9A
celery apio *m* 5A
censorship censura *f* 7A
century siglo *m* 3B
cereal cereal *m* 5A
certain ciertos 6B
chain cadena *f* 4B
chair silla *f* 1B
chalk tiza *f* 1B
championship campeonato *m* 4A
change cambio *m* 5A;
  cambiar 1B
character personaje *m* 1B
charge cobrar 6B (battery) cargar
  11B
charitable caritativo/a 12B
chart tabla *f* 7A
chat charlar 11B
cheap barato/a 8B
check cuenta *f* 5A

check in (luggage) facturar (el
  equipaje) 11A
checkered (plaid) a cuadros 5B
checking account cuenta
  corriente *f* 12A
cheek mejilla *f* 7A
cheese queso *m* 4A
chemical químico/a 1B
chemist químico/a *m/pl* 4B
chest pecho *m* 7A; (storage)
  baúl *m* 4B
chick pea garbanzo *m* 5A
chicken pollo *m* 5A
chief jefe/a *m/f* 6B
child niño/a *m/f* 2B
child development desarrollo
  infantil *m* 2A
children's infantil 8B
chirp (squeak) chirriar 10B
choose elegir 3B; escoger 2A
chores quehaceres *m pl* 6A
Christmas Navidad *f* 4A
Christmas Eve Nochebuena *f* 9A
church iglesia *f* 2B
cinema cine *m* 4A
cinematographer cineasta *m/f* 8B
citadel ciudadela *f* 10A
citizen ciudadano/a *m/f* 12B
citizenship ciudadanía *f* 4A
city ciudad *f* 2A
clarify aclarar 7B
classmate compañero/a de
  clase *m/f* 1B
classroom salón de clase *m* 1B
clause cláusula *f* 11B
clean limpiar 6A
clear claro/a 5A
clerk dependiente/a *m/f* 4B
clever listo/a 5A
client cliente *m/f* 5A
clipping recorte *m* 7B
cloak capa *f* 7A
clock reloj *m* 1B
close cerca 4A; cercano 2B
close cerrar 1B
close unido/a 2B
closet armario *m* 6A;
  clóset *m* 6A
cloth tela *f* 5A
clothes ropa *f* 5B
cloud nube *f* 3A
clown payaso *m* 7B
cluck cloquear 10B
clue pista *f* 8A
coat abrigo 5B
cobbler zapatero/a *m/f* 4B
cod fish bacalao *m* 5A
code código *m* 10A
coffee maker cafetera *f* 6A
cold frío *m* 3B
college universidad *f* 2A
college degree título
  universitario *m* 4B
color color 8B

comb your hair peinarse 11A
come venir 4B
come from proceder 3B
comfort comodidad *f* 11A
comfortable cómodo/a 6A
comfortably cómodamente 6B
command mandato *m* 6B; mandar 4B
commited comprometido/a 2B
commitment compromiso *m* 3B
common (everday) cotidiano/a 7A
commotion alboroto *m* 9A
company empresa 2A
compliment cumplido *m* 5B
compose componer 7B
composer compositor/a *m/f* 7B
computer computadora *f* 1A
computer science computación *f* 2A; informática *f* 2A
condiments condimentos *m pl* 5A
conference congreso *m* 5A
confront enfrentar 8B
consist of componerse 7B
container recipiente *m* 5A
contribute contribuir 4B
controversial controvertido/a 10A; polémico/a 10B
convinced; trusting confiado/a 8B
cook cocinero/a *m/f* 4B; cocinar 1A
cookie galleta *f* 5A
coriander cilantro *m* 5A
corn maíz *m* 3B
corn husk hoja de maíz *f* 5A
corner esquina *f* 7A
corner store bodega *f* 4B
corpse cadáver *m* 7B
costume disfraz *m* 9A
cotton algodón *m* 5B
count contar 10A
counter top encimera *f* 6A
country país *m* Pre
countryside campo *m* 7B
couple pareja *f* 2B
court (of law) corte *f* 4B
court, field (sports) cancha *f* 6B
cousin primo/a *m/f* 2B
cover cubrir 3B; (travel) recorrer 11A
covered cubierto/a 4B; tapado/a 8A
cow vaca *f* 1A
coward cobarde *m* 10B
cowboy/cowgirl vaquero/a *m* 3A
crazy loco/a 6A
credit card tarjeta de crédito *f* 12A
crime delito *m* 4B
cross out tachar 6A
cross-eyed bizco 5B
crossword puzzle crucigrama *m* 10B
crown corona *f* 2B

cruise ship crucero *m* 11A
cry llorar 4A
cup taza *f* 5A
cupboard alacena *f* 6A
curly (hair) rizado 7A
current actual 3A
currently en la actualidad 3B
curtain cortina *f* 6A
custom costumbre *f* 5A
customarily por lo común 8A
cut cortar 5A; picar 6B; partir 6B

D

daily diario/a 6B
daily newspaper diario *m* 4B
damage daño *m* 12B; dañar 11A
dance baile 4A; bailar 1A
dancer bailarín/a *m/f* 6A
dangerous peligroso/a 5A
dark moreno/a 7B; oscuro/a 5B
darkness oscuridad *f* 7B
data datos *m pl* 7A
database base de datos *f* 2A
date fecha *f* 1B
daughter hija *f* 2B
daugther-in-law nuera *f* 2B
dawn amanecer 4A
day dream soñar despierto 6B
days of the week días de la semana *m pl* 2A
dead muerto/a 2B
death muerte *f* 7B
debate coloquio *m* 2A
debit card tarjeta de débito *f* 12A
deceased difunto/a *m/f* 2B
December diciembre 3A
decency honestidad *f* 4B
decorate adornar 6A
decorum honestidad *f* 4B
dedicate oneself to something (esp. professionally) dedicarse a 6B
defeat derrota *f* 10B
defer diferir *3B*
deity, god divinidad *f* 10A
delay; become delayed demorar(se) 11A
demanding exigente 2A
demonstrate demostrar 10B
department store gran almacén *m* 12A
deposit depositar 12A
depth profundidad *f* 8A
design diseñar 4B; diseño *m* 8B
designer diseñador/a *m/f* 5B
desk escritorio *m* 1B
dessert postre *m* 5A
destroy destruir 1A
develop desarrollar 10A
deviate desviar 11A
device aparato *m* 5A
devil diablo *m* 1A
dew point punto de rocío *m* 3A

dial (telephone) marcar 11B
dictatorship dictuadura *f* 3A
die morir 7B; (games) dado *m* 1B
diet régimen *m* 2A
differ, be different diferir 3B
different distinto/a 3A
dimwitted (not smart) tonto/a 8A
dining room comedor *m* 6A
dinner cena *f* 5A
direct dirigir(se) 11A
disadvantage desventaja *f* 4A
disappointed desilusionado/a 8A
disappointment decepción *f* 3B
disassemble desmantelar 11A
disc disco *m* 4A
discomfort incomodidad *f* 7B
dish plato *m* 1A
dismiss (fire) despedir a 4B
displace desplazar 11A
disqualify descalificar 3B
distress angustia 2A
divorced divorciado/a 2B
do hacer 4B
do business hacer negocios 6B
do homework hacer la tarea 1B
do well/bad andar bien/mal 11B
do, complete realizar 2A
doctor médico/a *m/f* 6B
doctor's office consultorio *m* 3B
documentary documental *f* 1A
doll muñeca *f* 7A
donkey burro *m* 1A
door puerta *f* 1B
doorbell timbre *m* 11B
dough masa *f* 5A
download; unload descargar 11B
drain desagüe *m* 6A; drenar 6A
drastically dramáticamente 3B
draw dibujar 1A
drawing dibujo *m* 5B
dress vestido *m* 5A
dressing table, dresser tocador *m* 6A
drink bebida *f* 4A
drink beber 2B
drink (a beverage) tomar 1A
drinkable potable 3A
drive conducir 4A; manejar 1A
driver's license licencia de manejar *f* 2B
drunk borracho/a 8A
dry secar 6B
dryer secadora *f* 6A
due to debido a 7A
dunk hundir 8A
durable duradero/a 8B
dust polvo *m* 7A
dwarf enano/a *m/f* 1A

E

each cada 3A
eagle águila *f* 10A

ear (inner) oído *m* 7A
ear (outer) oreja *f* 5B
ear ring pendiente *m* 5B
early temprano/a 8A
earn ganar 4A
earn a living ganarse la vida 6B
earring arete/pendiente *m* 5B
earthquake terremoto *m* 3A
Easter Pascua *f* 9A
eastern oriental 8B
easy fácil 4A
eat comer 1A
edge borde 8B
educational educativo 1B
effect efecto 4A
effective eficaz 10B
effort esfuerzo *m* 11B
egg huevo *m* 5A
eigth octavo/a 6B
elbow codo *m* 7A
elderly anciano/a 7A
electric discharge descarga
   eléctrica *f* 3A
elementary school escuela
   primaria *f* 1B
email correo electrónico *m* 11B
embroidered bordado/a 5B
emerge surgir 3A
emotional afectivo/a 11B
emphasize enfatizar 4A
empire imperio *m* 10A
empty vacío 11A
enactment promulgación *f* 9A
enchanting encantador/a 7A
enclosure encerramiento *m* 8B
end acabar 11B
engaged comprometido/a 2B
engagement compromiso *m* 3B
engineering ingeniería *f* 2A
engraved grabado/a 8A
enjoy deleitarse 5A; disfrutar de/
   gozar de 6B
enjoy your meal buen provecho 5A
enjoyable ameno/a 6B
enough suficiente 3A
enrich enriquecer 11B
entail implicar 1B
entertain divertir 4A;
   entretener 8B
entertainment entretenimiento
   m 4A
entreé plato principal *m* 5A
environment medio
   ambiente *m* 8B
erase borrar 11B
essay ensayo *m* 4A
essentially esencialmente 2A
even incluso 4B
even though aunque 1B
event acontecimiento *m* 3B;
   suceso *m* 3A
example ejemplo *m* 1B
exchange intercambio *m* 2A;
   intercambiar 6A

exciting emocionante 9A
Excuse me. Con permiso. 5A;
   Perdón. 5A
exercise ejercicio *m* 5B
expel expulsar de 3B
expense gasto *m* 2B
expensive caro/a 4A
explanation explicación *f* 3B
exposed expuesto/a 11B
extend extender 10A
eye ojo *m* 7A
eyebrows cejas *f pl* 7A
eyeglasses lentes *m pl* 5B;
   anteojos *m pl* 5B
eyelashes pestañas *f pl* 7A
eyeliner rímel *m* 9A

F

fabric tela *f* 5A; tejido *m* 5B
face cara *f* 7A; rostro *m* 7A;
   enfrentar 8B
factory fábrica *f* 6B
facts datos *m pl* 7A
fair feria *f* 7A
fall in love enamorarse 1B
family related familiar 2B
famous célebre 7B
fan aficionado/a *m/f* 1A
faraway, far lejano/a 11A
farmer agricultor/a *m/f* 4B
fashion moda *f* 6B
fashion show desfile de
   modas *m* 5B
fast rápido 2B
fast food comida rápida *f* 5A
fat gordo/a 7A; grasa *f* 5A
father padre *m* 1A
father-in-law suegro *m* 2B
fault falla *f* 3A
fawn (mythological) fauno *m* 1A
fear miedo *m* 9A
features facciones *f pl* 12A
February febrero 3A
fee tarifa *f* 11A
feel sentirse 7B
feel ashamed avergonzarse 8A
feeling sentimiento *m* 3B
feet pies *m pl* 7A
fever fiebre *f* 10A
fewer/less than menos de/menos
   que 2A
field campo *m* 2A
fifth quinto/a 6B
fight combatir 1B; pelear 3B;
   luchar 3B
figures (numbers) cifras *f pl* 11A
filming grabación *f* 5A
finally finalmente 10A; por
   fin 10A
find encontrar 4A
find out averiguar 5B
fine (hair) fino/a 7A
finger dedo *m* 7A

fingerprint huella digital *f* 12A
finish terminar 1B
firefigther bombero/a *m/f* 4B
first primero/a (primer) 2A
first child primogénito/a *m/f* 2B
fish pescado *m* 5A
fixture instalación fija *f* 6A
flannel franela *f* 5B
flat plano/a 10B
flight vuelo *m* 11A
flirtatious comment piropo *m* 5B
flooding inundación *f* 3A
floor piso *m* 6A; (story of a
   building) planta *f* 6A
flour harina *f* 5A
flourish florecer 3B
flower flor *f* 4A
flower shop floristería *f* 6B
fly volar 4B
focus enfoque *m* 6B;
   enfocarse 12A
fold doblar 6B
folded doblado/a 8B
follow seguir 4A
following a continuación 2A;
   siguiente 3A
food alimento *m* 5A;
   comida *f* 3B
footwear calzado *m* 5B
for example por ejemplo 3B
for that reason por esa razón 4A;
   por eso 4A
force (someone to do
   something) obligar 11B
forecast pronóstico *m* 3A
forehead frente *f* 7A
foreign languages idiomas
   extranjeros *m pl* 2A
foreigner extranjero/a *m/f* 3B;
   forastero/a *m/f* 3B
forest bosque *m* 3A
fork tenedor *m* 5A
found fundar 3B
fountain fuente *f* 6A
fourth cuarto/a 6B
frame marco *m* 6A
free gratis 10A
free time ratos libres *m pl* 6B;
   tiempo libre *m* 2B
freeze congelar 5A
french fries papas fritas *f pl* 5A
frequently con frecuencia 2A
Friday viernes 2A
friend amigo/a *m/f* 1A
friendship amistad *f* 9A
frightening temible 9A
from de Pre; desde 6A
from where (interrog) de
   dónde Pre
frown fruncir 7A
fruit fruta *f* 5A
fry freír 5A
fuel combustible *m* 11A
fulfill (a dream) realizar (un

sueño) 6B
full lleno/a 11A
full time tiempo completo *m* 6B
fun diversión *f* 4A
funny gracioso/a 5B
furniture (piece of) mueble *m* 6A

G

gain weight engordar 5B
game, match partido *m* 3B
garbage basura *f* 3B
garden jardín *m* 6A
gardening jardinería *f* 6A
garment prenda *f* 5B
gather reunir 2B
geography geografía *f* 3A
German alemán 2A
gesture gesto *m* 1A
get along/not get along llevarse
  bien/mal 12A
get dressed vestirse 1A
get in debt endeudarse 12A
get up levantarse 7A
gift regalo *m* 5B
girl niña; chica *f* 2B
girlfriend novia *f* 3B
give dar 4B; regalar 5B
glass vaso *m* 5A
glass (of wine) copa *f* 5A
glove guante *m* 5B
go ir 4A
go bike riding andar en
  bicicleta 1A
go by foot ir a pie 11A
go into exile exiliarse 10B
go out; leave salir 3A
go shopping ir de compras 4A
go through customs pasar por la
  aduana 11A
go to bed; lie down acostarse 7A
go up subir 8A
goal meta *f* 4A
god/goddess dios/a *m/f* 9A
godfather padrino *m* 2B
godmother madrina *f* 2B
gold oro *m* 5B
good bueno/a 1B
Good afternoon. Buenas
  tardes. Pre
good grades buenas notas 4B
good manners buenos modales *m*
  pl 2B
good morning, good day buenos
  días Pre
good night buenas noches Pre
good taste buen gusto *m* 5B
goodbye adiós Pre
goodbye chau/chao Pre
good-looking guapo/a 8A
gossip chisme *m* 10A
government gobierno *m* 3B;
  gubernamental 6B
grab agarrar 3B

grade nota *f* 1A
grammar gramática *f* 1B
grandaugther nieta *f* 2B
grandfather abuelo *m* 2B
grandmother abuela *f* 2B
grandson nieto *m* 2B
grape uva *f* 5A
graphic arts artes gráficas *f pl* 8B
gray gris 5B
gray haired canoso/a 7A
great genial 1B
great grandchild bisnieto/a *m* 2B
greedy codicioso/a 10B
green verde 5A
green beans frijoles verdes *m*
  pl 5A
greet saludar 1B
grill parrilla *f* 5A
grinder molinillo *m* 6A
groom novio *m* 5B
ground tierra *f* 3A
grow aumentar 3A; crecer 3A;
  cultivar 5A
guard guardia *m/f* 12A
guerilla fighter guerrillero/a *m/*
  f 4B
guess adivinar 3B
guest invitado/a *m/f* 12B
guide guía *m/f* 4B
guilt culpabilidad *f* 4B
guy/gal chico/a *m/f* 2B
gypsy gitano/a *m/f* 5B

H

hair cabello *m* 7A; pelo *m* 3B
hairdesser peluquero/a *m/f* 4B
hairdressing salon peluquería
  f 4B
half mitad *f* 3A
half brother medio
  hermano *m* 2B
half sister medio hermana *f* 2B
half time tiempo parcial *m* 6B
hallway corredor *m* 6A
ham jamón *m* 4A
hamburger hamburguesa *f* 1A
hand mano *f* 4B
hand in entregar 5B
handbag cartera/bolsa *f* 5B
handling manejo *m* 6A
handmade artesanal 10A
handshake apretón de
  manos *m* 6B
hang colgar 6A
happening suceso *m* 3A
happiness felicidad *f* 11A
happy alegre 8A; contento/a 4A;
  feliz 4A
harm daño *m* 12B; dañar 11A
harmonious armonioso/a 8B
harvest cosecha *f* 9A
hat sombrero *m* 5B
hated detestado/a 10B

have tener 1B
have a good/bad time pasarlo bien/
  mal 6B
have dinner cenar 5A
have fun divertirse 7B
have lunch almorzar 2A
have to (do something) hay que
  + infinitive 4A; tener que +
  infinitive 2A
head cabeza *f* 7A
headache dolor de cabeza *m* 10A
headphones audífonos *m pl* 12B
health salud *f* 2B
healthy saludable 5A; sano/a 6B
hear oír 4B
hear escuchar 1A
heart corazón *m* 4A
heartland patria *f* 8B
heat up calentar 5A
height estatura *f* 5B
heir heredero/a *m/f* 2B
helmet casco *m* 9B
help ayuda *f* 2B
helpful útil 1B
here aquí 1A
heritage herencia *f* 3B;
  patrimonio *m* 10A
hi hola Pre
hide ocultar 9A
high heels zapatos de tacón *m*
  pl 5B
high quality fino 5B
high school bachillerato *m* 1B;
  colegio *m* 1B; escuela
  preparatoria *f* 1B
highlight resaltar 9A
highway autopista *f* 11A
himself/herself sí mismo/a 7B
hip cadera *f* 7A
hit pegar 3B
hobby pasatiempo *m* 6B
hold sostener 4A
holiday día feriado *m* 6B
Holy Week Semana Santa *f* 9A
home hogar *m* 4B
home-cooked food comida
  casera *f* 5A
homemaker ama de casa *m/f* 7A
homework deberes *m pl* 4A;
  tarea *f* 3B
honesty sinceridad *f* 6B
honey miel *f* 5A
horrified horrorizado/a 7B
horse caballo *m* 3A
host anfitrión/a *m/f* 7A
host family familia anfitriona *f* 2A
hot caliente 5A
house casa *f* 1A
how (interrog) cómo Pre
how much/many cuánto/a/os/as
  Pre
however sin embargo 4B
hug abrazar 5A
human being ser humano *m* 6B

human rigths derechos humanos *m pl* 10B
humble humilde 6A
hunger hambre *f* 8A
hurricane huracán *m* 3A
hurt daño *m* 12B; dañar 11A
husband marido *m* 2B
husband/wife esposo/a *m/f* 2B

I

agree. Estoy de acuerdo. 3A
I am … years old tengo … años Pre
I have a question tengo una pregunta 1B
I'm sorry lo siento 1B
ice hielo *m* 5A
ice cream helado *m* 5A
illegal indocumentado/a 3B
illness enfermedad *f* 4B
important relevante 3A
imprison encarcelar 10B
in en Pre
in a rush en tropel 3A
in addition además 2A; es más 3A
in case en caso de que 12B
in cash en efectivo 12A
in fact de hecho 3B
in front enfrente 7A
in light of a la luz 11B
in love enamorado/a 8A
in order that a fin de que 12B
in other words en otras palabras 4A; es decir 1A; o sea 1A
in random order al azar 6A
in spite of a pesar de 1B
in style de moda 5B
in that respect en eso 6B
in the background; at the bottom al fondo 7A
in the face of ante tal + *noun* 4B
in the same way de la misma manera 4A
in this way de esta manera 3B
in turn a su vez 10B
incident suceso *m* 3A
incidentally a propósito 7B
including inclusive 3B
income ingreso *m* 11A
increase auge *m* 11A
indigenous indígena 3B
indoors adentro 5B
inequality desigualdad *f* 8B
influence influir 12A
inform avisar 11B
inhabitant habitante *m/f* 3A
inherit heredar 3B
innocent cándido/a 8B
insert introducir 1A
inside adentro 5B; dentro de 5B
installation art arte de instalación *m* 8B

instead of en lugar de 10B
instill inculcar 2B
interests intereses *m pl* 7B
interview entrevista *f* 2A
introduce introducir 1A; presentar Pre
invest invertir 12A
involve involucrar 3B
iron plancha *f* 6B; planchar *f* 6B
isolated aislado/a 8A
isolation aislamiento *m* 11B
issue asunto *m* 3B
it (just) so happens that resulta que 11B
it turns out resulta que 11B

J

jacket chaqueta *f* 5B
jail cárcel *f* 12A
January enero 3A
jewel joya *f* 4B
jeweler joyero/a *m/f* 5B
Jewish judío/a 3B
job trabajo *m* 3A;
jog trotar 7A
join incorporarse 7B
joke broma *f* 8A
journalism periodismo *m* 2A
journalist periodista *m/f* 7A
journey viaje *m* 10B
juice jugo *m* 5A
July julio 3A
jump brincar 8A; saltar 3B
June junio 3A
jungle selva *f* 3A
junior high escuela secundaria *f* 1B
just + *verb* acabar de + infinitive 5A
just like; just as al igual que 9A

K

keep guardar 3B
key llave *f* 4A; tecla *f* 11B
kick patear 7A
king rey *m* 3B
kiss beso *m* 7A
kiss besar 7A
kitchen cocina *f* 5A
knee rodilla 7A
kneel down arrodillarse 7A
knife cuchillo *m* 5A
knitting tejido *m* 5B
knot nudo *m* 10A
know saber 3A; (be familiar with) conocer 1A
knowledge conocimiento *m* 8A

L

laborer obrero/a *m/f* 4B
lack carecer 7B

lack of falta de *f* 3B
lady dama *f* 8B
lake lago *m* 3A
land tierra *f* 3A
landscape paisaje *m* 6A
language idioma *m* 2A; lengua *f* 2A
last último/a 1B
last durar 1B
last name apellido *m* Pre
last time última vez *f* 10A
lasting duradero/a 8B
late tarde 4A
later más tarde 10A
laugh reír 4A
laughter risa *f* 5A
law ley *f* 4A; derecho *m* 2A
lawyer abogado/a *m/f* 2B
layer capa *f* 7A
layover escala *f* 11A
lazy perezoso/a 4B
lead to llevar a 11A
league liga *f* 5A
learn aprender 1B
learning aprendizaje *m* 7B
leather cuero *m* 4B; piel *f* 5B
leave dejar 5A; partir 6B
leave a tip dejar la propina 5A
left izquierda *f* 5A; (loc) a la izquierda de 3A
left-wing izquierdista 7B
leg pierna *f* 5B
legacy legado *m* 10B
legumes legumbres *f pl* 5A
leisure ocio *m* 4A
lend prestar 5B
leprosy lepra *f* 10B
less/fewer than menos de/menos que 2A
let go of soltar 11B
let's see a ver 7B
letter carta *f* 2B; letra *f* 1B
letter carrier cartero/a *m/f* 4B
lettuce lechuga *f* 4A
level nivel *m* 3A
liberal arts letras *f pl* 4B
library biblioteca *f* 1B
lie mentir 4B;
life vida *f* 1B
lift levantar 1A
light ligero 5A
light luz *f* 1B
lightning relámpago *m* 3A
like como 1B
likewise igualmente Pre; de igual manera 10B
liking, taste gusto *m* 6A
lip labio *m* 5B
lipstick lápiz labial *m* 4A
listen to escuchar 1A
live vivir 1A
living room sala *f* 6A
loan préstamo *m* 12A
locate ubicar 3B

long largo/a 5A
look mirada *f* 11A
loose suelto/a 5B
lose perder 4A
lose weight adelgazar 5B
lost perdido/a 2B
love amor *m* 1A; amar 2B
lover amante *m/f* 5B
loyal leal 4B
luggage equipaje *m* 7B
lunch almuerzo *m* 5A
luxurious lujoso/a 4A
luxury lujo *m* 5B
lying down acostado/a 7A

M

magazine revista *f* 4B
magician mago/a *m/f* 1A
mail correo *m* 4B
maintain mantener 3B
major (army rank) comandante del ejército *m/f* 6B; (course of study) carrera *f* 1B
make a stop/layover (at an airport) hacer escala 11A
make an appointment hacer una cita 6B
make an effort esforzarse 11B
make plans hacer planes 6B
make sense tener sentido 7A
make sound sonar 11B
make sure asegurarse 5B
make-up cosmético *m* 9A
malicious malévolo/a 4B
man hombre *m* 1A
manage manejar 12A
manager gerente *m/f* 4B
map mapa *m* 1B
marble mármol *m* 6A
March marzo 3A
mark marcar 11B
marker marcador *m* 1B
marketing mercadeo *m* 2A
marriage matrimonio *m* 2B
married casado/a 2B
marry casarse 9A
mask máscara *f* 7B
master's degree maestría *f* 1B
masterpiece obra maestra *f* 4A
match emparejar 1B
May mayo 3A
mayor alcalde/sa *m/f* 4A
mean significar 1B
meaning significado *m* 6A
measure medida *f* 12A
meat carne *f* 5A
mechanism dispositivo *m* 12B
meeting reunión *f* 4B
melt derretir 5A
member miembro/a *m/f* 2B
memories recuerdos *m pl* 7B
memory (mental function) memoria *f* 10B

merchandise mercancía *f* 6B
message mensaje *m* 11B
microwave (horno de) microondas *m* 5A;
middle child hijo/a del medio *m/f* 2B
midnight medianoche *f* 2A
military militar 10B
milk leche *f* 5A
mind mente *f* 4B
mini-skirt mini-falda *f* 7A
mirror espejo *m* 6A
misfortune desgracia *f* 7B
miss work faltar al trabajo 6B
misunderstanding malentendido *m* 1B
mix mezclar 4A; mezcla *f* 3B
model modelo *m/f* 8B
modesty honestidad *f* 4B
Monday lunes 2A
money dinero *m* 3B
monk monje *m* 6B
month mes *m* 3A
monthly mensual 12A
moon luna 7A
more más 8B
more than más de/más que 2A
moreover es más 3A
morning mañana *f* 2A
mortar argamasa *m* 6A
mother madre *f* 2B
mother-in-law suegra *f* 2B
mountain montaña *f* 3A
mountain range sierra *f* 12A
moustache bigotes *m pl* 7A
mouth boca *f* 4B
move (emotionally) conmover 8B; (from one place to another) mudarse 2B
movie película *f* 1B
movie director director/a de cine *m/f* 2A
mud lodo *m* 11A
multifaceted polifacético/a 10B
murderer asesino/a *m/f* 4B
music música *f* 1A
muslim musulmán 9A
must + verb tener que + infinitive 2A
my name is ... me llamo ... Pre
myth mito *m* 10B

N

nahuatl (indigenous language/culture) náhuatl *m* 10A
naïve cándido/a 8B
name nombre *m* 1A; nombrar 9A
napkin servilleta *f* 5A
narrow estrecho/a 5B
national anthem himno nacional *m* 3A
nature naturaleza *f* 2A

navegate the Internet navegar por la Internet 11B
navy blue azul marino 5B
neck cuello *m* 5B
necklace collar *m* 4B
need necesidad *f* 5B; hacer falta 11B; necesitar 1B
neglect descuidar 8A
neighbor vecino/a *m/f* 6A
neighborhood barrio *m* 9A; vecindad *f* 4B
neither tampoco 2A
nephew sobrino *m* 2B
nervous breakdown ataque de nervios *m* 8B
net; network red *f* 12B
never jamás 3B; nunca 3B
never-ending interminable 11A
New Year Año Nuevo *m* 9A
New Year's Eve Nochevieja *f* 9A
news noticia, noticiads *f, f pl* 2B; novedades *f pl* 6A
newscast noticiero *m* 4B
newspaper periódico *m* 2A
next próximo 4A
next to al lado de 3A
nice simpático/a 8A
nice to meet you mucho gusto Pre
niece sobrina *f* 2B
night noche *f* 2A
ninth noveno/a 6B
no one nadie 2B
nobody nadie 2B
noise ruido *m* 4A
noisy ruidoso/a 11B
none ninguno/a 4A
non-stop sin parar 8A
noon mediodía *m* 2A
nose nariz *f* 7A
note nota *f* 1A
notebook cuaderno *m* 1B
noted notorio/a 4B
nothing nada 4A
November noviembre 3A
now ahora 4A
number número *m* 3A
numbers (figures) cifras *f pl* 11A
nurse enfermera/o *m/f* 2A
nursing enfermería *f* 2A

O

obligation compromiso *m* 3B
obtain conseguir 4A; obtener 12A
occupation oficio *m* 4A
occur suceder 11A
October octubre 3A
of de Pre
offering ofrecimiento *m* 9A; ofrenda *f* 9A
office oficina *f* 1B; despacho *m* 6A
often a menudo 5A

oil aceite *m* 4B;
 petróleo *m* 10B
old anciona/a 7A; antiguo/a 5A;
 viejo/a 5A
old age vejez *f* 8A
older mayor 2B
old-fashioned anticuado/a 11B
olive aceituna *f* 4A
Olympic Games Juegos
 Olímpicos *m pl* 3A
on en Pre
on sale de oferta 9A
on the contrary al contrario 3B
on the other hand en cambio 1B;
 en contraste 8A; por otra parte
 11B; por otro lado 7A
on this point en este punto 12B
on time puntualmente 12A
on top of encima 3A; sobre 3A
once in a while de vez en
 cuando 3B
once upon a time... érase una
 vez... 10B
onion cebolla *f* 5A
online en línea 12B
only solamente 3A
only child hijo/a único/a *m/f* 2B
open abierto/a 4B
open abrir 1B
open accounts abrir cuentas 12A
opening abertura *f* 5B
operation funcionamiento *m* 11A
oppose oponerse 10B
opposite opuesto/a 3A
oppress oprimir 10B
orange naranja *f* 5A
order mandar 4B
ordinarily por lo común 8A
ordinary rutinario/a 7B
**out of
 proportion** desproporcionado 3A
outdoors al aire libre 5A;
 afuera 5B
outside afuera 5B
oven horno *m* 5A
overcome superar 12B
overview panorama *m* 3A
owe deber 5B
own propio/a 2A
owner dueño/a *m/f* 4B

P

pack suitcases/bags hacer las
 maletas 11A
page página *f* 1B
pain dolor *m* 8A
paintbrush pincel *m* 7A
painter pintor/a *m/f* 6B
painting cuadro *m* 6A
palm tree palmera *f* 3A
pan sartén *m/f* 5A
pantyhose medias *f pl* 5B
paper papel *m* 6A

parade desfile *m* 7B
parish parroquia *f* 9A
park parque *m* 1A
parrot loro *m* 11A
party fiesta *f* 2B
pass (a class, an exam) aprobar 7B
password contraseña *f* 11B
past pasado *m* 9A
pasture pasto *m* 3A
pat palmada *f* 6B
path camino *m* 10A; pista *f* 8A
pattern patrón *m* 3A
pay pagar 5A
pay attention prestar atención 4A
pay in installments pagar a
 plazos 12A
peace paz *f* 8B
peaceful pacífico 3B
peas guisantes *m pl* 5A
peasant campesino/a *m/f* 10A
peel pelar 5A
pen pluma *f* 1B
pencil lápiz *m* 1B
pendant pendiente *m* 5B
people gente *f* 1A;
 pueblo *m* 3B
pepper pimienta *f* 5A
percent por ciento 3B
perform (a task or
 job) desempeñar 4B
performance actuación *f* 10B
pet mascota *f* 1A
phone call llamada *f* 6B
pick up recoger 5A
pie tarta *f* 5A
piece trozo *m* 5A
pilgrims peregrinos *m pl* 7B
pine tree pino *m* 3A
pineapple piña *f* 6B
pink rosa 5B
pitcher of water jarra de
 agua *f* 5A
place lugar *m* 1B; colocar 5A
place of birth lugar de
 nacimiento *m* 2B
placement colocación *f* 11B
plaid a cuadros 5B
plains llanos *m pl* 3A; llanuras *f
 pl* 3A
plaintain plátano *m* 5A
plant planta *f* 6A
plate warmer calientaplatos *m* 6A
plateau meseta *f* 3A
play obra (de teatro) *f* 7B
play (an instrument) tocar 1A;
 (sports, games) jugar 1A
player jugador/a *m/f* 5A
player (CD, DVD,
 etc.) reproductor *m* 6A
pleasant agradable 6B
please por favor 1B
pleasing complaciente 8B
pleasurable complaciente 8B
plot trama *f* 8B

pocket bolsillo *m* 10B
poetry poesía *f* 10B
point punto *m* 4A
point of view punto de
 vista *m* 4A
point something out señalar 1B
poisonous venenoso 3A
political party partido
 político *m* 3A
political position puesto
 político *m* 10B
pollution contaminación *f* 7A
poor pobre 2B
poorly, not well mal Pre
popcorn palomitas *f pl* 10A
population población *f* 3A
pork chop chuleta de puerco/
 cerdo *f* 5A
port puerto *m* 7B
portrait retrato *m* 7A
positioning posicionamiento
  m 11A
postcard tarjeta postal *f* 7A
poster cartel *m* 7B
pot olla *f* 5A
potato papa *f* 5A
potato chips papitas *f pl* 10A
potato slicer cortapatatas *m* 6A
pottery alfarería *f* 8B
poverty pobreza *f* 1B
power poder *m* 4A;
 fuerza *f* 3A
powerful poderoso 9A
pray rezar 4B
pre-columbian precolombino 8B
pregnant embarazada 8A
preposition preposición *f* 3A
press (a button) oprimir 10B; pulsar
 11B; (apply pressure) apretar 8A;
 (iron clothes) planchar *f* 6B
pressure presión *f* 3A
pretty bonito/a 3A
previous anterior 3B
price precio *m* 3B
priest padre *m* 7B
prince príncipe *m* 2B
princess infanta *f* 2B
print estampado *m* 5B
printer impresora *f* 11B
produce producir 4B
profile perfil *m* 3A
projector proyector *m* 1B
promising prometedor 11B
promote promocionar 3A;
 promover 1B
pronoun pronombre *m* 3A
propose proponer 10B
proudly orgullosamente 3B
provide proveer 2B
provided that con tal (de) que 12B
pull jalar 3B
purple morado/a 5B
purpose propósito *m* 11A
push empujar 4A

put   poner   4B; (place inside) meter   12A
put away   guardar   6A
put in order   poner en orden   4B
put something on   ponerse   7A
puzzle   rompecabezas   *m*   8B

Q

quechua (indigenous language/ culture)   quechua   *m*   10A
question   pregunta   *f*   1B; cuestionar   3B
questioning   cuestionamiento   *m*   3B
Quiché (indigenous language/ culture)   quiché   *m pl*   10A
quiet   tranquilo/a   2B
quit (a job)   renunciar   6B

R

racecar driver   corredor de autos   *m*   7B
railroad   ferrocarril   *m*   11A
rain   lluvia   *f*   3A; llover   3A
raincoat   impermeable   *m*   5B
raise your hand   levantar la mano   1B
rate   tasa   *f*   5A
raw   crudo/a   5A
raw material   materia prima   *f*   11A
reach   alcanzar   6A
read   leer   1B
reading   lectura   *f*   2B
ready   listo/a   5A
real estate   bienes raíces   *m pl*   9A
reasonable   razonable   4B
rebut   refutar   12B
receipt   recibo   *m*   11A
recharge   recargar   12A
recipe   receta   *f*   5A
recognize   reconocer   3B
record   grabar   11B; disco   *m*   4A
recorded   grabado/a   8A
recorder   grabadora   *f*   1B
recover   recuperar   10A
red   rojo/a   5B
redheaded   pelirrojo/a   7A
redo   rehacer   10A
reduce   empequeñecer   11A
refinement   finura   *f*   6B
reflect   reflexionar   3A
regarding   en cuanto a   3A
reggaeton   reguetón   *m*   4A
rehearsal   ensayo   *m*   4A
reinforce   reforzar   10A
reject   rechazar   3B
rejection   rechazo   *m*   3B
relative   pariente   *m*   2B
relax   relajarse   6A
relaxing   relajante   6A
relay   relevo   *m*   10A
remember   acordarse   10B

remember   recordar   2B
renew   renovar   10A
repeat   repetir   4A
Repeat, please.   Repita, por favor.   1B
replace   reemplazar   5A
report   reportaje   *m*   10B
researcher   investigador/a   *m/f*   5A
resign   renunciar   6B
resource   recurso   *m*   12B
rest   descansar   4A
restaurant   restaurante   *m*   5A
restore   reivindicar   8A
resumé   currículum   *m*   6B
retire   jubilarse   6B
retired   jubilado/a   4B
return   regreso   *m*   6A; regresar   5A; volver   3B
review   repaso   *m*   6B; revisar   7A
rice   arroz   *m*   5A
rice maker   arrocera   *f*   6A
riches   riquezas   *f pl*   10A
ride a bike   montar en bicicleta   11A
right   derecho   *m*   2A; (loc) a la derecha de   3A
right now   ahora mismo   4A
right-wing   derechista   7B
ring   anillo   *m*   1A; sortija   *f*   5B; sonar   11B; (sound) timbre   *m*   11B
risk   riesgo   *m*   3A
river   río   *m*   3A
road   carretera   *f*   3A
rob   robar   6B
robbery   robo   *m*   9A
rocket   cohete   *m*   11A
role   papel   *m*   6A
room   cuarto   *m*   6A; habitación   *f*   4B; (Mex.) recámara   *f*   7A; salón   *m*   6A
roommate   compañero/a de cuarto   *m/f*   2B
root   raíz   *f*   3B
rough   rudo   10A
round   redondo/a   7A
roundtrip   ida y vuelta   11A
royal   real   2B
rule   norma   *f*   8B
rules   reglas   *f pl*   2B
rumor   chisme   *m*   10A
run   correr   1A
run late   retrasarse   11A

S

sad   triste   3B
sadness   tristeza   *f*   7B
sail   vela   *f*   11A
salad   ensalada   *f*   4A
salary   sueldo   *m*   6B
sale   venta   *f*   6B
sales representative   vendedor   *m/f*   6B
same   mismo/a   5A

sandwich maker   sandwichera   *f*   6A
satisfying   complaciente   8B
Saturday   sábado   2A
sauce   salsa   *f*   5A
sausage   chorizo   *m*   4B; salchicha   *f*   5A
save   ahorrar   11B
savings account   cuenta de ahorros   *f*   12A
saw   cierra   *f*   12A
scarcity   escasez   *f*   11A
scarecrow   espantapájaros   *m*   10B
scared   asustado/a   8A
scarf   bufanda   *f*   5B
schedule   horario   *m*   2A
scholarship   beca   *f*   3B
school subject   materia   *f*   2A
school/college of a university   facultad   *f*   1B
scold   regañar   8A
scrambled eggs   huevos revueltos   *m pl*   10A
scream   grito   *m*   11A
scream   gritar   4A
screen   pantalla   *f*   1B
script   guión   *m*   4A
sculpture   escultura   *f*   8B
sea   mar   *m*   1A
seafood   mariscos   *m pl*   5A
seaquake   maremoto   *m*   3A
search   búsqueda   *f*   3A
season   estación   *f*   3A; temporada   *f*   4B
seat   asiento   *m*   1B
second   segundo/a   6B
secondary school   bachillerato   *m*   1B
see   ver   4B
see you later   hasta luego   Pre
see you soon   hasta pronto   Pre
see you tomorrow   hasta mañana   Pre
seen   visto/a   6B
seize   arrebatar   11A
selfish   egoísta   8B
self-portrait   autorretrato   7A
sell   vender   1A
send   enviar   11B; mandar   6A
sense   sentido   *m*   1A
sense of humor   sentido de humor   *m*   4A
sensitive   sensible   8A
sentence   oración   *f*   5A
September   septiembre   3A
set   conjunto   *m*   7B
set the table   poner la mesa   5A
settle in   instalarse   6A
seventh   séptimo/a   6B
shadow   sombra   *f*   7B
share   compartir   1B
sharpener   afilador   *m*   6A
shave (oneself)   afeitarse   7A
shawl   manta   *f*   5B
sheet of paper   hoja de papel   *f*   1B

shelf   estante   *m*   6A
shirt   camisa   *f*   5B
shoe   zapato   *m*   5A
shoe seller   zapatero/a   *m/f*   4B
shoe shop/store   zapatería   *f*   4B
shopping mall   centro
   comercial   *m*   4B
short   bajo/a   7A; corto/a   11A
shortcoming   limitación   *f*   8A
short-sighted   corto/a de vista   7A
shot   disparo   *m*   4A
should + verb   deber + infinitive   4A
shoulder   hombro   *m*   6B
show   espectáculo   *m*   4B
shower   ducha   *f*   6A; (rain)
   chubasco   *m*   3A; (bathing)
   ducharse   7A
shrimp   camarón   *m*   5A
shrink   empequeñecer   11A
shrug your shoulders   encogerse de
   hombros   7A
shy   tímido/a   4A
sick   enfermo/a   4B
sign   firmar   1A
sign of protest   señal de
   protesta   *f*   3B
signature   firma   *f*   2A
significant   relevante   8B
silk   seda   *f*   6B
silverware   cubiertos   *m pl*   5A
similarity   semejanza   *f*   5B
simple; single   sencillo/a   6A
since   desde   6A; (because) puesto
   que   8A; ya que   12A
sincerely yours   (in a
   letter) atentamente   6B
sing   cantar   1A
singer   cantante   *m/f*   3B
single   (not married) soltero/a   2B
sink   hundir   8A; fregadero   *m*   6A
sister   hermana   *f*   2B
sister-in-law   cuñada   *f*   2B
sit down   sentarse   7A
sitting down   sentado/a   7A
sixth   sexto/a   6B
size   talla   *f*   5B
size   tamaño   *m*   2B
skin   piel   *f*   5B
skirt   falda   *f*   5B
skull   calavera   *f*   9A
slavery   esclavitud   *f*   10B
sleep   dormir   4A
sleeve   manga   *f*   5B
slender   delgado/a   5B
slice   rebanada   *f*   5A
slip   resbalarse   8A
slow   lento/a   5A
slowly   detenidamente   5B
small   pequeño/a   1B
smart   listo/a   5A
smell   oler   7A
smile   sonrisa   *f*   4B; sonreír   4A
smoke   fumar   4A
smooth, even   liso/a   5B

snow   nieve   *f*   5B
so that   para que   12B
so/so that   así que   7B
so/well   pues   7B
soap   jabón   *m*   6B
soap opera   telenovela   *f*   1B
soccer   fútbol   *m*   1A
social science   ciencias sociales   *f*
   pl   1B
social work   trabajo social   *m*   2A
socks   calcetines   *m pl*   5B
soft   blando/a   5A; suave   7A
softdrink   refresco   *m*   6B
soldier   soldado   *m*   10A;
   militar   *m*   10B
solve   resolver   3B
some   alguno/a/os/as   4A
sometimes   a veces   3A
son   hijo   *m*   2B
song   canción   *f*   2A
son-in-law   yerno   *m*   2B
soon   pronto   6B
sore throat   dolor de
   garganta   *m*   10A
so-so   regular   Pre
soul   alma   *f*   3B
sound   sonido   *m*   8B
soup   sopa   *f*   4B
source   fuente   *f*   7B
space   espacio   *m*   1A
space shutlle   transbordador
   espacial   *m*   4B
space suit   traje espacial   *m*   11B
Spanish omelet   tortilla
   española   *f*   6B
Spanish-
   speaker   hispanohablante   *m/f*   3B
sparkle   destello   *m*   8A
speak   hablar   1A
speaker   portavoz   *m/f*   8B
specialty   especialización   2A
speech   discurso   *m*   3B
spell   deletrear   1A
spend   gastar   12A
spend time   pasar tiempo   6B
spicy   picante   3B
splash   salpicar   8B
spool of thread   carrete de
   hilo   *m*   5B
spoon   cuchara   *f*   5A
sport   deporte   *m*   1A
sports jacket   saco   *m*   5B
sports related   deportivo   1A
spread   embarrar   5A
spread   untar   5A
spring   primavera   *f*   3A
square   plaza   *f*   4A
squeak   chirriar   10B
squid   calamar   *m*   5A
stainless steel   acero
   inoxidable   *m*   6A
stairwell   escalera   *f*   6A
stamp   estampilla   *f*   8B
stand   pararse   6B; soporte   *m*   8B

standing up   parado/a   7A
star   estrella   *f*   7A
start   comienzo   *m*   10B;
   comenzar   2A; empezar   2A
starting from   a partir de   11A
state   estado   *m*   2B
statement   declaración   *f*   3B;
   enunciado   *m*   6A
stationery store   papelería   *f*   6B
stay awake   desvelarse   9A
steam   vapor   *m*   11A
steam cooker   olla al vapor   *f*   6A
step   paso   *m*   1A
step on   pisar   6B
stepbrother   hermanastro   *m*   2B
stepchild   hijastro/a   *m/f*   2B
stepfather   padrastro   *m*   2B
stepmother   madrastra   *f*   2B
stepsister   hermanastra   *f*   2B
still   todavía   1B
stomach ache   dolor de
   estómago   *m*   10A
stone   piedra   *f*   1A
stop   (doing something) dejar de +
   infinitive   4B
store   almacén   *m*   4B
storm   tormenta   *f*   3A
story   cuento   *m*   1A;
   relato   *m*   9A; historia   *f*   5B; (of a
   building) planta   *f*   6A
stove   cocina   *f*   5A
straight (hair)   lacio/a   7A
strawberry   fresa   *f*   5A
street   calle   *f*   4B
strength   fuerza   *f*   3A
stretch   estirar   7A
striped   a rayas   5B
stroller   cochecito   *m*   4A
strong   fuerte   3A
stubborn   intransigente   10B
student   alumno/a   *m/f*   1B;
   estudiante   *m/f*   1B
student dorm   residencia
   estudiatil   *f*   1B
study   estudiar   11B
subject   (academic) asignatura
   f   2A
succeed   tener éxito   4A
success   éxito   *m*   1B
such as   tal como   3B
suck   chupar   7A
suffer   (an illness) padecer   11A
suffering   sufrimiento   *m*   8A
sugar   azúcar   *m*   5A
sugar cane   caña de azúcar   *f*   11A
suggestion   sugerencia   *f*   6B
suit   traje   *m*   5B
suitable   conveniente   4B
suitcase   maleta   *f*   4B
summarize   resumir   6B
summary   resumen   *m*   1A
summer   verano   *m*   3A
sun   sol   *m*   5B
Sunday   domingo   2A

sunglasses gafas *f pl* 5B
supplies suministros *m pl* 12A
support soporte *m* 8B; apoyar 4A; sostener 4A
supportive solidario/a 12B
surge subida *f* 3A
surgeon cirujano/ *m/f* 4B
surgery operación *f* 4B
surround rodear 4A
surrounded rodeado/a 6A
surroundings contorno *m* 8B
survey encuesta *f* 3B; sondeo *m* 11A
survive sobrevivir 2B
swear jurar 10B
sweep barrer 6A
sweet dulce 5A
sweet roll panecillo *m* 5A
swim nadar 1A
swimming natación *f* 8A

T

table mesa *f* 1B
tablecloth mantel *m* 5A
tableware servicio de mesa *m* 5A
take llevar 5B
take a nap echarse una siesta 6B
take advantage of aprovechar 11A
take care of ocuparse de 7B
take care of cuidar 2B
take notes tomar apuntes 1B
take off (clothes) quitarse 7A
take out sacar 5A
take place tener lugar, suceder 11A
take to llevar a 11A
take turns turnarse 5B
take up again retomar 6A
talk hablar 1A
tall alto/a 1B
tap pulsar 11B
taste sabor *m* 4B; probar 4B
taxes impuestos *m pl* 12A
taxi driver taxista *m/f* 4B
teach enseñar 4B
teacher maestro/a *m/f* 4B
team equipo *m* 4A
tectonic (geol.) tectónico/a 3A
teenager adolescente *m/f* 4A
teeth dientes *m pl* 7A
telephone teléfono *m* Pre
television televisión *f* 1A
television set televisor *m* 1A
tell each other contarse 7B
teller cajero/a *m/f* 12A
tend to be tender a ser 8B
tend to/usually + *verb* soler + *infinitive* 6B
tennis tenis *m* 1A
tennis player tenista *m/f* 4A
tenth décimo 6B
term término *m* 2B
test examen *m* 2A; prueba *f* 1B

that que 1A
that is to say es decir 1A
that's why por eso 4A
then entonces 10B; luego 10B
therapist terapeuta *m/f* 8A
there is/there are hay 1B
therefore por lo tanto 11A
thick grueso/a 7A
thief ladrón/a *m/f* 9A
thing cosa *f* 1A
think pensar 3B
third tercero/a (tercer) 6B; (quantity) tercio *m* 10A
thirst sed *f* 11A
through a través de 3B; mediante 2B
throw (away) tirar 3B
throw oneself tirarse 8A
thruth verdad *f* 3A
thunder trueno *m* 3A
Thursday jueves 2A
ticket boleto/billete *m* 11A; entrada *f* 12A
tic-tac-toe tres en raya 10B
tie corbata *f* 5B
ties lazos *m pl* 4A
tight fitting apreatado/a 5B
tile baldosa *f* 6A
time hora *f* 2A; (instance) vez *f* 7B
time of day hora del día *f* 2A
tin hojalata *f* 10B
tip (gratuity) propina *f* 4B
tire llanta *f* 11A; fatigar 11A; cansarle a uno 11A
tired cansado/a 8A
title título *m* 4B
titled titulado/a 6B
to a Pre
to this end con este fin 5B
toast brindis *m* 5A; pan tostado *m* 5A
today hoy 1B
together juntos 6A
toilet inodoro *m* 6A
tomar take 1A
tomato tomate *m* 5A
tomorrow mañana 1B
tongue lengua *f* 6B
tongue twister trabalenguas *m* 6B
too; too much demasiado 6A
tool herramienta *f* 4B
topic tema *m* 7B
tornado tornado *m* 3A
touch tocar 1A; toque *m* 5B
towards hacia 8B
tower torre *f* 4A
town pueblo *m* 3B
toy juguete *m* 9A
trade oficio *m* 4A
traffic tráfico *m* 11A
tragedy desgracia *f* 7B
trail juicio *m* 4B

trainer entrenador/a *m/f* 4A
traits rasgos *m pl* 5A
transfer traslado *m* 8B
translate traducir 4B
translation traducción *f* 12A
travel viajar 3A
travel agent agente de viajes *m/ f* 11A
treatment tratamiento *m* 4B
tree árbol *m* 3A
tribute homenaje *m* 8B
trick truco *m* 5B
trip viaje *m* 10B
truce tregua *f* 12B
truck camión *m* 11A
true verdadero/a 3B
try tratar 3B
t-shirt camiseta *f* 5B
Tuesday martes 2A
turn (age) cumplir 6A
turn off apagar 1B
turn on encender 9A
TV game show programa de concursos *m* 7A
twin gemelo/a *m/f* 3B
twist (part of the body) torcerse 7A

U

U.S. citizen estadounidense 1A
ugly feo/a 10A
uh…/um… este… 7B
umbrella paraguas *m* 5B
uncle/aunt tío *m* 2B
underline subrayar 5B
understand entender 3B
understanding entendimiento *m* 10A
unemployment desempleo *m* 2B
unexpected inesperado/a 8B
unforgettable inolvidable 8A
united unido/a 2B
university universidad *f* 1B
university directory guía universitaria *f* 2A
university school or college facultad *f* 2A
unknown desconocido/a 10B
unless a menos que 12B
unnoticed inadvertido/a 6B
unpleasant antipático/a 6B
unripe verde 8A
until hasta 6A; hasta que 12B
update actualización *f* 3A
uprising levantamiento *m* 12B
upset alterar 11B
upset (angry) enojado/a 8A
useless inútil 11A
user usuario *m* 11B
utensils cubiertos *m pl* 5A

V

vacuum cleaner aspiradora *f* 6A
value valorar 7B
value valor *m* 1B
vegetables verduras *f pl* 4B
verify comprobar 5A
video game videojuego *m* 1A
video maker videoasta *m/f* 12B
visit visitar 1A
vocational school escuela
  técnica *f* 1B
voice voz *f* 4A
vowel vocal *f* 4A

W

waist cintura *f* 7A
wait espera *f* 7B; esperar 11B
wait in line hacer fila 11A
waiter/waitress camarero/a *m/*
  f 4B
wake up despertar 6A
walk andar 8A; caminar 1A;
wall muro *m* 11A; pared *f* 6A
wallet cartera *f* 12A
want querer 4A
war guerra *f* 3A
warm cálido/a 6B
warning advertencia *f* 11B
wash lavar 4B
washer lavaplatos *m* 6A
washing machine lavadora *f* 6A
waste desperdicio *m* 12B
watch reloj *m* 1B; (look at)
  mirar 1A
water agua *f* 3A
wave ola *f* 3A
way manera *f* 2A
weak débil 10B
wear llevar 5B
wedding boda *f* 2B
wedding dress vestido de
  novia *m* 5B
Wednesday miércoles 2A
weekend fin de semana *m* 3A
weekly semanal 4B
weight peso *m* 6B
weights pesas *f pl* 1A
welcome bienvenido/a 1B
well pozo *m* 6B
well mannered bien educado 1B
well-being bienestar 6B
well-known conocido/a 6A;
  notorio/a 4B
westernization occidentalización
  f 12B
what (interrog) cómo Pre; qué Pre
wheel rueda *f* 11A
wheelchair silla de ruedas *f* 7B
when cuando 12B
where (interrog) dónde Pre
which (interrog) cuál/es Pre
while mientras (que) 3B

whistle pitar 6B
whistle pito *m* 6B
white blanco 5A
who quien/es 8B
who (interrog) quién/es 1A
whole grains granos enteros *m*
  pl 5A
whose cuyo/a 6B
wide ancho/a 5B; amplio/a 7A
widen ensanchar 5B
widowed viudo/a 2B
wild salvaje 3A
willing dispuesto/a 6B
win ganar 4A
wind viento *m* 3A
window ventana *f* 1B
wine vino *m* 5A
winter invierno *m* 3A
wireless inalámbrico/a 11A
wise sabio/a 10A
wish desear 2A
witch brujo/a *m/f* 10B
with me conmigo 2A
with respect to en cuanto a 3A
without sin 6A; sin que 12B
witness testigo *m* 7B
wolf lobo *m* 10B
woman mujer *f* 1B
wood madera *f* 6A; (for a
  fire) leña *f* 5B
woodcutter leñador/a *m/f* 10B
woodlands monte *m* 3A
wool lana *f* 5B
word palabra *f* 1B
work trabajo *m* 3A; trabajar 1B
work of art obra de arte *f* 7A
worker obrero/a *m/f* 4B
worker's strike huelga *f* 3B
workforce (personpower) mano de
  obra *f* 3B
workshop taller 4B
world mundo *m* 1B; mundial 3A
worried preocupado/a 8A
worse; worst peor 8B
worship culto *m* 10A
wrist muñeca *f* 7A
write escribir 1A
writer escritor/a *m/f* 2B
writing escritura 10A

Y

year año *m* 1B
yellow amarillo 5B
yet todavía 1B
young joven 7A
young person joven *m/f* 1B
younger; youngest menor 2B
youth juventud *f* 4A

Z

zoo zoológico *m* 7B

COGNADOS

Investigación preliminar
celular
civil
clase
código postal
dirección electrónica
divorciado/a
expresivo/a
femenino/a
formal
independiente
informal
inteligente
interesante
masculino/a
materno/a
móvil
número
origen
paterno/a
personal
profesión
relación
residencial
teléfono
término

Capítulo 1
Investigación A
acción
actividad
animado/a
asociación
atlético/a
colección
comedia
cómico/a
completar
complicado/a
comunicar
conciencia
contacto
contexto
copia
creativo/a
cultura
delicioso/a
descriptivo/a
drama
elefante
emocional
enemigo/a
estable/inestable
estereotipo
estilo
estudiar
eterno/a
experiencia
expresar
extrovertido/a
familia
famoso/a
fantasma
favorito/a
filosofal
físico/a
flauta

fotogénico/a
fruta
generoso/a
guitarra
hamburguesa
héroe
horror
imbécil
instrumento
intelectual
introvertido/a
investigación
laberinto
latino/a
leyenda
mexicano/a
modelo
mortal
musical
novela
observar
optimista
perfeccionista
perfecto/a
persona
personalidad
perspectiva
pesimista
piano
pirata
poema
popular
precioso/a
preparar
pronunciar
reacción
realidad
reportero/a
residente
respetuoso/a
responsable/
   irresponsable
romántico/a
sedentario/a
situación
sociable
suspenso
tímido/a
tomate
tragedia
violento/a

Capítulo 1
Investigación B
académico/a
acceso
administración
administrativo
antónimo
asociar
avanzado/a
básquetbol
bate
biológico
cafetería
capital
carpintero/a
computadora
concepto

conflicto
conversar
copiar
curso
definición
descubrir
destino
diccionario
diferente
directo/a
doctorado
económico
educación
electricista
entrar
escolar
especializarse
específico/a
estratificación
estrato
estructura
estudiar
explorar
fatal
final
gasolina
gimnasio
grado
guitarra
hispano/a
humanidades
imagen
inflexibilidad
información
innovador/a
institución
invención
jerarquía
lógico/ilógico
matemático
mecánico
motivado/a
mover
nativo/a
necesario
organizador
participar
perfume
persistir
posible
práctica
privada
problema
profesor/a
programa
pronunciación
público/a
repetir
repetitivo/a
resolver
seleccionar
silenciar
sinónimo
sistema
social
sociedad
socio-económico/a
usar
video

virtual
visita

Capítulo 2
Investigación A
actor
agricultura
anatomía
antropología
área
arquitecto/a
arquitectura
arte
artes gráficas
artes plásticas
aspecto
astronomía
atleta
básico/a
biología
ciencia política
ciencias
clínica
cognitivo
competitividad
comunicación visual
comunidad
crédito
criterio
departamento
describir
dictado
ecología
economía
especial
estrés
evento
excesivo/a
filosofía
física
geografía
geología
grupo
historia
ilegible
increíble
insuficiente
internacional
introducción
investigar
laboratorio
latín
literatura
matemáticas
medicina
música
norteamericano
obligatorio/a
potencialmente
presentar
presidente
producir
programación
psicología
religión
resistir
semestre
sistemático/a
sociología

teatro
tecnología
terapia física
turista

Capítulo 2
Investigación B
adolescencia
adulto
agresivo/a
arrogante
autoridad
aventurero/a
bautismo
carismático/a
celebrar
ceremonia religiosa
cliente/a
comprensión
comunión
condescendiente
condición
conectar
conexión
conservador
contemporáneo/a
contrario/a
convencional
convincente
cooperativo/a
cordial
decidido/a
determinado/a
diplomático/a
doctor/a
espiritual
estrategia
existencia
familia extendida
familia nuclear
financiero/a
flexible
frecuente
graduación
horóscopo
humilde
ideal
impaciente
importante
impulsivo
incluir
individualista
individuo
infancia
inocente
íntimo/a
intolerante
irresponsable
irreverente
jovial
mamá / papá
moderno/a
momento
moral
nervioso/a
obediente
obstinado/a
obtener
original

paciente
pacifista
papá/ mamá
persistente
persuasivo/a
princesa
proceso legal
radio
reservado/a
residencia
respetar
responsabilidad
sereno/a
sincero/a
solitario/a
sumiso/a
supervisar
típico/a
tolerante
tradicional
unido/a
unir
válido
valiente

Capítulo 3
Investigación A
acento
acentuación
actriz
animal
apropiado
atractivo/a
auditorio
autor/a
capitalismo
carácter
causar
centro
cigarro
circular
clima
colonizar
color
concentrar
concierto
constante
constituir
continente
continuar
contraste
costa
demostrativo
densidad
desastre natural
desierto
destruir
devastación
devastar
difícil
distancia
distinguir
diversidad
dólar
dominar
ecuador
eléctrico/a
escándalo
escena

este
excepción
exceso
existir
exótico
expansión
expresión
extremo/a
factor
figura
forma
formar
foto
frontera
general
golfo
grave
hemisferio
humano/a
humedad
impacto
independencia
infraestructura
instantáneo
instructor
integración
intenso/a
interior
isla
laguna
libertad
limitado/a
lista
mantener
máquina
mayoría
metropolitano/a
migración
millón
mineral
motivar
movimiento
nación
noreste/nordeste
noroeste
norte
objeto
observatorio
océano
ocurrir
oeste
ofrecer
palma
parte
particular
península
periferia
petróleo
planeta
plantar
plástico
prejuicio
preparado/a
principal
proceso
proteger
provincia
provocar
reciente

recurso
región
representar
resto
rural
sensualidad
separado/a
serie
serio/a
serpiente
servicio
sudamericano
sur
sureste
suroeste
tendencia
territorio
torrencial
urbanización
urbano/a
valle
varios/as
víctima
visibilidad
vulnerable
zona

Capítulo 3
Investigación B
análisis
anglosajón
árabe
artista
banco
bilingüe
café
celebridad
científico/a
cine
civilización
colectivo/a
colonia
combinación
compañía
compleja
común
consecuencia
conservar
considerar
construcción
contradecir
contratar
contribución
conversación
crisis
década
declive
definir
demanda
derivar
descendiente
detalle
dialecto
diáspora
diferencia
distribución
diverso/a
eliminar
emplear

estadio
europeo/a
evitable/inevitable
evocar
excluir/incluir
exclusivo/inclusivo
existente/inexistente
exploratorio/a
fenómeno
ferocidad
feroz
fusión
futuro
generación
generar
global
globalización
grupo étnico
iconografía
identidad
identificar
ignorancia
imaginación
influencia
inmigrante
justicia/injusticia
lingüístico/a
medios de
   comunicación
memorizar
milenio
mutuo/a
occidental
oficial
opinión
orden civil
parque
percepción
planta
polémico/a
popularidad
porción
positivo/a
predecesor
previo/a
protesta
raza
referencia
regular
representación
respeto
sacrificar
secreto
simple
sufrir
tabaco
taco
territorial
total
tradición
transnacional
unidad
uso
violencia
visión
visual

Capítulo 4
Investigación A
aceptable
actuar
admirable
afectar
agenda
alcohol
anestesia
ángel
animación
arma
beneficio
canal
caricaturas
chocolate
ciencia ficción
club
columna
composición
concentración
conferencia
congreso
corresponsal
criminal
decadencia
demonio
depresión
desaparece
discoteca
documental
drama
editorial
enorme
episodio
espectador
extender
frágil
futurístico
galaxia
generalización
género
guardia
hospitalidad
igual
influenciar
informar
ingrediente
jazz
mitológico/a
nocturno
obligación
organizar
participante
percibir
percusión
policía
pop
proyectar
proyecto
rápido/a
raramente
reflejar
reportar
resistencia
revelar
ridículo
rígida
ritmo

sándwich
servir
similar
sostener
tragedia
trompeta
validez
volumen
voto
xenofobia

Capítulo 4
Investigación B
absorber
activista
adaptarse
administrador/a
aire
ambicioso/a
antibiótico
antropólogo/a
arrestar
asteroide
astronauta
astrónomo/a
aventura
aversión
biólogo/a
catástrofe
cheque
columnista
comentarista
comercio
conductor/a
cruel
culinario/a
cuota
dentista
depósito
dictar
diploma
diptongo
director/a (de
   escuela)
documentar
elegante
empleado/a
evacuación
evidencia
excavar
farmacéutico/a
farmacia
filósofo
fotógrafo/a
geólogo/a
gracia
hospital
hotel
imaginativo/a
incidente
influyente
ininterrumpido/a
instituto
interacción
inyección
líder
lingüista
mecánico/a
mensaje

metódico/a
ministro/a
modesto/a
obvio
oficina
ordenar
pausa
perla
piloto
plomero
preciso/a
profundo/a
proyección
psicólogo/a
psiquiatra
recepcionista
reconstruir
religioso/a
restaurante
sal
secretario/a
sociólogo
sólido/a
temperatura
tenso/a
terrorista
transporte
vacaciones
veterinario/a
virtuoso/a
vitamina
vocación

Capítulo 5
Investigación A
abuso
ácido
acompañado/a
adorar
aire acondicionado
alterar
anticipar
asimilar
banana
botella
brócoli
cafeína
calcio
cáncer
carbohidratos
cardíaco/a
champaña
chef
chile
círculo
componente
condimento
consomé
consultar
contener
cortesía
costo
crema
cremoso/a
demostrar
desorden
diabetes
dieta
droga

COGNADOS

ejecutivo/a
enchilada
enérgico/a
ensalada
equivalente
espagueti
espinaca
fermentar
fibra
fresco/a
fundamental
gastronómico/a
limón
limonada
líquido/a
mayonesa
melón
mermelada
nutritivo/a
pasaje
pasta
pera
pizza
póker
porcentaje
preferido/a
proteína
puré
refrigerador
resultar
rico/a
rosa
salmón
segmento
separar
silencio
tamal
té
tipo
tortilla
transmitir
tribu
unificador/a
vasto
vegetariano/a
vinagre
yogur

Capítulo 5
Investigación B

accesorios
aniversario
artículo
aspirina
basarse
blusa
botas
cachemir
calidad
clásico/a
conclusión
costar
creador/a
diamante
esquiar
exhibir
extraordinario/a
idéntico/a
insistir

interpretar
lentes de contacto
léxico
lino
máximo/a
meteórico/a
neutro
pantalón
pieza
pijamas
poncho
sandalias
seguridad
silueta
sofisticado/a
suéter
texto
tráfico
uniforme
versátil

Capítulo 6
Investigación A

alarma
apartamento
apto/a
balcón
biografía
brillante
característico/a
centro de
   entretenimiento
chimenea
competitivo/a
condominio
confirmar
congestión
decoración
determinar
dispensador
doméstico/a
época
espíritu
estéreo
estudio
fachada
fama
formación
galón
garaje
granito
iluminar
importancia
importar
lámpara
límite
mencionar
milla
parcialmente
patio
privacidad
prodigio
protección
reducido/a
rentar
reputación
residencia estudiantil
sofá
talento

televisor de plasma
tostadora
velocidad

Capítulo 6
Investigación B

ambición
anacrónico/a
autorizado/a
balance
comparación
competencia
consistir
consumidor/a
contrato
correcto/a
cortés
crucial
decidir
defecto
depender
dócil
elemento
énfasis
equilibrio
establecimiento
evidente
expectativa
forzar
fragmento
impresión
inmediatamente
instrucción
insultar
inusual
medieval
metro
multinacional
negativo/a
obligar
obstáculo
paradójico/a
párrafo
periodo
práctico/a
preferible
preocupado/a
prestigioso/a
progresivo/a
progreso
prometer
protestar
puntualidad
raro/a
razón
recitar
salario
sección
sincronizar
superficial
supermercado
único
verificar
votar

Capítulo 7
Investigación A

abstracto/a
abundancia

abundante
adjetivo
antena
anticuado/a
apariencia
artificial
auténtico/a
brillante
captar
catedral
comentario
consenso
corpulento/a
ejecutar
emisiones
emoción
escape
espectacular
extraterrestre
fantasía
frase
funeral
galería de arte
geométrico/a
gimnasta
idealista
insecto
interpretación
karate
maduro/a
museo
notable
obesidad
obeso/a
opción
órgano
ozono
par
preocupación
proporciones
real
realista
recíproco/a
rectángulo
reflexionar
ruinas
sensual
símbolo
suspensión
torso
triángulo
trivial
universo
vampiro/a

Capítulo 7
Investigación B

afortunado/a
aliarse
aluminio
aparentemente
arlequines
armonía
ataque
atrocidad
béisbol
bombardeo
católico/a
circo

clarificar
compasión
construir
contemplar
cordialidad
cubismo
cura
deformar
desesperación
detectar
devoción
diálogo
dogma
entrada
entretener
escultor/a
espiar
evasión
examinar
externo/a
facial
ícono
ideología
ilustrar
imaginario/a
inconformidad
inhumano/a
interno/a
kilo
lotería
manifestar
miniatura
minúsculo/a
mural
panorama
pictórico/a
piedad
predominante
probar
prolongar
reciclar
recrear
reducir
revolución
semántico/a
sinfonía
soledad
surreal
surrealismo
técnica
tensión

Capítulo 8
Investigación A

accidente
actitud
adecuado/a
admirado/a
adquisición
agitado/a
amputar
ansioso/a
asumir
calmado/a
confesar
controlado/a
criticar
cromático/a
cronológico/a

desconcertado/a
desorganizado/a
diario
donar
equilibrado/a
estresado/a
exagerado/a
exhibición
fascinación
finalizar
frustrado/a
furioso/a
horrorizado/a
impecable
impetuoso/a
impregnado/a
inspirado/a
introducir
invisible
irritar
ópera
ordenado/a
personalizar
realismo mágico
refrescar
restaurado/a
satisfecho/a
trampolín
trascender
voluptuoso/a

Capítulo 8
Investigación B

abusivo/a
acumulación
alienación
ancestro
anónimo/a
apreciar
arte digital
arte visual
artes decorativas
artes musicales
audiencia
categoría
cerámica
cinematografía
colaboración
collage
complacer
controlar
convertir
cooperación
danza moderna
elevar
escultura
estatua
estelar
estético/a
excéntrico/a
exilio
fascinar
federal
filme
fomentar
fotografía
franco
grafiti
gramo

hipnotizar
homófono
hostil
injusticia
inmigración
instalación
manuscrito
marginal
masas
metal
montaje
orfanato
orquesta
panel
persistencia
prohibir
provocador/a
puro/a
rebelarse
sensación
signo
sinagoga
sonoro/a
superlativo/a
tatuaje
tema
templo
tenor
terrible
triunfo
universal

Capítulo 9
Investigación A
altar
autorizar
banda
carnaval
cementerio
ciclo
coincidir
conmemoración
conmemorar
coro
debate
decorar
fabuloso/a
festival
gastrónomo/a
gobernar
horizontal
horroroso/a
impresionante
intangible
invitación
invitar
magnífico/a
maravilloso/a
oral
ortodoxo/a
patriotismo
picnic
pingüino
procesión
respectivamente
ritual
ruta
santo patrón
simbolizar

sobrenatural
solemne
sorpresa
tono
tumba
variedad
venerar
vertical
violeta
virgen

Capítulo 9
Investigación B
acrónimo
adversidad
astronómico/a
boxeo
bravo/a
cámara
canibalismo
ciclismo
cohesión
condensar
crueldad
dedicación
dignidad
disciplina
discriminación
esencia
esférico/a
fortuito/a
fútbol
gol
golf
habitual
hockey
imperfecto/a
implicación
imponderable
kayak
lacrosse
medalla
metáfora
oposición
oxígeno
pistola
puntuación
raqueta
rifle
rugby
sitio web
tenis
virtud
voleibol

Capítulo 10
Investigación A
abandonar
aceptar
acueducto
adobe
alcohólico/a
alianza
alpaca
amplificar
armar
arquitectura
atacar
barbacoa

bola
búfalo
cacao
canoa
capturar
censo
champú
cíclico/a
civilizar
colador
cólera
comité
complejidad
conquista
conquistar
conservación
defender
defensa
desintegrar
detergente
devorar
diuréticos
dominante
dominios
eficiente
elaborar
elecciones
eliminación
eliminado/a
enumerar
epidémico
esplendor
ético/a
evitar
extenso/a
extinción
extinguir
fertilidad
fertilizante
firme
genocidio
hiato
higiene personal
imperio
imponer
influenza
insecticida
intolerancia
invadir
irrigación
jade
jaguar
jeroglífico/a
literario/a
malaria
masacrar
monarquía
monumental
mosquito
nómadas
ocupar
organización
palacio
papaya
presente
preservación
profecía
racismo
rayo

repelente
teoría
tolerancia
tuberculosis
utilizar

Capítulo 10
Investigación B
agrario/a
agresor/a
alergia
ambiguo/a
aristócrata
asma
autoritario/a
batalla
batallón
candidato
clemencia
comunista
democrático/a
deportar
dictadura
dimensión
embajador/a
escrúpulo
federación
feminista
histórico/a
inventar
liberación
mártir
opresión
pabellón
permitir
persecución
pionero/a
prisión
prohibido/a
rebelde
reducción
represión
revolucionario/a
rubí
segregarse
vainilla
venerado/a
visionario/a

Capítulo 11
Investigación A
abordar
aeropuerto
agente
aplicación
autobús
automático
barril
capacidad
contaminación del
   aire
control remoto
despachador/a
dividido/a
economista
emergencia
energía eléctrica
estadística
evolucionar

facilitar
firma
inauguración
litro
modificar
motocicleta
motor
moverse
mudo
orgánico/a
pasajero
pasaporte
plataforma
probabilidad
procesar
reservar
satélite
solar
solución
tanque
taxi
transformarse
tren
tropa
vehículo eléctrico/
   híbrido

Capítulo 11
Investigación B
ajustar
anormal
ansiedad
batería
cable
chatear
cibercafé
ciberespacio
consumir
contactar
cuestionario
déficit
disco compacto
estímulo
fotocopiadora
frustración
funcionar
inmersión
materialista
neurológico/a
página web
portátil
psíquico/a
rutina
situado/a
sofisticación
tridimensional
utilidad

Capítulo 12
Investigación A
acceder
biometría
cometer
competente
cooperativa de
   crédito
crimen
depositar
estabilidad

falsificar
financiar
finanzas
fraude
frívolo
impenetrable
inalterable
industrializado/a
interés
invertido/a
iris ocular
mínimo/a
mobilidad
nacionalismo
paella
robar
totalitario/a
útero
vena

Capítulo 12
Investigación B
abandono
acelerar
adicto/a
arsenal
autónomo
barrera
bomba atómica
clasificación
concreto/a
conectividad
democratización
destrucción
difusión de
   información
diseminación de
   culturas
dominación
escrutinio
espacio
estricto/a
expansión
   tecnológica
genérico/a
hipotético/a
imperialismo
interdependencia
líneas telefónicas
marginación
militarismo
modernizar
negociación
nuevas fronteras
posgrado
punto de vista
rapidez
reconfigurar
simpatizante
simular
solidaridad
sustitución
telecomunicaciones
transmisiones
   satelitales

ÍNDICE

ÍNDICE

CREDITS

PHOTO CREDITS

PRELIMINARY CHAPTER
Page 1: Laurence Mouton/PhotoAlto/Corbis. Page 11: AP/Wide World Photos. Page 13: (top right) Photodisc/Getty Images, Inc. Page 13: (center) Push Pictures/Age Fotostock America, Inc. Page 13: (bottom) Yellow Dog Productions/The Image Bank/Getty Images, Inc.

CHAPTER 1
Page 15: Kablonk!/Age Fotostock America, Inc. Page 17: (top left) Courtesy of Dolly Young. Page 17: (top right) Courtesy of Dolly Young. Page 17: (bottom left) Yellow Dog Productions/The Image Bank /Getty Images, Inc. Page 17: (bottom right) Courtesy of Dolly Young. Page 22: Ulf Andersen/Getty Images, Inc. Page 30: Courtesy of Claudia Montoya. Page 31: iStockphoto. Page 32: iStockphoto. Page 25: Moodboard/Alamy. Page 36: Courtesy of Jackie Muirhead. Page 48: (bottom left) Harper Collins. Page 48: (top right) Nikreates/Alamy. Page 48: (top left) Brooks Kraft/Corbis. Page 51: (top) iStockphoto. Page 51: (bottom) iStockphoto. Page 52: Courtesy of Pablo Muirhead.

CHAPTER 2
Page 61: aerialarchives.com/Alamy. Page 62: Moodboard/Alamy. Page 79: (top) iStockphoto. Page 79: (bottom) iStockphoto. Page 79: (center) iStockphoto. Page 84: Carlos Alvarez/Getty Images, Inc. Page 89: The Kobal Collection, Ltd. Page 92: Ariel Skelley/Blend Images/Getty Images, Inc. Page 98: (left) WireImage/Getty Images, Inc. Page 98: (right) Daniele Venturelli/WireImage/Getty Images, Inc. Page 100: Courtesy of Dolly Young. Page 101: (left) Courtesy of Claudia Montoya. Page 101: (right) Courtesy of Claudia Montoya. Page 102: Courtesy of Dolly Young.

CHAPTER 3
Page 107: Cris Haigh/Alamy. Page 112: (top left) John W. McDonough /Sports Illustrated/Getty Images, Inc. Page 112: (top center) Photo by Glenn James/NBAE /Getty Images, Inc. Page 112: (top right) AP/Wide World Photos. Page 112: (bottom left) Barry Gossage/NBAE /Getty Images, Inc. Page 112: (bottom right) TIMOTHY A. CLARY/AFP/Getty Images, Inc. Page 133: Courtesy of Pablo Muirhead. Page 138: Rahmaan Static Barnes, Chicago Public Art Group, 2008. Page 144: (left) Courtesy of Dolly Young. Page 150: Mark Sullivan/WireImage/Getty Images, Inc. Page 151: iStockphoto. Page 152: Courtesy of Dolly Young.

CHAPTER 4
Page 157: AP/Wide World Photos. Page 160: REUTERS/Sergio Moraes/Landov LLC. Page 163: Courtesy of Pablo Muirhead. Page 176: Courtesy of Pablo Muirhead. Page 177: (top) iStockphoto. Page 177: (center) iStockphoto. Page 177: (bottom) iStockphoto. Page 178: (top) Sony Pictures/Everett Collection, Inc. Page 178: (center) Courtesy of Dolly Young. Page 178: (bottom) Courtesy of Pablo Muirhead. Page 184: Javier Peraza/Getty Images, Inc. Page 185: Courtesy of Dolly Young.

CHAPTER 5
Page 203: Gonzalo Azumendi/Age Fotostock America, Inc. Page 206: REUTERS/Courtesy Food Network/Landov. Page 214: Blend Images/Getty Images, Inc. Page 218: AP/Wide World Photos. Page 222: Blend Images/Getty Images, Inc. Page 227: (top) Michael Buckner/Getty Images, Inc. Page 227: (bottom) Frank Micelotta/Getty Images, Inc. Page 233: (top) Dolores Olmedo Mexico/Gianni Dagli Orti/The Art Archive/The Picture Desk. Page 233: (bottom left) Courtesy of Richard Muirhead. Page 233: (bottom right) Courtesy of Richard Muirhead. Page 239: Barry King/WireImage/Getty Images, Inc. Page 244: Courtesy of Dolly Young. Page 246: (top left) Henry Spencer/Getty Images, Inc. Page 246: (top right) AGE Fotostock/SUPERSTOCK. Page 246: (bottom) Jed Jacobsohn/Getty Images, Inc.

CHAPTER 6
Page 251: Terry Vine/Blend Images/Corbis. Page 254: ROBERT PITTS/Landov LLC. Page 260: Courtesy of Pablo Muirhead. Page 261: Photo and Co/Taxi/Getty Images, Inc. Page 274: Courtesy of Claudia Montoya. Page 274: Courtesy of Pablo Muirhead. Page 275: iStockphoto. Page 276: (top) Courtesy of Pablo Muirhead. Page 276: (center) iStockphoto. Page 276: (bottom) iStockphoto. Page 281: Robert Fried/Alamy. Page 291: Courtesy of Dolly Young. Page 296: iStockphoto. Page 297: iStockphoto.

CHAPTER 7
Page 323: Carmen Lomas Garza, La Feria en Reynosa, 1987, Courtesy of Carmen Lomas Garza. Page 328: John August Swanson, The Classroom, 1992. Page 332: John August Swanson, The Classroom, 1992. Page 333: John August Swanson, The Classroom, 1992. Page 334: John August Swanson, The Classroom, 1992. Page 342: Edward Hopper, Nighthawks, 1942. Courtesy of SuperStock. Page 343: Pablo Picasso, Massacre in Korea, 1951. Courtesy of Réunion des Musées Nationaux/Art Resource.

CHAPTER 8
Page 349: Krzysztof Dydynski/Lonely Planet Images. Page 352: Francisco Jose de Goya y Lucientes, Time of Old Women, 1820, Courtesy of Musee des Beaux-Arts, Lille, France/Lauros/Giraudon/The Bridgeman Art Library. Page 357: Norman Rockwell, Day in a Life of a Little Girl, Printed by permission of the Norman Rockwell Family Agency ©1952 Norman Rockwell Family Entities. Page 364: Sonia Solanillo Morales, La Herencia, 2007. Page 366: Bettmann/Corbis. Page 367: (top) Juan Guzman/The Granger Collection, New York. Page 367: (center) Frida Kahlo, Self-Portrait at the Border between Mexico and the United States, Courtesy of Christie's Images/Corbis. Page 367: (bottom) The Kobal Collection, Ltd., The Picture Desk. Page 373: (top) Martina Lopez, Heirs Come to Pass, 3, 1991. Courtesy of Smithsonian American Art Museum, Washington, DC/Art Resource, NY/Art Resource. Page 373: (center) Irene Perez-Omer, Transplant, 1996. Page 373: (bottom) Maria Martinez-Casas, "Totem Negro: XVI," 1992, Gelatin Silver Print, Ed of 2, 54 x 10 inches. Courtesy of Julie Saul Gallery, New York. Page 381: Chris Jackson/Getty Images, Inc. Page 388: (top) Judith F. Baca, Triunfo de las manos, 1990/SPARC. Page 388: (center) Judith F. Baca, Resistencia sin violencia, 1990/SPARC. Page 388: (bottom) Judith F. Baca, Triunfo del Corazon, 1990/SPARC. Page 389: (bottom) Judith F. Baca, Balance, 1990/SPARC. Page 390: Courtesy of Claudia Montoya.

CREDITS

CHAPTER 9
Page 395: AP/Wide World Photos. Page 398: AFP/Getty Images, Inc. Page 399: Courtesy of Dolly Young. Page 406: AP/Wide World Photos. Page 408: (right) FilmMagic//Getty Images, Inc. Page 408: (left) Arnaldo Magnani/Getty Images, Inc.
Page 410: AP/Wide World Photos. Page 416: Courtesy of Carlos Jaurena. Page 432: Courtesy of Dolly Young. Page 422: (top) Pascal Guyot/Getty Images, Inc. Page 422: (bottom) Courtesy of Dolly Young.

CHAPTER 10
Page 437: Shirley Vanderbilt/Index Stock/Age Fotostock America, Inc. Page 446: Angelo Cavalli/Getty Images, Inc. Page 441: Nathaniel Tarn/Photo Researchers, Inc. Page 454: Courtesy of Richard Muirhead. Page 462: SuperStock. Page 469: NORBERTO DUARTE/AFP/Getty Images, Inc. Page 474: (top) Bettmann/Corbis. Page 474: (bottom) Bettmann/Corbis. Page 477: Bettmann/Corbis.

CHAPTER 11
Page 483: Alberto Paredes/Alamy. Page 486: Kord.com/Age Fotostock America, Inc.
Page 497: Scott Heiner/Getty Images, Inc. Page 496: Wendy Connett/Alamy.
Page 504: James Leynse/Corbis. Page 505: Keith Dannemiller/Alamy. Page 510: Courtesy of Dolly Young. Page 515: Tetra/Getty Images, Inc.

CHAPTER 12
Page 529: Rafael Campillo/Age Fotostock America, Inc. Page 532: Sebastien Baussais/Alamy. Page 546: Getty Images, Inc. Page 547: Efe Agencia
Page 552: Philip Reisman, God Bless America, 1940. Museum Purchase, Derby Fund, from the Philip J. and Suzanne Schiller Collection of American Social Commentary Art 1930–1970. Courtesy of the Columbus Museum of Art. Page 562: John Mitchel/Alamy. Page 563: Francisco Vazquez, Courtesy of Chiapas Media Project.

TEXT CREDITS

CHAPTER 2 Page 80: Reprinted by permission of Sociedad española para el estudio de la ansiedad y el estrés (SEAS), Págs. 159-172, © 1996.

CHAPTER 3 Page 126, 127: Reprinted by permission of H.J. de Blij and Peter O. Muller © 2002, Geography Realms, Regions and Concerns. New York: John Wiley & Sons, Inc., p. 238.

CHAPTER 4 Page 198: Reprinted by permission of the European Commission from Special Eurobarometer 237–Wave 63.4.

CHAPTER 5 Page 208: Reprinted by permission of EFE News Service, © EFE News Service (U.S.) Inc. Page 222: Reprinted by permission of Univisión Interactive Media, Inc., http://www.univision.com/content/content.jhtml?cid=945599. Page 225: Reprinted by permission of Latina Magazine, May 1999. Page 246: Reprinted by permission of EFE News Service, © EFE News Service (U.S.) Inc.

CHAPTER 7 Page 344: Reprinted from El Semanal, © 2004, by permission of The Times/ The Sun/ nisyndication.com.

CHAPTER 8 Page 366: Reprinted by permission of Diario La Prensa, Corporación La Prensa, © March 15, 2008. Page 375: Art and text reprinted by permission of Smithsonian American Art Museum, Washington, DC/Art Resource, NY.

CHAPTER 9 Page 416: Reprinted from El habitante by Carmen Villoro, Ediciones Cal y Arena, México, D.F., © 1997, p. 51, with permission of the author. Page 430: Reprinted by permission of Virginia García Zamorano, Rafael García Librán, and David García Liébana in Héroes de barro © 2006.

CHAPTER 11 Page 488: Reprinted by permission of © Miami Media LLC. All rights reserved. Page 512: Reprinted by permission of Tendencias21. Page 517: Reprinted by permission of Diario El día, © 2006.

CHAPTER 12 Page 546: Reprinted by permission of Univisión Interactive Media, Inc., Page 547: Reprinted by permission of EFE News Service, © EFE News Service (U.S.) Inc. Page 563: Reprinted by permission of Alexandra Halkin, Founding Director, Chiapas Media Project/Promedios, www.chiapasmediaproject.org, © 2006, Revista Chilena de antropología visual, número 7

REALIA CREDITS

CHAPTER P Page 7: Mosaico Subscription Form, reprinted by permission of © Bookspan: all rights reserved. Selecciones Subscription Form.

CHAPTER 1 Page 50: Reprinted by permission of Randy Glasbergen. Copyright © Randy Glasbergen: www.glasbergen.com. Book cover of Bulldog llamada Noelle by Gloria Estefan, illustrated by Michael Garland, © 2005, reprinted by permission of HarperCollins: all rights reserved.

CHAPTER 6 Page 282: Text and art reprinted by permission of María Renée